The Spell of the Song

Also by JOHN POWELL WARD

Criticism

Poetry and the Sociological Idea (1981)
Wordsworth's Language of Men (1984)
Raymond Williams (1984)
The English Line (1991)
As You Like It (1992)
Thomas Hardy's Poetry (1993)
The Poetry of R. S. Thomas (2001)

Poetry

The Other Man (1969)
To Get Clear (1981)
The Clearing (1984)
A Certain Marvellous Thing (1993)
Genesis (1996)
Late Thoughts in March (1999)
Selected and New Poems (2003)

The Spell of the Song

Letters, Meaning, and English Poetry

John Powell Ward

Madison • Teaneck
Fairleigh Dickinson University Press

Associated University Presses
2010 Eastpark Boulevard
Cranbury, NJ 08512

The paper used in this publication meets the requirements of the American National Standard for Permanence of Paper for Printed Library Materials Z39.48-1984.

Library of Congress Cataloging-in-Publication Data

Ward, John Powell, 1937–
    The spell of the song : letters, meaning, and English poetry / John Powell Ward.
        p.   cm.
    Includes bibliographical references and index.
    ISBN 0-8386-3987-9 (alk. paper)
    1. English poetry—History and criticism.   2. Alphabet in literature.
3. English language—Alphabet.   I. Title.
PR508.A45W37   2004
821.009—dc22   2003027480

in memory of
my maternal grandfather

H e r b e r t   E d w a r d   P o w e l l

who when parents lived abroad
took me under his roof
and whose exquisite handwriting
taught me to aim likewise
though the pupil never acquired remotely
the skill of the master

For Books are not absolutely dead things, but doe contain a po-
tencie of life in them as to be active as that soule was whose
progeny they are; nay they do preserve as in a violl the purest
efficacie and extraction of that living intellect that bred them.

—John Milton, *Areopagitica*

It seems precisely that this is what lends life a certain spectral
quality—the fact that everything that is denied reality, everything that is colourless, odourless, tasteless, imponderable and
non-moral, like water, air, space, money and the passing of time,
is in reality what is most important.

—Robert Musil, *The Man without Qualities*

I took the one less traveled by
And that has made all the difference.

—Robert Frost, "The Road Not Taken"

Contents

Acknowledgments

THIS IS A LONG BOOK AND IT TOOK SOME YEARS TO WRITE. THE NUMber of people to whom I owe gratitude is great. And, as so often in these cases, this applies whether they gave overt assistance on specifically named matters and issues, or whether their general conversation and their own work and ideas have been a valuable stimulus more widely. So all I can do here is to utter a sincere expression of thanks to all such people, while actually naming some of those whose support has been more specific and immediate.

Six of them were kind enough to read parts of the book at my request, and to give me their comments and advice. Five of these were Peter Larkin, Glyn Purseglove, Chris Stray, Mark Taylor, and M. Wynn Thomas, who each read certain sections of the book. The sixth reader was David Crystal, who read and marked the entire manuscript, and sent me comments as trenchant and exciting as they were detailed. The value of the help of all these six colleagues is incalculable. I can only hope that David Crystal and my other five readers will not be too disappointed at my use of their time-consuming efforts on my behalf. Not only errors, but also any failures or omissions of interpretation or understanding of their advice, are entirely my own responsibility. To all these six colleagues and friends, and many others, my deepest thanks.

My debt to the editors and staff of the Fairleigh Dickinson University Press is equally great. These especially include Julien Yoseloff and Christine Retz, Director and Managing Editor respectively of Associated University Presses; Harry Keyishian and Louise D. Stahl of Fairleigh Dickinson; others I know not by name but by their helpful work on my behalf; and not least the anonymous but most constructive and encouraging critical reader for Fairleigh Dickinson. He or she supplied me with a range of detailed and useful suggestions, all of which were of great value and nearly all of which have been incorporated. Finally, the support of Sarah Ward and all our family remains what it has always been; I here once again give my heartfelt thanks for it to them all.

The Spell of the Song

Introduction

Suppose you asked a cross section of people what they thought poetry is made of. I mean, in the same way that sculpture is made of metal or stone, film of celluloid and palpable events, music of noises, and paintings of paint. Most people would reply "words." I would agree with them. Some indeed would take the words for granted, and so would say metaphors, people, rhythm, or feeling. I would agree with all those, too. A few more might get technical and talk about stanzas or muses and we need not deny those things, either.

Very few would reply "letters"—the letters of the alphabet, from which words are formed. Yet letters—shaped ink-marks or noises—are the one thing we do actually hear on the airwaves or see on the page. As such, they might seem the closest parallel to the stone, metal, noises, and paint of the other arts. Of course, the reason why no one would answer "letters" to our question is that, of all the things just listed, like metaphor, people, rhythm and feeling, letters alone contain no inherent meaning. This observation points at once to an old aesthetic problem in literature. Literature differs from the other arts in using a medium that is public property anyway, and one not manufactured, as pigments or violins are, simply to create objects out of its own material. Indeed literature seems to have no physical material, for the letters of the alphabet, it is said, merely form into words that adduce the meanings, which are what really count.

This book examines many angles on a single question. It may be put thus: *what is it, to constitute or communicate all that we know, mean, think, and feel, and turn that into an art (poetry), by countless rearrangements of a mere twenty-six nonpictorial and seemingly meaningless material signs?*

Whatever the answers, the matter has struck more than one prominent thinker with wonderment.

> There is nothing so strange and at the same time so demanding as the written word. . . . (It) is the intelligibility of mind transferred to the most alien medium. Nothing is so purely the trace of the mind as writing, but

also nothing is so dependent on the understanding mind. In its deciphering and interpretation a miracle takes place: the transformation of something strange and dead into a total simultaneity and familiarity. This is like nothing else that has come down to us from the past.

That is Hans-Georg Gadamer, examining how truth is reached through interpretation of literature. Susanne Langer is equally impressed, using the same term to say so: "This pregnance of the physically trivial form with a conceptual import verges on the miraculous."[1]

The problem, perhaps the mystery, concerns both writing and speech. Letters make for silhouettes or textures both physical and mental by which writing and reading become what they are, and attain the presence we all experience. Writing and speaking, especially poetry, are acts not just of saying but of *say-ing*; doing inscription and utterance; and this raises further questions. What is it, to "say" a thing, how is that a transitive verb? Is the thing already there before I say it or do I say it into existence? Even if the process is not "miraculous," what would move evidently intelligent philosophers to such terms of praise? The question is even more cogent with writing as such. At one level it seems banal, for writing is merely what commits the necessary characters in the right order to paper. But what is the relation between "what I want to say" and the sets of letters that enable this to happen, outside of my mind and on a page? How far does writing, and, after three thousand years, our extraordinary facility at it, itself bring invisible mental activities together, firm them up as projection into the public domain? How far could we think, without the letters that make our words, and what sort of thinking does the letter-principle enable? Maybe we have ignored what that sterling contemporary journal the *Poetry Review* recently called "perhaps the most precious, although least vaunted code we possess."[2] An abecedary has characteristics; it is not just a piece of glass we look through at something else. These characteristics may shape that something-else, or even enable it at all.

It will be suggested later in the book that alphabets, and possibly other comparable sign-systems, seem to explain much about a currently prominent problem in neuroscience; namely, consciousness. Nonpictorial language may be a kind of mirror or sounding-wall, by which the neural system's work can be viewed objectively and so "bounce back," to be reabsorbed by its originator. But for this to occur, not just the structures of grammar and lexicon, but the physical way those are embodied is evidently important. A page of writing in an alien language still seems orderly and refined even though we can't understand it. Maybe these qualities have to be sufficient to mental activity, for that activity to assess itself and so be self-conscious in the first place. Humanistically this suggests the idea of "coming to terms," a three-way metaphor for what neurologists are seeking. "Coming to terms" implies finding a verbal formula that makes us comfortable with whatever problem confronts us. In extreme cases, it is a response to a blow to the self-esteem, a sad bereavement, an alteration in long-term plans, or something similar. At other times it seems like rationalization. But the metaphor is also legal and financial, the "terms" of an agreement; and that suggests a strong measure of precision. And thirdly, "terms" is of course cognate with "terminus," the idea of ends. The objective expression we reach—its exact rendering in words made of letters—clinches the problem that neural consciousness can only experience fluidly. The "terms" that make a situation bearable, or at least comprehensible, lock it into place by arranging their words as fixed, by their letters, to avoid any slippery modification. One can only wonder how this coming-to-terms was done before the alphabet was invented. Did people rationalize their positions in grammars bodied somehow differently? No doubt the authoritative and sacred worldviews that primitive peoples generated performed a similar service. And so maybe the abecedary itself, sacred or secular, has aided in individualizing human consciousnesses over the centuries.

The alphabet is a major halfway case between history and theory, the diachronic and the synchronic. Whatever language is generally, specific alphabets have histories and are used in certain palpable ways. Yet they are too long-lived to be explained by the features of any particular culture. The alphabet, much like the one we have now, was invented three thousand years ago. In human history that is recent; far more so than the development of "cognitive fluidity," proposed recently by Steven Mithen as the feature that distinguished us from Neanderthal man thirty thousand years back.[3] But the abecedary was still there well before what we now call the Western world, even if we also see it as itself a fountainhead of that civilization. The alphabetical idea is like the wheel and knife. Those things are also cultural of course. Yet they have seeped through different cultures for so long that they tend to rise above ordinary cultural analysis. The design of a letter may change—a, **a**, a, *a*, and so on—but the small circle with its overhead loop, that is to say the "grapheme" (the basic unit we will be considering), stays the same. Eras of enormous change, even of revolution, don't affect the principles of the wheel or the knife one jot. Furthermore, since the Renaissance at least, *no revolution political or technological, including those of the last two hundred years, has led to any serious suggestion that a single letter of the alphabet be added or discarded.*[4]

But, even granting all this, how can letters even be discussed? Aren't they still more or less meaningless signs; not especially magnetic; endlessly repetitive and usually tiny, too? Isn't it really the words alone that count? So it might well be argued. Is there anything more to be said?

Letters might seem very simple. In fact, and contrary to widespread belief, they were not invented to record speech. They were invented to combine speech and writing; that is to say, to combine two things—speech and graphicity—that both already existed. Indeed, letters would appear to have three aspects. They are visible signs themselves; they are associated with sounds; and their combinations as words evoke meanings without, however, the letters then falling away. These three aspects thus form a triangle, and if we take any one of them alone we discover that the triangle's center has gone missing. As merely visible signs, letters become word games, puns, calligraphy, print, letter-design, and so on; they seem to peel off the top. As merely sounds, letters disappear altogether into the continuous noise that picks up the word in toto. And as merely servants to meaning, letters leave meaning as a kind of mind-substance we think we possess (even of concrete things); naked of dress or fixable identity, which words themselves capture for us. The letters merely make up those words. All these versions of the letter, when isolated, leave letters as firmly secondary. They are either merely trivial, or are bypassed by speech altogether, or are just a tool of meaning itself.

But if we take letters as our starting point and work from them outward (this happened in medieval education), these parts need not merely separate. Yet the difficulty remains that the conglomerate of the three parts is elusive. The alphabet as it actually functions is the real entity. That is to say, the alphabet not just lying on the page, nor evaporating in speech's temporality, nor yet dissolving away from the meaning it evokes. Yet it is very hard to grasp in its threefold nature. It becomes like the air we breathe, or curved space, or number, or one's name, or death. So frail it seems, yet it might as well be made of cast iron so little chance have we of doing without it even when we can't grasp its reality; a mark in the air, a noise on the page, a group of mark-noises that are a thought. But the resulting experience, the materiality of the thought, is what the alphabet embodies. And this is what Gadamer and Langer saw as "miracle."

To the idea that letters might be important, two common objections can be considered at once. These are the supposedly "arbitrary" nature of alphabetical signs, and the fact that they are tiny. The first will be dealt with later in the book in more detail, but something can be said here. Letters are of arbitrary shape, and we have little idea what may have been intended by their inventors. You can look at a letter here and another there, and find no residue of meaning in them whatsoever. Individual letters may, over thousands of uses, give rise to possibly constant expectations, but it would be unwise to rely on it.

Yet the signs cannot be arbitrary pure and simple. If they were, they would be different sizes at different times and would unpredictably jump about—both techniques exploited by contemporary advertising. While each sign may first have been chosen arbitrarily—this is far from certain—they still evince constant features. The same few signs are always in use; they stray above or below the line only slightly and not in every case; they accrue horizontally in the same direction; a certain rough maximum, in any one language, is used for any word; and by their homogeneity they can be combined in countless ways. And letter-design is subtle; letters are simple enough for ready reading but complex enough to give each a unique flavor, making for the striking silhouettes of individual terms. *Happiness*, *tomorrow*, *emerald,* and *yourself* look and feel as they do because their parts allow it. Poor letter-design is often overornate, not allowing the letters themselves to get on with their work; yet equally a computer-alphabet made of plain dots or barcode stripes would lack in the opposite direction.

Equally though, any original arbitrariness is dispelled post hoc. What began arbitrarily takes on regular use and therefore expectation. True, as said, we cannot rely on this, but still clusters of letters accrue subliminal associations whether they make words or not. In English these spelling-clusters are distinctive because of our irregular spelling. But the post hoc dispelling of the arbitrary origin—if that's what it was—squares with a more general principle. In sport for example: it may be highly arbitrary to agree to kick a ball between posts at each end, or to run races of exactly four hundred meters. But consistencies then begin to appear; the kinds of skills and training needed for each activity, the usual kinds of score or time recorded, the most efficient placings on the football park, or the way to take the final bend. Arbitrary or not, an alphabet is not so utterly random as to fail to offer any qualities at all that are worth attention.

Second, letters are also usually very small. For books to exist at all, signs of microscopic size must appear in their successive millions, and for this very reason there might seem no point and much tediousness in examining them at that level. Counting grains of sand or the perforations of postage stamps evokes little of the sweep of an awesome beach or the place of communication in economic or domestic life. But scrutiny of the microscopic has underpinned virtually all the major scientific breakthroughs of our era. The identification of the DNA molecule and the splitting of the atom have had results so drastic that presumably no argument about them is needed. The most recent emanation of such devastating power is found in catastrophe theory, where John Donne's dictum that *If a clod falls from the main, Europe is the less* has a contemporary counterpart in the stir of a butterfly's wings which a thousand miles away ends in a hurricane.

The microscopic presses on us everywhere. The gene fingerprint means that bodies preserved in peat or ice from millennia back can be linked to living descendants today. Forensic science can trace criminals by identifying minute fiber particles from deposits on clothing far from the scene of the event. A pianist plays something like a hundred chords a minute with little conscious thought about them separately. Camilla Paglia has put it thus: "Had we time or energy to pursue it, each random choice, from the color of a toothbrush to a decision over a menu, could be made to yield its secret meaning in the inner drama of our lives."[5] Equally, then, when some thousands of letters impinge on the retina every minute in ordinary reading, the outlines, bends and straights, sharp angles, or cool curves will leave their traces on our nerve sensors in ways that could make a difference. Indeed, one might posit a kind of law, that small size of letter correlates with greater importance of signification. In simpler terms, books tell you more than posters or noticeboards. This isn't totally foolproof, but one warms to the view of Mike Baldwin of *Coronation Street* fame: "You know it's clever because it's all printed close together." And so maybe the poet touches in letters, like a painter with brush strokes, unconsciously but by the most delicate and rapid feel, dozens at a time. The text gets a texture, an aroma, in which the sets of letters, the murmuring and the hermeneutic tendency are all present, all delectable, and yet all inseparable, too.

There are signs that close analysis of this order is returning in literary criticism. For the past three decades Marxism, feminism, new historicism, biography, cultural studies, and most of the rest have largely neglected the text in its aesthetic provenance. The text has turned from artwork to information; there has been small sense that this matters, and it has seemed at times that some literary academics wouldn't know a poetics if they saw one. But maybe all this is beginning to change. There is for instance Helen Vendler's recent study of Shakespeare's sonnets. Tom Paulin—hardly an unpolitical critic—not only applauds Vendler's work in detail but even avers from its example that "critical accounts of poetry will never be the same again."[6] Paulin shows how Vendler sees "you" inside "youth" in sonnet 15, "sing" and "rings" in "despising" and "brings" in sonnet 29, and numerous further examples. Such close reading can be unpalatable for the reader, and the present book tries to avoid this by always relating the tiny sign and sound to whatever wider cultural emanations call for it. But there have been other reactions. When the Thatcherist response to critical disenchantment with Shakespeare was to cut grants to the Royal Shakespeare Company, Isobel Armstrong, among others, became understandably alarmed.[7] Terry Eagleton's extraordinary monograph on aesthetics itself, despite reservations we might hold toward it, did at least nod to the sense that the aesthetic pervades everything there is.[8] At a recent conference Kiernan Ryan stated unequivocally that criticism must now take back on board some of the activities, in some guise, that were jettisoned in the 1960s. Ryan was happy to hint that he liked some works of literature and admired others.[9]

But equally, a few poets have begun to use the abecedary overtly in our time. Two recent collections from the United States, *Sleeping with the Dictionary* (2002) by Harryette Mullen and *Blue Hour* (2003) by Carolyn Forche are notable in this respect. Both contain long poems whose lines are arranged in alphabetical order by first letter, and this makes for some remarkable effects. Mullen's huge verbal energy spills over into many inventive forms. That her two alphabetically arranged poems are both of the "nonsense" genre seems a key point, for it is the alphabet's ordering quality that brings such outpourings into fixed focus and gives them authenticity as language which is as valid in its place as any other we use. Forche's collection centers on her poem *On Earth,* a fine piece of well over a thousand lines that occupies two-thirds of the book. Its lines are also arranged alphabetically. Forche calls this poem a hymn, and notes its ancient genealogy; but to myself it is also, if surprisingly, Wordsworthian, with its beautiful limpid phrases and rich, natural, and gentle imagery. As with Mullen, though in different mode, the poem's abecedarial ordering anchors the great diversity of reference; yet those two features merge with no strain and effortlessly. With both poets, then, it is the use of the alphabet in its full, spread-out and orderly form—rather than with only local effects such as pun, anagram, neorhyme, and so on—that underlines the presence of this great cultural possession as a poetic means; and that is what is important in our context.

Finally, such close attention to the abecedary has a big payoff for anyone concerned for traditional standards of grammar and spelling in schools and universities. (Bernard Richards's discovery of poor spelling among undergraduates at his university in 1997 has now been followed by a Queen's English Society survey reporting similar findings.)[10] It is difficult to study the matter for long without being so affected, or so I have found. The recent view among some, that spelling doesn't matter, is not supported by people's practice, nor it is hard to refute in itself. To write *freedem* or *micrascope* may seem small errors, but *ortermobeel, perswaid,* and *kayoss* jar by destroying the words' very identities.

Suppose we didn't have the abecedary at all; suppose we did not read or hear words, but rather had the millions of thought-pulses that make up *Paradise Lost* or V. S. Naipaul or Ruth Rendell pumped intravenously straight into our neural systems. How would we experience those works; what would be their luminous presence in our consciousnesses? One might be deeply fond of anything from the Psalms of David through William Shakespeare and George Eliot to the novels of Toni Morrison or Alice Walker. What is the nature of this attachment? Some rows of letters and their evoked sounds, or some disembodied feelings? How can I even remember those feelings, or tell them to myself, without the over-there quality of the contrabodied presence of the letters themselves? My suggestion would be that the letters of words trigger neurological significances with each other, in ancient ways as well as current. New combinations of words, or old words in new rhythms, are themselves interventions into history that push history slightly aside. The actual terms, sounds, meanings, looks, and their stirrings, originating from long before the period in which they are used, are pleasureable in the brain because of what the brain has always kept, or has learned in childhood. Such resonances may stem from millennia before the reader's current awareness—who first said "weapon," "if," "love"?—and were originally not verbal at all. Literary criticism might begin to investigate such things.

Anyone who still doubts that letters have substance of their own might still read what follows as an "as-if" book. In the nineteenth century certain mathematicians invented geometries that accepted the whole of Euclid bar a single proposition. This they deliberately reversed. For example, they assumed that the shortest distance between two points is a curve, or that parallel lines do meet before infinity. In effect they knowingly constructed "as-if" geometries. And these strange geometries proved self-consistent, not the chaos that might be expected. This experiment proved, not that Euclid was wrong, but that his system was finite, limited.[11] Similarly, the arguments that follow in this book could, if readers wish it, be taken as treating letters "as if" they have valency visually as well as aurally, "as if" they affect meaning in other ways than just combining into words, and "as if" they were media somewhat like noise, stone, metal, or paint. The reader is invited to see whether this approach still yields results of interest, which couldn't have been reached from the orthodox position, just as those strange geometries did. Naturally enough, I myself believe that "as-if" is less than the full picture.

If the alphabet's essence is a matter mainly of relations between letter, sound, and meaning, we are likely to be able to get at it only by oblique approaches. For that reason this book has no linear argument moving to a Q.E.D. conclusion, but rather examines letters from many aspects, to find out how far they are at once both elusive and near our language's heart.

The book has four parts. Part 1 offers a selective look at historical attitudes. We go from the abecedary's invention and earlier up to and just after the Reformation in Britain, when the Bible had been translated into English and was widely distributed for the first time. This might seem superfluous to some, but I suggest it could be most valuable. In its early centuries the alphabet was still a remarkable invention, not yet the routine thing we take for granted today. To primitive religion, early recorded philosophy, and ordinary people, the invention was still most palpable, as gene, film, silicon chip, and even automobile are to us now, unaffected by familiarity and uncluttered by our recent civilization's associations with it. Early religion was profoundly concerned with what it saw as the sacred status of language, and the Greek philosophers, especially Plato, still found writing a disturbing intervention. We start then with what primitive people thought language was and where it came from. The invention of the alphabet was speedy, yet it took centuries to become fully flexible. It did not readily record linear speech from the outset, and the so-called "laundry lists" of gold, wheat supplies, armaments, and such were there from the earliest times.

Wisdom was encaptured in proverb form; the alphabetical was stiff, prominent, memorable. All this ties in with primitive belief. Early religions saw language as part of cosmic origin. Creation myths commonly centered on language, light, and water. Certain names were sacred. The alphabet can name nothingness but not the godhead. It can name some absent things and fail to name some present ones. It has unexpected qualities.

After Homer, who took flexibility to new limits, classical thought about the alphabet became possible. Plato was much influenced by Homer, but ambivalently. Plato's famous suspicion not only of poetry but of writing itself—writing as opposed to speech— suggests he did not value its permanence. Plato feared that writing would destroy memory, but also that it could secure falsehood as well as truth in ways that pictorial writing might not. Aristotle's more moderating position comes from an appraisal of Plato. Aristotle could assume that the alphabet was now sitting easily in culture and could take for granted that metaphor, a figure he much valued, depended on nonpictorial signs.

For some critics today the poetic canon of the last four hundred years has filled a hiatus between a full traditional theology of the Word and our own account, in nonabecedarial (for example, scientific) language, of a universe wholly material. On that view the theological argument here is central, though it has to be liberalized as far as possible. Jewish and Islamic sacred texts are touched on; but we necessarily attend to the Christian tradition most of all. In talking of Augustine, I use the relentlessly personal *Confessions*, not the philological or political works. Augustine is never still, and his bodily agitation leads to intrigue with time; he finds rest in Scripture's fixity. Then comes Thomas Aquinas's reasoned theology, exploiting the abecedary's power to render abstraction. Later medieval divines wrestle with the Augustinian body and the Thomist intellect in incarnational terms.

There follows the medieval notion of Nature itself as a great Book to be quite literally read. This needs to be seen in light of the absence of printing, which today we so take for granted. All writing prior to Johann Gutenberg and William Caxton was done laboriously and lovingly by hand, so that a book was a living thing. So to be "lettered" was educationally significant; *gramma* (our "grammar") is the Greek word for a letter. In the sixteenth century William Tyndale produced his English Bible. He translated for the most ordinary of people and drew on the tradition going back to *Beowulf* and the oldest ballads. Like many after him, Tyndale suffered death for his pains; and the whole struggle over the English Reformation, the Tudor revival, and the eventual civil war, can be seen in at least one major dimension as product of the new availability of the abecedary itself, no less, far outside the authority and edifices of the Church. Alongside came the growing humanist tradition of Sir Francis Bacon, Richard Burton, Sir Thomas Browne, Sir Philip Sidney, and their European counterparts. Thanks to writing and the permutable abecedary, conversation could be endlessly extended. The culmination is Shakespeare.

Before going on in detail to the poets, who wrote in the wake of these long periods, we need some analytical categories. So part 2 turns, temporarily, from the historical to the synchronic; we examine the abecedary itself. This is not a matter of treating it letter-by-letter, but of finding general characteristics. I suggest that letters, at least in our alphabet, are *few, stable, equable, physical, virtual,* and *distributive.* Each of these is treated separately in part 2. They raise many questions, and the following remarks merely sketch out the main areas in preliminary fashion.

The vast majority of world alphabets have fewer than thirty letters. Yet the nuances of sound they capture could have led to far more; *fewness* must have had advantages. It makes for easy learning; the alphabet was a democratizer. But much is entailed as a result. What we call alliteration, rhyme, and the rest, must be happening continually, at least in some form, so often are the same few letters repeated. Yet at the same time, as will be seen, the abecedary has ways of moving centrifugally away from this repetition. The abecedary is also both *stable* and *equable.* The standard order of the ancient Greek alphabet from A to T roughly survives in the Western alphabet to this day, the Roman even more exactly. A major outcome is that it is words, rather than letters, that are thus set free to change their meanings down the centuries, or to be ironized, or to let whole texts be constructed differently by different readers. All of this also survives technological advances in book production, print style, and electronic transmission. Abecedarial *equability* refers to the comparable demeanor of each sign. There is of course variety from letter to letter; yet all parts of human experience can be processed through this even channel. A calmness for civilization is achieved; everything can be named.

The *physicality* and *virtuality* of the abecedary take us toward the metaphysical. In one sense at least, letters are patently physical objects; curved, sharp, wavy, spiky, upright or angled, top- or bottom-heavy, simple or complex, and many other things. Sounds vary according to the positions of lips and tongue and power of larynx. Yet letters must strive away from this materiality if they are to render emotional, intellectual, and spiritual entities without grossness. A word is a virtuality, it intellectualizes or registers meaning to the bodily event. To write *arm* but *armed*, *city* but *capacity*, and so much more, enables virtual presences to surface that would be impossible if the abecedary were merely "arbitrary" as is so often said of it. This virtuality is also the enabler of metaphor, which eschews the solidities that would overpictorialize the things compared. *She brought sunshine to the whole garden* depends on the very absence of exact pictorial rendering. Virtuality seems the abecedary's contribution to, perhaps making of, civilization itself.

The sixth feature is the *distributive*. The distributive is the general method of the other five features, their mode of operation. It seminally depends furthermore on a deeper factor; namely, that letters are discrete. Unlike colors for example, letters do not merge into each other; they are an exact consignment of units and the nature of their distribution can be clearly examined in action. Yet this deployment of letters is also most various. It works via different levels, units, periods, modes, lengths, and kinds of word; yet some are banned, as though distribution must also show continence. In part 2 these six features of letters are looked at in readiness for part 3. This brings us to poetry. If we are concerned with the alphabet's very nature, then poetry seems a key place to look for that. Poetry is the art where the abecedary's texture is felt most prominently. In part 3 there are readings of five poets: George Herbert, John Milton, William Wordsworth, Emily Dickinson, and T. S. Eliot, as to how the abecedary appears in them. In the case of Wordsworth, I offer a detailed abecedarial study of *Tintern Abbey* as closely as that can be done while still I hope remaining readable. These poets all lived between the invention of printing and the exploiting of the electronic pulse in the digital computer. Harold Bloom once suggested that most strong poets are secret Kabbalists;[12] my own contention is that, however unconsciously, they have been working the abecedary over the centuries as surely as they have worked metaphor, rhythm, and feeling.

Every letter counts. The poet is responsible for every letter he or she writes. We shall not try to comment on them all! I have simply read selected poems in close detail, occasionally making an actual tally of certain letters by number or position, and reported the main results as approachably as possible. These seem to me intriguing and surprising, indeed at times they jump off the page once one notices them. Doubtless many readers, understandably, will remain skeptical in at least some areas. There are no computer analyses of any poem: when letter-counting occurs, readers will be forewarned.

Then there is the choice of poets. Specific reasons for choosing these five poets will be given at the start of part 3, so only a few brief remarks are needed here. The poets have been chosen somewhat intuitively; all have mattered to myself personally over the years, and between them they evince considerable variety. It seemed best, in the main, to avoid what might have been thought obvious; namely, to use the poets who exploit the abecedary most deliberately and overtly. These might have included such as Gerard Manley Hopkins, e e cummings, and to some extent David Jones. But this could have been a trap or a digression. Hopkins, for example, was so obsessed with the roots of words and their resulting alliterative connections—as his notebooks show—that we could easily have tried to prove a universal principle via a most exceptional example. Our whole point is that since, of necessity, every poet works the abecedary all the time, they must all tacitly evince the point in one way or other. As our major dramatist, Shakespeare would entail so many problems in what follows that it seemed prudent to leave his work out of the overall pattern. There is a two-page excursus on Shakespeare at the end of part 1, and I hope this may suggest how a detailed examination of him on these lines might start if one were so minded. Appendix 3 takes a preliminary look at Hopkins's *The Wreck of the Deutschland.*

When each poet's life and times are also considered, we find quite unexpected connections between their subjects, orientations, and personal lives, and the smallest textures of their verse. Gender, nature, politics, cultural movements, religious doctrine, lyric intensity, and epic scope, and the nervous palpitations of Modernism seem to lie in and through those masses of marks on the page and the sounds, subliminally or out loud, that they evoke. Metaphor, rhythm, and feeling inseparably mediate between these seemingly distant layers. Such, I suppose, is what I am suggesting might be one new if marginal direction for literary criticism, in light of what was said in the introduction on that subject.

In part 4 we enter the postmodern world. This takes the topic forward markedly. To wonder whether not only poetry but also language itself can ever be remotely the same again, may seem too apocalyptic or millennial. But certainly the culture of today throws former eras into a different light even more, it often seems, than has usually been the case at times of great change. Part 4 is retrospective on our language and literature in two ways. The cognitive sciences have upstaged language and consciousness as we knew them; but equally, postmodern culture itself appears to be realigning language as never imagined previously.

Structural linguistics, Chomskyan linguistics, speech-act theory, and psychoanalytic theories of language have all seen major advances in recent decades. To one seeking clues to the abecedary's nature there are interesting results. Little is said in this book—unexpectedly to myself—about Ludwig Wittgenstein or Jacques Derrida. Wittgenstein, who was much influenced by Augustine, is rich with ideas about the abecedary, but his casebook of examples isn't easily lifted from its unique setting in his work.[13] Something comparable happened with Derrida. Neither is wholly neglected here but they tend to appear as occasional references. But consciousness theory, also examined here, is something different again. It seems to x-ray itself; both language and mind disappear before arrays of nerval processes or electron pulsings. The question is how far, as suggested earlier, language remains as the very sounding board that consciousness needs, when it too is so evanescent, so that an ever more refined sign-technology is required to retain equilibrium with it and keep it in existence. The features of the abecedary—fewness, stability, equability, physicality, virtuality, and distribution—possibly each do a special job for consciousness. I also consider contemporary theories of aesthetics, because the abecedary's culmination in poetry itself seems one of its chief emanations.

Part 4 raises a further major matter. In our time there has occurred a letter-explosion with no precedent in human culture. The letters of the alphabet are thrown around in ways inconceivable even half a century ago. T-shirts, advertisement billboard, and news headlines carry them in all colors and typefaces. But they have also gone mobile. Via film, electronics, and aircraft, too, letters can be seen dancing, falling about, shimmering through glass, or trailing through the sky. They move on the screen in all directions, or materialize into place and vanish as quickly. They swing on hinges, become buildings, animals, or sex objects, and in such forms are now among the first experiences of most children. Along with this emerges a set of arts based on new technologies like film and amplified music, and cultural activities such as travel, design, and mass sport. All these are televised to the point that the personal video collection becomes playback of whatever lifestyle the individual viewer chooses. The poetic is no longer a main response to daily experience.

From another flank comes the computer. This writes with the ephemeral electronic pulse, but then generates a whole array of nonabecedarial signs for new generations to adopt as an entirely new mode of communication. Meanwhile, letters themselves traverse the globe in seconds, to be picked up on another screen in a different format and color, added to or subtracted from as the receiver wishes. The most vital, even governmental of messages is informally rendered. Language becomes the vernacular alone. But the computer may also be cutting the corner of language and making a new deal with mind direct. Later in this book my suggestion will be that the six features of the abecedary roughly match Alan Turing's five required features of artifical intelligence. But this could cut both ways. It could suggest that the abecedary has served its purpose or, on the contrary, that its calm and silent shapeliness is what these other violent manifestations of the modern world ultimately depend on, needed if they are to breathe at all. We wait to see what transpires.

Now for some technicalities, qualifications, and limitations. First, in the appropriate spots a bit will be said on calligraphy, printing, and the word processor; that is to say, the particular embodiments of the letter as general. The illuminated manuscript, Caxton and Gutenburg, and electronic writing and other changes now are the parameters of much of the discussion historically and culturally. But our main concern is the letter-as-such, the alphabet system in its nature. The *grapheme*—the letter as indivisible idea and smallest sign in the system—contrasts the "allograph," any different way of writing any one letter; and it is the grapheme that we need to attend to. Regardless of how one writes "m" (*m*, **m**, **m**, m, m, **m**, 𝔪), the three linked verticals must be present, or at least minimally suggested, or no "m" will exist. That is the grapheme, the letter itself, and along with its poetic use the grapheme is the real object of this study.

Then there are the key terms, "abecedary" and "alphabet." I confess to finding the former refreshing, and strictly it is the right term for English. "Abecedary" refers to English's first four letters, unlike "alphabet" which refers to the first two of Greek. It may then be helpful to keep "alphabet" for the general principle and "abecedary" for the alphabet of daily use and with which we shall often be dealing. In practice the word "abecedary" is correct for alphabets, including and, in our lineage, since the ancient Roman, which also begins a-b-c-d. The word "alphabet" is correct for all other systems, for example, Hebrew and ancient Greek. They use a sign for a separate sound. So the early part of part 1 tends to say "alphabet"; after that, beginning with Augustine and for the rest of the book, it is "abecedary." There are appropriate exceptions according to context in both cases.

I have also coined a few terms. These are *rolle, etaison, distance-double,* and *microbillion. Rolle* is a (feminized) acronym for "row of letters," by which is meant the letters of a word voided of its meaning. Thus: "the rolle *eerie* is almost entirely vowels, the rolle *strengths* almost all consonants." It becomes useful at certain points. Many readers will recognize *etaison* as comprising the seven commonest letters of the alphabet in English in order of their frequency. Fortunately, *etaison* is reasonably serviceable as a word in English. Our abecedary is distributed through the lexicon in very uneven rates, itself an aspect of the "distributive" as a feature of alphabets. The "etaison-factor" is a shorthand way of referring to the frequency of the commonest letters.

A *distance-double* will mean a word in which two different letters appear twice or more each, adjacently or otherwise; for example *character, follow, vivid, tumult.* They can be visually prominent and enhance a poetic effect. (Ordinary double-letter words such as *cattle, simmer,* and the like will be referred to as well.) Distance-doubles aren't so rare—we've just written *enhance* and *effect* in the space of four words—but they sometimes seem to matter in poems. Finally, *microbillion* is used to mean anything very tiny that exists in huge numbers of more or less identical size. Ants, cells, grains of sand, stars in the galaxy, even votes; and of course letters. The characteristic arises interestingly from time to time, and one wonders if all such items have something in common.

To refer to single letters without tedium, which will have to happen quite a lot, could also be a problem. To keep writing things like "the letters 'a', 'm,' and 's' are strong in this sentence, and the double 'p' is emphatic," would be hard on the eyes and soon become irritating. The linguists' conventional angle-brackets—<a>, <m>, <s>, and so on—are quite properly used in specialist texts, but they might also be out of place here. A word or name for each letter is required; yet terms like bee, aitch, tee, and so on seemed hazardous. My solution is simply to write each letter five times and treat the result as a word itself. So instead it would be "the letters aaaaa, mmmmm, and sssss are strong in this sentence, while the double ppppp is emphatic." This method probably seems most odd at first sight, but I have found that one gets used to it very quickly.

Sadly, there are also my own incompetences. I have no professional knowledge of biology, neurology, or genetics. Apart from high school and undergraduate Greek, I have had only the smallest acquaintance with any scripts other than our own abecedary. The pillars and doors of the Hebrew script, the sweeping waves and spray-dots of Arabic, and the wattles and reeds of Chinese are things I can only admire with incomprehension. (Incidentally, Western script looks to me like wheels, furniture, and tools.) I make a number of comments about pictographic, ideographic, and logographic scripts, but this is only in general contrast to our own. A fully pictorial script has signs that, if minimally, look like what they indicate. Ideographic signs refer to an idea without naming its sound, while in logographic writing each sign is a whole name, whether sound is included or not. There are other variants, but generally in this book the contrast is between the fully alphabetic script and all other systems.

As to authors, for this book I have used Plato, Homer, Augustine, and others in translation; fortunately I can claim at least some familiarity with the originals, but of course I have had to be watchful in those areas also. No comment is made on these authors' own use of their alphabets. I have little knowledge of Welsh, but gladly acknowledge, after many years in that country, that the strong power of the letter in Welsh poetry, by whatever hidden route, has influenced my thinking on these matters. Lastly, it was delightful and chastening at once to find that various things I thought I might have been the first to have stumbled on were long known to the medieval grammarians. As Ernst Robert Curtius noted half a century ago, the letter and more esoteric figures of speech have largely disappeared from most Western examinations of literature. Education worked from the letter up; to be "lettered" was to be educated, and to be educated was to know one's letters to a degree of thoroughness and implication that is now largely lost to us. A study of the countless medieval figures of speech in abecedarial terms would be a rewarding and informative exercise—but one I have not carried out here.[14]

Most important perhaps, though, are the obdurate matters of spelling, punctuation, capital letters, and the relevant texts generally. Of necessity the poems considered in this book are read in today's standardized texts. As said earlier, the letter survives its typefont or handwritten embodiment because the grapheme, the letter's essential shape, stays the same. But there are certain local exceptions. The notorious sssss, once written like our "fffff" today, can fortunately be ignored. The change to our own form came precisely because of the confusion that the old elongated sssss led to. (Our own sssss was always used at the ends of words anyway.) Capital letters are a different matter. Their common appearance—particularly in the eighteenth century—to start most nouns as well as proper names must have affected reading if anything we say in part 2 about the physicality of the abecedary is valid. Overall, however, the statistical count on capital letters in most mass printing today is low. But we shall occasionally refer to capitals.

The most serious difficulty lies with spelling. It can be exaggerated, and the major spelling changes in our cultural history were in place by about the middle of the seventeenth century. These were the fifteenth century's so-called Great Vowel Shift, sometimes called the Great Spelling Shift, the sixteenth-century fashion of reflecting the etymologies of Latin and Greek, and soon after that the spate of words entering English from other European countries. But everybody knows, even so, that Shakespeare did not write *perjured, murderous, bloody, full of blame* in sonnet 129. He, or his scribe, wrote *periurd, murdrous, blouddy full of blame*. Such differences level out in the centuries approaching our time but aren't altered for most of the seventeenth century, including in Milton and Herbert. So, if the claim is that letters on the page are germane to our feeling for the poetry they present, we must answer a serious challenge. If spelling is important, then a poem originally spelled differently from what we read now must to some degree be lost to us.

There are two main answers to this problem. The first is that the standard texts in modern print just are where the vast majority of reading of poetry old and new is done. The perusal of earlier books as artifacts, a much-growing and interesting study itself, is the province of the scholar, not the student let alone the layperson. We must take the texts as we find them, no matter by what route they reached us, and the merit of modern printing is that its very impersonality, devoid of medieval calligraphy, Victorian print capital-flourishes, and the poet's own handwriting, too, gives a generalized clarity in which the letter emerges in simple form. The grapheme, still materially based of course, survives all the more strongly. But of course, to those who think letters just record sound, this argument makes no difference. If the two renderings of Shakespeare's line are orally the same—not necessarily the case—it does not matter how they are spelled. This second argument calls for a separate answer.

The flaw in this second argument is that it applies equally to pronunciation. If sound in poetry were all—and it is of course very great, as will be much insisted in what follows—then regional and chronological variations in pronunciation would equally modify any supposed constancy the poem offered. To counter that too, we would have to say that neither writing nor sound mattered next to the meaning, a view that would kill off the gut visceral realities in which poetry's meaning is actually bodied. Furthermore, the argument would apply to most of the other arts. We find Greek statues beautiful yet we know they were originally painted in many colors. We admire portraits in art galleries, well aware that plucking them from the manor or castle they were painted for must modify them for their viewers. And we love Handel's *Messiah*, knowing full well that what we usually hear is simply not, or not exactly, what he wrote, nor are the accompanying instruments as he would have known them. Yet we still think of it as Handel's *Messiah* and credit it, surely rightly, to Handel. And we feel a continuing gratitude to both the composer and ancient sculptor for what they produced, even when we know it is now somewhat different.

How can this be? Aside from any pleasure's power to stir the impulse to praise, there is also, I believe, an organic continuum in a work of art that carries over these proportionately small changes and textual variants intact. This is not to mystify the matter. On the contrary, it says quite simply that often when we say that something has "totally changed" from what it was before, we mean that about 5 percent of it has changed and the rest stayed the same. This applies in the quite different context of, for example, revolution. During such crises most people continue to breathe, walk, speak the same language, experience night and day, summer and winter, and find the shapes of hills and rivers, and even tables, sidewalks, and cars around them roughly as they were previously. Of course, there are real local changes, in works of art (for example, newly discovered manuscripts) as well as by revolution. But if so, so be it; works of art, like laws of physics, are themselves in a state of glacially slow but still measurable, and slightly awesome, change. We live with this. At some deep level, our reference to "Sophocles's plays," accurate enough in one way, accommodates the metaphysical and practical flux that any understanding of existence has always had to acknowledge. The works we read just are the ones the poet wrote, even though they too are subject to the universal laws of reality that we can't do a lot about anyway. And textual scholars do much, of course, to restore works to the state in which their authors originally left them. There, it seems, the matter has to rest.

Finally in this introduction, we need to consider the "sight versus sound" debate, which still concerns linguists and which has run for so long. As said already, many people still think that letters simply record sound. So if written letters turn out to be important in poetry too, where sound is at its most potent, it might underline their place in language and literature more generally. But there is no denying

poetry's gut experience. Poetry would be nothing without sound—
dead mutton, a lunar world, lumps of inert matter on the page with
no power to catch the breath, enlighten, or give joy or heart. Poetry
would lack the very embodiment of feeling that was its primal impulse and has been ever since.

> Little think'st thou, poor flower,
>   Whom I have watched six or seven days,
> And seen thy birth, and seen what every hour
> Gave to thy growth, thee to this height to raise,
> And now dost laugh and triumph on this bough,
>   Little think'st thou
> That it will freeze anon, and that I shall
> Tomorrow find thee fall'n, or not at all . . .

*

> Forgive my grief for one removed,
>   Thy creature, whom I found so fair.
>   I trust he lives in thee, and there
> I find him worthier to be loved.
>
> Forgive these wild and wandering cries,
>   Confusions of a wasted youth;
>   Forgive them where they fail in truth,
> And in thy wisdom make me wise.

What possible worth would such pieces have without the aural
throb and hum of humanity that pervades them? Their very presence starts us murmuring. Nobody ever says, purely and simply,
"How beautifully the letters have been laid out, what harmonious
patterns they make for the eye." It is their resonance that matters.
The poet the late Ted Hughes deplored that few of us now know
poems by rote. Milton could recite most of Homer, as could the
novelists' father Patrick Bronte all of *Paradise Lost*. When Wordsworth read the whole of *The Prelude* out loud to family and friends
at Coleorton in the winter of 1807, they were delighted, none more
than Samuel Taylor Coleridge. (And they had no manuscripts on
their knees to follow, either.) One of my own major life experiences
was once to hear Wordsworth's poem "Michael" read aloud by
Angus Easson at the place it was written about—high up in Dungh-
eon Ghyll, a magnificent rising valley near Grasmere. Shakespeare
registered the basis explicitly:

> The man that hath no music in himself
> Nor is not moved with concord of sweet sounds,

Is fit for treasons, stratagems, and spoils;
The motions of his spirit are dull as night,
And his affections dark as Erebus:
Let no such man be trusted . . .
                    —*The Merchant of Venice*, 5:83–88

Composition often begins orally. A sentence or phrase resonates, or a topic, long mulled over, finds an oral movement within itself. But it is not just poetry. There are great speeches too, ancient liturgies, and that notable case that more than one contemporary British poet has exploited;[15] namely, the haunting list of the shipping weather zones round the British coast: *Wight, Dover, Thames, Humber, Dogger, Tyne . . . Viking, Finisterre, Forties, Cromarty, Fastnet, Rockall, Malin, Irish Sea . . .*

Even so there is an answer to all this. Shakespeare got it right, surely; the music is "in himself." In Octavio Paz's formula: "To read a poem is to hear it with our eyes; to hear it is to see it with our ears."[16] We usually read poetry rather than having it recited. There is no noise, no one watching us hears anything, for it is "in the head." We experience its sound, but in silence; and just what that contradiction means, and how it entails the written page, is the heart of the issue. This too applies beyond poetry and to ordinary people. We read on the train, in bed, on the beach; newspapers, thrillers, postcards from friends. If all poetry had to be read aloud, Poems on the Underground (a London subway venture) would have been not a success but a disaster.

Indeed, the common dictum that "all poetry should be read aloud" seems to call for rethinking. If poetry really had to be read aloud in order to be apprehended, students of honors English would spend most of their time chanting. They couldn't cover the Canterbury Tales or *The Dunciad* without it. In practice, they don't even get a play-through on tape. Music sales on CD and cassette number millions. Why then are there not comparable sales for poetry tapes? Beyond poetry, it is even more drastic. How often are *Middlemarch* or *Our Mutual Friend* read out loud, or Salman Rushdie or Joyce Carol Oates? And in an era in which the word has been made palpable, works emerge like Ezra Pound's *Cantos* or James Joyce's *Finnegans Wake*. Oral readings of these can be intriguing, but only by going against the grain of the work's evident presence.

Then there are the ways we refer to all our activities. We play tennis, cook gourmet food, and write poetry. *Write* poetry? There isn't a word to describe composing poetry orally, and "Do you compose poetry?"—a verb once apt for both typesetting and music[17]—would now sound a little antiquated. The same applies to reception. No one asks, "Do you listen to poetry?" They ask whether you read it. Of course, one might ask people if they go to poetry readings, and so underline a desirable element of the communal, exactly what silent reading could be said to lack. Yet although after attending a reading we may say, "I liked her poetry, I must get her book"; we don't say, on reading a collection of poems, "I liked that, I must listen to it sometime." Whatever the social reasons, the result is incongruous, and the suggestion remains that the relation between the subliminal sound and the printed page is where the real experience currently lies, most of the time. (The history of linguistics over the last half century evinces a remarkable change over the matter. We can't go into the specialist field here, but the whole issue is discussed in appendix 1).[18] In contrast to the earlier view that language is speech and writing is a linguistically irrelevant record of speech—itself a reaction to the earlier view still, that writing is everything—most linguists now regard both modes of communication as independent. Both have virtues apt to themselves and severally increase the richness of language. The view (discussed later) that the invention of the alphabet itself enabled speech to become self-knowing is particularly illuminating.

Rather than objecting to it, one might ask whether the power of letters to give us such beautiful sound-in-silence isn't pretty amazing. The harmonious signs on the page touch the murmurings in the mind that they evoke. This may be why the actual editions we use can become precious. Jerome McGann is at least partly right; there is a difference between one physical rendering and another, and our affections can get drawn in.[19] But the more general principle was put by John Keats: "Heard melodies are sweet, but those unheard / Are sweeter; therefore, ye soft pipes, play on . . ." Shakespeare's "sweet sounds" (from *The Merchant of Venice*, just quoted) is the same metaphor. It appears again in a recent statement. "The test of a poem . . . is the extent to which it lodges in the memory, not necessarily in word-perfect form, but as a kind of presence whose sweetness one recalls at times throughout one's life."[20] The sweetness lies in the rich mix of inscription, silent-sound, and meaning together.

It may be replied that all this silent reading is one of our time's great losses, connected to poetry's wider decline. Recent research implies that medieval literature was commonly read aloud, not just due to minimal literacy and the lack, then, of printing, but because the Middle Ages valued shared experience. It is not true that orality is somehow unanalytical and primitive or that everyone would turn to the book if they could.[21] The short answer to this is that silent reading needn't go unshared, either. The processes of connection lie elsewhere, in discussion, film, nuances of public implication. Most people value sex, and in some way or another religion, or at least the matters religion raises. But sex is (still) largely private in the witness, and religion equally in important ways, too. The decline of poetry as a leading art seems to stem from quite different causes, for film and television set the ethos and the pace, and literature either stays off deliberately or gets embroiled in the new media's terms.

As audience figures for culture and entertainment go, public poetry readings today can't be rated highly. Of course, technicalities are involved. Philip Larkin objected that you missed things like punctuation, shape, and enjambment, and you never knew how far an unfamiliar poem was from its end.[22] But it is more than that. Must we conclude that most poetry readings are pretty dreary events? The audiences sparse, the mode amateur, the surroundings unappetizing; the tentative "introductions" by the reader, apologetic, jokey, or defiant, the poets themselves too often seemingly unaware of the rift between the universality of their work and the particular timber of their own larynxes. So easy, and foolish, to mock, one might reply; we aren't here for glitzy entertainment, freebies, and the rest, and if you want the pure experience you accept its circumstances—let alone that poetry today lacks the funding to jazz up its readings in the ways consumer society likes. All true. But the point remains about the poem's universality and the reader's unique voice. The deliveries from soapboxes at London Waterloo railway terminus on National Poetry Day seldom enabled the poem; they more often prevented it. Reading the poem aloud presses it into a single time-strand and an overspecific rendering; it can destroy the very echo on which the poem depends. The voice can articulate each word only one way at a time. With silent reading there is a more saturated presence. This can only work out loud, therefore, when society itself is of one mind, so that the public voice can dominate the several inner ones, assuming, or forcing them into, unity. What is needed now is a kind of ethereal amalgam of voice, which the poem subliminally evokes in each reader personally and which the poem really is. The sound is in the mind; the sound, one might say, is the mind, and there is no discernible boundary, neurologically, between the visceral shift, the emotion, and the sound entailed by it. And we know that, with poetry, that is a stunning experience.

There are of course the great readings: Eliot's of *Prufrock*, Rich-

ard Burton of Dylan Thomas—and Dylan Thomas of Dylan
Thomas—even if they are not common. Professional radio readers
in Britain such as Joan Balcon, Hugh Dickson, and Peter Barker are
very effective, precisely because their quiet intonations leave room
for the reader. They seem to know how to be tactful, and touch off
our responses rather than imposing their own. The critic F. R.
Leavis practiced a deliberately flat monotone for like reasons, as
did the poet R. S. Thomas. But such examples only argue that reading aloud is possible and can be well done, not that it is essential.
The reading page is, it seems, the natural location for the poem in
our era. Poetry's sociality today lies in its very background quality,
its deeper presences.

The abecedary bodies our words; it gives them body. The written
form's permanence accommodates time in its briefest and longest
manifestations. In doing so it actually reverses the oral experience.
Orally the words are spoken and we statically wait for them. Visually the words wait, on the page, and we the readers move across
them. Reading silently for oneself allows time's varying speeds, its
doubling back, its dependence entirely on what occurs within it. It
is different with music, for music fabricates its time as it proceeds.
English irregular spelling lets one syllable or word slip easily away
after another, for the reader scans letters in groups, not individually.
Irregular spelling also sets different microspeeds of apprehension
going at once. The rolles don't just add up numerically to their
words; they follow each other, alternatively accumulating and leaving each other behind. And the letter, vvvvv for example, doesn't
just instruct or recall the sound "vee," it enjoins it in a certain way
according to context. This counters the time as "duration" that Augustine but also Henri Bergson noted as an invisible element we
push against. Without writing, culture's loss would have been ti-
tanic.

Letters have no physical depth in principle. They have no shadows; the meanings they evoke are their shadows. The printed page
is a surface, a receptor of light. The page's permanence lies in its
flat existence under the light. The relation between sound and light
in mythology is a profound one, and has been expressed by Geoffrey Hartman, among others.[23] The prototype form is the fiat: *Let
there be light*. This utterance of the godhead must have had speech
first, for it to be able to be said at all. But it then expresses a longing
for light; that is to say enlightenment, illumination. When the light
yields comprehension, then does sound come, and the poem's deepest resonances begin to stir themselves. The solitary reader is
moved to utterance, and may do that compulsively. But the joy too

lies in that the utterance has attained permanence. My own test case for this idea is W. H. Auden's elegy "In Memory of Sigmund Freud" (see appendix 5). One feels the poet selecting every word with the greatest care, dwelling on each in its choiceness; and as a result the poem stirs into aural life. Certainly Auden's alcaics were a prechosen form, but that was no guarantee of success in itself. Beneath the light, the letters' individual shapes suddenly, if modestly, assume great importance. The sculptor and letterist Eric Gill wrote that we like letters, not because they remind us of objects, bodies, sticks, fruit, or the like, but because their shapes are "connatural to the human mind."[24] Under the light's fixed gaze they have to be. It takes them as far from the arbitrary as is possible.

I want to say that the poem "shimmers" on the page, but it doesn't really; the look is more static. It is more like the effect of calm water, or a new-fallen sheet of snow. Where is the beauty when you look down through a perfectly clear lake and see every detail of the stones and weeds on the bottom? For few would deny how compelling that sight is. But it can't just lie in the stones and weeds, for when the water disappears in drought or fallen tide, the same stones and weeds just look gray and dull. But it can't be just the water either, for mere water is so transparent as to seem nothing. The relation of the two seems required. It is the same with a sheet of snow, which, one imagines, would not look especially attractive in a large roofed arena. Laid out across a field in open country, perfectly flat or with the most gradual curves on it, it contrasts the light we see it by. This can occur too, paradoxically, very movingly at night, when the relative lack of light is what all the more brings out the snow's awesome power still to be visible, so uncompromising and irresistible is its whiteness.

Of course, all this is mere analogy. Usually we don't see the page consciously. But people often don't see a landscape consciously either, yet afterward remember how beautiful it was. If the letters are the only route to the meaning, in what sense can we have not seen them in themselves, consciously or otherwise? Numerous people have praised the book and its pleasures; this is not new. The Elizabethans went into rhapsodies over it. With no doubt more professional motive, Harriet Martineau wrote of how "the lines burn themselves in on the brain" when you see yourself in print for the first time. In our time C. S. Lewis, Roland Barthes, Peter Redgrove, Jonathan Miller, George Steiner, and others have recorded similar sentiments.[25] The Welsh poet Saunders Lewis expressed the feeling as well as anyone:

You can contemplate words. By contemplate I mean stare at them. I appeal to a common experience. A line or verse of a poem comes to your mind. You speak it to yourself and relish its music or burden. But often that is not enough; you fetch the book and seek the page. You have a desire to see the line in its printed setting. The sight enhances the pleasure. The look of the letters, their spelling and arrangement between the margins of the white page, add a something to the enchantment of the heard poetry. I believe that is a quite common experience.[26]

The present book assumes this position.

I

The Abecedary: Some Historical and Cultural Foundations

IN THIS BOOK WE ARE GOING TO TAKE SERIOUSLY THE IDEA THAT, IN writing poetry, at least one aspect of the medium poets use is the alphabet or abecedary itself, the actual letters. Therefore, just as with any other aspect of writing, it won't be enough to take the alphabet simply at face value. We shall need, across several eras, to consider the alphabet's own cultural background; its origins and what went before it; its uses across centuries in different cultures and different circumstances; a little of the technology that evolved for the spread of it; and how it has been entailed in forming people's deepest beliefs. All this furthermore has to cover, or at least hint at, long eras from the beginnings up to not so long before our chosen poets lived and wrote. This is the aim of part 1 in this book, and such a survey will necessarily be both sketchy and selective. Yet we may still hope to find ourselves left with a number of principles, lines of thought, recurring practices, and attitudes that seem traceable to the alphabet itself. These ideas will be helpful when we come to the close-up analysis of the alphabet in part 2, and of its presence in a number of poets in part 3. Despite or because of the wide range of cultures entailed, our medium for this purpose is necessarily English. But wider principles need not be suppressed by the act of translation, as we shall see. Certainly it would be ideal to look at different languages, but the obstacles in practice seem insuperable.

Since this survey is going to try and cover two or three thousand years in some sixty pages—a tall order to be sure—it must be severely selective in its choice of eras, cultures, and texts for closest attention. Here then, first, is a brief preliminary summary of what is to follow in part 1[1]. First of all there is, broadly, the age-old period that led up to the invention of the alphabet at the very start, and some early consideration of what that implied for the alphabet when it did appear. The next era takes a large chunk of the first millennium B.C. in ancient Greece. The main start-and-finish writers here are Homer and Plato, and we shall give them the most attention along with a broad picture of the cultural events and changes behind the era's ideas. The third era for consideration is much of the first millennium A.D., and this will be considered exclusively as to the presence of the alphabet in the writings of major Christian theologians. Again we take two writers for main focus; namely Augustine and Thomas Aquinas, but with the wider background and some other writers also present. Finally we look at the first half of the second millennium A.D., in effect from the first English Bible translator William Tyndale up to and a little after the English Reformation. Here however there is some parallel attention to the more secular, political, and, in the end, humanistic features of this period. This last period brings us up to just a century or so before the three-hundred-year era of the poets we later consider in part 3. And it is now incumbent on me as preliminary to explain, as briefly as I can, why and how I have chosen these various eras and the items in them.

We are going to suggest in part 2 that the abecedary is not neutral; it has features and capacities. So it seems essential to start by looking at what the abecedary grew out of, what preceded it, and how it particularly seemed to add to and improve upon that earlier position. It is worth remembering at the outset that we can easily take the alphabet for granted, just because, in one sense, it has been with us virtually unchanged for so long. But of course, human beings neurologically identical to ourselves had already lived on this planet for some thirty thousand years minimum previously. They got by without the alphabet, just as we now get by—and find recently among us people like William Shakespeare, Isaac Newton, and Abraham Lincoln who got by—without whatever innovations appear in eras far, far ahead of our own times. For where genetic engineering, space travel, and the Internet will be at such times—if they aren't long superseded in their own turn—is to us almost inconceivable. A number of things emerge from those very early periods. It seems for instance that the alphabet was not merely a superimposition on something already in place but alone, namely human speech. Rather, graphicity (the making of any marks whatsoever both intentional and significant) and speech (the parallel making of intentional and significant noises from the human larynx) were both present from the start and then gradually came together. Prealphabetical writing methods gradually incorporated signs for sounds.

Furthermore, alphabetical writing, when it did appear, did not then merely record speech. As David Olsen has put it (in a work to be cited later), it quickly came to offer a model for speech. In hindsight we can see something of the conditions in which both writing and speech functioned before this merger occurred. We can also see what these early peoples themselves took language to be, and this too is instructive for our theme. Language is invariably prominent in creation myths. This suggests that people saw language, as we do, as a datum in human existence if "human" means humans whose capacities were as great as our own. Again if we think, as I do, that the different letters of the abecedary themselves have unique features—which the poets use—then it will be interesting at least to speculate on why the different signs were chosen and what weight was given them. We find too that writing sometimes continued, other times altered or enhanced, what people had already long noticed about both speech and prealphabetical systems of writing. Single words could become freighted with permanent value; they could be "sacred"; and single phrases or sentences as well, in what we have come to call proverbs. Unlike prealphabetical systems too, the alphabet found an important feature in repetition. The same words, phrases, or sentences could be reused in ways that added a different valence to what had been previously possible. There has also been speculation on how far the alphabet enabled the development of the earlier writing's rather limited "across-down matrix"—lists, tables, inventories, and so on—through to the extended sentence in which poetry and prose came to be able to be written. Finally, we encounter the primitive recognition that some things can't be named at all. This reminds us that, however long and pervasively the abecedary has been with us, it is still just one more human technology just the same. And yet, surprisingly, other things can indeed be named that might seem to have no obvious existence; in effect "the unknown." All these features of those earlier periods help build up a general context against which the more specific features of the abecedary can then be evaluated in clearer profile.

The second millennium B.C. saw the evolution and emergence of the high period of civilization in ancient Greece. If, as many believe, the Greek alphabet was invented just before the time of Homer—it may even have been invented to record those very poems—then clearly the question arises of how far the alphabet itself was key to that emergence. This is why we include this era, too, for attention here in part 1. But there is another, associated question. For we must also ask how far rationality itself, as it appeared in the flourishing of philosophy in Greece in approximately 500–350 B.C., was, in hindsight, actually enabled by the invention of the alphabet. There has been much discussion about the development of language and thought in this long era. It goes from the rich but single-paced Homeric poems through to the embodiment of logic; main and subordinate clauses as reflections of qualifying thought; the classical syllogism, and so on, with which Greek philosophy was marked. There are complexities here. The chief development was perhaps not just recorded thought itself, but dialectic; the statement-and-answer, or question-and-answer, by which thought of this kind evolved.

In that case it is not just a matter of a straight change from poetry to philosophical prose. The gradual appearance of the short lyric and the chorus; the appearance of classical Greek drama with its crucial addition of separate individual actors into the dramatic single-line chorus; the later emergence of dialectic into political and courtroom oratory in practical everyday disputes—all these went along with philosophy in the general development of the dialectical way of expressing events and ideas, and their recording or indeed creation in writing. As philosophy too multiplied its targets in this process, there emerged both the examination of reason and, also dialectically, the identification and classification of different areas of knowledge. Much of this will have to be dealt with only cursorily in what follows, and the main attention will be on Homer and then Plato himself. But the issue of dialectic taken broadly is clearly central. Things could gradually be studied, compared, rebutted, contrasted, over time. Consciousness of words as objects begins to grow, even if consciousness of that very consciousness itself came only very slowly. Finally, it will be intriguing to ask a couple of questions about the length of time all this took to happen. Only in about the sixth century B.C., some three hundred years after Homer, did science, philosophy, and, later, drama begin to appear in even rudimentary form. Furthermore and famously, Plato himself was still chary about the very existence of writing as late as four or five hundred years after Homer. All of this again, then, should deepen our sense of the alphabet's importance for the civilization from which, in broad outline and of course not exclusively, emerged our own.

And so to the next great era. It is hardly surprising that, if we are looking at the alphabet itself, then, certainly from Western civilization's viewpoint, the advent of the life of Christ raises huge issues of its own on the subject down those same centuries. These too claim our attention. To all Christendom, Jesus was and is "the Word made incarnate," while the alphabet is the very means by which, via words, we inscribe our immediate feelings and extended thoughts at all. Christianity is claimed to take ancient Judaism's emphasis on Scripture and the Law into a different kind of life; but equally it raises matters that were of little concern to ancient Greece. Perhaps these can be conveniently summarized under three headings; namely sin, will, and theological authority. The early Christians spread the new message into Mesopotamia and Parthia; Gaul and Spain; Syria, Arabia, and Illyria; and into the major cities of Antioch, Corinth, Carthage, and Rome. They were also victims of wholesale persecutions themselves. These two large events, along with the highly personal factors of both appeal and demand that the new faith made on individuals, soon led to the widespread phenomenon of heresy. Just what constituted the new canon, in effect the New Testament? Who was empowered with the authority to decide? And if Christ is alleged to have made all men free, and given us all free will, what is wrongdoing, what is sinful? Is heresy "sin," or merely a well-intentioned mistake, if mistake it be?

Such was the world—one whose memory still stretched back just to the ancients—in which Augustine was born in A.D. 350. In his lifetime the official creeds (the major response to heresy) were established by the Four Ecumenical Councils. By the time of Thomas Aquinas, born almost exactly nine hundred years later, the Church's superstructure virtually governed European culture. The greatest and most powerful popes, Gregory I, Leo I, Gregory VII, Innocent III, and others had established the near-impregnable papal system. The monastic system with its leading orders had been set up. The Roman Empire massively declined; in the eighth century Islam captured most of the lands east and south of the Mediterranean, and the sad story of the Crusades ran its course three centuries later. Though we can barely touch on it here, the influence of Islamic thought on the West was a major thread in the burgeoning of European philosophy and science. Meanwhile, pope continued to vie with emperor, with victory and defeat occurring on either side. In the world of education and thought more specifically, the chief texts of Aristotle were at last newly translated and disseminated; and, beginning with Bologna and Paris, the European system of universities from Naples in the south to Oxford in the north was established. Aquinas himself was an early student at Naples and twice studied in Paris.

So a key reason for selecting Augustine and Aquinas for closer treatment here is the long period they span. Loosely speaking, they are the start-and-finish theological peaks of this long millennium. No other Christian theologian or religious thinker or philosopher has had greater influence than theirs. But the great contrast between them, in their writings and personalities, is also suggestive. Aquinas, unique to be sure, is also the summit of a certain kind of thinking to which many could and did aspire. Augustine was his own man. Augustine attracted friends and enemies like a magnet; Aquinas embodied a more level serenity. Aquinas's writing is a model of consistent lucidity, while Augustine was a literary genius whose *Confessions*—to which we give main attention—has been described as the single classic by a Church father to retain that status in our own world. Augustine was also a doughty fighter, but also, paradoxically, a settler of violent disputes. Aquinas's life didn't lack for danger at times; even so, he was a scholar and thinker first and last. He produced a synthesis of Christianity with Aristotelian thought, while Augustine had no philosophical training, knew only Plotinus of the ancients, and lacked any major previous Christian intellectual guidance other than the Bible itself. Our comparison of the two men, then, and their notably different ways of writing, will surely also generate ideas for this book's topic.

Finally, our treatment of the period leading to the English Reformation and after perhaps needs less overt comment. It is more of a quick survey in cultural history, and so takes no main writer for close attention. But some readers might wonder about one or two choices. I have focused much more on Tyndale's Bible than on the King James Version. The later is more familiar anyway; but Tyndale's version is also so down-to-earth that it helps switch us finally from Latin text (though in translation here) to the English and indeed Saxon tradition. As is pointed out, and of course as with the King James version too, countless English expressions that survive today first appeared in Tyndale's Bible. Though briefly, we also take a quick glance at some preceding writing: *Beowulf,* Geoffrey Chaucer, and even Anon. I go on to cite passages from Burton and Bacon rather than the preferred Montaigne for the same reason, namely, that they are in English. And I hope the few comments offered on Shakespeare will provide at least an orientation toward how one might carry out an abecedarial reading of his work. Finally, in dealing with Tyndale, the Reformation, and the burgeoning of humanism, we must justify giving no more space than was given to just two writers, Augustine and Aquinas. The defense is dual. Literacy and language were effectively—and with great achievements attained—in the Church's hands for a millennium, and that had to be adequately considered. But equally, the later hundred years from roughly 1550 to 1650 is so rich that a whole book, or another part in this one, would be required to treat it properly. In any case, in part 3 we shall move into the equally humanistic period of the poets we there treat. It can be hoped that they will carry on the story there.

At the end of each section in this part 1, we shall also give a brief summary of how some of the main observations made and abecedarial features found in each section help set up the main categories of the abecedary to be discussed in part 2. There are six of these categories (listed in the introduction): fewness, stability, equability, physicality, virtuality, and distribution. I hope this brief summarizing will be a helpful preparation for what happens in part 2. Naturally enough, the interesting items we dig up in part 1 won't always turn out to fit conveniently into just one of these six part 2 categories. However, many of them do so readily enough, and I trust the exercise will be worth it.

1

Beginnings

THE ALPHABET WAS INVENTED ABOUT THREE THOUSAND YEARS AGO. It was a brilliant way of combining the two aspects of language that had existed in rudimentary form since Homo sapiens replaced Neanderthal man on this planet. As a result of the new alphabet, earlier attempts to denote speech in writing came to seem clumsy. The two aspects, the aural and the visual, were primal foundations; noise-of-throat and mark-on-material. Archaeological reconstructions of early human vocal tracts on the one hand, and the subtlety of the cave paintings from thirty thousand years back on the other, show that these two techniques had been present in human society millennia before the alphabet was invented.

Early in the twentieth century, linguists described the relation between the two aspects rather emphatically. Language is speech; writing is merely a record of it. Certainly they were responding to the preceding philological tradition that had made writing central. But Ferdinand de Saussure and Leonard Bloomfield, founding fathers of modern linguistics, flatly insisted on writing's rebuttal. "Language and writing are two distinct systems of signs; the second exists for the sole purpose of representing the first." When Bloomfield wrote twenty years later in 1933, he virtually borrowed Saussure's terms.[2] The obvious irony in this is that linguistics itself depends on writing for its very existence. This was not lost on them, nor on Walter Ong, who later wrote of writing's unfortunate—as Ong saw it—dominance of literate culture. Linguists today, by contrast, do not discount writing in this fashion (appendix 1 has fuller detail on this debate). Reams of printed matter record nothing that was ever spoken or ever will be. We can gather a word's meaning from its visual silhouette with no sound present. And as will be seen, language was never necessarily linear. None of this denies that letters were devised to indicate vocal sounds; it merely underlines that the relationship between the two is two-way and complex. However, our first aim, as far as the hazy evidence allows it, must be to consider both vocal and scriptive articulation—noise-of-throat and mark-on-material—as independent sources in language evolution toward the alphabet.

We don't really know how language began or developed. Indeed, there was probably no clear change from no-language to language over any relatively short period, any more than there was from no-eyeball to eyeball, as evolutionists since Charles Darwin have often pointed out.[3] But some general factors can be identified that may have predisposed full speech and full writing when each finally came.

Research has a couple of main themes as to speech. Speech stemmed from the human capacity to make noises and from daily social pressure to communicate. Mouth-emitted sound from the larynx of any kind whatever—coughing, sighing, roars of triumph—may have evolved into significant words over centuries. Recent work suggests that language and the brain emerged inseparably; the development of a signifying intelligence just is the development of a relationship between matter and humanity's capacity self-knowingly to apprehend it. And there are views as to how this may have happened. Early humans, whether Homo erectus or Homo sapiens later, reacted to natural or animal noises. There may be similarities to the trace patterns and top sounds of birdsong. The instinctual noises of anger, delight, or pain may have gradually gone formal, the grunts of hard toil turning into regular oral language via rhythm and chant. The sounds of sex and reproduction could occupy expression's heart because of what they are in fundamental fertility. From any or all of these starts, sound-symbolism generally was one likely outcome. There is a problem with all this, for by the nature of the case, speech left no record of itself. Furthermore, if such sounds and motions were the ultimate sources of speech, certain features of language would have been more prominent than they actually are. But as a general possibility it is reasonable, and in any event it is all that we have to go on.[4]

Equally, speech may have grown for social purposes, such as to convey vital daily information. But it isn't clear how the process could ever have launched itself. But a recent suggestion, combining two disparate pieces of evidence, may throw light on this. From archaeological studies of bone findings it seems that, as the human vocal tract developed and as compared to our close relatives the primate monkeys, breathing, chewing, and swallowing declined in efficiency. But breathing and eating are basic to survival, so communication must at some point have become rather important if those other functions could be put at risk. Along with this too, however, the fossil record shows that neocortex size predicts and correlates with group size. That is to say, the enlarging power of speech—putting breathing and eating at risk—came to be urgently needed for control and cohesion in larger human groups. Till then, physical grooming had been a main way of tightening social relationships. But grooming occurs between pairs of individuals and takes time, whereas you can address thirty or more people at once fairly easily. Since individuals at periods in their lives can, broadly, relate meaningfully to as many as 150 others (the figure usually given in sociopsychological research), clearly language might have displaced grooming when social coherence became a priority—for example, for defense against enemies. Mircea Eliade's famous suggestion was that early societies annually tried to regenerate the creation itself in order to stay close to their beginnings. This view squares with Robin Dunbar's argument that self-display among males, and social networking among females, spreads outward from the single aim of choosing mates to that of keeping the wider clan or tribe unified. As well as grooming and gossip, altruism and a specific language-gene have also been suggested. There is further evidence as to primitive brain size, intelligence, and speech capacity.[5]

But written language, too, may be cognate with human evolution. Maybe inscription of some kind, however rudimentary—and millennia before the invention of alphabets—appeared along with meaningful articulation. This is merely to say that adapting noises from the mouth to signifying ends is no more, though no less, fundamental than is making marks on the physical world lying about us. Both are part of how we occupy a material world. Scratches, marks, lines on the ground or on bodies, and rings round special territory or objects probably occurred as soon as meaningful communication appeared at all. Reaped plants would be laid out in rows, stimulating the idea of written regularity. Spilled blood could shape into forms that suggested a deep power to invoke. The earliest cave paintings already mentioned, such as those in Chauvet in France, are about thirty thousand years old; that is to say, from roughly when Homo sapiens superseded Neanderthal man as leading human species. Since these paintings show a high degree of sophistication and delicacy of line, it seems very likely that graphicity generally, as a tool of not only depiction but also expression, was there for humans almost as soon as they evolved as our own immediate forebears. Jacques Derrida's *ecriture* is "writing" in its most pervading sense. In Derrida's long-famous phrase, it is the mark, trace, hinge, rupture entailed in any intervention on bland unity of any kind at all. A gesture, a movement of twigs in the wind, a sound wave on the air, a sentence or paragraph or book, or poem, a sexual liaison, a building, a word left or erased, all mark the face of reality in a way that can be regarded as "writing" in this primal connotation.

Again the irony here is that writing has left its traces while speech has not. This means that we can say more about writing, and so need all the more care not to assume it is more important. That would be to refute Saussure and Bloomfield by going to the other extreme. Even so the position is not conclusive, for beyond about ten thousand years back tangible evidence for writing itself (as opposed to graphicity generally) peters out. With these reservations, interesting observations can be made. Protoalphabetic writing of one kind or another had appeared at least two thousand years before the full alphabet. From recent discoveries in China we learn that simple pictograms may have existed there as early as about 5500 B.C.[6] Written symbols appear on clay tablets or tokens from around 3000 B.C. in the Middle East. There is a long and slow process of development.

Four or five different stages have been identified.[7] They occurred at different rates in different places. "Proto-writing," the first real writing, was a pictorial shorthand with mnemonic implication. This then began to be arranged in linear form, that is to say sequentially. The "Linear B" text dates from about 1200 B.C. from the Mycenae in ancient Greece, and it seems the Ojibway Midewewin tribe of North America evolved linearity at roughly the same time. Next comes actual writing, still pictorial but with some regular word-to-sign correspondence along with some phonetic equivalence. Chinese characters and Egyptian hieroglyphics are the clearest examples. Syllabaries are then an important step by which signs stand for oral syllables. Clearly when the signs for *man* and *drake* together mean "mandrake," the two contributing items have nothing to do with the mandrake plant at all. A leap toward abstraction has been taken. With the penultimate step before the true alphabet, a sign could imply its first sound only. It is as though the four signs for *pole, apple, lion,* and *mouse* would mean "palm." This acronymic method is as near to the true alphabet as could be without making the final jump. One can see how ingenious yet still tedious it is, in light of the alphabetical principle itself. The alphabetical principle is that of a single small sign for a single sound. With that final move, all the encumbrances of previous methods are gone, and the simple slim-line alphabet has arrived. That crucial step forward brought—among other things—the full Greek alphabet, to which our own is still so close today, three thousand years later. The new principle had been found, and there was no need for further modification.

Most major inventions or breakthroughs work that way. The alphabet, with its spare, unburdening lucidity, was a long time in preparation. But it then discarded its forebears like an old skin no longer needed. No doubt the knife and the wheel had comparable starts. Humans had surely long noticed that the thinnest edge of a piece of mineral or stone could slice through softer substances. The idea of giving it a handle was probably quick and sudden. It had been equally clear that logs or boulders would roll, rather than slide, down slopes and inclines if they were roughly cylindrical or spherical. But someone then had to notice that the rolling piece could be not spherical but vertically flat, so enabling maybe the real invention, not just the wheel but the axle. In our own day the idea that the gene was helical had long occurred to scientists before James Watson and Bernard Crick realized that the helix was double. Computing had been tacitly in preparation ever since the abacus and the multiplication table. From Alan Turing came the unwieldy analog and arithmetical computers; but it was the silicon chip that miniaturized and so domesticated the computer into every corner of modern life. And as with all such breakthroughs, the applications in our lives go far wider than the inventor or first users ever envisaged.

So it is with the alphabet. And, as T. S. Kuhn showed in a famous study, once the innovation is in place, it appears so simple as to be mere tautology; almost boring. Maybe this is why writing itself, the alphabet itself, is seldom mentioned in literary criticism. The alphabet enabled a new kind of thought, and poetry, so diffuse in human life that we now virtually breathe it like air or walk it like land beneath our feet. It is largely taken for granted. One feature of the alphabet, which surely led to this great versatility and usefulness, was the very large number of combinations it can yield out of so few signs. This is why I am calling this feature a "microbillion," and in this respect it is like stars, grains of sand, or leaves in the forest. Some of the earlier writers just may have been consciously aware of this fact. For example, there is John's conclusion to the fourth Christian Gospel. He wrote that "There are also many other things which Jesus did, the which, if they should be written every one, I suppose that even the world itself could not contain the books that should be written" (John 21:25). The Buddha once said something similar. On one occasion he spoke to his followers in a forest.

When he had finished, he picked up a handful of leaves from the forest floor. He explained that this small handful was the equivalent of what he had just told his followers. All that theoretically he could have said, would be the equivalent of all the millions of leaves throughout the whole forest; so great is the province of truth.

The alphabet was a technological invention. That is refreshingly demystifying, and needn't refute a sense of language generally as—so far as the word still has relevant meaning—sacred. Language might be called sacred in that the capacity of matter to yield up sign or meaning, in fact anything other than matter, is a reality we can't get below, a datum of human existence. Henri Bergson wrote interestingly on that distinction as it pertains to language. "The word is an external thing, which the intelligence can catch hold of and cling to, and at the same time an immaterial thing, by means of which the intelligence can penetrate even to the inwardness of its own work."[8] This is what the present book later sees as "physical" and "virtual." But the classic accounts of this major human invention of the alphabet itself are found in David Diringer, *The Alphabet: A Key To the History of Mankind*, published in 1947, and then Ignace Gelb's *Study of Writing* in 1952. Later research has modified their work, and disagreement and obscurity remain over both detail and chronology. But there is agreement about the essential event. It occurred sometime in the second quarter of the second millennium counting back from the birth of Christ; in figures, 1700–1500 B.C. There are many observations to be made about it, and many questions to ask.

As Diringer points out (37), this period is roughly that of the Hyksos, invaders of Egypt from the Middle East. When the Hebrew Old Testament announces a new king of Egypt "who knew nothing of Joseph" (Exodus 1:8), it may be referring to the end of this dynasty.[9] The Greek poet Homer then flourished at about 850 B.C., some six or seven centuries later. By that time vowels had been introduced into the hitherto consonantal alphabet. All of which is to say that, for Western civilization at least, its foundation texts in Jewish and Greek society were written not so long, as human existence goes, after the "great event" as Diringer calls it, the means by which to write those texts at all. As we reach A.D. 2000 and further centuries and millennia are added—again, short periods as evolved human existence goes—so the way these huge writings followed on the heels of their very means will seem to have been quicker and quicker still. The alphabet enabled colossal openings of expression.

Diringer was fairly sure that the alphabet was invented once, as most inventions are. Even if it happened twice, the second probably merely modified the first. This view is still widely held. "Unlike other forms of writing, the alphabet seems to have been invented only once, and to have spread rapidly to other cultures." Recently Stephen Pinker has endorsed this view.[10] This raises our first and most intriguing questions—to which, of course, we have no answers. Who thought of the idea? How long did it take? One afternoon? Ideas are in a sense instantaneous; they are moments of total insight taking zero time. Perhaps an Assyrian priest in ancient Canaan was urged to find a less cumbersome way of notation than the ideographic and syllabic methods that had preceded. He passed his idea to a village draughtsman known for his liking for sketching huts, animals, or weapons. But this person was already responsible for the long-established "laundry lists" of stores of grain, tithes and taxes, and the like; maybe he was so enthusiastic about his idea, that by his new technique he later even wrote an account of that technique itself. If only we had such a record; but none is known to exist. Yet, suddenly, it was there, and the Bible, the ancient tragedies, the Homeric poems, *Beowulf,* Shakespeare, the modern realist novel, the personal diary, the letter home, the daily newspaper, the film soundtrack, and all the poems we shall consider, in that moment became possible. At least as the West knows these things, for they are of course differently present in, for instance, Chinese.

As to what the signs were drawn from, or what if anything they depicted, again we have very little idea. Many have thought letters depict mouth-positions for utterance. So, for our own letters, the (capital) BBBBB is a side-on silhouette of the lips in the required position, and the PPPPP half that to represent the same sound unvoiced. The OOOOO is the round mouth speaking that vowel: the runic sign for ooooo was named "os," the Latin for "mouth."[11] The TTTTT gives the upright tongue touching the horizontal roof of the mouth, while EEEEE might be the open mouth with tongue in the middle. And so on. Unfortunately, few of the other signs can be so regarded. If EEEEE is the open mouth with tongue in the middle, what is RRRRR? If kkkkk is merely an unvoiced ggggg, the mouth in the identical position for both, why do their signs look so different? And what are xxxxx, qqqqq, and iiiii?

There have been other accounts. Some find the sources of the signs in objects, for example domestic or military, which the first letter of the word naming them simply copied. It is as though hhhhh, ttttt, and ccccc came from houses, trees, and cups. The uppercase H has been compared to a fence, perhaps deriving from the Phoenician letter *kheth,* which as a word means "fence," too. But the lowercase h looks a little like an axe or hatchet; hence the French term *hache,* in English "aitch," our name for that letter. The sign for sssss in Greek—its letter "sigma"—looks somewhat like rows of teeth, which have to be pressed together for the characteristic sibilant sound to be made. The wwwww might be washing, waves, and water. Again, OOOOO and IIIII are two of the three single letters in English that are also words. They are also vowels, and among the most frequently used letters. They have been thought of as purity (upright line and pure circle) and as sexual (phallus and vagina). Indeed, the Renaissance letter-designer Geofroy Tory believed that the Greek myth of Io, whom Zeus loved, was an allegory to set forth the divine inspiration of all Greek letters.[12] Mmmmm and nnnnn look like many things; rigid columns or a calm wavy regularity. Maybe the sinuous and hissing sssss is the serpent. Much depends on the cursive hand and style of print. The symbol for the Egyptian god Heh was H; both arms raised.[13] According to some scholars, AAAAA may have been a tent, BBBBB has some look of individual cattle. For others AAAAA is an ox's head. A sixteenth-century depiction in Orvieto cathedral, of thirty Etruscan tools, has an ambience much like that of some early alphabets. Or none of these suggestions may be true at all, and the inventor just wrote down the first twenty-odd simple yet distinctive signs he could think of. When vowels were added to the Greek alphabet, the technician merely took five signs from the Aramaic alphabet that did not yet appear in the Greek one. That was "arbitrary" if anything was; yet the lowercase vowels are all written, still today, too, level to the line. Whatever the truth, if any, in these notions, it is lost to us.[14]

We learn a bit more from the earliest means of inscription, and from these two things—what the letters may have meant and how they were written—there is a possible inference. We can touch only a few details of this large and multifaceted topic. The first known case of prealphabetical writing goes back to the Sumerian (modern southern Iraq) civilization of about 3500 B.C. Their basis was stone, pebbles, and clay. Then in or just before the third millennium B.C. came paper, from the plant papyrus, which grew in abundance in the Nile Delta; indeed, Egypt was always central to writing's development. Thick black ink was made of water and soot. But because paper is a soft medium, cursive or "joined-up" writing could evolve, previously impossible on clay or stone; and this led to the distinction between capital letters (isolated) and lowercase (cursive). Yet in the Near East, at very much the same time, "The curves in the primitive pictographic signs disappeared" (Jean 1992, 14).

This resulted from the famous cuneiform method, the use of reeds as writing materials with their ends whittled into wedges (cuneiform = "wedge-shaped"). These were pressed on to wet clay, which takes curves only with difficulty. So there is a clear distinction between cursive and disjointed straight writing, depending on the materials used.

Such may oversimplify, but here is our inference. It is hard to imagine our own abecedary without curves, least of all in handwriting. The occasional font attempts it for display purposes; but for the modern world's needs, of hundreds of pages of prose reportage, accounts, documents, letters, printouts, and the rest, it would be hard on the eye if nothing else. But maybe these curves, and indeed straights, along with some possible origins of letters' shapes just suggested, imply something about letters more deeply. Perhaps there are subliminal archetypes lurking there, and the words that result from their combinations, with their unique shapes, have some sway in our unconsciousnesses. Meanings may become attached to the shapes of letters by neural processes as yet undetected. The materiality of the alphabet may yet be found to play an important part in the very formation of the meanings we see in, or impose on, our experiences of our world. One gradually becomes aware of just what it is that poets use, for the embodiment of their images and dreams. It spans time, ignores political thrusts and historical dynasties, and at the same time both liberates and constrains the shapes of the enabling thought, or conceives such thought itself. This will be looked at more fully in part 2.

There is another major factor. Contrary to belief often held, prealphabetical writing was not invented solely to record myth or tribal ancestral story that had thereto been passed down orally. The earliest writing commonly had mundane, logistical functions. It recorded grain and cattle quantities; numbers of employees (bakers, groomsmen, smiths) on a palace's staff; military personnel and armaments; letting out money at interest; records of the dead; and rudimentary educational tablets for teaching writing to children. Certainly, some less instrumental records are also found. The prealphabetic script of the Maya civilization of Central America, probably over two thousand years old, has accounts of military strategy, disputes over monarchical succession, and the creation of government systems after social collapse.[15] Yet these too are rudimentary, and such forms of writing usually don't evolve either the discursiveness or the innermind expressiveness of alphabets.

The anthropologist Jack Goody has examined this matter at length. Much prealphabetical writing is in "lists," the across-down matrix that speech, being sequential, could never encompass. The acronymic principle already referred to, like the common acrostic, equally entails the matrix. The matrix is essentially visual; what Goody calls the "grapho-linguistic technique of cognitive operation" (Goody 1987, 274). There is a major inference here; namely, that *thought itself doesn't have to be linear.* In our own world the chart or table pervades every aspect of organizational life, but ancient bureaucracy and administration used it from the beginning. A key innovation was the leaving of gaps between words; they could thus be arranged horizontally or vertically at will. The table or matrix is a kind of multiple list, with its columns and rows. Much mental and neural activity, including "mentalese" itself, is probably nonlinear in nature. In proceeding both across and down at once, the matrix is not orally renderable.

Items in matrices often come in similarities and categories; all fruit, all dead kings. They are exclusive too; fruit and dead kings alone. Again, much is still obscure here, but it has long been known that rudimentary languages, including written ones, went for long periods without syntactic markers. The script of the ancient Indus civilization (circa 2000 B.C.), still undeciphered, appears on nearly four thousand inscribed objects; yet they are extremely short, suggesting a lack of syntax or sentence. Since vowels were not yet there, either, it seems that oral fluency was not at first the paramount concern. Goody writes further: "What is significant about the use of language in early writing systems is that much of it displays a very different syntactical structure from spoken discourse" (274). "Matrices make it possible to manipulate, reorganize and reformulate [their] information in a manner that is virtually, one might say, inconceivable in the purely oral context" (276).

Could it be that the poem, certainly the short poem of regular form, descends in part from the matrix syndrome and its cognate mentality? Egyptian hieroglyphics and the ancient Chinese script had religious and poetic functions respectively. Hieroglyphics evoked the gods from which they came. Their great beauty, unlike the attractive but rather severe regularity of cuneiform, is often remarked on. With its watery applications on gentle paintings of misty hills with butterflies and delicate plants, Chinese poetry too is very beautiful, and the script was an integral part of the very idea of Chinese poetry. It may be that the matrical mentality survived into the era of the alphabet, emerging in traditional Western forms such as the quatrain, sonnet, and villanelle. The individual word, on which the list depends, mutates into the lyric poem's magnetic heart. Key terms appear at various points in the poem's mapped structure, and the (oral) echo back to an earlier occasion is matched by the visual placing "down," rather than "along" as in speech or recitation, when it is written and when we read it. Enjambment and other comparable features are hard to register orally; the centuries-old conception of "poetry" itself, as a kind of permanent transcendent item waiting to be given body, may stem from this material feature.

From these considerations one might suggest more general inferences. Maybe surprisingly, linguists occasionally point to the alphabet as not in every way adequate. We cannot phrase our minds' depths, nor does the thin, temporal shape of syntax actually match the obdurate world we experience. Joseph Graham has summarized the entire matter. "Words do not take the place of thoughts. They occupy a different space."[16] Numerous writers and philosophers have attested to this feeling, as will be recorded below. But for the same reason, the alphabet must have been much needed. It isn't perfect, yet the ability to record the sounds of speech, directly and with great simplicity, was an enormous step forward. But then, as so often with major new inventions, further unplanned effects and results began to emerge. Inventing the alphabet meant discovering its principle in all its aspects.

The question is of what this entailed. One recent suggestion seems of much interest. Our power to consider language at all, our self-consciousness of it, may itself have been enabled by the invention of the abecedary. Speech, which had existed for millennia, could only then become conscious of itself by being transposed into a different medium against which speech itself could be considered. The matter has been thoroughly examined by David Olsen.[17] Olsen suggests that writing does not merely report speech. Even if that is what first happened, writing didn't record already-present items like vowel, consonant, syllable, phoneme, verb, preposition, "correct spelling," or indeed word itself. Rather it generated the very idea of such things—and the possibility of such ideas—up to the surface from our subconscious. Nor was there ever some already existing, unchanging, and constant (oral) version of a poem, law, or domestic practice that the new method simply "wrote down." Rather, and for the first time ever, it enabled any such thing to become constant at all. And it was only the permanence of writing, a point of reference to look back to, that made awareness of such things possible. The moment writing is invented it then offers a model for speech. The thrust toward the invention may even have been powered by this impulse. For writing does not merely tell us what utterances are utterances of. Speakers knew that already.

Rather, writing "provides a basis for saying what, thereafter, utterances would be *counted* as utterances of" (my emphasis).[18] Rather than alphabetical writing being a (mere) record of speech, every separate utterance of a word is one more (superficial) attempt at uttering that word whose prototype, or perfect model, is now enshrined in written form. The new alphabet therefore enabled the very examination of language, because writing itself points to a range of utterances with which thereafter it will be associated.

The alphabet can all too easily seem merely the assignment of fixed sounds to already agreed words. But those words could not have been already agreed to in the first place, for in the oral world the nuance of both sound and meaning would vary, by however so little, on each occasion. But once the row of letters indicating sounds is fixed, the word is fixed, or at least can culturally be so regarded. Of course, it can change its meaning, but the sign whose meaning changes itself remains the same, or at least modifies very rarely and slowly. Thus the written word becomes a focus against which any subsequent use of a word can be compared or measured. Nigel Love points out (Love 1990, 113) that by virtue of this distancing of speech in the invention of writing, examination of that writing as a language became possible. Before that it was not possible. Perhaps literary criticism's formal beginnings lay here also.

Our surmise from all of the foregoing has to be that *speech and writing, voice and inscription, have been two interplaying modes of language that each support the other.* This has given language a sinuous resilience in its role in cementing human society, pushing out knowledge, expanding human imagination, creativity, and indeed ultimate longing and speculation. The way became open for elaborations far beyond what daily speech normally allows. Ordered thought, conceptual argument, the sustained poem or sacred text, philosophical theses, and the large-scale prose work generally, all unable to be "spoken" in the ordinary way, are enabled by exactly the mode of writing that records the simple spoken utterance.

THE PROVERB. THE SINGLE SACRED WORD. REPETITION. THE UNNAMABLE.

A major aspect of the oral word in the primitive world, cognate with poetry, comes with the saying or proverb. The proverb has some affinities with the role of the listed item or matrical entry.

Certainly it is linear syntactically but it cannot suffer continuation. Its end is an immediate closure of its start. As such, a society's proverbs amount to a kind of overall cultural matrix, broadly comparable to the economic and military matrices Goody records, in that proverbs too are a kind of huge list of separate items rather than a continuous text. In its proverbs a society's store of lore and wisdom could be embodied just as grain or gold were hoarded in the societies' monarchical treasure-houses. Once written, the proverb reveals how much it relies on alphabetical characteristics. *Look before you leap, no man can serve two masters, it's an ill wind that blows nobody any good*; a plotting of the letters of these reveals every character contributing its atomized part. George Herbert valued the proverb highly as we shall see, and his own are as dependent on individual letters as the older ones were.

The proverb was a key locus of traditional wisdom in primitive societies. Kwame Gyekye has made a study of the Akan people in Ghana in Africa, one of many communities that has had to move very suddenly from tribal life to modern-world conditions.[19] The thought and technology of intervening centuries were bypassed. Whatever the disadvantages, this has meant they could juxtapose traditional and modern thought in a number of strikingly fertile comparisons and contrasts. Gyekye's aim is to show that, contrary to much assumption, African traditional thought is properly called philosophical if seen on its own terms. But because Akan thought existed without writing until relatively recently, a key and widespread component of it is still the proverb.

In Akan thought the wise man's wisdom comes in proverbial form. Gyekye offers examples under the various philosophical headings his chapters discuss—being, cause, personality, free will, ethics, and so on. *Wonda a wonso dae* [You do not dream if you are not asleep] (i.e., realism is valuable). *Wo nsa nifa hohorow benkum, no benkum nso hohorow nifa* [The left arm washes the right arm, and the right arm the left arm] (need for humans to cooperate). Akan proverbs also deal with language, religion, proverbs themselves, and wisdom itself. *Asem kye a, nyansa ba ho* [If a problem lasts long, wisdom comes] (the virtue of patience). *Onyame bewu na m'awu* [Could God die, I will die] (dependence on God is total). *Aso mu nni nkwanta* [There are no crossroads in the ear] (principle of noncontradiction). And most tellingly, *asem nko, nyansa nko* [Speech is one thing, wisdom another]; or, similarly, *onyansafo wobu no be na wonka no asem* [The wise man is spoken to in proverbs, not in speeches or words] (Gyekye 1987, passim).

The Akan word for proverb is etymologically connected to that for palm tree. Palm trees yield their products, such as oil and soap, by distillation (Gyekye 1987, 16). The proverb is distilled, cryptic, and encapsulated; it does not spawn outward to self-critique or extended exegesis. Gyekye argues that this is one with Confucian and Heraclitean sayings like "He who learns but does not think is lost, he who thinks but does not learn is in danger," and "You never step into the same river twice." The Socratic "wisdom is virtue" is comparable too, but it gets much working over in Plato's dialogues, which are indeed "speeches and words" and not merely proverbial. But Gyekye's analysis is germane to our argument about matrices as they existed before the alphabet. Proverbs amount to a philosophy because they are a map or network—table or matrix—of parts of a wisdom not syntactically stretched into dialogue, paragraph, or extended thesis. They are of course oral; their aesthetically and alliteratively balanced form, like our own proverbs, shows this clearly and is, precisely, poetic; yet in a different branch of consciousness they amount not to debate or thesis but to philosophically diagrammatic schema. It is as though the proverb, like the poem, eventually depends on both oral and written forms at once. Equally like the poem, proverbial language tends toward the concrete. Akan language, Gyekye reports, remains physical even when referring to abstract or psychological topics. "I am happy" in Akan would be "My eyes are brightened"; "I am jealous" is "My eyes are red," and "a burning stomach" (167) would imply fear.

In short, the distinction between proverbs and speeches ("The wise man is spoken to in proverbs, not in speeches or words"), seemingly a self-contradiction, really refers to wider differences. If the proverb is cognate with the earlier kind of writing, that is to say the record-keeping and the matrix, then it and maybe by extension the poem too, are profoundly rooted in the prealphabetical form of writing as well as that which ties writing to sounds. Even when written in the alphabet too, the tension between written and oral is already built into them. In general then, the alphabet, certainly a system for notating sounds, was also used for forms of expression like lists, records, proverbs, and poems, which were more than just linear in structure. The alphabet enabled the spoken to be written, but it also enabled the inherently written to become a shaping power for speech. From that time on, neither would be complete without the other.

But a further major aspect of this arises. Poetry, it is said, touches the deepest primal chords. It requires our visceral feeling for language as well as language itself. This sense of language, as somehow forging the heart of human experience, has to be behind any idea of poetry as the age-old expression of that experience. But if that is so, then not only the origins of language but the understanding of that origin, by our earliest linguistic forebears, might point to physical features of language at poetry's center. What did the earliest alphabet-users think language was? Where did they think it came from? To the ancient and preancient worlds the answer was fundamentally religious. From the ways they saw language and religion implicating each other, we can see their deepest understandings of language and its resonances. In the earliest religious texts the primal chaos holds the embryo of language no less than it does the more palpable ingredients of matter; sun, air, sexuality, food and water, and their fertility for any one society. Creation myths are as permeated with language as they are with seed and light.

In such mythical accounts, language is present at, or emerges soon after, the first creation. Early beliefs held that primordial unity split itself in two. God sought fertile earth in chaos, such as swirling clouds or at the bottom of an ocean, or God generated it out of himself as seed or thought.[20] But language emerges most in beliefs as to creation ex nihilo. Commonly it came as sound. The gods themselves are already speaking, in soliloquy or dialogue; or the deep silence of eternity emits a voice. By Hesiod's account of the world's beginning, the *Theogony* of about 735 B.C.: "Voice (Chaos) was first to exist, followed by the rich mother Earth, the stable home of all forever, and then Eros, loveliest of the immortals. . . ." ("chaos"—gap, chasm—is the yawning gap of the mouth from which voice proceeded). If sound (here Voice) came first it must have preceded light. This pattern, and with it therefore the conditions of speech before writing, is common. *And God said, let there be light, and there was light.* The text of the Prasna Upanishad runs:[21]

> The sun shines not there, nor the moon and stars;
> These lightnings shine not, much less this [earthly] fire!
> After Him, as he shines, does everything shine.
> This whole world is illuminated with his light.

Similarly the ancient Maya text of the Popol Vuh:[22]

> The face of the earth was not yet to be seen; only the peaceful sea and the expanse of the heavens. . . . There were only immobility and silence in the darkness and in the night. Alone was the Creator, the Maker, Tepeu, the Lord, and Gucumatz, the Plumed Serpent, those who engender, those who give being, alone upon the waters like a glowing light. . . .

It is then that that the word came to Tepeu and to Gucumatz. . . .
Then light came while they counseled together; and at the moment of
dawn man appeared. . . .

Numerous early myths deploy the same three items of darkness and
silence (absence of language), and water. Darkness remains until
vocally called upon to illuminate itself. The Maori supreme being
(the Iho) evoked light by words as an agent of energy: "He began
by saying these words (that he might cease remaining inactive):
'Light, become a darkness-possessing light'" (Eliade 1967, 86).
Elsewhere the originary nature of speech is underlined in that the
god first talks and then gives that speech to man. In the creation
myth of the Winnebago Indians of Wisconsin, the Earthmaker notices that things appeared that he liked, such as water and light, and
he decides to add a being similar to himself. When he spoke to it,
however, it did not answer, not even when he gave it a mind and
then a tongue. Only when he breathed on to it did it speak (Eliade
1967, 83). This dimension of breath, spirit (Greek *pneuma*, Akan
home) also pervades later mythology. In India, the Brhadaranyaka
Upanishad has the Originator speak. The Originator longs for a self
and then a second self. By the mating of mind with speech the progeny appeared. "When it was born, Death opened its mouth on him.
He cried *bhan!* That indeed became speech" (Smart and Hecht
1992, 344. *Bhan* seems to be a newborn infant's cry.)

These are cases of the origin of speech. Of necessity they are recorded in writing, but the writings too are ancient, and they commonly recall prewriting myths handed down by tribal priests or
curators of religion and knowledge. In other cases, and with no contradiction, writing too has divine origin. "Hieroglyphics" means
"the writing of the gods," and so writing, of some sort, must itself
have already been invented for it to be attributed to the gods or anyone else. In Egyptian myth the god Thoth is creator of both speech
and writing. Brahma gave knowledge of writing to the Hindu people, while runic script, according to the Icelandic sagas, was invented by the god Odin. A heaven-sent water-turtle, with markings
on its shell, first brought writing to the Chinese (Crystal 1987, 384).
For all these cases writing had physical virtue, a kind of charge of
mythic energy. There are then two kinds of myth, some seeing
voice, others inscription, as originary.

The divine efficacy of writing and speech, however, is not shown
just by the claim that the gods first gave it to us. Aside from what
it declares overtly, there are countless cases of language's living
virtue in practice. Levi-Strauss cited the phenomenon of "umbilical

names" found among the Wik Munkan people of Australia.[23] When a child is born, a member of the tribe calls out a list of possible names for it according to certain fixed categories. The name called at the moment the placenta appears is the one adopted. Those concerned were not above the occasional rigging or fiddle; the umbilical cord could be pulled a little to make the birth coincide with a desired name at the right moment. Yet the practice itself is still what shapes the choice publicly. Levi-Strauss himself was once witnessed writing by some Nambikwara Indians in Brazil. They responded by drawing some squiggly lines and asking him to read them.[24] Equally a name's virtue-saturation could identify a murderer. A different hair on the head of the victim is pulled concurrently with calling out the name of each suspect. When a hair comes out, there is the murderer. Among the Nuer, names of birds that fly low were reserved for twins (Levi-Strauss 1972, 189). The reason for this might be intriguing; but why is the name the link?

Ezekiel was required by the Lord to eat the scroll of a book and then address the house of Israel (Ezekiel 2:9–3:6). In medieval Jewish exorcism, demons were recited by name with one letter omitted each time. This gradually shrunk the name, and so the demon too, to nothing. The story is told of an unlettered native who was sent to deliver some bread, along with an accompanying written note. When he stole some of the bread he first hid the note, so that it could not watch the theft and so betray him. The Berber medicine man still writes his healing words into a bowl, washes it with water, and gives it to the sick to drink. The ancient Celtic text the *Book of Durrow* was used in the same way to cure sick cattle. Water the cattle drank had first been poured over the book. In different context again, the earliest surviving Irish manuscript the *Cathach* [*Fighter*] was carried round the ranks of soldiers to show them before battle. The Tai peoples from Southeast Asia still tattoo themselves with words as a defense against enemy weapons.[25] In our own era, First World War soldiers sometimes carried Bibles in their breast pockets, across the heart, as a similar protection against bullets.

Then there is the fuller sacred text, and this too embodies divine efficacy. The sacred text is canonical. Once set, it does not allow change, for it had been bestowed from the divine source, just as language itself first was. The Ten Commandments given to Moses on Mount Sinai came in the form of tablets of stone, while the visitation to John of Patmos was dual. John "heard behind me a great voice, as of a trumpet, saying, I am Alpha and Omega, the first and the last: and, What thou seest, write in a book, and send it unto the seven churches which are in Asia" (Revelation 1:10–11). That is to say that John's experience, both oral and visual *(trumpet/write)*, was set in microdetail in the exact letters between the alpha and omega of the Greek alphabet.

But canonical status is not synonymous with exact divine donation. The Pali canon of Buddhism, for example, contains "much which does not claim to be in any sense Buddha's utterance . . . Nor is the Canon as it stands in any sense an authority for what is Buddhism. . . . Buddhism knows no 'authority', and the Buddha's exact words are the authority for this lack of it."[26] Rather, the decision on the canon in each religious tradition was taken on various grounds, not least political. Selected religious leaders came together in order to determine the relevant canon. The control and power such leaders had is clear from this; belief was enforced, with punitive sanctions often ensuing for the rebellious or wayward. Criteria for these decisions were reliability of authorship, the text's standing in spiritual terms, and the absence, as far as possible, of doctrinal dispute. Yet the sign's exactness remains. The text can change, but it is not fluid. At any moment it is one thing or it is another. It may be open, incomplete, or under dispute, or it may stay imperiously and awesomely unchanged for centuries, but the material conditions entailed by the alphabet do not alter. So a kind of shifting law seems to hold. Give or take degrees of interpretation in any one culture, a fixed canon makes for dogmatic belief, a looser canon leaves belief elastic and liberal. Indeed, a canon may be secular: Shakespeare, Karl Marx, and the American Constitution are all canonical for their societies. In *The Waste Land,* T. S. Eliot used scraps from European literature in a mode of decay and despair. The paradoxical result is a canonical poem whose fragments—the rubble of European civilization—themselves cannot be altered afterward.

Along with the sacred text come two other phenomena; namely, the single sacred word, and the universal feature of repetition. And of course, poetry's use of the single emphasized word and the repeated refrain hardly needs remarking. The single word may be sacred as name, for instance, Allah, Jehovah; or designation, as with the biblical I AM; but it also commonly gains verbal strength by the acronym of its initials. Acronym is central to the Jewish Kabbalah, which will be considered below. There is also the Christian *ichthus*, Greek for "fish" and acronym of the Greek for "Jesus Christ, son of God, savior: *Iesu Christos theou udor soter.* A major case is the mystic Hindu syllable *Aum* (sometimes *Om*), said to have been chanted by some priests thousands and thousands of times. Here is the well-known excerpt at length (*Aum* in Sanskrit is made up of a diphthong aaaaa, plus uuuuu, plus mmmmm):

> This is self in light of the word "Aum" and its components. The compo-
> nents (matra) and the fourths are synonymous; namely, the letters a,
> u, and m.
> The waking state, which is universal, is the letter a, the first component.
> It derives from apti ("getting") or from adimatva ("leading").
> Truly whoever understands this gets all he desires, and he leads.
> The sleeping state, the radiant, is the letter u, the next component, from
> utkarsa ("exaltation") or from ubhayatva ("the between").
> Truly he exalts the seamlessness of understanding: and he finds serenity.
> No one ignorant of Brahman can be kin or seed of one who under-
> stands this.
> The deep-sleep state, the aware, is the letter m, the final component,
> from miti ("setting up") or from mapiti ("emerging").
> Truly he who understands this sets up the entire world, and he emerges.
> But there is a last item with no component. It sustains no treatment or
> valuable evolution, without another component.
> And so truly is "Aum" the Self.
> And truly, whoever understands all of this, his own self enters the uni-
> versal Self too. (Mandukya Upanishad, author's rendering)

The letters' virtue here is comprehensive. It ties the three words of the acronym to the highly singular and interior body-mind experience of the word's actual utterance by anyone chanting it. *Aum* thus lends itself to a concentration of spiritual energy, perhaps moving toward ecstasy, by uniting the visceral throb of the sound with the meditation on the three abstractions of the Universal, the Radiant, and the Knowing as aspects of the virtuous and meditative life that attains nirvana.

It could not do this but by the letter; in Western culture, the abecedary. Clearly this practice descends from the protowriting mentioned above, where words were made up from the initial sounds of other words. But there is another curious feature here. There is an uncanny parallel between the mmmmm-sounding *Aum* and what Michel Foucault saw as "the murmuring of the ontological continuum" in nineteenth-century European poetry, the expression of self experiencing itself.[27] To the ancient world the nasals mmmmm and, although less so, nnnnn were nearly universal for first-person expression and to address family and close intimates.[28] These sounds, which seem to vibrate deep from the body, do seem to impose themselves naturally as most suited to expressing selfhood. Their presence survives in the modern world. In Wordsworth's poetry these consonants, along with the *-ing* ending, have a power of vibration on which much of his chief poetry is centered. Coleridge's I AM in the *Biographia Literaria* may have echoed this, and it was picked up by William Butler Yeats in his explicit use of the A, U, and M of *Aum* in *The Holy Mountain* of 1934. Both here and in the East an ultimate emptying-out or *kenosis* is embodied, in an aspiration to bliss and stability. In such cases the single word starkly contrasts that of the extended sacred text. The word as written, as opposed to the spoken voice evincing the god, embodies wisdom, divine but humanly written: "The wise man: a light, a torch, a stout torch that does not smoke . . . His are the black and red ink, his are the illustrated manuscripts" (Smart and Hecht 1992, 42).

This leads us to the second common feature of early sacred language; namely, repetition. The repeated word gathers meaning by qualification or expansion, but without definition. Definition, entailing further key words, would challenge the first word's holistic virtue. Definition gives the key word once, followed by an account of it. Repetition gives the key word many times, each filled out with a small new richness. "Love" for example is filled out in the famous epistle of Paul to the Corinthians, while in Confucianism the idea of *Li* (roughly, "ceremonial propriety") appears nearly forty times in a hundred lines of circling exegesis. "One who neither follows *Li* nor maintains *Li* is a man without the Tao: one who follows *Li* and maintains *Li* is a man with the Tao. . . . Hence one who persists in learning *Li* becomes a sage; one who fails to learn *Li* is a person without the Tao" (Smart and Hecht 1992, 309).

The proprietary qualities of *Li* are expressed by being interwoven with the name itself. The name itself is simply a syllable, neither pictorial nor syntactical. But repetition in religious speech, and writing in ancient cultures, often comes even without such discursive accompaniment. Whole phrases are chanted, often identical, or with a keynote word or phrase followed by variants. This frequent use depends on the same alphabetical principles as the one-word repetition. It is as though the *idem-in-alio* (same-in-other) principle was discovered early, and its powers exploited for teaching, ritual, worship, meditation, and other aspects of the religious life. In the Buddhist Discourse on the Eightfold Path the acolyte asks: *"And what, your reverences, is right view?" / "And what, your reverences, is right aspiration?" / "And what, your reverences, is right speech?" / "And what, your reverences, is right action?" / "And what, your reverences, is right mode of livelihood?"*—and so on. In the Koran, Allah is always "mighty and majestic is he," while any apostle of Allah carries the prayer "upon whom be peace." In the Anglican Prayer Book canticle the Benedicite Omnia Opera, every verse is the same basic phrase, with only the creatures and objects of the earth changing. "O ye children of the Lord, bless ye the Lord, praise him and magnify Him for ever." "O ye fowls of the air, bless ye the Lord, praise him and magnify Him for ever." "O ye whales, bless ye the Lord, praise him and magnify Him for ever." "O ye wells, bless ye the Lord, praise him and magnify Him for ever." And so on.

This rhythmic regularity is again sonorous, for aesthetic and easy-memory purposes. Elsewhere the exactness of formula can, to us, sometimes seem wearisome, but for different reasons. In an extraordinary Buddhist meditation, far too long to cite here in full, whole paragraphs are repeated, each adding only a single new phrase in the middle (Ananda is the young acolyte):

> A monk, not attending to the perception of village, not attending to the perception of human beings, attends to unity grounded on the perception of forest. His mind is satisfied with, pleased with, set on and freed in the perception of forest. He comprehends thus: "The disturbances there might be resulting from the perception of human beings do not exist here. There is only this degree of disturbance, that is to say, unity grounded on the perception of forest."
>
> "And again, Ananda, a monk, not attending to the perception of village, not attending to the perception of human beings, not attending to . . . (Smart and Hecht 1992, 259)

And so on, for some half dozen further paragraphs, each one almost exactly like the one we have cited here. In each case we learn what the monk does not attend to, what he is satisfied with, and what he comprehends. The final category in each new paragraph is, however, an addition for that paragraph, and it brings on its own "degree of disturbance" in each case. The new categories introduced into the base-paragraph one by one are as follows: unity grounded on the perception of infinite consciousness; unity grounded on the perception of the plane of no-thing; unity grounded on the perception of neither-perception-nor-nonperception; unity grounded on the perception of the concentration of mind that is without sign. Long before the end we know, each time, all of what's coming bar the one new phrase. At the close the monk "enters on the utterly purified and incomparably highest emptiness."

This recitation may, on first reading, seem monotonous. But it can be taken several ways. Maybe it knowingly imitates the tedium by which such wisdom has to be learned in life itself. Or it is just the ubiquitous "tunnel" effect of the alphabet, accepted here by whoever wrote it as inevitable. Or maybe, third, it is an early stage on the way to realizing the alphabet's "equable" nature (see infra chap. 7), its capacity to render anything at all—object, event, thought, thought about thought, connections between these, identity of speaker, and so on—in the one level medium. Whatever the reason, it sharply contrasts the sort of chanted repetition that heightens rhythm knowingly and joyously. This passage just quoted therefore shows further how adaptable the power of repetition by the alphabet or abecedary can be. The telephone directory, after all—certainly as far as (in Britain) Jones, McDonald, Patel, and Smith are concerned—works the same way, although there the number of instances does amount, like a purely pictorial script might, to the number of persons entailed.

But, even more disconcertingly, this passage's long and drawn-out message leads to Nirvana; nothingness itself; "the utterly purified and incomparably highest emptiness." It seems the writer is wittier than we may have realized, as he tapers his acolyte's consciousness out on the way to that extinction. This would point to another feature of ancient-world expression. This is the strange circling of the spoken/written alphabetical word with its opposite, with what cannot be said, must not be said, or, conversely, is desirably not said, and so in the end eliminates that need from the subject's consciousness. We articulate, or state an avoidance of articulating, the inarticulable. We name, or state the impossibility of naming, the unnameable. These opposites seem entailed with one another, and the development of the abecedary principle seems to dally with them and with what they make available to us from the invisible world.

It is curious that this one phenomenon, the alphabet's circling with its own opposite in nonexpression, can take these almost opposite forms. To blank out everything from my mind suggests that nothingness itself is the goal. But to encounter the unnameability of the godhead is to say the reverse; namely, that the godhead is larger and deeper than our power to express it. In the one, all life's details are extinguished, leaving pure existence and nothing itself as pure entity. In the other, a spirit or god lies beyond human power to apprehend, including by language itself.

The magnetism toward this strange duality is very great in the ancient texts. It stretches from the primitive sense of naming as dangerous, through Eastern mysticism that aspires to a peace where nothing nameable remains, on to the Western medieval mystic, author of *The Cloud of Unknowing*, who believed that encountering God meant removing all else including even God's named and good

qualities. Such things survive, at a more humdrum level, in our contemporary phrasing. To say "today's weather conditions" when
"today's weather" would be enough tacks on a final word but adds
little. In uttering it, my mind, however briefly, is a kind of blank
itself.[29] But conversely, to say "I know what I mean but there isn't
a word for it" is to use the abecedary to point the abecedary's limits. This last case emphasizes, too, that paradoxically both these
states are themselves named; the unnameable and the inconceivable. Since "unnameable" is a name and "inconceivable" is a conception, to suggest that the alphabet is warily circling its own
opposite in such ultimate formulations may touch an important
principle.

Buddhism frequently refers to this unnameable nothingness as
basis for reality. "There is, Brethren, an un-born, a not-become, a
not-made, a not-compounded. If there were not, Brethren, that
which is not-born, not-made, not-compounded, there could be no
escape for the born, become, made and compounded."[30] The Buddhist writer Lieh Tzu wrote of it as a knowing blankness of mind.
"He who has reached the stage of thought is silent. He who has
attained to perfect knowledge is also silent. He who uses silence in
lieu of speech really does speak. He who for knowledge substitutes
blankness of mind really does know. Without words and speaking
not, he really speaks and really knows. Saying nothing and knowing nothing, there is in reality nothing that he does not say, nothing
that he does not know. This is how the matter stands, and there is
nothing further to be said. Why are you thus astonished without
cause?" (Smart and Hecht 1992, 299). We are astonished without
cause, no doubt—as with the other passages from Buddhism already cited—by the play of repetition by which the gradual lulling
into cognitive nirvana takes place. Repetition is something the alphabet and abecedary are rather good at. If you draw a tree twice,
you suggest two trees; it can't be avoided. But if you write "tree"
twice, you may well have simply the same one thing but done a
second time. There is no addition of content, so the inherent rhythm
of the first pronouncement is reengrafted. It cannot give rise to further elaboration of itself without more words being brought in to
cover such ideas, and that would spoil the point of the singularity.
For this reason too, repetition has to be perfect. With alphabets, the
change of even one letter is total. If I mistakenly write "chief" instead of "thief," I haven't said "almost a thief" but something else
altogether. In a fully pictorial writing, a slight change in the sign
might make little difference; it would still be a house, tree, or man.
The endless repetition of the single word alluded to above, such as

Aum or *Li*, observes the same principle. The sacredness lies in the mystic ambiguity by which, again, saying all is saying nothing, saying nothing is saying all.

The unnameable as not nothing but all, what exists so much as to be beyond expression, equally pervades these texts. In Judaism the name Yahweh (Jehovah) "became so sacred that it was not spoken or written in normal circumstances" (Edwards 1976, 33). Sanskrit literature affirms the point strongly. "What cannot be spoken with words, but that whereby words are spoken. Know that alone to be Brahman, the Spirit."[31] "Not by speech, not by mind, not by sight can he be comprehended" (Katha Upanishad, cited in Bouquet 1951, 127). "All know that the greatness of the Lord is beyond words. Yet who can resist the attempt to express it in language?" (Ramayana, cited in Bouquet 1951, 225). Writing itself cannot express the ineffable condition, but it can express its own inability to do so. The abecedary, with its already virtual (nonpictorial, even nonideographic) signs, tempts the writer into apprehending the abstract, but a no-man's-land is all that can be reached; the evocation of the fact of what cannot be evoked.

From the Dream-Time religion of Aboriginal Australia, well outside the domain of the Indo-European family of languages, W. E. H. Stanner reported the same experience poignantly and firsthand. In the primal period of the Dream-Time, accessible to us only in dreams, the gods made the world for humans and then departed. An Aborigine took the researcher to a certain spot. He told him that this was his "Dreaming place" and that when he was young his father had in turn showed it to his son. The father told him that it was now the son's dreaming place, too, and that he should take care of it, hold on to it, and never let it go. As to what really was there, Stanner himself remarks that this cannot be known but that it is certainly something. "Like my spirit, like my brother, like my Dreaming . . . the father did not say *what* was there, only told him not to let it go. The Aborigine says finally, desperately to the researcher; listen! Something is there, we do not know what; *something*, like engine, like power, plenty of power, it does hard-work, it *pushes*." At last [the researcher] begins to understand, or thinks he does" (Stanner's emphases).[32] That is to say, he fits his own abstract, discursive, nonpictorial, in this case abecedarial set of signs to that understanding. Metaphor itself depends on the unnameable, for a few alphabetical or abecedarial words can leave a space into which some other fleeting, nonworded conception can richly glide.

This need, to go on expressing the inexpressible, seems connected to other primitive speech taboos. (They survive in our own

civilization. "There's never been a crash on this airline. . . ."
"Don't even say it.") A Bantu tribe in Southwest Africa, the Herero, has a named god, Ndjambi. But there are strong prohibitions.
"At best his name is invoked only in thanksgiving after some unexpected luck, or they pray to him when all other means of help fail.
For the rest, the utterance of his name is not allowed" (Eliade 1967,
9). Missionaries who had lived with the Herero people since 1844
did not hear the god's name until 1871, nearly thirty years later.
Equally common is the taboo on naming people for long periods
after they are dead. Indeed, sometimes the name is never used
again, and the offspring will take the title plus "dead," as with the
character Milkman Dead in Toni Morrison's novel *The Song of Solomon*. The Tiwi people forbid the use of proper names in initiation
or childbirth, a cognate custom though not quite the thing itself
(Levi-Strauss 1972, 191, 195).

The concern of tribal peoples and wider ancient civilization with
all these matters is very striking. The godhead spoke from nothing
and gave humans speech; there are sacred words and sacred texts;
total nothingness can be named, yet total wholeness, that is to say
godhead, cannot be named at all. The ultimate statement of it all
comes with great subtlety. The Hindu sacred text Rig Veda renders
the originary nonbeing of creation thus: "Then was not nonexistent
nor existent: there was no realm of air, no sky beyond it. What covered in, and where? and what gave shelter? Was water there, unfath-
omed depth of water? Death was not then, nor was there aught
immortal: no sign was there, the day's and night's divider" (Eliade
1967, 109). Not nonexistent nor existent; not even nothingness itself existed; it seems a conception still perplexing today to cosmologists attempting to grapple with the universe's origin ex nihilo.[33]
If nothing means just nothing at all, how can any negative-cancel-
ing-into-positive proposition be more than whimsy? This sophistication seems to grow as civilization progresses and as
expression—speech and writing both—moves nearer and nearer the
abstract in with the concrete together.

A final feature appears. In gradually more secular terms the alphabet's ever-widening uses, the enriched vocabulary, refinements
in syntax and its parts, carry with them the striking counter-sense
that speech and writing need their own restraining economy. We
have already cited the Akan proverb "speech is one thing, wisdom
another." The Tao Te Ching of Buddhism believes that "he who
speaks does not know; he who knows does not speak." Thomas a
Kempis stressed the importance "of avoiding superfluity in words,"
while in the nineteenth century Thomas Henry Huxley sensed the

glut in a too-linguistic education. In his poem "Point Rash-Judge-ment," Wordsworth discovers the need "to be reserved in speech," and in our own day Stanley Cavell notes how maturity in human relationships brings gradual and surprising sense that this cannot be expressed.[34] Between the extremes of all this nothingness and unnameability are the thousands of actual combinations of alpha-betical signs and human noises, and the things in the world, or the mind, they are associated with.

Summary. (As said earlier, these summaries in part 1 will point for-ward to the characteristics of the abecedary already identified for dis-cussion in part 2.)

This chapter has surveyed prealphabetical and early alphabetical societies in order to identify some main and, it seems, permanent features of the alphabet for our later discussion. Selection has been made on that basis—but, I think, such selection has managed to in-clude most of what has occurred. These features, then, do appear to be universal.

Letters are *physical*. They originate from noises in the larynx and scratches on the ground or elsewhere. Creation myth sees them as founded in light and water. The only nonarbitrary origins ever sug-gested for their design concern objects in nature, human artifacts, or parts or uses of human heads and bodies. Letters are also few in number in these first alphabets. This *fewness* seems to run deep; there is a profound early fear of excess, so that, as in acronym, proverb or the ubiquitous repetition in so much sacred writing, the same letters should be used again and again. Letters also quickly found the *stability* denied to words from the mouth, on the wind. Writing remained unchanged when its oral pronunciation—the very thing letters were at last supposed to capture—moved on. Through this longevity and constancy writing could be seen as capable of embodying permanent, that is religious truths. Both single words and entire texts could be conceived of as sacred objects. This began to provide a counter to letters' basic physicality. Letters could ex-press the nonphysical—what I am calling the *virtual*—whether the sacred, the intellectual or, as we saw, the unnameable, which doesn't need to exist for letters, combined as words, to attach to it. Creation myth saw letters as founded in the breath of the creator or divine spirit. People found that the acronym could embody the virtues of several words at once. We have also quickly identified the alphabet's flexibility. Performing all these tasks; ubiquitous repetition; switching letters to other words as in acronym again—these are only the wider cases of the *distributive* capacity of letters, the way they can be moved around in numerous combinations and in unexpected ways. Another and major distributive mode is the matrix, the "up-down" use of letters as in lists, tables, and poems, a practice that seems to go back to the earliest times. And letters can do all these things, catch all these meanings, but still at the same time and still remaining their own selves. They don't have to copy what they see, or vary themselves for different kinds of information, emotion, music, fact, or anything else. They are *equable* in nature.

2

Ancient Greece

HOMER. ATHENIAN CIVILIZATION. PLATO. THE SUSPICION OF WRITING

In about 1100 b.c. a non-Greek people from the southern part of what is now Greece was invaded by the Dorians from the north. Some time between then and about 900–800 b.c. the Phoenician alphabet came to these people. Earlier Phoenicians (Carthaginians) had probably inherited the idea of the alphabet from the Semitics, in their turn from its original founders or inventors (ca.3500 b.c.) in pre-Canaan. The powerful Phoenicians had pushed their trading empire outward until it stretched from Lebanon to Spain. The other great power, Egypt, was experiencing gradual decline. But this Phoenician alphabet that the Greeks inherited had no vowels. The now Greek (Dorian) tongue had particularly varied vowel-sounds, but it had no letters for these vowels. And it therefore appears that in about the ninth or eighth century b.c. the five Greek vowel-letters were added to their alphabet, the first occasion of this anywhere. The point of the Phoenician connection is that the five signs then added for the Greek vowels were chosen from those signs in the Phoenician alphabet that were not found in the Greek alphabet and therefore didn't duplicate them. And this date, perhaps around 850 b.c., is the one usually given for when Homer flourished. The late letters psi, chi, and phi, not found in the Roman alphabet or our own, may well have been added to the Greek alphabet at this time.

Homer

There is a significant consideration at the outset. Both the *Iliad* and the *Odyssey* have twenty-four books. One tradition holds that Homer chose this number because it was the number of letters in the Greek alphabet. But it has also been maintained, seminally and in great detail by Barry Powell, that the Greek alphabet was invented specifically to transcribe the hitherto oral Homeric poems.[1] This thesis is important enough for our topic to record briefly as to its main suggestions. Powell believes that a single Greek "adapter," assisted by a Phoenician invented the Greek alphabet all in one go for this purpose. Powell's evidence is massive and detailed, and so here we can only offer the barest outline of his thesis along with just a few brief comments. i) The Greeks could not read the writing of pre-Greek peoples. So they needed a writing system that could tell the reader a language's sounds even when they could not understand the meaning. This would have to be an "atomistic" system, one sign for each sound; that is to say, what we would now call an alphabet. ii) There is great similarity between the Phoenician and Greek scripts, even though the Phoenician is syllabic, not alphabetical. This could not have been coincidence. So a Phoenician informant and a Greek "adapter" probably worked together. The informant showed each Phoenician (syllabic) sign to the "adapter." The adapter then invented a sign, not now for each syllable, but for the separate sounds that make up syllables. These signs were all new except for the five vowel-sounds, which were taken from the Phoenician system at random. iii) No previous writing system— logographic, semasiographic, lexigraphic, hieroglyphic, syllabic— could record hexameters, in which the Homeric poems were written. The *aoidos*, the traditional "singer" or reciter of the epic poems, would have been highly motivated to get such a system. He just may have been the Greek "adapter" himself. iv) Given that 800 B.C. is the correct date, and that an individual poet was the likely inspiration, then Homer and Hesiod are the only realistic candidates. Powell assembles the evidence for Homer. v) Finally, Powell merges inventor of the Greek alphabet with whoever first wrote down the Homeric poems. "Once we accept that the adapter and the man who wrote down Homer are one and the same man, we will loosen the exasperating tangle of contradictions that has puzzled generations of Homeric scholars" (232). Powell even suggests this man's identity; namely, Palamedes the Euboian (the birthplace of Greek literacy), who is recorded by Euripides as claiming that "by making syllables out of consonants and vowels I taught men how to write" (235).

Powell does not insist that we accept all of this in its full detail. But the minimum conclusion from such evidence it would seem, and not only in the view of Powell, is that the new writing was used to record Homer soon afterward, even if it turned out that Homer himself was not the actual first case. As Powell puts it, "By any reckoning Homer's poems were recorded in the very earliest days of Greek literacy" (page 220). Furthermore—and quite aside from Homer—this attachment of a sign to a sound has great repercussions in the history of the alphabet. For the letters were few—for instance, we all speak far more than five vowel sounds—and the way we pronounce them changes over time. As a result, writing and speech drift apart from each other, for it would be totally impracticable to continually revise the spellings of long established written texts, or to keep on inventing new letters within an established alphabet. If any of this then is true, and much has to remain surmise, one has to wonder about the concurrence of this fully fledged and voweled alphabet with the appearance of Greece's first major poet, whose work later became the effective bible of ancient Greece's system of education. It is not even certain whether Homer wrote the poems himself or whether he amalgamated small poems and passages previously handed down orally. Nor it is known whether Homer used vowels, for the oldest surviving complete texts of the *Iliad* and *Odyssey* date to a couple of thousand years later. Nor is it clear that he wrote the *Odyssey* as well as the *Iliad*; this despite that any other writer of the *Odyssey*, agreed to have been written second, undoubtedly knew the *Iliad* thoroughly and its author, too. But certainly the appearance of the alphabet in Greek culture was recent as epochal cultural history goes, and so its freshness and undeveloped potential may well show itself in some of the poems' wider aspects.

We can look at the Homeric poems then in this light. The aim here is general; using the Homeric poems, to try and suggest the kind of thing the alphabet can capture. Although the style of both poems is often described as "leisurely," they differ markedly in atmosphere and scope. The *Iliad* is severely constrained in time and space. It deals not with the ten-year siege of Troy but its very last stages, and its action covers only a few weeks. The terrain is the open land between the city walls and the invading Greeks' ships. The poem omits several major features of the full Troy story. It is orientated toward its characters, their confrontations, their speeches, their lengthy debates over gifts and bargains, loyalties of the gods, and wider speculations; and their scores of individual duels and deaths in battle—all of which befit the oral tradition. The incessantly ghastly nature of the deaths ("the spear entered under his chin and up through the nose-bone; his eyeballs fell out and he screamed") contrasts the pathos of the wives and children as they witness these events. Richmond Lattimore, translator of both poems, believes that in the *Iliad* the poet had the problem of keeping accurately to the oral legends while giving his sophisticated audience the heroic status they wanted for the chief Greek figures, Achilles most of all.[2] The ingredients of the oral tradition had to be interwoven with tact, and the poem's human-interaction fabric dominates as a result.

The *Odyssey* by contrast deals with the homeward journey of Odysseus, thousands of miles via many countries over several years. He faces not one enemy but many, and of many kinds; monsters like the one-eyed giant Cyclops, the deadly wailing Sirens and enticing Lotos-Eaters, natural hazards like the death-dealing pair of rocks Scylla and Charybdis and the suitors of his wife Penelope when he returns to Ithaca. There are long sojourns with more friendly peoples. Odysseus's renowned "many wiles"—not just martial valor alone—are repeatedly needed. The poem ends up with an entire ecology—sea, weather, rocks, currents, sailing, and fishing; tending of flocks and herds, cattle, pigs, and also crops of wheat; female seducers, kings with opulent gifts; numerous stories each with a new kind of surprise.

In the *Iliad* the poetic descriptions are often clearly profiled set pieces; the richly developed yet curiously isolated similes ("as when a lion," "as when a huge oak," "as when the sea"), and superb descriptions of human artifacts, such as Hephaistos's construction of Achilles's armor and shield (18:478–607). The warriors come with no details of who they are. There is just the "rolle" or row of letters that is their name, often in fact only at the moment of their death, so that in any A-killed-B sequence, B (as object of the verb) is sometimes dead by the time we know he existed or what to call him. Formulaic repetition abounds without comment; snatches of the natural world, powerfully evoked, are wedged between the more widely layered languages of exhortation, defiance, strategy, consolation, and grief.

In the *Odyssey*, for better or worse, language's possibilities are pushed outward as to vocabulary and setting. In the *Iliad* one combat and debate is succeeded relentlessly by another until thousands are killed. In the *Odyssey*, one adventure follows another until hero and surviving members of the crew have met with all that earthly existence has to offer, and they at last reach home where everything begins and ends. The deeply moving quality of many passages has varying import. A character will reveal his thoughts in a kind of confession, heroically and naively at once, as when in the games in Book 8, Odysseus answers the brusque challenge of Euryalos. The challenger's own reply is fine, generous, poetically conceived, and underlines the oral tradition. "Farewell, father and stranger, and if any word was let slip / that was improper, may the stormwinds catch it away and carry it / off, and the gods grant you safe homecoming to your own country / and wife; since here, far from your own people, you must be suffering" (8:408–10). By contrast, in Book 14, Odysseus's account of his adventures to the swineherd Eumaios is a pack of lies, while his proof to his wife Penelope in Book 23 (183–204) that it really is he who has returned to her is profoundly touching. It is more enhanced by so many passages of her yearning answers to those who predict Odysseus's return (19:309–16), and later when she can hardly believe her nurse's report that Odysseus is here (23:310–41). Such passages mingle with very different events. These include Odysseus's plan to get his crew away from the Cyclops by having them cling under the stomachs of trios of sheep; the singer at supper who recites Odysseus's own story—this poem's story—back to him (8:499ff.); and the myth of the Old Man of the Sea who turns into lion, serpent, water, and tree successively. Odysseus tricks the Cyclops into thinking his (Odysseus's) name is "Noman"; puns have arrived, if still self-consciously.

Yet in this poem too all this feels fated, enounced. Language's potential is expanded, but not in the nuances of minds and their range of psychological response. The newly invented alphabet has enabled descriptive-power—which speech and writing already possessed—to amass further detail, grow more complex, and indeed get entailed in the action. Using the same marks—letters—to name objects, to instruct how to pronounce them and (by prepositions, conjunctions, and such) how they were part of human action, was a great step forward. But it was too early for this new alphabet also to unhook itself from the localized marks to which it had previously been tied, and so allow pure concepts to be presented as in effect fully fledged things themselves. So some of the parameters of what we call psychology and rational thought come to be hinted at, but without full consciousness.

There are glimpses. At 16:477, Telemachos "smiled as he caught his father's eye." At 17:290 it is the old dog that recognizes Odysseus first. When Penelope finally recognizes Odysseus, "her knees and the heart within her went slack." But so did the knees of many of Odysseus's crew, in the wholly different emotion of terror earlier in the voyage in quite other circumstances. Such formulaic repetition of course pervades the Homeric poems; the identical term or phrase for quite different people, places and action. This tendency to repeat comes from the same early tendency to repeat that we have already noted. The moot point then is whether consciousness is enabling language or language consciousness, and what degree and type of consciousness has been reached. To modern readers there is a curious, even dreamy, slowness in the battle with the suitors at the end, so that Odysseus and his son Telemachos, beset by dozens of opponents in a vicious fight, have time for a detailed interchange as to their next strategy (22:160ff.). The numerous practical tasks throughout the poem; the harnessing of horses (4:40); the cooking (3:453–63, lifted from the *Iliad*); the maids serving (7:172ff.)—all are given in a single level syntax of successive events, in which conditionals, qualifications, and subordinate clauses do not raise doubts about the main assertions, no matter what the event or occasion. "A maidservant brought water for him and poured it from a splendid / And golden pitcher, holding it above a silver basin / For him to wash, and she pulled a polished table before him. / A grave housekeeper brought in the bread and served it to him. . . ." (7:172–75). It is as though speech alone, as yet without writing, handles linguistic mimesis of fleeting or half formed mental states, or of departure from public address, however rich such things may be inherently.

Such writing sits easily with the repetitions alluded to as when Penelope recognizes Odysseus. These patterns abound, too, more than in the *Iliad* but in comparable form. Dawn with her rosy fingers; circumspect Penelope; Kalypso shining among the divinities; white-armed Nausicaa; thoughtful Telemachos. Refrains abound, of psychological import but again never elaborated. "See, I will accurately answer all that you ask me." "Sitting well in order we dashed the oars in the grey sea." "And their knees gave way beneath them." "What sort of word has escaped your teeth's barrier?" "What the heart within my breast urges." "And put away in your heart this other thing that I tell you." If "what the heart within my breast urges . . . escapes the teeth's barrier" (i.e., when the teeth are clenched with emotion) every single time, how is it spontaneous or individual, how is there initiative? When they are repeated, do we actually reread such lines, or just see them again? The real point is what such questions are asking.

The incidents of the *Odyssey* could be read today as dream. What are the Lotos-Eaters? Scylla and Charybdis? The Cyclops? They readily yield to interpretation to us now as escapism, dilemma, and one-eyed mania respectively, and the hero suffers, we are told, more than any mortal had ever done previously. Yet Odysseus seems to know none of this; no one asks who and what these hazards are, there is no questioning. Of course there isn't: they are sent by the gods, whose hands we are in; it is idle to inquire. In short, the poet still works by juxtaposing whole incidents, similes, set speeches and set duels, encounters with monsters and magic, in sequence with only large-scale flashback and so no explanation. It seems then throughout that the alphabet is being worked, turned around as to its own poetic possibilities, on a large scale certainly, but only for the first time, or certainly a very early time. Its capacity to remain "equable" while still embodying a rich range of mental, descriptive, and emotional registers, their qualifications and inscribed hesitancies and certainties, hasn't yet been grasped, maybe isn't yet needed.

The abecedary's equable quality is its capacity to refer to countless topics and their nuances through a single communicative channel. That last phrase is Goody's (Goody 1987, 72), who argues that later Greek skepticism became possible through the alphabet itself. Purely pictorial scripts have not this flexibility, because they have to depict the observed item on at least minimally its own shape and terms. They are mimetic, not virtual or arbitrary, while the syllabary script, as said earlier, has to confuse different registers of meaning *(man + drake = mandrake)* and so introduce extraneous concepts. Prealphabet cultures didn't lack either science or mathematics, nor proof and the elaboration of general skeptical reason and argument. But they did lack a full consciousness of these last two things, and it is argued that the invention of the alphabet is what gradually enabled this consciousness. It is this gradual evolution— and indeed there is no full agreement about it—that many believe reached its full flowering in the high period of rationality and philosophy in the middle of the second millennium B.C. in ancient Greece.

But alphabetical writing does gradually become subtle enough to speak doubt, and therefore investigation, of a kind Odysseus—let alone the Greek generals—can never stay for. Alphabetical writing could bring generality and high abstraction, yet with stunning power, and general proposition backed by concrete cases. The most diverse material, from warfare to philosophy, from narrative to syllogism, from astronomy to law, can be shaped down to the words' (letters') parameters, that is to say could be included without rocking the system of writing itself. As Goody puts it, "Try doing all this [syllogism, analogy, competing versions of stories] *without* writing, without the use of graphemes" (72; his emphasis). This isn't to say that nonalphabetical scripts like the ideographic can do none of these things, but that they will do them in a different way drawing on their own characteristics.

There is also the increase in self-consciousness that writing enables. Earlier we mentioned David Olsen's suggestion that writing does not merely report speech but also offers a model for speech. Olsen is quite clear when this happened. "[The] invention of the concept of mind . . . is thought to have occurred between the time of the oral poet Homer . . . and the time of the Greek philosophers Socrates, Plato and Aristotle" (Olsen 1994, 236). Homer's poetry lacks "the tender emotions of shame, embarrassment, sympathy, forgiveness, anger (as opposed to rage)"; it is bodily not mental. Terms like "decided," "thought," "believed," "doubted," or "equivocated" are markedly absent. "No one in the Iliad decides, thinks, knows, fears or remembers anything in his *psyche*" (239, Olsen's emphasis). Such things are fateful; they are the gods living in us. Olsen is not referring here to a self-consciousness as we understand that today; namely, the matter of one's fuller knowledge of one's own psychological makeup, with its aggressions, escapisms, drives, emotions, sexuality, subconscious, and the rest. That came much later. It is rather that the projection of ideas and feelings out into words could enable those ideas and feelings to be in some sense objectively identified and used as permanent entities. This is what the later classical Greeks meant by reason.

Athenian Civilization

Much then happened in Greece between Homer and Plato, both outside Athens and within it. Major cultural events and changes helped predispose the Platonic period. This is a long and often obscure story, so only general areas and issues can be addressed here.

The first question is a preliminary and can be treated quickly. If the alphabet was indeed invented at about Homer's time, then why did it take some three centuries to start developing its potential in the ways found in high Greek civilization? There are two possible answers. One is simply that the Homeric poems did not come into Attic, and therefore Athenian civilization itself, until about the middle of the sixth century B.C. The usual date given is 566 B.C., when a contest for recitation of passages from Homer was instituted at the Panathenaic ("all-Athens") festival. The impact was strong and immediate. "From being a culture-poor, backward land, Attica suddenly became *the* repository of the Homeric heritage."[3] The agent of this initiative was probably either the poet and political reformer Solon, or Pisistratus, a major patron of the arts. It is even arguable that Homer, so indubitably great, was in the end a partly constraining influence on the spread of dialectic and its diffusion into several cultural areas. Certainly Plato (if not always willingly), Aristotle,

Greek tragedy, and the later oratory had constant recourse to him. The second reason for the three-century delay is more general. Because we today take ease of dissemination for granted, we might well overlook how rudimentary such means were in early times. Even in our own fully aware technological era, advance from the first steam train to universal automobiles and popular air travel has taken nearly two centuries. Few in the ancient world were educated; they had no printing, no electronics whatever, and travel (and therefore the spread of cultural practices) was slow. Either way or both, things only begin to move in the mid-sixth century B.C.

Greek tragedy reached its peak in Athens in the fifth century B.C. Its origins and development have long been disputed. For many the key factors are the choric songs and religious rituals of earlier times; for others, tragedy was an invention of Athenian civilization alone. But even if it was the former in part, there is no denying the importance of the sixth and fifth century introduction of individual actors into the drama, and therefore their speaking parts, as distinct from the traditional tragic chorus. The first actor was introduced by Thespis. We know little of him other than that he won a festival contest in 534 B.C. The matter takes us back to the prealphabetical singer or reciter of the Homeric epic poems, the *aoidos*. The Homeric poems twice refer to *thespis aoidon* and *thespis aoiden* (divine singer, divine song); the *aoidos* survived into later centuries, and tradition has it that Thespis's father may himself have been an *aoidos*. But Thespis's innovation of the single actor allowed the reciter's self-impersonation of the epic hero to enter tragic drama. A century later Aeschylus and Sophocles added a second and then a third actor.

The significance of this, clearly, is that dialogue enters drama. This in its turn aids the advance of dialectic in its widest sense. Dialectic is the continuous interchange (of ideas, events, emotions, and so on) between different persons rather than their single uninterrupted statement; and this would clearly have an outlet in the dramatic arena. Aeschylus's plays admittedly take a long time to develop the potential of the actor. Only in his later plays is there a full dramatic development between individuals as we would understand that. But this brings us back to the idea of fate again. We have already suggested how, in the *Odyssey* particularly, the epic hero himself is still wholly in the hands of the gods; and we have suggested that this is result of the still-early development of the alphabet. As we put it earlier: in the *Odyssey* all still feels fated, enounced. Language's potential is expanded, but not in the nuances of minds and their range of psychological response. The achievement of Aeschylus, to reach its wider culmination most fully in Sophocles's *Oedipus Rex*, is to extend the vision to the point where fate itself is at last internalized, examined, and made comprehensive. In the traditional formula, *pathein mathein* [We learn by suffering]. So it seems reasonable to suggest that the gradual extension of dialogue, and therefore dialectic, within the drama is part of what led to this full, overt, written, and expressed encountering of suffering, the experience that comes only from endurance. And this too, surely, is furthered by the alphabetical mode. If the written form of a word can escape its own, unique material origin, in effect the detail of its "rolle," the word is then left free to associate its still-material but now unmoored sign with more universal and abstract notions. This "unmoored" quality is what I am later going to call "virtual." But the process is greatly furthered by dialectic. Dialectic is advanced when dialogue itself can be written down and so provide perpetual models or reference points for future occasions. Humans can exchange ideas, concepts, reasons, and evidence with each other via words, knowing that the same word always has a point of consistent focus in its written form that is unchanging no matter who happens to be using it at any one time.

And some modern commentators do tie this advance to the details of drama's development. Denis Feeney points to the emergence of actors' written scripts. Reviewing a work on classical literature, Feeney claims that "it takes only thirty seconds' thought to see that you cannot get twelve or fifteen people to sing the same (exceptionally complex and challenging) thing for fifteen minutes without a script. The same goes for Attic drama, which is inconceivable without scripts." Feeney favorably cites Barry Powell, and comments, "The impact of the new technology of writing was massive. . . . the creative power of alphabetic literacy [is what] made these new forms of immediacy possible."[4] The point does not apply to drama alone. There is also the newly rich work of the poet Pindar (born early in the sixth century B.C.) with his high-level thought, grand style, colorful language, and powerful and varied metaphor. It is difficult to see how this nonrepetitive work could have been constructed without writing, drafts, checking-back to what is already written, and so forth.

History as an intellectual discipline also begins in fifth-century Greece. From our point of view we can fruitfully compare Herodotus, known as "the father of history," with the Athenian historian Thucydides. Admittedly these two did not live so far apart in time that clear evolution can be deduced from their two lives too readily. Even so, there seems a progress from Herodotus's mode to that of

Thucydides. In the huge content of Herodotus's searching history of the Greek and Persian wars—and chronologically he does come down almost as far as Thucydides did—there are nevertheless features that still tie him to the ancient practice of essential storytelling. He digresses often, harks back to earlier stories without warning in the middle of a more recent one, is interested in a somewhat mythical world geography, and, although a genuine seeker after historical truth broadly, still accepts evidence from informers at face value. He was still hemmed in by an age "primitive in its religious beliefs and restricted in its general knowledge." His main aim was the somewhat epic one of maintaining "the memory of the great and wonderful deeds . . . of earlier times."[5] Thucydides by contrast was more nearly a historian as we think of that today. He reported both speeches and events meticulously, gave at least some credible basis of evidence—as Goody put it, competing versions of stories, not just one—and, again unlike Herodotus, sought causal connections between events and applied reasoning to political issues. He was also a specialist. Herodotus's story goes right back to Croesus, Babylon, and the conquest of Egypt by Cambyses. By contrast, Thucydides's entire work on the Peloponnesian War covers a mere nineteen years, each carefully labeled. Again then we see perhaps the entry into this genre of what the alphabet enables, or has been argued to enable. Reason, cause, collation, and most of all the support of main assertions by supporting material, qualifications, and other hypotheses; in terms of alphabetic writing, the support of main clauses by subordinates, parentheses, and qualifying prepositions.

Philosophy reached its peak only in the fourth century B.C., and, roughly contemporary with oratory and rhetoric, was the last major cultural form to flower in ancient Greece. Its sometimes imputed originator Thales (born 624 B.C.) not only left no writing—nor indeed did Socrates himself—but is remembered largely for thinking the earth floated on water and that magnets have souls. Greek philosophy matured when the dialectic in its many forms was able to recognize Reason with a capital R as itself a platonic Ideal Form. Reason was not, as we would think now, merely an important potential of organized psyches accurately noticing objective facts and events and recognizing their consistencies and inconsistencies. Reason itself was seen as an entity, and its medium was the interconnecting of fixed concepts. This is found in both Plato and Aristotle; and our presumption here, from what we have said earlier in part 1, has to be that the alphabet enables these concepts to be recognized with detachment. It is not that prealphabetical people lacked conceptual or logical thinking. But they had no means of objectifying them before the full alphabet system, with its aspiration at least to express the nonmaterial, was established. And so Plato came to believe that only when politicians were fully philosophers too, fully conversant with concept via reason, could a successful polity be run. Only when politically motivated expediency was removed could there be success. And the crucial interchange of concepts, via dialectic (itself via drama), was surely therefore greatly dependent on the alphabetical system. There are three logical stages in this argument. Reason could only germinate an intellectual community within the state when concepts could be voiced, from one person to another and back. Concepts could not be voiced until, as Olsen and others suggested, a consistent model for their voicing had appeared. And that model, in turn, could not remain consistent without being recorded in writing.

There has been dispute over the status of Plato's dialogues as to their public to private, outer to inner provenances. Some see them as close to the dramatic, others emphasize the inner psychology of the debates' participants. It seems to me to lie between these two extremes. The Greeks did not have the discipline of psychology as we understand that. Plato condemned action for selfish motive as ignoble, but only in light of the higher aim of Reason and the Good. On the other hand, as already suggested, the dialogue method was surely influenced in a general way by the actor-generated innovation of dramatic dialogue. Statement-and-answer and question-and-answer moved toward the center as a written as well as oral mode of communicating our most central feelings, opinions, and true knowledge. It seems then rather that the Platonic dialogues are philosophical conversations; social interactions certainly, but always on and because of a philosophical content. Nothing else is adduced. It has also seemed to me that both Plato and Aristotle, in their different ways, shared a common aim and one that was major. In the era's great blossoming of epistemological enquiry, the project of both men was to seek to establish what, on any topic, could be said as truth *regardless of who at any moment was saying it*. Socrates and his participants in Plato's dialogues subject their question-and-answer method entirely to seeing what comes out when you say this and then that, and who then is left with virtually undeniable verbal-conceptual (that is basically alphabetical) assertions. Aristotle assumes that language is tied, fundamentally and ab initio, to the items it names. He thus observes the material and animal world around him in light of these fixed concepts, and then interrelates the observation with the concept—neither having priority—in order to find what can be said as truth if this interrelating is accurate at both levels. Thus, when Aristotle compares hunger and thirst as examples of desire, or elucidates the difference between cutting and splitting, he reaches conclusions by tying the relevant physical realities to the permanent Reason-based concepts of these things he already possesses. Either way it is the alphabet—a material system, however, that a priori depicts nothing—that enables concepts both to stay at least consistent and be systematically relayed around an overtly dialectical community.

Plato. The Suspicion of Writing

This brings us to Plato direct. When Plato reads the Homeric epics some four hundred years after they are first written down, he is drawn by their beauty and power; but he is also dubious. For Plato the alphabet is almost too powerful; and here we encounter perhaps the central issue of this part of the whole topic. For if philosophy and Reason itself are the highest point of development from the original alphabetic invention, maybe its unique and greatest achievement, it is obviously paradoxical that its great exemplar, Plato himself, should remain suspicious of writing almost all his life. This is what we have to consider.

It must be remembered that Plato was born (in 427 B.C.) in a city at war; that he knew the older man Socrates personally, and that when Socrates was finally executed for his supposed anti-Athenian teachings, Plato left politics in disgust. But this is to jump the gun somewhat. As to Homer, and intriguingly, Plato finds much more wrong with the *Iliad* than he does with the *Odyssey*. At the start of Book III of the *Republic* he is looking to censor the poets who fail to control the moral import of their stories and descriptions along the lines the ideal state would want its young imbued with. There are twenty-three criticisms of the *Iliad* and only seven of the *Odyssey*, and this count omits the long barrage (*Republic* 3:4) against the *Iliad*'s opening. But this might seem counter to our argument. For it is the excessive and greater free play of poetic imagination that Plato fears, and this is stronger in the later poem if my reading is tenable. But, whatever the truth of that, this merely leads us to the interesting paradoxes in Plato's whole position, most exemplified by his renowned distrust of writing over speech even though so magisterial a writer himself.

The difficulty is compounded, for of course Plato opposed more than just writing as against speech. His much-debated disapproval of the arts generally has many aspects. The arts presented both falsehood and immorality; but equally, even when they did not, they presented reality twice removed from its true existence in its Ideal Form. Yet Plato has been thought of since, not just as a great philosopher, but one of essentially poetic nature. For Sir Philip Sidney, "[Plato] of all Philosophers, I have ever esteemed most worthy of reverence, and with great reason: Sith of all Philosophers, he is the most poeticall"; this in the very process of dispelling Plato's antipoetry arguments. For Shelley, "Plato was essentially a poet— the truth and splendour of his imagery, and the melody of his language, are the most intense that it is possible to conceive."[6] But we are talking about writing itself. In becoming the first major Western philosopher of the alphabetical era, Plato took its new capacity both to record debate and to express abstraction to fuller lengths than had previously been conceived of.

In the *Phaedrus*, Plato's characters first discuss love, and then examine that very discussion, that is to say, as to how love itself should be debated. And here comes the famous rejection of writing (*Phaedrus*, sects 274–75, 96–97). It is cast as a story about the visit to the king of Egypt by that country's god Thoth who, as was noted earlier, first brought writing to the Egyptian people:

> *Socrates.* "Theuth, my paragon of inventors," replied the king, "the discoverer of an art is not the best judge of the good or harm which will accrue to those who practice it. . . . What you have discovered is a receipt for recollection, not for memory. And as for wisdom, your pupils will have the reputation for it without the reality: they will receive a quantity of information without proper instruction, and in consequence be thought very knowledgeable when they are for the most part quite ignorant. And because they are filled with the conceit of wisdom instead of real wisdom they will be a burden to society."
>
> *Phaedrus.* How easy you find it, Socrates, to compose a story from Egypt or any other country.

Later Socrates continues (sect. 275, p. 97):

> *Socrates.* You might suppose that [written words] understand what they are saying, but if you ask them what they mean by anything they simply return the same answer over and over again. Besides, once a thing is committed to writing it circulates equally among those who understand the subject and those who have no business with it; a writing cannot distinguish between suitable and unsuitable readers. And if it is ill-treated or unfairly abused it always needs its parent to come to its rescue; it is quite incapable of defending or helping itself.

These are very fresh insights. The idea of writing itself "understanding what it is saying," and of staying the same when it is circulated, employs whimsy to get at truth. Socrates seems focused on writing, its actual signs, rather physically. He was fascinated; his dislike is double-edged. In Letter 7, to Dion's supporters in Syracuse and written probably at much the same period in Plato's life as the *Phaedrus*, Plato emphasizes writing's static quality even further. (Letter 7 is probably genuine, though by the strictest scholarship not certainly so.) "No intelligent man will ever dare commit his thoughts to words, still less to words that cannot be changed, as is the case with what is expressed in written characters" (sect. 343, p. 138). Since Plato spent much of his life apparently committing his thoughts to words that could not be changed, we might wonder at such puzzling remarks.

A clue may lie in Phaedrus's response to the account of Thoth. "How easy you find it, Socrates, to compose a story from Egypt or any other country." Isn't this also a touch whimsical, as though Plato is happy to let Socrates be teased a little? You defy the poets, Socrates, but you "compose" (*logous poieis*, "make words," act as a poet) so readily yourself, and with fine disregard of the source and perhaps little knowledge of it. What do you know about Egypt? For Socrates is referring to a writing-system; namely the Egyptian, other than the one he or indeed Plato is writing himself. And of course his smiling self-deprecations feature in many of the dialogues. Again and again Socrates disclaims ability to proceed, or says he has gone up a cul-de-sac in the debate. At the end of the *Thaetetus* he declares to Thaetetus that their conclusions as to knowledge's nature "are mere wind-eggs and not worth rearing." In the long debate between Cratylus and Hermogenes in the *Cratylus* on whether language is natural or conventional (cf. Graham 1992, chap. 1 and passim), Socrates seemingly can't decide which way the debate should fall. After a long speech from Protagoras in that dialogue he says he dislikes long speeches because of his wretched memory. This from Socrates, who blames writing for bringing such enfeeblement! Often too in the dialogues a point is painstakingly worried over and repeated to secure it, yet is still not written down in straight assertive form.

Of course, Socrates was not above affecting discomfiture he didn't feel, so that a sparring-partner's confidence could be exposed as misplaced. Socrates' apparent determination to antagonize the politicians he interrogated is partly why he was poisoned; but we can't examine that closely here. To the twentieth century and today which locate human behavior in personal inadequacy, Plato might seem congenitally distrustful of his own position and powers. But this would overlook the controlled harmony of most of the works.

Factors from birth or nurture might have disposed Plato toward such inquiry in the first place, but could not account for its evident maturation. The sunny irony and wit pervading the dialogues doesn't convey the residual neuroses that might disable the performance. But there is a big problem for Plato, as for any epistemologist who thinks knowledge cannot be expressed in words at all. Plato himself—for this is not in a dialogue but again Letter 7—expresses it thus:

> No treatise by me concerning (my subject) exists or ever will exist. It is not something that can be put into words like other branches of learning; only after long partnership in a common life devoted to this very thing does truth flash upon the soul, like a flame kindled by a leaping spark, and once it is born there it nourishes itself thereafter. . . . I do not think that the attempt to put these matters into words would be to men's advantage, except to those few who can find out the truth for themselves with a little guidance. . . ." (136)

The problem is clear. If Plato's subject forbids both philosophical record and the art of poetry, what sort of writing is left? I suggest again that alphabetical writing was still recent enough, as cultures go, for the earliest stages of collective self-consciousness about its use to have survived. It was about four centuries since Homer; a period, down to Plato, distinctly shorter than our own since the invention of print. Until quite recently—more or less up to the flood of postwar media, spread of higher education, and the later domestication of the word processor—for many people there was still a slight frisson at "seeing my name in print" and some awe shown to anyone who had achieved such a thing. Similarly in fourth century Greece and elsewhere, writing was still difficult and highly privileged. There may have been a comparable sense of writing itself as still not quite fully absorbed, the province of thinkers and intellectuals who stood out from the natural way of life of most people.[7] Indeed, strange as it may sound, Plato's very suspicion of writing itself seems like a turning point in the abecedary's history. It was the very moment at which it began truly to know itself, as, at last, a fully fledged and highly flexible medium, capable of poetry, drama, philosophy, history, oratory, and the various branches of epistemology and knowledge generally. There are a couple of pointers to this in the dialogues.

In the *Thaetetus*, the *Sophist,* and elsewhere—both quite late dialogues—Plato points to the "learning of one's letters" as a natural synecdoche of wider processes. In a discussion somewhat bizarre to us now (*Thaetetus,* sect. 203), Socrates and Thaetetus argue that while the syllable "SO" of Socrates (to us a morpheme) can be known about because it divides into the letters S and O (graphemes), yet those letters cannot be known because they divide into nothing lesser still. Socrates points out the fallacy; namely, that if letters are unknowable in themselves they must be knowable in use by other means—as words, of course. The real point of the debate is to see just how far anything can be understood by examining its components. But again, it seems that letters are still fresh enough to lend themselves to such an analogy. As Socrates says, they take letters not to examine *them*; "rather, let us examine ourselves, and see whether it was in accordance with this theory, or not, that we learned letters" (section 203). Even for many fourth-century educated Athenians, the "learning of letters" is still a foregrounded experience, reminiscent of childhood, not yet part of the depth-culture from the mists of time as with much later civilizations. Today we recall our first stumbling efforts on the word processor, or driving a car, in light of the future day when "driving" a car may mean setting electronic instructions and then sitting back to read the paper while the car does the rest. In the *Sophist* the debate is about how far entities within reality can be mutually exclusive, totally combined, or lie somewhere in between. Again the alphabet is the context; and here, significantly in light of their recent appearance, Socrates highlights the vowels. "And the vowels, to a greater degree than the others, run through them all as a bond, so that without one of the vowels the other letters cannot be joined one to another" (sect. 253). He goes on: "Now does everybody know which letters can join with which others? Or does he who is to join them properly have need of art?" This seemingly ingenuous question comes in a debate over philosophy and morality. Since Greek society changed somewhat less in the previous four hundred years than ours has in the comparable period, we feel here a cultural phenomenon, the alphabet, to be still not exhausted in its novelty. Three or four decades later Aristotle continues to spell out what letters are (Aristotle, *Poetics,* 22).

Furthermore, the *Sophist,* indeed these presently considered sections of it, is where Plato finally resolves his long-standing puzzlement over falsehood. To us now this debate is merely a curiosity; as Nicholas Denyer has argued it, a case history in philosophical progress.[8] That statements in language can be false has ceased to be a problem in philosophy long since. Yet it survived in Plato's time. This too seems part of the growing perception of the alphabet's capacities. The argument of the *Sophist* at this point, much simplified, is that not-being has its legitimate place in reality logically, and so it too must be able to be expressed. So the not-true, and so too the deliberately untrue in falsehood and deceit, must be able to be expressed in language as well. Clearly Plato is pondering what was adduced above, the power of speech and writing to name the unnameable, to refer to the inconceivable. Yet the mode of such expression, whether of not-being or of falsehood, turns out to be the familiar subject-predicate distinction (*Sophist*, sect. 254). Seemingly for the first time, Plato sees that nouns and verbs are quite different types of the genus "names," and so they can help express the similarities and differences within reality that the *Sophist* distinguished earlier. Nouns refer to things that just are, verbs refer to their capacity to act on or "mingle with" each other. Again this couldn't normally be done purely pictorially; it certainly couldn't be inflected syntactically, as letters with their ease of deployment can do it. The alphabet's equability is again invoked. So is its distributive capacity.

Plato also refers to the fact that letters are few, something almost lost sight of today by all but a handful of specialist linguists. So what arises from all of this?

Plato wants to keep expression fluid. Names themselves must mingle with each other, for "the complete separation of each thing from all is the utterly final obliteration of all discourse. For our power of discourse is derived from the interweaving of the classes or ideas with one another" (*Sophist*, sect. 259). Yet of all systems, the alphabet most enables such mingling. The same few letters, in combination, are used for all of a language's words however disparate their meanings. What then is Plato's complaint? Here, behind the bad effects on memory, lies the real objection to writing. What mattered to Plato was what he said about writing in the *Phaedrus* and in Letter 7 cited above. No matter what mingling is achieved, the letters just sit there on the page. In Letter 7, writing is "words that cannot be changed, as is the case with what is expressed in written characters." This fixity, absent from speech, is like the sacredness of the sacred text that also could not be changed. The literary effect of this fixity roots our own cultural history in the Bible, Malory, Pope, and beyond. But Herbert attempted to shift it, and the liberalism of the last two hundred years, from Wordsworth and the realist novel via modernism and Joyce to the centrifugal language of TV, film, endorsed vernaculars, and the rest, throws the matter wide open as we have it now. Plato never got near such a position, for uses of the alphabet had not evolved equivalently. He is left with only the alternative fluidities of oral dialectic and thought.

And in this, unlike writing, they are indeed fluent. I mean in the sense that there is often no clear boundary between thoughts or sounds. Written letters by contrast are separate from each other. In Letter 7, Plato goes from his argument against writing's fixity into listing the components required when thought aspires to knowledge and the necessary fluidity of thought as a result. Valid epistemology is itself seen to be fluid (sect. 343). Again this is no sticky interchange in a dialogue but Plato's defiant defense of his method to Dion's supporters in Syracuse, when they were trying to make him expound his philosophical method to them off pat. Yet this very defiance comes in continuous writing; in straight, alphabetical prose.

But the dialectical method, which aims to keep such fluidity of thought going, is still language. If many of the dialogues are open-ended, somehow unfinished, and as said earlier even on occasion anticlimactic, that may seem to underline that speech can't fully do the job. At the end of the *Thaetetus* it is knowledge as "true opinion with an accompanying rational account" that, however, still fails to be a satisfactory description of knowledge. It seems that Plato is not realizing just how near to, rather than far from, the truth of speech the new alphabetical mode of writing could be. It is almost as though Plato actually discovered abstraction, yet had to keep it as Idea—the Ideal Forms, not part of this world—being unable quite to trust the alphabet with abstractions' existence. There is something of a sad smile on Socrates' face as he goes through the various candidates for elimination from common life and thought in the *Apologia*, as though he is playing with the new conceptual power of the alphabet's way of mentalizing things. Evolving the abstract into an articulable system, and thereby postulating Ideal Forms of everything, left abstract and concrete in binary opposition to each other. Yet the alphabet can handle both. We saw earlier how the prewriting Akan people of Africa expressed even emotion and principle in physical terms. When language is still speech or thought, Plato could take this into further abstraction, but he went on disallowing the process in writing.

This finally suggests what the abecedary is "made of." Perhaps Plato did, eventually, begin to think of it so. In the *Timaeus*, a really quite late dialogue and a prosier one than most, nothing is said about language but much is noted about the basic material of the universe itself. If this material is to be shaped into all the things of the world we recognize, it must itself be originally featureless, without character. Only that way could it receive that multitude of impressions that themselves embody character. "That which is going to receive properly and uniformly all the likenesses of the intelligible and eternal things must itself be devoid of all character" (*Timaeus,* section 18). It is as though the new way of writing might stand to the Ideal Forms of Plato's thought just as base material stands to the myriad phenomena of the universe. The alphabet certainly doesn't lack character, as we shall argue; but it is equable, in part in that its few signs combine into the words of an entire language. If one is to be mimetic of the Ideal at all, then compared even to ideographic writing, let alone painting and (highly dangerous) music, the alphabet would best match that Ideal's unity. Maybe Plato finally realized this toward the end of his working life.

Aristotle must get briefer comment here. We have already touched on his particular contribution to the issue, via his scientific method of interrelating conceptual thinking with objective material observation. Here we turn to his literary criticism (more will be said of a third area, the political and ethical, when we come to Aquinas). In the fourth century B.C., along with oratory, the burgeoning genre of literary criticism entailed, among other things, an exhaustive and microscopic study of the possibilities of language. Hundreds of types of speech were identified; the grammar and spelling and shapes of words closely examined. E. H. Gombrich has said this was "perhaps the most careful analysis of any expressive medium ever undertaken."[9] The orators spoke for reasons of expediency that Plato condemned, but to improve their methods in heavy competition was always a pressure. The closest scrutiny of alphabetical words and what they were made of was a major result. Literary criticism however is more relevant to our topic.

Aristotle's work on poetics was in part a response to Plato, and that will be our emphasis. As member of the Athenian Academy that Plato headed, Aristotle doubtless brought his own angle to a set of problems and ideas already digested. In Aristotle, Plato's binary ideal-real distinctions went triple; namely, the mean between less desirable extremes, in an overall aim by stages at the naturally good (*Ethics* II, *Ethics* I). Aristotle's response is less idealistic, more an acceptance of things as they are. All arts and sciences aim at some good, the chief of which is happiness; but this aim emanates from our natures. It is equally natural to enjoy mimesis; one need not be suspicious of it. "We enjoy looking at accurate likenesses of things which are themselves painful to see" (*Poetics,* 4:3); this principle was resurrected by the medieval Italian painters as Vasari strongly underlined. The meeting between the object itself, however ugly, and the medium of the paint, words, or stone that reproduces it, just is satisfying to our constitutions. With drama likewise: the presentation of undesirable actions just does have the good and observable effect, in judiciously written tragedy, of cleansing our emotions rather than corrupting them.

All this connects to language and the alphabet, distantly but crucially, via Aristotle's easement of Plato's strong sense of falsehood. It is not a straight matter of truth versus lies. Rather, Aristotle characteristically moves from the Ideal to a belief that we may ask of any work simply what is proper to it. This can be found in our experience, which in the last analysis is biological. Art depicts merely what might happen rather than what does happen. In short, the inventive imagination, which is why Aristotle saw poetry as more beneficial than history; and that is another issue much alive with critics today. The epic poet needs "the art of telling untruths skilfully," and that alarming aim is justified by its preference for "what is convincing though impossible [over] what is possible and unconvincing" (*Poetics,* 24:19). This leads finally to metaphor, which Aristotle much admired. Metaphor could allow newly coined or strange words, riddles, or contradictions in its accompanying context, always so long as a sense of propriety reigned.

Metaphor is the "application of a strange term" from one category to another; and for the writer "by far the greatest thing is the use of metaphor. That alone cannot be learnt; it is the token of genius. For the right use of metaphor means an eye for resemblances" (*Poetics,* 2). That is to say, nature is a unity, yet we don't need to impose some Ideal constraint upon it beyond an everyday sense of what is suitable. Aristotle's position shows that, after and indeed thanks to Socrates and Plato, the alphabet's implication is loosening up. By permuting its nonmimetic signs, it can include all kinds of material in its one communicative channel, and this itself evinces the unity of nature. Metaphor most of all can introduce surprising comparisons without offending that unity, precisely because of the new alphabet's aptness for such a task. Being few and so more homogenous than in most other systems of writing, letters stay out of the way of the metaphor's items of strong comparison, which enter our consciousnesses with textures of their own. Nature is bounded only by what our own nature senses is proper. To evoke unnecessary criteria is to go against the new civilization's foundational writing system and what it was gradually showing it could achieve. The figurative results needed only to be checked against our instincts and the new sciences being developed by such as Aristotle himself.

Summary. The aim of this chapter has been, again, to bring out main features of the alphabet, but this time in the special context of the long development from the earliest alphabetically transcribed poetic writing (exemplified by Homer) to the later pervading forms of abstraction, logic and argument (exemplified by Plato). It has been interesting to see that, while they are not mutually exclusive, the poet and philosopher helpfully underline different alphabetical features. The growing drama was perhaps the key link between them, as we suggested.

The Greeks needed a system for recording languages they couldn't understand. The only way, obviously, was to record their sounds. That left the alphabet's letters "arbitrary," but it also freed them up to name the material as category or idea. The word "javelin" is a *virtual* javelin. The Greeks also found they needed only five vowels and little more than twenty consonants. The phenomenon of abecedarial *fewness* was reinforced.

Homer's poetry underlined linearity as a main aspect of alphabetical writing's *distributive* capacity. But Homer did not vary this; the poems' oft-noted fatedness seems entailed in the words themselves, how they just lie side by side, going on forever, like the stages of Odysseus's voyages. Yet poetry had another aspect. The first main use of the new alphabet was to record poems. It worked perfectly; the alphabet could say things that weren't true. (This is impossible, in one sense, with a pictorial script. If a sign for a tree doesn't look like a tree, it fails, however deceitful the writer's wider intentions.) This is a further *virtuality*, and it was one of Socrates' lifelong complaints about writing. The other was that writing lay woodenly on the page; it emitted no further questions or answers. Plato had unwittingly stumbled on abecedarial *stability*.

Drama brought dialogue and, later, philosophical dialectic. Dialectic generates and then examines concepts. Along with the unnameable and the lie, the concept is one more addition to our growing list of the nonmaterial items the alphabet can name. Hence Plato's Ideal Forms. So too is metaphor a virtual likeness in the mind, as Aristotle realized. But unlike sacred writing, dialogue is nonrepetitive. It has to be or there would be no move forward. Speeches get shorter and shorter; the discussion can change direction. Wider disciplines emerge; science, history, oratory. It is the Greeks' growing recognition of the alphabet's *equability*; so many things can be written and said via the same abecedarial means, with metaphor too now recognized as included; and this last was a stage Homer had not fully exploited. Widening thought and reason also derive from the abecedary's *distributive* capacity. Words stay the same or evolve; are like or unlike each other; both enable comparison. Words can also inflect, and so afford different angles on the same verb or noun. Plato sought fluidity, but didn't realize that writing does this by abecedarial distribution.

3

Augustine, Aquinas, and Others

AUGUSTINE

From here on, for reasons given in the introduction, the term "abecedary" takes over from "alphabet." There remain appropriate exceptions.

THE CHRISTIAN ERA UP TO ROUGHLY THE END OF THE SIXTEENTH CENtury A.D. is saturated with implication for language. It is often consciously recorded, equally often not. The status of Christ and/or the Bible as God's Word, Nature as a readable book, and some observations on language's supposed one-to-one match with nature are main outcomes. But there is more to it from our point of view than this. Three areas seem worth considering: the tradition of intense personal expression that stems from Augustine (A.D. 354–430), the very different structured scholasticism of Thomas Aquinas (A.D. 1225–74); and the English Reformation itself, most notably as to its translations and dissemination of the Bible.

If we are to consider Augustine we need first a brief account of some of the events and issues that had plagued the Christian Church from its beginnings up to Augustine's time. Many of the old pagan cults were coming to an end. In A.D. 66 the Romans put Jerusalem under siege and finally destroyed the ancient Jewish temple. The universality of the Greek language enabled the Christian story to be spread through many countries far and wide. (Augustine never knew Greek, only Phoenician, though he taught himself Latin.) Yet at this early period, Christianity itself was also constantly under threat of persecution. Justin Martyr earned his surname in A.D. 163 as result of his outspokenness toward the Roman imperial authorities. In the second, third and fourth centuries the Roman emperors Decian, Valerian, and Diocletian respectively were responsible for major persecutions. By the time of the capture of Rome by the Visigoth Alaric in A.D., 420 indignation was rife among pagans that

Christianity, in their view, had effectively ruined paganism's greatest achievement, namely, pagan Rome. This issue of persecution becomes important in Augustine's life in his long and difficult dealings with the Donatists. For the Donatists were not heretics; this was a vociferous and schismatic sect whose members identified themselves with the victims of Diocletian's purges.

Yet the church grew. In the second century the emperor Trajan counseled leniency toward Christians. Then major conversions to Christianity occurred, none more earthshaking than that of the emperor Constantine in A.D., 312 which effectively established Christianity as orthodoxy. Alaric was only one of many leading pagans who converted to Christianity, albeit of the heretic Arian variety. The picture gradually changes to one of the establishment of the new religion itself, as to its beliefs and structure. There was much to be settled in those early centuries, and it is also important that, until the fourth century, Christians were largely recruited from the uneducated. Authority lay largely in Scripture. Augustine himself had no training in formal philosophy and knew little of Plato or Aristotle.[1]

The three main issues can be summarized as sin, will, and theological authority. Consciousness of sin as a huge dark new conception stems from the very first century A.D. The new teaching stressed that human beings were lost if they relied on their own natures to direct their earthly lives. The famous epistle of Clement of Rome (A.D. 96) is uncompromising on this subject. Early in the second century Bishop Tertullian of Carthage, Augustine's own region, strongly emphasized humanity's timeless sinfulness.[2] Augustine's own work, the *Confessions* predominantly, is saturated with his strivings over this issue. It is probable that the other two main areas of dispute arose from this central concern. Whatever else it does, Christianity proclaims a kind of committed freedom to live in light of a new teaching—that of Jesus Christ—which sees goodness in espousing God's love rather than only adhering to the centuries-old Hebraic system of Law. An ensuing paradox is that this freedom itself entails an authority. For someone has to decide what this teaching consists of; and with that, too, someone decides who decides. As to will, as well as being the energy that fights sin off, it is also just what authority imposes in the public arena. Will reverses the Homeric fate and meets the circumstance of freedom from the old Law.

Struggle for theological and political authority was, of course, to continue for centuries, with papal power becoming at times wholly intransigent. The orders of bishop, deacon, and elder were established early, although the rank of bishop took a long time to reach the summit of its power, and a bishop might sometimes be little more than a small town's main cleric. But for the same reason, bishops were numerous. In the early years, when the life of the apostle Peter was, in historical terms, of recent memory, the real issue was of apostolic succession. As to doctrine, bitter controversies led to the final authority of the great fourth-century creeds.

It was the first age of the major heresies. This, too, paradoxically, resulted from the Christian dispensation of human freedom. "Vast and dangerous errors were made by interpreters of scripture confident of their own private inspiration."[3] The Gnostics believed that matter was the supreme evil, and out of the resulting asceticism there came the early monasteries. Arians believed Jesus Christ was lesser than God; this was widespread, but more urgent in any consideration of Augustine is Manicheism. Manicheans believed the universe contains two equal powers, evil and good, and "this element of psychodrama fitted [Augustine's] sense of his own internal contradictions."[4] The confessions are a dialogue with God. A renowned preacher, yet Augustine, it seems, was a poor teacher; the leadership role of authoritarian teaching no doubt modified the mode of dialectic too much.

All of these matters set up the background for Augustine's intense, fitful, lifelong concerns with, in effect, a single matter; namely, the existential relation between the individual's inner self and God. This is a strong contrast to the traditional Jewish sense of guilt before a godhead still mainly conceived of as external. We shall trace these topics through to that of writing and the alphabet itself. And yet, born and mainly living in North Africa all his life, Augustine was somewhat out of contact with the great trends and events just listed. The question then is of how he speaks from and for them with such literary vividness and compelling force. For we never cease to feel, for one moment, the presence of his restless but always approachable personality. Not everyone has liked it,[5] and indeed some Christian groups today emphasize what we would see as the more regrettable tendencies; easy tolerance of slavery, acceptance of the subordination of women, and most of all his anti-Semitism. Yet, whatever we think of them now, these were the institutionalized positions of the time, and they surely needn't compromise our regard for the man himself as his confessions reveal him. It has been said that while his contemporary St. Jerome—at one period they corresponded frequently—never had a friend, Augustine never lacked one. The eminent historian of the evolution of medieval thought, David Knowles, has put it for later times: "More than any other great thinker Augustine has seemed [to his readers] a personal friend."[6] Maybe this sense for people directly led to an exquisitely sensitive person's instinct for the movements of an age. Equally it may have been chance, and he just was the right genius who came along at the right time.

Augustine was born in Thagaste, a small town in North Africa, in A.D. 354 Apart from five years in Italy in his early thirties, he spent his life in that region. After Italy he returned mainly to Hippo, a seaport near Carthage, where he remained for forty years until his death in A.D. 430. The African church was never mainstream and we know little of its history before the start of the third century. Augustine's great rival of later years, Bishop Julian of Eclanum, once contemptuously referred to him as a "donkey-protector to his fellow-Africans." Indeed, although Augustine's influence was later to become huge and lasting, it was a long time emerging.[7] He left no school of disciples. His lifetime influence lay in Africa, later to be engulfed by Islam. His writings were long neglected.

The *Confessions* (A.D. 397–98) is an extremely personal book; far more so than the more intellectually structured—though still uniquely flavored—*City of God* (A.D. 413–26). Yet for that very reason it seems the one to consider closely, if we are to contend that the letters we write are humanly important in what we say. The *Confessions* is a major milestone in the long haul of humanity's attempts to express its relationship to God, and in the end our secular stance on the matter. It initiated virtually single-handedly that "unique and characteristic genre of Christian Europe, the spiritual autobiography."[8] Humanly and abecedarially, *Confessions* is a duality, and this quality, sometimes dialectic and sometimes a kind of double-layering, can show us how Augustine's personality touches and uses the abecedary's deepest features. The duality between Scripture and Augustine's personality, which struggles on every page of the *Confessions*, unknowingly continues the world-development of dialectic in all its emerging forms that began in ancient Greece. Greek tragedy had of course expressed personal obsession, ecstasy, and their bodily appearance, but as detachable tropes, built by the poet in dramatic character. Augustine used this same dialectic to speak of himself.

The first aspect to hit us is the incessant relationship struck between the writer and God. One man's stretched emotion, with all its convolutions, confessions, indecision, layers of event from his personal life, and profound awareness of human frailty revolve around the single word GOD, a kind of hub or anchor on which the writer can fully and permanently rely. Again and again, telling of some observation or crisis, Augustine adds that "of course you, God, already knew this would happen, or planned it," or such like. The book wheels round, departs from, and returns to that recurring reference. Today the contemporary theologian Rowan Williams, discussing *Confessions*, sees its mode as that of liturgy more generally: "a 'giving over' of our words to God . . . it is in this sense that good liturgy does what good poetry does."[9] In Latin, GOD *(deus)* inflects according to syntax but of course its first two letters don't change. How this relation of language to reality affects both the reader and Augustine himself is what matters.

On the human side of this duality we feel Augustine's language fused with his body. Like Donne and Herbert, later he talks of mouths, lips, sighs, and crying. When Augustine asks, before his conversion, "Who made me?"—and when he cites Scripture as saying that *the impulses of nature and the impulses of the spirit are at war with one another* (Galatians 5:17)—he is referring to the body he is forever entangled with. "During this agony of indecision I performed many actions . . . I tore my hair and hammered my forehead with my fists; I locked my fingers and hugged my knees" (8:8). And language is bodily too. "My voice was husky and I could not speak for long at a time" (9:2). As a boy he would "prattle away" at his prayers, boast at school, and fret about language and literature, not to mention the thieving, cheating, and carnality with which Books I and II of *Confessions* are laden. Later, "I wept bitter tears and found my only consolation in their very bitterness" (4:6). There are many more such examples. In *City of God* such expressions refer to other people: "This was the silly talk, or rather the delirious raving, of the Manicheans" (11:23). This is the stress of a man wrapped up in his era's consciousness of sin, and the resulting intertwining of the disturbed mind-body with the noises of language seems a kind of microcosm of the confusion of tongues at Babel, one result of humanity's fall from grace. Augustine is expressing the division of one Adamic language into many, but also how writing and utterance are entailed with the fallen individual.

But the contrast is with the one GOD, that lettered entity. This GOD is not only responsible for every incident of life large or small, but also has in grace given humanity a contrasting form of language, the Scriptures, which are static. One might imagine a colossal pyramid topped by the word GOD as the linguistically zero-size apex. It then spreads downward to every other alphabetical permutation we could conceive of. GOD in fact is monotheistically irreducible. Like the Buddhist *Aum* it is a monosyllable, but there's no acronym, so its power is its own. This argues that the alphabet helped not only monotheism's expression, but monotheism itself. This idea need not comment either way on monotheism as such, but rather on the place of the alphabet at the center of monotheistic theologies. Whatever happens to Augustine, or whatever he does, something summarizable, nameable, printable as *DEUS* or its inflections comprehends it all.

It might be replied that it is not the letters of GOD (or Latin *DEUS*) but the word GOD, on which Augustine so compulsively centers. Another selection of letters would have served, just as either GOD or DEUS does, depending on what country or era one dwells in. True, but the selection of some letters from the abecedary which, in the given language, provides the letters for all words whatsoever, means that the entity GOD is not signaled by some separate sign altogether, such as + + + + or [][]. Augustine's own language can cite the divine entity from within its own means. The word can have its unique meaning yet still be held in place syntactically. More important texturally, it is of the same cloth as what surrounds it. Such is the alphabet's equable and universalizing power, with the rolle "GOD," presumably, as a notion most likely to exemplify this. This equability is a key feature of Augustine's alphabet, and he exploited it for the first time in ways that it has never lost since.

Augustine's life was first carnal and dissolute, then more pious if still politically active and personally fraught, in the years mainly at Hippo after his conversion. But the duality just suggested doesn't just reflect these two periods. Rather it is a psychic gap between one inwardly disturbed man, and God. Instead of merely declaring God, Augustine pines for God. It intensifies when he resists God as conversion approaches. "I found no place where I might rest" (7:7). "It is to you that I sigh by night and day" (7:10). Years later, in the context of language, "Even though my tongue utters no sound, my heart cries to you" (10:2). But the fullest formula comes in the famous end to the opening paragraph: "You made us for yourself, and our hearts find no peace until they rest in you" (1:1). Augustine can write his conclusion at the beginning because he is remembering past years; yet the restlessness pervading the work still needs the God-word impressed on it, to give it a point of reference as we have said. The Hinduism's *Aum* tames turbulence by avoiding the linguistic syntax that admits human event, so it can simply be chanted. Augustine's searchings cannot just chant God. Instead, Augustine's GOD, supreme entity way out of our widest purview and known cosmos, can be named by an arrangement of letters within the abecedary itself.

This pining for God is paralleled by Augustine's perennial hope that God could be encountered by chance. Both types of event bear an instability unlike the flat statement of God's existence. Augustine's profound sense of chance underlay his wider belief that humans are too frail to resist sin alone; that is, without divine grace. Countless incidents in *Confessions* have the flavor of serendipity. Augustine's friend Alypius was wrongfully arrested for theft in the Carthage marketplace. He got off only because on being led away they passed an architect friend who, quite by chance—he hadn't witnessed the event—was in a position to show what must have happened (6:9). More important are the events that propelled Augustine's own life forward. His decision in A.D. 383, to travel to Rome for further study did not arise out of intellectual need, but because a group of students were so rowdy that his time in Carthage became unbearable. Again, he could hardly bear to leave his mother, but he boards ship and, again by chance, the wind is exactly fair for them to leave in the night without her knowing (5:8).

Of course, Augustine imputed all such occasions not to chance but to God's intervention. Of Alypius's arrest, "You allowed him to be arrested as a thief. . . ." (6:9). Of a man he rebuked, "I had not meant to rebuke him, but you use us all. . . ." (6:7). Most famously there is the key incident of Augustine's conversion, when he was in a garden and heard a child chanting *tolle legere* [take it and read] over the wall, over and over again (8:12). This is the quite different event of chance encounter with the Scriptures. Here it becomes rather specially relevant to language. On hearing the child sing, Augustine went straight back to Alypius sitting nearby on a bench, opened the Bible at random, and acted on the discovered text (8:12). Much earlier, a doctor friend interested in astrology had told him of the practice of opening poetry anywhere and pointing at any verse. This verse would then turn out to be highly pertinent to the issue at hand even if the poet hadn't been thinking about it at the time (4:3). According to Jacob Burckhardt, the practice survived in Renaissance Italy when the oracles had been superseded: "the fashion to open Virgil at hazard, and take the passage hit upon as an omen ('Sortes Virgilianae')."[10] The important distinction here lies between daily event and Scripture. You wait to see what daily events will come, but you open Scripture deliberately. Today this may savor of the mindless. But it is different when the culture preserves a clear distinction between the flux of daily language and the sacred fixity of Scripture. The formulation of Scripture is so static—the tiniest parts of the abecedary stay so firmly in place— that some spiritual nourishment is bound to obtain, however random the point of entry. This means, curiously, that when a daily event is chancy, Augustine almost believes in predestination. The same double-layered reality underlies it all: the seemingly chaotic life-process and the exactness of GOD and the Word of God.

All this is germane to Augustine's own incessant absorption with language as such. That he was a writer of immense talent if not genius seems incontrovertible. He combines metaphor with holiness without strain. He refers to "sacred ants and sacred bees." Baptism is a drowning from which we are rescued into a saved life. Augustine had a mistress, a former concubine, to whom he was devoted for fifteen years—indeed until only ten years before he wrote *Confessions*. When he finally had to let her go she seemed "torn out of my side." It was like Adam's rib: as Garry Wills puts it (Wills 1999, 15), Genesis haunts the entire *Confessions* text. But it is not just a metaphor. There is a kind of carnal savoring of direct description. Augustine describes cockfighting; noises in a drain; throwing a shoe at a rat; and a grim method of torture, in which the victim is bound tightly to a dead body, face touching face. Along with Augustine's first-person expressions in the simplest and most immediate words of language, *Confessions* becomes a text in which the writer is right beside us, in one gesture or another, at every moment.

But as well as being a great writer, Augustine came to examine and question language itself, as to what it can do and what it is. From our point of view here, it is as though he sensed that abecedarial writing holds the unifying key he wants that would close that gap between human life and God. At one point he states that he would be happier to forget the whole of Virgil than lose his literacy (1:13). Since the second seems to entail the first, this might sound extremely odd, except for precisely the fact that by knowing how to "read and write" Augustine means knowing how to spell, how to use letters and the alphabet. He couldn't learn about Aeneas without being able to read, but once having read about Aeneas, Augustine could remember it forever even if he lost the skills of spelling and letters. And he does not want to lose those skills. Yet there is another paradox here. Augustine so often seems to think of words as merely capturing mind, not constituting it or autonomously enriching it, even though his own writing talent works as though words and mind were autonomous entities. That is to say, words might affect mind as much as mind words. To cite Heidegger again: We don't speak language, language speaks us. Yet Augustine's statements about words and mind are quite clear, and he actually sees little relation between word and unexpressed meaning. "Wisdom and folly can be clothed alike in plain words or the finest flowers of speech" (5:6), a metaphor of clothing that survives in the modern era.[11] "Words are one thing and principles another. The words may sometimes be spoken in Latin and at other times in Greek, but the principles are neither Greek nor Latin. They are not language at all" (10:12). This paradox is what must have led him to become, very probably, the first ecclesiastic to probe seriously and at length the nature of language and its relation to thought and feeling. He sensed the dilemma as he sensed the contradictions in everything. His sermons are full of wordplay and verbal tricks, and his letters to political opponents use this verbal weaponry to their discomfiture. Augustine later eschewed such devices for serious writing, but even so *Confessions* is full of similar activity. Asking himself why as a boy in a gang he once stole some pears, he concludes, "What was not allowed, allured" *(eo liberet quo non liceret)* (Wills 1999, 11). Even the famous phrase that brought on his conversion is a kind of pun. *Tolle legere* can mean either "take it and read" or "pick up and sort out," a chant used by farmworkers when stacking bales at harvest. Augustine could coin a proverb seemingly without that overt purpose. "Thou hast made us for Thyself"; "Love God and do what you like"; "O God make me good, but not yet"—these and other aphorisms have long entered our language. Earlier he had written a treatise on language, the *Res Verba*; but what concerns us here is his obsessive probing—a formative influence on the later Wittgenstein—into how far the deepest realities can or can't be expressed. What levels of truth are entailed; indeed, are or are not nameable, that matter at the heart of the earliest sacred writings.

There is major implication for the abecedary here. It connects the deepest aspects of Augustine's personality to his language practice, and it suggests that he was one of the true pioneers in both grasping and using one of the abecedary's main features, namely equability, as we shall analyze those later in this book in part 2. The issue takes us back to the doctrine of sin itself, Augustine's understanding of it, and his practice of tolerance in his own life. It takes a little explaining, and I am especially indebted here to certain information from Garry Wills's sensitive and approachable account.

As said already, one of Augustine's chief problems in his public life as a bishop lay with the Catholic Church's relations with the schismatic sect of the Donatists. The Donatists' strong sense of martyrdom made them difficult and militant political opponents, and they were a strong force in Africa. Their long-term ambition indeed was to supplant the Catholics as the true Christian Church.

To cut this long story short, a showdown eventually occurred in a major convocation of the two churches in Carthage in the year A.D. 410 in order to settle the dispute. Augustine was the presiding adjudicator, and victory was won for the Catholics on this occasion largely by his skill. But despite the aggression he was forced to bear, he at once forbade triumphalism among Catholics and acted to cooperate with any Donatist who would accept the verdict with goodwill. He hated violence and sternly rebuked Catholics who spoke of Donatists uncharitably (Chadwick 1986, 79). Augustine's attitude was one of reconciliation wherever possible. He invited Donatists to join the Catholic Church on an equal footing; he presented the evidence with truth and scrupulous fairness.

A similar attitude pervades his official pronouncements on political suppression in cases of heresy or crime; despite that he has not always gotten good press on the matter in later centuries, including our own. His friend Bishop Ambrose denied churches to Arians and synagogues to Jews (Wills 1999, 101). Religious intolerance was normative, and, no doubt, for good reasons of necessary control. It fell to Augustine as bishop to produce a set of principles on doctrinal suppression. Despite Augustine's notorious formula of *compelle intrare* [force them to come in], in fact his document decreased the more punitive measures and opposed actual execution or torture. As part of the same events, when one of his own priests was tortured and another murdered, Augustine found himself pleading with the Roman tribune Marcellinus for leniency for the criminals. In a later irony he pleaded for leniency for Marcellinus himself, caught up in a purge soon after. Marcellinus was executed (Wills 1999, 109, 113).

Other matters relate to this same issue of tolerance. For example, with at least the more moderate-thinking Christians—among whom Augustine was a leader—it was quite normal to have friends in the pagan world. In fact, in the context of dealing with heresy, Christian authorities sometimes seemed less preoccupied with refuting paganism than with destroying their own faith's internal errors real or believed. The great Clement of Alexandria advocated the use of any source, any material, pagan or not, in reaching truth. Augustine's pagan friends included a very rich man named Romanian who allowed Augustine to walk freely in his orchards. There were also the Manichean students, who, he says, were cheerful and fun to be with (Wills 1999, 19, 26). Augustine's father was a pagan, though his mother's Christianity was deep and devout.

All this may seem a long way from language. But the connecting link, as in so many issues in this era, was through the matter of sin.

We might put it that there are two kinds of tolerance. One, maybe typical of our own times, is to regard all behavior including the worst as merely human by nature; the concept of sin grows redundant. The other tolerant view is that, although sin remains sin, humans are frail. Sin is so powerful an urge that we cannot hope to attain salvation by our own efforts. We therefore deplore the sin but have compassion on the sinner. This was Augustine's view. It led to his emphasis on the doctrine of salvation by God's grace; but the key factor here is his accompanying deep-seated belief that sin and virtue must be allowed to live along together. Indeed, his great rival, Bishop Julian of Eclanum, taunted him for always retaining his early Manicheanism at heart, always having the two principles of good and evil present within himself. But Augustine's precedent for his view lay in the biblical parable of the wheat and the tares (weeds). Wills describes this part of the story persuasively and intriguingly. The wheat and the tares are part of the same harvest. Ecclesiastical and civil order must be maintained, but for the individual it is never too late to repent.

But I would now suggest that Augustine applied the same principle to language. There could be more than one interpretation of any writing. The wheat and the tares lie hidden together in the same text. This comes out in Augustine's reading of the Psalms, an Old Testament book he deeply loved. Sometimes the psalmist might seem sinful, other times virtuous. There could equally be differential readings as between the theological and the secular, the public and the private. If we put this idea beside the fervid, changing, and indeed often tortured pronouncements and confessions in *Confessions,* too, we see the force of the contention that Augustine took a great step forward in using the abecedary itself in one of its greatest features: its equability. The abecedary is subtle enough to allow many things to run in its sentences along the same communicative channel. The theme perhaps prophetically recalls the firm view of the major nineteenth-century Catholic in Britain, Cardinal John Henry Newman, who held that there cannot be a sinless literature of sinful man.[12] (Newman was arguing for the study of secular literature within a Catholic university's curriculum.)

These considerations lead to another inference as to Augustine's development in his later life. We have stated that *Confessions* is a dialogue, that is to say a piece of dialectical writing. Early on, Augustine himself wrote fully fledged dialogues. As we have said, he did this knowing nothing of either Greek tragedy or Plato. It points further to the millennium-long zeitgeist; the deployment or distributive capacity of the abecedary was growing to absorb these forms.

But Augustine came to rate these earlier dialogues less highly than he had at first. His strong line on untruth and lying may have contributed to this. Dialogue doesn't necessarily lie, but it always allows two points of view, with the underlying presumption always available that one side if not both has to be faulty, or at least incomplete. Augustine turned more and more to extended prose, and therefore the unit of the sentence. The sentence is again an abecedarial feature.

The sentence (A does B to C) functions in the framework of time. Dialogue is always counter, but sentences in a single writer accrue. This is an early move forward into a deepening of what dialectic really is. Not just two people disputing, it is the structure of reason itself, though Augustine's temperament never let him get that far. But time is a feature that caused Augustine much heart-searching. There are long sections devoted to it in *Confessions*. It appears along with other troublesome abstractions, which we can deal with here briefly first. They include *forgetfulness, happiness,* and *evil,* for Augustine is concerned with the topic we raised back in part 1 as to just what can ever be named. (This capacity for nominal plurality is a further feature of abecedarial equability.) There is always some obscurity as to how far something exists but cannot be named (forgetfulness), or doesn't exist but can be named (evil). Of course, something is named in some sense; if the rolles exist they call up a meaning of some kind. But Augustine worries himself sick over, for example, forgetfulness. "I can mention forgetfulness and recognize what the word means, but how can I recognize the thing itself unless I remember it . . . ? What is forgetfulness but absence of memory? When it is present, I cannot remember. Then how can it be present in such a way that I remember it?" (10:16). He relates this to what linguists now call the "tip-of-the-tongue" phenomenon; but his problem arises from imputing an essence to forgetfulness and then finding it irretrievable by its nature. The problem with *evil* is the old theological crux that it cannot square with a benevolent God. Augustine, like many in his era, concluded that evil is an absence, an inadequate relationship between otherwise good things. But the name "evil" remains, and again an abecedarial rolle—the letters from the same alphabet that can name so much—can attach to a kind of nothing. It is as though Augustine were trying to turn the abecedary into a psychoanalyst.

But it is time that is central, and Augustine devotes by far his longest section to it (*Confessions,* 11:6–31). He also relates it to language directly. Both in *Confessions* and elsewhere Augustine pores over the fact that the syllables of sentences one by one pass away.[13] Orally he cannot compare one syllable with another, because when the next is uttered the earlier one has gone. (With writing, he can do that exactly.) As so often with creative people, Augustine worries away at a frontier whose nature he can't understand but whose existence he has detected, even if it turns out to be a nonproblem for a later age. The whole idea of time is explored. Humans occupy a world of time that language shares. In eternity by contrast "nothing moves into the past: all is present." But this means a problem for the nature of God's Word. When God said, "This is my beloved Son" (Matthew 3:17), it too was a sentence that passes away syllable by syllable. It cannot therefore be one with the Word as such, for the true Word itself is eternal (11:6). As the Swiss theologian Karl Barth has put it, the Bible itself is not the Word; rather it uniquely points to the Word.[14] There could hardly be a larger inference from the microworkings of mere letters and syllables.

This matter of time ties in with the distinction between sight and sound, writing and speech. As already said, scripture is static in that its words, its actual written rolls, lie there on the page unchanging and do not pass away like syllables on the wind. We can reread the line in front of us, look back at earlier lines, and so on. So much is familiar and it applies to any writing at all. That doesn't equate speech and writing with the temporary and permanent respectively, for of course both are imprinted on matter itself, and all will pass away in the end if not before it. But the distinction recalls a much-quoted passage from Augustine, often taken by later commentators as a turning point in human apprehension of language. Characteristically noting the corporeal, Augustine watches his friend Bishop Ambrose reading a book. "When he read, his eyes scanned the page and his heart explored the meaning, but his voice was silent and his tongue was still" (6:3). In short, Ambrose was an early case of reading "in the head."[15] Augustine became much intrigued by this, for Ambrose did it often and apparently did not mind people near him when he was doing so. Even visitors would be announced when Ambrose was silently reading.

Augustine's puzzlement led him to access Ambrose's method. Maybe Ambrose wanted to rest his voice, or didn't want to be questioned about his reading by visitors. But Augustine reached no conclusion and left it there. In later centuries the introduction of punctuation, among other things, made silent reading the norm. Did Augustine observe that Ambrose had crossed a boundary into seeing writing sui generis? Did it affect Augustine's own belief that the eye dominates the senses? "We do not say 'Hear how it glows,' 'smell how bright it is,' 'taste how it shines,' or 'Feel how it glitters,' because these are all things which we say that we see. Yet we not only say 'See how it shines' when we are speaking of something which only the eye can perceive, but we also say 'See how loud it is,' 'See how it smells,' 'See how it tastes' and 'See how hard it is' (10:35). Augustine seems prescient here; his observations, in detail, are uncannily close to those used by the American consciousness philosopher Daniel Dennett on the same topic.[16] They well illustrate Augustine's compulsive need to probe all the connections in immediate experience. In fact, Augustine is warning against the power of the senses as carnal temptation even as he knows our—and his own—weakness in resisting them. Eyesight, so convincing in its impact, tempts us into an easy curiosity. But writing, though material, is not a material item of knowledge as are water, skin, or chariots. It is an apprehension of knowledge as that entangles with a sign-system. Maybe—although Augustine would have been unaware of the fact—he is reversing Plato and seeing writing's fixity as valuable. The body is present when language is heard and spoken.

THOMAS AQUINAS

Augustine's influence has been great and continuous. Wittgenstein and Dennett go with such unlikely bedfellows as Samuel Beckett and John Cowper Powys as recipients. Thomas Aquinas made much use of Augustine. But Aquinas's duality differs much from Augustine's contrast between a messed-up mortal and the efficacious name of God. It is curious in one respect that while Aquinas disapproved of poetry, his debt was not to Plato but to Aristotle. Little surprise then that his work, and its linguistic texture, shuns such areas. Augustine's intense contemplation of God was the seedbed for medieval mysticism. Aquinas has no problem with a gut distinction between revelation and reason—and reason, too, could be fully put to service in human understanding of the nature of God. The events of scholasticism, the new learning, and the new universities place Aquinas in a quite different intellectual position from that experienced by Augustine nine hundred years earlier.

Eight centuries passed between the death of Augustine and the birth of Thomas Aquinas. It is ironic that the former was better known in the later period than in his own. Here we can just briefly touch on what are usually known as the Dark Ages—perhaps roughly A.D. 400–800—and must note only the obvious factors of the decline of the Roman Empire, the expansion of Islam, and the movements and conversions of barbarian peoples in the north. The question traditionally asked is when the Middle Ages really began. It has been put as early as 590 A.D., when Gregory I became pope, or as late as 1215 by R. W. Southern, who saw the *terminus a quo* as A.D. 970 and the eleventh century as crucial in the period's development.[17] In between lies the year A.D. 800, when the Frankish king Charlemagne was crowned emperor of the Western Empire by the pope. The event, and Charlemagne's commitment to education, inaugurated a process that, after ups and downs, culminated with the founding of the great monastic orders in northern France. If there is less dispute over these versions than there might be, it is because most historians now acknowledge that eras like the "Middle Ages" are to an important extent human constructions anyway.

Yet the great era of learning appeared, which is what must be looked at in dealing with Aquinas after Augustine. Not surprisingly, powerful popes had early been a key factor. Some, backed by what our own era would see as excessively central not to say tyrannous authority, established the Church as a wealthy institution capable of making large financial endowments, finally, to the building of monastic orders and universities. Late in the sixth century Gregory I gave away vast inherited wealth to become a Benedictine monk (the Benedictines were the first and only major order founded before the thirteenth century). He built six monasteries, extended major missions, and became a powerful administrative and political force (Renwick 1958, 64–65, 68–71). The church grew strong under his undeniably autocratic rule. He introduced not only new and stronger papal claims to papal power, but also new doctrines concerning the communion, purgatory, the adoration of Mary, prayers for saints and the dead, and confession. Five centuries later his namesake Gregory VII—formerly the monk Hildebrand— detached the priesthood fully from the ordinary life of most people, further consolidated church property, and won a power battle with the emperor Henry IV. This last event came to be seen as an unprecedented and valued example of real spiritual authority over secular. The pope immediately before Aquinas's own period, Innocent III, made a comparable impact. His papal letter of 1205, to the Masters and Scholars of Paris, was unfortunate in that it was written just after the disastrous Fourth Crusade. But its terms of encouragement of the reform of letters in the Eastern (Greek) Empire further under-pinned the advance of the liberal arts at the time.[18] Such various activities embodied the beginnings of the administrative structure without which the communal learning of the Middle Ages could not have developed. But they also contributed, in their doubtless politically slanted ways, to the stretching of minds over doctrinal ideas, and probably their promulgation and enforcement, on which the medieval advancement of learning was based.

Various factors then define the background of high scholarship and times in which Aquinas worked. According to David Knowles, for the three hundred years A.D. 1050–1350 Western Europe formed a single cultural unit. Clearly the lingua franca was Latin, despite that only a fortunate few comprised the community that knew it. Even so, "There was one stock of words, forms and thoughts from which all drew and in which all shared an equality. If we possessed the written works without their authors' names we should not be able to assign them to any country or people" (Knowles 1962, 1). This period sets in some 170 years before the birth of Aquinas.

The major monastic orders were all founded within this era. The growth of their distinctive traditions—scholarship, teaching, care for the poor and needy—interwove with the growth of the new universities as more fully educational and training centers of a wider nature. And of course, the monasteries housed the scriptoria, the big writing-rooms where countless copies of major texts were made, and the very idea of physical writing as a communal activity was established. St. Bernard of Clairvaux (1090–1153) was a leading light in the Cistercian order, and he probably founded it. Its mode of living arose from Bernard's emphasis on the spiritual warmth and focus of Christ that alone informed the systematic search for the soul. But Bernard was an intellectual force, too. His major treatises and renowned dispute with Abelard also contributed to the rise of the scholastic era. The Dominicans were a community that combined poverty and simple living with a vocation of teaching. St. Dominic (1170–1221) founded this community in 1216, as a burgeoning of his first project of bringing conversion to the heretical sect of the Albigenses. That medieval learning and monastic life were inherently close is underlined by Dominic's dispatch of over half his staff of brothers to the University of Paris only one year after his order's foundation. In A.D. 1210, St. Francis of Assisi (1181–1226) founded the rather contrasting Franciscan order, whose appeal to poverty and the unlearned filled a different role. Even so, in our own context it functions to demonstrate the link between the lives of soul, body, and mind to the detriment of none. The Franciscans, too, came to Paris early in the thirteenth century.

This was also the era of that prototypically medieval creation, the university. The tenth century had seen the revival of the study of logic. In the thirteenth century, especially at Paris and Oxford, Aristotelian logic—defined by Southern as "the listening to commentaries, the attendance at disputations, and the exercise in logical argument" (Southern 1953, 182)—arrived at the heart of the undergraduate curriculum. The church largely controlled the universities, but they were not monasteries but essentially academies. They flourished in Bologna, Naples, Paris, and Oxford, as did the scholasticism by which they were characterized. "Scholasticism" may be defined, perhaps, as the application of thought and reason to theological problems in formal and communal institutions of learning. There was no psychology or social science as we now understand those disciplines, nor was there professional belief in the academic autonomy or rights of the individual. Names associated with this great era, apart from Aquinas, include Bernard of Clairvaux, John of Salisbury, Peter Abelard, Aquinas's near-exact contemporary Bonaventura, Lanfranc, Anselm, Hugh of St. Victor, Duns Scotus, and William of Ockham.

But in any consideration of Thomas Aquinas the immediate key factor is undoubtedly the rediscovery of Aristotle. Aristotle's writings had been known in only a very small selection until the early eleventh century. The major texts existed only in Arabic, which is a historical irony. The thirteenth-century Crusades against the then Islamic fundamentalism mainly followed the great period in which, after more than a millennium of neglect, Aristotle became available again to the West via the Arabian route. The *Physics* and other works were translated from the Arabic in the late twelfth century, the *Metaphysics* and the *Ethics* at various times from the mid-twelfth to the mid-thirteenth century. Often, though not always, they derived from Arabic originals (Knowles 196, 196–202). In this context the great Arabian scholars Avicenna (980–1037) and Averroes (1126–98) put the Western Church permanently in their debt. Avicenna believed in the divine basis of the human soul, which also equated with its intellect. Averroes produced a major commentary on Aristotle. The Jewish scholar Maimonides (1135–1204) was an equally influential force whose life just precedes, and whose thinking on certain aspects of the relation between philosophy and religion much squares with, that of Thomas Aquinas.

Thomas Aquinas (1225–74) was born into a noble family. His early education was with the Benedictines but, after gaining his higher education at the University of Naples, he entered the Dominican order. This decision incensed his brothers enough for them to kidnap him and imprison him for a year. This act did not alter his decision, and after his release he worked and taught in Paris for seven years. From 1259 to 1268 he worked and taught in many parts of Italy—the Dominicans, of course, was a teaching order—and he then went back to Paris until 1272. The last two years of his life were spent back in Naples. His life didn't lack for other dangers. Bitter controversies between the Dominicans and the university in Paris in Aquinas's time led to more than one incident that disturbed his academic serenity and threatened his tenure and indeed his safety more widely.

Yet he worked on at his single-minded task. In summary this consisted, perhaps, of the application of one informing idea; namely, that human reason is an adequate instrument with which to elucidate the truths, including those of the divine nature, which are open to humanity to know. Aquinas's vast work, the *Summa Theologiae,* is a revision of an earlier work, the *Summa Contra Gentiles.* (In what follows they will be referred to as *Summa* and *SCG* respectively.) This "Summary against/directed to non-Christian people" depends exclusively on reason rather than revelation or faith, because of its targeted readership. Natural reason can reach only general and abstract conclusions about God. Things like the Incarnation, the Holy Spirit, or a people's chosen status could be felt only by faith and experienced. So it is useless to cite the authority of the relevant Scriptures to "Gentiles"; that is to say, those who do not accept that authority. Only reason, therefore, "to which all men assent of necessity" (*SCG,* 1:2), remains to carry out the theological agenda.

Aquinas is of course also famous for his attention to the Scriptures, but this too was an application of reason, even if with a different aim in view. In the medieval period, long-evolving processes of biblical interpretation had finally settled from fluidity into fixity. The sense of the fixed text, and the process of so fixing it, was finally achieved. Clearly this is parallel to what we have said about the unchanging nature of sacred texts in even earlier societies. Olsen locates the process for Christian Scripture as falling exactly into the period we are discussing. "The theory and practice of reading altered significantly from the time of Augustine (d.430) to the time of Thomas Aquinas (d.1274). During this time the very act of 'fixing a text' and 'establishing what it means' came to the fore" (Olsen 1994, 145). At and after Augustine's era, Scripture was held to contain intention, certainly, but only in that Scripture embodied the will of the Spirit. Divinely intended meaning was there but lay deep. Of course, the major difficulty then ensued of deciding how on earth God's eternal word could ever be contained in human language. The problem was resolved, in effect, by a binary division; precisely the one made by Thomas Aquinas. The text's surface intention could be fixed after all, including its allegorical and metaphorical parts and even as to its many genres (Williams 2000, 47–48), by the gradually evolving processes—human and rational—of hermeneutics. But what is *intended* by that intention, its deeper intention, remains in the hands of God. We may hope to see it but only through a glass darkly. Yet for Aquinas the application of human reason was fully adequate for the task of fixing at least Scripture's surface meaning, just as it was also adequate for the task of elucidating nonrevealed truths about God.

Our interest here, then, lies in how this reason is embodied by the abecedary. We have already discussed the role of the alphabet in the development of formal logic and argument in ancient Greece. Reason's abecedarial texture, especially in Aquinas, differs totally from the outpourings of Augustine and his successors. It embodies the pure and timeless quality to which reason's mode of thought ("to which all men assent of necessity") aspires. One might—with entire neutrality—call it noncharming; there are no highs or lows, no sudden emphases or vivid illustrations. To use the term we shall develop in part 2, it is virtual reason, virtual thought. Nor does Aquinas ever indulge in personal likings or reminiscence. Yet this gray continuity has its own virtues and indeed magnetism. There is a total absence of bias as the work grows within its ever-accumulating consistency. As David Knowles, having summarized some of these aspects, then expresses it, "The greatness is there. The judgement of [Aquinas's] contemporaries and posterity has not been false" (Knowles 1962, 255).

Such a mode had already appeared strikingly in the work of St. Anselm, born in about A.D. 1033, and in 1093 made archbishop of Canterbury. Here with translation is the renowned passage known as "Anselm's proof," of the existence of a being "than which nothing greater can be conceived":

> *Quod utique sic vere est, ut nec cogitari possit non esse. Nam potest cogitari aliquid esse, quod non possit cogitari non esse, quod majus est quam quod non esse cogitari potest. Quare, si id quo majus nequit cogitari potest cogitari non esse, idipsum quo majus cogitari nequit, non est id quo majus cogitari nequit, quod convenire non potest. Si ergo vere est aliquid quo majus cogitari non potest, ut nec cogitari possit non esse. Et hoc es tu, Domine Deus noster.*

[And it assuredly exists so truly, that it cannot be conceived not to exist. For, it is possible to conceive of a being which cannot be conceived not to exist; and this is greater than one which can be conceived not to exist. Hence, if that, than which nothing greater can be conceived, can be conceived not to exist, it is not that, than which nothing greater can be conceived. But this is an irreconcilable contradiction. There is, then, so truly a being than which nothing greater can be conceived to exist, that it cannot even be conceived not to exist; and this being thou art, O Lord, our God.] (Anselm, 8–9)

We need scarcely point to the presence of repetition here, which as we have seen is a strong capacity of any alphabet. Such repetitions as Anselm's had to be written out longhand with no carbon paper, let alone the word processor's repeat button. It reinforces the mind's retention of arguments. Aquinas knew Anselm's work and used this passage closely (Aquinas, 116). Anselm was no escapist bookworm; he was exiled in 1097, opposed slavery, and got into heavy trouble with the monarch for his stance on the politically sensitive matter of electing bishops. He was apparently an attractive personality, and Dante places him in the *Paradiso* among the spirits of light and power in the Sphere of the Sun—along with Hugh of St. Victor and Aquinas, too (*Paradiso,* 12:133–45). The Victorian historian James Anthony Froude described Anselm as "unquestionably the ablest man of his time alive in Europe."[19] Yet the recycling of key abstractions, carefully marshaled by copulative verbs and controlled by negating and conditional particles, shows what the abecedary becomes in this mode when its use has had time to mature. It exemplifies what Goody meant when he challenged us to even think such notions without the alphabet, without writing. The nouns and verbs seem pure abstraction and connection: it seems almost a syntax distilled. Any sense of aridity dies, in the passage just quoted, in the switch of the final phrase into a different register— rather as though Anselm turns to face his maker, an addition he later said came from love. And Aquinas, too, repeatedly writes sentences where triples incorporate this circling texture. *Quicquid recipitur, secundum modum recipientis recipitur* ([What is perceived is perceived in a secondary way of perceiving]): *cognitum est in cognoscente per modum cognoscentis* ([Anything is known only by a knowing by the mode of the knower]).

Aquinas discusses God's existence at length. He did not entirely accept Anselm's verbal proof of God's existence, and this argument shows further the writing's enabling power. The formula-statement "God exists" is made possible in one sense by the abecedary. But it means little if our understanding of "God" makes the statement self-evident. One might argue that any statement "x exists" must be true because the rolle "x" must refer to something; but this over-looks things like falsehood or self-delusion. Statements like "there are such things as bananas/eleven-legged dogs/God/olexgtnagjors" and such depend on prior acceptance of the noun-entity by reader or hearer. The problem lies in the term "exist." The verb "to be" will later turn out all-important in the classical post-Renaissance age, when ontological mingling between name and thing-named has dispersed (Foucault 1970, 34–44). The abecedary can postulate being, "to-be-ness," by arranging a few letters. But of course Aqui-nas sees through this. He points out that people may have merely heard the statement "God exists" from childhood and merely got used to it. Proofs are required.

The five proofs of God's existence concern change, causation, necessity, gradation, and design (Aquinas 1972, 122; *Summa,* 1:2:3). The first two are roughly Aristotle's Prime Mover and First Cause. The third and fourth derive from an incompleteness/com-pleteness distinction; the unnecessary implies a standard of neces-sity; gradation suggests ultimate perfection; and so on. The fifth argument is in effect the "argument from design." All these notions are abstractions the abecedary can, literally, inscribe with no picto-rial reference and so retain as parts of a unity. Yet they are some-how more than self-circling tautology too, not just signs followed by the word "exists"; and they are not poetry, either. What alpha-betical writing can articulate is underlined and exploited further by Aquinas's remarks about God's attributes. Aquinas endorses the traditional view that God cannot be qualitatively attributed. Saying God is wise is different in kind from saying Socrates is wise; the former is analogical.[20] But what silent shift then has taken place in the rolle "wise" *(sapiens)* by the change from God to Socrates? Yet at the same time, the claim to God's omnipotence, and the words of the claim, must have qualitative reference. In practice, divine om-nipotence isn't denied by a list of things God "cannot" do or be, if those are merely inconsistent with God's attributes. It is true, in a sense, that God "cannot" die, change, get tired, create another God, or alter the past; but it says more about our transfer of a few abeced-ary signs for "cannot-ness" to multiple predicates than it does about God.

Aquinas was aware of these negations. God is/has no time, parts, power not to exist, or finitude (Aquinas 1972, 139–41; *SCG,* 1:15–28). But Aquinas equally sees the dangers. "In apprehending the divine essence we do not know what it is. But by *knowing what it is not* we get some knowledge of it, and the more things we are able to deny of it, the nearer we come to know it" (Aquinas 1972, 139; *SCG*, 1:14, edition's emphasis). This would appear to raise the new dimension of negatives in language, the "not"-words. If God has no attributes, we cannot describe negatives of God by things God lacks, because they would merely attribute opposite qualities to God. Instead one can only state a (non)property of God and supply it with "not." The abecedary, then, can refer to what is not just as, we saw earlier, it can refer to the unnameable.

Yet Aquinas also states (Aquinas 1972, 143–44; *SCG*, 1:28) that God is/has perfection, simply because he has no defects. Here it is the syllabic modes of the abecedary *(perfect/defect)* that seem to make this argument circular. But they do allow the postulate even if it is inadequate. Aquinas later concludes that God's perfection is, in fact, infinite (Aquinas 1972, 144; *Summa*, 1:4:2), which again opens up or closes down one more abecedarial abstraction with another. This is not without its own interest, but we are still left with semblances, shadowy ideas of God, which raise the question of what language is for those who write such things. Again, God can be asserted by verb as well as by adjective or noun. God is to-be and unique (Aquinas 1972, 124–25) but is also knowing or, perhaps we should say, does knowing; does divine loving, choosing, providing, and communicating (147–62).

Clearly such examples amount simply to a process of evocation, difficult to achieve without a rarefied yet still human technique—the abecedary—by which to express this. Aquinas's rather negative conclusion about theological language, after these points, is that "nothing can be univocally said of God and of other things . . . nothing is univocally predicated of God and of other things" (*SCG*, 1:32). But the idea of a "rarefied yet still human technique" suggests the status of the abecedary as virtual, and which might be tied to Aquinas's conception of virtue itself. Whatever our own beliefs about God, it is useful here in suggesting just what sort of thing the abecedary, rather than a pluralized or purely pictorial script, can evoke when the poetic is ruled out.

This takes us back to Aristotle. It was effectively Aquinas who interpreted Aristotle's lately rediscovered texts at the start of the Renaissance to the Church if not the world (Kenny 1980, esp. 19–24), and who combined Aristotle's theories with Christian theology in a massive synthesis that still influences the world of philosophy both religious and secular. Naturally enough, Aristotle's views turn out formative in the present discussion. Two aspects are important as to both Aquinas and the abecedary. They are, the cause-ends process leading to happiness, and the relations of motion to rest. We have to be brief here but it is important to the argument.

In the *Nicomachean Ethics*, Aristotle argued a causes-ends philosophy that looks behind and ahead at once. Chasing the line backward brings us to the celebrated First Cause of all things, already mentioned. Conversely, coming forward to a present situation, there must have been a chain of causes. Something caused something that caused something that caused whatever is happening now. But, on ahead, causes are replaced by ends. I open the bottle to get the wine to entertain my guests to make business contacts to support my family to . . .—and so on. Some final, universal aim of these chains must be discernible. For Aristotle this is happiness, which we all aspire to by our natures.

Aquinas and Aristotle agree that this happiness is the end, and that it is not found in material wealth, pleasure, or even the nobler but still worldly attainments of high status or honor. Happiness is found in virtue, and that is intellectual virtue. This intellectual virtue does not at all preclude actual good deeds like raising one's children morally, feeding the poor, and so on, but those too cannot be fully understood but by intellectual means. Hence virtue is itself, as it were, abstract in nature, whatever its applications here on earth. Here Aquinas cites Aristotle direct (*Summa*, 1–2:9). To act virtuously one must act consciously; voluntarily or deliberately; and according to some principle capable of being universalized. In Aquinas's own words elsewhere: "As with all accidents there is no *matter* out of which virtue is formed, even though it has matter about which it is concerned and matter in which it exists, namely, the subject" (*Summa*, 1–2:55:4, edition's emphasis).

Now maybe we can appreciate the suggestion as to how the abecedary is virtual. Is not that sentence of Aquinas's close to Bergson's about words cited above (Bergson 1911, 168)? "The word is an external thing, which the intelligence can catch hold of and cling to, and at the same time an immaterial thing, by means of which the intelligence can penetrate even to the inwardness of its own work." And, in Aquinas's own sentence just cited, if we substitute "abecedary" for "virtue," it could exactly describe the abecedary. The point is not to dehydrate the robustness of self-denying human virtue, as when we attend our dying mothers, heroically drag someone from a fire, or anything else. Rather it suggests a structural transplant between what we do and the way, more and more refined, we devise to express it. As far as material existence permits, the abecedary moves toward the world of pure spirit by its virtual status. This status takes letters as near to nonmaterial signs as, bar in electronics, has yet been attained. So the abecedary may, at least minimally, aspire to membership with those "intellectual substances" (Kenny 1980, 10) that Aquinas believed to constitute the angels and other spirits and intellects who dwelt with God in heaven.

But Aristotle also underpins the cause-end chain, in material terms in the *Physics*, in his extensive sections on motion and rest. For instance, a stone falls because it desires the earth. Aquinas had used the *Physics* equally extensively in his own proof, contra Anselm, of God's existence. There are different kinds of motion in the same object. They include coming into being before being itself; coming to rest and being at rest; being kept moving; movement itself as imperishable; pushing and pulling; continuity and change; and so on (*Physics*, 4–8). Both Aristotle and Aquinas argue all this within the discourse of reason, and as hinted earlier there is some irony in Augustine's long sad search for rest, apparently without knowing that Aristotle had already formulated the matter.

But in linguistic and indeed abecedarial terms, the relation of movement to rest is the provenance of syntax and the sentence. The sentence moves—in most European languages from left to right—through subject to verb to object, and via satellite clauses, to a conclusion. But the conclusion is not merely the last bit of the sentence. Rather it is the sentence's whole import, only understood when the last bit has been reached. Similarly, rest is not just the last bit of movement, the place movement arrives at; it is also the overall condition of anything to which movement is contrary. Here Aquinas seems to have recourse to much of what Augustine discovered about language and its movement in time. This also relates to what was said at the start about Aquinas's discourse of reason, the circularity of phrases like "x exists," and the way we are forced to speak of God in opposites and negatives. For all these, therefore, turn out to be aspects of a kind of rest-state that the abecedary as material must attempt to express, but which, as characterized by virtuality and "fewness"—both to be examined in part 2 below—it is most fitted to express. Again this is different from ideographic or pictorial scripts, for they, in whatever fashion, depict actual things that without movement in the real world would be useless.

It is as though movement must be somehow put on ice for the nature of the godhead to be expressed at all. This puts a strain on any mode of writing; but the abecedary is best suited to meet such monotheistic demands. Aquinas's explicit views on language itself

seem to underlie these propositions. On the face of it he has a dual-
ist one-to-one view, static or synchronic in import, and pointing
forward to Saussure: "In us there are as many different words as
there are different things that we understand" (Aquinas 1972, 433;
Summa, 1:34:3). Yet it is more than that. Aquinas regards words as
counterparts of inner mental words that are somehow generated to
form definitions of the things they refer to. "In us this intellectual
concept is properly called a word, because this is what the spoken
word signifies. . . . It originates from the intellect through an act of
intellect, and it is the likeness of what is known. . . . So the word
originating from the intellect is the likeness of what is known. . . ."
(254). "The intellect of a man by the word he conceives in the act
of understanding a stone, speaks a stone" (432).

There is an astonishing inference here, namely, that the abecedarial word suits the thing it evokes. If this still holds today at all—a
point to be considered later in this book—it does so in quite different sense. Aquinas converts the Aristotelian movement-to-rest into
the medieval "great chain of being"—again a more static
image—in which everything in the real world is named by words
that are somehow appropriate. This, it was traditionally held, must
be because in some primal and pre-Babel language the signs ema-
nated from the same deep matter as the things themselves. But this
view must also apply to the intangibles and syntactical parts of language, the conditionals and connectives, the *if, exist, will be, not,
and, unless*, and so on, on which Aquinas's rationalistic work
equally depends. So they too come under the wider umbra of the
rational, the abstract, the permanent, to which both this world and
its (abecedarial) expression aspire. The whole linguistic structure
emanates from the real, rationally made order it signifies. One can
see then, not only that no system before the alphabet could readily
express such a philosophy, but also that the contingent alphabet, in
its albeit flexible fashion, was itself formative toward the very ideas
it itself enables to be expressed at all.

OTHER MEDIEVAL DIVINES

Later medieval divines returned to Augustine. Many of them belonged to the Order of the Canons Regular of St. Augustine. Walter
Hilton (d. A.D. c1395) and the author of *The Cloud Of Unknowing*,
the so-named Dionysus (floreat A.D. 1390) both lived after Aquinas.

But they were not composing theologies. Rather they were giving practical instruction to young acolytes entering the contemplative life. A few brief examples must suffice here. Using JESUS rather than GOD, Hilton fancifully elaborates and lightens Augustine's relentless one-term obsession. Hilton parallels JESUS with the coin in the biblical parable, first lost and then found in an exhaustive candlelit house-search. Dionysus deals similarly with prayer. "If [your prayers] are in words, as they seldom are, then they are very few words; the fewer the better." One word is even better than two, so exact is his emphasis. Noting one-word cries like "Help!" or "Fire!" (cf. Wittgenstein's "Slab!"; Wittgenstein 1958, 4–5), Dionysus enjoins "this little word "God." Fill your spirit with its inner meaning. . . ." Of the same period, Thomas à Kempis (A.D. 1380–1471), giving practical instruction to junior contemplatives, also recommends the "Avoiding Of Superfluity Of Words."[21] Such emphases on both economy and one-word succulence contrasts both the syntactical elaboration in "God exists" and any kind of figurative elaboration. It exactly parallels the idea of incarnation. The relevant author is Duns Scotus (John Duns the Scotsman, A.D. 1266–1308), probably best known outside medieval philosophy via the poet Gerard Manley Hopkins and seen for centuries as a vigorous opponent of Thomism.

Scotus's key emphases were on individuation and incarnation. "Individuation" is perhaps what a clone or twin has; identical to its pair but still another case with its own existence.[22] This too is just what an alphabetical rather than purely pictorial word does. The word "wagon" repeated doesn't have to mean a second wagon, as it might pictorially; it is a second use of the "wagon" word. Hopkins used the term *haeccaetas*, "this-ness," for this individuation, although it doesn't appear in Scotus's work. Aristotle had contended that individuation depended on matter, and Scotus—followed by Milton in *Paradise Lost*—wondered how nonmaterial and perfect beings like angels could differ from each other. Scotus's answer is incarnational and so related to the Incarnation itself. For Hopkins, poetry uses words as individual incarnations of language generally (cf. appendix 3 for a discussion of this aspect of Hopkins).

The alphabet is arguably closer to holding matter and spirit in union than any previous writing system; yet it can emphasize them apart as poetry, narrative, theology, and philosophy variously need. Since for Christians the Incarnation is central, "the Word made flesh," it was doubtless bound to find the analogy in language sooner or later. Despite having little time for poetry, a mere human invention, even Aquinas uses the comparison. That being so, how much more would the parallel of language and Word-made-flesh doctrine mean to lovers of the phenomenal world, such as Duns Scotus, Dionysus, and Augustine himself?

KABBALAH AND THE KORAN

The Jewish philospher Philo, who lived in Rome circa A.D. 40, attempted to reconcile Plato's Ideal Forms with Jewish Scripture. Philo's resulting theory of the Logos greatly influenced the writer of the fourth Christian gospel. Despite lack of space (and the present writer's competence) here are some brief observations on the Kabbalistic interpretation of Scripture, and the Koran of Islam. Both epitomize the canonical status of alphabetical sacred texts.

The Kabbalah, a mystical branch of Judaism, aspires to unmediated union with the divine source. Its own basic text, the thirteenth-century-A.D. document *Zohar*, is in its turn a commentary on the sacred *Torah* or "final account," the first five books (Pentateuch) of the Old Testament. All the light that God gave Israel is in the Torah. "Zohar" in fact means "splendor" while *sefirot*, the "ten" (ten aspects of the divine) is associated with *sapphire* and hence God's radiance. But Kabbalistic reading of the Torah is premised on the letters, the actual signs, in which that work is embodied. It is essential that the Torah is written. In exact reverse of the views of Saussure and Bloomfield, referred to in chapter 1 above, "The Written is first, the Oral is second, the second being the explanation of the first"; and, since the Torah is the "letter engraven in stone," it is unchangeable.[23] However, the oral interpretation is "like a hammer which shatters the stone." The American critic Harold Bloom has foundationally associated this shattering with poetic creation and its engendered critical response; and Bloom's own theories of poetic "anxiety of influence" depend heavily on these positions.[24] The implications for the centuries-long modification of sacred text toward poetic canon are great.

Indeed, the desired path to union with the divine is a difficult one. The ten *(sefirot)* aspects of God move from those most utterly distant from humanity down to those in which humanity participates. Thus the first is "crown" and the last three, roughly, are "glory," "balance," and "descent." Whether through human sin, or merely our unimaginable distance from the godhead, God's invisibility is what calls for interpretation in the first place. "My thoughts are not your thoughts, and my ways are not your ways, saith the Lord. For as the heavens are higher than the earth, so are my ways higher than your ways, and my thoughts higher than your thoughts." These words from the prophet Isaiah (Isaiah 55:8–9) epitomize the non-materiality of the godhead and its monotheistic unity, and again therefore suggest where the way of interpretation must lie.

On this argument, the God of one and all—rather than of the oak tree or the sea, for example—could ever be fully approached only by contemplating his word as alphabetically inscribed. "By his thought God creates all things. By his word, which is his first spiritual manifestation, he creates all things and at the same time reveals [i.e., to interpreters of Scripture] their reason for being. All expressible truths are comprised in this divine revelation" (Schaya 1971, 9).

In our own age, empirical science has got as far as neurology, and mentalese (inner brain-language) has been postulated by psycholinguistics. But until now, how could anyone approach God's "thoughts," whether they be like human thought or not, except by the most homogenous language, that is to say material expression of thought/feeling, that had yet been produced? This is surely behind the (to us) rather extraordinary attention the Kabbalists gave to the letter itself as key to the Scriptures. And since through sin or other limitation humans already lack full understanding, it must be that the Torah, no way imperfect spiritually or morally, is in some sense incomplete if it is to enter earthly existence. And so it turns out, for the Torah is held to be composed of an incomplete alphabet. It is a kind of divine lipogram; that is to say a work with a letter missing—much like George Perec's novel *La Disparition* which eschews the letter eeeee throughout.[25] With the Torah, the missing letter lies in the white spaces between the other letters. The Torah's would-be interpreter can therefore only succeed by zealous attention to the sacred texts' actual letters.

Here are two examples of the procedure. Like the Hinduist *Aum*, both depend on acronym. The Kabbalah reads Scripture by four basic modes of exegesis; *peshat* (interpretation), *remez* (allusion), *derash* (exposition), and *sod* (esoteric tradition). But the opening letters of those four, with vowels added, make *Pardes*, the "Paradise" of the divine knowledge sought. Subdivisions of such approaches include the *gematria* (the numerical value of letters—in Kabbalah the science of numbers is equally important); the *temurah*, or how letters are combined; and the *notarikon*, which examines the first and last letters of words. *Temurah* is especially important in this connection. It is a kind of anagram, because the sacred text is one huge but finite piece of writing whose secrets might lie in alternative arrangements of its letters. Both Umberto Eco and George Steiner have underlined its significance. "The Kabbalist could rely on the unlimited resources of *temurah* [anagrams] because anagrams were more than just a tool of interpretation; they were the very method whereby God created the world." Steiner has referred to the "language mystique of kabbalists [*sic*] and gnostics" as premised on "the supposition that the entirety of knowledge and experience is prefigured in a final tome containing all conceivable permutations of the alphabet" (Eco 1994, 28; Steiner cited in Firmage 2000, 51–52). If the cosmos itself, unified and therefore monotheistic, is indeed nothing but trillions of atoms, their combinations or "anagrams" are the multifarious phenomena we seem to see pervading it. *Notarikon* will be referred to later. Harold Bloom has averred that all poets are secret Kabbalists.[26]

Furthermore, the holy and ineffable name of Yahweh, without vowels, was YHVH, which is also acronymic. On the world: Y = world of emanation, H = world of prototypical creation, V = world of celestial formation, and H again = world of fact. On family and kinship: *yod* (Y: father) unites with *he* (H: mother) bringing *vav* (V: son), and the final H is the daughter (Schaya 1971, chaps. 1–2). To the modern mind in both science and theology it might strain belief that such procedures could ever explain anything, or that anyone could think they did. Yet given the fundamental principle, that the cosmos is somehow more than real estate, and is expressive in its very materiality, then prior to empirical science the only road to ultimate truth seemed to be language and its physical embodiments. If reality is a unity, as modern science believes, then language in toto must, somehow or other, body forth an ultimate unified spirit. It can't do otherwise even if it often strays and even if we haven't found the means to explain it. If man is special in the universe—a belief held by Orthodox Jews, Renaissance Christians, other religions, and a large number of twentieth-century scientists on wholly empirical evidence—then something very significant follows. The sounds our mouths make and the letters we catch that with, must aspire to comprehending (i.e., both including and understanding) every kind of "meaning" that our body-eviscerations can feel and sense in as unified a way as possible. The alphabet's equability allows this. Schaya ends his book by taking this signality to the extreme. He suggests that the "fine upper point" of created being which reaches down into the cosmic "ocean" (the upper layers of the *sefirot* or ten aspects of God), is analogous to that same pattern in Hebrew letters. They start at the top, turn into a horizontal stroke, and end up below (Schaya op.cit. 164). Analogy was a widespread medieval principle of apprehension of reality for Christianity, Judaism, and the newly secular worlds alike.

The Koran, or "item to be read," is a most striking case of a sacred book as to its written embodiment. Muhammad, born about A.D. 570, was forty before his visitation on Mount Hara by the angel Gabriel, who presented him with a text on silk that he was commanded to recite. Since Muhammad could neither read nor write, he was astonished to find he could recite this text perfectly thereafter. The completed Koran is to this day revered by Orthodox Muslims and recited whole in some mosques daily; and the power and poetry of its always unaltered language has influenced Muslims and others down the centuries. As Ninian Smart has put it, "No religion has stuck closer through its history to its scripture."[27] Nor was a major religious text ever derived so exclusively from the teaching of a single person.

Despite all this, the Koran was written in fits and starts—Muhammad was wandering and at war much of the time—and was neither assembled nor published until after his death. The answer to this paradox must lie in the single-mindedness of the Prophet and his total belief that the angel's text on silk was transcript of a tablet preserved eternally in heaven. It was the very words of Allah. Muhammad is said to have then written it out, illiterate as he was, in a style so beautiful and miraculous as to allow of no imitation or translation. Islamic belief that its poetry is what authenticates the Koran's divine origin, has established it as a potent force in molding Arabic thought and language (Smart 1971, 479). The elaboration of the major part of the Koran over the ensuing years was possible because of this divine authenticity. Like the Torah, it is written before it is spoken, a tablet not a voice, and is thus forever available for consultation. The importance of the Koran as unchangeable is at one with the Islamic tendency to play down church-type institutions. Since the one god Allah is invisible, an alphabetical text with its fewness and virtuality rather than pictorial quality is the earthly means by which his will is expressed and known.

Summary. This chapter has aimed to show how the constraints and opportunities seen in one dominant religion—and we briefly considered two others dominant elsewhere—themselves cause or are caused by the main alphabetical features in a way that becomes near-canonical or near-institutional. This may well be valuable for the next chapter, where we see how the breakout constituted by the Reformation as well as translation, expanding education, and indeed the invention of printing throw everything wide open even as these main alphabetical features continue and survive.

Abecedarial *stability* underlies the fixity of the sacred text. In Augustine's time, Scripture was Christianity's sole authority. Medieval scholasticism sought to fix Scripture exactly, while traditional Islam has perhaps the most noteworthy example of a sacred text, the Koran, being regarded as untranslatable.

Augustine's restless personality marks his writing. Sin and chance spread right out, and thus worked abecedarial *distribution* to its uttermost. Augustine saw words as affecting his mind (a virtuality) and body, too; his writing's carnal (not just sexual) relish incarnates abecedarial *physicality*. In later life Augustine eschewed these tendencies. As with the biblical wheat and tares, all strands sit together in his later texts. Abecedarial *equalibility* gives this full scope. Yet earlier Augustine had very often returned to the one sacred word, GOD. As with acronym, although differently, this singleness also makes for a saturation—or "sponging-up" as it will be called in part 2. It was central to Kabbalistic thought as to the Hindu *Aum* via the acronym, and to Duns Scotus (and Hopkins) with his *haeccaetas* or "this-ness." These are further virtualities. The Kabbalah highlighted other abecedarial principles. The anagram *(temurah)* embodies the whole principle of letter-combination, that is to say distribution; while *notarikon* (first and last letters) evokes abecedarial fewness, for numerous letters would make alliteration a rarity.

Both Augustine and Aquinas related language to time. The sentence moves along in linear mode; abecedarial distribution is crucial at the level of syntax. But time is an abstraction; it would name the unnameable; another *virtuality*. Again some things exist but cannot be named, or don't exist but can be named (Augustine's "forgetfulness" and "evil").

Aquinas reveals that reason has its own abecedarial texture. Here by contrast timelessness, contra Augustine, a state of rest, approaches pure virtuality. So do truisms, negatives, and impossibilities, such as "x exists," "God is not," "God cannot . . ." Letters are few. The Torah even has one missing. The workings of reason entail the recycling of the same terms—or their prefix-changes or inflections: perfect/defect, decide/decided—as an argument is worked through, and for this abecedarial *fewness* is a major asset. There are countless other applications.

4

The Reformation and Humanism

THE REFORMATION

THREE HUNDRED YEARS AFTER AQUINAS'S BIRTH, WILLIAM TYNDALE'S Bible appeared in English. It was only the second English translation ever, and the first from the original Hebrew and Greek direct rather than from the Latin Vulgate. The result was a rough, workaday texture putting Thomism to one side:

> And then they toke Ionas / & cast him in to ye se / & the se lefte ragynge.
> And ye men feared the lorde excedingly: & sacrificed sacrifices vn to the lorde: and vowed vowes.
> Bvt ye lorde prepared a greate fysshe / to swalow vp Ionas. And so was Ionas in ye bowels of ye fish .iij. dayes & .iij. nightes.
> (William Tyndale, *Old Testament*, Jonah 1:15–17)

Tyndale's outdoor-cum-homespun tradition is readily illustrated from its forebears:

> cwaeo Paet wilcuman   wedera leodum
> scapan scirhame   to scipe foron.
> Pa waes on sande   saegeap naca
> hladaen herewaedum   hringedstefna
> mearum ond maomum   maest hlifade
> ofer Hroogares   hordgestreonum

[They welcomed the people of Wederas, warriors who went to the ship with their armor glinting. Then on the sand the sea-curved boat was loaded up with war equipment, the ringed prow with horses and treasure, and the mast towered over Hrothgar's hoard of riches.]

—Beowulf

128

> sitting day-long
> at an oar's length clenched against clinging sorrow,
> breast-drought I have borne, and bitterness too,
> I have coursed my keel through care-halls without end
> over furled foam, I forward in the bows
> through the narrowing night, numb, watching
> for the cliffs we beat along
>
> *—The Seafarer*

> And then bespake Child Waters sister,
>   And these were the words said shee:
> "You have the prettyest ffootpage, brother,
>   That ever I saw with mine eye;
> "But that his belly it is soe bigg,
>   His girdle goes wonderous hye;
> And ever I pray you, Child Waters,
>   Let him goe into the chamber with mee."
>
> —Traditional Ballad

> He was short-sholdred, brood, a thikke knarre;
> Ther was no dore that he nolde heve of harre,
> Or breke it at a rennyng with his heed.
> His berd as any sowe or fox was reed,
> And therto brood, as though it were a spade.
> Upon the cop right of his nose he hade
> A werte, and theron stood a toft of herys,
> Reed as the brustles of a sowes erys;
> His nosethirles blake were and wyde.
>
> —Chaucer, prologue to *Canterbury Tales*

After such as Plato and Aquinas, we come down with a bump and are pulled up short by such passages. The scholar most responsible for the new interest in Tyndale today, David Daniel, has stressed the low profile of English at the time.[1] Yet Tyndale's version is more startling, direct, and pungent than many translations of today, even though English, as Daniel sees it, was never in better shape than now, from robust crudity to slimmest refinement and flexible for every cultural and technological use. Tyndale stuck to the indigenous language. His tremendously resonant version of the events in the Garden of Gethsemane, for example, as described by Matthew, is almost void of Latinate words. The King James Version of 1611 took it over almost unchanged. In Daniel's terms, Tyndale was willing to guess, and went for the cadence. He worked with the proverb, keeping the aphorisms of Jesus exactly as they were in the original Greek. "He was dead, and is alive again; was lost, and is found."

Proverbs enter the mind direct because of the equally direct placing of the abecedary, the letters that elicit the adage orally and poise it as a comfortably slim object on the page. Like the Akan philosopher, "Mary kept all these sayings, and pondered them in her heart" (Daniel 1996, 86).

Tyndale's version teems with down-to-earth phrases. "And the Lord was with Joseph and he was a lucky fellow." "When ye pray bable not much." "I was in the Spirit on a Sondaye" (Revelation 1:10). In other places the abecedary, just sighted as it were below the surface, shows itself by the change of a letter or two that makes all the difference. "We sailed away from Philippos after the ester holydays" (Acts 20:6). "Easter holidays" means something else for us now. In the King James Version, Ephesians 2:8 reads, "By grace are ye saved by faith." Tyndale wrote, "By grace are ye made safe through faith." "Saved" from "[made] safe" changes one letter and adds another, and the meaning alters a little. There is also the pattern of "the noun of the noun," found often in Shakespeare doubled: "the noun and noun of noun"—"the force and road of casualty" (*Merchant of Venice*, 2:9:29), "the files and musters of the war" (*Antony and Cleopatra*, 1:1:3), "the whips and scorns of time" (*Hamlet*, 3:1:70). It is a Hebrew structure that Tyndale adopted.

Many of Tyndale's vernacular phrases survive in our own everyday speech. Some were kept in the King James Version. Many people are still unaware of their origin. *The spirit is willing, God forbid, filthy lucre, faith that moves mountains, the fatted calf, fight the good fight, eat drink and be merry, the powers that be, the fat of the land, signs of the times, a man after his own heart, a fool's paradise, a law unto themselves*; all of these first appear in the Tyndale Bible. In Genesis, when the serpent tempts Eve to take the forbidden fruit, she replies with God's warning that if they eat it they will die. "Ye shall not surely die" answers the serpent in the King James Version (Genesis 3:4). Tyndale has it, "Tush, ye shall not die." Whether or not "tush" translates the Hebrew better than "surely" I cannot say, but it is certainly a different experience in English.

What Tyndale is doing here for the first time, and with some linguistic risk, is to apply the rough diversity of the profane Saxon language to a sacred text deemed by its nature to emanate from the unified source of God. Guttural and sibilant consonants, chiming vowels, and whole fleshy phrases can be hazarded because they are all selections of the same twenty-six letters. They may therefore be relied on not to endanger the integrity of what they are expressing. There is no way that a fulsome rendering of this Scripture could be allowed to invoke entities that might, in the last analysis, suggest polytheism or a plural cosmos. Like matter itself, all come from the single mind of the deity; and so the many idioms, vernaculars, regional dialects, educational levels, and the rest can be trusted with the scriptural message that is rendered in the same equable medium. Of course, this would not have been widely agreed, even when understood. The risk Tyndale took was more than linguistic; it was political.

As a result of his work Tyndale was captured, tied to the stake, strangled, and burned. His incessant railings against both Church and sacrament doubtless hastened his demise. But the long catalog of martyrdom in this period of the Reformation, in Europe even more than England, is only the extreme outcome of the impact of the many biblical translations of the era. Putting sacred text into words suitable for Tyndale's "Gloucestershire ploughboy" was always going to be provocative. The entrenched few acted violently to protect their privileged access to the sources of learning and to scriptural truth. Doubtless, but the linguistic and spiritual dimensions were inextricably enmeshed in this, and some deep soul-searching was entailed as the seismic shift in several cultures took place.

For up to Tyndale, none of the writers substantially addressed in the present book so far wrote in English. Literary scholarship has ignored the abecedary, as Curtius and others have noted, because the foundations of high English culture were laid from other languages from other places: Israel, Greece, Rome, and France, the first two even having a different alphabet. Yet the language of the English poets, from the English Renaissance to the silicon chip, emerged from the engrafting of Greek, Latin, and French on to the indigenous Anglo-Saxon. This rich mix and the marks it leaves on the page is what John Donne, John Milton, John Dryden, John Keats, Robert Browning, T. S. Eliot, and the rest have worked with. Indeed, poetry in Old English and Saxon has hardly survived, certainly not as a substantial poetic model, even though William Barnes, Gerard Manley Hopkins, Thomas Hardy, and W. H. Auden sometimes returned to them for linguistic stimulus. Poets up to Wordsworth would have expected to be as conversant in Latin, and maybe French, as in English. This postcolonial story has now been rewritten the other way around. Today English and "Englishes" are seen as the predominant world language resource. In such dissenting mood William Tyndale produced his English Bible early in the sixteenth century.

Dissemination of the Bible to all in their own tongue may have shifted the very idea of language. It was possible, we are suggesting, because whatever language was used, the abecedary was the common medium for all Europe. This medium in effect lay behind what had been called the Book of Nature. Both Curtius and Foucault have examined the traditional idea of the Book of Nature and the Book of Scripture in the centuries prior to the Reformation, Foucault in terms of his theories of cultural replacement, rather than slow evolution, of historical events.[2] This is relevant, for the question is of just what Tyndale changed.

The standard account runs as follows. Before the Fall, humans had access both to Nature and to God. Losing this and therefore the original Adamic language by their own disobedience, they were left unable to read Nature, and could see God only dimly. The Old Testament, notably in the Book of Job and the Psalms, is full of failures in face of plagues and earthquakes and our equal inability to see the face of God that is now hidden. But in his mercy God made two reparations. He gave us the Scriptures, and he left his own signature written into the world of Nature. These two came to be seen as "books." Reading and writing are gifts to enable this. The period of the illuminated manuscript, those beautiful and laboriously achieved objects that survive from the medieval period, implies that the sacred book as writing had to be secured in the noblest form that human techniques could attain, lest it should slip away from us.[3] Federigo of Urbino would have been ashamed to own a printed book (Burckhardt 1940, 117), much as some people today avoid plastic imitations of household objects and stay with wood or china. The idea of Nature as legible had existed for centuries. For Plotinus the stars are "like letters forever being written in the sky . . . he who knows the alphabet reads the future according to the figures they form." The plough is pen, the land is paper, the furrow is a line of writing. As late as the seventeenth century in Spain, says Curtius, "The sea writes letters with foam, dawn writes with dew on flowers . . . the sun (writes) on cosmic space, the ship on the waves, the birds on the tablets of the winds. . . . The rainbow is a stroke of the quill, sleep a written sketch, death the signature of life" (Curtius 1953, 307–8, 343–44).

The abecedary's universal application is clear enough. But one still asks, how are these things literally comparable to letters themselves, except in a most vaguely metaphorical way? Nature has features that of course can be watched and understood, but whence comes the call to compare this with writing? Jacques Derrida's notion of a primal *ecriture* expresses the point metaphysically, but it does not explain how nature's markings are not only material but signal; how there is anything to be interpreted. Even so, for medieval man red and white could not avoid evoking blood and purity, nor the twelve months and four seasons the apostles and Gospels.[4] On an ultimately mathematical metaphysic, in a prescientific age, one can see that this is explanatorily plausible. Galileo himself said as much. But as well as recalling the Trinity, a tree with three branches has its own existence as tough, green, fertile, and so on, aspects all with their own functions. If their combination with other hard phenomena could be read for a syntax of its own, either there must be a sign-matter unity in the created world, or we must sense such things by self-delusion or coincidence.

Foucault suggested that the system of signs from antiquity up to the Renaissance was triple-layered. These three parts are "the formal domain of marks [on the page], the content indicated by them, and the similitudes that link the marks to the things designated by them" (Foucault 1970, 42). These "similitudes" however also suggest entailment. Foucault cites the sixteenth-century grammarian Peter Ramus, who held that "words group syllables together, and syllables letters, because there are virtues placed in individual letters that draw them towards each other or keep them apart, exactly as the marks found in nature also repel or attract one another." "The names of things were lodged in the things they designated, just as strength is written in the body of the lion, regality in the eye of the eagle, just as the influence of the planets is marked upon the brows of men" (35–36). It recalls Aquinas's conclusion that words are appropriate to what they name. The great chain of being could not regard letters as "mere" signs alone. Letters were part of nature much as today cars for Richard Dawkins are biological objects (Dawkins 1986, 1–2). All things stemmed from God's creating source just as for today's evolutionists they stem from the primal matter that branches out into everything—the car as much as the bee's nest or the beaver's lodge. For pre-Renaissance observers "there is no difference between the visible marks that God has stamped upon the surface of the earth, so that we may know its inner secrets, and the legible words that the Scriptures, or the sages of Antiquity, have set down in the books preserved for us by tradition" (Foucault 1970, 33). Both merely needed interpretation.

The idea totally pervaded both the medieval period and antiquity. Certainly writing, word, and book were symbolic of God and ultimate things. But they weren't symbol and metaphor alone. The always unique act of handwriting was directly continuous with other craft processes that employed Nature's substances. But the fruit of the book, unlike that of the carpenter's bench or the apple tree, was meaning. To saturate the created world with the idea of the book is like our own tendency to see the computer in everything and everything in the computer. All can be subjected to or subsumed by the computer. Curtius's book is a mine of examples of this phenomenon. Plato likened the soul to a wax tablet imprinted by a seal ring. A poet thanks Nature for inventing writing materials in order to unite parted friends. Colors are entailed: the *album* is the white-paged book as yet unwritten, the *rubric* is written in red, readily suggesting blood. "My tongue is the pen of a ready writer" (Psalms 45:1): the oral and the written unite.

Letters came as insects in the Old Testament (Proverbs 6:6) and were taken up as such by Sir Thomas Browne. A human face is a word, most seriously for Dante: *The sockets of their eyes were like rings without stones: / Those who read "omo" in the human face / Would certainly have recognized the "m" there* (the drifting souls in *Purgatorio*, 33:31–3, Sisson's translation).[5] The ooooos are eyes and mmmmm the nose; *omo* means "man." The total parallels of writing, book, and creation later also appear in Shakespeare, Donne, Milton, Herbert, Francis Quarles, Henry Vaughan, and Richard Crashaw. Dante begins the *Divine Comedy* with the book reference (*Inferno*, 2:7ff.), repeats it sporadically throughout, and ends with his huge vision of ultimate reality's dazzling light in the same way: *I saw gathered there in the depths of it, / Bound up by love into a single volume, / All the leaves scattered throughout the universe* (*Paradiso*, 33:85–87). It is present, if less doctrinally and more as imaginative, in Shakespeare right through to Prospero in *The Tempest* (Curtius 1953, chap. 3 passim). We might put it then that the creation is "writerly," a conglomerate of messages and their embodiment where utility and communication meet. One could literally not act or breathe without writing in some sense, it seemed; the expression to "leave one's mark on life" stems from this.

Such things affected education, too, and in practical fashion. Writing has nature's disciplines. St. Martin would allow his monks only writing among the arts, because writing occupied mind, eye, and hand together. A monk would rule his lines before writing, an emanation from the entire created order. "Learning one's letters" and being a "man of letters" were cognate. The Greek for "letter" was *gramma*, and the early education of the monk entailed a stage-by-stage procedure from letters to words to sentences and on up to entire works; as Curtius put it, "the entire method of presentation" (Curtius 1953, 41–42). Such is what "literature" is made of. Printing eventually shatters all such things, though they survive in the writers named and elsewhere for quite a long time.

So it is no mystery that, before the Renaissance, words were entailed in what they named. Whether in the discourse of reason or the great chain of being, they could scarcely have avoided it. Within the discourse of reason their matter and form could not have been otherwise. Ramus's "virtues" are interesting, but in the terms of the present book, letters were seen as neither "physical" nor "virtual" but as indivisibly real. But Foucault's point is that with the impact of the Renaissance the middle term of the triple just referred to fell away. From the formal marks on the page, the nature they refer to, and the links between them, the links disappeared. As a result language turns into a network of marks and signs relating mainly to each other. By the abecedary's internal homogeneity this network remains intact and its words still have real outside reference, but now only by convention. The study of these relations appears as grammar. The question again is of what this led to.

Certainly manuscript was not swept aside, so for writers and poets to circulate work in manuscript among friends was itself to publish it, without benefit of print and in a procedure that would be unlikely now. But the invention of printing was an immense incentive to translate the Bible because of the new ability to distribute it. In England over a million copies of the hitherto guarded book had been published by the year 1640. But printing was itself cause or result of a shifting attitude to word as against thing in the first place. Giving spiritual prominence to word rather than other sacrament had deep implication. Bread, water, and blood in sacrament may remain bread, water, and blood, but the letters on the page come from nothing, or at most inscription itself; their pure form stems from the writer's intention. (Our word *cipher* is the Arabic *sifr* meaning "empty" or "zero." Again we glimpse the extent of Arabic influence on the medieval world.) In the early sixteenth century the Reformation process in Zurich was already well under way along lines later to reach Britain. Relics and organs were removed, pictures and icons smashed, altars stripped, clergy denied special robing. Everything had to be sanctioned by Scripture. Later empirical science, formally epitomized by the founding of the Royal Society in 1660 and its subsequent pronouncements, lightened matter of its mystery. Only sign and word were left as the remaining locus of God's will and nature. The Protestant emphasis on Scripture squares with its emphasis on science.

For with the arrival of printing the reformers could no longer see "word" as inscribed in some literal way deep within Nature. The

result was that they held on to the divinely given word all the more
tightly. The words of Scripture abecedarially on the page were
fused through and through in unchanging match with the will and
grace of God. The Reformation begins with Martin Luther; the first
issue, about indulgences, was over authority but Luther later translated the Bible into German. The concern of Jean Calvin, a generation after Luther, was not power either, for by then the reforming
movement had already thrown off the papal power. For the Protestant churches not to be merely anarchic or formless, the question
was of just what authority should replace that of the papacy. The
answer was already in place: Scripture; the Bible.

Yet the act of translation is also double-edged. As said earlier, a
Scripture once agreed upon is canonical. The abecedary in microscopic detail—the thousands of words and phrases, in their lengths,
inflections, and other distributions, syntax and meaning—is a precise and unified textural presence that can enforce huge authority.
So to translate a book, even a sacred book, into another language
paradoxically implies that the particular words are not uniquely
necessary to the full meaning after all. They only point through
themselves to that meaning. It is the fact of letters that remains
uniquely necessary. That is to say, the fixity of the alphabet can be
regarded as flexible in its use. Unconsciously or not, this is itself a
theory of the poetic. But it is again a statement concerning authority. Translating the Bible from its sacred origin (Hebrew, Greek) or
long-sanctioned institutional antiquity (Latin) into your own local
language is seen as taking its authority to yourself. This surely is
how Tyndale offended. In the Reformation the process begins to
diversify and spread. Not only churches but also individuals began
to translate and to issue scriptural commentaries. Commentary departed the scholastic, that is Thomist, mode of building theologies
because scriptural interpretation was now widespread. So it became
a paralyzingly close monitoring of every line, verse, and word; of
what, since it was sacred, might have been expected to radiate itself
to its readers without addition. This was so even though the "text"
was now translated and no longer the alphabetically exact canon-
ized original. To this day Orthodox Islam forbids translation of the
Koran. That book's perfection of style, it is said, is incapable of
sustaining such a process without loss. And the style, that is to say
the congruence of meaning with rhythm and abecedary, is what
counts.

It is equally paradoxical that individuals, rather than "the
Church," could then erect their own wholesale accounts of theol-

ogy, Scripture, and the desirable nature of the Church institution. Calvin's *Institutes of the Christian Religion* (1536), steeped in patristic learning from Augustine to Luther himself, gave exclusive place to Scripture. Yet in a sense not necessarily derogatory of Calvin, it was his own Scripture. His book had massive influence. In Francois Wendel's terms, it was "such a success that it established itself at once as the basic manual of dogmatic in the reformed churches. It can be affirmed without fear of error that when these Churches became Calvinist they owed it to the various French editions of the *Institutes*."[6] The Thirty-nine Articles of the Church of England are often regarded as essentially Calvinist in orientation. Adapting a phrase borrowed from late-twentieth-century literary criticism, one might say that the burden of faith in God-as-source risks becoming greater if there are as many Bibles as there are translators. Yet at the deepest level the alphabetical principle still integrates them all.

Of course, the King James Version of 1611 was in the end the chief biblical injection into English culture. Mary Tudor and Oliver Cromwell symbolize extremes of ecclesiastical belief and practice. The High Church devotee of the sacramental, Archbishop Laud, was beheaded in 1645 as was the Church's titular head, Charles I, in 1649. When the Protestants won the English civil war, they conducted their own forms of purge. Yet the King James Version won the scriptural victory and Cromwell's Directory of Worship fell out of favor, defeated by Thomas Cranmer's limpid Prayer Book cadences.

The old questions reassert themselves. What really caused the English Reformation? People still ask whether Henry VIII's sexual desires—and need for a male heir—detached the state from the Church, or whether that rift enabled him to risk going for broke on his personal aspirations. But if there was also a yearning for scriptural authority over institutional authority, was it more than that? Maybe there was some desire for fully literal scriptural interpretation and devotion over more liberal readings. Tyndale's wasn't the only relevant martyrdom. The first was that of John Rogers, burned at Smithfield in 1555. His translation of the Bible had been published in 1537 under a pseudonym. Thomas Cranmer, burned at the stake in 1556, was largely responsible for the English Prayer Book of 1552, still used in the Church of England today along with twentieth-century alternatives. Archbishop of Canterbury Matthew Parker published the so-called Bishop's Bible in 1568. The aim was to counter the Calvinist Geneva Bible. Parker survived, but himself damningly described Reginald Pole (Mary Tudor's chief organizer of the burnings) as *carnifex et flagellum Ecclesiae Anglicanae*: hangman and torturer of the English Church. It does suggest, paradoxically and aside from local variations, that the pressure of the word on institutionalized authority intensified as result of the very demystifying of the sense of language as entailed in nature as suggested by Foucault and Curtius. If the idea of language as merely one more aspect of the broad stamp of God on Nature dies away, then the remaining unique book regarded as "God's Word" may be asked to bear greatly increased responsibility. For it alone is taken to exemplify God-given language in the world that remains. What then is left of the other parts of Nature that are sacred within creation—in the Christian dispensation, bread, water, raiment, and wine? George Herbert's poetry is immersed in these questions.

HUMANISM

Meanwhile, a different discourse had been growing for two centuries in the nonradical but liberalizing thought-flow of a new humanism. It ran alongside, but a little way from, the more drastic confrontations of the period. Desiderius Erasmus's compromising character and sense of folly; Baldassare Castiglione's combinations of social grace, instruction, and laughter. Michel de Montaigne's easy self-knowing in the widest range of topics, and Sir Philip Sidney's impish affectation of argument within deeper implications. Richard Burton's happy-sad mingling of his digestive ailments with his reflections on all of life's local paradoxes. Sir Francis Bacon's project was more precisely structured, but the province he chose for himself, that of "all knowledge," is cognate with Montaigne's confession that there is no human act he has not at some time considered doing. Bacon's distancing, by and large, from hands-on scientific inquiry puts him too in this discursive tradition. Shakespeare runs all of this and more into a heightening of almost every kind of voiced abecedarial act one could imagine.

In the couple of centuries after Gutenberg, the humanist tradition burgeoned. Castiglione, Montaigne, Sidney, Burton, and others gradually saw how the speech of conversation—what Montaigne called "the most fruitful and natural exercise of our minds"—could be gently drawn out and elongated into writing like a spider's thread. Much more could be conversationally written than the same conversation's oral conditions allowed. And conversation's mode, the mix of courtesy, easy clarity, and willingness to change the subject before it becomes clogged, moves away from any fixed-text presence that holds when the Word is held sacred. In printing's abundance most texts neither need nor could be so resistant. The humanists laid their thoughts on the page like a watercolorist lays a wash. Their thought could be softly extended; and the calm evenness of the abecedary (its "stable" and "equable" features) in part made this possible. Printing took humanism beyond Plato by writing the tentative in means other than dialogue.

This connection between writing and the expansion of humanistic expression has an important origin in writing's nature. Earlier we cited David Olsen's view that the new abecedary did not merely record speech but offered a model for speech. But parallel with this, and of equal significance, Olsen pointed out that the new written mode had a need of its own. Spoken language carried indications of its intention within it. Stress, volume and tone of voice, body-language, facial expression, and so on give the speaker's intention along with the utterance itself. Any listener—as opposed to reader—can usually tell whether an utterance like "why don't you go home?" is intended to be threatening, helpful, cheerful, sarcastic, or just sadly sympathetic, from the mannerisms and tone of the speaker. And proverbs—*look before you leap*; *there are no crossroads in the ear*—usually originate orally and so normally bear their whole sense in their text; there is no interpretive problem. But writing, by contrast, lacks these means. Writing conveys only the uttered text itself.

As a result, over many centuries since the abecedary's first appearance, a huge effort went into evolving ways of wrapping into writing's material text its intention too, along with its more overt content. Following John Searle, Olsen calls this intention the text's "illocutionary force." The methods adopted by writing for this purpose are many. Explanatory phrases, qualifying clauses of many kinds, punctuation and emphasis markers, and figures of speech themselves may all enlighten the reader as to how what is written is also to be understood, when there is no author present to tell us or answer our questions. This is Plato's complaint once more. But the lexicon itself also expands to meet these needs. Adverbs describe an utterance's tendency and energy, conjunctions its purposes or changes of direction, repetitions its emphases, and reported speech or narrator-comment generally may lay a text wide open as to its underlying drift.

Olsen offers a list of terms that entered English before or during this period of humanistic expansion in Europe. Fundamental terms of telling and knowing were already in place in Old English: *believe*, *know*, *mean*, *say*, *tell*, and *think*. Later on, *claim*, *conclude*, *confirm*, *define*, *doubt*, *imply*, *interpret*, and *prove* arrived with Middle English; but *assert*, *assume*, *concede*, *contradict*, *criticise*, *explain*, *infer*, *predict*, and *suggest* do not appear until the sixteenth and seventeenth centuries (Olsen 1994, 109). These and comparable events broadly concurred with the medieval rise of scriptural interpretation. Ecclesiastical literacy opened up skills by which to establish exactly what the sacred text—the divine word, after all—must have meant and which, from then on, required something close to unquestioning acceptance. With Aquinas and others, particularly Andrew of St. Victor who was impressed by and consulted Jewish scholars (Olsen 1994, 149–50), came the aspiration to fix the text and discover its single possible interpretation. But writing's same feature, that of being marked with all kinds of explanations of itself and its nuances of stress, subtleties, deliberate hesitations, or multiplying possibilities, would inevitably then go further. This would be especially so if the sacredness of a text were no longer always the topic in hand. This is where our topic of humanism becomes relevant. The power of humans to enlarge their ways of identifying and expressing every aspect of what they thought, felt, and were—emotions, sighings, tiny separate items of thought, hesitations, jokes, figures—became multilayered by these means. And this itself over time could then become, or strongly feed into, civilized conversation's topics. As a broad act of enlightened self-consciousness and its expression to sympathetic others, humanism had arrived. We could read these feelings and intentions in texts concerned with quite other things such as art, politics, and manners. We could then write of such things ourselves, directly or otherwise, confident that civilized and educated readers would share this deep sense of an ongoing conversation and be glad and willing to share in it.

Here are two brief passages that may capture the way humanistic writing found it could use writing's self-explaining processes to stretch conversation very wide. Both, of course, are lifted out of much longer pieces; that is part of the point.

"Gentle reader, I presume that thou wilt be very inquisitive to know what antic or personate actor this is that so insolently intrudes upon this common theatre to the world's view, arrogating another man's name [Democritus], whence he is, why he doth it, and what he hath to say. Although as he said, *Primum si noluero, non respondebo, quis coacturus est?*—I am a free man born and may choose whether I will tell, who can compel me?—if I be urged, I will as readily reply as that Egyptian in Plutarch when a curious fellow would needs know what he had in his basket, *Quam vides velatim, quid inquiris in rem absconditam?* [Given you can see at least something, must you ask about what is hidden?] It was therefore covered because he should not know what was in it. Seek not after that which is hid. If the contents please thee and be for thy use, suppose the man in the moon or whom thou wilt to be the author." (Robert Burton [1577–1640], *Anatomy of Melancholy*)

"One of the later school of the Grecians examineth the matter, and is at a stand to think what should be put in it, that men should love lies; where neither they make for pleasure, as with poets; nor for advantage, as with the merchant; but for the lie's sake. But I cannot tell: this same truth is a naked and open day-light, that doth not shew the masques and mummeries and triumphs of the world, half so stately and daintily as candle-lights. Truth may perhaps come to the price of a pearl, that sheweth best by day; but it will not rise to the price of a diamond or carbuncle, that sheweth best in varied lights. A mixture of a lie doth ever add pleasure." (Francis Bacon [1561–1626], "Of Truth," *Essays*)

Almost every sentence in both passages contains overt hints as to exactly how we should take it. We can feel the writer as now calmly confident, now a little puzzled, now gently smiling. Not more human than Augustine, but less constrained by a single magnetic force, these writers can feel the abecedary as supple, light of touch, and sinuous. Plato feared that writing might lie, but in both these excerpts the unmalicious and indeed gently comic relish at deceit is itself too honest to offend us. Subordinate clauses do their work without growing cumbersome, yet the short words trip along without surfeit, leaving longer ones strong and clear. As in good conversation, one phrase can afford to wait for the next. Such passages would need closer analysis than that (my own favorite phrase here is Bacon's "but I cannot tell:"), yet surely we can see in them the seeds of later-seventeenth-century diarists like John Evelyn and Samuel Pepys, and writers of "Lives" like John Aubrey and Anthony à Wood. The master, I believe, was Montaigne.

Not surprisingly much of this development is tied to gradual changes in medieval education in the fourteenth and fifteenth centuries. Under the aegis of scholasticism, children were taught Scripture via the fixed interpretations laid down by the Church and its recognized scholars. Naturally enough, today we may see this as authoritarian; but books were rare, printing had not arrived, and at least something was getting taught to young people who otherwise might well have remained illiterate. Attempts toward at least some rudimentary education go back to Charlemagne and King Alfred. But the next step arrived when pupils were offered more than one interpretation to consider, for this induced the habit of making comparisons. Some individual fifteenth-century teachers, albeit rare, began to go further still. There is a change, then, from the early medieval view that, in Alberto Manguel's words, "a multiplicity of voices ultimately echoed one single voice, God's *logos*," through to the late medieval view that "the text . . . and the successive comments of changing generations of readers, tacitly implied that not one but a near infinity of readings was possible, feeding upon one another" (Manguel 1997,73–79; cited passage 86).

Handwriting, too, both enabled and responded to this new breadth and mental flexibility. It is intriguing that the invention of printing did not mean that handwriting was used less, as many at the time predicted. Rather, as print made reading a new experience for more and more people, handwriting spread very widely. It is like the way that television today, far from eliminating the book, takes viewers back to whatever cookbook, novel, or political biography is the latest TV adaptation's original. Again, as so often with new inventions, for a few decades printing did not at first seek to replace manuscript but to augment it (Jean 1992, chap. 5)—again just as, in our own time, early films were often conceived in the idiom of the stage. In a parallel development, handwriting itself attained a stretching, a liberation. The old calligrapher's gothic began to be replaced by italic and other cursive forms. As John Lewis has put it, "The gothic letter was fit only for the writings of the church. The strongly humanistic renaissance needed the open round letters to express the Florentines' new open-ended thoughts" (John Lewis, cited in Firmage 2000, 29).

Finally, a different though cognate kind of mental stretching occurred in the very different conditions of the English Reformation. Eamonn Duffy has studied in detail the uniquely discursive Church records kept by a Devon rector, Christopher Trychay, for four decades in the mid-sixteenth century.[7] The period covered three turnabouts. These went from Henry VIII's early loyalty to Catholicism to his later turning against the pope for his own reasons; the reaction under Mary Tudor; and then finally the settlement under Elizabeth I. Trychay's parish was small, rural, and domestic. Its parishioners were very human; grumblers but of goodwill, prudent with property and finance, and, while true enough Christian believers, as much concerned for their way of life quietly to continue as for exact doctrines always to be abolished or upheld. The relevance to our discussion here is that they therefore found themselves in paradoxical situations. They rebelled on behalf of tradition, and then they advanced with no progressive ideology. They fought for what they liked, yet quietly accepted change when it finally seemed inevitable. It is a case, one feels, of the spread of humanist values among ordinary people. The repeated changes couldn't avoid stirring the mind into thought and emotion, annoyance, sympathy, the making of arguments for and against, and the querying of their mildly pedagogic but mainly tolerant rector's shifting recommendations. So these and numerous other factors also underline the spread of humanistic writing, its stretching of English prose, and the abecedary's use to that end.

Certainly in any detail, Shakespeare must largely be passed over in the present book. Yet in context it is difficult to ignore him entirely. Here are just a very few observations. Sometimes the whole opus seems like a dream, from the early *Midsummer Night's Dream* whose audience is enjoined to "think that ye but slumbered here" (the unobtrusive alliteration is already second nature) through to *The Tempest* at the end of the poet's lifetime work. There the hypnotized conspirators can no more commit murder than John Keats's urn-lovers can make love. This pair is in the hands of Prospero/Shakespeare fully; at will he can lift his pen from the page as other artists can take their bow from the violin or their hand off the camera. In between are nightmares like *Julius Caesar* and *Macbeth*. Shakespeare's relation to words is deeply paradoxical. The Bible is to be read (Greek *biblos* = book), yet the secular world now more often hears it; but Shakespeare worked for the stage, yet the world of secular and mass education is commonly introduced to him as syllabus, as writing. It is his scenes and characters that must be preeminent, we feel, because great artists like Fyodor Dostoyevsky, Giuseppe Verdi, and Vincent van Gogh, whose first language was in no case English, adulated him so much.

Yet the Globe Theatre's lack of scenery, and so the near-total dependence of every character on just the words each utters, had an outcome that was perhaps only ever possible in world history soon after the Renaissance and printing. Shakespeare teems with human beings—kings, clowns, daughters, soldiers, assassins, fairies, courtiers, foresters, shopkeepers, shrews, and rabble—yet the abundance of his words *(What do you read my lord? / Words, words words)* seems to have wafted forward from the end of each play to the always-new start of the next. We end up feeling that the characters must be preeminent, must be bigger and noisier and fleshier than mere language, yet that only the language can so achieve it. The mature abecedary's homogeneity could expand forever without risk of collapsing into incoherence. Unsurprisingly the poet, like Macbeth, occasionally felt that "all is but toys"—in which phrase, toy-like, no word bar a plural has more than three letters—but always more came from that apparently bottomless source.

Especially up to and including the great tragedies, the plays are curiously loose-knit, as though sweeps of writing have a surplus that gives them autonomous existence. Sometimes it is the sheer repetition of terms. In *The Merchant of Venice*, for example, the caskets, pound of flesh, and gold rings etch their existence onto our minds, as though the physical things they are and the physical things that name them are one and inextricable. Shakespeare exploits the abecedary's power of subtle repetition within wider plurality to the utmost. Juliet's famous cry *Come, night. Come, Romeo. Come, thou day in night . . .* , with "come" twice more in two further lines, seems a willed sexual orgasm. Everyone knows the inscribed resonances from *Julius Caesar,* which the drama delivers up to memory forever: the *lean and hungry look; Friends, Romans, countrymen . . . ; Et tu, Brute;* yet the repetition of the farewell between Brutus and Cassius seals the words as things more than permanent. (Brutus) *If we do meet again, why we shall smile; if not, why then this parting was well made. . . .* (Cassius) *If we do meet again, we'll smile indeed; if not, 'tis true this parting was well made.* Elsewhere it is the mellifluous songs, from *As You Like It* and finally *The Tempest* itself, which stand off the play when the oeuvre is long closed.

Macbeth puts five terms before us insistently: light, dark, sleep, flight, murder. Macbeth does murther sleep, even though after life's fitful fever Duncan sleeps well. The contrast of light/dark matches that of long and short words—*the multitudinous seas incarnadine / Making the green one red;* varying word-length is a key alphabetical resource as will also be discussed in part 2. The play moves from light to dark to light again, and at its heart of darkness Macbeth loses contact with words altogether. *Wherefore could I not pronounce "Amen"? / I had most need of blessing, and "Amen" / Stuck in my throat.* Earlier he was more articulate, the words marshaled with black dignity along the line: *I am settled, and bend up / Each corporeal agent to this terrible deed. / Away, and mock the time . . .* In *Othello, King Lear,* and *Hamlet* variously, the words grow wonderfully too large for the characters. We find Othello's ooooos, *soft you, a word or two before you go; Hamlet* meanwhile was unfinished, leaving its power to depend much on its stunning soliloquies, *O that this too too sullied flesh would melt; To be or not to be; O what a rogue and peasant slave am I.* No one but Hamlet hears them, and he forgets them himself, but they then survive on stage and page for centuries afterward. Small hints are let loose; *O my prophetic soul* (how did Hamlet know his father had been murdered?), and his closest friend can take his leave with an utterance beyond his own usual powers: *Goodnight, sweet prince, and flights of angels / Sing thee to thy rest . . .* The words, their small letter-clusters, fly beyond the speaker into a timeless fixity.

Finally, words can overwhelm carnality itself:

> Age cannot wither her, nor custom stale
> Her infinite variety: other women cloy
> The appetites they feed, but she makes hungry
> Where most she satisfies . . .
> —*Anthony and Cleopatra,* 2:2:241–44[8]

How can Enobarbus, or anyone else, muster such expression, staying the flesh as it does at the moment of eliciting it? The songs most of all epitomize what happens all the time anyway. They touch a nerve in the poet himself, as though his pen is always outrunning the characters he gives body by speaking them, and where "characters" are humans and alphabet-units alike:

> Full fathom five my father lies
>   Of his bones are coral made;
> Those are pearls that were his eyes;
>   Nothing of him that doth fade
> But doth suffer a sea change
> Into something rich and strange.

We have now to look more systematically at the main characteristics of our letters. Maybe these are part of what takes familiar objects, routine thoughts, and feelings into communication's virtual world, also to become something rich and strange.

Summary. This chapter has aimed to round out our overall survey in part 1, by seeing how the long evolution of awareness of the abecedary's features by its users finally opened out into a general suppleness and flexibility. This was finally embodied in humanism; but the long constraints found in the earliest civilizations, in Greek epic poetry and later philosophy, and the textual power and authority of

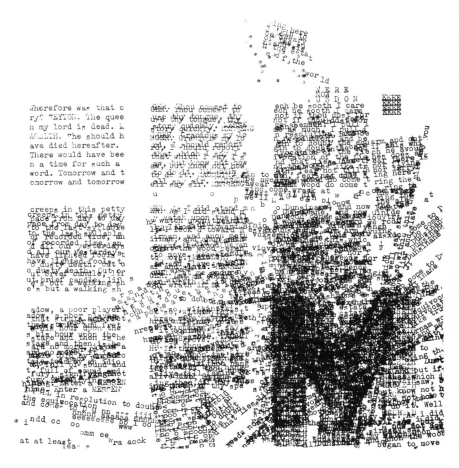

the Church, were important long-term enablers of this, by their very longevity and (with variations) consistency. So we are now ready to look at these main features of the abecedary in more systematic and synchronic fashion.

We arrive at our own language. It becomes easier to see how a single change of letter can alter a nuance, here by regressing across the centuries: Tyndale's "bable," "Sondaye," "ester." This is small-scale abecedarial *distribution*; in this case redistribution. Tyndale's earthy language also underlines its great *physicality*, but also the abecedary's capacity to be centrifugal, to distribute letters in countless combinations. This thwarts any reductive impact of the abecedary's *fewness*. These words too "sponge-up" or absorb their meanings, making words seem appropriate to what they name. This is a different kind of abecedarial *virtuality*. In so writing, Tyndale worked in the medieval tradition of the "Book of Nature," the belief that God's creation could itself be read and that language was cognate with it.

All this occurs in context of a new main idea: translation. With the invention of print, translation pervades the Reformation era, especially in England. This raises its own problems when central papal authority is challenged, for Scripture has all the more to embody that authority itself. Islam's belief, that its text is untranslatable, may not be inconsistent with this so long as the translation is into a language that uses the same alphabet. That way at least the letters remain the same; abecedarial *stability* is exploited. Meanwhile, education began with the learning of letters; all writing, all thought, is made in letters; and so their *fewness* is seen as essential to consistency and in the end cosmic unity. Peter Ramus similarly saw "virtue" in letters; a common virtuality is retained.

Yet when the sense of word as part of nature declined, as Foucault traced, words were left relating only to each other, and the age of the grammarian was inaugurated. In our terms here, the grammarian studied abecedarial *distribution* at the level of sentence structure. Later, with humanism, writing suddenly expands to converse with every aspect of human personality. Both abecedarial distribution and abecedarial *equability* become newly prominent. Distributions are multiplied by ever more ingenuity, wit, and understanding, yet abecedarial equability still conserves them all in the one communicative channel. They can spread across many societies with no risk, for the same medium of communication expresses them all.

II

Six Characteristics of the Abecedary

THIS PART SEEKS THE GENERAL PRINCIPLES BEHIND THE WESTERN abecedary, drawing examples largely from English. One may detect six such principles. Letters, I suggest, are *few, stable, equable, physical, virtual,* and *distributive*. The first five of these characteristics are basic to the abecedary. The sixth, the distributive, derives from the other five, but it is still an essential, because it is the dynamic of letters, their mode of operation.

In the brief summaries at the ends of sections in part 1, we drew out just a few of the main applications of these six features as we found them in the earlier eras, texts, and writers considered. The six principles offered may broadly apply to other world-alphabets, too, from which occasional evidence is cited, but any claim for general application would need to be guarded. It is now time to look at these six principles in their own light.

As was said earlier, the reason for carrying out this task here in part 2—and thus interrupting this book's otherwise mainly chronological sequence—is that we shall need some clear analytical categories of the abecedary when we come to look closely at specific poets in part 3. Of course, we hope too that this analysis will prove useful in its own right more generally.

5

Letters Are Few

In 1996 over ninety thousand new books were published in Britain. To produce just one copy of each of them meant printing some fifteen thousand million individual letters of the abecedary. If each of those letters was a grain of sand, the resulting heap would fill three or four large wheelbarrows. If multiplied by sales, we would have a good-sized stretch of beach. Laid end to end—as the phrase goes—and taking the text from only one copy of each book, the lines of print would stretch from London to Marseilles. Yet these fifteen thousand million signs were merely the same twenty-six graphemes repeated over and over. And there was normally no repetition of content, for, as we have said, we have counted only one copy of each book published.

People of average education, memory, and intelligence use something like fifteen thousand words in their lives but actually know as many as sixty thousand. Yet the same twenty-six signs report this vast vocabulary. If every sound used in English were captured by a different letter, our alphabet could contain sixty or even a hundred signs. Uuuuu has at least six sounds in modern English while eeeee has as many as fourteen (Firmage 2000, 227, 82). English lacks single signs for phonemes like *ai, ow, th, sh, ng,* and many more. But there are hundreds of further sounds, too, available on the voice and in the air, that English doesn't use at all. Our tongue has long eliminated them, just as for example Japanese does without a number of sounds found in English. Half a century back Ruth Benedict used this two-level selection process of sounds for speech as an analogy for all cultural selection.[1] Fewness, then, is a main feature of the abecedary.

There are good reasons why fewness is useful. It is practical and neat and so gives linguistic, aural, and scriptive control. It is also quite simply sufficient to its purpose, for its combinations run into millions. Any four letters combine twenty-four ways, and any eight combine in well over forty thousand ways, although of course in

151

practice, by convention or physical constraint, not all signs and sounds go with each other. A few letters, too, rather than many, are more easily learned. If immaturity is actually advantageous for early language-learning, as has been argued,[2] then fewness in alphabets was a step forward in language propagation. If languages are "under powerful selection pressure to fit children's likely guesses" (Deacon 1997, 110), then using so simple a writing medium is an advantage in any era aiming to spread literacy. The abecedary is thus a stimulus to democracy. All of this may well tie to a deeper, metaphysical feeling, which emerged in the Middle Ages. Education began with the learning of the letters themselves and worked upward from there. The sense was that all writing and therefore all understanding are expressed in letters, so that keeping them few is conducive to a consistency of mind, and therefore, maybe, a cosmic unity.

Almost all alphabets share this feature of fewness. In about 1500 B.C. the Proto-Canaanite alphabet had about twenty-seven letters, reduced to twenty-two in the thirteenth century B.C. Ancient Etruscan had seventeen letters, Phoenician had nineteen as did Old Hebrew, and early Greek had twenty-one (Crystal 1987, 202). In the fourteenth century B.C. an alphabet of twenty-two letters was developed in Syria (Jean 1992, 52). It was the eventual basis for both the square-letter Hebrew, the flowing Arabic, and the more miscellaneous Greek alphabet developed later. The fully abecedarial Izbet Sartah alphabet in Palestine had twenty-two letters in about 1050 B.C. (Goody 1987, 47). Depending how you count it, Arabic has eighteen letters, twenty-nine if one includes vowel-markers, and with some letters having two forms (Jean 1992, 58). The current Armenian alphabet, unusually, has thirty-eight letters.[3] Perhaps soon after 900 B.C., Greek appeared with its twenty-four letters, as we noted in part 1. Ancient Rome later adopted this Greek alphabet and reduced its number of letters to twenty-three. The traditional Gaelic alphabet, using the first letters of names of trees, had seventeen letters.[4] The runic alphabet of Northern Europe, dating from about A.D. 200–300, had twenty-four letters, although its British version added more to cope with the range of Anglo-Saxon sounds. The Ogam (Irish and Pictish) alphabet from about 400 B.C. had twenty letters, in four groups of five, and was based simply on the number of grouped strokes per letter. The highest-known number of letters in a genuine alphabet is the Khmer with seventy-four. But a Solomon Islands alphabet has only eleven, and the overwhelming majority of alphabets have between twenty and thirty letters (Crystal 1987, 203, 202). These numbers clearly contrast the numbers of different characters, commonly running into thousands, needed for logographic and/or pictographic scripts such as hieroglyphics or Chinese. At any one time the Egyptian hieroglyphic system contained about 750 signs; over its whole history there were as many as 6,000.[5] The debate over Chinese and Japanese systems, and how far to dovetail their use with Westernized (Roman-based) versions, still runs.

There is a pervading result of this alphabetical fewness, which would be hard to exaggerate as to its importance, and from which all else follows. You have only to speak or write a sentence or two and you will have already used most of the letters, up to four or five times each. With so few signs available, most words in a sentence, and usually all, will share at least some letters with other words in the same sentence. This homogenization is the opposite of a hypothetical other extreme in which every word would be made up of entirely different signs. Certain subfeatures follow from this main principle, some of which are perhaps surprising.

a) *Alliteration, assonance, and rhyme.* Usually seen as literally or poetic devices, in one sense these are ubiquitous in the nature of things. Since we repeat letters by the dozen immediately when we speak or write, then something close to alliteration and assonance will probably surface at least some of the time without overt intent. Alliteration as a literary figure then perhaps really means "strong" or "high" alliteration, or some such term.

What a miserable morning (alliteration), *she was going to bed, she said* (rhyme), *Robin Cook and Gordon Brown* (ooooo-vowel visually dominant); such pervade the language whether used consciously or not. The question is what happens to such uses, for heavy alliteration can be suffocating, even when not consciously poetic. An extreme case like *we wondered whether women would want weekend work* is disconcerting and would normally be avoided. It seems we have an instinct to keep the sign-system freely circulating, a fact that fewness statistically works against. But something else is of interest here. Initials evidently raise writing's main critical principles: and that remark took me some minutes to formulate. For in that very sentence, "initials evidently raise writing's main critical principles," the letter iiiii comes third in every word. No normally attentive reader will have noticed—why ever should they? *Katie sat eating nothing until late afternoon*—third letter again—it is seldom obvious, although with less frequent letters like kkkkk or qqqqq it would be far more so. One outcome is that first-letter alliteration is more visual, so that on the page a different letter for the same sound weakens it. On paper *the king's kind of knowledge* may well work better than *the king's cruel queen,* even though orally there is no kkkkk-sound in "knowledge." The second phrase's three different letters for the kkkkk-sound are a slight dilution. And one main inference is that a written word's first letter is prominent in our consciousnesses. The gaps between words on paper, absent orally, cause this enhancement. Kabbalistic thought was highly sensitive to these considerations. The "missing letter" in the Jewish Torah is concealed in the white spaces between words; but more important was the principle of *notarikon,* the study of first and last letters of words, as though those letters contained an important virtue. "The first letter owns the word": it becomes a useful formula and principle.

Alliteration isn't always playful. Same-letter alliteration, though not in every single word, was exploited for its relentlessness in fourteenth-century poets such as Langland and the *Gawain* poet. Of deer being hunted: *They brayed, and they bled, and on the banks were butchered . . . / and hunters with high horns hurried behind them* (*Sir Gawain and the Green Knight,* 1162, 1164). But that is a very specialized use. Consider too the recent spate of middle-class rhyming slang: *floating voter, Aga sagas, think-tank, culture-vulture, legal eagle, snail mail* (outdated by e-mail)*, put up or shut up, shop till you drop.* We seem to rely quite often on such effects, with the first letter not always the one at issue. Perhaps it's just as well, for letters tumble back upon each other in large numbers as sentences and paragraphs unfold, producing countless groups of words where the letters are similar (*roast/coast*), or identical but with different meanings (*fine*—good; penalty), or the same but inflected (*drive/ driven*). It surely argues that the sign-system has its own effects aside from meaning, and working upon meaning, too. And contrary to surface expectation, alliteration and rhyme enrich rather than impoverish. How can this be, if they increase repetition rather than reduce it? Maybe they proudly put forth the principle of homogeneity itself; the abecedarial fewness in action. Starting every single successive word with the same letter was a practice among the mannered poets in the Latin medieval period (Curtius 1953, 283). It was called "pangrammaticism," and wasn't alliteration's only use at the time. More important are the countless proverbs, adages, or merely general and lasting sayings, often scriptural or literary in origin, that pervade the language. It led Samuel Taylor Coleridge to state that "exclusive of the abstract sciences, the largest and worthiest portion of our knowledge consists of *aphorisms.*"[6] *No man can serve two masters, fortune favors the brave, it's an ill wind that*

blows nobody any good—these and others are based on a few letters much repeated and balanced by placing and stress. Such deeply
resonant phrases survive over long periods; they are part of our
thinking, and it is the abecedary's fewness that enables them. Proverbs in early language were considered in part 1.

Another common form of spontaneous alliteration and assonance
lies in inflection generally. This is properly a matter of abecedarial
distribution, discussed in chapter 10 below. But it is hard to conceive of an alphabet without the potential for inflection in the first
place, even though some don't use it. Clearly the frequent use of
-ed, -ing, and the rest act like rhyme, in that the same groups of
letters keep recurring. By inflection, despite letters being few,
words can flow into each other without the text becoming awkward.
The prefixes and suffixes, and the tense-markers in verbs, need no
modification by context, for "work-ed" adds pastness to "work"
whether the active subject was a student, a car mechanic, a cunning
plan, or a garden fertilizer. And the abecedarial signs can do the job
even when the same ones are already in play in the word's main
stem, so that *embedded* and *lingering* don't reject their inflection-
grafts. The language of reason is heavily dependent on inflections,
for by it logical relations can be established. Aquinas found God
"perfect" in having no "defects." Aquinas would often inflect one
word three times in the same sentence.

b) *The "near-miss."* In meaning, *window* is no nearer *widow* than
is *mayhem*, which has no common letters with either. Yet if we mis-
spelt *window* as *widow* it would simply become that different word
in the sentence. English contains countless words so similar in
spelling that they differ by a single letter, yet are quite unconnected
in meaning by topic, part of speech, or relevance more widely. Indeed, most words in English, apart from very long or exotic ones,
have some near neighbor of this kind; such is fewness in action.

Many such changes aren't very exciting: *marked/marker, plank/
prank*. At other times there are flickers of abecedarial interest even
with no change of part of speech: *reach/react, basis/oasis, gantry/
gentry*. The one-letter change can keep the same part of speech but
move to an entirely different part of the lexicon. But changes from
noun to verb, or verb to adjective, are very frequent: *avenue/avenge,
forbid/morbid, threat/thread, baronet/bayonet, waive/naïve, purr/
pure, least/leapt, fulminate/culminate, ski/sky, cover/cower, oath/
bath, quote/quite, divide/divine, petrol/patrol, goes/foes, longer/
lodger*. In this last example the single change from nnnnn to ddddd
changes the *-er* ending from signifying a comparative adjective to
signifying a role player. Sometimes the part-of-speech in question

is what makes the difference: *heavy/heady*—but not *heave/heade*.
Prepositions can get involved: *toward/coward*. For some reason
wwwww comes up often as a marked last-letter changer: *milder/
mildew, shred/shrew, three/threw, asked/askew, flat/flaw, squad/
squaw*.[7] Finally, adding or removing one letter, rather than changing one, has similar effect: *ought/nought, wench/wrench, best/
beset, astronomy/gastronomy, argue/ague, win/twin, eyes/yes, unin-
formed/uniformed, often/soften, ledge/fledge, we/owe, anguish/lan-
guish*.

All this may seem quite obvious. But the inference—which explains the small curious pleasure such pairings give—is that the
rails have run so close without the trains jumping track. A further
inference is that correct spelling, not always valued in our more
progressive classrooms, turns out to be important for this very reason. But there is no danger of "asked" meaning "rather askew"
any more than "raincoxt" means "almost a raincoat." The tolerance these near-misses can sustain may easily be seen from what
happens if they are misprinted for each other. "Tony Blair defined/
defied the whole of New Labour policy" might lead to a Cabinet
crisis, and "I forget/forged the records so easily" could mean an
instant police investigation. Error can result too when important letters are next to each other on the keyboard. So: *we were burdened
with unnecessary gear/fear* might happen, because ggggg and fffff
are adjacent on the keyboard. Equally with *a beast lives as a man
does/dies*: ooooo and iiiii are adjacent on the keyboard.

If abecedarial fewness entails such risks, what nano-experiences
may occur in the mind in our daily reading anyway? *Bruiser/
cruiser, feather/father, if/of, daytime/anytime*—these and thousands
of other clusters may underline the experience I had recently, in
idly scanning a report of a rugby match that seemed to have been
played in rough weather. But no: one player was *gutsy* and another
sleek, and I had carelessly paired the terms as "gusty" and "sleet."
Even when we are more attentive than I was, how far are these secondary meanings absorbed into the letters' records deep in our
memory banks, so that associations will inevitably be triggered?
The crucial question is whether, in instant neural reception, a hint
of the one meaning can carry across to the other when the letters of
the relevant rolles are nearly the same.

If it can, there must be a built-in safeguard. The text must be constantly controlled by writer and reader at the level of *intention*, that
term to imply both interpretation and purpose. It is an intentiveness
not merely passive but one on constant if minimal guard against

unwanted seepages of meaning. That *intention* is cognate with *attention* and *tension*, too, points to a microscopic but perpetual stress in all our reading. We can tolerate it easily enough but it never vanishes entirely. But if intention itself becomes a questionable category, as for example with poets who *attend* to their muses or have romantic or modernistic *tendencies*, then all these near-miss words may become important in different ways. Intention is clearly a key issue here, and will be considered in more detail later in this book.

c) *Overlap.* I use this term for cases where meaning as well as spelling is entailed. There was no overlap of meaning with *gantry/gentry* or *window/widow,* so the issue didn't arise. With other words it may be different. To the uninitiated, the words "imp" and "impious" might fairly seem etymologically connected. In Milton's *Paradise Lost* the reformed angel Abdiel strides forward to confront Satan in battle. He confidently predicts the slavery in hell Satan can look forward to, but then "mean while" [*sic*] he says—just to be going on with—"This greeting on thy impious Crest receive" (*Paradise Lost,* 6:188).

Abdiel then lands the devil leader a helmet-chop with enough force to send him backward ten paces. If this as "greeting" lends a sliver of comedy, then "impious" hinting "imp" might be an intentional pun belittling Satan. It could have suggested a primal verbal connection of the same sort as is found with *vice/vicious, joy/joyous,* etc. But of course there is no such connection. "Impious" has the common use of prefix *in-* or *im-* meaning "not"; "not pious," while "imp" comes from the Old English *impa, impe* meaning "young shoot," that is to say child, and so child of the devil, mischievous child. This case illustrates that what I will call the "centripetal" abecedary, as it cycles and recycles its precious store of so few signs, is bound to lead to such anomalies and may happily incorporate them.

Such matchings of meaning can occur by chance because fewness of letters makes for more overlapping spelling, too. Other pairs in English may equally deceive. *Obvious* and *evident,* almost synonyms, might seem to share a *vi-* root. But they don't; for the former comes from the Latin *ob* + *via* (a road), and so means "for the route," i.e., straight ahead; while the latter comes from Latin *e-* + *vid-* and so means "from sight"; as a result of seeing. Of course, those two Latin terms may have had a common root themselves in earlier centuries; that we don't know. Sometimes one rolle moves into another for semantic reasons. The *foxglove,* whose name seems so apt for its mittenlike flowers, was originally the "Folk's Love," a favorite or a sign of tryst. The word *miniature,* meaning a small painting, did not come from the Latin root *mini* referring to all things small, but from the verb to *miniate*, to paint with vermilion, an extract derived from lead *mining*. If an eagle-eyed person also seems eager, or a small terrier dog a tearaway, or to loathe is to have poisoned love, or a new job perk ("perquisite") makes one perk up, the closeness of the two spellings may urge or even first suggest a link semantically when actually there was originally none. As far as I can tell, there is no etymological tie between "sin" and "sinister" (originally "left-hand side"), but someone new to the tongue could be forgiven for imagining there was. One might wear regalia for a gala, but the former is *regal*, the latter derives from the Arabic *gila*, a presentation garment. *Sleaze*, as general quality of political corruption, is like its cognate group *slosh, slop, slurry, slurp* in suggesting an unpleasant mire, yet its root meaning was "cloth from *Silesia*,, of a wet and fragile kind. Such cases are sometimes known as "folk-etymology." *Devil/devious* and *mist/mystery* are further suggestive cases.

Bizarre outcomes of letter-and-meaning overlap generally are there in numbers, and can be oddly unsettling. There is anagram, that strangely happy occurrence that, as the seventeenth-century grammarian George Puttenham put it, can "breed one word out of another, not altering any letter nor the number of them, but onely transposing of the same."[8] The abecedary tolerates anagrams by the thousand, and the commoner and shorter the word, and the more frequent its letters in the language, the more likely the anagram is. *Late/tale, thing/night, north/thorn, went/newt, fibre/brief, end/den, on/no, moor/room, flow/wolf, rail/liar* (the last three are exact reversals)—the list is endless. Whole phrases can sometimes anagram neatly: *twos and threes/short and sweet*. However, the single word is the classic prototype. When the anagram depends on mere inflection it scarcely seems to qualify: *formed/deform: fresher/refresh*. More unlikely anagrams retain their attraction: *dialect/citadel, Monday/dynamo, crocus/occurs, thirst/T-shirt, tedious/outside, pistol/spoilt, neigh/hinge*. Others have entirely chancy but nonetheless usable connections of meaning when context allows it: *treason/senator, canoe/ocean*. But they remain isolated curiosities with no tie to the meaning, and the author can't assume that the reader will spot them. So their use in poetry or prose is unlikely to be fluent. Yet anagrams illustrate exactly, perhaps more than anything else, the remarkable tolerance-level of the abecedarial fewness, where to the linguistic space-visitor so much muddle and confusion might have been expected.

Almost as neglected are the words that encompass smaller words, irrelevant to both themselves and the sentences they are part of. So we find *foreigner (reign), kitchen (itch), haunting (aunt), overseas (verse), thankless (ankle), detached (ache),* while across two words lie *ming vase (looming vasectomy), psyche (gipsy cheers),* and *cycle (policy clearance).*[9] Again the point may seem trivial; again it underlines, though, the abecedary's powers of absorption and toleration, its easy digesting of what it doesn't need, while keeping such in store for poets like George Herbert who notice such things. There is a figure of speech known as *tmesis* that places whole words inside other words consciously. But it is rare, and usually archaic or clumsy: *where then soever;* "don't be so hypo-bloody-critical!" What we are pointing to here is rather the presence of words within words as a natural offshoot of the abecedary's principles. Again this would be impossible in most other systems. Last, there are of course puns, found finely in poems and excruciatingly around some dinner tables. Many commentators, such as Joseph Addison, seem contemptuous and fascinated at once.[10] In ambiguity and double-meaning generally, abecedarial "overlap" is total. As seen in part 1, the abecedary's tolerance of pun was valued in early societies. The Kabbalah system depended profoundly upon it, and the acronym, a kind of pun at a different level, famously yields words of great spiritual saturation at the heart of sacred writings as we have remarked. The riotous prevalence of puns in slogans and headlines, on hoardings and T-shirts, pervades the postmodern world. This will be discussed in part 4.

As said already, there may be a deeper significance behind abecedarial fewness. Johann Wolfgang Goethe once noted that, in Arabic, near-same spelling for words of very diverse meaning was underpinned philosophically (Curtius 1953, 303). Cosmic unity held all meaning together despite local differences. For English, linguists justly emphasize that many words must bear multiple meaning, otherwise we would need an intolerable number of signs to convey everything by.[11] *Mine, air, paper, party, brook, pound, swift, wake,* the list could go on for pages, both from words where a primal common meaning can be traced and those whose spelling is identical only by chance. Sometimes the two meanings of the same rolle are as different as oil and water, with no overlap in syntax, lexicon, or function: *inter* (between, bury), *stern* (severe, aft of ship), *flatter* (blandish, more level), *does* (some female deer, takes action), *shy* (diffident, throw), *smack* (fishing boat, hit with hand), *rung* (used bell, step of ladder), *moped* (motor-scooter, was gloomy), and *spoke* (uttered, wheel radius). There are indeed some weird puns such as *atom* which, written spaced out, means "the first half of the alphabet"; and *oomph* which contradicts itself as thrust or punch, and zero miles per hour. There are also curious rolles of two meanings where the ambiguity is purely syntactical. For example, "multiply" can be both verb and adverb, suggesting that "multipally" might be clearer for the latter; yet that longer form is seldom found.

d) *The centrifugal effect.* All these cases just discussed, alliteration, rhyme, near-miss, overlap, anagram, and so on, consciously or otherwise put "fewness" to use. It is done by the process we have just called "centripetal," for the letters attract repeats of themselves. But we now come to the very opposite. This is what I call the centrifugal effect. Far from putting fewness to use, the centrifugal effect works by striving away from it. The tendencies found in our other categories seem to be annulled, and the pull is the other way. We noted that *window* and *mayhem* have no common letters at all. More aptly, nor do *day* and *night*. And as we found earlier when looking at Tyndale's Bible, this centrifugality can help thwart any danger of abecedarial fewness being overreductive.

A curious feature is associated with this. Using words for more than one meaning does not arise from any lack of letter-combinations by which to make new words. The supply has certainly not run out; not remotely. Here are just a few words:

CARD	cerd	cird	CORD	CURD
BARD	berd	BIRD	bord	burd
fand	FEND	FIND	FOND	FUND
galf	gelf	gilf	GOLF	GULF
HALT	helt	HILT	HOLT	hult
LARD	lerd	lird	LORD	lurd
nane	nene	NINE	NONE	nune
OAST	oest	oist	oost	OUST
PATH	peth	PITH	poth	puth
rade	rede	RIDE	RODE	RUDE
RATE	rete	RITE	ROTE	rute
SAWN	SEWN	siwn	SOWN	suwn
taft	teft	tift	toft	TUFT
tane	tene	TINE	TONE	TUNE
WALL	WELL	WILL	woll	wull

Clearly the capitalized words are those in use in English today, the lowercase words are (usually) possible forms in English but not in use. Many never have been. This is surely curious, that so many elementary monosyllables lie idle while other equally simple words double or treble up in signification. Or, if that is answered by the point just made—that is to say, the need not to have too many words—then one might have expected some of these simpler forms to replace unnecessarily longer ones in the language. Nor is there any principle as to which vowel-forms, and how many from each set of five words, are going to be in use and which not. And one could compile similar lists for words of three, five, or any number of letters. Why should three-letter words ending in -ar be so frequent in English—*bar, car, ear, far, jar, mar, oar, par, tar,* and *war*—while all four other vowels together offer only a single more word in total: *her, per, air, fir, sir, for, nor, tor, cur, fur,* and *our?* Again, we could as easily have used the consonant rather than the vowel as basis, yielding such groups as *daily, dairy,* and *daisy,* but not *daiby, daimy, daity,* and so on. The word *tuft* is not only the sole case of *t-ft*; it is also the only case of *-uft*, for no other consonant precedes that combination in English four-letter words at all.

The inference seems rather like a fundamental law; namely, that *abecedarial homogeneity hovers continually between saturation and zero.* While "fewness" is basic, it has no power to grant unused rolles, however simple, priority of employment when an unattached meaning seeks a home and needs it. This is what I mean by the centrifugal effect. There is a counter-pull outward, which can take words' spellings away from each other as well. The cause of this outward-moving tendency must be obvious. As said already, there is much toleration of near-miss words: *each/etch, vein/vain, home/come,* and the like, and it is valuable. But if spellings were centripetal in every case, all our words would be too like each other; it would make difficult the instant recognition that speech and reading depend on, and so result in confusion. The principle seems to have been recognized by humans deeply, and very early. It compares with totemism in primitive tribal life. Any child, by its birth, would belong to a near family in its own tribe, with no outward pull to wider reality. So whatever totemic group it was then allotted to—leopard's paw, sunrise, woman's smile, top of oak tree, saltwater, silent time—it would never be one that any member of its immediate family belonged to as well. Rightly or not, Freud related this to the primitive dread of incest.[12] By some profound cognate instinct the same principle informs the lexicon. *Mass* can mean volume or (Catholic) sacrament, and *miss* can mean young lady or fail to hit; but neither could possibly be allowed to mean the other, for muddle would ensue at once. The language can tolerate synonym, but not between terms of near-same spelling.

But the centrifugal tendency has another, and major, outcome. At its extreme, it leads to the "exotic" word, which exploits letters less frequently found in the general vocabulary. Here is a standard frequency-table for English:

ETAISON   HRDLCF   BGMUPWKYV   JQXZ

(Here then is our "etaison-factor," one of the terms specially coined for this book.) The frequency rate is split into four groups because, apart from eeeee—almost universally the commonest letter in English—the ratings within them are approximate. However, the individual ratings for the first group, and the membership of the other three, are agreed by most measurements (Crystal 1987, 86–87). Unevenness of letter-use in English is itself a "distributive" factor, arising from the abecedary's fewness but associated with it. But lacking a more or less even spread of use, some letters and sounds must come into play less often than others, and when the rarer ones combine, they stand out, in a small ripple or shimmer on the page: *amazed, judge, quiddity, phlox, gazebo, joke, quaver, larynx.* All these words contain jjjjj, qqqqq, xxxxx, or zzzzz, plus some other letter of the third group in the frequency table.

Other factors, as well as infrequency, make for the "exotic" feeling. The item referred to may be exotic itself, rare, or special in some small nuance, quite aside from the letters employed. Here are two lists of words: 1) *although, maybe, well, quite, just, being, thinking, considering, quick, exist.* 2) *banquet, onyx, kings, lick, jewel, gliding, thou, biscuit, sting, hithe, marquee.* The first list is humdrum and everyday, the second list is opulent and a touch exciting. Yet exactly the same sixty letters are used in both: eight iiiiis, four ggggg, two qqqqq, one jjjjj, mmmmm, wwwww—and so on. Again, letters common enough in themselves may be found in rarer combination. As we saw in the list above, *sawn, sewn,* and *sown* are found in English while *siwn* and *suwn* are not; in English *iwn* and *uwn* never are. But some combinations appear, but seldom, such as eeeee + wwwww + consonant, as in *lewd, newt, pewter.* Willa Cather's Mr. Giddy has a garage that is being dismantled, and Thea sees some cheap soft-porn in it. "Underneath the picture was printed the title, 'The Odalisque.' Giddy was under the happy delusion that this title meant something wicked—there was a wicked look about the consonants" (Willa Cather, *The Song of the Lark,* 1:16). *Odalisque* has only one "etaison" consonant, two moderately common ones, and the infrequent qqqqq. But *odalisque* also contains all five vowels, a rare phenomenon in English. Most of all though is the rarity of combination: ooooo at the start followed by only one ddddd; the "alis" combination—as also in *talisman*—and so on.

Another effect from centrifugality is words of mutually exclusive letters. The pairs *bath/file, maybe/trunk, fledgling/tomorrow* have little connection in meaning, and such might be valuable in context for a particular text's enrichment. But a sharp profile emerges when opposite meanings are also entailed. *Light* and *night* share most of their letters, but *light/dark* are mutually exclusive in both meaning and letters. So are *white/black, open/shut, funny/grave, clean/dirty,* and any amount more, including *late/soon,* employed by Wordsworth in his sonnet "The world is too much with us" and contrasted at once by the more homogenous pair of semantic opposites *getting/spending.*

Of course, exact contrast can also appear centripetally, as when the identical stem carries a tiny negating prefix: *appetizing/ unappetizing: advantage/disadvantage.* Shakespeare was fond of this use, with *un-* his commonest. He apparently liked to have the meaning-item he was negating also present.[13] Near-opposite meaning can even come in near-same letters or full anagram solely by chance: *deft/daft, aliment/ailment, united/untied,* or something more like a mirror-image: *maximum/minimum: backward/forward: cellar/attic.* But going back to the centrifugal effect, there is also the synonym, whose spelling can differ from other words of like meaning considerably. *Enjoyment, pleasure,* and *happiness* are by no means semantically identical, but are close enough to make the point. Finally there is the case where words of very different root in both spelling and import have an identical prefix or suffix attached, making for a satisfying kind of list: *fighting, bathing, swaggering, dreaming, yellowing, walking, voting, harvesting.* The small pleasure we gain comes perhaps from the collocation of "the one and the many" in the same few words. Thomas Hardy's poem "Lines to a Movement in Mozart's E-Flat Symphony" exploits the technique in each of its four stanzas.

There are a couple of final inferences from alphabetical fewness in general. The first might be called a modified or flexible conservatism. Our words can be very like each other, or markedly different from each other. When by virtue of common letters they are like, they can risk running into each other even semantically, and this makes at least parts of the lexicon into a large and deep network of linked thoughts, and so may encourage a kind of neural/cultural consistency. The somewhat homogeneous set of signs literally underwrites this. While this aids social unity, a degree of conservatism may also be entailed. This can again be guarded against by authorial intention and reader attention; yet, at least in literary criticism, to believe in "authorial intention" as paramount is itself often thought of as conservative. Reader attentiveness, however, can ensure that the line between two meanings when words "overlap" or are very like—*imp/impious, eager/eagle,* and so on—can remain both clear and subtle at once. We enrich our language by retaining both the overlap and the distinction. With homonyms, *career/ Korea, shore/sure,* the words' visual profiles can warn us that the meanings differ, too. And our expectation that different words mean different things is deep-rooted. As Pinker says, the infant does not expect *battle* and *cattle* to mean something similar.[14] Another factor making for good and quick word-identification, considered more closely later, is the word's unique outline and shape, its silhouette in both sound and writing. In Wittgenstein's terms, we feel "the familiar physiognomy of a word, the feeling that it has taken up its meaning into itself, that it is an actual likeness of its meaning" (Wittgenstein 1958, 218). I shall call this the word's "sponging-up" quality; it can absorb its meaning into its appearance. This is again exactly what Aquinas concluded: the abecedarial word suits the thing it evokes. So the risky side effects of fewness are countered by the word's individual profile. The word's uniqueness, like that of a fingerprint, can help resist ambiguity; and when its letters are also infrequent in the alphabet, so that the word is "exotic" as we suggested, then its look and physiognomy are even more sharply marked. And personal factors such as handwriting, regional accent, oral emphasis, layout on the page, as well as English's famously irregular spelling all affect the outcome locally. The results can be aesthetic, and it is the poets who resort most to such flexibility, thereby intensifying the reading experience as a visceral as well as plainly emotional or cerebral act. This of course applies to other abecedarial features.

The other major inference is that fewness cannot tolerate excess. From the very beginnings, acronym, proverb, and repetition were widely deployed. Of course, this was in part because the abecedary's equable tolerance and distributive capacities had not been evolved and indeed were not yet appreciated. But there was probably also a healthy sense of prudence. It wasn't wise to say too much, let alone write it; not only the gods might be offended. The stand against excess in words goes back to Ezekiel and the psalms of David. It concerned Thomas à Kempis as to his charges and Thomas Traherne for himself; is embodied by Shakespeare in Antonio's voluble friend Gratiano in *The Merchant of Venice;* is found in William Wordsworth and Thomas Henry Huxley as we saw; and set Pound's scalpel to cutting away the debris surrounding T. S. Eliot's *The Waste Land*.[15] If the linear unrolling of the same twenty-six letters gets out of hand, the feeling of surfeit may be greater than in systems where signs and sounds were numerous from the outset. This is not a matter of cliches and hackneyed phrases. Those are merely done to death by overwork. Rather it is when simple phrases carry a dead freight of words and letters beyond semantic requirement. In English, brackets can often be put around elements often strictly extraneous; viz: *at this (particular point in) time; (on a) daily (basis); in the laboratory (situation); for a (period of a) year; a good (track) record; not enough income (coming in); an(other) alternative; reduced traffic (levels); improved weather (conditions); in the summer (months); she was (emotionally) moved by this; when he said it, he meant it (for real); (so) how are you (doing)?; that's what sport/politics/culture is (all about); the toilets are (located) outside;* and, *maybe the sofa could be moved upstairs*, where *maybe* already means *could be*.[16] Single words have comparable fungus: *wast(ag)e, us(ag)e, u(tili)ze, import(ance), transport(ation), method(ology)* ("what methodology have you adopted?"), and that most strange case *part(ial)ly*, almost ubiquitous in even the most fastidious writers. Why do we call an obsession "pathological" rather than "pathial"? A pictorial or ideographic system could not make such additions without signal change.

Small ergs of energy are consumed that could be used elsewhere. One might speculate on the hours that could be saved in offices and typing pools if such ubiquitous baggage were discarded. Every excess letter adds its tiny but cumulative dead weight on the reading brain. This is why we are warned to avoid too many abstract or Latinate terms when we write. For it is those that pile on the suffixes or are sometimes superfluous altogether. More directly superfluous are successive words of the same stem: *except in exceptional circumstances, the actual action*. Similarly, that great mouthful *institutionalization* suffers not from being encrusted on to a stem already sufficient (for there is no word within it that would do alone), but from a pile of inert suffixes. A plethora of prepositions has also entered English in our own time; *miss (out on), meet (up with), head (up)* (an organization), *getting something (for) free, next time (around), where it is (at)*. All such phenomena are curious, for they seem to contradict John Searle's contention that there is a kind of law of minimum speech effort for maximum resulting content. Searle ties this to Zipf's laws of frequency.[17] If Searle is correct, then the reason must lie in some kind of current cultural pressure, which certainly seems likely. One recalls the primitive instinct that naming is dangerous. And, heeding Thomas à Kempis's warning, I'm all too aware of my own probable excesses in this book, much as I have tried to reduce them. Poets spend their lives pulling against this tendency.

Summary. In almost every culture that has an alphabet, it seems, only a very few letters are wanted or needed. There are almost invariably fewer than thirty letters and sometimes fewer than twenty. As a result these letters are brought multiply into play from the start. The resulting repetition can be exploited on the surface in many ways. Alliteration, rhyme, inflection, "overlap" and "near-miss," anagram, acronym, pun—all these suggest an underlying centripetal pull or magnetism. But these features need not limit our powers of expression. The centripetal pull is opposed by a centrifugal tendency that uses various ways to keep letters apart. The abecedary's rarer letters may be used often, or words of mutually exclusive spelling may be juxtaposed. This process seems deliberate, or at least socially instinctive, for many simple combinations fully appropriate to the relevant language—*nate*, *daimy*, *gelf* plus countless others—are never used at all. A richness results, a range of exotic terms becomes available. Words of mutually exclusive spelling can be juxtaposed with vivid results, and synonyms like *enjoyment* and *pleasure* feel right because their spellings are largely different.

Wider laws seem to emerge, like "the first letter owns the word" and "abecedarial homogeneity hovers between saturation and zero." There is also a fear of excess, which may entail a modified conservatism, but it might be hoped that the "centrifugal effect" would take care of that sufficiently. We noted a couple of instances of these various uses from the poets, and will consider many more in part 3.

We shall find the poets exploiting these aspects of fewness in almost every line they write. Of course, if they are bound to move toward either the centripetal or the centrifugal tendency, this is a something of a truism. Nevertheless, it still underlines the material the poets do work with. Some indulge in "wordplay" frequently while others ring the changes on similar words and changes in order to express the circlings of an often melancholic feeling and thought.

6

Letters Are Stable

Mᴀɴᴜᴀʟs ꜰᴏʀ ᴀᴘᴘʀᴇɴᴛɪᴄᴇs ᴏꜰ ᴄᴀʟʟɪɢʀᴀᴘʜʏ, ᴀᴘᴘᴇᴀʀɪɴɢ ɪɴ ʀᴏᴍᴇ and Venice in ᴀ.ᴅ. 1522 and 1524 respectively, give their models as follows, in the order stated:

A.a.b.c.d.ee.f.g.h.i.k.l.m.n.o.p.q.r.s.s.t.u.x.y.z.&.

The writing is as easy to read as if it had appeared yesterday. The alphabetical order is our own, with all letters present bar jjjjj, vvvvv, and wwwww, all three surplus to requirements in Latin. Hence our word "doubleyou" for that letter now; and jjjjj always was a consonant version of iiiii, that letter written with a tail. The two aaaaas seem to have been merely an opening flourish, for the first is the only capital. The first eeeee includes an optional serif available to all other letters; and the second sssss is the well-known fffff-like sign, simply the standard sssss elongated. By 1549 in Cologne in Germany the jjjjj has appeared in a comparable manual, and in two manuals from London (1587 and 1618) the wwwww has appeared also.[1]

Our alphabet and its familiar order were fully in place five hundred years ago. Melanchthon and Luther played alphabet games on a journey in 1539; alphabet parlor games existed in ancient Greece and Rome (Curtius 1953, page 58). As said earlier, there has been no really salient change since the Greek alphabet was established well over two thousand years earlier still. One of Socrates' lifelong complaints about writing was that it lay woodenly on the page; it emitted no further questions or answers. But Plato had simply and unwittingly stumbled on abecedarial stability. The abecedary does not change, it seems, unless by some kind of overwhelming cultural crisis. That might be the influx of a new language and script altogether—perhaps from colonial or economic invasion—or a technical invention such as printing itself. Yet even printing only introduced—later—the idea of alphabetical order as conventionally agreed.

It was clear from what we said in part 1 that the sacredness of a sacred text depended on this stability, but that stability also, from the very beginning, helped ensure this sacred status. Letters quickly revealed a longevity denied to words from the mouth, on the wind. As Barry Powell pointed out in his study of the Greek alphabet's likely connection with Homer, it was seen early that writing remained unchanged when its oral pronunciation—the very thing letters were at last supposed to capture—moved on. "There is no growth, in the history of the Greek alphabetic script, from a system less complex and well adapted to one more so. No one has added anything important to the original system." Powell attributes this to the "rigorous conservatism that characterizes a writing within any culture" (Powell 1991, 66, 63). Firmage extends this point to our own system—which of course continues the Greek one. "Although our writing tradition is only a convention, it is one that is so strongly ingrained as to remain virtually unthreatened by all attempts over the centuries to contravene or supplant it" (Firmage 2000, page 226).

Both single words and whole texts could become lastingly sacred. In Augustine's time Scripture was Christianity's sole authority. Medieval scholasticism sought to fix Scripture exactly, while traditional Islam has been chary of the Koran ever even being translated. A millennium later, with the invention of print, a huge new issue arose with the advent of biblical translation. This raised its own problems when central, that is papal, authority was challenged, for Scripture has all the more to embody that authority itself. Islam believed that its text was untranslatable, and one accepts that as far as it goes; but there is a further consideration too from our point of view here, if any translation is into a language that uses the same alphabet. That way at least the letters remain the same; abecedarial stability is exploited.

Since language is a living and changing thing, this fixity of its signs must mean something pretty basic. In part of course it is simply a practical matter. In practice, no one has the power to enforce any such change. The rewriting of every single previously existing text would itself be an insuperable obstacle. But it seems rather more even than that. If abecedarial fewness reveals anxiety lest too much be written or said, so does abecedarial stability guard against cultural change occurring too quickly. Plato feared precisely that the method could not vary to meet its readers. Yet its reliability seems more positively a premise upon which other things can happen. Alphabetical order itself becomes a cultural icon. Any lasting human activity needs items to work with but that can also be taken for granted; and these are likely to be material objects of neutral significance. The most basic inventions are such: knife, chair, glass, or wheel. So are natural things in human use, like stone or water. The knife may commit murder or cut nourishing food, and we go in vehicles as samaritans to the hospital or as robbers to the bank; but still the simple cutting edge and symmetrically curved wheel remain impartial and functionary. In the arts it is the clay, pigment, musical set of sounds, or the letter that resiliently survive. This underlying base must itself be stable; perhaps in motion like water but still constant in its nature.

Jerome McGann's recent projects on the ways that texts change do not refute these principles. Rather they depend on them. McGann has stated that "the law of change declares that [the life histories of different texts] will exhibit a ceaseless process of textual development and mutation" (McGann 1991, 9). True, but such changes play variations upon a more or less identical abecedary. Calligraphy, illegible personal scrawl, old bent portable typewriter, fine Times Roman print, vellum and mass-produced A4 copy bond—none of these change the basic grapheme. For that must remain recognizable; and when authors or editors make changes, they do so merely by rearranging, adding, or omitting in their own kind. The same answer applies to McGann's view that "to read, for example, a translation of Homer's *Iliad* in the Signet paperback, in the edition published by the University of Chicago Press, in the Norton Critical Edition, or in the limited edition put out by the Folio Society (with illustrations) is to read Homer's *Iliad* in four very different ways" (115). How different is very different? Certainly McGann points to an important material ingredient, and one recognizes the experience. But the basic requirement of literacy, to "learn your letters," stays basic.

The sense of the grapheme as an ideal form needn't entail an unworldly idealism. Linguists have addressed the matter in detail.

> The most striking characteristic of the language signal is its perceptual *invariance*. . . . [There is] tremendous physical variation in the actual sounds produced from (our) vocal tracts; but against this, what we typically perceive is a standard, normative language signal, and only secondarily may we notice such contingent properties as husky voice quality, slow delivery, nasality and so on.

The same invariance applies to writing. The individual word is still a stable item, characteristically black on white, and the many different ways or styles in which that may be done do not shift that basic reliable form or grapheme.

> The "same" letter, or word, may be easily perceived against a range of physical differences that may derive from the sort of writing implement used, the type of letter form aimed at, individual styles of handwriting, imperfections of execution . . . and so on. (Garman 1990, 8; his emphasis)

The letter's ideal form is an aspect of what later will be called its virtuality.

Wheels, knives, and abecedarial signs straddle cultures between which ideologies have altered markedly if not wholly. In the 1970s, Raymond Williams used to complain about the word "ideology," then in high profile in political and sociological debate. Ten years previously it had meant an askance view of some fairly specific set of social and political beliefs. It then became so diluted under intellectual scrutiny of belief's contextual factors that it now meant almost everything that the word "culture" meant. The one notion missing, ironically, was the most central thing that culture itself employs; namely, the material practices, based on the constraints of planetary existence, by which any such belief could ever be reached or enacted. This valid observation is uniquely intriguing in the matter of signs, which are only—though basically—material as a means to self-presentation for whatever purpose. Indeed, if we say that the forms "eeeee" and "EEEEE" stay constant, no matter what color or font they are embodied in, then we have something nearer to the Platonic pure form. It is the first and final "eeeee" which supervenes all its occasions; something incidentally that Plato doesn't seem to have remarked himself. What is the main characteristic of "eeeee"? Its eeeee-ness, perhaps we have to say.

This is a paradox, one that conflates the letter's metaphysical status with its great practical usefulness. We can rely on the letter staying on the page now, remaining there in the future, and being recognizable from pages centuries back. This paradox is also close to what will be later referred to in the abecedary as "virtual," and which, it seems to me, has too easily let such signs be pushed aside as "arbitrary." One might wonder whether the longevity of the abecedarial sign, like that of knives and wheels, aligns it equally with ethical imperatives in the idealist realm, which also seem to outstay the flux of time. Thou shalt not kill, tell the truth, we ought to be kind to each other. These have their own counterclaims, such as that the fittest must survive; but in reality both positions are long-term. More practically, the abecedary retains stability by not aiming for too much. If the physical world is three-dimensional and mobile, the written word at least can remain two-dimensional and stable by not trying for every single oral intonation. That is why alphabets contain only a few letters even though the relevant language uses many more sounds. Furthermore this has its own time-dimension. The phenomenon of what we now call intertextuality is enabled by abecedarial stability. People from different regions and countries meet each other and whole cultures intermix. Equally in practice, books, libraries, and now electronic recordings can be passed on unchanged over the generations, their reliable signs intact even if locally paper burns or a book rots. In these ways letters differ from the comparable materials in other arts. "Words will not dribble like Jackson Pollock's paint, or blur like Ornette Coleman's sax."[2] Later we shall call this the letter's "discreteness."

But this very stability of letters, of course, is precisely what allows change of meaning. If the letters kept changing too there would be no basic fulcrum against which changing meanings could be known or compared. All would be total confusion. Words' meanings get shifted—that is to say, rolles allow different meanings to attach to them—usually in evolution from what held before. Henry Vaughan's notorious line, "How brave a prospect is a bright *backside*!" (his emphasis: the north view of a sunny hill) is merely an extreme case of what always happens. In 1855, Harriet Martineau wrote that when the poet Mrs. Anna Barbauld visited Norwich "she always made her appearance presently at our house."[3] To us, "presently"—already becoming an obsolete use itself—would mean "soon," but at the time it meant "immediately." "Infantry" once referred to the mere boys—infants—shoved into the front line untrained. Within our own time "gay" has changed drastically. Examples of such catachresis permeate the language, which moves like a glacier, different parts at different speeds. Equally, roots survive, in words whose meanings have moved apart. So "experience" and "peril" are etymologically connected; the link is now lost but we enrich our understanding of "experience" by considering the risk-element it once must have connoted.

And change of meaning, though often locally irritating, does seem inevitable if not essential. Henri Bergson thought that the ever-changing meanings of language were a product of biological evolution itself. Words not only may, but must, be constantly on the move if humans are to adapt to their changing environments. "There must be a language whose signs—which cannot be infinite in number—are extensible to an infinity of things. This tendency of the sign to transfer itself from one object to another is characteristic of human language. . . ." (Bergson 1911, 166–67). The infant adapts words readily and ubiquitously from the start; it seems a biological adaptation. And only in motion from one solid item to another could words ever have come to signify image; things and also recollections of things; fleeting moments; but most of all abstraction. "It is only because the word is mobile, because it flies from thing to another, that the intellect was sure to take it, sooner or later, on the wing, while it was not settled on anything, and apply it to an object which is not a thing and which, concealed till then, awaited the coming of the word to pass from darkness into light" (168–69). But obviously again, such shifting verbal intelligence would become chaotic if the material signs of such volatile language kept on changing also. There would be no consistency left in language for there would be no reliable point of reference. (Some scribes of the Middle English period did indeed vary letter-forms at the same time as meanings were changing, making for serious difficulties in interpretation of M.E. manuscripts.)[4]

The cultural or social occasion of such change of meaning is various. Crystal cites geographical movement, appearance of new technical inventions and processes, social prestige, and aspiration to membership of a more dominant culture (Crystal 1987, 332–33). Such changes rely totally on the consistency and longevity of the abecedary and would be impossible without it. Whole literary and intellectual movements such as Augustinism and Romanticism, modernism and postmodernism, still take the abecedary with them, with near-identical views on it, insofar as they trouble to formulate any such views at all. At a more day-to-day level, a general slippage is at work as concepts, fashion, and other social rearrangements ease into place; always the abecedary survives unaltered. Ideological views on the matter both respond to it and affect it. Jean Aitchison's Reith Lectures of 1996 for BBC radio carried on the long-standing challenge to the idea that change of meaning is somehow automatically bad, ruinous to fine or educated expression. At other times and places, some form of Academy, as in eighteenth-century France, and Germany today, will attempt to attain fixity well above the abecedarial level.[5] Certainly spelling has become standardized in the last couple of hundred years. Occasional attempts like this are of course understandable. Such fixity might yield some advantages in both reliability and clarity. Sadly, it is a lost cause in face of our necessarily ever-shifting meanings, and indeed the richness and power that this movement enables. A stronger challenge is posed by theories like Ferdinand de Saussure's, who aspired to see language as a fixed system by which match of word and meaning could be seen as synchronic and static. This view, taken to an extreme (for Saussure of course contrasted synchronic with diachronic, too) would isolate linguistics as itself a closed system. But such views as Saussure's are bound to go out of favor when language-use itself, now known as pragmatics, comes to be seen as the necessary object of study. Curiously though, Chomskyan linguistics, often seen as a mirror-rival to Saussure by its emphasis on language as instinctual, makes little comment on the alphabetical element.

Linguistic pragmatics has grown up largely in response to Chomskyan linguistics, though it hardly seems a return to Saussure. As Geoffrey Leech has put it, "By accepting ambiguity and synonymity as among the basic data of linguistics, Chomsky opened a door for semantics. . . . But, once meaning has been admitted to a central place in language, it is notoriously difficult to exclude the way meaning *varies from context to context*, and so semantics spills over into pragmatics."[6] Leech contrasts linguistic pragmatics with traditional semantics. Traditional semantics sees language as rule-governed, formal, conventional, and discrete and determinate. Pragmatics sees language as principle-controlled, functional, variable, and continuous and indeterminate respectively. The inference, though maybe obvious enough, is fundamental. The flux implied in the second set of terms would be impossible without the guarantee of a stable alphabet over very long periods.

Broadly, if traditional semantics asks "What does X mean in itself?" then pragmatics asks "What did you/she/they mean by X?" We can rephrase the distinction in the terms we have been using. Abecedarially, the first question just cited implies that a rolle has an exact match in meaning. The second question implies that the rolle stays reliably fixed, so that a more fluid question can still, nonetheless, be usefully asked. Leech offers a scheme by which we see how utterances are pragmatically governed. They make the answer to that general question (What did you/she/they mean by X?) as ready as possible in ordinary occasions. His scheme starts with and revises Grice's "co-operative principle" of language and adds to it a "politeness principle," elaborating both into four categories for each (Leech 1983, chaps. 1 and 4). The co-operative principle requires that any speech give no more or less information than is needed; attempt truth; be relevant; be perspicuous. The politeness principle has maxims of tact, generosity, approbation, and modesty. Leech develops the scheme on many fronts; for instance, suggesting how hyperbole can offend, how phrases become clichés, and so on; yet even these support language's general fluidity and openness.

But we can add a further consideration. If Leech contrasts the questions raised by (orthodox) semantics and (new) pragmatics as

"What does X mean in itself?" and "What did you/she/they mean by X?" respectively, then a middle question between those two might be the real one commonly implied. This would be "What does X mean usually?" That is to say, in most everyday cases but not all. This intermediacy goes deep to the heart of the abecedary as stable. If the approach of pragmatics is both valid and yet non-conventional, continuous and indeterminate rather than discrete and determinate, then the stability of the abecedary is crucial in retaining any social interpretation whatsoever. If pragmatics is to examine language by flexibly interpretative rather than fixed-structure categories, these won't be underpinned by a set of coherently interlocking principles. Rather there will be sets of ideological positions and oppositions, all moving gently or sometimes more energetically around each other.

As to whether the abecedary is a conservative force, as is sometimes suggested, the answer as far as its stability is concerned seems clear. In holding us to a continuous literacy and perhaps literature, it is conservative. In enabling meaning to be forever in flux, it is not. However, both these positions stand back from a wider possibility altogether, which one might refer to as general indeterminacy. Indeterminacy of the literary text has been a key tenet of postmodernist criticism.[7] But in its extreme form this possibility evokes something far more drastic; namely, late-twentieth-century theories of catastrophe and chaos. Catastrophe theory, applicable to both fundamental physics and more everyday existence, avers that the deepest realities are not the regularities. The deepest realities are the infrequent and unique events that nevertheless change everything. These may be cosmological like the Big Bang; one-off revolutions or civil wars; earthquake or flood; or irreversible invasion. Or they may be wholly original works of art. What then ensues is the acting out of seemingly more law-controlled events but within a brand-new paradigm, to use T. S. Kuhn's term. On this view, history is a series of nonrepeatable, nonrecurring, noncyclical events, an idea on which the theories of Hegel and Marx were momentously based.

But maybe language changes this way, too. "It has been proposed that change might be essentially unpredictable—the result of arbitrary changes in fashion or chance errors in articulation" (Crystal 1987, 333). If one current view is correct, namely that "language is languages," that is to say, no language's system can be deduced from any other, then this will affect the contacts between any two languages. Such contacts will themselves lead to change, they are more likely to be random, or they may ensue from factors outside the language system itself. Maybe our assessment of literary works is "catastrophic" in a parallel sense. The really major books may not conform to the prevailing criteria; rather they are themselves the few works in literary history that rewrite the criteria altogether. They move previous canons aside to launch their own.

Opinions of the last four hundred years seem to encourage such a view. Critics have often rejected earlier peaks, not merely as falling short, but as not qualifying as literature at all. Samuel Johnson believed that, by the criterion of Aristotle, poets of the school of Donne had "lost their right to the name of poets." Harriet Martineau said that despite their feeling and charm, few of Wordsworth's pieces could really be called poems. Arnold called Dryden and Pope "classics of our prose," and Somerset Maugham thought that in writing poetry, Hardy had left his natural medium behind him.[8]

Beneath it all lies the abecedary. A characteristically offbeat story by Jorge Luis Borges, "Pierre Menard, Author of the *Quixote*," expresses the issue clearly.[9] Borges imagines an early-twentieth-century author attempting to write Cervantes's novel independently. Menard doesn't read the novel itself, but puts himself into as exactly Cervantes's own (early-seventeenth-century) cultural position as he possibly can. He finds out everything about Cervantes's life, reads all that he read, and so on. It can't be done; the result, says Borges, is still two very different works. For example, Cervantes writes of "truth, whose mother is history, rival of time, depository of deeds, witness of the past, exemplar and adviser to the present, and the future's counsellor." Borges sees this as a typical seventeenth-century piece of routine rhetoric on history. But look how differently it is written three hundred years later! Pierre Menard writes: "Truth, whose mother is history, rival of time, depository of deeds, witness of the past, exemplar and adviser to the present, and the future's counsellor . . ." "History the *mother* of truth—what an original and very modern notion!" says Borges (his emphasis). Not a single abecedarial sign has been changed.

There is just one other outcome of abecedarial stability; but it is important. As we have seen, in any language some sounds, and therefore letters, will be used more than others. Indeed, there will be a range of frequencies. Since these are letters, not common or scarce raw materials, there is simply no need to spend time and trouble making sure each letter is used as much or little as any other. But this differential may then increase. If, via the law of abecedarial stability, an abecedary's letters remain the same while culture, meaning, and forms of expression change, then it may turn out that the original abecedary no longer exactly matches what the later situation requires. We have already spoken of this differential under the heading of abecedarial fewness. There will be "exotic words" that poets can and do exploit. Furthermore, a few letters—via the words that contain them—may gradually be found only marginally useful or even redundant. This can occur quite simply when two or more letters end up being used for overlapping purposes. Even so, and again by the law of abecedarial stability, these letters will still survive. It can happen—though it hasn't wholly yet in English at present—that a letter survives in the alphabet but is "dead." Strictly, English could work without qqqqq and either ccccc or kkkkk, and even—if we were content always to write *ph*, an unlikely eventuality—without fffff. Names like Kwik-Save (a British cut-price goods chain) make the point. Yet *qu*——— has its character; perhaps its quality as quaint. These rarer letters, and "letter-frequency" generally, will come up in other parts of this part 2.

Summary. The key first factor in abecedarial stability was the sacredness of the sacred text. Abecedarial stability both enabled it and was enabled by it. This sacredness may be cognate with other lasting components of human life. Human inventions like the wheel, the chair, and the knife equally survive the largest cultural changes, and they, and the alphabet, can come to seem as basic to our lives as do parts of nature like air, stone, and water. But abecedarial longevity occurs at least partly for practical reasons. Any major change of letters would render previous texts almost unreadable. No one has the authority to make these changes, and such few and small attempts as have occurred have usually failed.

There might seem to be advantages and disadvantages in abecedarial stability, although the former probably outweigh the latter. We can read centuries-old texts with fairly clear understanding. Paradoxically, words can change their meanings without semantic chaos resulting. Shifts of human intelligence and culture would be hazardous indeed if the sign-system itself was also constantly on the move, for there would be no fulcrum against which anything could be compared. Literature can thus survive the largest cultural, political, and even military upheavals; and the poets, too, thus have a tradition to work in. "Linguistic pragmatics" is the study of these variations in everyday language-use. It posits the two extremes of fixed linguistic law and actual language variation. But again, the poets make use of these variations. Imagination, variation, and innovation of phrase, lexicon, and imagery can all proceed on the basis of this stability of letters. In the extreme case—on the "catastrophe" theory—entirely new ways of writing poetry can appear, which alter all that follows them. Greek tragedy, Chaucer, John Dryden, and *Finnegans Wake* are clear cases.

The major disadvantage, if it is one, is that the basic sign-system, the actual physical medium, does remain fixed. Changes in innovations in both handwritten and print forms do not and cannot alter the grapheme. So there is no exciting challenge to compare with the invention of wholly new instruments in music, or the use of new materials, like industrial waste, in sculpture. Twentieth-century poets such as e e cummings have experimented with radical spellings, and with some success, but even they can't coin utterly new words. There must be some connection with previous ones for any understanding to be possible. A more neutral factor is the survival of underused or even, at times, "dead" letters. However, even qqqqq and kkkkk in English haven't yet reached that state.

7

Letters Are Equable

BENEFACTOR, CRISIS, JEL, JAIL, GAOL, GOAL, GOLDEN GOAL, GOAL OF the month. Birmingham, Birmingham City Council, Birmingham day return please, Bunyan, Babylon, subliquity, entechomy, our partner, those girls, my op, your heart-surgery techniques, their second house, hands, unhand me gentlemen, she'll bundle this.

This; after this, between that, I said that, or at least I thought I said that; I meant that. Was it I that said that? If, of, oftentimes, "of" ten times. Care, did care, sure was able to care, wasn't fit to care, was never going to be fit to care, but if on the other hand they, but if only they; mazy, jazzy, zany, yuh, yeah, yeh, yet, not yet . . .

Gardening, swimming, artillery, snow, kitchen, kitchen politics, fiscal planning prithee, sound fiscal planning, get that sound, undecided, nondeducible alchemick. The norm, we'll sue, herb garden, peg it back, strike it rich, so say Norm, Sue, Herb, Peg, and Rich. Door-to-door the hourglass turneth, supernova, interflora, the opposition is in disarray, oh mistress quickly, I spake to my gossip and she did mirth so . . .

A, I, O, me, he, we, to if, an, on, in of, box, the, why, day, four, five, crow, free, door, true, mouse, twice, house, garden, burden, abroad, insist, insisting, lighting, bargaining, hoping, capturing, sneezing, singing, sing, bring, thing, cling, azalias, take the fight to them, carefully explain our strategies, he rejoyceth in himself unto the last, carefully, care.

In *Ulysses* and *Finnegans Wake* alike, Joyce did it richly for seven hundred pages. It is hard to convey the import of it all except by yet another list. Facts, feelings, thoughts, thoughts about thoughts, hesitations, qualifications, changes, objects, dreams, animals, people, places, stars, gods, events, activities, titles, and exotica—all convert to the same thin, one-plane language. The abecedary's twenty-six signs are, among other things, a system for recording, evoking, or hypothesizing spoken sounds. Over the centuries these sounds have come to suggest countless thousands of items that the abecedary can convey in roughly even format in print. The abecedary labels all such items, the sound-element largely omitted. The printed page accounts for the vast majority of all letters ever written. The exceptions, from medieval illuminated initials through to the spate of technologized advertising seen now turn out in the upshot to confirm rather than deny the abecedary's equable characteristics.

Aided by fewness as we have seen, the signs are equable. There is a principle of equity by which they belong with each other, each being deployed in the same way in word and line. Yet clearly they can't be identical, as the Greek inventors found; each has to be different from the next for combinations to evoke words at all. This is equable in a different sense; the abecedary is tolerant. It bears small distinctions within the wider demand of same-size standardizing, and it tolerates whatever dispersals of human expression, however ultimately remote, that call upon it.

It does this via the tiny sign—hardly a tenth of an inch each way in most ordinary print—diversified along three paths. The lowercase version has proved more legible than uppercase capitals, perhaps because of its ascenders and descenders. Even single names blown-up often use the lower-case, as in motorway signing. The upper-case or capital was necessary for stone carving, before the arrival of the more flexible stylus and papyrus; pen and paper. The signs vary between three groups of alternatives:

a) single-stroke or multistroke (optional serifs are ignored here)

   c l o s n u
   a b d e f g h i j k m p q r t v w x y z

b) all straights, all curves, or straights-and-curves mixed

   i k l v w x z
   a c g o s
   b d e f h j m n p q r t u y

c) protruding above the line ("ascenders"), below the line ("descenders"), or remaining level to the line. (No letter protrudes both above and below the line unless we count jjjjj with its dot or the handwritten fffff).

b d f h k l t
g j p q y
a c e i m n o r s u v w x z

And so, in that last group, we can see that some words stand out a little by containing letters with little or no variation from one or other of those three types. *Forbid, truth,* and *kills* all lack descenders, while none of *jogs, preying,* and *quay* contains any ascender. In between, *vision, eerie,* and *cream* have neither ascenders nor descenders. Because no vowel has either ascenders or descenders, very few words in English lack at least one "level" letter. One such word is *fly.*

There is some common membership across the three sets of lists just given; but not much. We know that vowels were added later, so their lack of ascenders and descenders is intriguing. Even so, as also said earlier, we have little idea on what basis our signs were first devised. But the result is certainly effective. The system is impressively subtle. The signs are distinct from each other but not distractingly so. The interplay of the three criteria just named leaves all the signs sufficiently same-size to unify our overall experience, yet different enough that combination into words leaves each word's overall silhouette instantly unique.

Here is a small experiment that might illustrate this. Taking at random, let's use John Keats's sonnet "When I have fears . . .":

> When I have fears that I may cease to be
> Before my pen has glean'd my teeming brain,
> Before high-piled books, in charactery,
> Hold like rich garners the full ripen'd grain;
> When I behold, upon the night's starr'd face,
> Huge cloudy symbols of a high romance,
> And think that I may never live to trace
> Their shadows, with the magic hand of chance;
> And when I feel, fair creature of an hour,
> That I shall never look upon thee more,
> Never have relish in the faery power
> Of unreflecting love;—then on the shore
> Of the wide world I stand alone, and think
> Till love and fame to nothingness do sink.

Letterwise the poem is a standard piece of writing. It contains mainly fairly short words with a few longer ones, one or two that might seem archaic to the modern reader, but nothing unduly exotic. The least frequent letters of English, jjjjj, qqqqq, xxxxx, and zzzzz, are all absent, a quite common event in English in short passages.

We might try seeing what this would look like in a blander abecedary. On the ordinary keyboard, the nearest way I could devise this was to take the thirteen visually least elaborate letters, repeat them italicized, grade them all by decreasing simplicity, and then allocate them to normal letters in order of frequency in English. (Despite their ascenders, lllll and ttttt are preferred for simplicity to iiiii with its intrusive dot, and to xxxxx and zzzzz because of their sharp angles and, perhaps, infrequency in English. Doubtless these impressions are partly subjective.) The resulting alphabet is as follows, with the standard frequency-rate for English given above:

E T A I S O N   H R D L C F   B G M U P W K Y V   J Q X Z
o o c c n *n* u   *u* v *v* r *r* s   s e *e* w w *m* m *a* a   l *l* t *t*

The Keats poem comes out like this:

mu*ou c* ucao socvn *ouco c* eca rocno *on so*
sosnvo ea *wou* ucn erocu'*v* ea oooecue *svccu,*
sosnvo uc*e*u-wc*r*ov snnmn, cu ru*cv*croova,
un*r*v r*c*mo v*c*ru ecvuovn *ouo* swrr v*c*wou'*v;*
mu*ou c* soun*r*v, ww*n*u *ouo* uc*e*uo'n nocvv'*v* so*r*o,
u*w*eo *rr*nw*v*a naesn*rn* ns *c* uc*e*u vnecuro,
cuv *ou*cum *ouo c* eca uoaov rcao *on* ovcro
*ouo*cv nucvnmn, m*c*ou *ouo* ececr ucuv ns ru*c*uro;
cuv mu*ou c* soor, sccv rvocowvo ns cu unwv,
ouco c n*ucrr uoaov *r*nnm ww*n*u *ouoo* wnvo,
uoaov uc*a*o vor*c*nu cu *ouo* scova w*n*mov
*n*s wuvosro*r*ocue *r*nao;—*ouou* nu *ouo* nunvo
*n*s *ouo* mcvo mnv*r*v *c* nocuv cr*n*uo, cuv *ou*cum
oc*rr rn*ao cuv sceo *on* un*ou*cueuonn vn n*cum.*

Making all allowance for absence of meaning, the effect is surely rather more homogeneous than is Keats's already unremarkable (in letter terms) proper version. There is, maybe, an unusual calm, a reposeful ease about the experimental version; but the words are less distinct. If there is any doubt about the matter, one would only have to introduce an even simpler set of signs, for in the end we would approach pure sameness. Indeed, we could have gone the other way and invented a rougher and more jagged alphabet by using the ascender/descender letters like fffff, ggggg, kkkkk, and qqqqq for the most frequent ones. I think the result would have been temporarily exciting but in the end intolerable. This experiment does seem to support the suggestion that the abecedary is even enough for sustained reading, while still offering enough hooks and curves and corners to make the individual word memorable. More will be said about this later, including the question of whether individual letters are in some microfashion well served orally and even semantically by the signs they have.

In virtually all mass printing, the signs bear no difference of size, color, or position. Apart from the rather larger capital sometimes placed at the opening of a whole section—usually just a formal announcement of opening—the letters stay uniform size. Like a mass of frog spawn, or leaves on the forest floor, they parade their identity at all times unless some special effect is required. Special effects, as with glossy magazines, advertising headlines, T-shirts, and so on cannot sustain much extension; their text is brief. It is the same with color, and the black-on-white page is almost universal. The signs also retain their position, consistent and usually upright; they can't be rotated, sit on their sides, or anything of the kind. They also march together; individual letters cannot suddenly appear wholly above or below the line, or appear in a box or circle, nor are some suddenly three-dimensional and others not. No system, in our language at least, has devised any such variations for other than, again, temporary special effect, that exception that always has to be noted but which proves little in terms of the abecedary's diffusion across our culture. Always there is the retrenchment to simplicity and homogeneity. So each letter's own individuality becomes a special contrasting burden.

But there is a final negativity, perhaps most important of all. *The abecedary has no center.* Certainly some letters are used more often than others, as the frequency table showed, and this stays remarkably consistent over long passages. But statistically, none bar eeeee really stands out from the rest, and it is at the bottom end, the rare letters jjjjj, qqqqq, xxxxx, and zzzzz, where infrequency is marked. Those letters can intrude rather suddenly, and indeed interestingly, but in general they have little power over the broad outcome. But even eeeee has no special privileges. On the contrary, it seems fated merely to do more donkey-work; it can be somewhat colorless, or "silent," or simply a survival, or it modulates other letter-sounds near it. Eeeee is perhaps comparable to flake white in oil painting, commonly used to dilute other hues as well as for itself. (Huge amounts of flake white are used, at least by traditionalist oil painters.) The lack of any center to the abecedary—for example, by insisting that a particular letter inhabited every word in the language—preserves its equable one-planeness, and this would seem to be at the heart of our experience of reading and indeed of meaning.

Certain qualities seem inherent in this equability.

a) A modest calm and control are achieved. When we read, mind, and emotions receive the hard-knocks world of real experience, however powerful or moving, under a kind of transfiguration. The strongest feelings, the most wonderful or appalling events, the most authentic dialogue and the deepest philosophies, impinge in their fullness yet are appraised by a second-order detachment at the same time. In his later life Augustine eschewed his more restless tendencies, and his dialogues. Sin, chance, body, mind and virtue all had to live in the same text harmoniously together. As with the biblical wheat and tares, all strands sit alongside each other in his later texts. Abecedarial equability gives this full scope. Little of this kind of thing is likely with film, painting or in its different way music, where up-and-down movement seems the very mode of the medium. The strong writer has to struggle uphill against this calm, to express the sway of emotion, scene, character, or their sudden disruptions. If successful, the effect is all the greater.

b) Thought itself feels manageable. This was quite essential if, as Olsen argued, any worker in writing was to convey intentions to the reader that, by contrast, the worker in speech had hitherto conveyed by tone and body language. Such intentions were one more layer, one more dimension of meaning that the equable alphabet had to incorporate within its one mode of signification. This was quite aside from the many-faceted qualities of the projected message itself—the facts, conditionals, metaphors, questions, indirect reportages, inferences, and so on. In Olsen's terms, the alphabet's equability allows the text's overt propositions to merge easily with the illocutionary forces that underlie it. This general stipulation applies to expressions of thought in a more specialized sense. The language of concept and abstraction is subject to the same rubrics. Hence traditions such as Western philosophy can burgeon into whole libraries, as notion after notion, principle after principle, however diverse, can be laid out as belonging to the same universe, rendered in the same leveled mode. Equally with post-Renaissance humanism, writing suddenly expanded to converse with every aspect of human personality. The individual writer began to play the combinations of his own responses in with every aspect of the perceived outside world. It would have been difficult to control this as cogent discourse without the abecedarial equability that united and tolerated such combinations. They could spread across many societies—the whole of Europe—with no risk, for the same medium of communication expressed them all. The even texture passed into the mind by a single channel, and it is only deliberate subversions such as Modernism that break this up, in eras when thought itself has come to seem unreliable.

c) Yet paradoxically, the same features permit endless extension and addition. New words and new combinations of words may always be added. The subtle mixes of tiny signs on the basis of a single combinatory principle means that countless permutations— many of the simplest still unused as we saw earlier—are always available. In the nature of the system's homogeneity, no group of letters is banned from entry. Of course, convention and pronunciation can prevent this, and certain groupings are "not permissible in English." But this arises by sanction of time rather than inherently in the system itself. And, while there are tendencies in certain directions, there is no exact prohibition on length or syllable-count bar either. For example, words like conjunctions and pronouns tend to be short, yet *themselves, notwithstanding,* and such need not jar on the reader. Homogeneity itself is democratic—equable—in its open-endedness.

d) Language generally strives for distinction. So if the abecedary is equable, looking homogeneous even when every word is different, then an undercurrent away from that is needed for diversity to be expressed. And the equable abecedary allows this, too. Many linguistic studies are classifications of modes of statement or expression. R. H. Robins' study is a comprehensive textbook of such hierarchies. D. A. Cruse's work on semantics refers, lexically, to hierarchy, opposition, meronomies (parts for wholes), legitimate and illegitimate membership (Westminster is "part of London" but Westminster abbey is not), and points where overlap makes for ambiguity.[1] So, *spotless/filthy* and *lion/lioness* are both oppositional, but differently, and the nearly common letters of the latter, in this case, make their contrast actually a close pairing. Equally *table, triangle,* and *gold* have no opposites; but if *silver* and *gold* have come to seem both oppositional and paired, it may be that the vowel + lllll in both aid that embodiment. One of Cruse's examples, *I love proverbs, cats and Sylvia,* gets its zeugma-like effect by having no pluralizing sssss on the final item; but here too the rolles along the line in grammatically equivalent places contrast their categorical differences. Without such placing, a novice in English would not know that *purloins, poplars, peoples,* and *perhaps* are very different kinds of reference. But syntax and lexicon must win this against the ever-present tendency of the abecedary to pull all back into a single medium.

e) Finally, all is named. The abecedary is not colored but provides words for colors. It is not biologically alive nor kinetically mobile, yet can express those things. The gathering back of all entities into an equable medium means that the resulting words all have the one function of reference, whether to palpable world-matter such as *wisdom, poison, carry, eight,* or wisps of significance like *didn't, if,* and *before.* At the height of Greek civilization, when sacred writing had passed through dramatic dialogue, it burgeoned further outward. Wider disciplines emerged; philosophy, history, oratory, literary criticism, science. But they remained in contact with each other. This was the Greeks' growing, if unconscious, recognition of the alphabet's equability. So many things could be written and said via the same abecedarial means, with metaphor too now recognized as included—a stage Homer had not fully exploited. Again, the oft-cited myth of Adam's naming of the creatures in Eden was a recovery of everything into a linguistically closed system—except that the abecedary, too, as we are laboring to suggest all along, of necessity remains an entity in the same palpable world. But it is a homogeneous, one-dimensional entity. The more or less figurative pictogram can always keep some connection with the real world it presents. By contrast, the abecedary is free to elaborate its own palpable presence in that world, with its own distinctive characteristics, and it can do so only by severely maintaining itself as a single mode or method.

Control of what is diverse via homogeneous naming while granting that same diversity—that is the province of the equable abecedary. These features seem definable characteristics. Yet that finitude itself implies further features which, by contrast, the equable system can't tolerate. That is to say, even the universally usable abecedary has its parameters.

For example, in part 1 we said the abecedary is good at repetition. Yet there are limits on that, too. The sports page report, "The marathon was won by half a mile by Liz McColgan by sheer guts by three o'clock" is perfectly possible, but can't avoid seeming mildly whimsical. A sentence in Stephen Hawking's best-seller *A Brief History of Time* runs: "There are something like ten million million million million million million million million million million million million million million (1 with eighty zeros after it) particles in the region of the universe that we can observe."[2] Knowingly indigestible, this tour de force conveys all the more how unimaginable is the number referred to.[3] Equally, naming can turn into cliché. Remarks like *that's just elitism/chauvinism/blackmail* or *they're all yobs/vandals/layabouts*—single abstract noun as total argument—can replace thought by a row of letters gone empty. The letter-resonance or rolle-silhouette can seem like an entity when it isn't. Such naming is dangerous, too, by this very fact; for since the abecedary can do nothing but name, it may intrude into areas reluctant to receive it.

Finally, the abecedary can't let words be too long. Of course, this varies from language to language. Longer combinations occur in German than in English, while some African languages sustain what seem extremely long coinages to English readers. But they too have their limits. In English we grow uneasy with *unintelligibilities*, *antidisestablishmentarianism,* and the *institutionalizations* already mentioned. Indeed, words can't be too short, either, and if all the twenty-six letters each at times stood for a word, as alone do "a", "I", "O," and perhaps "x" in English, this might become equally intolerable. There is also the common phenomenon of "limited subjacency," the way the horizontally one-plane language can't support a Chinese-box structure of subordinate clauses. Thus: *The member who had invited the secretary whose husband whose few remaining colleagues whose wives were shopping had gone to the gym was in Tokyo back to his flat chickened out of it.* The sideways movement of the abecedary breaks down. Of course this is really a syntactical matter, but the linear mode of letters is part of it. Most famous is the weird catalog of animals, again devised by Jorge Luis Borges, and cited by Foucault at the start of *The Order Of Things*: "Animals are divided into a) belonging to the Emperor, b) embalmed, c) tame, d) sucking pigs, e) sirens, f) fabulous, g) stray dogs, h) included in this classification, i) frenzied, j) innumerable, k) drawn with a very fine camelhair brush, l) etcetera, m) having just broken the water-pitcher, n) that from a long way off look like flies" (Foucault 1970, page xv). As Foucault points out, each entry is quite clear in itself. The problem lies in the anarchic discreteness, made to seem uniform by the spurious act of classification. But only the equable alphabet allows such an act at all. In a wholly pictorial writing it could hardly have appeared in the first place. The alphabet can seem to offer such a list, the words can be written, but it collapses as sense unless the items are literally given as lists of words themselves, deictically (as in a dictionary), or given as the equally equable signs of syntax.

However, these limitations still leave the abecedary intact. It is so because, right at the start, a few working principles had to fall into place as to what rolles were permissible. Most of them, though not all, were probably noted quite soon after the alphabet was invented. The following rules seem necessary—but they are enough: i) rolles may refer to other rolles, ii) to themselves referring to other rolles, iii) to their own parts, iv) they may contain other rolles without referring to them, v) they may refer to the outside world by naming it, vi) or without naming it. So, under i) *a politician*, but then *a parliamentary politician*. Under ii) *he was offensive* but *I felt like calling him offensive*. Under iii) *gardening* but *garden*, and under iv) without ambiguity, *kitchen* but *itch*. Under v) we might say *point the knife with the blade outward*, but then under vi) *point the knife so, like this* (an example of John Searle's). From such principles the equable abecedary can be arranged and rearranged to cover most contingencies.

It can negate by including *no* and *not*, and name the unnameable by such terms as *the unknown, zero, falling upward*. It can make time-gestures, by what George Steiner calls the psyche's "monstrous and liberating power" of referring to the future.[4] So we can combine yesterday and tomorrow: "If Jenkins resigned last night—I haven't heard yet—we'll be moving to the North." And we can distinguish between language-time and real-time. Novelist Ian McEwen in *Enduring Love*: "What takes a minute to describe took two seconds to experience." Walter Scott was particularly fond of this touch. "This scuffle, though it takes up some time in the narrative, passed in less than a single minute." "While these things passed through her mind, much faster than pen and ink can record, or even the reader's eye collect the meaning of its traces, Jeanie found herself in a handsome library, and in presence of the rector of Willingham."[5] The "handsome library" presumably contained countless such cases, and we might wonder whether Scott meant us to notice this. There will be another interesting case of this when we come to consider John Milton.

The equable can make suppositions by "if"—"much vertue in if," as Touchstone in *As You Like It* put it. And as Plato, Jonathan Swift, and others felt so strongly, it can tell lies. This is the strength and the limitation of the abecedary. Central here to its equable character is how it presents or fails to present thought itself. For all of this stems from the abecedary's self-referring capacity, how it can articulate the thinking of its utterer and his or her subject. This is our number ii) above, and without that motive power no writing or articulation would have developed much beyond its first uses. We notice something, reflect on it, reflect on our reflection, and also that such reflection has taken place. This, the realm of consciousness, is a pole area of neuroscientific research at the present time.

But, even if we deem language to be an instinct or a set of genes, the abecedary is certainly a cultural construct; and the question then arises of how its equable, noncentered system can reach into the mind, or whether it can at all.

In an exhaustive study of naming, Joseph Graham has delved into various layers of this issue. There are categories of apprehension the abecedary must deal with, right before cultural considerations come into it. First of all, things referred to are already separate from ourselves referring, even when we don't put that referring itself up for formal contemplation. So there is necessarily reference and predication. "You always have to say something about something (i.e., you don't just say something; it is always about something, too), and to do that you need at least two different kinds of expression" (Graham 1992, 24). As Wittgenstein put it of objects, "I can only speak *about* them; I cannot *speak them*."[6] Equally though, nothing is true without also being capable of falsification. So there is not just "oak/beech" but an articulation like "there's an oak and a beech out there in the park." Bound by abecedarial linearity rather than drawing, we may then wonder how we chose oak before beech when both trees are there without priority.

Next, we think about ourselves thinking these very things. But there is a further consideration. For all these layers have not only to be expressed by the equable abecedary; they are also themselves moments of active thought or response in active minds. The short account of this would be that grammar itself is generative, a la Chomsky; but, as Graham stresses (67), grammar is not a truth and it does not know its utterances. It merely generates them. We do not intend thinking; thought itself does and is that. How and where then was this motivated, in living motion, from the start? And so finally, we refer, represent our referring, represent our own response to that, but also vainly gesture toward, or perhaps merely conceal, its irretrievable origins and purposes. How can the abecedary express the intention shot through it by its own author?

All of this, too, this spurring into expressive action, is somehow interwoven into the abecedary. It is its ultimate province. Its character as equable may then seem to be problematic. Perhaps it is simply inadequate to thought and feeling by its nature, and the daily experience of being "unable to express what I feel" is endemic. In Graham's terms again: "Words do not take the place of thoughts. They occupy a different space." One might equally say, though, that it is like the two-dimensional TV screen. From behind, the screen receives objects of considerable depth, such as foregrounded people and distant landscapes, and their movements, colors, gestures, and the rest. The viewer sits watching in front. Similarly, the paper-thin abecedary serves the same two sides, and author and reader meet at as transparent a barrier as one could imagine. Reading does not just go from left to right and nothing else. As Garman and others have pointed out, the reader scans in all directions; "collects" terms that seem prominent; moves in "sweeps" of perhaps seven words at a time; circles around; recapitulates; and so on.[7] These are all skilled attempts by native readers to meet from the far side what the writer has written, via the leveling abecedary, from his own irretrievable psychic origin in the first place. Poetry seems to accept the inadequacy; but poetry then also gives at least the illusion that the one-plane medium is itself doing the thinking, feeling, and talking, and that its surface reactivates the multilayered realities that evoked it. Either way, the origins of what is uttered feel dark and mysterious; as yet beyond the reaches of neuroscience to extricate.

Summary. Everything, just everything, is expressed through the one communicative channel. This is possible because the letter-signs are moderate; not too like or unlike each other, not too simple or complex. They can protrude above or below the line or remain along it. Deliberate departures from these principles, as often in ads, have to be the exception. Along with this moderation is a deeper one; namely, that the abecedary has no center. To privilege one or a few letters above the others would compromise one of the abecedary's most valuable characteristics.

As a result, several general qualities of meaning can be expressed. There is an overall sense of calm and control regardless of what material is in hand. Thought itself, whole intellectual disciplines and the most extreme personal feelings, remain manageable. Yet for that same reason any material at all is capable of expression. Furthermore, new phrases and new coinages of words can be tolerated and indeed welcomed. So long as it retains a general consistency, the language structure itself, its lexicon and grammar, can grow outward from the central tolerant homogeneity. Everything, in short, can be named.

There are a few caveats. Extreme repetition, like extreme or anarchic discreteness, is seldom possible. Cliché can burgeon. Words cannot be excessively long or indeed short. But these reservations are few. The lettered language can negate, name the unnameable, refer to present, future, and past, and their combinations. It can distinguish between rates of time. Via terms like "if" it can express condition. It can express thought and feeling, but it can also express thought and feeling about thought and feeling themselves, and it can refer to its own speaker/writer doing so, too. It can go right out and far away or it can be utterly self-referring. The linear movement "left to right," found in most European languages is part of the equability. The language and its letters do not suddenly jump up, down, or sideways.

The poets do it all, and it is their business in fact to highlight it. It is their medium, just as pigment, stone, and sound are the media of painters, sculptors, and composers.

8

Letters Are Physical

LETTERS ARE INK ON THE PAGE AND SPOKEN WORDS ARE SOUNDS IN the air. They originated from noises in the larynx and scratches on the ground and other places. Those are the aspects of language we physically confront, and no other. Equally, neural events cannot find a local habitation and a name without a concomitant medium. As Mary Shelley put it in *Frankenstein*:

> Invention, it must be humbly admitted, does not consist in creating out of void, but out of chaos; the materials must, in the first place, be afforded: it can give form to dark, shapeless substances, but cannot bring into being the substance itself.[1]

Mary Shelley's reference to "chaos" recalls our comments in part 1 about the place of language in early creation myth. Creation myth sees language as physically founded in light and water. But for "chaos" we might also read the "arbitrary" character the abecedary is usually held to have, although, as with the primal chaotic matter, it may turn out not to stay arbitrary for very long. The only nonarbitrary origins ever suggested for letters concern objects in nature, human artifacts, or parts or uses of human heads and bodies. The physicality of letters goes deep symbolically. High wind in the trees or echo in the mountain pass; phallic pen with paper as the bedsheet stained by the ink's menstrual blood; truth as permanent when "carved in stone": all these suggestions, which have all been made at times, underline what it is to speak and write.

All the later stages of the abecedary's development had their physical aspects. Early Greek drama necessitated dialogue, along with the names of the speaking roles; and the gaps between their different speeches. Even more than Thomas Aquinas, Anselm perhaps most among the medieval theologians reveals that reason has its own unmistakable abecedarial texture. Tyndale's earthy language underlines its physicality at every phrase; they are near-palpable.

Writing furthermore is solid; *pace* John Keats one cannot write on water, at least in any ordinary sense. One talks on air, something now recordable electronically. And the abecedary is physical firmly; effectively it is mineral, not organic. Derrida added the term *signifix* to Saussure's *signifier/signified*, to designate the actual mark—the rolle—as opposed to the linguistic sign that called up the meaning. But therefore, like all physical things the abecedary has finite characteristics, which may modify writing or speech. This modification does not simply leave any communication somehow less than perfect. It also embroils the physical in with the mental such that one can't imagine the latter ever being fully extricated.

There is useful evidence here in the well-known "tip of the tongue" phenomenon, much adduced by linguists. It is worth asking just what happens on such occasions. We say "what's that word . . . ? It means wandering, oscillating, hesitating . . . it's on the tip of my tongue but I can't think of it." And someone kindly says "vacillating," and we are duly grateful. The question is, what exactly had we forgotten? Clearly not the meaning, for that was adduced in the three orbiting words that were near synonyms, *wandering*, *oscillating*, and *hesitating*. What we had evidently forgotten was the rolle, the row of letters or sequence of sounds that would run parallel to what the brain had only hazily recalled. Until we find not the meaning but the row of letters or its sound, we are unsatisfied. It is interesting in this connection that from time to time in *The Confessions*, Augustine seems to be teetering on the edge of the tip-of-the-tongue phenomenon. That phenomenon is a form of restlessness, and Augustine's early work was nothing if not restless, as so many have noted. But this characteristic went along with his incessant anxiety about the workings of his own restless body, including in the context of language. His writing's carnal relish incarnates abecedarial physicality.

In some ways this physicality is very simple. The Greeks needed a system for recording languages they couldn't understand. The only way, obviously, was to record their sounds. When they came to add five vowels to their alphabet they simply borrowed five at random from the Phoenician. That was "arbitrary" beyond question, it might seem—and the signs were just physical marks. Maybe it wasn't so arbitrary after all, for as we noted above, all the five vowels lack both ascenders and descenders. But then so does half the entire alphabet. Either way, arbitrary or not, it was physical. I look out of my window here at an outer-suburban, near-rural landscape. There are iiiiis in every vertical building and every horizontal field, hhhhhs in doors and windows, oooooos and pppppps in the fruit and trees. The up-ended wheelbarrow is a WWWWW, the open stepladder is an AAAAA—and so forth. Our letters just are selections from simple shapes, in combinations that end up with a unique appearance. Letters are then a kind of child's toy building-kit from which the shapes of unique words can be made. The shape of each separate word is different by definition, otherwise it would be simply the same word again, though a different occasion of it. The materiality of these signs furthermore means that their general form, aaaaa, dddddd, yyyyy, or whatever it is, must be particularly embodied. This may occur in formal print, gothic script, the electronic derivation of every letter from the figure 8, or just plain handwriting. Alfred Tennyson and Dante Gabriel Rossetti both said they couldn't begin to feel their poem's presences until they appeared in print. W. H. Auden and Noel Coward differed on just when to transpose their work from their own handwriting to the typewriter, but they both saw it as important.[2]

It isn't easy to know what sort of physical thing-in-the-world to compare the abecedary with. In his book on consciousness, already cited, Daniel Dennett frequently uses the phrase "rather like" as a near-fixed grading term. Because consciousness isn't directly available for scrutiny, parallels to it would be difficult to light on; yet some kind of comparison must be made. So focus can be achieved by the "rather-like" designation. The nearest things I can suggest letters are rather like, would be anything which a) is very small, b) comes in millions or billions, c) has members highly similar to each other; "equable" as we have said. I am calling such things "micro-billions." We mentioned the point in part 1 when we cited certain words of St. John and the Buddha. So, letters are "rather like" grains of sand or salt, cells, stars, ants, leaves in the forest, and so on. But the similarity is far from exact. These other things are sui generis; just themselves, they represent nothing. Written letters, like grains of sand, differ from each other under the microscope in any one embodiment—they too are "just themselves"—but when a letter is repeated, the two occasions are identical. Yet they are still physically embodied.

Does this physicality mean anything? Did the abecedary's designer mean his marks to represent anything from the physical world? Unfortunately such speculation has usually led nowhere. However, it is not entirely valueless. It does seem likely that more than mere whim settled into the alphabets in at least some of their incarnations. On that front, a more promising approach would be to ask whether the rolle can attach itself to the meaning in the neural system scanning it. This could be a post hoc happening. Even if the signs were originally arbitrary—or might as well have been, for all we now know about it—this does not mean that, in some way, they had no power to accrue associations later, which we go on using, time after time, over the generations.

Surely the brain cannot avoid entangling the rolle's physicality with the "meaning" it attaches to or finds there. The response of many to that, as usual, will be that "the linguistic sign is arbitrary." Nor can we debit this to a supposedly outdated Saussure. To Steven Pinker the sign is "utterly" arbitrary, and he wastes no further space in discussing it (Pinker 1995, 83–84). Yet neuroscience grows ever more sophisticated. Why need the character of the ab-ecedarial sign, "rather like" cells, insects, and the rest, be immune to the investigative techniques long prevalent in the natural sciences? If a particular letter-shape can be part of a hook on to this or that kind of meaning, then that will become as conceptually knowable as any other neural engagement with the environment, however microscopic. Maybe the receiving brain-sensor, working microscopically, can't avoid matching the features of letters—curves, wriggles, uprights, angles, forks—on to things a bit like them in nonletter items already in the memory bank. It will do this when it scans that bank for whatever form is taken by the recalled item that the word containing these particular letters is naming. The present book can only speculate on such possibilities, but they are worth considering briefly, for they turn out more intricate than has usually been suggested. Here are two letters taken for illustration.

The letter kkkkk has a spiky look and feel about it, with its four stark prongs sticking out at all angles. By contrast the letter uuuuu—ignoring the optional serif—is mainly a single sweeping curve. Let's take kkkkk first. At least three hundred monosyllabic words in English either end with the letter kkkkk or have only a silent eeeee following. Many have ccccc preceding. Orally kkkkk is almost redundant in English, for it does little that the hard ccccc does not do, although it still distinguishes pronunciation as in *lace/lake*. But it has long fallen away from certain terms in culture and knowledge: *metaphysick, musick, physick,* and others. So one has to ask what value it retains. A remarkably large number of words ending in kkkkk or kkkkk-eeeee connote abruptness. There are the numerous fully or nearly onomatopoeic words like *kick, click, crack, strike, knock,* and probably *clock*; but dozens of others, too, have a sense of short-sharp-shock about them. Leaving certain vernacular (and much-used) terms modestly unprinted, these include *quick, quirk, check, fleck, speck, nick, trick, shock, pluck, fake, quake, choke, poke, puke, creak, peek, brink, slink, skunk, skulk, stuck, hark, bark, nark, quark, jerk, irk, cork, fork, murk, crank, hank, yank, prank, stink, yank, bunk, clunk, funk, punk, stalk,* and *sulk.* The expression "a stroke of luck" captures the gut sense of such words. That something is a "fake" is a sudden realizing, and to be on the "brink" is to be at a marked edge. A "fleck" is a brief touch of color in clothing, paint, or light. We choke, check our stride, and yank a rope in a more or less immediate moment; a dog's bark is a sharp sound; one could continue.

Of course, this is often what is called sound-symbolism. Yet sound is not entailed alone. If the retinal impression of the sign has a counterpart in neural scanning, as seems likely, then that may enter the parallel scanning of the meaning. But – and here is the interesting qualification—what makes this both difficult and yet re-assuringly more acceptable (because more complex and subtle) is that many other words ending with kkkkk or kkkkk/eeeee have no such touch of abruptness. No such reading could be obviously ob-tained for *lack, sick, lake, make, sake, like, duke, weak, oak, seek, dark, clerk, ask, desk, dusk, musk, monk, milk, silk, talk, think,* or a number more. And if we now take words containing the vowel uuuuu, something comparable seems to hold. A clear uuuuu-lexi-con hints at curvature: *curve* itself, *curl, turn, urn, lurch, churn, hurl, under, up, hull, gull, bush, cup, pull, bun, spun,* while words ending in *ump: bump, lump, jump, rump, tump, hump, sump,* and *dump* all suggest some kind of rounded movement up or down. What of *gun, fun, mush, usual, fund, full, pure, true, usurp, suc-cumb, unity, dull, null, tumult?* Maybe these have a deeper, less vis-ible curvature with the neural self-representation of such nongeometrical items still needing such form. Perhaps *purity* en-tices the perfect form of the curve for its neural register, and *null-ness/dullness* can't sustain sharp interruption. In that event only the curve, which has no angles, satisfies that requirement. Adding the ooooo to the uuuuu may increase roundness: *round* itself, *about, mound,* and *wound* when past tense of "wind."

But again, as with kkkkk, even if such ideas have indeed sedi-mented into uuuuu over the centuries, there is still a large stock of uuuuu-words hardly accountable this way by any reasoning at all: *but, hut, put, shut, us, bus, fuss, sue, adjust, stun, abrupt, stuck, skunk, mutter, stutter,* and the rest. A more salient point addresses this whole issue. Suppose for argument's sake that uuuuu just does evoke curvature in the brain's nonverbal representations. So maybe *sun* evokes a curvature of abundance. How then does the brain cope with *stun,* the same word but with ttttt added? What tells the brain what it certainly does know, that the semantic component has wholly changed? If *spun,* what of *spin?* And the same applies with the list of kkkkk-words. Suppose the spiky kkkkk does fittingly trigger the suddenness of so many kkkkk-words: *jerk, quake, creak, kick, pluck.* One word there, *kick,* elicits abrupt activity with the feet. How does that entirely semantic difference enter the same word, furthermore by adding yet another kkkkk? Similar considerations arise with other letters. Many words containing bbbbb twice seem somehow comic: *babyish, bubble, rhubarb, baboon.* But this can hardly be automatic, for *blackbird, absorb,* and *bibliography* escape it. And if *babyish* does evoke a mild hidden grin, why doesn't *babyhood?* So why should the trend be there at all?

We could suggest that, sometimes, different consonants modify the uuuuu's curvature while not removing it entirely. Lists like *such, much, munch, mulch, lunch* or contrasts like *bung* and *buzz* are suggestive. Equally we have cited *stuck* and *skunk.* It would seem that here the kkkkk dominates the uuuuu. Yet overall, attempts to tie individual letters to objective realities seem doomed as either incomplete or never fully reliable. They leave tensions that offer no clear semantic way forward. Indeed, even if such exactness were available, it is hard to see how it could be used. For it would reduce meaning to the crudest levels of interpretation, the match so exact as to be clumsy. Yet the semantic clusters we have traced do carry some conviction. There may be a middle way here, which might be called "weak regularity."[3] The materiality of letters and sounds is just one resource among many for the brain to make use of. The abecedarial sign works like a mnemonic, in the same way as words of like meaning and spelling but from diverse etymological origin *(sin/sinister, imp/impious, gala/regalia, mist/mystery)* can come to absorb their chance connections powerfully. The neural sensor will use the letter's physicality when it can, and seek other correlations when it can't. Or it won't bother with the letters' physicality if those other correlations are already in place. The letters' physical attributes flow with the words' meaning like water seeping to a lower level. If the gaps for seepage are there, they are used; if not, not. There are no precise guidelines, just an option that never departs.

This is no problem; rather it enriches language. The search for exactness of one-to-one evidence has fallen away from much empirical research in our era. This too is not surprising, indeed it seems fundamentally easeful, in that probability rather than dogmatic certainty has become a general criterion in epistemology, too. Relations between components offer themselves not only for interpretation but also as mental resources, mental furniture. The written and spoken word waits as a resource, outside the neural system, by which that system can be enriched. This is the clear distinction between, for instance, abecedarial language and any purely pictorial one. It seems a profound observation on the very nature of verbal language.

Risking overdoing the point, here more briefly are three examples of a different kind. There is a "common-cluster" phenomenon. Such clusters include -ion, -ity, -ing, and the oft-cited -ceive, morphemes that seem to contain meaning even though they are not words themselves. But there are other common groupings that are not even meaningful, like -ough, -tch, and -ght. These irregular spellings end up as familiars, "old favorites" as we might call them, to which the brain's response is probably something like "I've seen this before; this is the kind of thing I know about." The topic raises incidentally the observation that in English our supposedly irregular spelling, especially inflection, commonly characterizes the very oldest words. They survive from earlier languages, usually Old and Middle English (Pinker 1995, 274–75). Proto-Indo-European languages inflected by changing the vowel; *grow/grew*, *fight/fought*, or they pluralized by means other than the sssss ending: *child/children*. There is also what one has to call general difference of texture. *Moon* and *stretch*, *passable* and *horticulture* evoke palpably different responses at both visual and oral levels, as do their meanings. The vowel-spread provides an admittedly unusual example. A description of someone as *adamant, extreme, illicit, orthodox & untruthful* might seem either a notable coincidence or stylistics run riot. Such extreme effects ask to be avoided.

Next, words vary in length.[4] *As, if, by, he, it, so,* and *of* palpably contrast *extension, flyover, geological,* and *miraculous.* Longer words may also contain exotic rarer-letter combinations as seen earlier; *odalisque, hexagon, ukulele, rhizome,* where mixes of letter and combination dominate. Since the rarest letters in English are all consonants—jjjjj, qqqqq, xxxxx, and zzzzz—they cannot comprise whole words by themselves by definition. *Od-, hex-, uk-,* and *rhi-* are already rare in English, let alone with the additions of qqqqq, zzzzz, etc. One variant of the short word commands attention, namely the monosyllabic range of the form aaaaa + yyyyy: *bay, day, gay, hay, jay, lay, may, nay, pay, ray, say, way.* Less often another vowel is used: *fey, hey, boy, coy, joy, toy, buy, guy,* and in a very few cases none at all: *by, my.* When a consonant replaces the vowel, the open-ended effect shifts fractionally: *cry, dry, fly, fry, ply, pry, shy, sky, sly, sty, thy, try, wry.* Emily Dickinson deployed three-letter words to great effect, as we shall see. Where consonant and vowel both appear in the middle there is an ambivalent effect: *ahoy, ploy, gray, whey, fray, spry, stye*.

Finally there is the double-letter configuration. Orally this shortens the preceding vowel; visually, *mutter, trigger, accent, pebble, barrow* and countless more examples seem to impress the retina by reinforcement. This doubling-up has its own variations. These are what I would like to call "distance-doubles," words with two or more pairs of letters, not just one, and in which these pairs reinforce each other while not being necessarily adjacent: *tumult, vividly, cataract, proportion, mesmerize*. When the double pair is a central double flanked by the same vowel on each side, there is a comparable but more symmetrical impact: *fetter, sorrow*. *Murmur* is a triple repeat, beautifully exploited by Wordsworth in *Tintern Abbey* as we shall also see. Another form in English, which the eye readily lights on, is double-consonant + consonant/ vowel or vowel/consonant. There is little in common semantically between *prattle, battle, cattle, settle,* and *spittle*; there is *mutter/stutter*, but *butter, gutter,* and *shutter* are largely discrete. Again, though, the abecedary system seems to leave grouping options open. *Waffle, piffle, baffle, muffle, skiffle,* and even *soufflé* all suggest the lightly evanescent or spurious. Differently but cognately, is there not something in common between the mmmmm/aaaaa-starting terms *majesty, masterful, maharajah, magnificent,* and the British all-conquering soccer team *Manchester United?* Again the neural sensor feels, "This is the sort of thing I recognize; maybe I can use it."

Perhaps there are some really wide generalities. On the page the five vowels eschew ascenders and descenders. Aaaaa, eeeee, iiiii, ooooo, and uuuuu never stray above or below the written line. But the same also applies to the "soft" consonants that sometimes function as vowels, rrrrr and wwwww, although yyyyy does go below the line. The "hard" consonants (plosives) go firmly above or below the line; thus ggggg/kkkkk, ddddd/ttttt, bbbbb/ppppp, and the fricative fffff; or else they cut the page as with zzzzz and vvvvv; or wriggle around on it, as with the sinuous sibilant sssss. At least some sounds of sharply physical edge are matched by angular signs: kkkkk, xxxxx, and zzzzz most obviously. There are subtle features in the nasal consonants mmmmm and nnnnn with their regular but calm vertical uprights, giving a visual presence to words like *common, minimum,* and *moon*.

Indeed, as a final illustration of all these tendencies, let's take one word often thought of as beautiful: *moonlight*. Among other things it contains the consonants mmmmm and lllll, held by some theorists of phono-aesthetics to be inherently attractive. But maybe the word's physical beauty, if it has that, lies in joining a level word made of symmetrical letters, *moon*, with the "old favorite" form of consonant + *-ight*. Attached to the meaning of a lovely object in itself, this makes a beautiful word in our language. But the same form of four-letter word + five-letter word—often containing double-letters, too—is also common in English. So what do we make of *beefsteak, woodlouse,* and the like? Again, these components are resources for the neural sensor to sift and sort and choose or reject as it will.

By such means the visual abecedary stands back from what it means and what it sounds like while retaining an angular relationship with it. I suspect such things could be microscopically researched although it hasn't been done yet. I wonder too how far poets have always instinctively used this. Many poets compose orally in the head before writing, or indeed while writing, too, dashing off the words and hardly noticing what they look like. But poets of the era we shall consider had usually already encountered huge amounts of print in their earlier lives, most of it in massed small-type settings like magazines or books. Could there not be a visual dimension within the oral activity? My own feeling is that they mutually activate each other.

Summary. Letters are ink on the page and spoken words are sounds in the air. Most of the many suggestions for what originated them refer to physical objects natural or man-made, or parts of the human body. Letters then symbolize, or look like, physical objects. The familiar "tip-of-the-tongue" phenomenon, which Augustine among others encountered, makes the point well enough for it suggests that what we forget is not the word's meaning but its physical embodiment as noise or letters. Our cursory history of letters in part 1 revealed other examples of this materiality more widely. We are calling the physical letters of a word its "rolle."

As a result this materiality may be picked up by the brain when the latter apprehends any one rolle or group of rolles and neurally attaches it or them to the words' meanings. The letter's shape, its curves, straights, or angles, may be helpfully embodied. In considering examples of this, we then suggested that there is no exact match between letter-signs and meaning, but even so some general congruence might often grow up. This congruence might be called "weak regularity." Obvious cases to consider were single letters (we discussed kkkkk and uuuuu), lengths of words, double-letter formations, and typical clusters or "old favorites" like *-tch* and *–ght*.

By such means the abecedary seen as physical retains an oblique relationship with the meanings of the words it composes. It seems that this could be researched; but also that poets, often though not always, have probably been instinctively while not consciously aware of it. There are numerous instances of the care that poets take of their manuscripts as well as the look, shape, and layout of their poems on the page.

9

Letters Are Virtual

IF LETTERS ARE PHYSICAL, WHAT ARE THEY PHYSICAL CASES OF? Signs and sign-sounds no doubt, but what in turn are those? The frequent answer is that they are arbitrarily chosen marks that indicate sounds, and those sounds too are arranged by mere convention into rolles that match meanings. The meanings are conceived of as somehow there already, so that the signs for them are arbitrary completely. Saussure's system was obliged to see the sign as arbitrary, so that its quite separate meaning could stay fixed. In fact, it is the reverse. It is the abecedarial system, not meaning, that is fixed or "stable," and that is what leaves meaning valuably flexible.

By taking this stand on arbitrariness—which of course has some truth behind it—some linguists have dodged the matter of the sign altogether. For these linguists the matter is simple. The word "duck" doesn't look like a duck, walk like a duck, or quack like a duck. The sign "duck" for that bird is therefore arbitrary. But as Derrida has somewhere pointed out, the idea is a truism. If "duck" did look, walk, and quack like a duck, it would actually be one. Hayley Davies, although she draws a different conclusion from my own, suggests that if the sign is arbitrary, then we cannot claim objectivity for linguistics as a science (Davies & Taylor 1990, 2). Deacon, also arguing against the "merely arbitrary" view, states that language-signs must have some fit with human cognition and aptitude more generally, because "the correspondence between words and objects is a secondary relationship, subordinate to a web of associate relationships of a quite different sort" (Deacon 1997, 59). But a preferable view to that of arbitrariness would surely be that, while certainly physical, letters seem also to need to be in a permanent state of reaching across to their nonphysical meanings, striving to slip the chains of their physicality. When the Greeks recorded languages they couldn't understand by simply recording their sounds, the process left their newly invented alphabet's letters "arbitrary," but it also freed them up to name the material as category or idea. This freedom released the aspiration that makes the abecedary "virtual."

We can now see that many features of the first alphabetical societies pertain to this virtuality. The first users quickly found that letters could express the nonphysical in many forms. These included the sacred, the intellectual, the unnameable, or that which doesn't even exist. The acronym, too, could embody the virtues of several words at once. We noted similarly that both Augustine and Aquinas related language to time. That relation is material or physical in its visceral rhythms. But as an idea, time is an abstraction. As Augustine saw, in that context it is more cogent with other abstractions like happiness, forgetfulness, and evil. Aquinas's writing reveals throughout that reason has its own abecedarial texture. Here indeed it is a timelessness, a state of rest that approaches pure virtuality. Aquinas's truisms, negatives, and impossibilities; "x exists," "God is not," "God cannot," are equally such virtualities.

And in order to attain such ends, there is a rationality and order across the abecedary generally that accrues from the many features of it we have looked at. These features are far from arbitrary. Letters remain the same over centuries; are of roughly homogeneous size; are different but not too different; group into recognizable clusters; have their vowels level in shape; and end up with the consistent, easy, and homogenous presence that writing must possess for so many thousands of pages and books to be palatable at all. Letters are arbitrary, if at all, only in their separate states and their origins. As soon as they bind to sounds, meanings, and each other, their unique shapes set up real relationships via reasonably consistent routes that, hypothetically at least, could be known. In one way or another, consistently or not, their fewness, physicality, and equability begin to be glued to their meanings in ways that, however unconsciously, poets and others use and rely on. This aspect of the abecedary is the most elusive yet, but thereby the most subtle and intellectual by its very nature.

The letter is not so much arbitrary but virtual. This is what I take it the new linguists like Hayley Davies may be asserting in their claim that linguistics cannot be a science. Naming can't look like what it names, for in some cases that can't be rendered physically at all. Yet naming must equate with what it names in some virtual sense, and must have some kind of mental presence itself both appropriately and adequately impressive. The resulting device, the abecedary, has this elusive quality that I call virtuality. Here is what I mean.

The previous section suggested that letters are physical and therefore presumably solid. Yet they are nearly always linear, not solid, in the actual writing of them. Commensurate with visibility, their lines are as thin as possible. Curved letters like ccccc and ooooo are boundaries, but boundaries of nothing; straight letters like lllll or vvvvv are edges, but edges of nothing. By their nature they cannot strictly avoid solidity, for example they can't be zero width, but they approach that as far as possible. Big public hoardings, or the occasional capital at the start of a chapter, thicken them up for special effect, but this can't be sustained for any long-term reading experience. Letters are equally two-dimensional on a different plane. They lie on surfaces and seem to offer themselves up to the light. Letters have no shadows, for they are their own shadows; as noted earlier, in the vast majority of cases they are printed in black. White letters printed on a black background are strangely unacceptable. Such rare occurrences are mainly confined to glossy theater programs (theater operates precisely in a dark place, locally lit up), or school blackboards where the writing is transitory, wiped off after a couple of hours. Writing is surface, and again when hoardings ink in the shadow for special effect, the practice can only be temporary. As to both width and surface then, writing thus observes the literal sense of Euclid's geometric laws. Euclid wrote that *a point has place but no magnitude, a line has length but no breadth,* and so on, through to *an area has length, breadth and width, but no depth.* The lines that make letters have length, but minimal breadth, and in any formal sense, no depth at all.

But all these, one might reply, are merely fanciful notions. Yet the absence-but-virtual-presence of the word's referent in its letters lies in deeper factors. Because the signs are virtual, not copying what they stand for but rather naming it into existence outside the neural system, they can refer to virtually anything, any level of meaning at all. Indeed, it can often be more than one thing or dimension of mental activity at once. The linguistic distinctions between lexical, syntactical, and function words *(garage, invested, won't),* as to which the abecedary is equable, are brought into virtual existence in the same way, even though their existences in the real world are quite different. So we can touch a tree; and sit or stand "by" a tree; but we can't touch "by" at all; and we may do nothing physical with "perhaps-ness," either. The pronoun "I" is often taken as the central case of such ephemerality. The referent of "I" is revealed entirely by the occasion of its use; it means only the person who is using it.[1] Yet all these have virtual presence in the virtual world of the sentence.

Real existence and nonexistence are also found in near-same

words, compromising the words' own existence further. For example, differences of level as between lexicon and syntax exist in the
same term at once. With words like *unfenced*, we envisage the
fence clearly, but what do we envisage with the negation, and what
is the difference between what the two rolles do for this? The rolle
"bottle" visually calls up a glass cylindrical object. But in "she bot-
tled the plums" there is a ddddd on the end of the rolle. Do we call
up the bottle alone and leave off the ddddd, or what? In ordinary
reading there is no difficulty, because the name is only virtual, so it
does not compromise the bottle by adding the extra letter. This example is of course just inflection, but language is saturated with
such dual-level phrasings. They exploit the equable nature of the
abecedary to keep both "naming" of things and talking "about"
them all on the one plane. "I've planned the garden, but, well, if
it's going to rain down in bucketfuls . . ." This would be quite beyond our apprehending if letters were only objective real-world
phenomena of the same kind as selves, futures, gardens, thoughts,
and rain. For *thought, well, if,* and the rest would not be able to live
with the physical objects they do in fact easily consort with in the
sentence. Not to press this too far, we can see what might be entailed in such odd contrasts as *giant/extremely small person* or
dwarf/extremely large person. The two ways of writing are of inherently different kinds. One seems vivid and the other elaborated;
one is materially brief and the other materially extended; neither
has priority, so both are virtual still. All these layers of expression;
statements, orientations, hesitancies, namings, questions, bits and
pieces of utterance generally, are not just copies of events. They
are virtual events themselves, virtual divinity, virtual polity, virtual
sexuality, virtual humanity, virtual reality.

 This virtuality cuts across another duality in the debate about language; namely, as to whether language is autonomous and opaque,
or a transparency through which thought and feeling may be
glimpsed behind. The debate has had its protagonists. Some students of language attribute opacity to the abecedary, others attribute
transparency. The traditional hermeneutic view is that we go direct
"through" the written signs by interpretation to their place in the
mind. The contrasting poststructuralist version, going back to Walter Pater and others, stresses not writing's penetrative tendency, but
its sideways or deferring movement, one word or phrase always
adding to another. There is thus a gulf behind the whole to which
the reader must just respond as best may be. But there is no solution
to this debate, for it turns out illusory. Rather, it is a paradox. Abecedary signs are nothing in themselves, only in what they evoke;

yet they are nothing like what they evoke, so if they exist they can't be nothing after all. Letters are things, yet they aspire not to be. This is the riddle of the virtual. The notion of abecedarial arbitrariness does not resolve it. The view of the abecedary as virtual, however, allows us to be both more unified and more flexible.

It is true that "Words do not take the place of thoughts, they occupy a different space." But this does not leave them in static opposition to the mind or feeling to which they are orientated. It is more a matter of degree. The issue is of how far the sign system can coax the reader/hearer forward into receiving what the intending subject wants to utter. As just said from our examples about fencing, bottles, and wondering about gardening in the rain, our utterances aren't merely external parallels to something inside, for there are too many layers being expressed or captured. We think something, we then think about it or around it, and we then think of ourselves doing such reflection. Indeed the "then" is dubious, too, for all this may be entailed in identical time. And all of these layers can be captured homogeneously, too, by the abecedary in its capacity as equable. The process is wrapped in with the other relationship between "naming" and "talking-about," that is to say the subject-predicate distinction. If—too crudely to be sure—syntax is a property of mind while lexicon refers to items in the real world (mountains, tantrums, birthday wishes, surgical operations in hospitals), then the interplay between these two in verbal language is also always a leaning-forward or yearning by the abecedary in use. It is not a fixed one-to-one set of referrals. From the examples we have taken, Augustine and Tyndale maybe evince this yearning most overtly, but it is always present. And finally, these elusive suggestions point to further layers of mind that may not be retrievable by language at all. Language does not always go all the way down.

For right down at the mind's base there are what the philosopher R. M. Hare once called "bliks."[2] "Bliks" is a deliberate nonsense-word for fundamental dispositions incapable of articulation. It is akin to those everyday silent orientations you have that, in words, might be expressed as something like "yeh . . . yeh . . . that . . . that 'n' that . . . that . . ."—well knowing what you mean and yet still needing no words for it. It may be a relationship, a yearning, or a memory generalized. In a different context, the Confucian *Li*, discussed earlier, offered such a case. This again recalls the primitive awareness of the unnameable; it also touches on the idea of mentalese, although that term implies a brain-language to be considered later. It is cognate with Wittgenstein's famous reference in "whereof we cannot speak, thereof we must remain silent" (Wittgenstein 1961, 74:7). Notably it is incapacity to speak, not lack of understanding, that Wittgenstein refers to. More generally Stanley Cavell has written of the common experience of being unable to express one's general self-knowledge.

> The more one learns, so to speak, the hang of oneself, and mounts one's problems, the less one is able to *say* what one has learnt; not because you have *forgotten* what it was, but because nothing you said would seem like an answer or a solution: there is no longer any question or problem which your words would match." (Cavell 1976, 85; his emphasis)

T. S. Eliot wrestled with the problem in *Four Quartets* (East Coker 5) and William Faulkner wrote of a time when he "learnt that words are no good; that words don't ever fit even what they are trying to say."[3] Again we see the tradition of suspicion of excess in language. Again one recalls Plato's doubts; writing itself doesn't know what it is saying. We don't inaugurate thought ourselves. Thought itself does that, and we are thinkers because that is where evolution has brought us.

The transparency-opacity distinction, then, seems too oppositional. On this theory, and if this doesn't sound too bizarre, the difference between language and mind would be more like one between "yesterday" and "tortoise," where the two things simply don't evoke each other at all. Language and mind occupy different terrains. The abecedary is just itself in the air or on the page, yet it has no existence at all without matter like ink or voice, and mind-feeling; and so it is virtual. The oft-noted contrast between the abecedary and the media of other arts emphasizes the point, and constructively so for what follows next in our argument. Apart from technical services like electric light, elevators, and plumbing, an architect's model of a building matches the real building on several dimensions; solidity, color, shape, proportion, and even texture. It just is the building in miniature. Paintings narrow that down to the two-dimensional and visual, with some textural feel in support, while music works through pure sound. Yet all of these are still palpable. So what is the corresponding product of abecedarial language? What fills the spaces that the grosser—though still "fine"—arts fill with bricks, film, and paint, reaching the areas of mind that ink marks and noises can't reach?

It seems to be figurative language. Figurative language turns out central to virtuality in language. At first look, figurative language seems the most palpable and solid area of discourse. In metaphor, a savoring and relish of the physical are commonly evoked in the reader. "My hopes vanished like melting snow"—"he seemed ablaze with emotion." Yet if figurative language achieves this, it seems to do so exactly by sliding the relevant rolles out of the way, and surrounding the central figurative experience, which has no rolle of its own, with subsidiary terms that leave a space in which the powerful and vivid, or hidden and elusive, event occurs. This is what makes figurative language cognate with, or perhaps a living substitute for, the inarticulable neural experiences just mentioned; that is to say the "bliks," the feelings of not being able to put our deepest selves "into words." Figurative language finds the rolles that draw the meaning off. This is why rightly or wrongly figurative language, and most centrally metaphor, was for centuries since Aristotle thought to be at the heart of poetry, and poetry itself was enshrined as the most gut form of human expression available. The well-known debate over metaphor two or three decades back had much to say about these matters. It can usefully focus the issue of figurative language generally, and we can therefore draw useful conclusions from it as to the abecedary also.

Theories in this earlier debate, such as those of I. A. Richards and Max Black, outlined the process of metaphor as that which keeps literal terms at the periphery, to allow a vacuum at the center into which the metaphor-experience then flows. The "tenor" or "focus" was the anchor-word in sentences round which the "vehicle" or "frame," the sentence itself, circulated. This set up the missing experience.[4] This theory was carried further by Winifred Nowottny.[5] Nowottny suggested that a sentence based on a metaphor could be written out as two nonmetaphorical sentences. So the sentence "The ship ploughed through the waves" actually merges two sentences. These are, "The ship did something-or-other to the waves" and "The tractor-harrow unit [literally] ploughed the soil." By understanding the second sentence, the reader/hearer supplies what was missing from the first. But the key point here is that the word for "something-or-other" could never be found in the language's official lexicon. If it could, it could simply have been used in the ship-waves sentence. Developing Nowottny's terms in our own context, we might say that "something-or-other" is the vacuum or gap in the middle that holds the exciting new meaning, yet which can have no abecedarial rolle of its own. And the outcome is, that metaphor is what moves our experience forward. This is because metaphor is always making available new experiences the lexicon is not yet equipped for. Later still Paul Ricoeur widened the discussion considerably, taking it from word-level to sentence-level and indeed discourse-level, and from transference and resemblance to metaphoric reference more generally: such is the power of metaphor to adduce meaning beyond lexical reference locally and literally.[6]

The inference of all of this is that it can be achieved only by the abecedary, no other medium. This follows from the character of the abecedary as virtual. Film, television, music, and other art-media, of course, generate their own impressionistic and imaginative methods and techniques that alphabetical language lacks. But as expression in day-to-day intercourse, only by language can the mind attain a new, nonembodied or virtually embodied experience in the ways described. Take the case of painting. Unless it is either abstract or surreal—both of which have their own quite different and entirely valid agendas while still embodying the palpable medium of paint—painting must, in some way or other, always capture physically what the ship does to the waves. But when language does this, it does it "virtually." All the quite literal language that surrounds the "missing" word is also virtual, too, and so the "missing" word, the "something-or-other" word, can fit into the sentence's meaning felicitously. As a result we get the entirely new metaphor itself. No wonder that back in the sixteenth century Peter Ramus found "virtue" in letters. This also ties in with the objective existence, outside of mind, that the abecedary offers, by which mind can project and hence objectively evaluate its own spontanous utterings by mouth. It is the abecedary as virtual, remaining as diaphanous as it can while still embodied in the ink-paper of palpable rolles, that achieves this radical experience.

Connected to this there is also the ancient view of metaphor as plain lying. The first main use of the new Greek alphabet was to record poems. It worked perfectly; the alphabet could say things that weren't true. This is a further virtuality, and again it was one of Socrates' lifelong complaints about writing. This older suspicious view of metaphor as lie is cognate with the notion of something "inside" the mind or feeling that refuses to acknowledge the abecedary, leaving the latter as arbitrary event only. Holders of this view nullified it not least by their own glorious failure to write metaphor-free prose themselves. Plato and even John Locke abound with fine vivid metaphor, A. J. Ayer only less so because he was writing a treatise on logic.[7] Metaphor is not lie but, precisely, virtual truth.

In more recent years the debate on metaphor has moved on in other ways. The range of metaphorical utterances was already seen to go from Cohen's "full-fledged" metaphors through to what is called dead metaphor; but, as Davidson suggested, dead metaphor is not in any sense reprehensible.[8] Rather, even fully vivid and realized metaphors were merely rather more memorable cases of quite ordinary statement. A dead metaphor is merely a word that has come to be used in a different way, availing itself again of the abecedary's stability, which allows meaning to be flexible. So an innocuous remark like "your shirt's in the linen cupboard" can ignore the fact that cupboards were once boards for cups, not linen. But we couldn't say "I've started woodwork classes in metal," because woodwork has never become a general metaphor for other crafts.

There is a final point about living metaphor in writing that should not be overlooked. Indeed, it seems a capacity unique to language, and so is perhaps the most important, even the most valuable, of all. The very fact that the process is virtual and nothing more, not pictorial fully, is what also allows the two parts of metaphor to accommodate each other in a merging comparison. We could never think literally that the ship plows the waves, or that the heavy artillery bristled with anger, or that Juliet is the sun. We can only have a shimmering sense of that merger. But we can at least have that finally elusive sense as far as it goes, which we could not with literal painting, sculpture, or photography. Of course, I appreciate that these other arts, quite legitimately, have their own meanings for the term "metaphor" in their practices, and that these meanings express something important in those contexts. But the merger of the two parts of the metaphoric expression—the tenor and vehicle, the focus and frame—can reach its unique, curiously compelling unity only because of the virtuality of the medium by which it is expressed.

One could launch comparable discussions about simile, metonymy, and other figures of speech. Accent, tone, emphasis, and other human-oral accretions also require the virtual body of the abecedary as their place of reference. Figure-of-speech, then, supports the view of the elusive nature of all that the abecedary attempts to express and articulate. It succeeds, not by being right or wrong, accurate or inaccurate, but in rendering such images, ideas, or hesitant possibilities as virtual. It is one more attempt at the negotiation our language always makes between the neural system and the physically objective abecedary which, even so, hang always "virtually" in the air. Neither can be fully at one with each other, yet each is always mutually and inextricably entailed.

Words are virtual grammar, virtual thought, and virtual object-in-the-world. They must render up what they equate with but not get in the way of it. Rather aside from Touchstone's "virtue in if," the virtuality of *-ness, -ceive, -ity,* and such often feel like a receding target (is there "ness"-ness or "ity"-ity?), leaving us only to inquire what this virtue consists of, and why that term is useful. This point leads to some final rather important observations. Abecedarial signs seem able to absorb or "sponge up" their meanings; or perhaps, they are saturated and stained with them as by a dye. Each separate rolle has its unique silhouette that neurally intermeshes with its signified, with what it is intended to convey. In Wittgenstein's term again, words have a "physiognomy," a look about them, like a person's face does. It is more than merely the sum of the letters that make them up, for that remains the same even when the context shifts the word's meaning (Wittgenstein 1958, 181, 218).

Of course, these suggestions, of "physiognomy" and "sponging-up," are themselves mere metaphor. But so are ideas about looking "through" the printed page as through a pane of glass, to the meaning reposing "behind." In my own experience at least, words—let's say *milk* and *battleship*—don't literally look like milk or battleships. Yet in their physicality they seem able to give hooks to those things' silhouettes or their felt presences. The very word *milk* seems to attain a blue-white-gray-liquid quality: while *battleship*, possibly via its ascenders, one descender, and double-letter, can attract the hull, body, and funnels of that vessel. We have a virtual experience of milk and battleship. Again Tyndale's richly physical lexicon lends itself to this virtual "sponging-up" process, as indeed did Homer's. Here Tyndale's writing evinces the medieval tradition of the "Book of Nature," for material Nature too has absorbed or "sponged up" the divine meanings with which God has implanted it. At a somewhat different level, Augustine's oft-repeated GOD, and the acronyms central to Buddhism and the Kabbalah, are similar one-word absorptions. Duns Scotus's idea of *haeccaetas* or "thisness" was a clear attempt to conceptualize this characteristic of absorption.

Words like *milk* and *battleship*, though, are palpably material. That *seldom, nevertheless,* and *tomorrow* are less easily realizable this way, and *well, tomorrow, maybe, oh my gosh . . .* even less so still, only underlines their functionality, their power to stay loyally at work and so epitomize their relating purpose. Yet they too are still realizable as a kind of version of the mind-emotion stuff we, as material beings, need to envisage in some form or other. Some abstractions seem pretty flat at any time; *expect, relation,* and the like. But others, just as heavily Latinate on the face of it, absorb a tang, a vividness, some kind of feeling. The sad eyes of *disappointment*, the gory *execution* (guillotine or firing squad), and the *conservatory*, a glasshouse in which to catch the sun. All these take on their physicalities and atmospheres in combinations of the same few signs. And all of this is "virtue" in an older sense that still just about survives in English.

The reader won't have ignored the conception of "virtual reality" as it currently pervades advances in electronic communication and computer graphics. This new meaning, I suggest, is a secular cognate of the meaning of "virtue" that pertained prior to the Enlightenment. Again Peter Ramus's remark is relevant here. Virtue was once thought of as almost a substance, if a spiritual one. But it also suggested moral goodness as it does today. If there is still a live etymological link between "virtual" and "virtuous," it lies in the traditional belief in human fallibility as measured against some ultimate standard. Fallibility lay in the absence or insufficient quality of those substances—ichor, elixir, spirit, virtue—that alone could take us up to perfection, by willed self-improvement against the grain of our earthly natures; in short, by virtue itself. Indeed, it is pertinent here that those creation myths we considered earlier saw language as emerging not just from light, water, soil, and so on, but also from the creator's spirit or living breath. But this virtue is unreachable as self-knowledge without the self-articulation made available by external language. The abecedary externalizes our minds, and this gives our minds reflexive opportunity for spontaneous utterance to know itself. It does so by "coming to terms" with a problem or situation; we find the adequate terms or words, and thereby reach a terminus, an end, in the rolles that satisfactorily draw it off. Phrases like "the ring of truth" express something comparable in the oral sphere. In being "virtual" the abecedary gets as near to the expression of the spiritual, and the wider virtuous, as any sign-system does that has ever yet been invented.

The Socratic recognition was that self-improvement was tied to self-knowing, and that self-knowing had to be monitored by articulation of one's merits or failings via a system of external expression. This recognition projected one dimension of virtue out into this marvelous distillation that humans found they already had at birth and societies had possessed from time immemorial; namely, language. Verbal language didn't have to be grown like plants or get found like minerals or water. It just was there; never, it seemed, had it not been. As with the Aborigine view of the world, the gods had made it for us and then gone away, leaving their imprint all over it. Hence language has always been thought central, a gift from the gods, in at the creation from the start.

Finally, the response of some to all this "virtuality" may be that it is simply spurious. There is no flesh and gore in the rolle *execution*; we just put it there. There is merely an associational connection, however complex in its manifestations, between the signs or "rolles" and the meanings the neural system has internalized. Signs trigger recalls within the brain, both lexically as to experience and in the neural structure that is already instinctually syntactical. But this view is self-circling. It simply swallows itself. The words we have just used to express it, *associational connection, signs, neural system, trigger, recall, lexically, instinctually syntactical*; all of these, too, are ideas already projected out into the rolles they need which are drawn from the abecedarial system. They too are already virtual, already encapsulations with which the neural system has to interact. The neural system's view of itself is already obliged to find (virtual) expression in something that works in its own way with its own palpable embodiment. It is not a mechanical tool suborned to neural nature and therefore servile to it. It is none the worse for that, nor is the neural system; rather the two interact, the DNA-based coding and the sign-meme out in the culture, with fruitful and virtual result.

It is noticeable how written embodiment has correspondingly re-fined itself over the millennia. In the progress from animal blood and charcoal to finer dyes, to purpose-made ink, to the felt-tip pen, and now to the electronic pulse, the formal shapes of the abecedary nevertheless remain constant. The inference is not that they will one day somehow merge with the neural system totally. Rather, both will remain virtually autonomous, each ever more refined, to their mutual advantage.

Summary. The alphabet's virtuality is the obverse of its physicality. It names even physical objects as conceptions, and it names non-physical objects like thoughts and abstractions, too. Letters are "arbitrary" in only a limited sense, for rolles quickly accrue complex associations with meaning that remain constant. The teleology of a whole text is not at all arbitrary. The *Odyssey* is a virtual voyage while Aquinas's *Summa* is virtual reason.

Written language cannot look like what it means, yet must in some sense equate with it. It does so by its aspiration to the virtual. So the width of the line that draws any letter and the vertical depth of any word is notionally zero. The letter aspires away from its underlying physicality, such as ink or pencil, and it lies as pure visibility under the light. Gross physicality's minimal presence gives letters lightness and air, so the rolles they comprise can absorb or "sponge up" meanings of the objectivities, physical or abstract, in the real world. Many parts of language beside full abstractions, such as particles and inflections, are also virtualities.

Similarly writing is never a copy of events and nothing else. It is also its own event, always also "occupies its own space." So, while by its virtuality it wraps itself into the layers of our thoughts, it never reaches their inner center. That remains the province of "bliks" or the fully unnameable. This is a dual aspect of writing. It is its independent self, yet without some relation to nonlinguistic realities it too would cease to exist. This always present but never complete relationship is writing's virtuality.

And figurative language has a special place in this virtuality. Metaphor well illustrates this. Metaphor generates new notions without needing new words, for it juxtaposes old terms unexpectedly, leaving a space in which a new virtuality can appear. Equally, metaphor is not lying but virtual truth. Dead metaphors survive as useful virtualities via the abecedary's stability. Perhaps most valuable of all, metaphor is found uniquely in language. Only language's virtuality can achieve its compelling if elusive presence.

Finally, if communication is fundamental to civilization and a harmonious world, then this virtuality is in some sense also virtuous. In at least this sense the two terms are still cognate today.

10

Letters Are Distributive

So the abecedary is marked by fewness, stability, equability, physicality, and virtuality. But what translates these five features into actual words on the page? How are the letters deployed, how is it done? Obviously, by some principle or principles of distribution.

Distribution is the abecedary's general mode of operation. The letters just are arranged in thousands of different combinations, and many different kinds of combinations, to evoke the meanings of the texts they end up in. Abecedarial signs in English are also capitalized, italicized, and punctuated, and appear in different typefonts. But within all aspects of grammar, lexicon, syntax, and the rest, it is the grapheme—the letter regardless of how it is written—that is distributed. In general, this distribution can occur because letters are discrete.[1] Written letters and words cannot dribble into each other like colors do in painting, or lie across each other like notes in musical chords. This discreteness is related to abecedarial fewness. The fewer the signs, the more must they remain distinct from each other for their combinations to flourish. But this same discreteness also enables distribution, the mode of operation of letters in all their aspects. The richness of our language suggests that distribution is markedly varied in practice. There is not just massive distribution. There are many modes of it.

In a general way we have already seen many of these modes at work in the earlier eras of the alphabet and the abecedary. There were the earliest matrixes or "up-down" lists, tables and charts before our own kind of alphabet was invented; many examples of repetition from religious chanting to Homer's single-line repeats; a sacred device like the acronym; Homer's line-after-line way of capturing his voyages—and so on. In all such cases the texture and tendency of the language was enabled by the great flexibility of deployment of the letters that make up its words. The widening-out of thought and reason to the high point of Greek philosophy was also made possible by the abecedary's distributive capacity. Words

214

remain as they are or else they evolve; they are like or unlike each other; and both these features then enable comparison, which is at the heart of thought. Single words inflect, or have prefixes or suffixes, and so give different intellectual angles on the same verb or noun. Plato sought fluidity, but couldn't yet realize that writing does this by abecedarial distribution.

Augustine's restless personality marks his early writing. Curiously intense feelings of both sin and chance spread across it, making for a kind of distributive eccentricity at the written level. But both Augustine and Aquinas also related language to time. The sentence moves along in linear mode, and this is abecedarial distribution in the service of syntax. When in the Renaissance the sense of word as part of nature declined, as Foucault traced, words were left relating only to each other. The age of the grammarian was inaugurated. In our terms here, the same abecedarial distribution that Augustine and Aquinas had seen as a matter of time, the grammarian then saw at the level of sentence structure. And cutting across this sentence-movement within time itself are the verb-inflections or tense-markers. They tell the reader what time periods are being named by the sentence's language.

The Kabbalists' idea of anagram (temurah) embodies the principle of letter-combination—distribution—as an emblem of the very structure of the universe. As we noted in chapter 3, if the material cosmos is at base nothing but trillions of atoms, then the combinations or "anagrams" of those atoms are what give rise to the countless palpable things we see about us in the universe, nature, and our own man-made world. That is to say, the "distribution" of cosmic atoms was seen as an underlying model for the distribution of letters that make for language's seemingly endless richness of expression. At an altogether tinier level: a single change of letter, by mere shift of convention over time, can alter a nuance. Tyndale's "bable," "Sondaye," and "ester" became our "babble," "Sunday," and "Easter." This is small-scale abecedarial distribution, that is to say spelling. But Tyndale's earthy language also underlines the abecedary's capacity to be centrifugal; that is to say, to distribute letters in countless combinations, rather than remain with just a few basic ones, as more in the manner of the writing of rational thought. Finally, with the new Renaissance writing of conversation distributions are multiplied by ever more ingenuity, wit, and understanding. This is so much so that abecedarial equability has to strain hard to conserve them within the one communicative channel still.

The five features of letters we have considered evince this general distribution. Because they are few, the same letters are deployed countless times, making for overlaps, deliberate centrifugality, and other features. Because they are stable, letters allow meaning to change, but they therefore then need new coinages, new spellings, and new imports, in effect new distributions, against that secure basis. Because they are equable, letters can tolerate distributions of several kinds; lengths of words; varying frequency of different letters; inflections, irregularities, and symmetries, and so on. Because they are physical—and discrete—all this distribution is clear and unhindered. Because letters are virtual, the countless word-silhouettes that result from distribution can seem to "sponge up" and almost symbolize the meanings they evoke. There are further subdivisions of all these features.

Language is always a system of signs. Whether letter-distribution contains some kind of overall, hidden, final system would be hard to say. Maybe there is merely great variety. Distributing letters in a single word is what we call "spelling" that word. Distributing letters in a sentence or longer unit may seem more a matter of grammar or meaning. But the relations between letters across words and sentences then immediately makes for abecedarial textures of other kinds; the alliterations, tiny-word particle connections, exotic terms, and the self-circling repetitions of inflected reason. Furthermore, each aspect of distribution doesn't simply trace back to just one of the five abecedarial characteristics. There will be layers, mixes, and different kinds of boundary between each. All this takes place at many times and in many places, consciously and unconsciously, collectively and individually. A rich organic mulch results, and its life nurtures the life of language.

Here follows, then, a résumé of distributive principles for the abecedary. They are drawn largely, though not entirely, from the previous sections. The aim here is to group them in a clearer overall picture. The apparently main predisposing features of abecedarial distribution are given in brackets in each case, but these are somewhat notional.

The principles are listed in five groups. The first gives the general disposition of letters on the page. The second focuses on letters within individual words. The third is like the second, but arising from some semantic consideration. The fourth is also like the second, but arising from some syntactical consideration. The fifth reveals the limits of abecedarial distribution. There are overlaps.

1. General Dispositions

a) *Letters are distributed in short rows (rolles), which evoke meanings* (distributive)
This is what we call "spelling."

b) *Distribution separates words, by the white spaces between each rolle on the page* (physicality, virtuality).
   The abecedary's words divide seamless reality into discrete parts. For example, a "tall green vase" has three rolles, but really there is only one object with three aspects, a point much discussed by philosophers.[2] Idioms are an important case here. Since idioms are "indivisible" *(kicked the bucket, swept the board)* their white-space markers suddenly change significance. With an added subtlety, in "Peter went to work on his motorcycle (project)," the addition of the bracketed word not only changes the sense overall, but also shifts "went to work" from literal to idiomatic. There are many cases like this in English sentences. "Betty's dressmaking firm made all Martha's new wardrobe seem old-fashioned." If we omit "seem old-fashioned" we change the meaning of "made" radically. Incidentally, this could be a special case of why interrupting is held to be socially bad manners.

c) *Distribution moves mainly horizontally, but also vertically* (equability, physicality).
   The "Linear B" text dates from 1200 B.C. Saussure thought of language as linear. Distribution arises from grammatical word order, but not via the word unit alone. Although as readers we "scan" words and as listeners put them "on hold," we can still only speak or hear one word at a time, so words must follow individually along the line. In a sentence like *there's an oak and a beech in the garden*, the choice of which tree to name first is not affected by grammar. In everyday life this may entail important choices for emphasis. Should we say *He's conceited but he works hard* or *He works hard but he's conceited*? It's as though the whole chiasmus is needed. There are deep preference-principles fixed in the culture controlling such things; for instance, left before right, near before far, female before male. Letter-clusters, and single letters, all take spatial positions along the line.
   There is also downward distribution. This principle was cited in chapter 1 in context of the matrix. It doesn't arise just because of margins. A horizontal scrolling, a paragraph going forever to the

right, or indeed forever and only downward, would be intolerable even if practicable. In special effects like advertisements downward distribution often applies only to single words.

2. Letters in the Individual Word

d) *There is a distribution of letter-shapes* (equability, physicality).
   Individual letters are shaped in several ways. They may have ascenders, descenders, or neither on the line. The words *truth* and *gipsy* each omit one, *eerie* omits two of these three possibilities. Most words contain two or sometimes all three variations. Letters are shaped in other ways, too; straight or curves, simple or angular/spiky, and so on. All make for a word's own silhouette and so secrete its "sponging-up" capacity.

e) *The twenty-six letters are distributed with varying frequency* (equability).
   Again here is the frequency list for English:

E T A I S O N   H R D L C F   B G M U P W K Y V
J Q X Z

It applies reliably to almost all texts in English, although it can vary markedly in, for example, very short poems. *Zebra, quizzical, waxy, jewel* use far rarer letters than do *tenant, noise, season, estate*. The first four words all use letters from both the third and fourth group in the frequency list, while the last four words draw entirely on the "etaison" group, the seven most frequent letters. Semantically, common letters usually mean mundane words, rare letters more exotic words; but there are many exceptions both ways: for example *aeon, quick*.

f) *Some letters can be distributed twice in succession* (fewness, physicality, virtuality).
   The "double-letter." But this itself is subject to distribution down the abecedary. In English b, c, d, e, f, g, l, m, n, o, p, r, s, t and z can be doubled; a, h, i, j, k, q, u, v, w, x and y cannot be. Exceptions come from imports, onomatopoeias and slang: *radii, pukka, baa, flivver*. Other things being equal, the double-letter has above-average visual impact. Orally it affects vowels directly, while doubled consonants commonly affect the vowels next to them.[3] Words can contain more than one pair of double-letters, for example *committee*, and not necessarily adjacently, for instance *cataract, proposal*.

g) *Vowel-consonant ratio is also subject to varying distribution* (physicality, virtuality).

Extreme cases are *strengths* (one vowel in eight consonants) and *eerie* (one consonant—and that a "soft" one—in four vowels). There are nuances of sound and sight symbolism here. Equally words can begin and end with consonants, or with vowels, or with one of each. This difference makes for different textures of writing, often roughing up or softening the effect. *Tough jobs make staff work damn hard* has a rougher texture than does *A raw air lay over the new era.* Of course, there are exceptions the other way here, too; for example, *extra* crowds its fricative consonants between two vowels.

h) *Distribution highlights a word's first letter: "the first letter owns the word"* (virtuality).

The white gap between words enables this and perhaps insists on it. English goes from left to right, so we enter a word from the left. This is highlighted culturally. Children are taught that "A is for apple, B is for bear," and so on. We capitalize names and opening words of sentences and commonly use "alphabetical order" for various listings. Alliteration usually operates most strongly through words' opening letters, with both visual and oral results. Kabbalistic studies were well aware of the first-letter phenomenon. The *notarikon* is the examination of first and last letters, just as the *temurah*, roughly, is the study of distribution itself.

3. Semantic Applications

i) *Distribution makes for more or less abecedarial homogeneity* (fewness).

This is the "centripetal/centrifugal" distribution. Centripetal movement ends in sameness itself; pun or ambiguity. Centrifugal movement occurs through infrequent letters as already said; infrequent combinations of letters (*-rhi, -odda,* etc.); or rarity of the word semantically. Centrifugal distribution thus aims at a kind of "incest-prevention." From the language's outset there have been, or would soon have had to be, words like *feeling, emotion, mood, temper, impulse,* and *by, to, near, from,* rather than something like *feeling, feelong, feelang, feelag, feelun,* or *by, yb, byb, yby,* etc. Such clusters would surely generate confusion.

j) *Distributions may be irregular and indeed weird (in English), yet still occur frequently* (fewness, stability, virtuality).

The result is our "old favorites": *-tch, -ough, -ight, -attle,* etc. Although English's irregular spelling can be frustrating, we are more irritated when words are misspelled. *Sammon, nayber, sikey,* and *kee* seem to lose a bit next to *salmon, neighbor, psyche,* and *key,* and it would take much liberality to accept "a motarweigh dryve to Heethroe." The same applies to silent letters, as in *sword, halve.* All these enable reading—scanning, parsing, "collecting"—to go ahead easily, and for rolles to secrete meanings readily because uniquely. English spelling is "compositionally phonographic only *post lexically*" (Garman 1990, 38, his emphasis).

k) *Distribution may be altered by elision and disappearance* (physicality, virtuality).
   Pram (perambulator), *perm* (permanent shampoo), *pub* (public house), *con* (confidence trick), *fax* (facsimile), *hype* (from hypersensitive, hyperactive, and such). Is this simple economy, or is it an urge to make the Latinate feel Saxon? It affects the average of distributions.

l) *Distribution seems constrained by both economy and excess* (fewness, equability, virtuality).
   Rolles can add length with little extra sense: *a longer (space of) time.* Yet some repetitions can produce equal unease: *we were expected to respect the inspector.* But equally the same group of rolles used in many contexts can dwindle into cliche or become fixed as standard phrases. There is often balance or alliteration in such oft-used utterances: *take it or leave it/a bloody bore/friends and relations/back to basics/I've started so I'll finish.*

m) *Distributions from diverse linguistic roots may end up rather like each other* (fewness, stability, virtuality).
   We mentioned *imp/impious; gala/regalia; mist/mystery,* and other examples. But there may be a chance semantic attraction, too: *a disheveled dishcloth, a huge deluge.* Individual cases are of course coincidences, but the principle of abecedarial fewness makes them more likely to occur.

n) *Distribution can leave "words" inside other words with no semantic trace* (fewness, virtuality).
   Kitchen/itch, fundamental/amen, foreigner/reign, detached/ache, and similar cases. The word *jeweled* contains successive words for: a member of a Middle Eastern people; a female sheep; ourselves; an obsolete measure; the French for "she"; being taken or induced;

abbreviated "editor." Yet the overall rolle alone congeals into its semantic significance.

o) *Similar distributions of a single letter both may, and may not, be attached to similar semantic groupings* (fewness, equability, virtuality).

This is the "weak regularity" feature. We cited kkkkk words, which do or don't suggest short sharp impact, and uuuuu-words, which do or don't suggest curvature.

p) *New distributions may occur at any time* (stability).

These may come from imports, technical terms, acronyms, colloquial spellings *(gotcha, tonite),* abbreviations and elisions, and names *(saxophone, Thatcherism, tantalize).* A jazz musician named Sax invented the saxophone, and a whole economic policy became known by the name of the politician who inaugurated it. The final case named goes back to the ancient world; to *tantalize* is to treat someone as Tantalus was treated. In all such cases, the cause of the word's origin may eventually disappear from the view of all but specialized philologists.

4. Syntactical Applications

q) *There are regular distributions for the main inflections of syntax* (fewness, stability, equability).

These of course vary internally. They include tenses and plurals; *-ing, -ed, -s, -en;* but also gender: *man/woman, male/female, he/she, priest/priestess.* In such ways can a language be marked with its users' ideologies. The stems of words tend to vary distributions *(house, luggage, skeleton, Philadelphia)* while inflections usually repeat them *(inconveniently, incessantly, impossibly; section, position, auction);* but neither principle is exact. Tendency to variation in words is modified by the "old favorites" phenomenon: *light, night, fright, sight;* the familiar case of varied pronunciation for *bough, rough, cough, ought, through,* and more.

Distribution by prefixes, suffixes, and inflections can visually and orally link words of very different meaning. *Reading, fishing, meditating, caring, blushing, murdering, woolgathering, electioneering, bathing, frying.* This is the medieval *homoioteleuton* or "same endings" (Curtius 1953, 44, 74). Of course, the very act of listing such words may emphasize the effect.

r) *Letters are distributed in varying amounts; there are short words and long words* (equability, physicality).

Letters are few, so if rolles were all the same length, too, the homogeneity might well become intolerable.

Inflections of syntax, and additions by prefix and suffix, affect this feature. English has several one-letter and two-letter words, but almost none is a noun or adjective (one exception is *ox*). Three-letter and four-letter words may be nouns, adjectives, and verbs, but if so they are "nondeducible": *cat, sky, hit, run, big, red: hair, tree, push, fill, wide, blue*. Much longer words, being usually compounds or inflections, seldom refer to simple or "basic" items.

Length of rolle is less important in speech. The speech-stream lacks the gaps found between words on the page. With sound, different lengths of words are known mainly through their meanings. However, monosyllabic words, especially nouns and adjectives, have more stress orally than do longer ones (Robins 1993, 420). This slows passages containing many such words, and a gravitas—compelling or ponderous—may result. Short words can be wittily concise: *Dear Me* (title of comic actor Peter Ustinov's autobiography); *Now Then* (a beginner's guide to history).

Length is unimportant with multifarious and visual characters, as in Chinese; indeed there the same-size regularity is a kind of traffic-calmer in such a welter of signification. With the abecedary, by contrast, length-variation is the ubiquitous and easing device.

s) *Similar meanings can be distributed into several short rolles or one long one* (fewness, physicality).

For example, *inconveniently/in an unhelpful way*; *several/quite a number of*; *giant/extremely large person*. Of course, this overlaps the semantic criterion. But it supplies a variant of texture, both visually and orally.

t) *The same distribution aesthetically may have very different effects grammatically* (virtuality).

> *Why should Tory love Labour, or Labour Tory?*
> *Night precedes day, day follows night*
> *Not the man in my life but the life in my man* (Mae West)

In these three cases of chiasmus, the second half elegantly reverses the first half at the verbal level. But in the first case subject and object simply change places. In the second, via the change of verb, the second half repeats the first but with altered emphasis. In the third case the reversal changes the meaning of "life."

5. The Limits of Abecedarial Distribution

u) *Distributions into rolles, though both physical and virtual, can refer both to nonthings and to self-generating entities* (stability, physicality, virtuality).

We noted Augustine's *forgetfulness* and *evil*. There are also *zero, the unknown*; terms for the future *(we shall be going . . .)*; but also the familiar "I" (first-person pronoun) and terms like *pain*, much discussed by philosophers and which seem to name whatever it is that the rolle in question uniquely refers to each time (Wittgenstein 1958, 89–104). Just possibly comparable—because of abecedarial sequencing in time—is *aposiopesis*, a figure of speech by which an expected outcome is missing. "They rushed up the stairwell, ran along the corridor, broke down the door and—well, you can guess the rest."[4]

v) *Some things seem untouchable by any distribution at all.* (stability, physicality).

The "ineffable" or "incommunicable" seem not subject to naming by any rolle. They can only be evoked. Examples include the inner space or missing term in metaphors; some mental attitudes or spiritual positions; and the like.

Summary. (This chapter's summary is followed below by a general appraisal of this whole part 2.)

Distribution is the abecedary's general mode of operation. The discreteness of letters, unlike that of paint, or sound in music, allows this. Obvious earliest examples vary from the "up-down" matrix via the acronym to many sorts of repetition. Humanism, human restlessness and philosophical reason alike evince different abecedarial distributions, and the Kabbalists saw letter-combination as matching the very structure of the universe.

Our five other features of the abecedary—fewness, stability, equability, physicality, and virtuality—evince this distributive feature in their various appropriate ways. Distributing letters in a single word is what we call "spelling" that word. Distributing letters in a sentence or longer unit concerns grammar, meaning, and a wide range of more local features. We listed these as a set of principles, as follows: 1) *General dispositions*. Rolles (spelling); white spaces between rolles; horizontal and vertical distribution. 2) *Letters in the individual word*. Shapes (ascenders, descenders, etc.); frequency;

the double-letter; ratio of vowels to consonants; the first letter ("the first letter owns the word"). 3) *Semantic applications*. The "centripetal/centrifugal" distribution; irregularity ("old favorites"); disappearance (colloquial abbreviations); the economy-excess factor; similarity from diverse roots (imp/impious, etc.); words inside other words (kitchen/itch, etc); "weak regularity" (e.g., kkkkk, uuuuu); innovation (imports, technical terms, acronyms, colloquial spellings). 4) *Syntactical applications*. Distributions by syntax (tenses, plurals, prefixes, suffixes, inflections); long and short words; number of words for same meaning (several/quite a lot of); balances (night precedes day, day follows night). 5) *Distribution's limits*. Nonitems (abstractions, zero, the unknown, the future, first-person pronoun); the ineffable or incommunicable.

So concludes this part 2 and our survey of these six features of the abecedary. But before putting them to work on the poets just as they are, perhaps we might first pause for a brief general appraisal.

Such might begin by asking whether these six aspects of the abecedary are merely miscellaneous, things we just happen to notice, or whether they are rooted in something deeper. Is there some coherent pattern behind them? Will it help, when we come to look at the poets? I think we can see a couple of possibilities. Some of our answers to this, at least in these first few paragraphs, may seem excessively theoretical, but they could be useful none the less. First of all, it seems that these six aspects are of two kinds. One kind tends to yield up close, detailed, specific examples of letter use. These are what we called abecedarial fewness, physicality and distribution. The other kind concerns the wider, background ways in which the abecedary can be counted on to function reliably and attain human expression at all. These aspects are what we called abecedarial stability, equability, and virtuality.

We can describe this pair of differences in a little more detail. Again and again we have noted in a line, a phrase, or a single word that letters either repeat themselves or veer deliberately away from that, with varying results. Or the letters' shapes and design (whether alone or—as with double letters or mutually exclusive spellings—with each other) seem to press upon us. Or the different ways letters can be deployed seem to merge into an especially rich texture. And these results come from the three aspects of fewness, physicality, and distribution. But just as often we were on a broader front. We found that texts could last over centuries, and that words' meanings could safely change without confusion. Or texts could sustain many meanings at once, and shift their moods and tone likewise, without difficulty arising for the act of reading. Or more teleologically, physical letters have a strange capacity to go beyond themselves and become one with resultant meaning, emotion, and spirit. These results come from the three aspects of stability, equability, and virtuality.

This is a rough division and there are exceptions of detail. But it works reasonably well. It is true that equability straddles both these groups somewhat, particularly via the tolerant nature of letter-design via ascenders and descenders. But, with equability, the result is less often a technique applied for local effect—when that does happen it is "physical"—and more often the resulting overall quietude and moderation of the whole system; to be varied, but not too much.

But if this pattern does hold, then it may also point to a deeper and more permanent system. For these six aspects also fall into three pairs, each of which matches some important aspect of communication in the widest sense of a necessity of human living. I would see these pairs as fewness/distribution: stability/equability: physicality/virtuality. Fewness/distribution refer to the letters as a self-contained system. There are few letters, yet they can be distributed many ways. This is "the one and the many" of abecedarial writing. The other two pairs are more metaphysical: they each concern fundamental conditions of our existence. Stability/equability offer reliability in the respective domains of time and space. The abecedary lasts indefinitely, and it can also tolerate whatever needs to be expressed in the present. Physicality/virtuality, clearly, refer to our human body-mind distinction. That is a complex area, and we should again say then that the medium of material letters allows expression across the range of human spirit, intellect, and emotion.

All these considerations would bear further expansion but are adequate for our needs here. However, for readers interested in the deeper metaphysics of the matter, it may also be noted that these two patterns can be further related to each other. We now have two trios, one that broadly controls local surfacing (fewness, physicality, and distribution); the other that controls wider reliance (stability, equability, and virtuality). We also now have three pairs: fewness/distribution: stability/equability: physicality/virtuality. But if we also take each term from the first trio and match it with a term from the other trio, we get an elegant system capable of bearing further examination. As we have said, fewness and distribution (from the first trio) combine to arrange letters into the texts that actually get written. Stability and equability (from the second trio)

combine to make that opportunity permanently available. But physicality and virtuality alone cut across those two trios, and so they
make the link between writing's immediate material means (which
fewness and distribution act on) and the resultant long-term value
of the text (to which stability and equability give permanent existence). This is not the place to pursue these ideas further, but we
might well conclude that the abecedary speaks to, and from, the
most lasting aspects of the interaction between people and each
other, and people and the conditions of planetary existence. And
those, after all and whatever else, are the ultimate topics of the
poetry we usually most value.

*

Now to maybe more workaday considerations. One can see the
force of John Ruskin's contention that a fuller education is to be
had from perusing ten pages of writing with minute care than from
reading several books casually. We asked earlier, what sort of thing
is the abecedary? By now, surely, we may insist that it has features;
it is not merely a set of anodyne marks that do our communicating
but with no presence of their own. We also suggested the abecedary
is "rather like" grains of sand, leaves in the forest, and so on; but
one might also note its place in what Bergson called the *duree*; time
as something we strive against. As an invention, subject in part to
its culture's way of using it, the abecedary is not timeless. But, invented so long ago, it shares to some degree the status of timeless
things. The abecedary is at least something like, comparable with,
land, sky, thought, love, perhaps death, in its constancy. Knife,
wheel, cloth, and door often also seem to transcend routine or casual time. On a biogeneticist view of reality this places letters,
knives, cloth, and the rest not so far away from ears, legs, nostrils,
and other human-grafted implements as similarly perennial. As Steven Pinker has put it, language is an instinct, but an instinct to acquire an art (Pinker 1995, 15). It is an interesting inference.

This is the physical medium the poet uses. In matching vision or
emotion to the language that evokes it and may have first suggested
it, the poet steers, strokes, caresses, eases, nudges, cajoles, bullies,
invites, forces, or tricks each letter into place, to achieve the effect
of inevitability that enduring works of art possess. Here, written
sign and in-the-head echo merge. This may be barely conscious, but
many daily actions are the same. We don't even notice, let alone
decide upon, every touch on the steering wheel, each finger-move-
ment on piano or guitar, each step on a full day's trek or hike. Yet
they are our responsibility, and overall we feel they are our achieve-

ment. Acquired skill has been defined as the capacity to do something well without noticing how. Every instant is an instance; every letter is part of the poet's work. The successful poem defies the reader or hearer to improve on a single part. Every letter counts.

Barely conscious of the many tiny distributive categories on the surface, rather the poet will be attuned to the possibilities on offer. There is the length-of-word constraint. A line would look heavy and sound weighted, or look thin and sound shrill, if every word had more than around nine letters or fewer than four or five respectively, though such can arise for special effect. There is the centrifugal/centripetal constraint, which we have now mentioned frequently. There is the "may or may not" constraint, by which a word may seem to absorb its meaning through its silhouette or individual letters, or may not, and this will probably depend on degree of precision or elusiveness. There is the across/down constraint, which modernism exploited and which holds traditionalist poets to forms like the quatrain. There are constraints of irregular spelling or uniquely shaped sign. There are the combinations of all these resources. There are the constraints of economy and excess, and of what can only be inferred askance, not written at all.

What many writers have seen as the poetic dimension of language is thus enacted at the abecedarial level. It is "the maximum foregrounding of the utterance,"[5] or, put more fully: "the object of poetry is to display the textual condition. Poetry is language that calls attention to itself, that takes its own textual activities as its ground subject . . . poetical texts operate to display their own practices, to put them forward as the subject of attention" (McGann 1991, 10–11). This doesn't demote the role of political or moral materials, nor, one might add, the imagistic. Rather, poetry merges with those very things by its practice. Roman Jakobson's famous if technical definition was that "the poetic function projects the principle of equivalence from the axis of selection into the axis of combination."[6] In simpler terms, and confined here to this book's topic, lexicon and syntax are poetically arranged as much from what the abecedary is as from what lexicon and syntax are, too. The implication is that poets have led in putting the abecedary to work in its own kind, as that cuts across or blends in with image, feeling, and meaning. We now need to look in some detail at how certain poets have wielded the abecedary as part of their medium. They are chosen from the last four centuries, beginning roughly in the period where our account in part 1 finished and ending up at the twentieth century.

And so we turn to the poets.

III

The Abecedary in the Poets

AND SO WE TURN TO THE POETS. IF POETRY IS THE LITERARY ART that most foregrounds the medium of language, then it should be of interest to see how far poetry uses and foregrounds the aspects of language and the abecedary we have just discerned. That is the aim of this part 3. We need a couple of preliminaries. The first concerns poetry itself, which moves to a kind of independence when printing is invented. The second is our reasons for choosing these particular five poets.

The invention of printing, in broad historical terms, preceded and thus allowed the four hundred years of poetry that, through the work of five poets, this part will broadly consider. Poetry is a special kind of writing, and when it entered the age of print, its inner compulsion had to accommodate to the new technology. But in so doing it opened up vast possibilities through the abecedary itself. The very reductionism of printing—of many handwritings to one if not from highly ornate to simple—gradually forced the poets' sensibilities outward. Different scripts such as uncial, carolingian, gothic, and humanistic had already brought some degree of standardizing, but the first printing styles are still the basis of our modern lettering. The question then might be of how poets were to go on varying their work when calligraphy found its idiosyncratic but unchanging continuity—the constant basis of any one society's established canon—no longer acceptable. As Barry Powell has put it: "An important instrument of the magico-religious use of writing in opposing change is calligraphy, meant to stir an emotional, primarily aesthetic, response in the beholder. Calligraphy is indifferent at best and sometimes hostile to a need to facilitate thought or communicate information" (Powell 1991, 108). That is to say, it renders an already fixed sacred text in a form suitable to its revered status. Printing standardizes, but in that very fact it is a great liberation for poets, too.

David Olsen's views on writing, already cited, can be related to this issue. In answering the question of why intention was omitted from language before writing was invented—why, that is, intention wasn't built into the sounds themselves, as well as into gestures, accent, and so on—he cites the illocutionary force itself, "the most primitive part of language" (Olsen 1994, 113). But poetry itself is usually seen as the most primitive part of language. As we saw in part 2, one outcome of the abecedary's equability is to wrap the intention and the result into the same expression; that is part of its function. But poems are just such writings, for they declare no intention external to the poem itself. Again then the poet draws on writing's physical nature—and the aspects of physicality—within the initial inspiration and then the development of that within the poem, too. As Olsen repeatedly insists, writing when first invented presents "only some aspects of what a speaker has said" (60). With speech the illocutionary force, the gut thrust, is in the stress, tone, accent, and body-language of the speaker. So if the poet, like everyone else, lacks this dimension in writing, and his/her actual starting point is writing itself, then writing's own features have both need and opportunity to move into that vacated gap, and become part of the final meaning directly. Barry Powell also added this point. "Writing, in sum, attracts to itself complexes of emotional meanings unconnected directly with facilitating thought or communicating information" (Powell 1991, 108). In the context of a particular and epochal case, "The moment of recording of the *Iliad* and the *Odyssey* is also the moment of their creation" (189). The achievement of the poem is its final writing, and that alone. How do our far later poets handle this? Is it the very basis of their poetry's possibility? More and more the poets of the past few hundred years aspired to produce a poem sui generis; not just a recording, however inventively and vividly, of a society's established stories and myths, but rather ones invented and imagined by the poet himself. This comes out in John Milton's radical rewriting of *Genesis*; in George Herbert's wrestling with Scripture rather than any straight—if poetic—presentation of Scripture; in William Wordsworth's overt adoption of the first person—his own self but poetically transformed—as his topic;[1] in Emily Dickinson's utterly new and unique expressions, with which it seems nothing else we have can be compared; and in T. S. Eliot's total revision of how poetry can be written at all. One key point here is that once printing appears, poets can read all the time, and much of their incentive comes from that exercise.

For Alberto Manguel an important moment is the increase of education, that is to say the teaching and learning of letters and so the interpretation of writing, in the fourteenth and fifteenth centuries.

But these too were the eras of Johannes Gutenberg (c1395–1438) and in England William Caxton (1422–91), and the invention therefore of movable type and the first printing presses. The spread of printing led to widening practices of interpretation. Over decades, pupils gradually came to be taught the contents of texts; then their authorized interpretation; then the possibility of many interpretations; and finally the idea that readers could find their own readings. All this pushed the poets of the last four hundred years outward in creativity, to discover more of their own things to say and more ways of saying them. They decreasingly transcribed established belief or legend, and increasingly responded to the changing world: industry, technology, new agriculture, the mingling of the religious with the secular, a psychologized philosophy, world travel, new colonies, and science. Putting that alongside Powell's view cited, that "writing attracts to itself complexes of emotional meanings unconnected directly with facilitating thought or communicating information," this must mean that the abecedary itself became more and more subject to poetic invention, more and more part of what the poet wielded as medium.

Now to the choice of poets. These were somewhat intuitive, and this poetry has played some part in the present writer's own life and work: so much should be acknowledged at the outset. But we can be more considered than that. The choice must not beg questions about the aspect of the subject in hand. The main criterion was variety; but variety itself can be measured in various ways. First, there are obvious background criteria by which to secure such variety; occupation, genre, dates, and so on. The bald facts may seem dull and hardly relevant to our language's alphabet; but, given the subliminal nature of universal connection overall, they may still be worth stating. By occupation the five poets, in the order treated in the next few chapters, were a Church of England priest, a parliamentary secretary, a full-time poet of nature (but also Distributor of Stamps), a domestic recluse, and a London bank official (later publisher's editor). By nation and region we have two Americans— one took British citizenship—and three Britishers; these comprise (in order again) an England-Wales borderer, a Londoner, an English Lakelander, an American New Englander, and an American Southerner of Northern ancestry. By gender and family there are four married men and an unmarried woman; Milton and Wordsworth both had several children while Herbert and Eliot were childless, although Herbert virtually adopted Katharine, his orphaned niece. By education, Herbert, Milton, and Wordsworth were all Cambridge-educated, and Eliot was a graduate of Harvard and Oxford. Dickinson briefly attended Mount Holyoke Seminary, but also came from a highly literate family that had strong associations with the university of Amherst. By social rank and politics? It depends what you count and at what periods of their lives. George Herbert was a liberal-conservative of aristocratic birth, John Milton a lower-middle-class but public-school-educated radical. William Wordsworth's middle-class background took him from young revolutionary to high monarchist, and T. S. Eliot was a staunch Tory of well-reared background all his life. Emily Dickinson alone eludes convenient political categories, even that of feminism. Finally religion, and here the complication is that any pre-twentieth-century poet of necessity lived in a milieu before that of high secularism. Given this reservation, clearly Herbert, Milton, and Eliot were still religious poets as that phrase is normally understood. Although Wordsworth shifted somewhat in later years, both he and Dickinson found the visionary and metaphysical largely in moving outward from the natural world rather than via the traditional Scriptures or ecclesiastical institutions.

I do believe that such features crucially form the aura in which a poetics in all its detail is nurtured. Such is the mainstream historicism of our critical times. But it is seldom easy to trace the routes by which the process travels. As Wordsworth once asked, in comparable enough context, "Who . . . shall point as with a wand and say / 'This portion of the river of my mind / Came from yon fountain?'" (*Prelude* 1805, 2:213–15). In any event the poetic gift, whatever that is, may not be tied down by such general and social categories. Psychological dispositions, bodily characteristics, genetic data, and chance life-events all sully or enrich the picture further, perhaps in the end invisibly. But we have been trying, up till now, to reveal more in the abecedary than meets the eye scanning the page; and in the chapters that follow, certain things seem to emerge, and in every case. The raft of dispositions granted to or accruing for each poet gets into the written text as much as the musical score or rectangle of canvas seems to exude, or secrete, similar wider and deeper origins.

Even so, the crucial choices must also lie in the kinds of poetry each produced, backed by the prevailing genre and conventions of their respective eras. Again then; we have a writer of short religious poems and devotional hymns; an epic poet (our chapter deals only with *Paradise Lost*); the author of numerous first-person Romantic effusions; an eccentric acid lyricist of unique genius; and a founder-Modernist who modified into more limpid mode in later years. The chapter on Wordsworth is different from the others, for we subject a single though longish poem to a microscopic analysis of, in effect, every letter the poem contains. The special reasons for choosing *Tintern Abbey* are given at the start of that chapter.

As far as any five poets could, the range given by these selections seems likely to cover most of the abecedarial possibilities. But the criteria listed above also point to why we chose each poet individually from those of similar period or type. Herbert was preferred to John Donne because—as well as for his lovely lyrics—conveniently Herbert exploits the abecedary deliberately. His religious intensity is as great as Donne's, but his concern with the sacred Word is different from Donne's passionate sexual love, and tendency to take the period's vogue for metaphysical imagery to extreme lengths. Milton had no serious contenders as an epic poet. Edmund Spenser's *Faerie Queene* contains such a wealth of diverse material phenomenologically presented that it could have been a distraction. *Paradise Lost* by contrast has been a byword—sometimes notoriously—for poetic consistency, and its power stands alone. The Wordsworthian mode is unique among the Romantic poets. The Romantic first-person effusion was clearly interesting for its own reasons. But poets of such texture, no matter their period, are more likely to ignore the alphabet they use, and so Wordsworth was a good way of testing the view that the abecedary is necessarily exploited whether the poet thinks of it or not. From a mainly but not wholly male-dominated half millennium it seemed accurate to include one woman, no more no less. Like Milton, Emily Dickinson had few challengers. In her chapter we consider the way nineteenth-century women poets perforce followed the male poets' models. It took extreme originality to disturb that trend in the way Dickinson's extraordinary poems did. T. S. Eliot was preferred to Ezra Pound as—despite the length of Pound's *Cantos*—the more varied poet, and as one whose work, highly experimental as it was, still drew on his deepest personal preoccupations. If Pound attained the Modernist quest for impersonality more successfully, it was (to use his own term) programmatically so; his interest in typography and allied subjects was great, but that fact itself affects his work perhaps too much from the outside.

There is a hiatus, though, in the periods selected. There are two seventeenth-century poets, none from the eighteenth, two of the nineteenth, and one of the twentieth, with none from the later part of that century. That last point is shortly justified by an instinct to avoid getting too close to our own times; but the missing eighteenth century may need more explanation. The problem, if it is one, lay in the dominance of the heroic couplet in that period. It seemed, intuitively, that the flattish mathematics of that form might limit what was abecedarially possible, and even interesting. In case that is a mistake there is a brief appendix on Alexander Pope and Oliver Goldsmith (appendix 4).

But the key issue must be how far the poets chosen exploit the abecedary overtly or more surreptitiously; and that pairing might equally mean deliberately or subconsciously—or indeed unknowingly. It was important to select a wide range of forms, styles, and modes of writing, and not be tempted to pick just those who most overtly use the alphabet for their purposes. If we had dwelt solely on Herbert, Gerard Manley Hopkins, David Jones, e e cummings, and perhaps even—stretching genre—James Joyce, it would not only beg questions totally, it would also narrow our attention away from the countless highly elusive ways in which the abecedary does get used. Many such are hidden in both everyday vernacular and the polite mannerisms of formal convention. All poets exploit the abecedary, knowingly or otherwise. In a key sense they do so equally, no matter how much one seems to more than another on the surface. For readers who would have liked more special attention to an overtly abecedarial poet, appendix 3 provides a few notes on the letters that make up Hopkins' poem *The Wreck of the Deutschland*.

Maybe this point is also why we can't easily place the poets along any sort of continuum in this respect. In any event we do not want to anticipate our readings of each poet here. George Herbert leads the field by being a clear and highly skilled player with letters, and he refers to this compulsion here and there in the poems. In *The Waste Land*, T. S. Eliot broke up and rearranged European texts and lines in ways that couldn't fail to shatter them into their component parts, too, though how far he thought of it so is a different question. After that it is more difficult. John Milton's powerful and (as we have called it) centrifugal lexicon vies with Emily Dickinson's frequent abecedarial quirkiness, as to which of them seem to wear the abecedary most on their sleeves. By contrast William Wordsworth's 'Tintern Abbey,' like most of main Wordsworth, appears unconcerned with overt philologies. His "language of men," as his 1798 preface put it, survives in his own philosophical meditations even if the "man" thus evinced is evidently no longer an unlettered peasant but educated and middle-class. Eliot's *Four Quartets* is the same if for different reasons. Within the poem he repeatedly asks how his language is getting along, and he unwittingly expresses abecedarial equability in that *Four Quartets*, too, as we shall see, walks round and round an unattained and invisible center. Neither Wordsworth nor the Eliot of the *Four Quartets* are much troubled by the abecedary consciously; I doubt that it much occurred to Wordsworth as an item of linguistic interest, though it may have. And yet none of this need disturb us. This continuum, first and last, expresses the issue of how far exploitation of the abecedary is overt or casual. It is not a range from much exploitation to little, for such exploitation occurs universally.

11

George Herbert

Love bade me welcome: yet my soul drew back,
    Guiltie of dust and sinne.
But quick-ey'd Love, observing me grow slack
    From my first entrance in,
Drew nearer to me, sweetly questioning,
    If I lack'd any thing.

A guest, I answer'd, worthy to be here:
    Love said, You shall be he.
I the unkinde, ungratefull? Ah my deare,
    I cannot look on thee.
Love took my hand, and smiling did reply,
    Who made the eyes but I?

Truth Lord, but I have marr'd them: let my shame
    Go where it doth deserve.
And know you not, sayes Love, who bore the blame?
    My deare, then I will serve.
You must sit down, sayes Love, and taste my meat.
    So I did sit and eat.

THIS IS "LOVE (III)," ONE OF GEORGE HERBERT'S BEST-KNOWN AND best-loved poems. Though perhaps not written last, it comes last in his collection *The Temple* and has a maturity in that the torments found elsewhere in his writing are here laid to rest.

A traveler arrives tired, dirty, and downcast at an inn and is fed and comforted. But equally, a person of low self-esteem and strong guilt-feelings discovers that calm can ensue from another's love or a perceived spiritual love. These two versions lie over each other, as though written on tracing paper; the two become one in an abecedarially equable text.

Herbert is a poet of both turbulence and peace, but "Love (iii)" is exceptional. There are other serene poems, but usually the turbulence predominates. This part of the present book, if rather briefly in each case, will touch the historical background of each poet; and the account we left at the end of part 1 ended on some of the conflicts and anguish in religious and political life, when Herbert's vocation was also practiced. Something, though not much, is known of how they affected him personally. He was born in 1593 and died in 1633. Of course, the Elizabethan settlement left an easement. But the civil war lay ahead, barely a decade after his death, and being close to the court of King James I when young must have deepened his sense of those violent oppositions, which seem to convert to psychic energy in his poems.

Such turmoils pressured the individual clergy, for they were about ecclesiastical practice as that symbolized God's authority. That authority was claimed by the English monarch, by the European dissenters in line of Martin Luther and Jean Calvin, and by Rome. Litmus tests for this question included the status of bread and wine in the sacrament; the wearing or discarding of priestly vestments; bareness or ornament in church buildings and their contents; whether clergy could marry; and exact or more liberal interpretation of the Bible, including whether it could be translated. Depending on one's viewpoint, such practices were or weren't the "outward and visible sign of an inward and heavenly grace"; and to pronounce on them, from either side, was to insist on where truth lay in relation to its earthly embodiments. Right or wrong stances toward what counted could make the difference between salvation and death, both in this world and the next.

And despite the myth, not wholly unfounded, of the "peaceful country parson," Herbert's talents and connections were such that he could no more be free of the time's pressures than could anyone else. Much of his poetry may have been written before he went to the rural living at Bemerton. University Orator at Cambridge for many years, he later briefly stood close enough to the throne to entertain "Court-hopes," at least on Isaac Walton's admittedly unreliable testimony. Yet his mother Magdalen Herbert married Sir John Danvers, an eventual regicide, though the marriage happened late in the poet's own life. Henry, brother of John Donne who closely befriended Magdalen and perhaps Herbert, too, was imprisoned for harboring a priest and died in Newgate. Herbert's own elder brother Henry was also imprisoned, although this was censured by King James himself.[2] Exactly why Herbert suddenly opted for ordination into the priesthood in 1624 is also still obscure.

Yet with Herbert, one seldom feels that these dilemmas—body and blood of Christ or not, Bible as literal truth or not, and so on—

were based solely on fear of reprisal, depending on whose side you were on. John Donne's dilemma, between punishment in this world by remaining a Catholic or in the next by becoming Anglican, often led to thoughts of suicide (Carey 1981, 51–57): Herbert felt such problems more compromisingly. The poems boil up with inner agonised struggles born of the very complexities into which they got twisted. One issue overlapped another; the anxiety, the expression of it, the emotion about that expression; all come from a set of personal oppositions that most of the poems strain and writhe to embody verbally. Here we have abecedarial equability in force already. These oppositions were the "contradictions" and "contrarieties" of the poem "The Crosse," which Herbert typically resolves in four short words at the close to match the cross's four extensions: *Thy will be done*. But as his more experimental poems show, his language had a dark center too. More than most poets, Herbert needed abecedarial stability. Many of the dilemmas were insoluble.

There was Scripture, for example. According to Nicholas Ferrar's preface to *The Temple*, Herbert said of the Scriptures that "he would not part with one leaf thereof, for the whole world, if it were offered him in exchange."[3] But it brought its own nest of pressures. A century after Tyndale's martyrdom, the Bible could be liberally interpreted, and translated. But as Chana Bloch has said, Herbert's obsession was also to enter it, remake its stories, and thus fragment it just as his experimental poems break up individual words.[4] As to icons and images, Herbert's instinct was to domesticate, to see "furnishings" as not just dangerous distractions but also as the humble comforts by which, in church and home, one is surrounded. This is seen for example in the poems "Church-monuments," "Mortification," and "The Banquet." This domestication in turn contrasts the public world of state and politics, country rather than town, even though Herbert is never a pastoral poet of field and shepherd. And finally the body-spirit dilemma of all traditional renouncers of this world comes out in Herbert as body-centered. The body is more than carnal; it is the arena in which everything is fought out. If meals recall eating the body of Christ, then how eating should be valued becomes a problem, too. According to John Aubrey, Herbert's marriage hastened his death, for his wife Jane Danvers (Aubrey's kinswoman) was "a handsome *bona roba* and ingeniose"—a lovely and intelligent woman with red cheeks. The word *lust* appears in Herbert's poetry sixteen times.

"Love (iii)" feels like a sigh of weary relief after such burdens. It is a near-perfect poem in which every letter counts. Take the letter hhhhh. In the first stanza hhhhh occurs only once, and that in the final word "thing": *If I lack'd any thing*. Yet in the first three lines of the next stanza it appears six times:

> A guest, I answer'd, *worthy* to be *here*:
> Love said, You *shall* be *he*.
> I *the* unkinde, ungratefull? *Ah* my deare . . .

Perhaps the gentle aspirate gives Love itself something to match in loving empathy. The sad poet makes up for what was "lack'd" at the start by that mild ejaculation, *Ah my deare*, which feels like a truth. Orally it varies, but to say that the hhhhh in *Ah* is "silent" would miss the point, for the word itself is the aspirate sigh. Hhhhh equally softens the sssss and ttttt here by its soft breath through them.

The letter bbbbb appears ten times. Curiously these come in five pairs:

> Love *bade* me welcome: yet my soul drew *back* . . .
> *But* quick-ey'd Love, *observing* me grow slack . . .
> . . . worthy to *be here* . . . Love said, You shall *be he*.
> Who made the eyes *but I*? . . . Truth Lord, *but I* have marr'd them . . .
> And know you not, sayes Love, who *bore* the *blame*?

Again the poem is unimaginable without its (sometimes inner) pronunciation, but again the bbbbb in *back* is not a mere instruction to make the noise "b". It also engenders the emotion, whatever that is for each reader, to feel the answer to the same mark/sound in *bade*. *Back* is the poet's response to Love's bidding in *bade*, while Love in turn answers the poet's reluctance to be guest and so *be here*, by telling the poet to *be he* and so be both. The double *but I* reinforces the contrast in both assonance and meaning between *made* and *marr'd*; "bore the blame" is straight alliteration; and with *But . . . observing* the two words come first in their respective phrases. Consciously or not, Herbert uses bbbbb to help reach points of equilibrium—and he uses it for nothing else.

The letter ppppp (bbbbb unvoiced) appears only once in the poem, in *reply*: "smiling did reply." Maybe it answers the equally sole qqqqq of "sweetly questioning," the two phrases so beautifully balanced. But it is more, for gentle human interchange is this poem's very arena, enacted in the dusty forecourt of an inn perhaps, and this letter-sound ppppp may have been kept to nudge the idea into consciousness at that one moment. It may also adjust the unusually frequent yyyyy, which appears in all but four of the poem's lines. The ever-present sense of *my* and *you* is backed by *yet, sayes, worthy*, and so on, and the proximity of *ey'd* and *eyes* to those uses, deepening the sense of intimate personal interaction. The letter vvvvv is also written unusually often by standards of English frequency. Of its ten appearances, six are in the name *Love*. But this merits a gentle echo it seems, strong itself but not distracting. So, apart from the innocuous *have*, the other three vvvvv-words are of lengthened vowel and cognate stem: *observing, deserve, serve*. It restrains, dignifies, and aligns them.

Aaaaa appears thirty-two times. They gradually increase, with eight, eleven, and thirteen coming in each stanza respectively, woven into a texture of sound and meaning as this happens. In the first stanza aaaaa is often strongly stressed: *bade, back, slack, lack'd*. Evidently it works in tandem here with kkkkk. But after that it has a burden of sadness. *A guest, I answer'd . . . ungratefull? Ah my deare, I cannot . . . Love took my hand. . . .* Then comes the sorrowful contrast already mentioned between *made* and *marr'd*, leading to the gently conceded guilt in *shame, blame*. Aaaaa wins recompense at the close though, at the heart of the very embodiment of sustenance: *. . . and taste my meat. / So I did sit and eat.* These last two phrases will prove key to the poem.

In many poems the letter ddddd accrues the finality one would expect from English's main past-tense marker. Here it is the permanence of arrival. So many phrases, however short, end with, accentuate or move to a ddddd-word: *. . . If I lack'd anything . . . I the unkinde . . . Ah my deare . . . Love took my hand . . . Truth Lord, but I have marr'd . . . Go where it doth deserve . . . You must sit down, says Love . . .* Ddddd appears in every line of the poem bar one, much higher than its standard usual rate.

Lllll as "owner" of Love—the first letter owns the word—itself gets lexical support throughout via terms of contrasting spiritual charge. There is *welcome, sweetly, Lord* (Love's only other name), but also *guiltie, slack, ungratefull, blame*, and one or two others.

Eeeee is ubiquitous in English; but in "Love (iii)" the letter ooooo, rather, is key provider of level stretches of one-vowel presence. The poem begins, *Love bade me welcome: yet my soul . . .* ; thirteen letters of the alphabet with no repeat bar eeeee until the lllll in *welcome*, but even so followed quickly by first entrances for yyyyy, ttttt, and uuuuu. But ooooo is the guiding vowel, making smooth transition into several more ooooo-run phrases: *. . . Love, observing me grow . . . I cannot look on . . .* (followed at once by) *Love took . . .* (then later) *Go where it doth deserve. / And know you not, says Love, who bore . . . ?* Eeeee does this seldom: *Drew nearer to me . . . My deare, then I will serve.* Ooooo's perfect circle aids serenity in a poem with its strong undertow of past guilt and present fatigue.

The letter iiiii, with quite different resonance, seems tied to this feeling. The poet is *guiltie of dust and sinne*, we are abruptly told, yet in the preceding opening line *Love bade me welcome: yet my soul drew back*, iiiii has not appeared at all. This *guiltie . . . sinne* is riposted quickly in the flash of *quick-ey'd Love*, enhanced in that the vowel is not repeated in that line again. The commonly noted intermerging of "I" and "eye" joins the general vowel iiiii, enabling the sense of sin to tie with that of lack, *If I lack'd any thing . . . I the unkinde. . . .* This guilt gets strong and "kind" reassurance in Love's answer; *smiling did reply*, where the visually different yyyyy in "reply" is made fully cognate with iiiii, because iiiii's triple in "smiling did" has been so recent.

The nasal letters move in and out of this texture. Mmmmm finds due employment in the regular *me* and *my*, but it too shifts from *welcome/smiling* to the guilt of *marr'd, shame, blame* before resolving itself in *meat*, the sustenance it earns with aaaaa. Nnnnn crops up whenever relations between one thing and another are especially sinuous: *observing, entrance in, nearer, questioning, lack'd any thing*, and so on. But this is sharpened by the connection with the double-lettered *sinne* itself, emphasized in the double confession *I the unkinde, ungratefull—?* to which the answer is that Love took my *hand*, and that word bears the line's stress. Neither nasal darkens the lucidity of the final line: *So I did sit and eat*, and only one does in the line on that meal's recipient, *A guest, I answer'd, worthy to be here.*

The poem's last line turns out to be more significant the more we consider it. *Meat* has been previously balanced in the line by *must*, which contains the two vital and key letters sssss and ttttt. For many critics the poem turns on this; it is based on a hidden pun "host," a term not actually present but which means both the landlord of the inn and the bread consecrated in the Eucharist. The word's other connotations of "army" and "enemy" *(hostile)* contrast pointedly the pervasive sense of a love-encounter that the poem embodies. The combination sssss-ttttt has been run through the poem from the outset, and it is cumulative. *Guiltie of dust and sinne*—not one of Herbert's sixteen uses of *lust*, then, and the presence/absence of that word in "dust" sharpens the attention at once.[5] Then via the *first* entrance, the need for a *guest* and the *sweetly questioning* welcomer this *-st* form viscerally transposes into the group of echoing words in the poem's last lines.

Must begins it; the injunction is to receive the ultimate goodness at Love's table and it is *tasted* there. But the final line *So I did sit and eat*, seeming to end Herbert's entire quest, may derive from his early upbringing. It is a modification of *cynhanedd sain*, one of the standard forms in Welsh regular verse.[6] The form is a + ab + b, with *sit* combining the sssss of *so* and the ttttt of *eat*. This structure varies the pattern of the phrase wherein lay the traveler's trouble, *Guiltie of dust and sin*, where the form was b + ab + a. So the sacramental *host* is verbally present, as in some way or another it is, or longs to be, in all Herbert's poetry.

We have looked at fifteen letters already. That is two-thirds of the quota, for jjjjj, xxxxx and zzzzz don't appear at all. The poet is sensitive to every word, which slot into place as though lubricated with oil of the subtlest refinement. Helen Vendler's summary seems to strive for Herbert's own abecedarial feeling. "Like some decorous minuet, the poem leads its characters through steps in a delicate hovering: a pace forward, a hanging back, a slackening, a drawing near, a lack, a fullness, a dropping of the eyes, a glance, a touch, a reluctance, a proffer, a refusal, a demurrer insistence—and then the final seating at the feast."[7] Naturally, some poems succeed more than others, but one still feels Herbert working every single letter; he is never unwatchful of this, however unconscious it may be or habitual it has become. The question is of how and why he did so.

"Love (iii)" is one of a handful of Herbert poems in which complete calm—albeit here from fatigue—is in place before the poem starts. In such poems the letters form an equally serene matrix, most evident perhaps in the poem "Vertue," whose content and mode as well as title let it evince the abecedary's virtuality discussed above. We can't comment in detail here, but the reader might care to try reading "Vertue" by a method that brings out both its unique qualities and those of letters generally (the poem appears in appendix 2 along with "The Elixer"). Its unusually equable nature makes it perfect for this. If we read it a number of times, the first time gently stressing one particular letter, the second time another, the third time a third, and so on, we reveal a subtly different facet each time. The letters that most make "Vertue," I would say, are vvvvv itself, ccccc, ddddd, lllll, mmmmm, and sssss.

But in very different poems the first agony stands alone. As said, in Herbert this is far more commonly the way. He is tortured, rants and raves, cries aloud, abortively seeks God, and changes tack in bitterness and self-abasement. The sardony can be painful: *Joy, I did lock thee up: but some bad man / Hath let thee out again* ("The bunch of grapes"), or plain screwed up: *O spitefull bitter thought! / Bitterly spitefull thought!* ("Assurance"). Elsewhere it ails (*With sick and famisht eyes . . .* : "Longing"), is vigorous (*I struck the board, and cry'd, No more. / I will abroad . . .* : "The Collar"), or rueful (*Kill me not ev'ry day, / Thou Lord of Life . . .* : "Affliction (ii)"). The desperate search for peace seems part of its own suffering, for in Augustine's restlessness Herbert found his own experience: "Thou has made us for thyself, and our heart knows no rest until it rest in Thee." As with Augustine, the compulsion to express the struggle is also its arena. Herbert tries to calm himself: *Peace mutt'ring thoughts . . .* ("Content"), *"Peace pratler, do not lowre . . .* ("Conscience"). As with Augustine, too, this very compulsion to voice one's condition finds language and the word at the visceral heart of human existence.

This turbulence marks such poetry's shape and structure as well as its overt emotion. Every poem tries out something new, some further way of deploying the contents to express the agony. Here are three examples.

The poem "Deniall" contains a spread of words of mutually exclusive or near-exclusive spelling; part of what in part 2 we called the centrifugal capability of the abecedary.

> When my devotions could not pierce
>   Thy silent eares;
> Then was my heart broken, as was my verse:
>   My breast was full of fears
>   And disorder:
>
> My bent thoughts, like a brittle bow,
>   Did flie asunder:
> Each took his way; some would to pleasures go,
>   Some to the warres and thunder
>   Of alarms.
>
> As good go any where, they say,
>   As to benumme
> Both knees and heart, in crying night and day,
>   *Come, come, my God, O come,*
>   But no hearing.
>
> O that thou shouldst give dust a tongue
>   To crie to thee,
> And then not heare it crying! all day long
>   My heart was in my knee,
>   But no hearing.

Therefore my soul lay out of sight,
Untun'd, unstrung:
My feeble spirit, unable to look right,
Like a nipt blossome, hung
Discontented.

O cheer and tune my heartlesse breast,
Deferre no time;
That so thy favours granting my request,
They and my minde may chime,
And mend my ryme.

The last rhyme in each stanza veers sideways from its preceding pairs, with a perverse skew in the repeat of *But no hearing* in stanzas 3 and 4. By contrast, the monosyllabic and italicized plea to God *Come, come, my God, O come* briefly homogenizes the terms and therefore the spelling (four mmmmms and five ooooos), and the calm at the end lies in a similar leveling: *They and my minde may chime, / And mend my ryme*. In those six mmmmms and four nnnnns Herbert murmurs himself back into calmness, takes himself down. But if that were all it might be just an exercise. What is marked, is that this glancing of one word away from another abecedary-wise, goes all through the poem, unnoticed in the gaps as well as at line-ends and key points. For example, the visual/resonant difference lies not just between *thunder* and *alarms* but between *thunder, warres*, and *some* that precede. The poem is steeped in such violent yoked juxtapositions. Again and again these pairs have almost mutually exclusive letters. *Devotions/pierce: silent/eares: heart/broken: bent/thoughts: flie/asunder: crying/benumme* (this a vertical juxtaposition): *night/day: shouldst/give: feeble/spirit: unable/look/right: nipt/blossome/hung: cheer/tune: favours/request*. The anger that "My heart was in my knee," prefiguring Eliot's decomposed Prufrock whom we never see in one piece while hearing his plaints, briefly shows what is going on throughout. In referring to Herbert's "successive fireworks of contradiction, and a mind jumping like a flea," William Empson underlined something that the writing makes, as well as conveys.[8]

In other poems a single letter runs down the poem as a kind of cable for others to gather round. The singularity is less feverish, more melancholic. "Sepulchre" is about the stone where Christ's body lay after his crucifixion. As Bloch puts it, the stone moves through the poem. First it is a cold receptacle for Christ; it is then exonerated from blame for this; we use stones for stoning people;

the ancient laws were carved in stone; etc. The vowel ooooo suffuses it all:

> O blessed bodie! Whither art thou thrown?
> No lodging for thee, but a cold hard stone?
> So many hearts on earth, and yet not one
>   Receive thee?
>
> Sure there is room within our hearts good store;
> For they can lodge transgressions by the score:
> Thousands of toyes dwell there, yet out of doore
>   They leave thee.
>
> But that which shews them large, shews them unfit.
> What ever sinne did this pure rock commit,
> Which holds thee now? Who hath indited it?
>   Of murder?
>
> Where our hard hearts have took up stones to brain thee,
> And missing this, most falsly did arraigne thee;
> Onely these stones in quiet entertain thee,
>   And order.
>
> And as of old, the law by heav'nly art
> Was writ in stone; so thou, which also art
> The letter of the word, find'st no fit heart
>   To hold thee.
>
> Yet do we still persist as we began,
> And so should perish, but that nothing can,
> Though it be cold, hard, foul, from loving man
>   Withhold thee.

The monosyllabic words, of great importance in the poem's texture, outnumber the polysyllabic by more than four to one. Among them furthermore, ooooo is fractionally more frequent than eeeee itself. Here we need a statistical paragraph for which I beg the reader's indulgence. There are 168 words in "Sepulchre." Only 32 of them, even including *quiet, brain,* and *findst,* have more than one syllable. The monosyllabic words thus total 136. Silent eeeee ending a word is not counted as a syllable; yet even so there are still 42 monosyllabic words containing the vowel ooooo and only 41 containing eeeee. A further nine contain both vowels, all of them having a silent eeeee at the end: *stone* four times (one is *stones*), *store, score, doore, lodge,* and *toyes.* And there are 44 monosyllabic words containing only the remaining vowels, aaaaa, iiiii, uuuuu, or yyyyy. This makes up the 136 monosyllabic words. The count of vowels in all the poem's words, including polysyllabic, is eeeee 88, ooooo 66, aaaaa 41, iiiii 40, and uuuuu 17. Ooooo is very high there on the normal counts for English. Although eeeee dominates as usual, that makes ooooo's count among the monosyllabic words alone, all the more striking.

Such analysis may seem pretty desiccated. The point is that in English the poem's effect would be almost impossible without deliberate contrivance, even if such is a degree unconscious. If as Chana Bloch contends the stone's movement "remarkably, does not strike us as a succession of dizzying leaps" (Bloch 1985, 59), it is because Herbert is putting stoniness before us in the circular ooooo itself, kept purer by the emotion yet gravity of monosyllabic slowness. I believe that writing and sound here support each other. Monosyllabic writing has a cold spacing on the page that the perfect circularity of the ooooo, repeated again and again, mingles with. Orally the ooooo lends constancy to sadness; it is a continuous level lay. It is so different from the irate and crusty look of "Deniall." In "Sepulchre" the ooooo-texture is enhanced in the poem's first two and last three lines. The lexicon there of *not one, room, good store, lodge, score, doore, rock, holds, stones* (repeated), *order, old, word, hold,* and the rest needs to be read in context to be experienced.

Finally, here is just one stanza from the poem "Ephes. 4.30," a more complex case of consonants struggling with each other and achieving only a knotted articulation:

> And art thou grieved, sweet and sacred Dove,
>   When I am sowre,
>   And crosse thy love?
> Grieved for me? the God of strength and power
>   Griev'd for a worm, which when I tread,
>   I passe away and leave it dead?

In the poem, a play on the title's biblical verse, the consonants ggggg, sssss, wwwww, mmmmm, vvvvv, and ddddd are deployed to saturation point. Three-quarters of the stanza's words contain at least one of these letters, the only remaining words being the tiny particles *I* (three times), *thy, for* (twice), *art, thou, the, of, a,* and *it.*

Five of these six letters form chains of consonants, oral connections, and little visual maps that knot the tortuous meanings of the poem together. *Grieved* repeatedly weighs in on three of these letters; for sssss the common double-letter binds *crosse* to *passe*, while *sweet, sacred*, and *sowre* tie each other in also. The past-tense ddddd goes from *grieved* right past the consonantal strength of *strength* and through *God* to the deadness of *dead*, an eerie quality of ddddd we shall find in other poets.

It leaves the sixth letter, mmmmm, isolated. Mmmmm appears only three times and in three very short words. It shares a word, once, with the two near-vowels wwwww and rrrrr, and otherwise only with vowels and itself; and the result is a bleak sentencing of self-abasement: *me, am, worm*. And this seems the key to the stanza. For it is not an exegesis of the Ephesians text ("Grieve not the holy Spirit of God. . . .") but a response to it. This happens in light of the poet's disturbed sense that he both causes such grief and yet, apparently, is valuable enough that he can do so, and therefore wretchedly undercuts that value by being "sowre." His response to this sour quality then compounds it by his being a "worm" (*me, am, worm*) via the letter mmmmm. The word *worm* itself appears in the New Testament at only one point. This is not in the letter to Ephesus, but in the Gospel passage where Christ tells his followers to cut off their feet and hands if they offend, and to tie a stone round their necks and jump into the sea rather than be unkind to a defenseless child. This verse is twice more repeated, *where their worm dieth not, and the fire is not quenched* (Mark 9:44, 46, 48). Herbert probably had it in mind when he wrote the poem. The syntactical parallel of "Grieved for me / Griev'd for a worm" unites the mouthing of the mmmmm-exclusive *me/worm* (with *am*) as one in a visceral as well as a mental event.

Herbert's poetry contains such variety—such is his distributive saturation—that one would need dozens of cases to show what forms self-abasement and peace could take. He seldom repeated a technique. The poem "Nature" has a proliferation of words containing double-letters: *full, rebellion, travell, suggestions, will, bubbles, smooth, rugged, saplesse, fitter*, and (twice) *thee*. In context their symmetrical geometry seems to yearn for human artifact to counter nature, our own and that of the green world, in its fallen state.

"Constancie" sets up a pillar of capitalized WWWWWs in a "who" stem vertically down the page, indented to open each of the seven stanzas. Looking at the poem, it is impossible to miss the logo of durable strength needed to thwart the lifelong temptations each stanza then relates:

> Who is the honest man?
> Whose honestie is not . . .

> Who, when great trials come, . . .
> Whom none can work or wooe . . .
> Who never melts or thaws . . .
> Who, when he is to treat . . .
> Whom nothing can procure . . .

There is not an exception in sight. "Faith" by contrast plays around the letter ttttt but with less certainty, as though constancy is a fixed state while faith must forever be on the watch. "Sinnes round" is rendered impotent and perhaps onanistic (line 12) by repeating the last line of stanzas 1 and 2 as the first of stanzas 2 and 3, and then ending where it began, with the opening line "Sorrie I am, my God, sorrie I am" also ending stanza 3. The word *lewd*, mentioned earlier for its very rare vowel-plus-wwwww/ddddd, jumps right up out of all this into our faces. Refrains on paper rather than recited force the abecedary right on us, for we have to choose their degree of permanence as to whether we reread them fully, or merely see them again.

"Clasping of Hands" approaches pure personal relationship with one-tone transparency:

> Lord, thou art mine, and I am thine,
> If mine I am: and thine much more,
> Then I or ought, or can be mine.
> Yet to be thine, doth me restore;
> So that again I now am mine,
> And with advantage mine the more.

This transparency is abecedarial. Quickly, just a few more statistics. Of the 147 letters in the passage, 129 come from only 10 different letters of the alphabet. These are eeeee (19), nnnnn and ttttt (16 each), iiiii (15), aaaaa (14), mmmmm and ooooo (12 each), hhhhh (11), rrrrr (8), and ddddd (6). The remaining 16 letters thus get only 18 appearances between them. Much the usual order of English frequency is found, with only sssss and lllll dropping noticeably below their usual rankings. But the general demeanor of the passage is maintained, in that there is a sharp count-gap between the more frequent and the much fewer letters. Only rrrrr and ddddd form a small middle wedge between the higher group ending at hhhhh with eleven, and the lower group starting with ggggg and uuuuu with only three each[9]. This playing down of any exotic or centrifugal presence is paralleled in the lengths of the words. No word has more than five letters—and there are only four of those—apart from *restore* in the fourth line, and that one distinctly longer word, the strong calm *advantage* in the last line. Those two words bear a certain quiet weight, with *advantage* seeming to clinch the passage's import with its surprisingly strong consonants which, however, we aren't disposed to feel make for any upturn. Rather, and paradoxically, they confirm the direction in which the dialectic movement between speaker and Lord has been moving. Christina Rossetti, a devotee of Herbert, was to use this relentlessly monosyllabic and short-word technique in her sonnet sequence *Monna Innominata* two centuries later.

"The Collar" is a brilliant tour de force of vowel-shifts on a phonetically "I-or" base, beginning with *I struck the board, and cry'd, No more. / I will abroad* and arriving back at *My Lord* at the end. In between are a series of attempted escapes from faith's spiritual tether via every variation on these two vowels possible. *Board* turns to *rode, loose,* and *winde,* then back to *store.* Then come *restore, sure, wine, sighs, drie, corn, before,* all stressed against the contrasting vowels around them, until just before the end when *forbears* and *load* presage the inevitable return; "And I reply'd, *My Lord.*" Ddddd's common finality aids this hampering constraint.

Finally, the letter sssss feels like a Herbert signature. It saturates "Easter," the second half of "Christmas," and several other poems. So many poems begin with its hallmark:

> *As men, for fear the starres should sleep and nod*
> *False glozing pleasures, casks of happiness*
> *How sweetly doth My Master sound! My Master!*
> *Lord, I confesse my sinne is great*
> *Oh all ye, who passe by, whose eyes and minde*
> *Philosophers have measur'd mountains*
> *Rise heart; thy Lord is risen. Sing his praise*
> *Sorrie I am, my God, sorrie I am*
> *Sweet day, so cool, so calm, so bright*
> *Sweetest of sweets, I thank you: when displeasure*
> *Sweetest Saviour, if my soul*

—not to mention keynote phrases like *a glasse of blessings* in "The Pulley." Herbert's vocabulary of *Jesus, Christ, son, soul, Saviour, spirit, salvation, cross, sin, ascension, praise, sacred, psalm, rise, Sunday, Easter, saint, Satan,* and his ubiquitous *sweet* might seem coincidental. But it is noteworthy how many sssss-words in English, surprisingly, convey not the hiss of serpents but calmness and peace. *Soothe, bliss, rest, leisure, ease, hush, sleep,* and the aural *peace* itself could be countered by opposites; but the "weak regularity" of letter-potential as a resource generally may be underwritten here.

One might wonder, though, how far such means are merely the surface emanation of the confusions Herbert experienced daily and which we listed at the start of this chapter. Scripture was language as against the differently physical icons of sacrament—vestments, crucifixes, stained glass, bread, and wine—but it was also holy language as against daily language. If Herbert revered Scripture so much, how could he allow himself to enter it, modify its stories poetically, and indeed "relish" the "versing" ("The Flower") that this entailed? How could a whole poem's wordplay on "sunne" and "The Son" be other than frivolous? And just as pressingly, the icons, too, the church "furnishings" as Herbert called them, were sacred and domestic at once; the table, clothes, glass, and food of everyday life. The group of "church" poems near the start of *The Temple* focuses this other theme of Herbert's churchmanship in the contemporary and crucial Laudian-Calvinist debate as to the relative theological status of the sacraments and the Scriptures. The poem "The British Church" expresses exactly the via media Herbert seems to have opted for on the matter. He is deeply drawn, we often feel, by the things the Laud school wanted: clerical dress, stained glass, church organs, stone altar, and red wine. Indeed, even this is abecedarially expressed. When Herbert writes that *Thy glorious houshold-stuffe did me entwine* ("Affliction (i)"), the very long words almost suffocate the two little ones near the end. Yet on the status of the Sacrament he is guarded. In a poem omitted from *The Temple* as perhaps politically risky, Herbert wrote that the debate about transubstantiation, as to whether bread in Eucharist rite is truly changed into Christ's flesh or not, "concerneth bread, not mee." The Calvinist exclusive regard for the Scriptures, as containing all that is needed for salvation and not found elsewhere, may not have attracted Herbert fully, but his devotion to Scripture is written all over his poetry.

So he could revere Scripture at the very moment of raiding and changing it, and when writing about not language but physical objects, flesh, and blood. As a result he would often disrupt the very idea of a poem's sequence, so that his grapplings with language's inked embodiments on the page in front of him—his "dictionarie" as he termed it—are ensnared in the making of the poem itself. Helen Vendler is insightful as to how his instabilities may have affected his way of working. Her statement is virtually a comment on abecedarial equability in practice. "At any moment, a poem by Herbert can repudiate itself, correct itself, rephrase itself, rethink its experience, reinvent its topic"—all this within the finished poem as it appears. Yet "a different sort of poet would have written one version, felt dissatisfied with the truth or accuracy of that account, written a second, more satisfactory version, then rethought that stage, and at last produced a 'truthful' poem. . . ." (Vendler 1975, 56, 29). Perhaps these last would be such as "The Elixer," "Vertue," and "Love (iii)"; but more usually Herbert's angular efforts meant mixing it with the very substance of language itself.

For, of course, Herbert delved into the intestines of the abecedary explicitly, as though he could find there, down in the actual marks and signs, the secret of the Word they expressed. I think his famous pattern-poems and other more formally experimental work should not be overemphasized. Excessive focus on the letter is as deleterious as that on the meaning; it is the triangle of letter, resonance, and meaning that merges as poetic utterance. In fact, there are not many fully pattern-poems in *The Temple*. They draw unusual attention to abecedarial features, even by Herbert's own standards, but can hold up the full flow of meaning and emotion. However, such attempts provoked fascination as well as ridicule in the highly language-conscious seventeenth century. In *The Arte of English Poesie*, George Puttenham wrote scathingly of "emblem" poems, verbal tricks, and comparable activities. Yet he could hardly conceal his intrigue that they lie deep in the abecedary's nature, and he wrote long and detailed sections, with many illustrative drawings, about shaped poems and other forms of explicit rhetoric (Puttenham 1936, 91–112). Herbert's small group of highly visually experimental poems does reveal something about his sense of his medium, and many critics have taken them very seriously for that reason.[10]

Among these, it is less in the shape-poems like "Easter-wings" and more in those that break off letters individually that George Herbert can be seen shut in his study, examining the particles of the words he was obsessed with. In the poem "Jesu," the beloved name is written on a slab of stone that is dropped and breaks. The three pieces are inscribed "J", "ES," and "U", which the poet reads to himself as *I ease you*. But this is more than pun; the broken stone is the poet's broken heart. The poem begins uncompromisingly: "J E S U is in my heart, his sacred name / Is deeply carved there," and even when the heart is shattered, Christ's saving power still offers spiritual help. The poem "Paradise" is about the care of a garden by pruning it. Herbert mimetically prunes the rhyme-word in each three-line stanza: *grow-row-ow(e), charm-harm-arm, start-tart-art*, and so on; a kind of part-repetition. Paradise seems impotent in its very perfection, lacking the sinful vigor of the real if fallen world.

The poem "Coloss 3.3" writes a version of that text down the poem diagonally. The poem can be understood only visually. From *My Life Is Hid In Him That Is My Treasure* we find *My* beginning the first line, *Life* the second word in the second line, *Is* third in the third line, and so on. Of course, this is mimetic of "hid." The line has to be discerned by a conscious act from the poem that contains it. It is an extreme form of what always happens in Herbert; the abecedary hovers and, in the present case, when physically moved can shift its meanings without changing its letters. So it embodies and enacts rather than merely shows the abecedary's own nature as physical and virtual as well as just a piece of glass through which to see the hermeneutic. As Helen Vendler has put it more generally; by such poems "it is shown that by linguistic manipulation (pronouncing sounds in one case, interpreting initials in another) the speaker may come to wisdom" (Vendler 1975, 68). The parallel with the Kabbalah is obvious.

Cognate with this interest is Herbert's absorption with proverbs. Proverbs deploy abecedarial fewness overtly and were popular and valued in Herbert's time. Randle Cotgrave's *Dictionarie of the French and English Tongue* (1611), much used by George and his brother Henry, uses numerous proverbs to illustrate colloquial language. For the Geneva Bible of 1560 a proverb is "a grave and noble sentence, worthy to be kept in memorie."[11] The circle of Herbert's friend Nicholas Ferrar compiled a list of nearly five hundred proverbs, while Herbert himself collected well over a thousand in *Outlandish Proverbs selected by Mr G.H.*, published in 1640 after his death. Herbert later wrote in *The Country Parson*: "exhortations, which though earnest, yet often die with the Sermon . . . but stories and sayings they will well remember."[12] That dual emphases on memory and worth, as in Gyekye's work on the Akan people, too, puts the visceral resonance of wisdom's voice right at the center of what we morally value. Gyekye's conclusion was that what Westerners might call a society's formal philosophy can itself be proverbial, and the more memorable for that reason. The Bible itself is full of such sayings, not only in the book of Proverbs but also in Christ's teaching. There are for example *no man can serve two masters, let the dead bury their dead*, and many more. For its continuous storage as a society's lore, such aphoristic sayings depend on the abecedary's existence.

Herbert's poems contain many proverblike phrases. *Kneeling ne're* [sic] *spoil'd silk stocking* ("The Church-porch") has thirty letters, but uses only thirteen of the alphabet, and a mere five appear only once. Of these five, rrrrrr is silent in many pronunciations, leaving the other four paired in two words: ppppp and ddddd in *spoil'd* and ttttt and ccccc in *stocking*. The proverb's ethical force— you needn't worry about your best hose when praying to God—is visually and orally empowered. Again there is *the best-bredd child hath the best portion*, which appears in Herbert's collection of proverbs. Out of fourteen letters only five appear once; but again, four of those come in only two words, *child* and *portion*. What is more, those two words are "centrifugal" to each other, overlapping only in the letter iiiii. One child gets the portion; it is clear, memorable, and lasting.

Deep within the whole enterprise remains the probing, the search for interpretation. And the image of glass, which pervades the poetry, seems a precise metaphor of Herbert's sense of language as both opaque and transparent; a thing in the created world yet a medium to penetrate to the truth behind it. Since glass is itself a domestic item, Herbert may have attained stillness by it for just this reason. The famous "glasse of blessings," after all, is where the poet found rest after the long weariness that also took the traveler to the inn in "Love (iii)." There is a pair of glass-images in the poetry that repay brief examination as to this matter.

In "The Windows," Herbert starts off:

> Lord, how can man preach thy eternall word?
>   He is a brittle crazie glasse:
> Yet in thy temple thou dost him afford
>   This glorious and transcendent place,
>   To be a window, through thy grace.

Surely it is no fancy to see the stained glass itself in the angular lettering of *brittle crazie glasse*. These are among the "exotic" words we suggested in chapter 5 arise from abecedarial fewness. I can't help seeing the ABC itself in the first ("owning") letters of the three words *a brittle crazie . . .* , and the way they introduce the rare and final letter zzzzz, enhanced by the doubled ttttt and sssss in the words flanking it. The zigzagging zzzzz itself hits like a splinter of stained glass, and the consonants then regather in the softer rounder term *glorious*, which is what the preacher becomes with God's grace in the actual church. But this splintering does not merely imitate the splinter of glass. Splintering is as characteristic of zzzzzs as of pieces of colored glass, and our eye sees both. The colored-glass effect is enhanced further by the *glorious/transcen-*

dent pairing, where all five English vowels are present but with none appearing in both words. The two eeeees and two ooooos support that as do the almost mutually exclusive consonants.

The other glass image comes in "The Elixer" (full text in appendix 2):

> A man that looks on glasse,
> On it may stay his eye;
> Or if he pleaseth, through it passe,
> And then the heav'n espie.

The idea clinches the poem, pointing to its magnificent final stanza, for every other stanza has also had a double import: said something, and then said it again differently. And how calmly this suggests that we may either look at language, or look through it. Equally, too, if glass is opaque and we can "stay [our] eye" upon it, it may be a mirror. Though not in this poem, Herbert may literally reflect on his self-agonizing. But again there is the further, different dilemma between church trappings and the simple word of God. It is not just "at language" versus "through language"; it is also language seen any way at all, as against other icons altogether. We look at the palpable body of bread, cloth, or picture; but we look at the words of scripture twice, both at them direct and through them to their meaning. In "The Windows" the difficulty came in the first two lines. There too the transparency of the first line—preaching, Scripture, language—was countered by the opacity of the second; Sacraments, furnishings, body, and blood. But for a poet, or anyone else for whom language was paramount, the problem was that language itself, in its fallen state outside the Holy Word, had a compromised virtue.

For as Richard Todd has expressed it, in a study of the basis of Herbert's language, we cannot even express language's incapacity, for by the nature of the case we have only language by which to do it.[13] This problem was discussed in part 2 when we spoke of "bliks"; but it also of course ties in with the matter of the two great "books," the Book of Scripture and the Book of Nature, neither of which, as fallen creatures, can we properly read. God in his providence gave us Scripture by which to know such things, but only in part, "darkly," and this is the Pauline glass Herbert refers to in "The Elixer." According to some critics Herbert resolved the difficulty by writing in (necessarily) fallen language but consecrating the results to God.[14] Hence the much-noted addressing of God direct in so many poems. Herbert searched this created/fallen language down as far as the letter. Louis Martz has written of the "stanzaic letter-bag" that Herbert played about with in sheer frustration.[15] Herbert had to suppress his brilliant poetic gifts in his involvement with theological issues. He gave no formal account of his views on poetry as far as we know, but the poems teem with clues on the matter. In "The Flower" he writes that *Thy word is all, if we could spell*. In "The Temper (i)" he wonders how his "rymes" would *gladly engrave thy love in steel* if only his soul was always in fit condition. "Providence" formally posits the human as *Secretarie of thy praise*, the only creature granted that gift, but only after a typical Herbert entwining: *shall I write, / And not of thee, through whom my fingers bend / To hold my quill?* In "Obedience" the poet would be most happy *if some kinde man would thrust his heart / Into these lines*. His question in a note of 1610, "Why are not *Sonnets* made of thee?" (Charles 1977, 81; Herbert's emphasis) becomes more curious the more one looks at it. It has a remorseless sense of the inextricable.

The letter is itself part of creation. But is its origin Scripture or nature? If Christ himself is literally "the letter of the word," as Herbert called him in his poem "Sepulchre," then via Scripture, word/letter and God/Christ were inseparably one. Although nature is divinely invested with significatory power—in simple terms, every line or mark in nature could become part of a letter of some kind—the languages we design from it are inadequate. We can only do our limited best with them even in worshiping God himself, or crying our suffering to God, however sincerely. Yet language is physical, of nature; it must be written on paper or stone and in ink or blood. From that starting point, from the pen of the penitent sinner and dedicated to God, it is virtuous, "virtual." It can at least aspire to virtue. But if language, the abecedary, is "stable" (and equable), too, then that permanence is not subject to the seasonal and other chances to which nature is subject, at least not in the same way. It all suggests that Herbert's love of the Scriptures, devout and sincere as it was, was touched with the divine eroticism of the earlier mystics. He believed that God's Word was not only Scripture, but the letter itself.

12

John Milton

Herbert made abecedarial fewness a virtue, that is virtual, and relied on its stability even as he broke it up. In *Paradise Lost*, John Milton also distributed letters centrifugally, but with rare confidence, feeling their stability and physicality as one and the same thing. The result is an abecedarial variance found across whole passages at a time.

The poem abounds with great passages and periods. There is Satan's fall from heaven and the debates in hell; the love scenes between Adam and Eve in Eden; the mighty battle; the temptation and Fall itself. But another passage, though acknowledged as striking, is less often remarked:

> The Earth obey'd, and strait
> Op'ning her fertil Woomb teem'd at a Birth
> Innumerous living Creatures, perfet formes,
> Limb'd and full grown: out of the ground up rose
> As from his Laire the wild Beast where he wonns
> In Forrest wilde, in Thicket, Brake, or Den;
> Among the Trees in Pairs they rose, they walk'd:
> The Cattel in the Fields and Meddowes green;
> Those rare and solitarie, those in flocks
> Pasturing at once, and in broad Herds upsprung.
> The grassie Clods now Calv'd, now half appeer'd
> The Tawnie Lion, pawing to get free
> His hinder parts, then springs as broke from Bonds,
> And Rampant shakes his Brinded main; the Ounce,
> The Libbard, and the Tyger, as the Moale
> Rising, the crumbl'd Earth above them threw
> In Hillocks; the swift Stag from under ground
> Bore up his branching head . . .

—7:453–70

The angel Raphael is describing the creation to Adam and Eve, its first human inhabitants. In this astonishing picture, the plants and animals rising into existence before our very eyes, Milton reveals his essential imaginative compulsion. "Creatures" emerge from gross matter fully formed. The mutually near-exclusive names letterwise—Cattel/Meddowes, Tawnie/Lion, Ounce/Libbard, Tyger/Moale, Hillocks/Stag—give them sharper profile on the page, as do their capital letters, and we are gripped by the sense of watching a new start at every moment of its occurrence. This section of Book Seven follows the Genesis seven-day creation story fairly closely; surprisingly, for Dryden said that when Milton was virtually transcribing Scripture, he would run into a "flat of thought."[1]

Milton goes even further. He descends next into the world of the insects; one of the "microbillions" (grains of sand, leaves, stars) with which one might compare the letters of language:

> At once came forth whatever creeps the ground,
> Insect or Worme; those wav'd thir limber fans
> For wings, and smallest Lineaments exact
> In all the Liveries dect of Summers pride
> With spots of Gold and Purple, azure and green:
> These as a line thir long dimension drew,
> Streaking the ground with sinuous trace; not all
> Minims of Nature; some of Serpent kinde
> Wondrous in length and corpulence involv'd
> Thir Snakie foulds, and added wings. First crept
> The Parsimonious Emmet, provident
> Of future, in small room large heart enclos'd,
> Pattern of just equalitie perhaps
> Hereafter, join'd in her popular Tribes
> Of Commonaltie: swarming next appeer'd
> The Female Bee that feeds her Husband Drone
> Deliciously, and builds her waxen Cells
> With Honey stor'd; the rest are numberless . . .
>
> —7:475–92

The creation teems with microscopic creatures, just as the newly created poem teems with millions of tiny signs. The meaning strives to wrench itself free from the black signs entrapping it, like the "tawnie lion" does from the soil. Yet the small has emerged from the vast; the abecedary as major epic:

> there Leviathan,
> Hugest of living Creatures, on the Deep
> Stretcht like a Promontorie sleeps or swimmes,

And seems a moving Land, and at his Gilles
Draws in, and at his Trunck spouts out a Sea.

—7:412–16

Samuel Johnson's response to *Paradise Lost* was that "an un-learned reader, when he first opens the book, finds himself sur-prised by a new language."[2] Very true; indeed it is "limn'd and full grown" from the outset. But it therefore had to be written, not spo-ken, because a virtually new language can't be imposed on people orally, ephemerally on the air. Such would have to be evolved grad-ually by recital as it was prior to Homer's time. For the poet who was to rewrite the provenance of epic almost entirely, the abeced-ary's stability was needed in support. Milton succeeds, because thanks to his blindness he had to dictate to his amanuenses ready-made; the result is superbly sonorous. But it still had to be written down, and Milton is one of the few to succeed with epic innovation since the alphabet was invented.

The sense from the passages just quoted, that Milton confounds God's act of creation with his own, is hard to escape. Milton be-lieved in God's providence, one feels, almost more centrally than in God, whom the poem notoriously hardly characterizes. Milton's libertarian instinct was to replace the official authority of the church, not by a better one, but by original creation, ex nihilo, "self-begot, self rais'd," like Satan himself. If Milton was of the Devil's party without knowing it, as William Blake averred, it was not just through siding consciously or not with Satan. Possibly he even believed he could match God's sacred Scripture. Of course, this new language aspired to replace the Adamic, prelapsarian lan-guage.[3] But it equally aimed to take Scripture radically forward. Milton's abiding longing in *Lycidas* for "fresh woods, and pastures new" is repeated in the last lines of *Paradise Lost*, where Adam and Eve walk out into a new world. This view doesn't dispute Milton's true belief in God's ultimate authority. But such authority has infi-nite scope: though hardly so in the poem, God is fount of all and so has no boundaries. With no irreverence then the poet could still be originator, poetically, of the entire universal story, for God's even greater authority would still survive it. It is from there that "above th' *Olympian* Hill I soare, / Above the flight of *Pegasean* wing" (7:3–4).

Whether this last is the voice of total freedom or of a despotic tyrant who would control all depends on our own imaginative re-sponses. This, of course, turns from the religious and poetic issue to the political issue. One political trope within radicalism, that of those who will not brook authority precisely because they would impose their own, seems at the heart of Milton's long change from straight pamphleteering to the writing of an epic about the universe itself. This was accompanied, to be sure, by the events of the Restoration when he found himself in great peril. But he also gradually got disillusioned with the idea of the English as God's chosen people, and so the original plan to write an Arthuriad gave way. Yet Milton still wanted to free his epic from the earlier tongues Norman, Saxon, and Latin, and in effect make an English tongue anew.[4]

Milton's lasting oppositional stances politically can't be denied. The three pamphlets of 1644 on areas of freedom are all "freedoms from": from censorship *(Areopagitica)*, from the banning of marital breakup *(Doctrine and Discipline of Divorce)*, and from the conservative resistance to vernacular translations of scripture *(On Education)*. Insofar as Milton was an Arminian, that too was a stance against institution. Arminians took the Church to be the body of believers whoever they are, whether formal Church members or not. Although the Church of England contained all shades of opinion by this time, it was still essentially Calvinist in doctrine.[5] Later, Milton saw Cromwell too as a tyrant.

But the radical instinct went further up than politics. The ode "On the Morning of Christ's Nativity" was written early. In *Paradise Lost* and *Paradise Regained,* Milton plays down the crucifixion, resurrection, ascension, and indeed Christ generally, never so named in *Paradise Lost* and always the Son. Some commentators sense that Milton had a curiously limited attachment to Christ himself; indeed, was "much more at home in B.C. than A.D."[6] Milton's gut intuition was that no orthodoxy, political or otherwise, could be right because it cramps the style. There seems no problem, in the end, in feeling that Milton moved away from overt earthly politics in *Paradise Lost*, for it packs its own punch so powerfully that we do not need to trace parallels with civil war or interregnum figures living or dead in the persona of the epic.[7]

Much depends on the texture of the language. It is strongly material in substance, form, and content as the creation passages cited above illustrate, and it emanates from deep belief about the creation itself and poetry within it. Its materiality is always an oral imperative, yet always a terrain, too; always, in both, a presence. It is neither atheist nor inhuman; Milton's cosmos is not the lifeless lump of real estate it is held to be by some twentieth-century scientists. Milton believed that matter is good and contains seeds of all goodness, and that God made matter neither from zero nor from chaos but from God's own self.[8] The world's creatures come up out of the ground. What the ground is like linguistically may be our real question.

The poem has a number of strong abecedarial characteristics. First, it is common knowledge that Milton's language cuts corners on grammar, inverts word order both natural and conventionally in-grained, and proffers substantives as assertions. But that way of writing brings a feature of its own; it omits connectives. This pervades the poem. In the lines on the ant already cited:

> The Parsimonious Emmet, provident
> Of future, in small room large heart enclos'd . . .
>
> —7:485–86

In prose the last six words might read "(which has) in (a) small (space) (a) large heart enclosed." Ten words instead of six. At 5:855–56 Satan jeers at Abdiel's contention that no one is independent, all were created by God. *Strange point and new! Doctrin which we would know whence learnt. . . .* Again a full version: "(A) doctrine (of) which we would (like to) know whence (it was) learnt." Countless such cases in *Paradise Lost* contain longer and more solid substantives than either of these two passages. Lexically thin words are blown away, leaving what Matthew Arnold called "this pressure, this condensation, this restraint."[9]

But it is not purely lexical. The omitted words are always the short ones. In the examples just given, all but two of the seemingly absent words have three letters or fewer. As a result, the average length of word in all but special passages is decidedly longer in *Paradise Lost* than in most other poetry. The exceptions, such as the intimate exchanges of Adam and Eve, or lines like *Rocks, Caves, Lakes, Fens, Bogs, Dens, and shades of death* (2:621), are the more telling as a result. But the more general firming up of the text, in eye and mind, is very great. Orally the speaker sounds terse and abrupt; on the page it is lexical, cognitive. Because of these connective omissions, the one-word-one-thing ambition of seventeenth-century epistemology and science is enhanced. Quantities of explanation or qualification in barely four or five words, are possible; and, curiously enough, at one point in the poem Milton gives us what may be a motive for such writing.[10] He makes the point Walter Scott and current novelist Ian McEwen also made (see above, chapter 7), on the fact that it can take much longer to describe an event in language than for the event itself to take place:

Immediate are the acts of God, more swift
Than time or motion, but to human ears
Cannot without process of speech be told,
So told as earthly notion can receive.

—7:176–79

So Milton's ruthless excision of short connectives, never breath-lessly or in uncontrolled haste, speeds things up; but it may also be an attempt to render the creation story as near to statically for all time as language allows. Matthew Arnold saw Homer's epics as rippling forward while *Paradise Lost* always consolidates its ground. It is the very efficiency of Milton's means that impresses, as though his language itself is of his own design. He can rely on the abecedary's equability to sustain his unusual linguistic econo-mies. The result, though, is that a main distributive principle of the abecedary, that rolles may be long or short, permeates the text throughout. It stiffens meaning and solidifies its physical embodi-ment as the shorter connectives go missing.

And it might become intolerable to read and strange to hear—we recall that the abecedary has no center—if the poet didn't also vary it by other means. In *The Odyssey,* Homer used masses of small-scale detail, marine, military, and domestic, in the more lightweight meter of the hexameter. In *The Iliad* the epic homogeneity befits the claustrophobic scene in front of the walls of Troy in any case. In our own century, Modernism's visible fragmentation works the epic in exactly contrary direction. Milton's conception was archi-tectonic from the start. When T. S. Eliot said that Milton worked less with the word than "the period, the sentence and still more the paragraph," it was the last-named that Milton's sentence led to most emphatically.[11]

There is a texture of different lexicons for different topics. The clearing away of the usual small connectives enhances these differ-ences. Here are two passages to set alongside the ones already cited as well as beside each other:

```
              . . . nor stood at gaze
Th'adverse Legions, nor less hideous joyn'd
The horrid shock: now storming furie rose,
And clamour such as heard in Heav'n till now
Was never, Arms on Armour clashing bray'd
Horrible discord, and the madding Wheeles
Of brazen Chariots rag'd; dire was the noise
Of conflict; over head the dismal hiss
Of fiery Darts in flaming volies flew,
```

And flying vaulted either Host with fire.
So under fierie Cope together rush'd
Both Battels maine, with ruinous assault
And inextinguishable rage; all Heav'n
Resounded, and had Earth bin then, all Earth
Had to her Center shook.

—6:205–19

O Adam, one Almightie is, from whom
All things proceed, and up to him return,
If not deprav'd from good, created all
Such to perfection, one first matter all,
Indu'd with various forms, various degrees
Of substance, and in things that live, of life;
But more refin'd, more spiritous, and pure,
As neerer to him plac't or neerer tending
Each in thir several active Sphears assignd,
Till body up to spirit work, in bounds
Proportiond to each kind.

—5:469–79

A martial evocation, and a piece of philosophical abstraction.
They sound different, and look different on the page. Compared in
some detail we find, for what it is worth, the following. The battle
passage has distinctly more hhhhhs, wwwwws, and yyyyys, although the latter two are still low absolutely. It has far fewer ppp-
pps, but also, more to the point, notably fewer mmmmms—the
"meditation" letter, as we shall see later in the context of Wordsworth. But there is one other difference, which we have classed as
a distributive mode. While the martial passage's abrasive consonants are, surprisingly, far fewer than those in the philosophical
one—an unexpected finding in such clamor of battle—it also has
significantly more words with a strong consonant at each end. This
disperses the passage's terms into the hard entities that brook no
dilution. Gerard Manley Hopkins and David Jones were later to
practice the same thing in different poetic contexts. Milton's battle
is vigorous enough in all conscience, but this feature enhances what
it gives us; namely, a sense of the strength of all the participants
and their armoury, such as to withstand the peril of plunging the
made world into chaos; the *Horrible discord . . . with ruinous
assault / And inextinguishable rage: all Earth / Had to her Center
shook.*
    Of course *Paradise Lost* consists entirely of spoken passages,
even if one speaker is the author himself. This differentiates the tex-

ture further within the overall epic sweep. The formal introductions
to and closures from each speaker, *and in the midst thus undismai'd
began* (6:417); *no sooner had th'Almighty ceas't* (3:344), and so
forth, encase each speech as a block of its own rather than as part
of dialogue, even though of course each remains dialogue within
the wider frame. Some critics have suggested that each speaker's
individuality is limited. All have the one meter and syntax, the same
"promiscuities," inversions, extended parentheses, delayed verbs,
and so on.[12] But there are variants within that. For example, the intimate or confessional passages:

> But who I was, or where, or from what cause,
> Knew not; to speak I tri'd, and forthwith spake,
> My tongue obey'd and readily could name
> What e're I saw. Thou Sun, said I, faire Light,
> And thou enlight'nd Earth, so fresh and gay,
> Ye Hills and Dales, ye Rivers, Woods, and Plaines,
> And ye that live and move, fair Creatures, tell,
> Tell, if ye saw, how came I thus, how here?
> Not of myself; by some great Maker then,
> In goodness and in power praeeminent;
> Tell me, how may I know him, how adore,
> From whom I have that thus I move and live,
> And feel that I am happier then I know.

—8:270–82

This is Adam discovering his very existence. It sounds so gentle
and looks so delicate. It cues the out-loud or inner-mind oral reader
by its subtle texture. There are the very short words, the near-dozen
"I"s backed up by yyyyys and small iiiiis, the many ooooos common in emotional dialogue of all kinds in *Paradise Lost*, and the
sssss's, which by the end have all but gone. As in the animal creation passage cited earlier there is the list of capitalized nouns, as
though Adam can name what he sees, but breaks it up when he
turns to himself. And in a vast universe the passage's short words
match Adam's lowly stature. The passage differs markedly from
Raphael's lines just before (66–178) about the unity and power of
the godhead from which all things proceed and to which they return.

The poem has another curious feature. I call it "singling-doubling." The larger unity expressed by both the solitary Satan and
the voice of the poem's author permanently strains against the pairing intrinsic to dialogue. This feature itself might profitably be
compared to the advance of dialectic widely, which we saw in the

development of the civilization of ancient Greece, a subject with which Milton was fully conversant. But the pairing element in this "singling-doubling" is matched verbally by all kinds of word-repetitions even when dialogue itself is not the reason. That is to say, singling-doubling is perhaps a special case of the centrifugal-centripetal distinction that we suggested arises from the abecedary's fewness, its paucity of letter-signs for any one alphabet. There is a great example of this in Book Four. Perennially famous in gender debates on the poem, it brings out these features clearly. Satan has arrived at the Garden of Eden. There, among *all kind / Of living Creatures new to sight and strange*, he also sees:

> Two of far nobler shape erect and tall,
> Godlike erect, with native Honour clad
> In naked Majestie seemd Lords of all,
> And Worthie seemed, for in thir looks Divine
> The image of thir glorious Maker shon,
> Truth, wisdome, Sanctitude severe and pure,
> Severe, but in true filial freedom plac't;
> Whence true autoritie in men; though both
> Not equal, as their sex not equal seemd;
> For contemplation hee and valour formd,
> For softness shee and sweet attractive Grace,
> He for God only, shee for God in him:
> His fair large Front and Eye sublime declar'd
> Absolute rule; and Hyacinthin Locks
> Round from his parted forelock manly hung
> Clustring, but not beneath his shoulders broad:
> Shee as a vail down to the slender waste
> Her unadorned golden tresses wore
> Dissheveld, but in wanton ringlets wav'd
> As the Vine curles her tendrils, which impli'd
> Subjection, but requir'd with gentle sway,
> And by her yielded, by him best receivd,
> Yielded with coy submission, modest pride,
> And sweet reluctant amorous delay . . .

—4:288–311

Broadly, at least at first, they are a pair. Adam and Eve are introduced to the reader for the first time. They are majestic, unsullied, unreprehensibly different from the rest of us; not merely "superior" as in our social-distinction term of today, but romanticized, etherealized, spiritualized as of a different order; in short, prelapsarian. Much is also uttered twice, as though to underline the pairing of gender and dialogue together:

erect and tall, / Godlike erect
seemd Lords of all, / And worthie seemd
thir looks Divine . . . thir glorious Maker
severe and pure, / Severe
true filial . . . true autoritie
For contemplation he . . . For softness she
by her . . . by him
yielded . . . Yielded

Even *not equal* is repeated—equally; and even the notorious key line of all, *He for God only, shee for God in him*, balances in its very difference, as though even such gender roles might bear equal weight and worth. One asks today, could Milton really mean this? We must return to that, but the coupling, doubling balance supports the introduction and conclusion of Adam and Eve together, first as "two," last as "hand in hand" near the end of the passage:

> So hand in hand they passd, the loveliest pair
> That ever since in loves imbraces met,
> *Adam* the goodliest man of men since borne
> His Sons, the fairest of her daughters *Eve.*
>
> —4:321–24

Hand in hand and *man of men* are the last of many repetitions here. There are also the parallel descriptions of hair, motivated doubtless by Milton's puritan leaning. The epithets are paired; Adam has contemplation and valor, Eve softness and grace. Finally in Book Four, when they take leave of us and enter their bower for lovemaking, the poet himself chants the pairing: *Thus at thir shadie Lodge arriv'd, both stood, / Both turn'd, and under op'n Skie ador'd / The God that made both Skie . . ."* (720–22). It is subtle, the matchings not always obvious; they slide in and out of each other, yet are there undeniably. Dialectic itself has become a mental habit, an inner structure.

Yet it is more than it appears. First, Satan by contrast is single and solitary. When he first secretly spies on Adam and Eve, he is agonizingly brought into the same verbal-doubling mode:

> Sight hateful, sight tormenting! thus these two
> Imparadis't in one anothers arms
> The happier *Eden*, shall enjoy their fill
> Of bliss on bliss . . .
>
> —4:505–8

Sight hateful, sight tormenting! . . . bliss on bliss. But later, in the fateful Book Nine and now more confident, Satan seduces Eve into visiting another great singularity, that phallic object that menaces and forbids, and which fittingly Satan himself had most strongly named. *One fatal Tree there stands of Knowledge call'd* (4:514): it is the Tree of Knowledge. And when Satan describes it, he doesn't repeat himself once:

> Till on a day roaving the field, I chanc'd
> A goodly Tree farr distant to behold
> Loaden with fruit of fairest colours mixt,
> Ruddie and gold: I nearer drew to gaze;
> When from the boughes a savorie odour blow'n,
> Grateful to appetite, more pleas'd my sense
> Then smell of sweetest Fenel, or the Teats
> Of Ewe or Goat dropping with Milk at Eevn,
> Unsuckt of Lamb or Kid, that tend their play . . .
>
> —9:575–83

The objective prose singularity Aristotle used in his works on empirical science, and which thus contrasted Plato's dialogue technique, is cognately applied here to the comparable "tree of knowledge." Satan does repeat himself later, but only because narrative then requires it. And now one can notice the shifts within the supposed gender-equality impression. We recall, for instance, that when Eve described her own first self-awareness, unlike Adam's cited above (8:270–82), it was seeing herself reflected in the water, and her centripetal verbal doubling-up was narcissistic:

> As I bent down to look, just opposite,
> A Shape within the watry gleam appeerd
> Bending to look on me, I started back,
> It started back, but pleasd I soon returned,
> Pleas'd it returnd . . .
>
> —4:460–64

Here the issue is not that of dialectic, for the event itself is narcissistic; there are no opponents. It recalls, rather, a question we asked in context of Herbert, and which always arises when alphabetical rather than wholly pictorial writing is repeated. Do we read it twice, or merely see the first time again? In a male-dominated world, is Eve her own self, or merely Adam again? Returning to the long passage cited above (4:288–324), we see anew that those pairings were occasionally flawed; not always what true parity might warrant.

They are not only *not equal, as their sex not equal seemd . . . He for God only, shee for God in him*; there is also the telling abrupt enjambment at the heart of it: *His fair large Front and Eye sublime declar'd / Absolute rule . . .* But it is the final couplet that so subtly shifts away from exact balance. Adam gets just more than a line, Eve just less. *Adam the goodliest man of men since born / His sons, the fairest of her daughters Eve.*

We are drawn in at the deepest level of response. The words offer—have "sponged up"—the mental shapes that come, not just as statement, but from the psychic patterns that prose must draw out into statement but which poetry and the abecedary can embody. The debate can't be pursued here, but it seems Milton's position on gender in *Paradise Lost* is not one that ascribes dialectic to that relationship. Rather it is deliberately ambiguous and deliberately implicit. Satan's final comment returns to doubling, but this time with deep irony:

> Sleep on
> Blest pair; and O yet happiest if ye seek
> No happier state, and know to know no more.
>
> —4:773–75

Singling/doubling is not confined to gender. And naturally one can always find counterexamples, because no artist is going to use the same means mechanically all the time. So singles include Satan and the Tree of Knowledge but also Raphael and Abdiel, while doubles cluster round the devils' debate, Adam/Eve, God/Son, and Night/Chaos. Yet the pattern is deep in the written universe Milton has created and cuts across the solid materiality of the text itself. The lines where the fallen angel Abdiel recants his new allegiance and leaves the ranks of Satan to return to God seem to leap off the page; they are among the most commonly cited by critics. And they are not just doubles but triples:

> So spake the Seraph *Abdiel* faithful found,
> Among the faithless, faithful only hee;
> Among innumerable false, unmov'd,
> Unshak'n, unseduc'd, unterrifi'd
> His Loyaltie he kept, his Love, his Zeale:
> Nor number, nor example with him wrought
> To swerve from truth, or change his constant mind
> Though single.
>
> —5:896–903

Abdiel's singleness rests within trinity. The *faith*-root comes three times. The three *un*-words all tell of some single failing that Abdiel resisted, and the three very different capitalized nouns in the next line do the same positively. The vertically doubled and thus matrical "Among" contrasts the singularity by enhancing it. Abdiel too contrasts Satan here in merit against sin and in loyalty against disobedience; but he matches him in singleness. There is power, one senses, in the word "number" for that reason; Abdiel's integrity is etymologically supported.

Everything suggested so far—the omitted connectives, the short and long words, the blocked-out passages, the nondialectical singling/doubling—shows how the material was shaped up to take Milton's energizing drive. We haven't yet referred to that as Milton himself defined it. In his prefatory Note of 1668 he wrote: "This neglect then of Rime so little is to be taken for a defect, though it may seem so perhaps to vulgar readers, that it rather is to be esteem'd an example set, the first in *English*, of ancient liberty recover'd to Heroic Poem from the troublesom and modern bondage of Rimeing" (Shawcross 1970, 73). This well-known passage undeniably ties a social and political ideology of "ancient liberty" to what might seem a mere mode of executing verse, but there is little doubt of Milton's emphasis.

It is what rhyme stands in the way of, that Milton was concerned with. As the same Note puts it, this was "sense variously drawn out" from one line into another, without either having to find a rhyme-word or being left with its visual and aural presence when he has done so. Rhyme often, though not always, makes the line a separate unit of feeling and thought as well as meter. Milton wanted the swelling passage. For the same reasons he usually avoids successive-word alliteration. But as well as the absence of an end-stopping rhyme, the process of being "drawn out" also entails some kind of *enjambment*, the uninterrupted dogleg turn around the corner to the next line, which the reading eye, however instantly, must follow. *Enjambment* therefore is also in part an abecedarial feature. Having no rhyme lets the poet split a grammatical unit at the line end, forcing the reader to think less in lines than in longer periods. Internal dialectic subsides the more we look at it.

Enjambment is sharpest when the next line has a full-stop or comma straight after the first word. In the lines already cited,

> Shee as a vail down to the slender waste
> Her unadorned golden tresses wore
> Dissheveld . . .

—4:304–6

At first it seems mainly that Eve wore her hair as a veil. But the next line's first word gives the real significance; she wore her hair disheveled. It is a virtuality like the case given in chapter 10: "Pete went to work on his motorcycle (project)." The enjambment can also take us far beyond the first word—the sense is "drawn out"—to the point where three or four lines at a time are caught up in a structure of movement across the line and then sweep round into the next. Again the across/down matrix is recalled. Thomas de Quincey called the whole result Milton's "solemn planetary wheelings," and Empson "the sliding, sideways, broadening movement, normal to Milton." Both critics were obviously thinking of periods longer than just a couple of lines.[13] But this suggests more than just extended sense. For Milton's powerfully oral poetry replaces rhyme with another effect, by deploying all five vowels and their various subdivisions in great circles of rhetorical movement.

I call this Milton's vowel-clock. It pervades almost every passage and usually almost every line. All the passages cited so far contain it. This "clock" could not occur without the language's vowels having long been fixed in separate written letters rather than swaying along a continuum, much as the musical octave marks out eight pitches from a single high-to-low sweep of sound. If one thinks of the vowels moving around a dial in visualized sound, if that oxymoron is allowable, then one can work up a mnemonic for it like *level, raise, high, up, on, over, down, through, beneath.* Said out loud, those words force the mouth into positions that indeed seem level, raised a bit, high, up—and so on; while writing them, as I have just done, argues the effect before one's eyes. Of course, the words as meaning alone prove nothing. Instead of *up, over* we could have said *under, below.* But the point is conveniently illustrated. The poem rolls ever forward with these circles of vowel-sound:

> Was never, Arms on Armour clashing bray'd
> Horrible discord, and the madding Wheeles
> Of brazen Chariots rag'd; dire was the noise
> Of conflict; over head the dismal hiss
> Of fiery Darts in flaming volies flew,
> And flying vaulted either Host with fire.

—6:209–14

> Why sleepst thou *Eve?* now is the pleasant time,
> The cool, the silent, save where silence yields
> To the night-warbling Bird, that now awake
> Tunes sweetest his love-labor'd song; now reignes

> Full Orb'd the Moon, and with more pleasing light
> Shadowie sets off the face of things . . .
>
> —5:38–43

It is not only that rhyme has been replaced with something that spirals around and around the clockface: *bray'd, Wheeles, noise, hiss, flew, fire.* With each line's final word no longer a privileged hinge, as with rhyme, these circlings occur within the line, too, wherever imaginative emphasis needs them. It is marked in the second passage just quoted, for the first four words actually level off the emphasized vowels, "Why sleepst thou *Eve?*" In strong contrast *time, cool, save, yields, Bird, song, Orb'd,* and *things* then come rolling in, magnetizing us to the variant points on the circumference of the vowel-circle, and so increasing the stress they already have.

This, then, is what Milton really substitutes for rhyme. Rhyme is a dialectic of its own. It squashes the wheel flat, and makes it go along in pairs. Milton's sweep forward enables the nuances, both repeated and unexpected, which Stanley Fish examined (Fish 1971, chap. 1). It is aided and abetted by an equal swing of consonants. In the great debate in Book Two, Belial argues that they could be a lot worse off than they are, down here in hell but at least unmolested:

> What if the breath that kindl'd those grim fires
> Awak'd should blow them into sevenfold rage
> And plunge us in the flames? or from above
> Should intermitted vengeance arm again
> His red right hand to plague us? what if all
> Her stores were opn'd, and this Firmament
> Of Hell should spout her Cataracts of Fire,
> Impendent horrors, threatning hideous fall
> One day upon our heads; while we perhaps
> Designing or exhorting glorious warr,
> Caught in a fierie Tempest shall be hurl'd
> Each on his rock transfixt, the sport and prey
> Of racking whirlwinds, or for ever sunk
> Under yon boyling Ocean, wrapt in Chains;
> There to converse with everlasting groans,
> Unrespited, unpitied, unrepreevd,
> Ages of hopeless end; this would be worse . . .
>
> —2:170–86

Belial wants to seem suasive and powerful when he is really being idle and cowardly. The threats of dire event come in a kind of chain, discernible as to content but linked to each other in a general surge of conviction, albeit a merely affected one. We suggested that Milton doesn't much use formal alliteration. Instead, here the consonants come in overlapping waves; what Christopher Ricks called "two kinds of movement, forward and spinning."[14] In each case the letters are the ones stressed in the poem. Kkkkk in *kindl'd* . . . *awak'd*, ggggg in *grim . . . rage . . . plunge*, vvvvv in *sevenfold . . . above . . . vengeance*, rrrrr in *red . . . right*, ppppp in *plunge . . . plague . . . spout . . . impendent*, hhhhh in *hell . . . horrors . . . hideous . . . hopeless*, -ing in *threatning . . . designing . . . exhorting*, ddddd in *hideous . . . day . . . heads*, kkkkk again in *rock . . . (transfixt) . . . racking . . . sunk*, ppppp in *Tempest . . . sport and prey . . . wrapt . . . Unrespited, unpitied, unrepreevd . . . hopeless*, and the more spaced marker-phrases throughout premised on the wwwww in *what . . . what if . . . while we . . . warr . . . this would be worse. . . .*

Such considerations could settle some old debates. Whether Milton must be read in broad sweeps "without resistance" as Dr. Johnson put it (followed by F. R. Leavis and C. S. Lewis though refuting each other as to its worth), or whether his grand style can be appreciated close-up, as Ricks set out to prove—this one has run for a long time. But, it seems, mere rhyme and ancient liberty turn out to be connected. You remove the rhyme but replace it with the same material from which rhyme was made. In constructing the large-scale, I think Milton kept his sense of the small-scale components that made it, which themselves had to remain sturdy and focused. The issue ties in with the other factors we have just identified, and is one of reading practice. Hostile critics objected precisely to being swept along by Milton and so, they considered, putting at risk the right critical detachment required if proper evaluation of a literary work is to be achieved. But the interest for us here is exactly in the way Milton's poem only enhances—perhaps exaggerates—the way reading is done normally. As suggested earlier when discussing abecedarial equability, we commonly read in just the way Milton seems to want. We scan around and about, "collect" what seem to be the main terms, "sweep" seven or so words at a time, recapping, circling, and so on. Any kind of enjambment is thus more likely to be picked up within the swing of the verse without losing its power and even surprise. The "vowel-clock" gets up a head of steam, the swaying consonants follow suit, and, when this continues for a paragraph at a time, we see in action the most ancient mode of writing of all, the matrix form, as the mode of overall poetic presentation. It is then perhaps political after all, if only generally so, and readers are obliged to decide for themselves whether this mode does indeed release "ancient liberties," or rather stifles the dialectic of reason so that opposition is not brooked. Perhaps both are present, and the battle is on to constrain the very opponents who would quash liberty itself.

Milton dictated forty lines of *Paradise Lost* each morning, then spent the day cutting them down to twenty. That time/work ratio points to scrupulously close attention. Jonathan Richardson commented early: "a Reader of *Milton* must be Always upon Duty; he is Surrounded with Sense, it rises in every Line, every word is to the Purpose; There are no Lazy Intervals, All has been Consider'd, and Demands, and Merits Observation."[15] To "every word" we could add every letter, but the point has been made enough. Certainly this seems to go against the views of Samuel Johnson, C. S. Lewis, and F. R. Leavis, at least on this particular aspect of the matter. Milton's blindness may even have taken a form—commoner among the blind than is sometimes realized[16]—in which visualization is possible. Milton once stated that "the Constant and Settled Darkness that is before Me as well by Night as by Day, seems nearer to the Whitish than the Blackish" (Richardson 1932, 262). Richardson's observation that "*Homer* [Milton] could Almost repeat without Book" (211) doesn't preclude a memory of the "book" as its first source, although it can be done just as readily by practiced oral repetition.

Further local examples of letter-use pervade *Paradise Lost*. We can only note a few of them. The play on the word "fall" and its letters in Book One has been noted by Stevie Davies, whose study is a gold mine of perceptions on these matters.[17] Recognition dawns: *Farewel happy fields / Where Joy for ever dwells: Hail horrours, hail / Infernal world . . .* (1:249–51). *Horrours* is one of those "distance-double" words that is also symmetrical, like *fetter* and *sorrow*, although the seventeenth-century spelling still contained the uuuuu that compromises that effect. The same applies with *assault*, cited above from the battle scene passage. Both are strong forces on the page, *horrours* especially after the preceding double-letter words and alliterating hhhhhs. Words contain the letters of other words. In *So glister'd the dire Snake, and into fraud / Led* Eve *our credulous Mother . . .* (9:643–44), Ricks notes the bright "glister'd" playing against the dark "dire," and how "our" and "Mother" pinion "credulous" between them (Ricks 1963, 75–77). But "glister'd" contains the letters of "dire"; so the latter rolle has no new sign and little new sound, so can exist as sheer meaning. "Credulous" contains the letters of the immediately preceding "our" and "led"; Eve's credulity is prelapsarian and large. At 9:385–86, where Eve's hand *soft she withdrew*, the preceding five words all begin with the equally soft aspirate: "Thus saying, from *her Husbands hand her hand* / Soft she withdrew." The first letter owns the word indeed.

Mutually exclusive spellings recur powerfully. Raphael pairs off the beasts by decreasing fitness (8:389–97). "Lion with Lioness" may happily consort, "Bird with Beast," and "Fish with Fowle" much less although they still alliterate; but Ox/Ape come nearest in the text to "Man with Beast," which match "least of all." The hint of hideous couplings matches the increasing abecedarial difference. A wider, astonishing diffusion comes in Book Nine with the letter zzzzz. In the first five hundred lines it appears only four times, at lines 34, 52, 161, and 429. It then comes eight times in only the next eighty, in strong association with the serpent. The serpent stands up *on his reare, / Circular base of rising foulds, that tour'd / Fould above fould a surging Maze, his Head / Crested aloft, and Carbuncle his eyes, / With burnisht Neck of verdant Gold . . . .* (498–501). Eve has to *gaze* on this mesmerizing form—of the tempter who *gloz'd* (549)—four times in the following forty lines, being *not unamaz'd* as well. When Satan returns triumphant to hell, he and his codevils all become hissing serpents; the zzzzz is seen and heard at once. The zigzagging serpent rises swaying in the air; it is something the reader is drawn to. Whether Milton intended this one can't say, but certainly he was "Always Careful in the Printing . . . and This After he was Blind as well as Before" (Richardson 1932, 306). From all we see in *Paradise Lost* it seems quite credible, for the effect is very powerful.

It all recalls how much of *Paradise Lost* is not only dark but darkness's opposite:

> Hail holy light, ofspring of Heav'n first-born,
> Or of th'Eternal Coeternal beam
> May I express thee unblamed? since God is light,
> And never but in unapproached light
> Dwelt from Eternitie, dwelt then in thee,
> Bright effluence of bright essence increate . . .

—3:1–6

Milton the nonrhymer ends a line with "light" twice. In the first fifty-five lines of this third book he ends on a strong ttttt eleven times; and he concludes the long paragraph accordingly:

> . . . there plant eyes, all mist from thence
> Purge and disperse, that I may see and tell
> Of things invisible to mortal sight.
>
> —3:53–55

Ttttt saturates the line-endings of the first fifty lines. Our "old favorite" the common cluster -*ight*—"light" (four times), "bright," "Night(ly)," and "sight" (twice each)—dominates them. In these un-Miltonic endings the wretchedness of his blindness is evoked by a sharp click, as though in subliminal longing that eyesight, if it ever returned, would be a sudden reappearance. This is the book in which the "Son" appears, his effulgence punning of course the source of all light, which Milton would never see again. But perhaps he remembered it, as he surely remembered so much of the written page from the time before his eyesight deserted him.

13

William Wordsworth

This chapter differs from the others in this part 3. We make a close and detailed analysis of a single fairly short poem, *Tintern Abbey*.

Wordsworth did not create a new English from earlier vernaculars as did Chaucer, or invent his own as did Milton, or absorb a whole way of life via a linguistic renaissance as did Shakespeare. Wordsworth made a new poetry from personal utterance itself. His subject matter, the basic triangle of language, nature, and childhood, was dynamic. The growing child, at least this one born in the Lake District and returning there, drew on its origins in nature to nurture a poetic speech that essentially moved from inward to outward. One senses an evolutionary trajectory predating Darwinism. Hence Wordsworth's rejection of mythical and heroic theme as epic topics in *The Prelude* Book One; hence his belief, albeit temporary, in the language of "humble and rustic life"; and hence, too, *pace* today's historicist critics, his return to his native surroundings on painfully finding as a young man that he wasn't cut out for mobile politics or civic position. Nature evolves living beings that grow to utterance from the "one human heart," as Wordsworth felt impelled to insist on several occasions.

First person as subject had already appeared in other long discursive poems, prototypically Goethe's *The Sorrows of Young Werther*. But there was always a fictional, and so in part objective, figure as protagonist. Wordsworth uses his own self, William Wordsworth, as that figure. It culminates in his long autobiographical poem *The Prelude*, but had already appeared substantially in *Tintern Abbey*, and more shortly in the Lucy poems, the 1802 sonnets, the *Poems on the Naming of Places*, and elsewhere. Short lyrics, though of centuries' standing, had usually been thought of as externally visitant to the subject rather than emanating from it; from the muse; from religious devotion; or from the inspiration of sexual love. For poetry and self-expression to shape each other in a single process was a major change for language.

It brought on a personal anxiety Wordsworth probably never got over. The lasting impression is of vulnerability, hesitation, deferral, unanswered questioning, and therefore this indeterminancy of expression and even lexicon, too. Such come to seem the very cast of his writing. Wordsworth knew what he was undertaking. In 1805, when *The Prelude* was nearly finished, he wrote to his patron Sir George Beaumont that it is "a thing unprecedented in Literary [sic] history that a man should talk so much about himself." With characteristic defensiveness he goes on that "it is not self-conceit, as you will know well, that has induced [me] to do this, but real humility: I began the work because I was unprepared to treat any more arduous subject and diffident of my own powers. . . ."[1] Of the completion itself, two months later, he told Beaumont that "it was not a happy day for me . . . [the result] so far below what I seem'd capable of executing, depressed me much" (Wordsworth 1967–69, 1:594).

Wordsworth was a strong personality at all levels, yet these uncertainties permeate his life. Dependent on women, changing direction, always thinking about himself and his past, worrying away about family and property, and bearing endless headaches and illnesses; all these find their symbol in the "motion" that pervades so much of what he describes. Whether hanging on the cliffs birdsnesting or skating on the lake, it is the foundational movement of land, sky, and water that besets him. How characteristic of him, then, to see and feel the restlessness of Augustine and Herbert as a deep theme of universal nature itself and to calm it to that level. This vulnerable motion is expressed by Wordsworth's language. And if, for the first time in a major poet, expression also comes direct from the self-experiencing subject, and just is that utterance, it raises problems for the poet about the language employed. The poet may utter from the heart, which is voice, but must commit it to paper, which is writing. All we have said about the abecedary is brought into new question. Wordsworth composed much while out walking; that is to say, orally. The whole of *Tintern Abbey* was so created; his wife, sister, and later his daughter were his amanuenses, and text at the time was often careless of precise abecedarial rendering. Spellings would vary; the ampersand for "and" appeared frequently. But like many poets Wordsworth sought immortality—"a work that might live" as he said of the never-completed *Recluse*.[2] This brings hindsight irony for ourselves, for he was looking for a collected poetry that would in effect join the great volumes of the world in the great libraries. That is to say, its final state would be as writing. And so a near anguish over these comparable states of language as sound and language as markings ends up running through the autobiographical *Prelude* like the underground river with which the poet finally compared that great work. This matter of language's material nature is central to the discussion.

The autobiographical story repeatedly lurches or dips into the matter of language as nature's marks or as eerie resonance. In Book One of *The Prelude* the "presences of Nature . . . haunting me . . . on caves and trees, upon the woods and hills, / Impressed upon all forms the characters / Of danger and desire," as a result making the earth's surface "work like a sea" (Wordsworth, *Prelude* 1805, 1:490–501). The solid dry earth sways like water. Yet the metaphor's vehicle is not sound but writing. The print-metaphors of "character," "type," and "impress" appear both here and in most of these passages about material Nature's mark-receiving capacity. It recalls again how the "Book of Nature" seemed a set of readable signs both before and after the European Renaissance. Yet by Book Two of the same poem the impulse has turned toward sound. Walking alone one night "in storm and tempest," Wordsworth ponders on life, love, and society in a maze of abstractions. But then in the dripping of water from a rock and the movement of twigs in the breeze he hears "the ghostly language of the ancient earth" and sounds that "make their dim abode in distant winds" (Wordsworth 1805, 2:322, 328–29). These seem to express Wordsworth's acute sense that language did originally emerge from matter's oral potential, via living and then sapient forms such as ourselves, and so utterance from the larynx.

But the dilemma grows. Language is voiced from the mouth but Nature and matter seem made for imprint. In Book Five, Wordsworth cries out with one of his most eloquent passages:

> Oh, why hath not the mind
> Some element to stamp her image on
> In nature somewhat nearer to her own?
> Why, gifted with such powers to send abroad
> Her spirit, must it lodge in shrines so frail?
>
> —1805, 5:44–48

The "shrines so frail" are the durable written word as well as the ephemeral voice on the wind. The context is Wordsworth's famous (if invented) dream about the stone and the shell in the desert, which turned into books. The general import is that, even though at the earth's final destruction "would the living presence still subsist / Victorious" (33–34)—presumably in some spiritual dimension—still all human works in this world must perish for lack of some "element" of more eternal nature. This again means print, for certainly permanence, before electronic storage appeared, meant writing rather than speech.

Wordsworth's obsessive dilemma continues with the apocalyptic description of the Simplon Pass in the Alps (6:549–72). He passed through the gorge after the uncanny event of crossing the Alps without knowing he had done so. He was thus thwarted of an anticipated sublime experience. At first this passage seems to run sight and sound together. Rocks mutter, crags have a voice in them, waterfalls are stationary yet we hear their "blasts." Decaying woods are never to be decayed, and all is "tumult and peace" at once. Yet the outcome seems visual. For all of this was

> like workings of one mind, the features
> Of the same face, blossoms upon one tree,
> Characters of the great apocalypse,
> The types and symbols of eternity,
> Of first, and last, and midst, and without end.
>
> —6:568–72

Again the "characters" and "types" seem unavoidable. There are two further effusions about language in *The Prelude* that can't be discussed in detail here. But the emotional impact of seeing a blind beggar in London who carried a piece of paper saying who he was (7:608–23), and of meeting a young woman by a murderer's gibbet in open country when he was a boy (11:278–327) both left the sight-sound matter wide open still. The street beggar can't read his own writing, and the poet by the gibbet would need "colours and words that are unknown to man" to "paint" the dreary scene of the beacon, naked pool, and the woman's garments "vexed and tossed" by the strong wind. Both stories are captured visually, yet both express that as inadequacy. I think that in confronting the awesome mountainous presence back in the Simplon Gorge, Wordsworth stared at the apocalyptic "writing" as something massively eternal, unchanging, and fixed; the written word metaphysically or archetypally conceived, yet always unattainable even as it hung there forever possible.

Wordsworth never overcame the difficulty. His pervading "indeterminacy" is one outcome of it. The trouble may have lain in his lifelong sense that language couldn't actually express full truth. Effusions from the "human heart"—via the larynx—were necessarily passing, yet their more permanent fix in "writing" was somehow a grim absorption into the static; somehow a dead thing, out there in the minerals and on the rocks. In the end this is of the nature of epitaph, as his essays on that subject suggested. Wordsworth was left with a permanent compulsion somehow to fall short, never to say it all. We have only "the utmost that we know," whatever that is, as summary of his huge emotional surge on seeing the London beggar; the "fallings from us, vanishings" of the *Immortality Ode*, whatever they are too, that humans must bear when childhood fades away; and the "silent unobtrusive sympathies, / And gentle agitations of the mind / From manifold distinctions" which he was thinking of when he heard the earth's ghostly language (2:316–18) on his walk at night. These successive and frequent abstractions, Wordsworth's indeterminancies, are surely where his abecedary rises fading gently into virtuality too.

Tintern Abbey is a good poem in which to examine these features. It is the first major case of Wordsworth's writing in the discursive mode that became one hallmark for romanticism. As is well known, the poem was written when William and Dorothy Wordsworth went on a four-day walking tour in the summer of 1798. This took them from the mouth of the River Wye at Chepstow some thirty miles inland passing the ruins of Tintern Abbey en route, and then back again to cross the Bristol Channel and return home. The poem went to the printers less than a week later. It was just in time to be last, and last-placed, in the *Lyrical Ballads*, Wordsworth's joint expression with Coleridge of their revolutionary view that poetry should use the language of ordinary people. Among the *Lyrical Ballads* of 1798 *Tintern Abbey* most departs that norm.

Tintern Abbey is central to the Romantic canon; it has also engendered heated debate, including some hostility, in the past decade between radical critics, feminists, and traditionalists. Yet it is massively and meltingly resonant, a view agreed by virtually all readers both pro and anti. Scarcely a phrase fails to move us, suggesting, for me, that among its other qualities it distributed the abecedary to near saturation. I have carried out an examination of every letter, both of the alphabet and in the poem. To report the exercise fully would be impossible; to report even a selection has its attendant risks. We need to avoid congestion, but also to guard against too-obvious patterns, small pleasures that turn out largely inconsequential, and worst of all, a kind of manic detection of empty regularities.[3] There are also those letter-distributions that may be real enough, but that reflect only their syntactical or semantic roots. One has to hang back and then, intuitively though backed by reasonable evidence, go for what seem to be key and/or unexpected clusters, the main group of abecedarial deployments. The debate and criticisms referred to above will be addressed afterward.

Here is the poem's text in full. The reason for providing it is solely the reader's convenience, enabling him/her to check back to the text as we consider the examples it offers. However, if any reader cares first to use it differently, for instance to test his or her own levels of alertness to features already considered in part 2, then of course they are free to do so. At the end of the text we shall go direct into close analysis with, at first, no further general comment.

Lines Composed a Few Miles above Tintern Abbey, on Revisiting the Banks of the Wye during a Tour. July 13, 1798

> Five years have past; five summers, with the length
> Of five long winters! and again I hear
> These waters, rolling from their mountain-springs
> With a soft inland murmur.—Once again
> Do I behold these steep and lofty cliffs,
> That on a wild secluded scene impress
> Thoughts of more deep seclusion; and connect
> The landscape with the quiet of the sky.
> The day is come when I again repose
> Here, under this dark sycamore, and view   10
> These plots of cottage-ground, these orchard-tufts,
> Which, at this season, with their unripe fruits,
> Are clad in one green hue, and lose themselves
> 'Mid groves and copses. Once again I see
> These hedge-rows, hardly hedge-rows, little lines
> Of sportive wood run wild: these pastoral farms,
> Green to the very door; and wreaths of smoke
> Sent up, in silence, from among the trees!
> With some uncertain notice, as might seem
> Of vagrant dwellers in the houseless woods,   20
> Or of some Hermit's cave, where by his fire
> The Hermit sits alone.
>
>   These beauteous forms,
> Through a long absence, have not been to me
> As is a landscape to a blind man's eye:
> But oft, in lonely rooms, and 'mid the din
> Of towns and cities, I have owed to them

In hours of weariness, sensations sweet,
Felt in the blood, and felt along the heart;
And passing even into my purer mind,
With tranquil restoration:—feelings too   30
Of unremembered pleasure: such, perhaps,
As have no slight or trivial influence
On that best portion of a good man's life,
His little, nameless, unremembered, acts
Of kindness and of love. Nor less, I trust,
To them I may have owed another gift,
Of aspect more sublime; that blessed mood,
In which the burden of the mystery,
In which the heavy and the weary weight
Of all this unintelligible world,   40
Is lightened:—that serene and blessed mood,
In which the affections gently lead us on,—
Until, the breath of this corporeal frame
And even the motion of our human blood
Almost suspended, we are laid asleep
In body, and become a living soul:
While with an eye made quiet by the power
Of harmony, and the deep power of joy,
We see into the life of things.

                    If this
Be but a vain belief, yet, oh! how oft—   50
In darkness and amid the many shapes
Of joyless daylight; when the fretful stir
Unprofitable, and the fever of the world,
Have hung upon the beatings of my heart -
How oft, in spirit, have I turned to thee,
O sylvan Wye! thou wanderer through the woods,
How often has my spirit turned to thee!

And now, with gleams of half-extinguished thought,
With many recognitions dim and faint,
And somewhat of a sad perplexity,   60
The picture of the mind revives again:
While here I stand, not only with the sense
Of present pleasure, but with pleasing thoughts
That in this moment there is life and food
For future years. And so I dare to hope,
Though changed, no doubt, from what I was when first
I came among these hills; when like a roe
I bounded o'er the mountains, by the sides
Of the deep rivers, and the lonely streams,

Wherever nature led: more like a man   70
Flying from something that he dreads, than one
Who sought the thing he loved. For nature then
(The coarser pleasures of my boyish days,
And their glad animal movements all gone by)
To me was all in all.—I cannot paint
What then I was. The sounding cataract
Haunted me like a passion: the tall rock,
The mountain, and the deep and gloomy wood,
Their colours and their forms, were then to me
An appetite; a feeling and a love,   80
That had no need of a remoter charm,
By thought supplied, nor any interest
Unborrowed from the eye.—That time is past,
And all its aching joys are now no more,
And all its dizzy raptures. Not for this
Faint I, nor mourn nor murmur; other gifts
Have followed; for such loss, I would believe,
Abundant recompense. For I have learned
To look on nature, not as in the hour
Of thoughtless youth; but hearing oftentimes   90
The still, sad music of humanity,
Nor harsh nor grating, though of ample power
To chasten and subdue. And I have felt
A presence that disturbs me with the joy
Of elevated thoughts; a sense sublime
Of something far more deeply interfused,
Whose dwelling is the light of setting suns,
And the round ocean and the living air,
And the blue sky, and in the mind of man:
A motion and a spirit, that impels   100
All thinking things, all objects of all thought,
And rolls through all things. Therefore am I still
A lover of the meadows and the woods,
And mountains; and of all that we behold
From this green earth; of all the mighty world
Of eye, and ear,—both what they half create,
And what perceive; well pleased to recognize
In nature and the language of the sense,
The anchor of my purest thoughts, the nurse,
The guide, the guardian of my heart, and soul   110
Of all my moral being.

        Nor perchance,
If I were not thus taught, should I the more
Suffer my genial spirits to decay:

For thou art with me here upon the banks
Of this fair river; thou my dearest Friend,
My dear, dear Friend; and in thy voice I catch
The language of my former heart, and read
My former pleasures in the shooting lights
Of thy wild eyes. Oh! yet a little while
May I behold in thee what I once was,   120
My dear, dear Sister! and this prayer I make,
Knowing that Nature never did betray
The heart that loved her; 'tis her privilege,
Through all the years of this our life, to lead
From joy to joy: for she can so inform
The mind that is within us, so impress
With quietness and beauty, and so feed
With lofty thoughts, that neither evil tongues,
Rash judgements, nor the sneers of selfish men,
Nor greetings where no kindness is, nor all   130
The dreary intercourse of daily life,
Shall e'er prevail against us, or disturb
Our cheerful faith, that all which we behold
Is full of blessings. Therefore let the moon
Shine on thee in thy solitary walk;
And let the misty mountain-winds be free
To blow against thee: and, in after years,
When these wild ecstasies shall be matured
Into a sober pleasure; when thy mind
Shall be a mansion for all lovely forms,   140
Thy memory be as a dwelling-place
For all sweet sounds and harmonies; oh! then,
If solitude, or fear, or pain, or grief,
Should be thy portion, with what healing thoughts
Of tender joy wilt thou remember me,
And these my exhortations! Nor, perchance—
If I should be where I no more can hear
Thy voice, nor catch from thy wild eyes these gleams
Of past existence—wilt thou then forget
That on the banks of this delightful stream   150
We stood together; and that I, so long
A worshipper of Nature, hither came
Unwearied in that service: rather say
With warmer love—oh! with far deeper zeal
Of holier love. Nor wilt thou then forget,
That after many wanderings, many years
Of absence, these steep woods and lofty cliffs,
And this green pastoral landscape, were to me
More dear, both for themselves and for thy sake!   159

The poem has 159 lines containing 1237 words. Of this number of words, 514 are different from each other; the rest are repetitions. The poem contains 5,252 letters. Their appearances total: eeeee (681), ttttt (474), ooooo (409), aaaaa (395), nnnnn (369), hhhhh (367), sssss (343), iiiii (340), rrrrr (317), lllll (238), ddddd (208), fffff (165), mmmmm (153), uuuuu (146), wwwww (115), ggggg (114), yyyyy (99), ccccc (81), ppppp (80), bbbbb (64), vvvvv (54), kkkkk (19), jjjjj (9) and qqqqq, xxxxx, and zzzzz (4 each).

The poem's punctuation, as modern texts give it, is unusually self-effacing. Only four lines are end-stopped, including the last. The poem's five sections end with stops of course, but all bar two end at midline, and one of those two ends the poem. The end-stopped lines are 8, 18, 57, and the last line 159. Three of the four end-stopped lines are exclamation marks. Furthermore, there are only thirty-one punctuation stops in total; the poem's average sentence is five lines long. The movement is periodic not staccato. These punctuation stops are exclusively full stops (twenty) and exclamation marks (eleven); in this most hesitant of poems there are no question marks, as though the meditative flow, however uncertain, must be integral to itself, its own breath, unfolding and internal. The rhetorical questions of the *Prelude* and *Immortality Ode* are absent. Finally, in the standard versions of today, only seven words other than line-openers are capitalized. These are *Friend* and *Hermit('s)* twice each, *Wye*, *Sister,* and *Nature.* The contrast with Hopkins for punctuation and Milton for capitals is great.

This continuity is enhanced by the 159 line-openers. It is surprising to note, once one spots it, that all but a bare twenty are among the most unobtrusive words in the language. Fifty of them are prepositions, thirty are articles or article-pronouns like *his* and *these,* just on twenty are conjunctions, and sixteen others are further join-words like *here, wherever,* and *though.* About ten others come from the simplest verb forms such as *have, be, is, do.* What is more, two-thirds of the line-openers have only three letters or fewer, and more than twenty more have only four letters. Only eighteen lines in the whole poem begin with words of any palpable presence, including the first, *Five years have passed . . . ,* from which we see the contrasting force of even innocuous terms when they are longer. *Until* and *almost* start their lines in one of the poem's two famous crescendo passages:

> Until, the breath of this corporeal frame
> And even the motion of our human blood

> Almost suspended, we are laid asleep
> In body, and become a living soul
>
> —43–46

Of the twelve lines immediately preceding this excerpt, all but one begin with a word of only two letters: *of, as, on, his, of, to, of, in, in, of, is, in.* But the common feature isn't the part of speech; namely, preposition, though that is frequent. The common feature is the small number of letters. The word *of* appears in the poem over fifty times; half of them start their lines. The poem's opening passage of twenty-two lines, describing the pastoral scene, trees and cottages by the river Wye, has only four line-openers which are not prepositions, pronouns, or the simplest verbs *(do, are)*; namely, *five, thoughts, green,* and *sent.* The seemingly deliberate self-effacing of these opening words also leaves well over two-thirds of the poem's lines starting with only five different letters of the alphabet.

What is a line-opener? Literally where one writes the first letter, it is also where enjambment does or doesn't occur, and where, if needed, a strong nominal term can reinforce itself. Clearly article or conjunction might well start many lines in any poem. But with Wordsworth consistently leaving the preceding line unstopped, these played-down openers can take the meditation forward without jerkiness, however hesitant this poem's meaning is in most of its phases. Yet the contrasting and famous passages of swelling inspiration and vision (35–49 and 93–111) use exactly the same process. Indeed they homogenize the openings even further, by the successive two-letter words in the first passage as already pointed out, and by the seven successive lines starting with AAAAA in the second:

> And the round ocean and the living air,
> And the blue sky, and in the mind of man:
> A motion and a spirit, that impels
> All thinking things, all objects of all thought,
> And rolls through all things. Therefore am I still
> A lover of the meadows and the woods,
> And mountains; and of all that we behold . . .
>
> 98–105

Tintern Abbey is limpid, fluid, and internal, its mental quality offering itself as it were in the hands, undulating gently up and down rather than arguing with itself in open and strictly controlled dialectic. The poem is certainly one of changeover: *I cannot paint / What then I was . . . That time is past . . .* Yet this most preoccupied of poems constantly replenishes itself; Wordsworth's deep motions of thought and feeling are constant; the page is quiet and the music gentle and rotund; all is continuous. That is what the short opening words enable. This brings us to individual letters. The abecedary has no center and the poet doesn't force one. Yet Wordsworth's change, when at last he puts his sad years in France and after behind him, realizes youth is gone but hasn't yet reached the adult haven of Grasmere, finds its moment of discarding in a memorable utterance:

> Not for this
> Faint I, nor mourn nor murmur; other gifts
> Have followed; for such loss, I would believe,
> Abundant recompense. For I have learned
> To look on nature, not as in the hour
> Of thoughtless youth; but hearing oftentimes
> The still, sad music of humanity,
> Nor harsh nor grating, though of ample power
> To chasten and subdue. And I have felt
> A presence that disturbs me with the joy
> Of elevated thoughts; a sense sublime
> Of something far more deeply interfused,
> Whose dwelling is the light of setting suns,
> And the round ocean and the living air,
> And the blue sky, and in the mind of man:
> A motion and a spirit, that impels
> All thinking things, all objects of all thought,
> And rolls through all things. Therefore am I still
> A lover of the meadows and the woods . . .
>
> —85–103

The key is the letter mmmmm, the meditative mmmmm. Its imprint comes in a phrase of such sonority that few readers are ever likely to forget it: *Not for this / Faint I, nor mourn nor murmur . . .* For there is *abundant recompense* in the unlikely but so right form of *hearing oftentimes / The still, sad music of humanity,* neither harsh nor grating yet of *ample* power to chasten and subdue. Those two phrases, *the still, sad music of humanity* and *abundant recompense,* like many others in the poem have well below the abecedarial norm of ascenders and descenders. More remarkably still, *nor mourn nor murmur* has no ascenders/descenders at all. Even if this is chance it is undeniable that it enhances the phrase visually.

There is another mmmmm-feature. Mmmmm appears in just over a hundred lines in the poem. In no fewer than a third of them, a word containing mmmmm ends the line. As *Tintern Abbey* averages eight words a line, this is a very high rate. Again it gives continuity;

the emotion builds and deepens along the line, and there is then a kind of regular unnoticed enjambment as the self-aware welling of feeling proceeds. Here are some of the phrases with mmmmm in the line's final word: *these pastoral farms . . . my purer mind . . . that blessed mood . . . that serene and blessed mood . . . burden of the mystery . . . this corporeal frame . . . the lonely streams . . . more like a man . . . a remoter charm . . . are now no more . . . hearing oftentimes . . . a sense sublime . . . the mind of man . . . and this prayer I make . . . for she can so inform . . . so impress . . . Therefore let the moon . . . shall be matured . . . a mansion for all lovely forms . . . from thy wild eyes these gleams . . . this delightful stream . . . hither came*—until the very last line of the poem which, although not for the first time, reverses this, putting mmmmm at the beginning: *More dear, both for themselves and for thy sake!*

Ancient-world languages often used mmmmm in the first person pronoun, and only less often in the second person. It is the one letter in our alphabet that we can utter continuously with the mouth always shut. As such it can keen and hum for it has no sharp edges, and by using no open orifice seems to come from the whole mind-body; it is near to the indivisible thought-ribbon of mental and emotional experience. Its visual rendering, with verticals gently curved at the top and with no ascenders or descenders, eases its reading on several occasions. Wordsworth's lexicon abounds with mmmmm through his entire work: *meaning, mood, moon, man, mind, mourn, mountain, gleam, murmur, element, memory, motion, dream, moment, imagine, time, calm, theme, melancholy, home* and many more.[4] *Unremembered* comes twice in *Tintern Abbey,* and within only four lines: *feelings too / Of unremembered pleasure . . . little, nameless, unremembered, acts / Of kindness and of love* (30–35). Even when absent this lexicon is felt running just below the surface. Stephen Gill, knowingly or otherwise playing the letter himself, says the poem's "impassioned music is magnificent and not magniloquent."[5] But then too there is Foucault's wonderful phrase, or his translator's, which we cited earlier; the "murmur of the ontological continuum." Foucault believed the nineteenth century was first to detect such a dimension, one this poem so strongly embodies. Foucault's wider views on historical discontinuity needn't appeal to everyone for us to see the force of the suggestion. When traditional epistemologies broke down, along with belief in language's power exactly to match them, language was left as just one among many orders of knowledge, not its overall sign. Language was left to express fairly primitive entities, wants, hungers, and aspirations, and the very self. Foucault cites Destuut de Tracy writing at the beginning of the nineteenth century: *"To think,* as you see, *is always to feel,* and is nothing other than to feel." The interior was hidden, organic, and powerful. The outward symptoms are "fragments, outlines, pieces, shards" (Foucault 1970, 207, 239–41). The ontological continuum murmurs, the poet turns it into verbal utterance. The abecedary has no center, as we have noted, but occasionally it seems to aspire to one—and, to do Wordsworth justice, in *Tintern Abbey* at least it is not the word-letter "I." In the list for frequency of use of English letters in *Tintern Abbey*, just four letters move up three or more places from their positions for all English usage. Mmmmm is one of them.

The letter nnnnn is cognate with all of this. It appears in the poem, as in English generally, more than twice as often as mmmmm, yet the two nasals are deeply harmonized. Their relationship peaks in the phrase already cited: *hearing oftentimes / The still, sad music of humanity.* Nnnnn then takes over in a counterpoint:

> And what perceive; well pleased to recognize
> In nature and the language of the sense,
> The anchor of my purest thoughts, the nurse,
> The guide, the guardian of my heart, and soul
> Of all my moral being.
>
> —107–11

Nnnnn now, not mmmmm, provides the line-end words, leading finally to that striking phrase *the guide, the guardian of my heart* which introduces the ggggg to join with nnnnn in *-ing,* the passage's last syllable. Indeed, three of the entire poem's five paragraphs end on an nnnnn-word, each a Wordsworth penchant word: *alone, things,* and the ontology of *being* itself. Nnnnn was also second letter in six of the eleven short line-openers before the climactic line already cited: *We see into the life of things.* It hums the line into consciousness; the slight pause from each previous line proceeds with a visible marker and no oral hiatus. By notable contrast, in the opening paragraph about the Wye landscape (1–22), an outward subject, there is not one case of nnnnn as either first or second letter, and only one line-opener *(sent)* contains it at all. That opening passage is external, projective.

If mmmmm utters with the mouth shut, other letters add to the poem's fluency by being open. The vowels are naturally so, but some consonants are open-ended too. Microscopically the physical shapes of rrrrr and yyyyy allow the brain a cumulative association with this openness. The lower-case rrrrr, comparably to ccccc, has a loop swinging to the right, so leaving a space for what is to come yet still seeming part of its own form. Yyyyy's long diagonal tail and its two angled lines above, like antennae to the "sky" whose spelling it ends, makes openness more complete, larger, vigorous. *Tintern Abbey* finds both letters at the ends of their words often and significantly.

Rrrrr earns an atmosphere in the poem's first four lines:

> Five years have past; five summers, with the length
> Of five long winters! and again I hear
> These waters, rolling from their mountain-springs
> With a soft inland murmur.—Once again . . .
>
> —1–4

If rrrrr appeared as often as this throughout the poem, its total overall would increase by a hundred. The first five rrrrrs in the poem, *years, summers, winters, hear, waters* are all open whatever their pronunciation, followed only by the pluralizing sssss if even that. In most British accents the uttered rrrrr, as in *rolling*, differs from the silent one, as in *former years*. If Wordsworth rolled all his rrrrrs when he spoke, as his fellow-Cumbrian poet Basil Bunting believed, then he uses that for the smallholding landscape by the river (*cottage-ground, orchard-tufts, unripe fruits, green, groves, hedgerows*). It is all clinched by the visually and aurally wonderful word *murmur*, surely anticipating its repeat in line 86. Then follow two lines with no rrrrr at all down to *impress*, a rare gap for English:

> Once again
> Do I behold these steep and lofty cliffs,
> That on a wild secluded scene impress . . .
>
> —4–6

Rrrrr is English's comparative letter. Many expressions in *Tintern Abbey* are marked with it. *More deep seclusion . . . my purer mind . . . aspect more sublime . . . coarser pleasures . . . remoter charm* leading to *something far more deeply interfused* and finally paired and emphasized: *rather say / With warmer love—oh! with far deeper zeal/Of holier love.* A space is opened for the reader to fill in, or in which to wait for a word which is never forthcoming. It led Marjorie Levinson to ask, with some exasperation, "deeper *than what*?; purer and holier *than what*?";[6] and indeed there even seems a carryover to other quasi-comparative and rrrrr-marked words: *another gift . . . my former pleasures . . . future years . . .* Other *-er* words with no comparative sense at all get in on this look

and echo: . . . *the power / Of harmony, and the deep power of joy*
. . . That even further *-er* words like *winter* would accrue no such
effect, merely evinces the "weak regularity" of letter-distribution
mentioned earlier. Such are available resources, as well as letter/
meaning fixities.

With yyyyy, the paramount example is another "distance-double" *mystery*—by which of course *the heavy and the weary weight /
Of all this unintelligible world, / Is lightened . . .* Yyyyy ends its
word in nearly four-fifths of its fifty different appearances: *beauty,
betray, day, decay, deeply, dizzy, dreary, gloomy, gently, harmony,
joy, lofty, lovely, solitary,* and *weary.* Hardly surprising in English,
with its yyyyy-ending adjectives and adverbs; yet the place names
of *Tintern Abbey* and the *Wye* themselves literally underwrite it.
The unique *Wye* is the poem's most open sound. This characteristic
seems to touch Wordsworth just as *joy* will as a key line-ender in
The Prelude not so long after. Equally yyyyy can absorb antithesis
in the poem. In the brief paragraph by the river, yyyyys in successive words go from the *joyless daylight* of London rooms to the relief of the *sylvan Wye* that brings such gratitude. The *heavy and the
weary weight* of city life yields to *the deep power of joy* by which,
from nature, we see into the life of things. The time of *thoughtless
youth* is gently displaced by *the music of humanity.* The double-
yyyyyed *mystery* bears this contradictory burden, from which however the affections gently lead us on, until within a dozen lines
yyyyy brings a cluster of tiny peepholes, glimpses of pinprick light:

> . . . A presence that disturbs me with the joy
>
> .   .   .   .
> And the blue sky, and in the mind of man:
>
> .   .   .   .
> Of eye, and ear,—both what they half create
>
> —94, 99, 106

The three-lettered *joy, sky,* and *eye* are all followed by line-break or
pausing commas. Late in the poem (125) we can go *from joy to joy*
with no further interruption.

Rrrrr, yyyyy, and other letters bring change but not total contrast.
So do formations such as *un-,* frequent in this poem as in Shakespeare. To say *unintelligible* (40), rather than for example *opaque,*
retains the intelligibility it contrasts. This kind of low-key contrast
keeps the hesitant meditation within the bounds of unity and allows
progress. But against all this—the punctuation, humming nasals,
open vowels and consonants, and many other things—there are

counter-effects. For there must also be some change of pace or cutting edge present, if the whole was not to be merely seamless or blandly self-examining. One way is by certain sharpened effects, local or widespread, quick or slow, but which are not adversarial. Let's call them "suddens."

For example, there are the rarest letters of both the poem and of English generally; kkkkk, jjjjj, qqqqq, xxxxx, and zzzzz. In small ways, knowingly or not, Wordsworth heightens them all. The nineteen kkkkk-word appearances either entail some sort of repeat (*banks, sky,* and *kindness* twice each; *like* three times in quick succession; *dark/darkness*; *knowing/thinking* linked semantically); or, of the six remaining, five end the lines in which they appear. *Joy* and cognates account for seven of the poem's nine jjjjjs. They come in groups; in lines 48 and 52; then three from lines 84 to 101; then three (two in one line) from 125 to 129. Then a final "joy" at line 145. Wordsworth isolates the quality of *joy* by promoting it. The other three letters all appear four times each. Xxxxx comes only in *half-extinguished, perplexity, exhortations,* and *existence.* Again they are grouped, this time in pairs, at lines 58/60 and 146/9. Possibly the second pair was stirred by the strongest xxxxx-sounding word in the poem though it has no xxxxx itself, Dorothy's *ecstasies* eight lines previously, with which the poet identifies. All is quiet for qqqqq's four appearances; just *quiet, tranquil, quiet,* and *quietness* at lines 7, 30, 47 and 127. There is no question, quickening, quality, or anything else. Of the four zzzzzs, two are in *dizzy,* which with *zeal* give it some presence we possibly *recognize,* even visually, in that elsewhere the voiced sssss would sound like zzzzz without appearing that way so obviously.

The commonest letters, too, supply their "suddens." Eeeee and aaaaa are the poem's first and fourth most frequent letters. We have already cited the aaaaa-sequence of line-openers in the major passage in which *a motion and a spirit . . . rolls through all things.* Added to this, of the sixty *ands* in the poem, exactly a quarter begin their line. Here John Barrell sees lists connecting natural objects, "islands of fixity and clarity in the troubled currents of Wordsworth's syntax."[7] In this whole passage (lines 98–111) *and* is a marshaling agent, *all* a universalizing of categories; and while Wordsworth or his amanuenses often wrote "&" instead of *and,* this did not apply when *and* began the line.

Another passage has aaaaa working even more prominently, and suddenly indeed. It is where the oft-cited hearing/seeing contrast in Wordsworth's experience of nature is most strongly evoked:[8]

(. . . . .And their glad animal movements all gone by)
To me was all in all.—I cannot paint
What then I was. The sounding cataract
Haunted me like a passion: the tall rock . . .

—74–77

There are eighteen aaaaas in four lines, but only nine eeeees. This is a truly extraordinary ratio in English. The lines jump off the page; once noticed, they become visible inseparably from the poem's import. That Wordsworth *cannot paint* the thing he was, is itself like painting, with the three-aaaaa "distance-treble" (plus two cccccs and ttttts) *cataract* immediately underlining it. This sense of aaaaa as fitting for the optical seems to come instinctively to Wordsworth elsewhere in the poem: *In darkness and amid the many shapes . . . As is a landscape to a blind man's eye.* In both these cases eeeee is eclipsed by aaaaa. As to eeeee itself, enough to point out that, when the only two words of the poem containing as many as four eeeees appear, each has a two-eeeee word adjacent: *of unremembered pleasure. His little, nameless, unremembered, acts . . .* Such distributions are way over the poem's normal rates.

Finally of our "suddens" there are the double-llllls and double-sssss's. The distinctively sinuous sssss seems to claim its hiss more than the simpler ccccc can. It is a dangerous letter for the poet of melancholy, and no poet can easily avoid its plurals, particles like *as, thus, his,* or endings of singular verbs. The poem instinctively dwarfs these with sssss's strong double-letter appearances. They subliminally amalgamate the Wordsworthian tropes of abstraction, negation, and passion, and often meet in the same or neighboring lines. The list is: (internal) *passed, passing, blessed, passion, blessings;* (endings) *impress, weariness, nameless, kindness, houseless, less, darkness, joyless, loss, thoughtless, impress, quietness, kindness.* The liquid lllll comes and goes and comes again; the ripple of that compelling idea *felt in the blood, and felt along the heart* rides in the four lllll in the line, the unexpected *along* containing the last. Unusually, there were no lllll at all in the previous two lines. But the poem throughout compounds this by its double-lllll words. Lllll has more of these than any consonant bar sssss, and both are exceeded only by the "etaison" vowels double-eeeee and double-ooooo. In *Tintern Abbey* these four letters have five times as many double-letter appearances as all other double-letter words put together.

Double-lllll is distributed through the poem to quite amazing effect. There are only two anywhere before line 40, when we get the climactically burdened line *Of all this unintelligible world.* This is one of only four lines in the whole poem to contain lllll six times (and no line has five). Here it is a kind of outrider, for there are then no more double-lllls until line 67, when we suddenly get nineteen, no less, in the next forty-odd lines. There is *all* eleven times, interspersed with *hills* at line 67, *tall* (77), *followed* (87), *still* (91), *dwelling* (97), *rolls* and *still* (102), *well* (107), with *all* finally again both clinching and breaking open the whole passage; . . . *soul / Of all my moral being.* This is where *all* swells and spreads, but—like Milton with his *Fall* and its reverberations—Wordsworth has mingled it, consciously or otherwise, with other words of like feature. The same word is comprehensive in Yeats, but with Wordsworth a huge sense of something pressing is relieved.[9] Yet in the poem's last twenty lines, after the last of the poem's six-lllll lines *Shall be a mansion for all lovely forms*, there is no line with even four lllll and only one (line 155) with three. The effect has slipped gently away.

As well as these "suddens" the poem also contains, in one of its own terms (line 53), an intermittently feverish quality that counterpoints the meditative melancholy. Again for continuity, this meditation has to be held in tight grip even as it pursues the poet's alternating sadness and elevation. The key letters are the breathy and feathery fffff and its voiced vvvvv, combined in *fever* and preechoed in the poem's opening word *five*, which is then repeated in a kind of sigh twice in the next line. But fffff's key passage is easily guessed at:

> If this
> Be but a vain belief, yet, oh! how oft—
> In darkness and amid the many shapes
> Of joyless daylight; when the fretful stir
> Unprofitable, and the fever of the world,
> Have hung upon the beatings of my heart—
> How oft, in spirit, have I turned to thee,
> O sylvan Wye! thou wanderer through the woods,
> How often has my spirit turned to thee!
>
> —49–57

If fffff's twelve appearances in this short paragraph recurred in the rest of *Tintern Abbey* at the same rate, it would appear over seventy further times. Fffff borders on such fret elsewhere. Kenneth Johnson has suggested that, despite the "still, sad music of humanity," the poem's sufferings don't really echo the large tragedies of poverty, famine, war, and love's irrecoverable losses. They are sim-

ply one sensitive person for whom things aren't going well.[10]
Throughout *Tintern Abbey* fffff intwines itself into such phrases:
the sneers of selfish men (not the poem's most attractive moment),
the dreary intercourse of daily life, and *if solitude, or fear, or pain,
or grief.* From the Sylvan Wye passage itself, if *the fretful stir /
Unprofitable, and the fever of the world* is the strongest case, then
that paragraph's opening sentence, *If this / Be but a vain belief, yet,
oh! how oft,* has nervously anticipated it.[11]

Elsewhere fffff has a different import. As already said, the preposition *of* appears over fifty times, half of them starting their lines.
It is curious that many of these introduce some nobler feature. *Of
unremembered pleasure . . . Of kindness and of love . . . Of aspect
more sublime . . . Of harmony . . . Of present pleasure . . . Of elevated thoughts . . . Of something far more deeply interfused . . . Of
all my moral being . . . Of tender joy . . . Of past existence . . . Of
holier love.* Is this gentler fffff, voiced in *of* like a vvvvv, trying to
sublimate feverish qualities into worthier areas? They are suddenly
refreshed by the *oft* and *often* in the effusion that ends the Sylvan
Wye paragraph: *How oft, in spirit, have I turned to thee . . . How
often has my spirit turned to thee!* It is as though the preceding *ofs*
had precipitated it. Fffff seems the site of surface expressions of
deep emotion. The short and voiced *if*, which starts the passage,
seems to add to the fffff's fever while the unvoiced quiet fffff
moves alongside the connotations of the vvvvv with its river and
love.

Vvvvv turns out lexically pervasive itself. It is the rarest letter in
the poem bar five. Yet it is in there at the start: *Five years have past;
five summers, with the length / Of five long winters! . . .* and for a
while it stays: *and lose themselves/'Mid groves and copses . . . Of
sportive wood run wild . . . Of vagrant dwellers in the household
woods, / Or of some Hermit's cave . . .* Later it carries both the
heavy and the weary weight of the world, and the resonant *living
soul* the poet becomes when the mortal coil temporarily eases. In
the *sylvan* Wye lines the maybe *vain* belief and the *fever* of the
world—precursing Matthew Arnold's scholar-gypsy—recall the as
yet unwritten *river* to his aid. But it is strongest in the poem's last
section where lies, possibly, what this poem is really about; the
river, evil, believing, living, and *love. Love* and cognates (four of
the poem's eight) overshadow the *evil* (once) whose overlapping
letters it almost shares, powered by Dorothy's *voice* and *service.*

Dorothy enters the poem when the *river* does, cited thus as a singular for the only time, with increasingly biblical resonance. Terms
echo Psalm 23:

> For thou art with me here upon the banks
> Of this fair river
>
> —114–15

and are followed by the poem's moral and emotional outcome;

> Knowing that Nature *never* did betray
> The heart that *loved* her; 'tis her *privilege*,
> Through all the years of this our life, to lead
> From joy to joy . . .
>
> —122–25

None of the catalog of ills, "evil tongues," and the rest *shall e'er prevail against us*. The stress on the equally biblical *prevail* makes it one of the poem's node points. The letter of love—vvvvv for Wordsworth, not the first letter this time—has introduced the denouement of Dorothy's future—from which it then departs:

> Therefore let the moon
> Shine on thee in thy solitary walk . . .

We have a few letters still to go. I realize all too well that this welter of microscopic examples makes for difficult reading. Indeed "reading" may hardly be the word; rather one just has to work through it. But how much more one could say of the lettering of *Tintern Abbey*! We haven't even touched on the dourer consonants, ttttt, ddddd, ppppp, and bbbbb. Those voiced and unvoiced pairs, no doubt coincidentally as believers in the "arbitrary" sign will say, use the same sign, suitably shifted, for three of the four of them. The sign ddddd is the sign bbbbb turned over, like a page, while ppppp is the sign ddddd rotated clockwise through half a circle. In *Tintern Abbey* ddddd ends lines as tellingly as Auden made it do in "In Memory of Sigmund Freud," whose names end accordingly. This is the medieval grammarians' *homoioteleuton* (similarity of endings) which has affinities with the Kabbalists' *notarikon* which no doubt influenced its investigation. *Five years have passed*, Wordsworth's poem begins, and numerous more phrases end on ddddd either at line-end or by punctuation. *These plots of cottage-ground . . . Of sportive wood run wild . . . the deep and gloomy wood . . . other gifts/Have followed . . . For I have learned . . . far more deeply interfused . . . Felt in the blood. . . . / And passing even into my purer mind . . . of all the mighty world. . . .* and others. At one point in the famous elevated passage ddddd ends four lines in eight: *Of aspect more sublime; that blessed mood . . . Of all this*

unintelligible world/Is lightened:—that serene and blessed mood,
. . . And even the motion of our human blood . . . As to ttttt, it
interplays with and without a following hhhhh, the former escaping
towards the poem's end. The added hhhhh perhaps makes ttttt
somewhat cerebral, as though years of close reading have semantically sensitized us to expect that. Hhhhh, notably, is the one letter
from outside to enter the "etaison" group in letter-frequency in the
poem. The eight most frequent letters are the "etaison" seven plus
hhhhh in sixth place.

Bbbbb is the letter of *being* for the poem entire, and its provenance is divided. That word's sole appearance ends a major passage, *of all my moral being*; but such existentialism then turns to
the poet's sister. What Dorothy will come to *be*, under nature's be-
nign care, seems to matter greatly: *. . . .be matured / Into a sober*
pleasure; when thy mind / Shall be a mansion for all lovely forms, /
Thy memory be as a dwelling-place / For all sweet sounds and har-
monies . . . (138–42). The poem has *be* only seven times and three
of them are here. Ppppp, the other plosive consonant, climbs upward; *passing even into my purer mind* till *almost suspended . . .*
(29, 45); later culminating in a spate: *haunted me like a passion:*
appetite . . . by thought supplied . . . and all its dizzy raptures (77–
85); two of the only three double-ppppps in the poem, so close together (the third is *worshipper,* line 152).

Examples of rich letter-distribution abound; no letter or line lacks
them. There are the periodic absences, with no two-eeeee words appearing in the major lines 97–102, for example (the *rolls through*
all things passage), a very rare absence. Surprisingly, too, only the
letter ccccc fails to appear in the Sylvan Wye passage, that is bar
the four usually infrequent letters of English jjjjj, qqqqq, xxxxx,
and zzzzz. Ccccc features heavily in the poem's opening landscape
description; *once* (twice), *cliffs, secluded scene, seclusion, connect,*
landscape, sycamore, cottage-ground, orchard-tufts, clad, copses,
silence, uncertain, and *cave*; but its appearances then decline by a
third in the next paragraph (lines 22–49), to disappear altogether in
the one after (lines 49–57) as already said. In *Tintern Abbey* ccccc
works in risings and fallings.

Sometimes called the alphabet's "thin" letter, iiiii has its saddest
moment while opening four lines out of six, when it whitens the
poem's longest single word:

> that blessed mood,
> In which the burden of the mystery,
> In which the heavy and the weary weight

> Of all this unintelligible world,
> Is lightened . . .
>
> —37–41

Is lightened alleviates *all this unintelligible world* by the same letter. Uuuuu, after its distance-doubles in *murmur* and *subdue*, has a joint distance-doubling with ggggg: *the guide, the guardian of my heart* in a grand double alliteration, a climax to its passage. In the list for frequency of use of English letters in *Tintern Abbey*, as noted earlier, only four letters move up three places or more from their positions for all English usage. Uuuuu, our letter of curvature it will be recalled, is one of them.

Ggggg is hard *(guide)*, soft *(gently)*, silent and visual *(light)* and nasal *(tongue)*.

The poem's -*ing* lexicon seems to become a habit in the way noted in chapter 5, when words of remote meaning share a common letter-cluster: *rolling, passing, pleasing, flying, something, sounding, aching, dwelling, setting, thinking, being, shooting, knowing, healing, feelings, greetings, blessings, wanderings.* Feeling is injected into diverse lexical contexts. No coincidence that again Wordsworth's most heightened transcendental expression has four of these words in three lines:

> Of *something* far more deeply interfused,
> Whose *dwelling* is the light of *setting* suns,
> And the round ocean and the *living* air . . .
>
> —96–98

After *all thinking things* it ends the fifty-line passage on a word found in the poem only once: *of all my moral being.*

Finally wwwww, the poem's nomad: *O sylvan Wye! thou wanderer through the woods* . . . The same metaphor seems close to Dorothy's sexually-charged envelopment:

> And let the misty mountain-winds be free
> To blow against thee . . .
>
> —136–37

The *winds . . . blow*, and after the *waters* at the poem's start wwwww moves like air through the two most elevated passages (lines 35–49, 93–102) as well, centering on the plural *we* of all humanity and backed by the connectives of English: *in which* (three times) *while, what, well,* given added power by *the power / the deep power* until the conclusion firms up, no longer needing this feather-weight letter of the breath, not even once:

> The anchor of my purest thoughts, the nurse,
> The guide, the guardian of my heart, and soul
> Of all my moral being.

—109–11

The final *wanderings*, in the last line but three, bring the poem home. In the frequency list for use of English letters in *Tintern Abbey*, only two letters have moved up four places—no letter moves higher—from their positions for all English usage. Is it coincidence that these two letters are the wwwww and yyyyy of the named river?[12] We have touched at least briefly on all twenty-six letters.

But this is enough of such details. Wider considerations arise. It might seem risky even to try to relate the poem's mere letters to its more controversial interpretations.

In recent years *Tintern Abbey* has been attacked by a number of politically oriented critics. The poem is an evasion of Wordsworth's political past, his disappointment at the failure of the French Revolution, and his consequent suppression of the poverty he and his sister Dorothy witnessed at the abbey in July 1798 (Johnson 1983, 7, 1998, 591–93). This poverty took the form of the starving wretches and poor vagrants who cowered under the abbey's ruined walls. The references to "Nature" studiously avoid the unlovely and dirty coal barges and other industrial activity common on the river at that time, defacing the Nature Wordsworth cherished. The poem sublimates a deeper topic.

The extreme critic of this kind is Marjorie Levinson. Anything Wordsworth doesn't name he "suppresses." He suppresses the poem's historical significance and consciousness, the formulation of the important questions, and of course the abbey itself. Wordsworth variously sells out, erases, glosses over, conceals, and is defensive; the poem in the end is "this great escape" (Levinson 1986, chap. 1 passim). Naming the abbey only by deflection *(a Few Miles above Tintern Abbey . . .)* concedes the true missing topic. The title's date, *July 13, 1798*, ninth anniversary of the eve of the fall of the Bastille, was also eighth anniversary of Wordsworth's arrival in France for a visit both politically and personally unforgettable. To suppress the abbey was to suppress poverty and its revolutionary

response. McGann, too believes that Wordsworth lets slip his com-
pulsions in citing edifice—the "houseless" woods, Dorothy's mind
as a "mansion," and Wordsworth as a "worshipper" of nature, presumably in some kind of church.[13] But as said already, "houseless"
is a Wordsworthian term of opposition, like *nameless, houseless,
joyless, thoughtless,* and so on, and the "smokeless air" in the
Westminster Bridge sonnet. "Mansion" is one of his mmmmm-
nnnnn words, and the context of "worshipper" lies elsewhere.
Whatever else, it recalls that words are things and not merely meanings, a point McGann himself has frequently made.

Gender critics bring a different charge. Anne K. Mellor, John
Barrell, and others note Dorothy Wordsworth's delayed entrance
and Wordsworth's elder-brotherly tone towards her, which at times
is undeniable. For Mellor Dorothy is a "silenced auditor . . . a less
conscious being whose function is to mirror and thus to guarantee
the truth of the poet's development and perceptions." Barrell, making astute points about the poem's language, sees it as working on
two levels. The poet's "thoughts" are for the poem, the simplicities
of nature for his dumb sister.[14] Putting the political and gender
views together, Wordsworth is suppressing his own political past,
and his sister's voice in the present.

Such one-strand views bear their own psychic contradiction. For
it would be as easy to argue that Dorothy's late entrance is the
poem's structural climax, with her *dea-ex-machina* arrival illustrat-
ing the wider Worthworthian theme of love of nature leading to love
of humankind. In saying the poet suppresses one topic, whether it
be political or of gender domination, these critics themselves may
too readily suppress everything else. For instance, they universally
ignore the tour's actual target, another ancient edifice. This was
Gooderich Castle, three times as far again upstream as Tintern is
from Chepstow, where also "five years past" in 1793 Wordsworth
had met the little girl of the poem "We Are Seven." The memory
of this little girl may have become equally pressing. Wordsworth
was still looking for her in 1841, nearly half a century later; she
clearly made some impression on him.[15] How far this memory was
evoked by his "dear sister" of "former years"—that is to say, his
closest sibling throughout his own infancy and childhood—one
might well ask, but it opens up possible readings of lines 114–21,
none of which these critics touch on. Then there is the poem's network of literary echoes from poets of diverse orientation; William
Cowper, John Milton, Mark Akenside, James Thomson, Thomas
Warton, Samuel Taylor Coleridge, and Charlotte Smith.[16] To highlight, as some critics do, only the poem's few phrases from William

Gilpin's guidebook to the Wye, which makes so much of the Tintern poverty, is again selective. Wordsworth had written a lot on poverty in the Lake District, France, London, and on Salisbury Plain; he didn't need to add to it. We might even dare to feel the poem evokes nature; the poet's childhood in a region of beauty and permanence, and his rootless experience of it here, when he and his sister were still unsure where finally to live. Pressures on him at the time were many as Levinson rightly concedes (Levinson 1986, 18). One is left with no single matter culpably left covert, only the complexity of events, people and things from past and present which anyone lives with at any time.

Johnson's recent study (1998) contains a monumental attempt to bring all the poem's explanatory sources together, while still recognizing that so valuable a work as *Tintern Abbey* needs to transpose such manifold material poetically if it is to reach a final and coherent form. Yet we still can't know the micro-occasions of phrases, notions, words, or how their shapes or rhythms haunted the poet's mind; they aren't retrievable. Those days, that weather, that water, those faces, food, walking, small girl remembered, vagrants remembered from all periods, political dates recalled with their telling coincidences, trees, colors, echoes, that wonderful sound, and the phrases from other poets long read and digested. Paradoxically, the more we know of the poet's childhood, background, anxieties, loves, and earlier biographical incidents of life both public and personal, the more inextricable they are from the outcome that matters: the poem itself.

One phrase in the title many of these commentators ignore is "on Revisiting the Banks of the Wye during a Tour." Levinson asks, "Why would a writer call attention to a famous ruin and then studiously ignore it?" One can only reply: why a famous river likewise? The family and circle, especially William and Mary themselves, knew the poem not as *Tintern Abbey* (as some have stated they did) but as "the poem of the Wye."[17] Standing "on the banks of this delightful stream" is where Wordsworth sees himself as "worshipper of Nature" two lines later.

Our abecedarial analysis bears out this presence. It reveals the subdued punctuation, the absence of endstops and harsh contrasts, the flow of the letters, the occasional special use of some hard or feathery consonants, the distribution and increased use of the more open, nasal and liquid letters, and many other effects. The river Wye, with its varying and endless rhythms, would have entered the poet's consciousness deeply. They were beside it, or on it, for the entire trip. The shifts, turns and hesitations noted by all critics keep the poem constantly in gentle motion, itself a common word in the Wordsworthian lexicon. Nature is a stillness around this motion, as are the political memories, local penury, childhood disturbances, sisterly companionship, and everything else in the sad music of humanity that Nature won't betray. The poem is riverine. Its opening four lines set it on the river; the "sylvan Wye" passage (lines 49–57) returns to it and names it—the main text's only place name—and on its banks the poem ends. The poem is hesitant, meditative, fluid, sometimes feverish, beautifully murmuring, continuous.[18] In such respects the poem of the Wye retains its secrets.

14

Emily Dickinson

EMILY DICKINSON WROTE IT "SLANT." THE LINE WHERE SHE STATES this, *Tell all the Truth but tell it slant*—(Poem 1129) is so sharply injunctive that it feels as if she stumbled on it at the moment of writing. Numerous poems startle with their abruptly weird openings. *Split the Lark—and you'll find the Music—* (P861); *'Twas just this time, last year, I died* (P445); *One need not be a Chamber—to be Haunted*—(P670); *I like a look of Agony / Because I know it's true* (P241). Internally a bird stands aside on a path "to let a Beetle pass" (P328); and who would have expected *That odd old man is dead a year* to continue with *we miss his stated Hat*? (P1130). The angular sightings, the comic-irate voice, the sudden disturbing words out of context, the oddly static renderings of garden and house, the terse lines in equally terse poems, the capitalizings and dashes; all these and much else are a seminal originality glancing across rather than directly at its targets. All the more then are the hits against expectation, as to an unwary defender who thought a sniper was aiming elsewhere. Dickinson's stature is debated today; yet her eminence was acknowledged earlier than is sometimes now recognized.

In 1891, only five years after her death, William Dean Howells wrote that "If nothing else had come out of our life but this strange poetry we should feel that in the work of Emily Dickinson, America, or New England rather, had made a distinctive addition to the literature of the world, and could not be left out of any record of it." This despite that Dickinson had had only seven poems published in her lifetime. In the *Boston Herald* the year before, Louise Chandler Moulton had drawn attention to one aspect of this strangeness. "Madder rhymes one has seldom seen—scornful disregard of poetic technique could hardly go further—and yet there is about the book a fascination, a power, a vision that enthralls you, and draws you back to it again and again . . . It enthralls me and will not let me go." For Harold Bloom a century later Dickinson "manifests more cognitive originality than any other Western poet since Dante." And there were numerous accolades in between—and some dismissals too, as by R. P. Blackmur who thought Dickinson happened upon "success by accident" in her output of nearly eighteen hundred short lyrics.[1]

But the gut response, that here is a true and outstanding poet of our civilization, hasn't made it easier to see in just what the greatness lies. Feminist critics have led in acknowledging the stumbling block. Jan Montefiore sees Dickinson's love poems as "so elusive as to escape final definition," and her poems overall as "too ambiguous and contradictory to be read as purely woman-centred texts." Helen McNeil acknowledges that "It is easy not to know Emily Dickinson . . . the type she manifests—the great woman poet—is still in the root sense not known by our culture . . . I also do not know Dickinson fully . . . I have also had to find my way out of assuming that because I am a woman I would know automatically what Dickinson would think, and accept instead the surprise of what she truly thinks."[2] Such generous comment is also astute. The sense of an abyss beneath the poems, of a plot we don't know, itself holds the key to the atomizing of the whole oeuvre. Dickinson's profound awareness of the abecedary, of words as rolles as well as meanings, permeates her poems in several ways as will be suggested. But just what it all amounts to is much harder to say.

The life story holds tantalizing clues. Dickinson was born in Amherst, Massachusetts, in 1830 to a Protestant family of considerable local distinction. Her paternal grandfather was instrumental in the founding of Amherst College where her father Edward Dickinson, a lawyer and eminent public figure, was treasurer for nearly forty years. He was elected to the U.S. House of Representatives in 1852. Like other much observed literary fathers such as Edward Barrett and Patrick Bronte, Edward Dickinson was liberal over both his daughters' education; he was also a dutiful and conscientious citizen. Yet he was also apparently a cold, traditional figure of little imagination or affection; Emily once described him as "pure and terrible" (Kirkby 1991, 3, McNeil 1986, 48). Neither Emily nor her sister Lavinia married. In 1855 their mother, an ineffectual figure it seems, sank into a long and terminal illness. Aged twenty-five Emily took over the running of the household.

In 1862 she was visited by Charles Wadsworth, a clergyman she had met in Washington some years previously. This aroused, in all probability, a deep love human and sexual and to the end of her life in 1886 she became the recluse of popular legend. She seldom left the family house The Homestead or its garden; did not come downstairs to meet callers or for social occasions; did not recite her poetry even at home; and would listen to others playing the piano only through the ceiling. She wouldn't look at the doctor or let him near her even when she had summoned him herself. Mabel Loomis Todd (mistress of Emily's brother Austin) called her "The Myth." Famously she took to wearing the white dress which, many still feel, symbolized the adopted role of child. She would give a flower or a poem to callers, both to avoid speaking to them but also as an ironic way of playing the delicate female. In that same year 1862 she responded to an article by a local columnist, Thomas Wentworth Higginson, calling for poetry by young aspirants. They corresponded for years, but with instinctive insight Dickinson did not act on Higginson's advice. Wadsworth may not have been the only love, though Dickinson's Brontesque and so-called "Master" letters of some years earlier—probably never mailed—may reflect no more than self-abnegation. Emily Dickinson died in 1886.

But countless women in patriarchal societies have endured such constraints. Was Emily Dickinson's poetry her way of coping with them? We need to consider this briefly for our present topic. For three decades now feminist critics have sought the authentic tradition in women's poetry in face of a hitherto male-dominated literary form. Broadly, three strategies have been suggested (I take the "madwoman in the attic" pattern of Sandra Gilbert and Susan Gubar to be not a strategy but a generalized response). Elizabeth Barrett Browning, a heroine for Dickinson, met the male tradition on its own ground. Her Wordsworthian poetry—his portrait always hung in her room at Hope End—culminated in *Aurora Leigh*, the five-book social epic in which the traditional-male hexameter narrative is fused with "woman's" content. Aurora's vocation as poet resists marriage to her suitor. An opposite strategy, commonly associated with the American poet Adrienne Rich, is that the only models for women poets are other women poets. There is a strong enough female canon going back to Sappho, and there is intertextuality at any time. A third approach, from the psychoanalytic critic Margaret Homans, examines the duplicitous roles women use to enter the male tradition. Women can equal men as poets, but ideologically cannot espouse the male stance; so they must find a way in pragmatically. Homans's model is thus Eve, first woman whose deceit is itself prototype of creative imagination in literary form. Homans believes this was Dickinson's strategy, and for McNeil too Dickinson deliberately wrote against the prevailing Emersonian ("Orphic") American tradition of male-orientated poetry.[3]

These views are compelling. But my own sense of it, which is adopted here, is that Dickinson was wary of all these things. Much as she admired Barrett Browning she never attempted poetry of that expanded and discursive order. She can't have taken Rich's position because she absorbed and cherished the male poets. And she may have adopted a pose in her life, but surely not in the poetry, which compels sui generis. Dickinson is perhaps closer to those women poets who disclaim the title "woman poet" altogether and aim for authentic poetry of whatever kind. By writing her poetry as she did and avoiding performance and publication, Dickinson eluded the traps of either competing with males or too obviously opposing them.

In the main Dickinson avoided making ideology explicit. She wrote tersely and askance about the man, the male God, and the "Wife," but these were hardly a main topic—she had none as such—and they could well have swamped the poetry's freshness if she had made them that. Rather these allusions too are "slant." When she says *God preaches, a noted Clergyman— / And the sermon is never long* (P324), she is recording a Sunday morning, but not in church. She is at home, with her orchard and birds, where she "keeps the sabbath" with "God," simply her own thoughts. Elsewhere her humble confession to God ends a terse poem with terser irony:

> More respectful—"We are Dust"—
> We apologize to thee
> For thine own Duplicity—
>
> —P1461

God the father—not a hundred miles from Edward Dickinson—peers out through his Scriptures. *The Bible is an antique Volume— / Written by faded Men* (P1545). Yet in other much-quoted lines we aren't even clear whether she is being flatly caustic about marriage, or literally espousing Christ of whom she is the bride, as was the Church in traditional theology:

> Title divine—is mine!
> The Wife—without the Sign!
> Acute Degree—conferred on me—
> Empress of Calvary!
>
> —P1072

Rather, in wilier fashion, Dickinson swapped pronouns to the point where gender was confounded. Here we start to look at the work more close up. In the poem *I died for Beauty* (P449) lines like

He questioned softly "Why I failed"? are said to refer to Elizabeth Barrett Browning. That might seem straight disguise, like calling oneself George Eliot or George Sands, both of whom Dickinson admired. Elsewhere she wondered about being *Myself that easy Thing / An independent Man* (P801), which may just be irony. But in *Going to Heaven!* (P79) the line *And yet it will be done* seems in context the male-deity reference "thy will be done," strangely shifted. In just as tiny a word though not a pronoun, in one poem she is "Boy", completely in passing (P389). Neutral items may be gendered: *Day—got tired of Me— / How could I—of Him?*; as indeed may language too: "Sometimes I write [a word], and look at his outlines till he glows as no sapphire" (McNeil 1986, 28). Throughout poem 462 she calls herself "it." Her letters bear the same traces. Her "Master" is also "it," and writing to Higginson about "Awe" she said cryptically, "He was an awful Mother but I liked him better than none" (Gilbert & Gubar 1979, 602, 589). Most diluted is an early recollection of days at home: "Ladies call, and evening, and some members of another sex come in to spend the hour . . ." (Kirkby 1991, 9).

These examples indirectly reveal a ubiquitous Dickinson strategy; the microscopic. In the phrases just cited the tiniest words are made luminous as their shifted—or "slanted"—direction dawns on us. *He, Man*, and *Boy* (both herself), *it* instead of "thy," *Him* (for day), "his" (gendering "word"), "it" for herself and her Master, and "he" as a mother are all thus highlighted. The switch of just two or three letters, as with "another" for "the other" here, alters an entire perspective. And this strong tendency to the microscopic marks the poetry in two ways, both surprisingly overt. These are the three-letter word, and the insect. Words of three letters abound. They seem to jump off the page when capitalized, which is frequent, especially when they are nouns. This feature is so prevalent as to be worth looking at more closely. Here is a list of Dickinson's three-letter words. They name domestic objects, basic parts of nature, and simple emotions. The list is far from complete but, apart from staple terms like *she, and, his*, and so on it is representative. The words are given in miscellaneous order so as to capture their quirky and strangely violent presence in the poems: *Key, Boy, Gem, Sew, Log, Sea, Arc, Sky, Woe, Box, Dew, Hat, Sod, Day, Lip, Jug, God, Owl, Hem, Bun, Rip, Eye, Bed, Pod, Gap, Air, Ear, Bee, Sun, Egg, Fly, Bog, Awe, Gun*, and *Doe*.

I have usually tried to keep overt statistics well out of sight in this book, but here perhaps is a chance for a bit of more than usually interesting counting. This sample of thirty-five three-letter words evinces a curious and idiosyncratic distribution of letters. The letter-frequency ranking turns out to be:

E O G A D B Y   S W L P R U I N   H K M C J T X F   Q V Z [4]

The change is remarkable. Instead of our normal "etaison factor" of E, T, A, I, S, O and N, this gives us a first seven of E, O, G, A, D, B and Y. These are followed by a group of five which includes W, L and P. The normally very frequent I and N come down in the middle of the list and the usually second highest T has only one appearance. Furthermore, one hundred and five letters is not too low a sample for at least some normality to be expected of it, and we also find two of the usual "bottom four" appearing, J and X. Further common English words she uses could have included *but, boy, why, job, fix*, and others, all of which contain less frequently used letters. So, in the count for the list we have chosen, there really is something a little weird in finding O above A and more than three times as frequent as I; the trio B, Y, and W all well above R, N, and H; and G nine times as prevalent as T.

In the poems the effect of this strange letter-distribution is exploited and even heightened. In the famous *I'm Nobody! Who are you?* (P288) the tart contempt of telling her name *To an admiring Bog!* ends the poem. Elsewhere, between the form of life and life itself *The difference is as big / As Liquor at the Lip between / And Liquor in the Jug* (P1101). The bird that *let a beetle pass* (P328) a moment later *drank a Dew*, where the indefinite article rather than "some" dew atomizes it even further. *A Window opens like a Pod* (P389) comes in a poem about a neighbor's death. We have already cited the *odd old man* whose "stated Hat" was missed after his death, too. Of the eighteen lines of *Answer July*—(P386) eight end in three-letter words, all capitalized, and no other line-ender has more than five letters. The poem *I went to thank Her*— (P363) contains forty-nine words. Almost exactly a third of them have three letters, twelve capitalized. There are many more cases.

As said earlier, bar a very few exceptions three letters is the usual minimum for any palpably naming term in English, noun or adjective. Three-letter words have certain features. Almost any word of any length bar the single-letter exceptions "a", "O", and "I" must have at least one consonant, and words of vowels plus half-vowel consonants (like *ewe* or *way*), though hardly exotic, are statistically few by definition. So the ratio of consonants to vowels is notably higher in a typical list of three-letter words than it is for longer words. Furthermore, capitalizing such short words increases their unfamiliarity even further. The rolle becomes visible, the sign's physicality all the more "sponges up" its meaning to embody its virtual presence. And by using letters of strange infrequency too, next to their usual appearances in English, Dickinson presents us both semantically and visually with a curiosity. She veers toward the tiny end of the material world-spectrum, and there makes it strange.

This strangeness is both intentional and compulsive. Excess of words both tiny and overtly dull could just make the poetry feel inconsequential. Shakespeare gives Macbeth the sad feeling that "all is but toys" in maybe a toy-like phrase. Only one word in that phrase has more than three letters, and that one only has four by virtue of being a plural. Dickinson's persona has its childlike dimension sure enough, but she has a couple of ways of eluding that as an easy pigeonholing. These two ways turn out to be connected.

One is the intriguing fact that many of her three-letter words name insects. Their place in the world of nature is tiny yet compelling, bizarre, and both affectionate and stark at once. Again and again Dickinson turns to insects. The famous fly in *I heard a Fly Buzz—when I died—* (P465) is a stark focus against the eerie emptiness of dying, until when the light fades *I could not see to see.* The buzzing alone remains;[5]

> I heard a Fly buzz—when I died—
> The Stillness in the Room
> Was like the Stillness in the Air—
> Between the Heaves of Storm—
>
> The Eyes around—had wrung them dry—
> And Breaths were gathering firm
> For that last Onset—when the King
> Be witnessed—in the Room—
>
> I willed my Keepsakes—Signed away
> What portion of me be
> Assignable—and then it was
> There interposed a Fly—
>
> With Blue—uncertain stumbling Buzz—
> Between the light—and me—
> And then the Windows failed—and then
> I could not see to see—

—Poem 465

So much happens, but it is the Fly's zany randomness that closes a stanza, and its capitalized three-letteredness, beating on the windowpane, blocks the light.

The Fly comes and goes in the poetry, along with the Worm, the Beetle, and the Gnat. In the last two lines of Poem 534, "Gnat's" and "Giants" starkly poise tiny with immense in a near-anagram. Unlike that of Herbert, Dickinson's worm is peremptorily dismissed with no hard feelings, by the bird who "ate the fellow, raw" (P328), and by the poet who "secured him by a string" (P1670). The Spider, not strictly an insect, is just as prominent (Gilbert & Gubar 1979, 633–42). The Butterfly is common, as indeed rather differently is the Bird, often in its many species. But most astonishing is the Bee. The Bee occurs nearly ninety times in the whole work. Even terms like "know" and "day," Dickinson's commonest noun, only occur about three times as often. The Bee—a very few times "Bumblebee"—is always capitalized. What is more, it is almost never plural. Since bees live in colonies of some forty thousand members, its lonely state in Dickinson implies a strong focus. Dickinson's insects are rather different from Milton's in the passage we cited from *Paradise Lost*. Milton's insects march forward together, as though to announce how great a multitude they are even if that isn't always obvious on the surface. Dickinson's insects come one by one, randomly and even chaotically, and none more so than the Bee itself. The Bee is variously *saintly, drunken, abstemious, booming, prowling, blameless, delirious, Goblin Bee*, and *Meadow Bee*. It is also "Helmsman," "a Traitor," and "Fame," and it "rows" as in a boat. It gets among the flowers and grass in the garden, associated with both "Noon" and sunlight. Yet although the Bee is evoked—*A Bee his burnished Carriage / Drove boldly to a Rose* (P1339), *Of Silken Speech and Specious Shoe* (P896)—it is never really described. If there is a main connotation it seems to be freedom, to *visit only where I liked . . . With no Police to follow . . . What Liberty!* (P661). Yet this freedom is still mainly confined to visiting the flowers of its choice: *Auto da Fe—and Judgement— / Are nothing to the Bee / His separation from His Rose / To Him— sums Misery—* (P620).

The insect trope touched a chord for Adrienne Rich, who sought Dickinson's personality compulsively by both reading the work and visiting The Homestead. "For months, for most of my life, I have been hovering like an insect against the screens of an existence which inhabited Amherst, Massachusetts between 1830 and 1886 . . . Here [in Dickinson's bedroom] I become again, an insect, vibrating at the frames of windows, clinging to the panes of glass, trying to connect."[6] Insects are tiny; but their angularity, their leggy efficiency, their lack of sentimentality, their beauty, and their flight square with Dickinson's weird perspectives and Rich recognized it.

Across all these three-letter words the obsession with singularity is tied to its abecedarial highlighting. By capitalizing she makes vivid things more vivid; and her ubiquitous dashes, dividing up her discourse into small stabs, adds to the force of the mark on the page. These tiny significations leave beyond them the large abyss they also evoke.

With four-letter words the provenance alters. Sometimes they simply name wider general and natural entities: *Home, Noon, Time, Year, Snow*. But, to take just one feature here, Dickinson commonly used the four-letter word as rhyme, and we needn't go outside the poems already cited to underline the point. There were cases at the start of this chapter: *Split the Lark—and you'll find the Music—* (P861); *'Twas just this time, last year, I died* (P445—where every word bar one has four letters)—and *I like a look of Agony, / Because I know it's true* (P241). Other examples include the last three lines of poem 465, which end with *firm, King* and *Room*; the endings *As cool . . . As numb. . . .* in poem 496; and *the very nearest Room* in poem 1760. In some variants the four-letter rhyme word is preceded by another close to or actually beginning the line in a seemingly pointed balance, and followed by another four-letter rhyme in the next line. Poem 1461 has *More respectful—"We are Dust" - / We apologize to thee*, and poem 1072 reverses that order with *Title divine—is mine / The Wife—without the Sign!* Two poems about the three-lettered Bee juxtapose it with the same rhyming flower: *A Bee his burnished Carriage / Drove boldly to a Rose* (P1339), and *Auto da Fe - and Judgement—/ Are nothing to the Bee / His separation from His Rose* (poem 620), while a third looks down at her feet: *Of Silken Speech and Specious Shoe* (poem 896), as we have seen already too. Poem 79 with its *and yet it will be done* seems to echo Herbert's "thy will be done" at the end of his poem "The Crosse." And in the final stanza of poem 1104, the nearly mutually exclusive spellings of the starting-words *A Vastness. . . .A Wisdom. . . . A Peace* are followed line for line by the four-letter rhyming words *came, Name*, and *Home*. In two poems the four-letter rhyme dominates overwhelmingly. In the well-known *She rose to His Requirement*, already cited whole, six lines out of twelve end with four-letter words, while in the equally famous *I felt a Funeral, in my Brain* (discussed below) there are nine four-letter rhyme words in twenty lines, five of them in the last eight. To curtail this discussion here I will only suggest that a certain calming is achieved by these words, just as, briefly, even Dickinson's chaotic world must be briefly mollified. And yet even there the lasting impression is of the strange contrast with that great range of teeming insectile three-letter terms.

But this absorption, not to say obsession, with the tiny has its polar opposition. Again and again it is contrasted with immensity. This is the second way in which the three-letter prevalence avoids the risk of mere child-expression. Dickinson faces up to contexts increasingly vaster, unattainable and, at times, more ominous; next to infinity all sizes are relative. In one key pattern the microscopic stands over against the immense, the small to the large, with no intervening middle-size term. *My Basket holds—just—Firmaments* she begins one stanza (P352). When another poem starts with *The Missing All—prevented Me / From missing minor Things* (P985), we sense the adduced "All" is only "Missing" in not having palpable objects nearby; animals or furniture by which to name it. Instead, there is the tiny though alliterating *Me*, right in the middle. In a kind of characteristic oxymoron Dickinson called all this "a nearness to tremendousness" (Reeves 1959, xxix). She spent most of her life in the same house, whence she probed into the big things that assailed her; religion, the cosmos, eternity, love. This forced her to a perspective, which she capitalized on, by which the small stood to the large as a main source of metaphoric comparison or metonymic juxtaposition. In their different ways the "All," the immense, the spiritual, the hidden, and the dark are as omnipresent in her poems as is the immediate. Slicing across from one domain to its opposite like this, without wearisome journeying between them, gives her poems the quirky feeling that critics have often noted.

Late in her life this formula was cleanly expressed in terms of mythological distance: *Elysium is as far as to/The very nearest Room* (P1760). The context is a sickbed. But the small/large dichotomy comes out long and strong in another well-known poem, also on the theme of gender:

> She rose to His Requirement—dropt
> The Playthings of Her Life
> To take the honorable Work
> Of Woman, and of Wife—
>
> If ought She missed in Her new Day,
> Of Amplitude, or Awe—
> Or first Prospective—Or the Gold
> In using, wear away,
>
> It lay unmentioned—as the Sea
> Develop Pearl, and Weed,

> But only to Himself—be known
> The Fathoms they abide—
>
> —P732

Ironically—for the "Wife" seemingly had to give up both—the "Playthings" are a long way from the "Amplitude, or Awe" and the "fathoms" where they abide. Yet there is no movement between them, for Dickinson's nondiscursive mode allows the syntax no extension. There is a slight curiosity in the word-length distribution in this poem. There are fifty-three words in the two-to-five-letter range, only four words in the six-to-eight-letter range, but six in the nine-to-eleven-letter range. Four up to six may not seem much increase, but word-counts normally drop away considerably as they get past eight or so letters. This finding here is no more than a hint of Dickinson's penchant for the small-large discrepancy in her imaginative orientation, but it is borne out by the single lines already quoted, and others too. Another "tiny-immense" poem keeps the large-scale infinities firmly for the last stanza:

> The Crickets sang
> And set the Sun
> And Workmen finished one by one
> Their Seam the Day upon.
>
> The low Grass loaded with the Dew
> The Twilight stood, as Strangers do
> With Hat in Hand, polite and new
> To stay as if, or go.
>
> A Vastness, as a Neighbour, came,
> A Wisdom, without Face, or Name,
> A Peace, as Hemispheres at Home
> And so the Night became.
>
> —P1104

After the near and small Crickets, Workmen and twilight like Strangers "Hat in Hand," the engagement with the unnameables sits on the page in a vertical, centrifugally split list of words of almost mutually exclusive spelling:

> A Vastness
> A Wisdom
> A Peace

Vastness and *wisdom* overlap only in the sssss. *Vastness* and *peace* have a common overlap in the aaaaa and the eeeee. But w*isdom* and *peace* have no overlapping letters.

Many poems in the oeuvre make the tiny-immense issue specific and overt. Two of them succeed each other in the standard text; poems 737 and 738, so they only shortly follow poem 732, one of the two poems just discussed. Poem 737 compares the moon to a small human mortal. It begins, "The Moon was but a Chin of Gold / A Night or two ago," and it ends:

> Her Bonnet is the Firmament—
> The Universe—her Shoe—
> The stars—the Trinkets at Her Belt—
> Her Dimities—of Blue

Four very large items, four very small ones, each paired neatly off with no intermediaries. Again there are four-letter words at the ends of lines. This is an interesting closure, for in the intervening stanzas the aim had been rather more to give the moon a human personality. The moon looks down at earth, could smile if she so wished, and thinks of her "privilege" at being the "remotest" star—this last a curious designation for what, to the eye, is the nearest. Once more we sense the deep instinct to insert space or even an abyss between perceived entities. The other poem, 738, is worth citing entire, for it takes the same instinct for tiny-immense duality into a love context:

> You said that I "was Great"—one Day—
> Then "Great" it be—if that please Thee—
> Or Small—or any size at all—
> Nay—I'm the size suit Thee—
>
> Tall—like the Stag—would that?
> Or lower—like the Wren—
> Or other heights of Other Ones
> I've seen?
>
> Tell which—it's dull to guess—
> And I must be Rhinoceros
> Or Mouse
> At once—for Thee—
>
> So say—if Queen it be—
> Or Page—please Thee—
> I'm that—or nought—
> Or other thing—if other thing there be—

With just this Stipulus—
I suit Thee—

Precisely because this no longer has a cosmic provenance the strong small-large division is the more notable. Dickinson seems to be wrestling with an inner dilemma. The love she feels threatens to overshadow the deep division that is her normal urgency. It is resolved by herself being in the end "nought," which reinstates that opposition in that the lover presumably remains very sizable. The poem moves back and forth between her two feelings in a controlled anguish. It begins by clearly setting up the great-small contrast, but at once moves to the qualification "or any size at all," which is particularly minimal in eschewing her usual capitalizings. This lack is repeated almost at the poem's end with "I'm that—or nought— / Or other thing—if other thing there be—," where two lines with no capitals at all bar the line-beginnings are a rarity indeed. But meantime the irresistible instinct to pair off small and large must have its expression too. So Stag/Wren and Queen/Page intervene; but the one that really opens up space between its sizes, "Rhinoceros/Mouse," is firmly announced right in the poem's middle. Dickinson is thus set free to declare her love's subjection at the end as she properly must—via the seemingly overriding stipulation that "I suit Thee"—but with her own mode of saying so, as indeed usually of saying anything at all, also fully inscribed.

Yet it seems clear too, that although the universe contains large and small, the poem's speaker rates herself firmly in the latter category. Of the poem's ninety-four words only six have six or more letters. Exactly half the poem's lines begin with a two-letter word. The one line beginning with a one-letter word, the first-person pronoun for herself, is the last. The longest word by far is of course the mocking "Rhinoceros," and this is pointed up further in that the other names, Mouse, Queen, Page, Wren, and so on are all down in the middle-length or small-length group. If I seem to be pressing this point rather far, it is only because length of word in Dickinson turns out so very important; more so even than in Wordsworth for example, despite his equally brief line-openers and his contrasting lengthy negatives *unremembered* and *unintelligible*. And it isn't solely length. The strong vowel aaaaa appears in this poem twenty-two times. Yet when Dickinson speaks of herself rather than quoting her lover, it nearly disappears. "Or lower—like the Wren—," "And I must be Rhinoceros / Or Mouse / At once—for Thee—", "I'm that—or nought— / Or other thing—if other thing there be—/ With just this Stipulus— / I suit Thee—"; three appearances in almost half the entire poem. This is a kind of freak, but so much of Dickinson's abecedarial use feels like freak.

Overall, then, this holding apart of the tiny and the immense has important significance. In general it suggests a massive mind in a frail body secluded and untouched, and this is expressed in a similar contrast more widely; a vast collection but of short and often tiny poems. But it also underscores the size of the cosmic in Dickinson's apprehension. Just as important though, in maintaining the distance between them, it leaves the vast gap in which nothingness reigns, and where therefore, perhaps, chaos, and catastrophe may enter, too.

Dickinson is not averse to letting the long words accompany each other, or stand against smaller ones, when abstraction is entailed. Abstraction is a different angle on the small-large axis. The immediacies of small things like jugs and bees may stand opposed not only to the universe but also to the human capacity, more than that of the animals, to go some way toward at last apprehending our dual situation in its presence. We are tiny but we can feel that limitation. Again we need only refer to already-cited excerpts. In the lines "More respectful—"We are Dust"— / We apologize to thee / For thine own Duplicity—" the statement about God's nature is clearly marked by the three longest terms. The same word-length appears in lines like *He questioned softly "Why I failed"?* where there are just two midlength words, while theology's location in Scripture itself is underlined in *The Bible is an antique Volume— / Written by faded Men.* A strong contrast between duty and the pleasures of childhood appears in the assertion that "She rose to His Requirement—dropt / The Playthings of Her Life," a poem we have already adduced in this small-large connection. Far the two longest terms make the conceptual contrast very sharp. And even when the fly buzzes and Dickinson in a convoluted mental state "could not see to see," the King (no less) is "witnessed—in the Room," and a "portion of me" is "assignable." The Bee's one presumed value gets the line's longest term too: "With no Police to follow . . . What Liberty!" Just possibly when she says that "God preaches, a noted Clergyman— / And the sermon is never long" the final word, again a four-letter one, is an ironic comment on this whole issue. Most intriguing though are the lines cited earlier about difference. "The difference is as big / As Liquor at the Lip between / And Liquor in the Jug." The notion of difference itself—far the longest term here—finds the homeliest point of comparison imaginable. "Difference" as a general motif behind all Dickinson is uttering gradually turns out quite revealing.

Other signs are foregrounded, too. Taken together, these seem to evoke the chaos already referred to. There are the rhymes for example, which almost wilfully mismatch within common letter-clusters: "Things/Hinge" (P985) and "inch/Experience" (P875). These are no doubt some of the "madder rhymes" Louise Chandler Moulton focused on. But there is also the centrifugal tendency of the letters of prominent words. They exploit the fewness of the abecedary discussed above and already particularly seen in George Herbert. Frequent trios of adjacent words contain nearly mutually exclusive letters. They come either three in the same line or two together with the third just above or below them on the page (there are occasionally intervening particle-words). For example: *Gamblers/Toss/dice* (P21), *swamps/pink/June* (P22), *Oozed/crimson/bubbles* (P28), *dusk/boat/gurgled* (P30), *purple/Host/Flag* (P67), *Woods/exchange/smile* (P74), *Bee/quaffing/Hock* (P230), *Dimity/Horror/freckled* (P401), *paused/Swelling/Roof* (P712), *Yesterday/Girl/school* (P728). The phrase "Rower and Yacht" begins a line in poem 453; the phrase "Empress of Calvary" was already cited above, with its nearly different consonants and its balance of two doubled vowels bridged by just one "ooooo" between them. In the same poem this phrase followed, and so contrasted, a mass of iiiiis: *Title divine—is mine! / The Wife—without the Sign!* The abyss between nonrelated terms, themselves thus also suggesting the chaotic, is again evoked.

The precept that "the first letter owns the word" is strongly highlighted by the capitalizings. Centrifugality of spelling is pointed up further by the many contrasting cases down the left-hand margin, when the same word or letter starts several lines in succession. In poem 43 "Could" begins four lines out of six, and in poem 154 "Except" begins five out of six. In the first nine lines of poem 46— only eleven lines long—IIII begins four of the first five lines and BBBBB the lines 6–9. In one poem of eight lines (P107) the first six begin with TTTTT, and in another of eight lines (P113) the first four begin with OOOOO. In the twelve-line poem cited above (P1104) every line bar one begins with TTTTT or AAAAA. One senses here Dickinson's urgent energy, for her identification with the set of signs that writing entails meant that successive lines could shoot out of the same signal source quite naturally.

Sometimes the centrifugality and its opposite effect in centripetal repetition are closely combined. Poem 91 has successive lines starting *So bashful/So pretty/So hidden*, where only eeee and hhhhh are repeated. In poem 496 the word "As" starts seven successive lines, but these include the succession *As far . . . / As cool . . . / As numb*

. . . / *As if* . . . Only fffff is repeated, and that by both starting the sequence and finishing it. This is an unusually interesting case, for it is an example of the medieval figure of *anaphora*, in which successive different lines are introduced by the same word. Curtius (page 44) sees anaphora as belonging to the medieval category of "figures of language", as opposed to that of figures of thought, but Puttenham (cited and in Taylor 2002, 121) saw it as symptomatic of dance, in which a first step leads to many variations. This seems like the *idem in alio* principle we noted in chapter 1, and one has to ask how far Dickinson was taking it to extremity by so ensuring that not only the words but the very letters, apart from those in the one opening word, were as varied as possible. It is still maybe not quite a "figure of thought," but certainly the nuance of plurality and abundance on a common base seems part of what the phrases express.

Telling it slant, it seems then, is a unique case of abecedarial distribution, and the unconvinced reader may like to look for further cases. But the question is of what all this amounts to. Helen McNeil sees Emily Dickinson as striving for "a curious kind of *written* silence" (McNeil 1986, 63; her emphasis). The centrifugal trios, the capitalized letters, and the dividing dashes charge up the individual word, and they enact the discontinuity of Dickinson's atomized sense of reality. This atomizing functions at the levels of letter, word, phrase, and short poem itself; each is a multiple subdivision of the next stage moving outwards. It all recalls the catastrophe theories of contemporary physics as a real-world challenge that, as we have mentioned earlier in this book, abecedarial stability might have to resist. Clusters of law-like events may occur together but entirely separately from any other similar local cluster. On this view, the peaks of the literary canon are a series, not of continuities as T. S. Eliot believed, but of wholly new beginnings. It is not that earlier literature was not read or absorbed, but that its reformulation is fresh. The abecedary's stable nature, furthermore, is what allowed Dickinson to risk her catastrophic mode of expression. McNeil sees the periodic citing of the "Gem" (consonant at each end) as itself symbol of the diamond-hard term that doesn't merge with its neighbors. As cited already, "Sometimes I write (a word), and look at his outlines till he glows as no sapphire." Gems are not the only comparisons. Insects, flowers, bits of furniture, stars, and other items equally stand out. Dickinson's statement to Higginson that after her tutor's death "for several years my lexicon was my only companion" (Reeves 1959, x) answered a question of his, not about words but about her books; the tome of individual words was her last resort.

Indeed, Dickinson may have internalized the alphabet as a medium. In the year she entered Mount Holyoke Seminary, required reading for students who sought admission included Isaac Watts's *The Improvement of the Mind.* In effect, Watts cites the medieval educational practice of attaining literacy by starting with the letter and working on upward. "Beginning with A, B, C, and making syllables out of letters, and words out of syllables, has been the foundation of all that glorious superstructure of arts and sciences, which have enriched the minds and libraries of the learned world in many ages" (Kirkby 1991, 21). Dickinson finds solace in this precious thing that could never be taken from her:

> Might someone else—so learned—be—
> And leave me—just my A-B-C -
> Himself—could have the Skies—
>
> —P418

Perhaps this compulsion can leave the abecedary itself as the one text that won't deceive us, because it utters nothing we could then falsify. But it is also the final atomizing. There is an extrapolation here that may seem fanciful but is perhaps worth adding. Gubar and Gilbert connect Dickinson's virginal white dress with the cold "Snow" that ends some important poems (for example, P135), and with other aspects of white's meaning, too. White is a blank space to which Gubar and Gilbert give some emphasis. In Dickinson's poetry white is "both the energy (the white heat) of Romantic creativity and the loneliness (the polar cold) of the renunciation or tribulation Romantic creativity may demand . . . [White] paradoxically represents both a divine intensity and a divine absence, both the innocence of dawn and the iciness of death, the passion of the bride and the snow of the virgin . . . It is the colour of the lily's foot and of the spider's thread, of the tender Daisy's petals and of the experienced Pearl's tough skin" (Gilbert and Gubar 1979, 615). Everything in fact bar the blank page on which Gilbert and Gubar write; Emily Dickinson likewise. Her blank page and atomized letters leave her with only the chaos to express and any way she wants by which to do it.

Of course, naming-words must be connected syntactically, too, to have life at all. Roman Jakobson suggested that aphasia disturbance in clinically committed patients was of two types, on the two principles of metaphor and metonymy.[7] Patients with blockage in the "selection principle" (similarity/metaphor) could not initiate a dia-logue. They could intervene only in one already started by others. Loosely speaking, they couldn't use nouns, only link-words like copula verbs or conjunctions. The opposite kind of blockage, which pertained via the "combination principle" (contiguity/metonymy), left the afflicted with a word-heap. Loosely speaking, they couldn't use link-words, only the nouns, which needed to be linked. In *I heard a Fly Buzz—when I died—* (P465), also cited earlier, the syn-tax is firm enough for its purpose, but the verbs are static. This allows the mysterious allegoric connection between the nouns to surface strikingly. Bar "Signed," the very term of signification (and bar of course some lines' opening words), all the capitalized words are nouns: Fly, Stillness, Room, Stillness, Air, Heaves, Storm, Eyes, Breaths, Onset, King, Room, Keepsakes, Fly, Blue, Buzz, and Windows. The only sense of motion comes from the "uncertain stumbling" of the Fly itself.

But even so the vacancy, along with maybe the plot we don't know, remains. And when nothing tangible is present and feeling alone is at issue, the syntax itself steps forward. It is sometimes in a state of collapse, a further instance of the atomizing urge and its expression of catastrophe or the chaotic. In the love poems a furtive obscurity suggests the illicit. This poem was probably written in 1862 shortly after Charles Wadsworth visited The Homestead in Amherst:

> "Why do I love" You, Sir?
> Because—
> The Wind does not require the Grass
> To answer—Wherefore when He pass
> She cannot keep Her place.
>
> Because He Knows—and
> Do not You—
> And We know not—
> Enough for Us
> The Wisdom be it so—
>
> The Lightning—never asked an Eye
> Wherefore it shut—when He was by—
> Because He knows it cannot speak—
> And reasons not contained—
> —Of Talk—
> There be—preferred by Daintier Folk—
>
> The Sunrise—Sir—compelleth Me—
> Because He's Sunrise—and I see—

Therefore—Then—
I love Thee—

—P480

A sequential meaning can just be traced, but there are barriers. The obdurate world is there in Wind, Grass, Lightning, Eye, and Sunrise, but such terms are few and dispersed. There are actually more capitalized words in this poem than in *I heard a Fly buzz* (twenty-four as against nineteen) even though the poems are of almost identical length (ninety-one and ninety-two words respectively); but these words are more fugitive. They denote less firm entities in the real world. Ten of them are pronouns. The apostrophe between verb and object in line 1 is disconcerting, and the referents of "He" and "You" in the second stanza are unclear. If "You" is as in line 1, then "He" may perhaps be God, granting the grammatically incomprehensible phrase "The Wisdom be it so" at least a kind of gnomic status. Yet the struggle to reach the unequivocal final line entails three preceding lines of incoherent syntax, so that any other clear avowal of identity may be firmly denied. Unlike in *I heard a Fly buzz*, the dashes and capitals now just muddy the waters, which of course must be exactly what she intended. While relying on the abecedary's stability, Dickinson tests its equable tolerances and its general distributive capacity to the limits.[8]

Was she aphasically disturbed—eccentric, a child, mad, as no few critics seem at times to protest against or wonder (Gilbert and Gubar 1979, 58, 594)? If not, did she affect such for her own good reasons? Two well-known poems with curiously matching titles, *I felt a Cleaving in my Mind—* (P937) and *I felt a Funeral, in my Brain* (P280), suggest that Dickinson herself had such fears. But this need not go beyond what any solitary person might feel if prone to depression. Rather, a final question is raised, of Dickinson's capacity for intellectual activity. Earlier Dickinson criticism sometimes tied this to gender difference.

The American poet Allen Tate wrote of Dickinson: "She could not in the proper sense think at all . . . we must conclude that her intellectual deficiency contributed at least negatively to her great distinction" (Reeves 1959, xliv). Yet this preposterous chauvinism comes in context of some admirable defenses. Much as she was constrained—and Tate was surely right in at least some ways—Tate goes on to assert that "all pity for Miss Dickinson's 'starved life' is misdirected. Her life was one of the richest and deepest ever lived on this continent." That might narrow the "deficiency" down to a specialty, presumably the structured reasoning proper to abstract thinkers of either sex. But Dickinson herself was more than capable of such reflections, even if they came sparingly. *I reason, that in Heaven— / Somehow, it will be even— / Some new Equation, given— / But, what of that?* (P301). There are other cases, for example the poem *A Thought went up my mind today—* (P701). But in the main her mental work was knowingly more immediate. Dickinson discovered what she called "the truth's superb surprise" by writing down hitherto inarticulated experiences. *By intuition, Mightiest Things / Assert themselves—and not by terms— / "I'm Midnight"—need the Midnight say—?* (P420).

Such examples seem clue to the great void that we have suggested is often felt behind Dickinson's writing. It is not enough to say that her signifiers have no referents, no signifieds. On the contrary, the signifieds leap up on to the page with tremendous presence and force, capitalized, isolated, and abecedarially radiant, as I have hoped to illustrate. Rather, there is still a space in which she (ambiguously) "finished knowing" (P280) even when the poetic event was consummated. The poet "distills amazing sense / From ordinary meanings." The ordinary is the small, the amazing reaches out for the vast or infinite. Dickinson has to seize and secure the words, the "rolles" or rows of letters in front of her, because in the "slant of light" where in broader sense she might be said to have lived, she found "internal difference, / Where the Meanings, are" (P258). And again the longer words in the abstract context are suggestive in both these cited sentences.

A century before Derrida this "difference" brings to mind the difference which lies at the base of any marking, any inscription on bland primal reality whatsoever. But Derrida's "difference" was conceived in the face of a metaphysical absence to which however, as he averred, his thought is always a necessary supplement.[9] Dickinson's "internal differences" may compare rather with the sets of binary differences that Derrida's structuralist predecessor Claude Levi-Strauss found at work in tribal life. Rather than extrapolate abstract verities from a Platonic universal source, the organising principle of tribal life was that of clear distinctions between general but perceived categories experienced in the palpable worlds of plant life, kinship, language, food, human events such as war, and the like. Levi-Strauss posited five binary pairings from which tribal thinking drew its own classifications of reality. These were earth/ sky, life/death, animal/human, male/female, and raw/cooked.[10] Clearly this pattern formally arranges the kind of thing Kwame Gyekye found in the networking pattern of Akan philosophy. Any everyday phenomenon could be assigned to the subdivisions of these pairings.

One could read Dickinson via such clear binaries. There is the small/large already mentioned; the "insect/immense." There are also the overt oppositions of house/outdoors, riches/poverty, man/wife, writing/speech, and noon/night. But no such implied classification would fit exactly. The chaos remains, and the turbulence of her syntax and impulsive voice would turn any tidy scheme into a grandly messy one. The difference between Allen Tate's "thinking" and this Levi-Straussian difference is not a difference of level of intellect but that between philosopher and anthropologist. Dickinson's four-square poems recall the ancient origins of across-down writing, her dash-separated phrases are comparable to the proverbial, her long-short terms give body to her relentlessly binary orientation, and her abyss or void asserts what we earlier called the unnameable. As was observed in chapter 1, peoples without distancing technologies and close to earthy reality also experienced the unnameable as a boundary category in a way our own world does not. Dickinson approached, but still always drew back from, finally articulating what language couldn't inscribe. The British poet the late Ted Hughes recently referred to this in her: ". . . something unnameable at the heart of her poetry . . . the subject of some of her greatest poems."[11] The more Dickinson was aware of her own mental processes, and their sometimes endangered condition, the more she ended up with clear stories of a kind of chaotic annihilation round this unreachable articulation. She entered this void herself, but also held it at bay by the rows of capitalized nominals, huge and microscopic, that she herself could touch and hold in relation to each other. One of her most famous poems (P280) articulates this:

> I felt a Funeral, in my Brain,
> And Mourners to and fro
> Kept treading—treading—till it seemed
> That Sense was breaking through—
>
> And when they all were seated,
> A Service, like a Drum—
> Kept beating—beating—till I thought
> My Mind was going numb—
>
> And then I heard them lift a Box
> And creak across my Soul
> With those same Boots of Lead, again,
> Then Space—began to toll,

As all the Heavens were a Bell,
And being, but an Ear,
And I, and Silence, some strange Race
Wrecked, solitary, here—

And then a Plank in Reason, broke,
And I dropped down, and down—
And hit a World, at every plunge,
And Finished knowing—then—

Funeral/Brain, Drum/Mind, Box/Soul, Boots/Space, Bell/Heavens, Plank/Reason—a physical object or event stands for or beside a mental or spiritual idea in every case; and Emily Dickinson "finished knowing" when this binary way of thinking, the "difference/ where the Meanings, are," itself ended. The unforgettable voice through all the poems lies close to the equally distinct flair for abecedarial distribution. She knew herself, it seems, as exactly as any poet ever did; perhaps therein lies what we value in her work.

15

T. S. Eliot

W<small>E CAN STILL RECOGNIZE THE FAMILIAL AND PROVINCIAL SETTINGS</small> of Wordsworth and Dickinson. But they aren't remotely urban, and scarcely mechanized. With T. S. Eliot we glimpse the modern urban world. *The Waste Land* and *Four Quartets* were written just after World War I and during World War II respectively. Those mechanized wars are still aped in countless films and TV features. Transport, business, media, medicine, and political protest from those periods look like early runs of our own. Our times are now moving on further still, into total electronic information, cultural/racial relativity, and a foundationally threatened environment, but those things come later. Of the five poets considered here, Eliot's life alone overlapped those of many people still living. The twentieth century underwent a seismic shift since previous eras, far exceeding the usual rates of change, and the texture of its poetry was equally made new, as the Modernists intended.

The Waste Land relies heavily on the abecedary's stability, for it alludes to poetry and Scripture from hundreds of years earlier. Yet it also fully exploits the abecedary's distributive nature and threatens its equability at every turn. In the poem, the abecedary must tolerate every difference of tongue, patois, line-length, fragmenting or continuity, syntactical mode, presence and absence of punctuation, clusters of capitals, and naming itself. One result is a text that draws its virtuality from the very physicalities it seems burdened with. *Four Quartets* sits more easily with the abecedary's equable nature. Its distributions are wider but more orderly, and it has more flow between modes of discourse, enabled by the softer consonants such as the semi-vowels and nasals. It searches for spiritual resolution under equal pressure but in a more continued meditation. One result is a text that asserts its virtuality over its physicalities, even though it resorts rather desperately to the latter as named symbols at regular points. *The Waste Land* uses the two ends of the "fewness" continuum (sameness and total centrifugality) more than does *Four Quartets*, but both poems are laced with "incremental repetition," as it has been called, awkwardly spurred as that was by Eliot's early reading of Jules Laforgue.[1] *The Waste Land*, one might say, is littered with letters—litter itself figures strongly as an image—yet both poems are profoundly sonorous, so much so that they raise that to consciousness and speak throughout of their own chanting. They are then a redoubled challenge to us to see how the abecedary locates or even calms such echoing and re-echoing. It gives it somewhere to reside, thus holding out the hope of equability as lasting.

One such echo and re-echo in *The Waste Land* comes right at the start as, apparently, agent of April's latent but cruel power. The *-ing* verb or participle ending, referred to more than once in this book already, ends five of the very first six lines. Of course, this has often been noted. Even the exception, *spring rain*, uses the same syllable and underlines the seasonal theme. The gentle spondee of *spring rain* eases and refreshes what had been nervous in the participles. Each participle comes jerkily after a comma yet at the end of the line, as though to express the sharp, successive leaps in the renewed fertility. But after *breeding, mixing, stirring, covering,* and *feeding*, the eighth line's participle is different. *Summer surprised us, coming . . .*—but the line doesn't end there. It continues *over the Starnbergersee,* the fashionable lake resort near Munich. This is emphatic, for as early as line eight *Starnbergersee* is the poem's longest word, equal first with *Shakespeherian* at line 128. It is as though, in some obscure fashion, spring is aborted, for the key letters of *-ing* then rather curiously rearrange themselves in the accentuated words in the lines that follow, *sunlight, frightened, tight, night*. There is no more *-ing* bar *staying* (at the arch-duke's) in this paragraph, and then none at all until the group at lines 27–30, when it is suddenly prominent again:

> And I will show you *something* different from either
> Your shadow at *morning striding* behind you
> Or your shadow at *evening rising* to meet you;
> I will show you fear in a handful of dust.

We noted a similar case of ggggg's confinement to the *-ing* syllable in successive lines in *Tintern Abbey* (lines 96–98). Here, too, the letter ggggg appears in the participles but not once anywhere else. Some might call this the merest serendipity. In reply one can only point to the lines after the arrival at Starnbergersee about coffee and talk in the colonnade, and the memories of the clear-aired but eerie winter: *And I was frightened . . . In the mountains, there you feel free* (15–19). These lines look and ring quite differently from the sonorous and "spellbound" lines of nature's fertility at the start.[2] The speaker is switched, the presumably male narrator giving way to "Marie" who speaks these next lines. The opening lines are "spellbound"—literally by the—*ing* refrain—because the feeling of participle is as of a verb on hold or arrested. It can't get into a real action as, for instance, in a sentence like "I am fighting, we are working, they are planning." And it is this block on the action that recurs in the lines 27–30. The threatened companion in the desert, who has been called under the red rock, has no power to resist the handful of dust that so menaces.

All through *The Waste Land* what could have been firm action is, in the event, a participle, a constraining condition, as though to withhold the spring's fertility that the opening lines so coldly—as we now see—promised. The hyacinth girl is fertility embodied, her arms full and her hair wet, but the voice addressing her is not: *I was neither / Living nor dead, and I knew nothing* (39–40). The -*ing* of participle and negative are the same, and in this most voiced of poems there can hardly fail to be semantic seepage between them. The crowds of people Madame Sosostris sees are *walking round in a ring* (56) like those on London Bridge only six lines later whom death has undone. The -*ing* marker usually appears in clusters. It informs the suffocating luxury of the woman's opulent surroundings at lines 91–93, and it swamps all communication between the nervous woman and her voiced companion at lines 111–26. This nihilism, still with the -*ing* marker, recurs in the canoe at Richmond in an equally sterile sexual partnership (301–2). And so on. The soulless combustion engine will *bring / Sweeney to Mrs. Porter in the spring* (197–98) while at lines 217–18 the human engine, like the androgynous Tiresias, is a *taxi throbbing waiting*, still not on the move.

What is notable here is that the two "Unreal City" passages (60–76 and 207–14) are almost entirely free of the -*ing* cluster. There is only *crying* to Stetson at line 69. Instead, the *un-* prefix is itself repeated round its opening phrase a number of times in both cases. There is *unreal/under/undone* at the first and *unreal/under/unshaven* at the second, with *under*, of course, not a negative prefix at all. Before the first of these, and apart from *under* twice at lines 25–26, this prefix is not found in the poem; and before the second of them, the last previous case, *unheard*, was back at line 175, only the third line of "The Fire Sermon." It seems as though negation in *The Waste Land* is bound deeply to the level of sterility engaged with at each point. Numbed urban existence is embedded in the deadlier sterility pervading nature.

But this visceral sound of *-ing*, so cardinally emotional in *Tintern Abbey* and so stillborn here, is a little too deep for even the larger parts of modern planetary existence. The voicer of *The Waste Land* utters and writes those aspects differently, informed undoubtedly by the then sick Eliot's own experiences. The nervous breakdown that took him to Lausanne for psychiatric care in winter 1921–22 was symptomatic, it seems, of the social conditions from which the poem draws much of its power. These specifics are prominent through the juxtaposition of discrete kinds of writing; fragments, perhaps; the hallmark of Ezra Pound's programmatic decade. There is a clear case in one of the poem's most decisive symbols. "Water" is deferred from the start. Spring fertilizes, if coldly; but only after twenty-five lines, when we are blistered by the sun beside the red rock and *the dry stone* (gives) *no sound of water*, is the rolle *water* actually written. In the first paragraph there was rain, a shower, and snow, but not abecedarially *water.* This is a very striking feature of the poem. It abounds with water in the memory, but water's emanations are strangely insulated from each other, and the term itself is never used when water itself is present in what must be called its natural state.

The clairvoyant warns against death by water. There is *hot water at ten*, that is to say, nonnaturally heated for civilization's purposes. The Porter ladies *wash their feet in soda water* (55, 135, 201), and the *waters* of lines 182 (Leman) and 257 (Ferdinand's words) come ready-written from the Psalms and *The Tempest.* Yet when water is naturally present in river and sea, and directly engaged, it is not named as *water* in the poem's lines even once. The dead Phoenician sailor is immersed in it but only the section-title names that horror. The passages about the Thames and the canal at the start of "The Fire Sermon," the short-lined wailing song about the barges on Greenwich Reach, the Thames again at Richmond, and the final imminent burst of rain after the thunder has spoken, use every term bar "water" itself. *River, wet, bank, canal, fishing, tide, wash, drifting, swell, stream, "Margate sands," sea,* and most tantalizingly *a damp gust bringing rain* but, in the naming process, no "water." We might even ask if water is temporarily "unnameable" in some deeper sense. The equability of the abecedary, we can recall, reinforces and ensures naming, and language has been inseparable from naming since writing was invented; yet here it seems deliberately withheld. Centrifugality of spelling—every rolle for water except *water* itself— seems ironically turned to impotent purpose. Elsewhere the word tries to get itself said and fails. The Greenwich Reach song (266–91) offers the materials to anagram *water* in its very first three words: *the river sweats*. The chant *Weialala leia / Wallala leialala*, in the middle and at the end, sounds like someone trying to utter that word, "water, water," when parched to the point of delirium.

Again one could call that sheer chance. More likely surely, the poet is subliminally sensing it from the hyperconcentration by which such poetry is ever written at all. And certainly the poem's thirst for the water of life does gush out unrestrained, precisely when its voicing throat is dry and there is simply no water to be had. Here "water," the word's naming power, is evoked frequently. The two passages in "What The Thunder Said" that long for water repay close attention and intuitive empathy at once:

> Here is no water but only rock
> Rock and no water and the sandy road
> The road winding above among the mountains
> Which are mountains of rock without water
> If there were water we should stop and drink
> Amongst the rock one cannot stop or think . . .
>
> —331–36

Of course, one's response is personal. But to my eye the abecedary's "sponging-up" power here is overwhelming; it virtually does look like rock and sand and dry yellow dust. There is hardly an active main verb, and there is no punctuation and so no energy or direction. But most of all is the near invisibility of the letter eeeee. English's elementally vital vowel is well down the "etaison" letter-count, fourth on the list behind ooooo, nnnnn, and ttttt, and only above aaaaa by a single appearance. This is quite extraordinary in English. For eeeee to be anything other than the most frequent letter is rare enough, but to have three other letters ahead of it means a passage of very distinct texture indeed. (Anyone can verify this for themselves by checking virtually any handy passage of writing. Cf. the tour de force novel already alluded to, *La Disparition,* by George Perec, written entirely without eeeees.) If eeeee itself gives so little nourishment, what hope is there for articulation? And the hissing and bubbling sssss has a mere eight appearances, eleventh only, well outside its own normal "etaison" ranking.

The short-lined passage that follows—*If there were water / and no rock . . .* (346–58)—is subtle in construction and phrasing and we can only touch on its details here. It seems to be Eliot's most direct attempt to enact the primitive spring rites he had learned of from Frazer's *The Golden Bough* and Levy-Bruhl, and which, with Jessie Weston's book, led to the so-called "mythic method" around which so much criticism of the poem has centered.[3] With one exception, the lines in this passage always introduce either no fresh letters, or two at a time. It is as though the voicer is desperate to inject a bit more life-giving semantic component in each added short phrase. After *water* alone in three of the first five lines, he tries a *spring*, a *pool*, and then a *sound of water*, even *where the hermit-thrush sings in the pine-trees*, a line with no ooooo or aaaaa in it. This long line is a kind of preliminary enticement-by-detail to the gods before the full sympathetic magic of the line following: *drip drop drip drop drop drop drop*—yet still to no effect, for the hard truth follows at once: *but there is no water*. The visual "distance-doubles" of *the cicada* and *(dry grass) singing* were equally abortive attempts to turn a dry sound into a wet one.

All of this is critically significant in many directions. The poem is alphabetically and abecedarially rich, as one would expect when so much is drawn from already written material from a wide range of places, eras, and works. This richness sets up the aridity at the heart all the more, for the richness is spiritually worthless. Yet there has been much debate about the poem's ending, which for many recent critics is negative, too. For some, *shantih shantih shantih* is heavily ironic, while others believe that the "I" of *These fragments I have shored against my ruins* is Eliot himself. The latter might well nullify the famous/notorious intention to write impersonally on the end of a tradition.[4] But we can read the ending differently. Immediately after the three pronouncements of the thunder, the first line of that final section unites the *-ing* cluster with the theme of water in something at last active:

> I sat upon the shore
> Fishing, with the arid plain behind me

> —422–23

Fishing, a symbol of Christianity, stands in for *water*. Water is still unnamed, but naming it here could have been too pat a finish. The aridity is behind, and water is at least imminent.

Then there is the poem's sexuality. Ezra Pound's excisions removed much of the earlier version's supposed "female stench"; the phrase appeared in "The Fire Sermon" before Pound cut it.[5] What remains still gets trenchant critical comment. But the sexuality sits within the larger sterility. This comes early with the clairvoyant

(43). The name *Madame Sosostris* backs Tiresias in its bisexuality, in that the title is female but the surname male. Eliot took it from Aldous Huxley's *Chrome Yellow* where it is an Egyptian pharoah. But Huxley spelled it "Sesostris." Eliot's change to ooooo provides a second "distance-double" to go along with the four separated sssss's, matching the distance-doubles of mmmmm and aaaaa in the title *Madame*. It makes the bisexuality rather exact. His/her warning is to "fear death by water," and this turns out valid for the sailor; but its irony lies in its voicing by a bisexual person and in the fact that, in general, spiritual death comes from water's absence.

Sexual sterility has no issue. Eliot never had children. Apart from Marie and Mrs. Porter's daughter, both somewhat notionally present and perhaps now adolescent, the only whisper of children in *The Waste Land* is "young George" whom Lil "nearly died of" (160). Admittedly, George had four siblings, but this left his mother all the keener to abort any further embryos. The voicer's question *What you get married for, if you don't want children?* (164) is already tersely answered—the question itself is abortive—by Albert's sexual requirements (148). The man in the canoe at Richmond can "connect nothing with nothing" (301–2), hardly the sexual route to a bounteous next generation, while the typist who succumbs to the "young man carbuncular" is equally "glad it's over" (252), again a phrase to cut off a flowering future. The woman beset with perfumes and ornaments at her dressing table is associated only with the speechless Philomena, her tongue cut out after rape, yet another "withered stump of time" (line 104). Instead of offspring there is only waste matter, litter on the river banks, stony rubbish, and fragments literary or otherwise. The same bodily organs serve both sex and excrement, occasion of satire and disgust for centuries.

In all these cases the text bears close inscription of the import. The language that opens "A Game Of Chess" is opulent; exotic and abecedarially centrifugal. There are the semantically suffocating *marble, golden, glitter, satin*, and the many terms beginning and ending with consonants, which separates them as objects from their neighbors. The alphabet's rarest letters and vowel add their exotic touch prominently in *unguent, jewels, laquearia*, and *antique mantle*. This centrifugal quality ought to bring what *The Tempest*— much adduced in the poem—saw as "something rich and strange." But as always there is a counterforce. The only slightly more frequent letter vvvvv works through to a different connection. After the *vines, sevenfold candelabra, vials of ivory, carved dolphin*, and *sylvan scene*, Philomena now turned nightingale sings with *inviola-*

ble voice. As Maud Ellmann points out, the only "inviolable" voice can say nothing but *la la.*[6] The woman speaks: *"My nerves are bad tonight . . ."* The key three letters of *nerves* underline the hysteria. *"Why do you never speak? . . . I never know what you are thinking"* . . . *"Are you alive?"* she finally asks; the hoped-for grace of the civilized surroundings has collapsed. Vvvvv is remarkable in *The Waste Land.* It divides itself into the lexicons of opulence, extremity of tension *(reverberation, endeavours, nerves, strives),* and a traditional elegiac vocabulary of *evening, river, lover, lives,* and *graves.* Yet the vvvvv-lexicon of good-evil—*virtue, value, evil, devil, vile,* and *vicious*—does not appear in the poem anywhere; nor indeed does *very,* as though to say that banal sterility is the poem's only scale of moral worth.

The pub dialogue about Albert and Liz (139–72) is one of the poem's most often cited pieces, testimony to its memorability for many readers. Here the textural contrast is even stronger. The passage is one of basic articulation, and has been thought most to underlie the social-class division from the opulent "Cleopatra" passage (Trotter 1984, 42). It is certainly that, but the poem's sexual sterility seems rather indifferent to class distinction. The "young man carbuncular" might as easily be a callow public schoolboy of a well-to-do family as the Leonard Bast-type clerk he is in fact, and the Richmond canoe couple are "humble people" at Margaret Sands as well as Tom and Viv Eliot. This last incident collapses into incoherence when of all people Augustine and Buddha, the "two representatives of eastern and western asceticisms" as Eliot himself put it in the poem's Notes, are adduced together (307–11). The Eastern doyen of spiritual teaching by repetition and the most articulate personal confessor in the West have dwindled to a few letters sprinkled on a page with no length, punctuation, or consequence. The poem's infertility is rooted deep and far back in civilization's history with great poignancy.

The thin vowel iiiii is highly and numerically prominent in the Lil-Albert passage. This occurs not least via the "I said" refrain, which makes the supposed dialogue into an insistent monologue without response. The iiiii also recurs in "it," which David Trotter believes is sex, although phrases like *I can't help it* (158) scarcely suggest that. Iiiii's prominence is underscored further by the first-person pronoun and no less than nineteen apostrophes, a kind of visual "iiiii" themselves (apart from quotation marks, there were only two apostrophes in the twenty-eight lines before the Lil-Albert monologue, which also has twenty-eight lines). The invariant "I said" not only brooks no reply but also underscores the lack of educated vocabulary. "I said" might be seen as one of the poem's countless allusions, though here to Cockney speech generally rather than to any work of literature. Furthermore, of just over two hundred and fifty words in this passage, nearly half are of three letters or fewer, and a third in fact have one or two letters only. Indeed "mince my words" (140) is just what the speaker does. She positively shreds them. It is miles from Emily Dickinson's robust three-letter lexicon. But this is no dumbing-down, for the speaker knows the score where it matters; what the chemist thinks, what demobbed soldiers want, and what you can do to smarten up. She is hardly being despised either, and has far more to say than (presumably) Eliot's wife, or even Augustine. But like the nervous woman's desperate insistence on talk ("Speak to me . . . Speak"), although all is ostensibly addressed to a listener, it goes out into the air of the faceless pub unanswered.

The very different formal couplets of the young man's dry seduction at lines 231–48 pound the deadening ddddd. There was something comparable but to very different effect in *Tintern Abbey* and we have alluded to the letter in Auden's "In Memory of Sigmund Freud" (see appendix 5). The eighteenth-century couplets hint at satire, but it would be a weary one leaving no way forward. *The meal is ended, she is bored and tired*, and in those eight lines, 235–42, ddddd is the fifth most frequent letter, a very high count for that letter in English. Ddddd's voiced partner ttttt, commonly English's second most frequent letter, is way down at tenth, right outside the "etaison" group altogether. The lover's *bold stare*, and that he grotesquely *assaults at once*, lends little finesse to the scene, for the ddddd makes a *welcome of indifference*, it fatigues everything it touches. Edmund Wilson put these lovers among the poem's "people whose pleasures are so sordid and so feeble that they seem almost sadder than their pains."[7] Modernism had more to say on this deadness of the ddddd. Following and associated with T. E. Hulme's belief in the essential badness of humanity, Wyndham Lewis averred that "deadness is the first condition of art; the second is absence of soul . . . good art must have no inside: that is capital."[8] But the deeply moving sadness of *The Waste Land* lies partly in Eliot's futile resistance to Lewis's idea which, as here, he also voices. Again, as with any letter-use, we cannot say that ddddd must inevitably resound with or write death; but it can lend itself to that. There is no relief in an inner melancholy, no marked presence of mmmmm, rather it is the sssss, the second most frequent letter here, which makes love strident and which *bestows one final patronising kiss*.

There are, of course, many voices. *He Do The Police In Different Voices*, a snatch of speech from Charles Dickens's *Our Mutual Friend*, was Eliot's early choice of title. But just how these decentered articulations alternately stay off and merge isn't always critically emphasized. The poem's drifting people, who never hear each other, never know of each other's presence and are never answered, seem to move below the level of the poem's main vision. They aren't aware of that vision nor take any part in it even when on the surface someone seems to be addressing someone else present. Yet in curious fashion the poet's voice remains continuous with these other voices even as it sharply demarcates them. The voice from the pub talking about Albert and Lil, the nervous woman, Madame Sosostris's *One must be so careful these days* (59); all of these are somehow also Eliot's voice. It utters within those voices yet also seems to be hearing them. It points up those separations by juxtaposing passages with no warning and without modulation in between. This response, which Eliot will develop strongly in *Four Quartets*, grants the poem a profound unity so that it can survive in the canon, while remaining the grouped fragments and voices it is also.

Clearly all of this is to do with Eliot's renowned views about impersonality in the poet. But there is also his attested unease about the poem's lack of a "single narrator" and his attempt to develop that in the poem's original versions. I share the view of Ellmann, Eric Svarny, and others that Tiresias and the poet are not synonymous, however much Eliot wanted that, as his footnote on Tiresias suggests. Eliot admired the electrifying unity that Baudelaire shot through late-nineteenth-century decadence by his symbolic "correspondances"; but with Eliot it is voice, not symbol, that achieves this correspondence. Peter Ackroyd asserts that Pound's cuts were drastic because he had "heard the music" of the poem.[9] If that is so, then Pound was able to sweep away the complex structure Eliot originally wanted, by removing much of the first-time-round baggage of symbolism: the primitive mythology, the rainmaking, and the Fisher King. Pound saw, or heard, that the voice itself was the adequate substitute. The result was a poem of ritual rather than recycled myth; the ritual of litany, of echo and repetition.

Just a few more observations, at the microscopic level, before we summarize. Abecedarially they are always seminal of course, the "microbillions" that make the text what it is. In great poetry, as here, they are so subtle that it would take the closest analysis to elucidate them: we have to be brief. Here are a couple of cases where an innocent pair of letters, looked at closely, suddenly turn out rather important.

After the opening passage, the tone suddenly deepens into the voice of the narrator. *What are the roots that clutch, what branches grow / Out of this stony rubbish?* (19–20). Then at line 30 comes *I will show you fear in a handful of dust*. The *-tch* in "clutch" has not previously appeared in the poem (though "echt deutsch" and "arch-dukes" at lines 12 and 13 came close). The very common *-st* ending of "dust" had not appeared at a word's end previously since "cruellest" in the very first line. Then, right at the poem's end when the Upanishad is cited, the poem responds *I have heard the key . . .* (411), and "key" is repeated twice in the next three lines. Again the kkkkk and yyyyy of "key" had not previously appeared together in a word anywhere in "What The Thunder Said," despite the frequent yyyyys and the repetitions of *rock*. Kkkkk-yyyyy is not a hard combination to avoid, yet ninety lines have gone by. To be brief, I would suggest only that "clutch" tightens the reader's muscles defensively, as though in alarm; it is hardly surprising that Evelyn Waugh heard "a handful of dust" for his novel's title. And the "key" Eliot lighted on may be those of Dante and Milton's Lycidas, and perhaps too James Joyce's *Ulysses*, which so impressed Eliot when he read it in journal-episode and manuscript that he feared it might influence his own work too obviously (Ackroyd 1984, 112).

Origins have been suggested for the tiniest particles of *The Waste Land*. The first of the Upanishad spiritual injunctions, *DA* (line 400), comes from one of the earliest written (Sanskrit) records of religious experience in existence. Here it is also said to echo Freud's "fort/da," or Dadaism, or both. If *she smooths her hair with automatic hand* (255) cites Tourneur's "She soothes with Leucrocutanized sound," a single letter or two if it was visual *(soothes/smooths)* was the pre-echoing stimulus. *Co co rico co co rico* (392) may allude to either Jean Cocteau or to "a broken Coriolanus," twenty-five lines later. "Phlebas" in "Death By Water" could be the Greek *phles/phlebos* meaning a vein or (colloquially) phallus; the Latin *flebas* ("you were weeping"); *Oedipus* along with the warning against hubris at line 321; or even "fleabag." This last was a term of jocular abuse current at the time, and just the kind Eliot would have liked. It remains only to mention the occasional knowingly banal dry tone, usually with few ascenders or descenders (for instance *which is not to be found in our obituaries*—nine out of thirty-two: line 406): and the ubiquitous refrains of repetition, frequently noted by critics. These last come to the poet subliminally, or even constitute mind with no remainder. *Shadow/shadow/*

shadow/ shadow (25–29), *What shall I do/What shall I do/What shall we do* (lines 131–33), twit twit twit/*jug jug jug jug jug* (203–4) . . . *walks always beside you/walking beside you/on the other side of you* (359–65), and numerous others. If repeated phrases are abecedarial rather than pictographic by their nature, as was argued in chapter 1, then we can see here their profound power in setting up the poem's chant even when we aren't always certain of the allusion. In the Road to Emmaus passage, for example, (359–65) it may be either the resurrected Christ or the cowled figure of Death (Smith 1983, 115). Where repetition is traditionally doctrinal, it underlines that continuity. In a decadent and nonrenewable civilization, by contrast, its tone is wearied, and if truly poetic nonetheless, deeply saddening. There are endless further examples of these and other microscopic categories.

What do we conclude from all these considerations? Here is a totally different kind of passage. "The general opinion, is, I think, favourable to the demands of the strikers, but strongly opposed to their summary methods. There is also some evidence of the growing resentment of the bourgeoisie at the continual demands and continued higher wages of the 'working class.' Certainly the bourgeoisie has turned out amazingly quickly to take the strikers' place; all the underground railways, and a surprising number of trains through the country, are running more or less thanks to volunteers. What is also notable is the cheerfulness with which people have insisted on going about their business." It could almost be from a formal committee report: it is actually Eliot writing to his mother.[10] The tone and jargon of officialdom reveal a strong inner reticence. Eliot's letters insist on secrecy frequently. "I need hardly say that this is a *confidential* letter—what I have said would be certain to be *misunderstood* by most people" (Ibid., 554); *"please keep it to yourself till I let you know it may be revealed"* (Ibid., 467; his emphases) are just two cases. There is a clear reluctance to commit the psyche's central impulses to the permanent page. It is some way from the voice of *The Waste Land*.

Eliot was aware of this block in himself. He knew it influenced his poetry and he distinguished it from inspiration. Instead of a positive input from an unidentified and elevated source, there is a "long incubation" and then a "breaking-down of strong habitual barriers . . . some obstruction is momentarily whisked away."[11] The blocked material could then find immediate expression: "a piece of writing meditated, apparently without progress, for months or years, may suddenly take shape and word; and in this state long passages may be produced which require little or no retouch" (Eliot 1951, 405).

Again to cite Ackroyd; Eliot's genius lies in his "ability to resist the subversive tendencies of his personality by fashioning them into something larger than himself" (Ackroyd 1984, 335). The "subversive tendencies"—the right-wing leanings, the sexual needs, the love of cheap thrillers and low life—are attested by Eliot himself, and "the more sordid aspects of the modern metropolis" were among four or five things he lists that he learned from Baudelaire.[12]

The "something larger than himself" is a network of voices plural in source: Eliot's own, his affected voice, his personae's voices, his literary allusions, and his echoing repeats. But the question then must follow, of how it could all then emerge in overt words, as though the inner material was already linguistic, secreted so from the start, and mental activity and material language were synonymous.

The poem's masthead, from Petronius on the Sybil, concerns her wish for eternal life without allowing for ageing. But it also recalls her oracular practice of writing single words on separate leaves, for her suppliants to arrange themselves for their meaning to emerge.

I suggest Eliot wrote separate letters, too, "on leaves," leaving the reader to trace their interconnections. *The Waste Land* is a fragmented text. There are sharply different line-lengths; presence or absence of punctuation; clusters of capitals; phrases in italicized foreign tongues; short-word and long-word clusters; lexicons opulent and penurious; solid pentamenter couplets and stabs of writing almost in collapse; and repetitions so frequent that we hardly reread them but more or less just see them again. It is an intuitive practice, for the poet will not usually clumsily decide upon this or that letter's recurrence or omission—although even that is occasionally possible. But the poet nudges the writing into place, and the result has to feel exactly right for both reading and resonance. Nothing less would do, for someone with Eliot's erudition and ear; and he was so uncertain of himself that only such a text could be trusted to stand in for the inner personality he apparently so distrusted, and may have not much liked.

Four Quartets must be treated here more briefly. It was written a generation later. Modernism's peak flood had abated; Eliot had written and seen staged his first poetic drama; and while his first marriage left permanent scars, their immediacy was behind him. The group of four quartets was not conceived as such. The first poem "Burnt Norton" was published well before World War II actually broke out; and the rest, considering what bomb-ravaged London was then like, were written in fairly calm conditions. Eliot didn't shirk his responsibilities; he went daily to work in the city like everyone else and served as an airraid warden for long periods. But he was able to spend four nights a week out in Surrey, and the rest at the house of his publisher Geoffrey Faber in Hampstead, hardly a target of enemy raids (Ackroyd 1984, 259). Now in his fifties, Eliot was also involved in a low-key yet close relationship with a long-standing American friend, Emily Hale, who spent time with him at Burnt Norton, the country house in Gloucestershire, in 1934 and 1935. Finally, the opening poem, "Burnt Norton," which established the quartet's mode, had grown naturally from passages withdrawn from *Murder in the Cathedral*.

The poem is about quietness and silence; about time; about the interruptions of both; and about inadequacy of language and expression. The abecedary has no center, so if it seeks one it will find only silence. Yet it engenders the philosophical attitude, pointing humanity to a still centre that will never desert us even though we can never attain it. So, for a poem so resonant, *Four Quartets* could still begin with this quietness that ensues upon sound perhaps desirably, and quite often. The unheard is everywhere. In the opening passage of the opening poem, "Burnt Norton," *Footfalls echo in the memory*, very early. In the next lines the lotus rises *quietly, quietly,* emerging with watery clarity, while *unheard music* is secreted in the shrubbery, along with the sounds of children and birds. *Words, after speech, reach / Into the silence* (BN sect. 5: for convenience line numbers are omitted, as the standard Faber edition *Collected Poems 1909–1962*, which is widely used, does not give them, although they appear in the 1959 edition that is used here). In "East Coker" church the tattered arras, shaken by the wind, is *woven with a silent motto*. Though houses decay and crumble and factories and bypasses replace them, *the dahlias sleep in the empty silence*, and *heat and silence* come the next day at dawn (all EC 1). When the subway train stops unexpectedly between stations, *the conversation rises and slowly fades into silence* (EC 3); the passengers' alarm is at their own self-confrontation, but the solution repeats what was just said: *I said to my soul, be still . . .* One stares at the rolle, *silence*; it is different from staring at *sound*, or *dancers*, or *water*.

The slow movement from sound into silence gets sharper profile from injections of sudden sounds elsewhere. "Dry Salvages" is set against the vivid and resonant background of the sea off Cape Ann, Massachusetts. Around the buoy:

> The future futureless, before the morning watch
> When time stops and time is never ending;
> And the ground swell, that is and was from the beginning,
> Clangs
> The bell.
>
> —"Dry Salvages" 1

The centripetal *future futureless* is followed by the fully centrifugal *morning watch*. Then comes the chiasmic sequence, to ear and eye, of *swell/beginning/ clangs/bell* in which literally every letter plays a key part. We have just unforgettably heard *the sea howl / And the sea yelp*—again *sea / sea* wholly centripetal, *howl / yelp* nearly centrifugal; it is so common in *Four Quartets*—and the reader's ears are pregnant with oral expectation. The double enjambment of the two lines *Clangs / The bell*, each virtually a tolling word, emerges directly from the echo of an older liturgy in the line before, to be given place in a created world of which sound itself is nakedly a part. It is the material from which noises are constructed.

These sharper sounds are associated with time. Time is brought to consciousness in the very act of being arrested. This tolling bell *measures time not our time,* as the heave of the tide seems to measure that, but *a time / Older than the time of chronometers . . .* And the measurement of time, its moving on and then falling back before moving forward again, is abecedarially articulated by the seemingly endless repetitions. But unlike in *The Waste Land* these repetitions are not simply sequential. There is a further dimension. In *Four Quartets* the repetitions loop over themselves or fold back on to what they have said previously, with an extra qualification or else a reversed hesitancy, as was appropriate. *Quick, said the bird / Go, go, go, said the bird* (BN 1) *. . . The time of the seasons / The time of milking / the time of harvest / The time of the coupling of man and woman* (EC 1) *. . . The river is within us, the sea is all about us* (DS 1) *. . . If you came this way / If you came this way in may time / If you came at night / If you came by day not knowing what you came for* (LG 1)—the poem is saturated with these re-phrasings and self-echoes. Some of the last few lines of "East Coker" 3 address this self-echo overtly: *You say I am repeating/ Something I have said before. I shall say it again. /Shall I say it again?* The unexpected reversal of the last two phrases there, leaving the question still hanging, ensure its ongoing continuation in the poem. Nothing is settled.

By such subdued yet compulsive repetition Eliot copes with Henri Bergson's *duree*, the duration-component of time. Eliot was chary of Bergson's work—which he knew well—but retained this dimension. Time is not a kind of featureless vacuum, but rather a hidden pressure against our own movement forward. Bergson had been intrigued to observe that, although the cube of sugar he put in his glass of water dissolved completely, this reality couldn't be summarized by a nontime scientific formula such as "sugar + water = syrup." He had to wait some minutes for it to happen; it had to press forward against some hidden resistant force of time itself (Bergson, 1911, 10). *Four Quartets*, too, pushes against time with a time-consuming, that is to say syntactical phrase, but then repeats it, sometimes identical and sometimes modified, in order to take the poem's rhythm onward. Again we hear the reflections of Augustine and Thomas Aquinas on the sentence as time, across the same time-consuming centuries. The nonpictorial and virtual alphabet alone makes this possible. The end, reached only by an effort *costing not less than everything* (LG 5), is maybe not possible in our world.

The poem's very first paragraph walks round the idea of time, tests its feeling and echo, and then places it in context of the house and garden where the idea was evoked in the first place. The search is on for *the still point of the turning world* (BN 2) where, perhaps, Word itself exists though unreachable by humanity. And in "East Coker" kinds of time are tried out along the back of words locked into time's rhythm:

> . . . there is a time for building
> And a time for living and for generation
> And a time for the wind to break the loosened pane
> And to shake the wainscot where the field-mouse trots
> And to shake the tattered arras woven with a silent motto.
> —"East Coker" 2

Such poetry is then led into questions. They culminate in the lyric in "Dry Salvages" 2: *Where is there an end of it, the soundless wailing . . . ?* straight after the salt-wind evocation of the sea off Massachusetts. This lyric briefly attempts to firm up the process by fitting a common Eliotesque trope to the lyric's regular form. The five six-line stanzas start with lines ending with -*ing* and close with lines ending with –*ion*. When Virginia Woolf was shown various parts of *Four Quartets* in manuscript, she said she thought that too many lines ended with a present participle. Eliot accepted the criticism but made few alterations as result of it.[13] In *The Waste Land* this participle suggested an impotence. Here it murmurs of the philosophy of abstraction's nature. But the lyric's attempt at firming up fails, not poetically but metaphysically. The poet ends where he began: *There is no end of it, the voiceless wailing,* which is the first line of the lyric's final stanza.

In another strand of the poem this expression of time runs into the inadequacy of language. Time is soundless, so in our world it needs sound to measure it; but in the passage already cited, about the buoy's clanging bell out in the ocean, time fails to match consistently the forward movement of grammar. "Our time" (object of the verb "measures") has just been elaborated and extended in "Dry Salvages" 1 for nine lines. *Anxious worried women* lie awake at night relating past to future, *the past . . . all deception, / The future futureless,* at which the bells clangs finally. But by then we have almost forgotten that this long apposition is a verb's object at all. This curious blurring of ordinary syntax occurs elsewhere. In "Burnt Norton" the pool with the lotus-flower is evoked without a verb, just as the pool then itself fills with elements that do not mix:

> Dry the pool, dry concrete, brown edged,
> And the pool was filled with water out of sunlight. . . .
> —"Burnt Norton" 1

Other sentences are repeated with no addition. *If you do not come too close, if you do not come too close . . .* (EC 1). Yet more have no verb at all. *At the still point of the turning world. Never and always. In my beginning. Dung and death. Who then devised the torment? Love.* This last is the poem's only single-rolle sentence; complete in its truth-bearing nature, the absence of main verb has utterance fall short of fullness. The arrival here is that *Every phrase and every sentence is an end and a beginning, / Every poem an epitaph* and both the waterfall and the children are only "half-heard" against the background of the sea's movement. The theme is consummated at the end of "Dry Salvages," (and so just before the total resolution of Little Gidding): *. . . music heard so deeply / That it is not heard at all,* albeit that we ourselves merge with the music for its duration. The time-dimension can never be grasped long enough for a straight grammatical injunction to be laid hold of: *Quick, now, here, now, always—/Ridiculous the waste sad time . . .* (close of BN 5). The short words stutter along: the commas point up the abecedarial entities; they are all we have.

These strains and incompletions point to what the liturgically meditating voice is seeking coterminously with the poem in all dimensions. And this feature leads us to the renowned passages in

Four Quartets where Eliot stands back and looks at his work in a very ordinary discursive kind of tone, usually once in each of the poem's four parts.

That was a way of putting it—not very satisfactory (EC 2). It is noticeably retrospective; it occurs, too late, a moment after the expressions it is dissatisfied with. That notion is expanded elsewhere, in context not just of language but temporal experience. As "Dry Salvages" 3 has it, travelers are never the same people they were earlier in their journeys, whether by train or boat, for time has inexorably both moved them forward and left them behind. But this is also true of language, for when the poem is explicit about language, it is always the too-late element that is emphasised:

> Because one has only learnt to get the better of words
> For the thing one no longer has to say, or the way in which
> One is no longer disposed to say it. . . .
>
> —"East Coker" 5

This sense of the "too late" also marks much of Thomas Hardy's poetry; it is a deep preoccupation of the period. Again Eliot's very long sequence of very short words seems to capture the time-blocked inarticulation he is talking about. This was the problem that plagued Augustine and Aquinas about sentences. A sentence's conclusion is not its last bit, it is the whole import once the last bit has been reached—but by then the sentence is complete, and so is "too late" to change. Legal "sentencing" no doubt has comparable inevitability. The idea is part of how an alphabet works, and here quite simply Eliot is twining the abecedary around it. Curiously this relapsing, so to call it, means a conversational and approachable tone, unlike the formal lyrics it commonly follows. It stands oddly next to what Eliot had said of language back in a much-cited passage in "Burnt Norton":

> Words strain,
> Crack and sometimes break, under the burden,
> Under the tension, slip, slide, perish,
> Decay with imprecision, will not stay in place,
> Will not stay still.
>
> —"Burnt Norton" 5

Words will not stay in place, will not stay still, yet by the stable abecedary their rolles are held still and can at least remain identifiable. Small wonder that for centuries language was thought sacred. *Four Quartets* is also fundamentally "equable" in the sense earlier

defined. The symmetry of the five parts of each of the four poems—
the discursive openings, short lyrics, and explicit engagements
with writing itself—emerge naturally from Eliot's concerns. It is
"not very satisfactory" but that is the way of things. The poem's
sources metaphysically, whether in language, sound and music,
time, loved places remembered or forgotten, or ultimate belief
could at least arrive together, none seeming more pressing, more
the main point, than the others. The abecedary has no center, just
as the lotus flower could rise silently in the pool with no pragmatic
(Western) "purpose" other than the local embodiment of whatever
existence may be.

The problem for Eliot was how to wind off such a poem, which
circled round and round the still center of the unnameable, an un-
ending process by its nature. The last poem, "Little Gidding," gave
him by far the most trouble to finish. He told John Hayward that it
lacked a "personal reminiscence" (Gardner 1978, 24). This is intriguing if indeed the poem moves toward the subjective, as some critics have thought, and away therefore from the impersonality Eliot
had earlier espoused. Yet the poem stems too deeply from Eliot's
keening meditations on Indian mysticism, to understand which he
thought would entail "forgetting how to think and feel as an American or a European."[14] That might be a personality-loss fully; yet the
poem still lacks the nub it constantly wheels around, content at this,
yet sadly so. Eliot couldn't just write the word GOD as the "still
point," as Augustine could throughout the *Confessions*. Indeed,
Stephen Metcalf has proposed that "between" is Eliot's word for
"God" in *Four Quartets*.[15] The religious commune of Nicholas Ferrar (patron of George Herbert) at Little Gidding itself is only a setting for "Little Gidding," not its center or its resolution.

Eliot's brilliant solution was to insert an imitation (his own term)
of a Dantesque encounter with a ghost of the past. The meeting was
to occur in a 1940 London air raid. This is the main content of "Little Gidding" 2. Eliot's problem then became the technical one of
imitating Dante's *terza rima*, a matter on which he expounded at
length in a lecture on Dante at Leeds in 1950, five years after *Four
Quartets* first appeared as a single work. Eliot ended this lecture
saying that our first major lesson from Dante is his sheer attention
to "the *art* of poetry, [there is no] more scrupulous, painstaking and
conscious practitioner of the *craft*."[16] This implies a change from
the view that "Little Gidding" lacked personal reminiscence, stated
back in 1941. If the ghostly figure in "Little Gidding" 2 is Yeats,
as is the strong inference (Gardner 1978, 64–69), then it does seem
as if Eliot is binding in the ancient poet who most influenced him,

along with the poet most recently encountered. Again time's parameters are invoked, but differently. Yeats died in 1938 and Eliot delivered his lecture "Yeats" in Dublin in 1940. Yeats's symbolic mode aspired to be anything but personal. But how extraordinary, too, that Eliot should resort to the letter we have adduced often already; the deadening ddddd, when Eliot actually meets his mentor-poet, in one of the most resonant lines "Little Gidding" contains. That line, *We trod the pavement in a dead patrol* (LG 2), was only reached after many corrections and changes. It had earlier read *Stepping together in a dead patrol*. With characteristically flippant defensiveness, Eliot wrote to Hayward that "a reminder of the surface of the Cromwell Road is timely" (Gardner 1978, 181). In fact, for a fractional moment, the poem attains planetary stoppage. It is the nearest we can get to the stillness the poem seeks.

Summary of Poets' Letter—Uses in Part 3

As well as words, metaphors, rhythm, meaning, and emotion, poets use the abecedary. They do so like other artists use soft clay, black ink, glass, waste industrial metal, a palette of pigments, crayons and chalks, the flute and harp, two baritone voices, a choir, and so on. They interweave this with meaning and image by touching the letters subliminally into place, pushing them a little in front of themselves as they write, sensing the next kind of cluster coming up when it will be needed and having earlier groupings "on hold" to be capped, contrasted, or resolved. They see and hear their letters into place. Many poets, including Wordsworth, Tennyson, and Dante Gabriel Rossetti, have become quite neurotic when seeing their work through the press, checking each character, and changing their minds on seeing how handwriting has turned out in print. The poet is responsible for every letter. Every letter counts.

The poets in English of the last four hundred years have at their heart a kind of quiet beat of the abecedary. Herbert and Milton used it with firm explicitness; Pope's use, with great skill, was mathematical; Wordsworth (though he couldn't avoid it) reacted against this foregrounding, writing as much as he could with the sounds of the inner self—as he put it, from the heart. With those two dimensions achieved, the outer and the inner, there has been nothing for poetry to do since bar the third major intervention, the abecedary's fragmentation in Modernism, dada, T. S. Eliot and Ezra Pound, e e cummings, concrete poetry, and media techniques such as advertising. In now summarizing what we have noticed about these poets' uses of their medium the abecedary and what conclusions we draw from it, we need to bear in mind this new age.

George Herbert works every letter of the abecedary exhaustively and hard. Of these five poets he does this the most overtly. The double letter and the round ooooo, the near-puns and anagrams and words of mutually exclusive spelling, the deployed inflections, the consonants at the words' extremes and the words' varying lengths; these and many other features all appear at the surface of the effect. We saw very short words in "The Crosse," "Sepulchre," and "Coloss 3.3."; unusually high letter-frequencies to special effect in various poems; the centrifugally spelled words in "Deniall" and the centripetal in the proverbs and elsewhere. Consonants are a main fabric of "Ephes 4.30" and double-letters of "Nature"; regular first-letter capitals in "Constancie" and abecedarial physicality in "The Windows." Individual letters take turns for prominence. Among many others here are the balanced bbbbb in "Love (iii) and the roundness of the ooooo in "Love (iii)" and again "Sepulchre." Yet these examples are of much the same small size from poem to poem, and whatever the poem's theme. Herbert's uniqueness lies in the homogeneous blend he makes of these uses across the whole body of his work. In overall terms he has little variation in poem-length or sentence-length in his poems. As a result these small-scale uses of the abecedary are distributed in a similar degree of consistency from poem to poem. Their mode varies here and there along with the emotion expressed, but not the basic short-lyric form. Indeed, the really quite few experimental poems, like "The Altar" and "Coloss.3.3.," stand all the more clearly apart because of this more general uniformity. Although a few poems do get quite long, in their cases the length seems not merely an extension of each poem's theme by detail but a formal metaphor and embodiment of it. So there are "The Search," "Love unknown," and "Longing," whose title itself is a pun. Otherwise only the opening two poems "The Church-porch" and "The church" go to really unusual length, as though to set the scene for the book's theme overall. This homogeneity appears, too, in the mix of abecedarial effects from the categories we have suggested. Uses arising overtly, as from the small number of letters, their physical natures, and their modes of distribution, are all merged in together in the same poem. There is variation of course, but the texture of a Herbert poem doesn't depart from its own average norm very far. "Love (iii)" and "Vertue" are as much and as little of the same oeuvre as are "Deniall" and "Ephes.4.30."

The reason for all of this in Herbert's poetry is that its virtuality depends for its existence on the same constant point of reference throughout; namely, Scripture, the Word. Since that is also a written text, any Herbert poem can spin off it, walk round it, echo it, challenge it, or even seem to avoid it without there ever being any doubt as to its nearby shadowing influence, its hovering presence never far off. For the same reasons Herbert can rely upon the other wider characteristics of the abecedary in its foundational aspects, namely its stability and equability, as themselves secreting features of the Word's provenance and its infinite permanence. The equability of the abecedary lets a Herbert poem see a reading on the surface and a deeper one "through glass"; its virtuality is near-totally embodied in a poem like "Vertue." As a result, though all of a piece as said, at the same time it is never bland, invariably intense. His calmer poems like "Vertue" and "The Call" always seem written over against such intensity. In being more overtly a poetry of letters than is most English poetry, Herbert keeps before the reader the presence of Scripture as itself a divine emanation inscribed via a human invention in all that invention's smallest details. That seems to have been his entire purpose.

John Milton's mode in *Paradise Lost* is different. His apparent aim was not just to make new effects in an old language but to make something like a new language altogether. From the parts of the old one of course; the stability of the abecedary is essential to any such project. But the construction of a new creation before our eyes, mirroring that which God made at the dawn of time, is also like the building of a new edifice. The "microbillions" of letters, like the insects seemingly evoked by them, offer Milton his first material. He seems large of scale because, uniquely, his unit of abecedarial distribution is a particular form of the ancient matrix, namely the paragraph. Milton keeps different modes for different passages. Noisy battle, speeches in debate, natural description of the Garden of Eden, and the domestic talk of its two inhabitants, vary in their use of the language including how the abecedary embodies that. Yet unity is achieved, via the inexorable pentameter and the ever-powerful poetic voice. Omitting small connecting words, and so depending on participles and inflections, makes the passage strong and hardy when that is called for. So does the special case of words with consonants at each end—a technique also used by Herbert—which gives them identity and obduracy at once. The battle scenes and heavier debates are of this kind. The omitting of connectives is also epistemological; longer words are lexically more saturated, and the "tree of knowledge" is thus thrown before us with all its tempting possibilities. Satan's "singling," as opposed to the "doubling" when the innocent Adam and Eve are described, is a nondialectical suggestion that knowledge for humans would be dangerous because it is unquestionable and unanswerable; and this in a poem that offers knowledge of the creation itself. So Adam and Eve match each other with small variation for gender, while Satan's solitary state is marked by words that avoid each other centrifugally and so never pair off at all—except, of course, when he sardonically refers to Adam and Eve themselves. Elsewhere, as in Adam's speeches, the words are shorter, the monosyllables more prevalent, the vowels more rounded. Milton's eschewing of rhyme paradoxically allows a more powerful bond. He plays upon our deepest practices as to the very act of reading; a swinging process in clusters, scanning, gathering several words at once, and so on. Rather than use ordinary alliteration, Milton brought waves of consonants on in batches. He used the enjambment to thwart our expectation of a sentence's meaning, and so shifted the provenance of former rolles in the sentence. He deployed a "vowel-clock" that would wind round through a whole passage. He planted words within words, and he alliterated words after gaps of whole paragraphs or even hundreds of lines. And in a single context Milton works an abecedarial "old favorite" as he invokes the divine *light* on which any mortal achievement must depend.

This is a virtual building and virtual world. It is a large and, unlike Herbert here, highly continuous act of abecedarial distribution. Milton's language is massively physical. Yet he doesn't just convert abecedarial physicality into a virtual counterpart. That happens, but only as deliberate contrast to his own theological belief that God made matter out of his own self; that is to say, made the physical out of the divine virtue. As a mere mortal Milton has to reverse this; but as concomitant, and as might befit such total creation, Milton goes further with the abecedarial stability and equability than do most poets. For by working for an edifice he not only relies on the stability but also enhances it; by varying his paragraphs so pointedly he not only depends on abecedarial equability but stretches it out in front of him, takes it further. It is not coincidence that Milton's different creatures are often grouped by the criterion of their mutually exclusive spellings. These animals, insects, and reptiles, coming up out of the ground distinct from each other and ready-formed, hint at something unnatural; but in the same phrasings they symbolize the parts of the structure their creator is building. Milton's virtual creation leaves its physical materials in clear evidence, underlining now one aspect of them, now another, a passage at a time, but always with the interweaving clear in its interlocking power. This is epic, and if he was to challenge the creating power of the deity even when he knew such deity would outlast him, little else would suffice.

In marked contrast to Milton—his hero and rival at once—William Wordsworth never resolved the question of how his inner voice should convert to writing on the page. But since he wrote not so much about nature as his responses to nature, one result was that he imprinted his voice upon nature's materials. Yet he hesitated to do this, and so his poetry is always a falling-short; not in deleterious sense, rather such is his very mode of expression and what we value his work for. It isn't particularly noteworthy that Wordsworth deploys the many features of letters we have been at pains to describe in part 2. What is remarkable—in *Tintern Abbey* as elsewhere—is that he should do so to such special effect, and in so many cases, when his own ambience seems to stand back from any such overt intention. His perpetual motion, so to call it, is thus gentler than the restlessness of Augustine, Herbert, and the Eliot of *The Waste Land*, and this procedure is cognate with his deep sense of nature as the source of humanity via the latter's earliest earth-experience in human infancy. Wordsworth's uniqueness lies in reversing the usual arrangement of the abecedary's features in terms of their degrees of overtness. His own Romantic mode of thoughtful first-person effusion exploits fewness and physicality very quietly indeed; but the depth of that understatement evokes our silent sense of the abecedary's stability, equability, and quality of virtual expression and truth so evident in Wordsworth's work.

And so, in most cases, we find his letters deployed in a kind of moderation. Incidental distractions like punctuation and capital letters are kept to a minimum. His poem moves forward as does Milton's, but his two-letter line-openers have a markedly quieter effect than do Milton's intellectually challenging enjambments. These two-letter words join up with "be" in a soft existentialism, while the single-letter opener AAAAA runs in successive lines to add further to the poem's steady and easy continuity. AAAAA is for "and," which lines up with other three-letter open-ended words in inscription or meaning: *and, joy, eye, Wye, all*. Physically powerful double-letter words are frequent, but they accrue subdued lexicons down the poem rather than coming as sharp local effects. These double-letterings are confined to the soft letters eeeee, ooooo and lllll—along with the harsher sssss as in the *-ess* ending, but that is

paradoxically a connoter of abstraction. "Distance-doubles"—
murmur, mystery, cataract, guardian/guide—are especially telling.
The ending *-ing* underlines this permanent presence. Rrrrr and
yyyyy are equally and interestingly open. Some letters, like fffff
and vvvvv, briefly modify this continuity and so give it all the
clearer profile. All of this centers on that watery letter wwwww;
but, even more so, on the poem's culminating abecedarial feature
the pervasive ubiquitous mmmmm, the letter of meditation.
Mmmmm eases line-endings throughout, it expresses the inner self
by its open-voiced humming, and with its supporting nasal nnnnn
it offers the most level phrase (no ascenders or descenders) found
in any of these five poets: *nor mourn nor murmur*. Surely those
words seem to say what the poem is always doing even as the poet
is half-trying to avoid it. The poem is more open than any other we
find in these five. The river Wye, I argued, is the poem's true topic,
and not any heavy political issue supposedly lying behind it.

Emily Dickinson breaks, if not all the rules, certainly all the expectations. Some aspects are much like those found in the other poets.
Words move away from each other centrifugally, and there are frequent exoticisms, jewels, tools, animals, stars, even if sometimes
just by context. The same first letter starts not just the word but the
line, in certainly weird sequences. Words of "overlapping" spelling
are used as rhyme. But Dickinson adds much of her own. As soon
as she mixes up male, female and neuter pronouns we sense something is afoot. For surely this could as well apply, if she so chose,
to copulative verbs, conjunctions, and prepositions. Later on whole
poems collapse syntactically. The mutually exclusive spelling clusters—even when of sympathetic meaning to each other (*rower/
yacht*; *wisdom/peace*)—are unusually frequent. Wordplay evokes
an ironic fairyland: *log, frog,* and *bog* could unite in a child's magi-
cal learn-to-spell sentence, while *gnats* and *giants*, similarly evoca-
tive, are just one case of many near-anagrams. Letter-frequencies,
especially of three-letter words, are often highly unusual for standard English. This issue of word-length seems one key to the enterprise. It is not just "short v. long," for the tendency to keep three-
letter and four-letter words for special purposes seems to mark them
off not just from longer words but from each other. The three-letter
word makes for, among other things, a bold lexicon commonly of
tiny insects, while four-letter words group as rhymes at the ends of
lines. But there is also a curious staggered relationship between
other different lengths at different times. Much longer words are
sparse; very deliberately selected and carefully placed, often close

to very short words and with few or no words in the middle-length range near to them, if present at all.

These details may express a worldview. The relation between short, long and (fewer) middle-length words suggest a pervading vision of smallness and immensity. No other poet here, not even Milton, makes so clear-cut a distinction. The clear difference—a Derridean or Levi-Straussian difference—between the tiny and the immense is central to a group of binary concerns that seem to underlie that cosmic structure. But this absent middle is also reflected in Dickinson's entire oeuvre; a huge collection, yet of very short poems. As is sometimes maintained of Thomas Hardy, too, though for quite different reasons, there is no middle-length poem and no central group of connected poems that seem to define or control the rest. Dickinson's short words name palpable entities, the long ones refer to the authorities or abstractions from which she could presumably have constructed a system if she had been so minded. But the short words have another, profound effect. The shorter the word, the more its first-letter capital and often its rare letter, too, stand out. But equally, the more blank spaces there are on the page. This space is supplemented by those endless dashes, which leave more white space, themselves naming nothing. This blank space, the "white page" like the famous white dress and white flower given to visitors, may stand in for the abyss that so many critics have noted. The abecedary, which Dickinson apparently valued for itself, is thus atomized. But this effect is supported by the treatment of each word—all her words of all lengths—as individual. It is as though each word itself must be kept as, or made into, a unique object. The alphabet's most infrequent letters, the many juxtaposed words of almost totally different spelling, the commonly very short words, their capital first letter, the far longer ones isolated, and the thin dashes between words too—all these features give nearly every word isolation, prominence, and self-solidity on the white page that surrounds it. The short word is thus somehow prototype for the whole lexicon. This is further atomizing at the verbal level. If it is indeed aphasic, it seems very strongly controlled. And so we can reach some kind of conclusion about her. Dickinson highlights the small-detail features of the abecedary, its fewness, physicality, and overt distributions, just as George Herbert did so prominently, too. But with Herbert there was always the lurking, fleetingly appearing sacred Word of Scripture behind the poems he made from it. In Dickinson's seeming chaos that scriptural Word is replaced by a blank, a vacancy or abyss. Rather each single word of our language could have its sacred quality independently, and become its own jewel, divinity, bee, or just scrap of writing. This is not at all to say Dickinson believed in nothing. Rather it may be that this great space expressed a lifelong act of waiting—for a lover, for nature or God. The alternative is that it covered over a plot we still don't know and may perhaps now never find.

T. S. Eliot was represented here by two poems that differ markedly from each other. On the face of it their differences might seem clear and opposed, according to the distinction suggested at the end of chapter 10 earlier. With exceptions, it is the local small-detail aspects of the abecedary (occasioned by fewness, physicality, and varied distribution) that most mark *The Waste Land*. It is the basic principles behind letters as a cultural invention at all (occasioned by stability, equability, virtuality) that emerge quietly revealed in the more philosophical poem *Four Quartets*. And that is indeed so; we aren't going to start complicating things at this point. But reading the two poems together also brings a sense of how one followed the other in one poet's career. For while the poems' textures are indeed different, we suddenly see that neither mode, despite the different way of each, seems capable of escaping the poet's same concerns, early and later in his life though each was.

The verbal impotence expressed in *The Waste Land*—the sterile present participle, the sudden disappearance of the most frequent letters, the speeches addresses to no listener, the inability to utter "water," and so on—suggest the poet's profound anxiety in face of his task, both in this poem and in his vocation in a world hostile to his particular art. But the same resurfaces in *Four Quartets*, in the poet's regular sections in which he questions that same art at the level of fundamental poetics. "Not very satisfactory," "Words strain, / Crack and sometimes break, under the burden / . . . will not stay in place, / Will not stay still," and so on. The mode is now self-conscious, but the problem remains. Equally the many voices of *The Waste Land* turn into the silence of the *Four Quartets* where all is "unheard" and echoes endlessly die away. The rattle of different activities in the London poem, the sound of car horns, the splashing on the Thames, and the snatches of song come up, if differently in *Four Quartets*, in the wind shaking the rafters, the howl and yelp of the sea, and the clanging of the bell. The short-word refrains in *The Waste Land*, "twit twit jug jug," "co co rico," "drip drop drip drop drip drop drop" and the like, find a calmer and more subdued outlet in the equally monosyllabic lines of *Four Quartets*. For there the poet seeks a way forward by probing tentative possibilities: *if*

you came this way / If you came this way in may time / If you came
at night / If you came by day not knowing what you came for. . . .
The fragmented blocks of past literature from which much of *The*
Waste Land is drawn give way to a comparable though more regular
and settled blocking in the orderly arrangement of *Four Quartets'*
five sections in each of its four parts. The *-ing* present participle in
The Waste Land, devoid of action, fertility and future, transmutes
in *Four Quartets* as the perpetual human anxiety in face of the constraining power of time itself. And the poems overlap just a little in
mode, too. *The Waste Land* has its more discursive sections while
Four Quartets doesn't eschew staccato monosyllables: *Go, go, go,*
said the bird . . . Quick, now, here, now always . . . Who then de-
vised the torment? Love. Even the ending or "deadening" ddddd—
found too as we saw back in Herbert and Wordsworth—makes its
curtailing mark in both poems. It aborts joy in one of *The Waste*
Land's few more luxurious sexual moments, while in *Four Quar-*
tets the two poets find firm but temporary ground as they walk London's streets in nighttime and wartime. Most of all though, neither
poem has a center. That is an appropriately overt expression of the
abecedary's lasting equability, though it is diversely expressed, in
the *The Waste Land's* fragmentation and the endless circling of
Four Quartets. But the later Eliot has only—though it is some
achievement—expressed this lack in terms of a reconnection to the
mainstream of traditional human philosophy and humanity's modern existential experience.

Perhaps indeed the lines in "East Coker" 3 refer beyond their
immediate context. *You say I am repeating / Something I have said*
before. I shall say it again. / Shall I say it again? (Again a long
word, "repeating", makes its necessary emphasis.) Perhaps the
context is not just internal to *Four Quartets* but to both poems, as
indeed to Eliot's entire poetic career. Certainly both poems move
from main despair and voices of lamentation toward briefer but
more positive conclusions, *The Waste Land* in "What The Thunder
Said" and *Four Quartets* in "Little Gidding." But that is not the
main outcome. Rather Eliot is wrestling with modernism itself;
with how, in an increasingly mechanized and electronic world,
poetry can be written at all. Eliot tried both ways, with great success. Yet some would still say that modernism itself had its demise
built into it while *Four Quartets* is no more than a temporary resort
to something like a traditional, discursive, even nineteenth-century
mode of writing. I would be more positive on both modes. But the
modern world had arrived, to which this book must now turn.
Overtly we shall say less about poetry itself (although it will remain

the underlying concern); and the main aim, in part 4, will be to look at the utterly new conditions of language in our time. This will be as to language itself, that as poetry's medium, and the many ways that scholars and intellectuals of all kinds have been forced further and further to examine it.

IV

The Abecedary, the Mind, the
Aesthetic, the Postmodern

So to our own world.

This part will move a little differently from the others. We are going to have to introduce material from several disciplines and areas, serially and one at a time; so there will be a number of restarts. Furthermore, it may take a little space, in one or two cases, to outline the material itself and explain its relevance to our topic. The reader is thanked in advance for his or her kind patience.

There are three major areas to be considered. This would seem so if we are to reach any sensible conclusions on poetry, the abecedary, and the modern world together. The three areas are: twentieth-century conceptions of the language/mind relation generally; that relation aesthetically; and the wider topic and practices of postmodern communication culture. The abecedary is inextricably entailed in meaning; yet is also a physical artifact in its own right and so a medium for art; and it is massively modified by developments in electronics, in film, and in television, and in usage such as advertising and popular culture generally on all fronts.

First, there are the general areas of language, mind, and meaning. There are numerous schools of thought and research on the language-mind relation. Not surprisingly, they don't all agree with each other. For some, descending from Chomsky and long before, language is an instinct. Its outward embodiments are mere detail. Neural dispositions toward reality have their own structure that the sign-system, whatever that may consist of, presents post hoc. Others, such as Jean Aitchison, prefer to see the lexicon as a language's heart; what the lexicon contains and how minds learn it and store it. By contrast to both of these, the traditional intentionalists, the most famous being J. L. Austin and John Searle, looked at utterance as the expression of, in effect, a single person intending. We have already touched on this via the work of David Olsen. This "intending" exists aside from both the general instinctual capacity to generate a neurally structured grammar, and the particular set of cultural entities that the language lexicon refers to. The psychoanalytic approach is a kind of subversion of the intentional. Finally comes the range of neurological and cognitive sciences and the responses they get from philosophers. The terms here are brain, mind, and consciousness.

The abecedary is entailed in meaning and developed for that purpose. The disciplines that explore meaning, namely, philosophy and psychology of language and of mind and where those meet, have been transformed by contemporary advances in biochemical and neurological research. Current consciousness theory seems crucial to language; in fact, the connection has been little explored as yet. And theories of language and mind generally have seldom treated the alphabet as part of the material to be examined. Some don't think the sign matters, or is other than "arbitrary" at all. Other theories, even if sometimes only implicitly, do offer ways forward. Theory and research of both kinds are relevant to any view of the abecedary, and to whether its role, in poetry especially, has been neglected.

Our second main topic here is the aesthetic specifically. This elusive matter lies within wider general meaning. It is the poets who most bring the abecedary to the surface while losing nothing— indeed gaining all—in the intensity and poignancy and power of such meaning. Long dormant in literary studies, the aesthetic has recently been rediscovered, as though political attempts to cower the victim and humiliate the prisoner all the more reveal an obduracy in it that just can't be defined out of existence. One can hardly be ungrateful for the important political and historical literary work of the last few decades. Yet several critics prominent in those very areas have turned back to the aesthetic.[1] Maybe they are aware of the void within political theory itself, an elusive heart where tensions of matter and meaning are consciously highlighted. The consumer world consumes; no message lacks power to disturb, delight, or both at once. Surely this feature is perennial even if no longer necessarily transcendental.

Third, there is the new aura of the postmodern. New eras commonly believe they are undergoing greater changes than the world has ever seen previously. Maybe they are always right, and after Eliade's "eternal return" the rate of change merely increases. But there is a real sense that our age is especially unusual. The heart of postmodernism, what everything comes back to, is the perceived shrinkage of the planet. For centuries, indeed millennia, the world had seemed for all practical purposes of infinite size. This pertained even after its actual finitude had been discovered. Today it is quite different. The world is not merely finite; it is too small, shrinking fast, a tiny piece of real-estate hardly able to support its rapidly burgeoning and demanding population. From any point on the earth's surface we can now reach its apogee in little over twenty-four hours. We can in fact destroy the planet by detonation or pollution. Meanwhile, scientific study of our own mind-bodies reveals a material base within range of full discernment. We can transfer bits of our bodies to each other, carbon-date our ancestry, genetically trace our most distant ancestors individually, abort our embryos, and probably clone ourselves from other DNA material. Yet, despite these advances, we still have no in-built rules of a reliable metaphysical nature. We may learn everything about our workings, yet we live on a tiny globe and don't know why we are here. The outcome is an implosion of thought, technique, cultural interchange, and communication saturation, for none of which is there any precedent. The postmodern sense of carnival within catastrophe expresses the awareness of what presses upon us.

Such changes, by various routes, have intervened in language and communication. Gore Vidal has put it that we are at a "great hinge in history, where we are going beyond writing."[2] Even if we don't go so far, various elements seem important. The electronic era is one. The planet-shrinkage comes not only by population increase and superfast transport, but also in the communication revolution whereby everything is brought nearer to everything else. But language itself is at issue. Speaking and writing may be in process of switching medium. The change from voice and paper to computer, word processor, and Internet challenges the very idea of inscription as we have understood it. But if those challenge the idea, the visual media challenge the need. The book has not disappeared as many predicted it would. But the shift of cultural investment in humans' interpretation and image of themselves, from page alone to page and screen together, is a new cultural keynote. Television and film furthermore have come of age. From birth two generations of adults have never been without it, and film classics and forms are now long established and will gradually become distant history. Traditional literary genres proportionately diminish and some, such as poetry, may be pushed to the margins. All this is familiar.

There is another new aspect of the postmodern, though, and it is perhaps the most important here. There has been a letter-explosion, a blowing apart of the alphabet, unlike anything seen since its invention three thousand years back. Letters—the actual familiar letters of the abecedary—are thrown around in ways inconceivable even a century ago, probably far less. News headline and commercial slogan have adapted traditional proverb by pun and brand name respectively. Letters are worn by the million on T-shirts and leather jackets in every color and typeface, rendered in huge size-variations in advertising and headlines, and made mobile on television screens and elsewhere in ways that might seem to leave their foundation-feature of "equability" deeply undermined. Letters can be seen dancing in pairs, falling into pieces, crying and laughing, shaping photo-images, shimmering through glass, floating in the air or on the seabed. They march on screen right and go off left, or they move up from bottom to top as the credits roll. They materialize into place as the newscaster calls upon them, or they shrink from oversize down into visibility and then into nothing. They can be made to seem to curve and fall into place on the screen like litter wafting through the air down on to the street. They are towed through the sky behind aircraft or form names on tip-up seats in huge stadiums. They appear and disappear before our eyes, turn into ghosts, animals, sex objects, swirls of smoke, or other strange vapours. Letters in such condition are the early experience of millions of children in the modern world and a continuing one for adults. This deeply psychic violence to an old mode of inscription suggests an equally deep move, across the whole of civilization, to the permanent and exclusive adoption of a new one.

What poetry might become in such circumstances is not predictable. We won't attempt any detailed examination of contemporary poetry or poets. But my own (unoriginal) feeling is that a major era of poetry is now closing, one that began with the spread of education and articulation via the Renaissance and its seminal technology the printing press, and ended similarly with the equally new media referred to above. This era depended upon the stability of the abecedary; its equability, and its disposal from the physical to the virtual by a combination of its members in thousands or millions. But further, there is the exponential explosion of literary criticism today into factions who don't even know each other's agendas.[3] This parallels, and perhaps at some deep-structure level is cognate with, the explosion of the abecedarial system in which criticism is written.

We now need to go into some detail as to all these areas.

16

Language-Mind Theories

THE LANGUAGE INSTINCT

THE LANGUAGE-INSTINCT BELIEF HAS BEEN THAT LANGUAGE IS merely an aspect of mind, or body-mind. It may be an innate faculty, as Chomsky first saw it, or an instinct, as do the biogeneticists; either way it is simply a product of mental life. Only a couple of observations on Chomsky are needed here. His "generative grammar" elaborated the inherent divisions of mental structure that matched and were continuous with comparable divisions in reality. And so we had the familiar tree-diagrams, made up of noun-phrase, verb-phrase, and so on, with their major auxiliaries such as adjectival or adverbial phrases. That nouns, verbs, and abverbs are "words"—never mind letters—is incidental. Their true nature is as events that reality is made of, and which we cognize as such: matter (noun and adjective), matter in action (verb), and matter in action in certain ways (adverb).

Discussion of just a few examples from Chomsky may help highlight what we are seeking. In his original scheme the generative drive was so dominant as to severely constrain even semantic considerations, let alone any material ones. Chomsky's selectional rules for lexical choice could be narrowed down as closely as a house address could be by a zip code. So for example the noun *boy* was a) a quantitative noun (not a mass noun like *butter* or an abstract noun like *sincerity*), b) a common noun (not a proper noun like *John* or a pronoun like *him*), c) an animate noun (unlike *book*) and a human noun (unlike *bird*).[4] Two or three more steps would have left "boy" the only candidate for the job. The same process was available to verbs. It was still in the nature of the case impossible, and so an "ideal dictionary" is needed to attain each unique sign; in our terms its "rolle." But even there, the actual meaning could only be reliably obtained by consulting the linguistic deep structure. The rolle-sequence *visiting aunts can be boring* (Chom-

357

sky 1971, 103) remains ambiguous until we know whether "visiting" is adjective or participle; more humanly, whether aunts are being given a characteristic or someone else a familial chore.

By insisting on the place of instinct in what is grammatically allowable, Chomsky could further argue that grammar does not depend on meaning. Sentences like *the situation called for reappraisal* and *I missed the train* (110) refute the standard view that the grammatical relations subject-verb and verb-object correspond to a previous "structural meaning" of actor-action and action-goal respectively. Equally *the man has an arm* is possible while *the arm has a man* is not (124). This last is plausible semantically but not instinctually; the whole includes its parts, not the reverse. Even more extremely, we can tell without consulting semantics that *John elapsed the book* doesn't work because we already know from habit that *to elapse* is an intransitive verb. And so on.

But if grammar doesn't depend on meaning, then any link between meaning and sign is irrelevant. Typeface, rhyme, or the pleasurable savoring of words such as *murder* or *moonlight* is of no interest. Whatever the real "meaning" of *boy*, or *visiting aunts can be boring*, its letters are merely incidental. Steven Pinker (1995) has vividly presented a view much like Chomsky's although closer to the biogenetic way of thinking. Pinker's view it seems to me has to be questioned, but his countless day-to-day examples "feel poetic," they have the power to stir that one associates with poetic expressions. But his comments about English spelling—for example oronyms *(The stuff he knows/the stuffy nose)*, or how anything at all can be pluralized (trees, ideas, blues, Darwinianisms, New Yorks, even "Get-out-of-heres!")—pull in the rich flavors of the very language-expressions whose essence he tries to undercut. His points though are pertinent. For example, why can we say "Henry dined" and "Henry devoured the chicken," but not "Henry dined the chicken" or "Henry devoured"? Why can we say "She put it in the garage" but not "she put in the garage," "she put it," or just "she put"? As Pinker has it, the correct renderings "keep the verb happy." In the headline *Mothers on way to Jaunt among Dead* (these cases aren't always jokey) some verb like "were" or "found" is needed between *Jaunt* and *among*. True, but why is it needed? And how can verbs be kept happy?

Pinker's general theory is that language in outward expression is based on two items. These are a) a discrete combinatorial system, b) the arbitrariness of the sign (pages 83–84). The discrete combinatorial system has a basic structure of noun-phrases and verb-phrases, and subparts of the system include connectives, copulae, prepositions, and so on along with prefixes, suffixes, and other inflections. Nouns are not necessarily things/persons/places, nor are verbs only actions. Nouns can be actions (for instance "destruction"), qualities, events, abstractions, and parts of idiom ("raising the roof"), while verbs may be mental states like "know," possessings like "own," or abstract relations like "falsify." In a sentence like *the situation justified drastic measures*, "justified" is not something that was done to the measures. It follows that a part of speech (noun, verb) is not a kind of meaning; it is a kind of token that obeys certain rules (Pinker 1995, 106).

This inference is important for the theory. As with Chomsky, parts of speech don't belong to a lexical system. For Pinker they stem from instinct. The sentence about the garage keeps the verb happy because it just feels right. Similarly, the "discrete combinatorial system" works not in a chain-structure—the (alphabet-type) linearity of visible sentence or sequential speech—but in a tree-structure. We say *the director of operations with the bald head* and not—though with equal sense—*of operations the director with the bald head* or *the director with the bald head of operations*.

And the arbitrariness of the sign, for Pinker, keeps these outward expressions, written or spoken, effectively featureless. In our context here what is most marked is that Pinker stays largely off the nature of language's signs. They are "utterly arbitrary" he says (152), with barely a page of justification. Pinker supports his contention with a few offhand examples passim. "Babies should not, and apparently do not, expect *cattle* to mean something similar to *battle*, or *singing* to be like *stinging*, or *coats* to resemble *goats*" (152). That seems fair enough, and indeed we emphasized the point in part 2, but Pinker also explains that he uses the words and letters *Socrates is a man* solely as a courtesy to a reader. He "could just as easily have used a star of David, a smiley face, and the Mercedes-Benz logo, as long as [he] used them consistently" (page 74). And finally, as noted earlier, "the word *dog* does not look like a dog, walk like a dog, or woof like a dog, but it means 'dog' just the same" (83). George Steiner, with some subtlety it should be said, has said the same for "rose" (1989, 95–96)—and they both cite Shakespeare's "What's in a name? That which we call a rose / By any other name smells just as sweet."

The rose might smell just as sweet, but under another name it would have taken the heart out of Edmund Waller's poem "Go, Lovely Rose," Robert Burns's "Oh, my luve's like a red, red rose," and numerous others. The first line of Waller's poem depends on the repeated vowel ooooo for its cool wooing power, its rhyme *knows* (so the lady can't fail to get the rose's message), and its opening out into the ever more varying rhymes down the poem: *me, be, young, spied, worth, forth, rare/share/fair.* We have already alluded to the "near-miss" and "overlap" phenomena as in *notes/ votes* and *cattle/battle,* and the tension they can leave in language when meaning is diverse. Language can move in and take up available letter-combinations even of near-same spelling. The outcome may be irony, extra emphasis on intention, or some further effect. As to his other example, if Pinker had indeed used a star of David, a smiley face, and the Mercedes-Benz logo instead of *Socrates is a man,* consistently or otherwise, he would have brought strange looks to the faces of his readers. For those signs have already accrued deep associations in their uses, and so the signs themselves, the actual marks, have become woven in to the neural texture of any observing receiver. No mentalese could blot out these associations. The signs Pinker names—star, face, logo—are anyway quite unsuited to extended cursive writing and would be distracting in practice to say the least.

In all these cases the dual principle mentioned earlier remains. The signs may have been arbitrarily chosen at their origins—though we don't really know even that—but use over centuries then builds up relationships between them, psychological nuances, sets of associations, and ways of incorporating them neurally. These features are hardly arbitrary—they could be called postarbitrary perhaps—and that reliable consistency is supported by the abecedary's general appurtenances; its roughly consistent size, its process along the level line to the right, its normal homogeneity of typefont and color, and all the rest. The sign has its own uses.

The same applies to abecedarial distribution when viewing language structures not as chain but as tree. (*The director of operations with the bald head* results from such a tree.) Abecedarial distribution is necessarily linear, but that only contrasts it to the tree-system of the instinct; it does not make it arbitrary altogether. This is not to espouse a science of signs. Anything at all can be used as a sign by being so intended. But within any one cultural system, order can be discerned. The deployment or distribution of the abecedary has explicable principles as we have seen. The point about abecedarial distribution is not that it necessarily has no system, but that any such system would be independent and intrinsic to itself.

Terrence Deacon (1997) gives far more weight to the sign. He sees language not as mental but as an input to the mental from the outside: language is made of matter beyond ourselves. Intelligence, articulation, syntactical structure in the brain, and so on came from language as much as they caused it. Language is easily replicated, so it correlates with easier learning in early childhood, and this is especially true of the alphabet. Language structures have always adapted preferentially to children, because languages that are easier to acquire early will tend to replicate more rapidly and be passed from generation to generation with greater fidelity. For one's native language to take twenty years to learn would be highly extravagant of time. And if the child's feeling about the alphabet is sensual and libidinous—if it just likes playing around with letters—and later becomes a poet, it will be a poet of a special kind. It may even have been more likely to become a poet in the first place.

Mind and the Lexicon

Other language theorists and psycholinguists, such as Aitchison, give more weight to the lexicon.[5] The question is of how the lexicon is stored. The average educated person has a store of about fifty or sixty thousand words. Since we can say "there's no such word" to a nonsense-term almost instantly (Aitchison 1994, 8), the whole lexicon obviously isn't scanned right through to reach that conclusion. Rather, a sense of what actually counts as a word seems entailed; and that in turn argues that the "sponging-up" theory suggested earlier in the present book is part of this. But equally, the mind/brain is not a dictionary; it doesn't use alphabetical order, and it stores far more information about words' uses than any dictionary could. Maybe there are deep semantic "primitives" that can be subliminally used as storage categories, or maybe words are stored in webs or networks. Maybe some abecedarial clusters even lend themselves to storage more easily than do others.

Aitchison records various findings. Most revealingly, lexical storage may be independent of the language instinct. Recalling Jakobson's distinctions, we find that some speech-disorder patients with aphasia have a sizable lexicon but with no structural control, while others can string together syntactical rudiments but with no palpable content. So syntactical and lexical features are perhaps stored separately; but if so, we might deduce that it is the syntactical aspect of language, rather than its vocabulary, that language's instinct is instinctive about. Of course, not every linguist agrees that instinct can "select" one area of language and ignore the others, as Chomsky's example of *boy* might indicate. But one inference for poetry is that in poets like Milton and, at times, Dickinson, who are sparing of syntax, lexical storage may have dominated. It gives credence to the idea that, as Wallace Stevens once put it, poetry is not made with ideas but with words. If all this is so, too, and of course here we risk oversimplification, other things fall into place.

For example, in word-association tests people relate words most to their pairs or coordinates, such as *salt/pepper, butterfly/moth,* or *red/white/blue/green.* The second likeliest pairing is between words commonly used with each other; *salt water, butterfly net, bright red.* This is what produces the collocations of cliché or standard phrase: *agonizing decision, wide awake, a hearty breakfast, buxom barmaids, blissfully ignorant.* (The last-named comes from Thomas Gray; poets avoid clichés but often inaugurate them.) Equally, mistakes don't usually confuse parts-of-speech categories. People might say "I sent a table" (instead of "cable"), but "let's color it seen" (for "green") would be most unlikely. People seem to know that you can *pursue knowledge* but not *pursue wasps* (Aitchinson 1994, 90), even though the latter could physically happen while the former is metaphor. For this very reason, of course, a poem could use the latter expression, and a surreal pursuit of wasps would result. We are also less likely to associate category members with their generic heads. *Butterfly/insect* or *red/color* would seldom come up in word-association experiments.

Aitchison gives further examples. Verbs cluster by general type of reference (110–21) and people know this even when context brings exceptions. Activity-verbs like *cook, sew, read, change* (your clothes) imply an object but it can be omitted; yet removal-verbs like *brush, extract, dislodge, wipe* normally need one. Risk-verbs, *risk, threaten, endanger, gamble* are interesting. Only a sophisticated, or pedantic, person might say "So Hilary risked a phone call, a bad cold, and her job, too," but any native language-user would sense, even without knowing the term, that this was a zeugma; that—as we might put it here too—it "felt poetic." By pointing the verb to three different objects at once, both it and they are abecedarially highlighted in their apprehension. Yet despite the surface oddity there are hidden rules covering each use. Risk-verbs risk *an item* (valuables, loss of job), *for* gain or beneficiary (good health, not having a cold), *through* a deed (getting home late, or a phone call). On the view of Aitchison and others, the categories come from the structural demands of the language-instinct, and the strange juxtapositions come from the lexicon.

This matter of word-storage may be closely connected to the abecedary's stability. The mind lets words constantly shift their meanings by the catachresis that keeps languages living, and it depends on abecedarial stability for that process to remain coherent. If words change their meanings in popular use, and indeed many words are ambiguous anyway, questions arise as to how rolles and meanings remain connected at all. The oft-cited "tip-of-the-tongue" phenomenon, discussed earlier and which Aitchison also considers, suggests that the connection, though usually reliable, is not fully welded. Ambiguity, metaphor, and multiple meaning (*she felt unhappy with her new felt undercarpet*) all disconnect the rolle from one-to-one mental relation; it must know what different things to trigger, and when. Maybe words are not always stored individually and whole, but sometimes in clusters, or even in syllables or other bits (121). It seems, for example, that in compound words— *provision* or *pro-vis-ion*? —inflectional suffixes are not stored at all but added by rule as needed, while derivational suffixes, and prefixes, are already attached. This is how we know not to say *computeredize* for *computerized* or *wash upped* for *washed up*, and that *repertoire* and *replenish* are words but *pertoire* and *plenish* are not (124, 127). Abecedarial stability may allow for many such possibilities.

All such seems like a straight answer to Chomsky and Pinker, or at least as to Chomsky's earlier position. Even if there is a "language-instinct"—and there may be—our view of it must stop seeing the lexicon as "a collection of bric-a-brac," "superficial trivia . . . that may be picked up but not absorbed" (Aitchison 1994, 232). Indeed, Chomsky too later modified his view of the syntactic/ semantic relation. He came to recognize that it "evidently offers many mysteries, both of fact and of principle" (Chomsky 1971, 126). But our general inference has to be that all such examples evince the abecedary's place for lexical storage, in its capacity to "sponge up" the meaning of the word, absorb what it ontologically stands for in its written and, if differently, oral palpable presence. I suggest this is how *red* and *green* can support each other while *red* and *color* can't, as collectively can *buxom barmaid* and *hearty breakfast*. *Pursuing wasps* is awkward but still gives us a picture.

Aitchison strikingly if indirectly gives credence to this view when she refers to theories of generic-categoric typification. According to one survey, people see sparrows and robins as "birdier" birds than ostriches or parrots. Aitchison quotes a TV commentator: "legs are leggy, fruits are fruity, newspapers are newspapery" (65). That sentence's abecedarial impact on the page itself gives point to what would otherwise be mere tautology. Finally there are innovations like *unmurder, beatnik, stayputnik, iffy,* as well as new combinations such as *glue-sniffer* and *woman astronaut,* and whole phrases depending on a newly introduced term, like "Do a Napoleon for the camera"; put your hand inside your jacket. In all these cases, of course, we feel very immediately what is meant, but it is partly because the abecedary compels by its presence. Bar codes would be equally unique and indeed "arbitrary," but bar codes offer no easily grasped silhouette with which meaning could become identified. In short, what the mind stores lexically is, in important part, *not just words but abecedarial rolles.* The word's physiognomy may also be part of what is stored. There seems no good reason to say that somehow a (disembodied) "meaning" is retained in the brain, when that same brain has the capacity to provide connections drawn from the palpable world, between what the word means and what it looks or sounds like. What the abecedary's distributive modes do *not* do, is to match either the meaning or the syntactic structure in any reliable one-to-one way. There will be match on occasion, in fact often, but just as often not. Length of word, presence of the commoner or rarer letters, familiar clusters or "old favorites," vowel-consonant proportions, and the rest fail to correlate exactly with either syntactical or lexical emanations; yet equally they may come to do so. As we have seen, the poets are alive to all these things.

INTENTION AND ILLOCUTION

Speech-act theory, associated with J. L. Austin and John Searle, introduces the crucial aspect of intention. It was suggested in an earlier chapter that intention is what allows the writer normally to exploit abecedarial fewness without danger of misunderstanding and, indeed, with some increase of tension and excitement. The reader will not confuse *garden/harden* or *appealed/appeared* if the sentence's intention is always adhered to. However, the term *intention* in contemporary cognitive science means more than just what directs an action with a clear will and for a clear purpose. Common-root terms in English like *intention, attention, tendency, tension, intensity,* and (in both senses) *content* are all germane to this matter. They reveal "intention" as more than a subject-intender deploying an inert body of material.

Yet both Austin and Searle did adopt a purer model of intention.

Speech-act theory centers on verbs, "the pump which drives sentences along" as Aitchison put it (111); and with Austin and Searle the emphasis is not on the clustering of verb-types in semantic areas of practical life, but as to how intention powers their illocutionary force. Austin's theory came first.[6] His performatives *(I promise, I congratulate you)*, verdictives *(I reckon, I take it that)*, executives *(I appoint you as, I bequeath, I sentence you to)*, behavitives *(I apologize, deplore, drink to)*, and expositives *(I postulate, I concede that, I begin by)*—these too "feel poetic" when listed this way. They evoke not just meaning but a kind of common energy in what they do, which the abecedary absorbs. Wordsworth's "-ing" lexicon in this connection: *rolling, passing, pleasing, flying, thinking, being, shooting* and so on, is a similar case structurally. As with Wordsworth, Austin's unusual glut of terms, gathering various meanings and abecedarial combinations under a common syntactical form, sets the lexicon throbbing.

Searle's greater elaborations, however, uncover a whole range of inferences for any one verb as to just what each sets in motion. Clearly we have to keep this brief, and we can't remotely do justice to the thoroughness with which Searle detailed specific cases; for example, the rules for *requesting, asserting, questioning, thanking, advising, warning, greeting,* and *congratulating.*[7] Again the list from Wordsworth is cognate.

Searle first distinguishes the three parts of any speech act. These are utterance (the physical act, which could include writing); proposition (reference or predication; the "content"); and illocution, which he too also refers to as "tendency," that term of course belonging with our list of intention—words, given above. For his prototype example, *promising* (57–64), Searle then lays out a set of conditions and a set of rules. I have to give my own brief summary here, but these would appear to run along the following lines. The speaker must have something to promise and will predicate it in the speech act. The hearer must want the promise to take effect and the speaker must believe the hearer so wants. It must not be obvious to either party that the promised act would occur in the normal course of events (whether it actually would or not), otherwise no promise would be needed. The speaker must really intend to carry out the promise (otherwise there is bad faith), but must also intend that the speech-act that promises, is itself what commits him/her to carrying the promise out. The speaker must also intend that the hearer will learn, from the speech-act of "promising," that the commitment is now in place. There are a few further details, for example that I can't promise a past act. This last is not just a syntactical impossibility. If I have carried out an act already, then to promise it after the event would be an affectation. The further rules that Searle then appends—and which we have to omit here—derive from these conditions.

It is interesting that earlier (22–53) Searle had given a set of rules for plain statements, as opposed to commitments, performatives and the rest, along comparable lines. The double-import in English of the word "mean" surfaces here. if I make the assertion that *When I said "Wembley" I didn't mean the stadium, I meant the suburb* I signify a neutral intention to refer. But *I mean to get that promotion, I'm really going for it* is more loaded. Yet in speech or writing the two strongly overlap. If I say *hey, that's a big house*, a) I mean that I think it is big, b) I mean you to know it is big and that I think so, too, c) I mean you to know that I intend you to know it—and so on. In the act of promising at least three levels of intention were entailed. Yet all that was said, the actual abecedarial presence, may have been merely *OK, I promise to meet the kids*, just as here we only say *hey, that's a big house*.

Again the abecedary does its equable and distributive work, along a linear plane. But there is no match between the details of that distribution and the various levels of Searle's rules and conditions. Yet this still does not make the linguistic sign "arbitrary," for as said all along, it has its own internal system. The abecedary as virtual, however, emerges in speech-acts rather strongly. This is clear from the many cases where the illocutionary thrust is achieved without its verb even being present. The above promise could omit the rolle "promise" entirely; it could have been *OK. I'll meet the kids* in a certain tone of voice; or, in writing, with a period-point between and not a comma. *There's a bomb alert in the High Street* could well be an act of warning; that is to say, one of Austin's "performatives." *He went home?* can be a question—with the question-mark certainly, but only an intonation in speech—while *he's just hit a four* (in the game of cricket) can "mean" to tell you—who have just arrived at the game—that the batsman has just hit a four, that I am aware you are familiar with cricket and so know what a "four" is, and that I would not offend you by implying otherwise. The speaker might assert, inform or reassure, or all three at once, with no singly identifiable term (or abecedarial cluster) tied to those meanings at all.

So we might next ask how illocutionary acts stand in poetry itself. For Searle the speaker must not be "telling jokes or acting in a play": Austin had said they mustn't be in a poem (Searle 1969, 57; Austin 1971, 9). Debates about the poet's "intention" and the supposed "intentional fallacy," as against the poet's subliminal drives and social background, or the potential multiple readings of the resulting text, go back a long way.[8] Richard Ohlmann has suggested that literary works are "discourses with the usual illocutionary rules suspended, or . . . acts without consequences of the usual sort." Stanley Fish has taken both Ohlmann and Wolfgang Iser to task for such assertions. Fish's emphasis is that an illocutionary act simply produces a recognition that it has in fact been produced, so that to consider it alone is to remove it from its real source of value; in effect, the intention behind it. But that seems just a difference of genre. Iser and Ohlmann understand Fish's inference but are thinking largely of the structure of fiction. Iser's belief is that "fictional language does not lead to real actions in a real context, but this does not mean that it is without any real effect."[9] On this argument there would be, in effect, two layers or stages. First there would be a kind of outer intention, of one sort or another, to produce the literary work at all. Then, within that frame, would come the "inner" intentions or tendencies of the statements, promises, questions, joyous outbursts, or wailings of grief that the literary work's own parameters, and its characters, throw up. But in poems it works differently. In poems the alphabet is itself thrown forward as palpable artistic medium with a double intensity, double presence. *Intention* and *intensity* here merge with each other. David Olsen's suggestion, already cited (Olsen 1994, 113), that the illocutionary force is itself "the most primitive part of language," is clearly germane here.

For a feature of the speech-act view is the implied "central intender," the single "I" or ego who intends, knowingly or otherwise. The central intender, consciously, unconsciously or by instinct, lurks somewhere at back of many language theories, though not all. This does not necessarily—though it may—follow from Olsen's view, for that view emphasized solely that the text, whatever the source of its intention from "behind," must then convey its intention within itself. The writer no longer has to be present. But this central intender is certainly a nineteenth century stance behind traditional hermeneutics. This traditional hermeneutics declined, maybe because it assumed too often a single interpreting reader making sense of a single intending utterer. The linguistic sign lay between them like a piece of glass to be penetrated. Herbert, as we saw, was all too aware of this "piece of glass" as was the biblical coiner of the phrase "through a glass darkly."

Actually the chief hermeneuticists of the nineteenth-century period, Freidrich Schleiermacher and Wilhelm Dilthey, were both aware of wider context, of what was unsaid behind the work, as well as of the subtleties and grades of understanding to be sought within it. But the two differed a little from each other, too. Schleiermacher most looked to the balance between the grammatical and the psychological in seeking which texts most excited human interest— and so were worth interpreting anyway—while Dilthey encountered more nakedly the apparent cul-de-sac of the concern with the "hermeneutic circle." One can only read the whole by knowing the parts, which themselves first need an overview if they too are to be understood.[10] This went along with giving greater weight to longer works; in effect, those which could not merely be spoken (we saw in chapter 4 how Montaigne, Castiglione *et al* were able to "stretch" conversation by getting the genre down in print). It also paradoxically penetrated the text as text while endangering the sense of knowing the author. This last point seldom troubles the more extreme political critic, who sees precisely the text—not the author—as the place where its ideology furtively lies. But the relevance of Wordsworth is that his endless hesitations, qualifications and indeterminacy themselves show him to be always at the behest of the play of his own language. The "I", the Romantic first-person who of course lay behind much nineteenth century hermeneutics, hovers on the surface of the Searlian listings of illocutionary action; *I promise, I bequeath, I warn,* and the rest. But with Wordsworth it is as likely to be *I may have owed . . . I dare to hope . . . I cannot paint (what then I was) . . . Not for this faint I . . . I would believe . . . for I have learned*—all from *Tintern Abbey*. The poet is drawn in as subject of already formed expressions and to feel vulnerable under such power. What Wordsworth himself called "the charm of words in tuneful order" also informed his intentions.

17

Unconsciousness and Consciousness

PSYCHOANALYSIS

THE MATTER WAS DIFFERENT HOWEVER FOR THOSE WHO SAW ANY "intention" as driven by powerful factors within the individual but unknown to him or her. At that point "intention" became mere surface consciousness and, in language terms, articulation. The unconscious, at bottom the libido, was the driving force behind it. Much of psychoanalysis has been reformulated in light of cognitive science, genetics, and Darwinian evolution of more recent date, and might seem redundant here. Freud, Jung, and Lacan have also been subjected to the most bitter attacks in recent years, on grounds that link their professional theories inseparably, it is said, to their own highly questionable practices. Psychoanalysis itself is not merely wrong but personally and intellectually corrupting. Yet since the insights of psychoanalysis were often poetic and mythmaking (the terms are used neutrally) in their nature, and remain to this day part of Western educated discourse, they need attention here, and their connection to signs remains impressively cogent. Imaginative insights can and do outlast the fallacies of their origins.

Freud's location of the subconscious also presumed a single "central intender," but it was one who didn't know of these intentions or where they came from. This at once means the (abecedarial) sign is not necessarily secondary to the intender using it. The intender may have been gripped by signs encountered in some drastic context. A couple of Freud's well-known observations relate to language, in quite different ways in each case; namely, his researches into dreams, and into everyday mistakes. Both areas imply a quasi-intentional resistance to pressures in the subconscious. Freud variously suggested that we dream for wish-fulfillment, to off-load unwanted material, repress deep earlier traumas, or simply in order not to wake. But the means to achieve this, namely condensation and displacement, image rather than concept, and the dream-scene's near-stasis, all entailed a kind of syntaxless import by which troublesome unconscious movement could be annulled.[1] When language itself appears in dreams, it too is static not discursive: a looming document, a single repeated refrain, the "writing on the wall." In linguistic terms though, the immediate question for Freud was what happened in dreams to the connectives of language which can't find a dream-image; *because, just as, not, perhaps, either/or* and so on (op.cit. sect. C, p. 422). Such terms are among the "virtualities" the abecedary can express. Why should these be what is suppressed rather than only the loved persons or bad digestion that the dream did, if indirectly, allow in?

In the event, said Freud, *because* was expressed by dreamed chronological sequence, *just as* by a unification or merging within the dream picture, *perhaps* by various kinds of fade, and *not* by sharp or sudden change. *Either/or* however could not be represented, as though to say the dream couldn't be two things at once, and could only displace the realities it was suppressing by straight substitution. Although the dream suppressed something, the replacement was firm and insistent; there was no "either/or" about it, even if the substitute was complex. The question is of what we make of all this in present context. Cognitively it recalls the contention of Aitchison and others that syntactical and lexical features may be stored separately in the brain, and suggests that the lexical ones are somehow more strongly wired into or available for whatever is itself the source of the dreaming process. Whatever the truth of that, the abecedary's equable and virtual nature is again underlined. In the unconscious, at least in dreams, the syntactical and the lexical are separate. In the broad light of day our code of language renders them homogeneously, by the same set of letters in the same sentence-forms moving from left to right. The abecedary's virtuality is equally emphasized. The unconscious doesn't rise to abstraction and reason, which can only be attained by the power of physical signs to ascend to virtuality.

The lexical-syntactical distinction surfaces equally, if differently, in verbal errors in everyday life. These were Freud's "Freudian slips." The cases he collected were again usually a matter of the referential lexicon. Furthermore, when they were verbal they were commonly puns. If one said "I am going in September" instead of "I am going in disgrace," there might be a repression; yet some ordinary element of decision would be entailed, however fleeting. There would be no verbal problem to investigate. But when Freud reported an informer writing "anectode" instead of "anecdote"—a clear case of our "near-miss" (see above, chapter 5), he surmised that a certain gypsy called Tode, under sentence of death and important to the writer, was being subliminally suggested.[2] Among many other cases a woman became *klapperschlange* (rattlesnake) rather than *Kleopatra*; children were called *Juden* (Jews) not *jungsten* (young people); and a speaker said he was *geneigt* (disinclined) rather than *geeignet* (unqualified) to comment on an esteemed predecessor. In English *endurable* might go to *incurable, adulating* to *adulterous,* and so on; there are numerous such examples in chapters 5 and 6 of *The Psychopathology of Everyday Life.*

Because the sound and/or writing of the rolles in these pairs were close to each other, the unconscious had an easy route to the surface. Abecedarial fewness therefore, which is what yields and indeed selects such near-puns, is itself a force in the psyche, and other students of the unconscious discover it. With Jung, the infant is not merely sexually potent, as with Freud, leaving it as a "single intender" however much that came from early parental attention. Rather, the infant is already born with an array of symbolic archetypes—the collective unconscious—somehow already installed in the sexual and neural systems. Although their outward expression varies from culture to culture, these archetypes cannot be merely cultural in origin, for they are found universally. The child knows, or recognizes on first acquaintance, gender, tastes, color, air and light, plant/animal characteristics, narrative, human prototypes such as "stranger" and "wise old man," and language.[3] Jung took this to mean that each person has several potential personalities and these have to be integrated. There wasn't, as for Freud, a single personality requiring cure, but rather multiple selves needing resolution into a unity. In this respect some current consciousness theory is closer to Jung than to Freud, for it too eschews the idea of a central "clearinghouse" of neural operations. It was Jung, too, not Freud, who first used the term "complex" for a cluster of associated aspects of behavior. The task is then not, as with Freud, libido repression on a reward/punishment axis, but rather a mythmaking on which to base individuation for each unique human case. This last furthermore is the task of middle life rather than postinfancy, and again Jung's term "midlife crisis" has entered our language.[4]

Jung researched Western myths, dreams, religion, alchemy, sexuality, mantra, painting, and arcana of various kinds for materials from which to reach this desirable individuation. But one inference for Jung was that language itself is not just a record of the naturally emerging system, perhaps "instinct," by which all these things are related. Rather, language itself is one more item, one more large symbolic area within the set of resources that individuals draw upon to construct the myth that suits them. But again then the abecedarial rolles are of consequence. For language here, symbolic and meaningful to its heart of course, would then be effective from its own palpable presence just as would the bodies and canvases of sex and painting, the actual waxed and gilded icons of religion, the bottles and retorts of alchemy and the rest.

From all such considerations it is tempting to match the Freud-Jung contrast with two kinds of poet. Those like Wordsworth and Frost seek a form for their inner, turbulent but self-contained thrusts, and come to find the language that "spontaneously" (Wordsworth, *Preface to Lyrical Ballads*) seems to fulfil that. Those like Herbert, Hopkins, David Jones, and indeed James Joyce begin with the language itself, then work it into the shapes that symbolize the many deeper realities in themselves that feel inherently inexpressible. For whatever reason, the latter group prefers the stored lexicon to syntactic continuities, and most highlights the abecedarial features of alliteration, pun, new coinage, "sponging-up," and the rest. Most important, such poets also use a markedly more "exotic" or "centrifugal" language as we have defined those terms abecedarially. Joyce himself said, of his meeting with Jung, that he could "psoakonaloose" himself perfectly well without help from anyone. In *Ulysses*, which mystified Jung when he read it and which anticipates the letter-explosion of the postmodern world, Jung may have found Joyce's surface manipulations simply destructive.[5] Even so Jung's poet would seem to be Yeats, whose life-project was also, as Yeats put it, to "hammer his thoughts into a unity"; that is to say to weld an integrating myth from many sources rather than uncover something deep and organic. Yeats too achieved this best in middle and old age.

Jacques Lacan saw it all a third way. Although Lacan's work is rooted in Freud, his key reversal of Freud's view of language and the subconscious takes him part way toward Jung's position. His view is not evolutionary but teleological. But Lacan gives more weight to language overall than either Freud or Jung, and also eschews the parent. In his renowned "mirror stage" the child first sees itself in a glass and experiences itself as separate from the parents, as independently real. The child can then posit a generalized Other to which its future life-activity is directed.[6] In terms reminiscent of Emmanuel Levinas, Lacan suggests that desire's first object is to be recognized by this Other. This desire is not simply sexual but pertains to language and to speech. The "Name of the Father," so often cited by Lacan commentators, is thus not the usual paternal prototype but language itself; for "the law is that of language." All this removes Freud's primary unconscious, the dark force that Freud himself declared he so feared. To Lacan it is not that language—via, for example, the Freudian slip—expresses the unconscious, nor does the unconscious immobilize language as in dream. Rather, the unconscious is itself structured like a language, and language is primary.

The aim of Lacanian psychoanalytical treatment thus becomes quite different from that of Freud. Freudian psychoanalysis would search the patient's discourse for what was prior to it and suppressed by it. For Lacan, treatment is an attempt to restore the patient's speech from neurosis back to its proper role in ordinary life; namely, that of joining the past to the future. The aim was not to find and eliminate some trauma or blockage in the past. It didn't matter what caused the blockage in the past. "The effect of full speech is to re-order past contingencies by conferring on them the sense of necessities to come . . . In order to be recognized by the other, I utter what was only in view of what will be."[7]

This link from past through present to future is embodied in discourse because language is linear—an aspect fully and completely accounted for by abecedarial distribution. The signifier anticipates meaning by unfolding its dimension before it.[8] Again one recalls Augustine and Aquinas on the sentence and time. This turns "intention" into both *content* and *tendency*. The patient's signifying chain is thus what the psychoanalyst should *attend* to, so that the patient can reenter *verbe*. All this, along with its clear language of intention, is possible precisely because the source of speech is not in any unconscious. Rather, the source of speech is in language itself. Lacan reversed not only Freud, and indeed Chomsky, too, but also Saussure. For Saussure the signified, a real house, calls up "house," the signifier. For Lacan it is the signifier that does the summoning. In Heidegger's terms again, we don't speak language, language speaks us. We may decide what thoughts to think about, but we cannot decide what thoughts to have, for thought does not consult us about what it is to be or when to enter consciousness. Thought is already decided by what is named.

If language does motivate us in this way, it has great power, and its palpable nature in the real world must be of some significance. For Lacan it has such presence. "Speech is in fact a gift of language, and language is not immaterial. It is a subtle body, but body it is" (Lacan 1997ii, 87). But Lacan's "subtlety" here matches the abecedary's virtuality. Much seems to follow from this for our present concerns. If signification is a linear chain, then what is needed is the presentation, in language moving steadily to the right, of every level of desire, object, connective, denomination of speaker, second-order and third order of implication, and so on. And for this the equable and distributive nature of the abecedary could hardly be more appropriate, or more in evidence. The unchangeable form of each letter, regardless of handwriting style, typeface, or electronic pulse, is what the patient can relearn to rely on. And something else follows. "The elementary structures of a culture" are laid down "long before the drama of history is inscribed in it," and this is "inconceivable outside the permutations authorised by language" (Lacan 1997iii, 148). In the relation between language and humanity, for Lacan this makes the poet the key figure. The poet has the gift of language prior to its present modifications in the temporary life that surrounds it. The chain of history the patient reenters by joining past to future in discourse comes via the language that encompasses the smaller eras which we call historical periods. Again the centuries-old abecedary is not just "arbitrary," no longer mere chance. It is more than a trivial set of sounds or marks that could be substituted tomorrow without effect on our lives, histories, or psyches.

Currently, psychoanalysis has a heavy question mark hanging over it. This too turns out relevant to our topic. It has long been recognized that psychoanalysis forces the consultant into complicity with the patient in at least some way or another. If the consultant is merely neutral or inert, then that itself lessens the chance of the patient uncovering his/her own repressed orientations whatever their nature, or reentering the flow of language. The consultant may inflame comparable tendencies in his own self, and predispose the patient toward his own theories, while himself unwittingly regarding those theories as invulnerable (the male pronoun is deliberate throughout). Psychoanalysis is insightful and risky at once; its material evidence is reportage in language, which is always to some degree figurative. The unconscious can't normally be explored, let alone relived, under foolproof laboratory conditions. The analyst is therefore always tempted to read his patients' stories in the light of his own speculative insights. A group of early insights leads to a satisfyingly elegant theory; this leads to figurative elaboration, to fitting future patients' reports into those theories, and to widening the whole to apply to the entire human condition. The more gifted, and linguistically gifted, the analyst and theorist, the more the situation deteriorates.

Denials by patients are taken all the more to confirm that something is being resisted. The analyst's need to dominate will itself attract achievers of overbearing personality into the profession; or else those who feel sick and want to project that on to others or explore it there. The urge to trace psychic sicknesses back to the patients' parents descends from the analyst's faulted relationship with his own parents. The paranoia found in patients' personalities is entailed. The analyst becomes paranoiac about paranoia itself. These are the averred dangers.

Jung, if briefly, became a Nazi sympathizer. Raymond Tallis has called Lacan crackpot, lunatic, and charlatan in a single review article, and even Freud the master has been termed dangerous, mendacious, ruthless, messianic, demented, "intrinsically comic," perpetrating a "labyrinth of errors," and having the "nerve and effrontery" to call such work science. Richard Webster, Anthony Clare, Frederick Crews, and others are the accusers.[9] Such detractors, it has to be said, can be somewhat unctious in their outrage at times, and Freud continued to be vigorously defended by such as Adam Phillips and Anthony Storr. It depends what you expect from a theory. Insights such as that we dream in order not to wake, that Hamlet envied Claudius for usurping his own Oedipal position, that there are symbolic archetypes in the unconscious, that where you were I will be—such insights aren't refuted or upheld either by empirical testing or by the unimpeachable behavior of their originators. They depend on the society in which such work is practiced, the linguistic gifts of the practitioners, and their degree of insight into the human condition into whose darkness they enter.

The insights of psychoanalysis have become part of the bloodstream of Western culture, and are thus subject to the ordinary sifting process by which any orientations to, or expressions of, our condition are evaluated. But they were also unattainable without risk. Something as seemingly innocent as the abecedary has its profile in the subconscious as surely as, if less glamorously than, food, sex, or aggression. The signality of matter is as effectual as its libido. The psychoanalysts' explorations of language could not have avoided insolently probing into the language-mind connection—in all three writers as we have tried to show, the abecedary-mind connection—with attendant results. Their findings overlap the things that poets have transmuted and the ways they have done so with language. As Freud said, the poets were there before him.

CONSCIOUSNESS THEORY

Whatever the truth of all this, a main feature in the game was clearly the unconscious or subconscious, the bit the patient is supposed to be unaware of. In recent years disciplines have addressed the other side of the coin; namely, consciousness. Consciousness is the self we feel we have and are. There is major disagreement about consciousness on all fronts; what it is, whether it is material exclusively, partly, or not at all, and indeed whether its nature can ever be known or is inherently irretrievable. Again we must simplify in this account; even so, it will take us a little while to reach language and the abecedary. I have to ask the reader's indulgence here, for some few pages of comment first, before we get there. When we do, the mutual relationship of consciousness and the abecedary can be suggested.

Two aspects of the matter are agreed on by all. First is consciousness's overwhelming presence to the individual. The massiveness of the ME is universally held to be both impressive in itself and the subject that needs explication. As Thomas Nagel has emphasized, it is a "subjectively stupendous event" even though in the flow of the whole cosmos it "produces scarcely a ripple" (Nagel 1986, 55). Consciousness is quite simply inseparable from anyone experiencing it, embodying it, simply being it—something expressed with rare vividness, incidentally, in a prose text by the poet Gerard Manley Hopkins.[10] For John Searle consciousness is never plural, always singular; a perspective private to myself. Others from Gilbert Ryle to Daniel Dennett have believed consciousness might someday cease to be private. To many, a key element is the "qualia," experiences such as of redness or pain that seem irreducible. Dennett denies their existence, while others see them as "mental representations," a topic we shall come to. To Dennett the sense of a ME, the "central intender" already mentioned, is just a mechanism evolved in the interests of survival. The brain's activities are many and not necessarily strongly connected, so the brain must at least seem to be monotrack to its owner even if it is not, for its survival to be installed as a long-term concern. This mere "seeming-ordering" (Dennett 1991, chaps. 5, 13) is, perhaps, itself the phenomenon we call consciousness. Yet it is still there. Consciousness is, so to speak, nonconvertible.

The second agreed factor, however, again among many who elsewhere disagree, is that mind and brain are basically different. Mind and brain seem inseparable yet still irreconcilable. Our experiences, memories, emotions, hopes, self-knowing awareness, and the rest are one thing; the neurons, the synapses that carry electrical brain circuits, the cortex and so on, where all these subjective experiences must "happen," are of a different order. Mind is somehow entailed with brain yet floats above it. This follows from the consciousness experience.

Neurons—"gray matter"—are specialized cells that have projecting fibres. The cell bodies can integrate inputs and so generate electrical impulses. They receive other impulses from other neurons via other fibers (dendrites), and transmit electrical impulses to other parts of the nervous system via yet more fibers (axons). The axon from one neuron goes to the dendrite of another via the synapses. There are events such as neural synchronization and oscillation. The brain's frontal region, the cortex, seems especially important. But the gap between brain and mind is not bridged by such knowledge. Is "mind," that is to say consciousness, the spur to or the result of such things?

Dennett, as so often, has expressed the matter as vividly as anyone. As consciousness, our brains are undeniably aware of such things as love, "I", purple cows (nonexistent in the real world), and much else. Yet if we literally dissect a brain in the laboratory, we find no trace of such things. As Dennett puts it, *"there's nobody home"* (Dennett 1991, 29, his emphasis). Yet the array of mixed and strange items we are conscious of, the "phenomenological garden" as Dennett calls it, subsists. We can "have fun," imagine being burned alive, and understand Conan Doyle's reference to "that day Holmes met Watson at Paddington" without needing to know if it was a Wednesday or a Thursday, about which there is simply no fact of the matter (Dennett 1991, 43–59). One might add that we can draw a picture of our Uncle Bill but not of "an uncle," less still of a yesterday; yet we understand, are conscious of, uncles and yesterdays as concept. The fact remains: the brain reveals nothing of it, the mind shows it all.

Numerous explanations of this strange abyss have been put forward. Dennett himself believes there are no minds, only very wonderful, refined, capability-endowed brains. David Chalmers, on the same grounds of observation, believes the reverse. Because the mental is not logically supervenient on the physical, so mental and physical experience are literally independent entities. Chalmers believes that consciousness is a real, nonphysical feature, an additional fundamental property of the universe.[11] Indeed it may be present in proto form in inanimate matter. This view has been called "pan-psychism." An even stronger view is idealism, which holds that consciousness is all and matter the illusion. Between such views there are the many quite content to hold that mind and brain are autonomous. Both are real and independent, but they are mutually influential, too. Much of this, needless to say, is variation on the Cartesian duality.

Some theorists are still a touch reluctant to accept a mind-brain separation, and it is certainly upheld only by a major difficulty. Surprisingly, it will turn out important for our own discussion of language and the alphabet. Again, on all sides it is accepted that research into mind-brain connection has yielded virtually no returns whatsoever. The problem is that of how subjective states can be mapped on to the brain. The results are not encouraging. Susan Greenfield has stated that "No single neuronal mechanism has as yet been identified which functions only during consciousness and on its own causes consciousness." She states elsewhere that "even if you buy into [her model of consciousness], you must recognize that it is still only one of correlation, not cause."[12] Others agree, none more insistently than Jerry Fodor:

> There isn't one, *not one*, instance where it's known what pattern of neural connectivity realizes a certain cognitive content, innate *or* learned, in either the infant's nervous system or the adult's. To be sure, our brains must somehow register the contents of our mental states. The trouble is, nobody knows how—by what neurological means—they do so. Nobody can look at the patterns of connectivity (or at anything else) in a brain and figure out whether it belongs to somebody who knows algebra, or who speaks English, or who believes that Washington was the father of his Country . . . because *nobody knows how the cognitive brain works.* (all Fodor's emphases)

Elsewhere he tersely summarizes: "Nothing is known about the way the structure of our minds depends on the structure of our brains. Nobody even knows which brain structures our cognitive capacities depend on."[13] There's nobody home indeed.

But after that, opinion becomes divided. For some, the lack of results merely confirms that consciousness is mysterious and must forever remain so. For Searle, the privacy inherent in the first-person perspective means it can never be accessed by third-person research or computer models, and clearly this ties in with Searle's single-intender of speech acts. This also applies to "qualia." As Wittgenstein put it, when I call out "pain!" what am I referring to but—pain! That is to say, the word or rolle "pain" has to be adduced even to say what pain is if no such word were available. The literature expended on pain, by philosphers and others, as "qualia" or not, would fill libraries. Both Colin McGinn and Jerry Fodor have declared that "the brain *is* more complicated than it is smart . . . consciousness will forever be a mystery to us."[14] But others, usually empiricists, believe it is still early days and success will come. Research and subsequent theory construction alone, not speculative philosophizing, will bring results. Via chemical action of various sorts, it may become possible to trace how changes in consciousness relate to changes in brain states. Dennett claims to have actually established what consciousness is, although even the optimists regard this with skepticism. For a few, the road to understanding goes via examination of eyesight and particularly the "blindspot"; and film, after all, has had some imaginative success in presenting first-person inner states. The car from the viewpoint of the driver; autobiographical flashbacks; sudden cuts to a subject's nervous imaginings.

Every kind of question has been asked and every kind of suggestion put forward. All, *pace* John Locke, now assume at least some degree of innateness. One view of the brain is modular, plural. For Dennett there is no "Oval Room in the White House" which receives messages and emits instructions. The brain is multitrack, a set of connectionist networks by which information, impulses, memories, and practical techniques are stored in different ways and locations, ready for different responses to outside stimuli, at any time. This has derived from evolution. Humans across the millennia have responded to countless small expedients with no long-term plans attached. Survival-tricks grew to meet every kind of expedient imaginable; dodging mechanisms to avoid predators, berry-picking, itch-scratching, friend/foe discriminators, knowing that one has been wounded or that it is too cold, and the like. Later elaborations are more complex and more sophisticated, including that of how we select language (Dennett 1991, chaps. 5 and 7).

The survival drive idea, however, doesn't tell us how this is more mental, more a process of thought than the sheer reaction of, say, a plant that has "learned" to conserve water. For many, including both Fodor and Dennett, this is computational. Again the mind-brain dichotomy appears, and the question is of how the structure of computational networks in some way matches the structure of brain tissue to become conscious at all. Their answer is Turing's model of computation, which explains how "mindless" objects—computers—can nevertheless order items in logical sequences. If A is greater than B and B is greater than C, then A is greater than C; computers can draw such logical inferences, and far more complex ones, with no conscious intention whatever.

This still lacks a description of qualitative meaning, which has to come in from the outside. This next element, "externalism," reassociates brain-learning with experience as well as internal definition. The true belief that holly trees have prickly leaves comes from the user's contact with holly trees. Expanded to its necessary conclusion, externalism introduces the whole range of experiences known now by Richard Dawkins's term "memes," recently expanded by Susan Blackmore.[15] A meme is anything that can be copied or "replicated." In Dennett's random list: wheel, wearing clothes, vendetta, right triangle, alphabet, calendar, the Odyssey, calculus, chess, perspective drawing, evolution by natural selection, Impressionism, "Greensleeves," and deconstructionism (Dennett 1991, 201). But most of these are "cultural", and not all sound good for survival. Classical symphonies, returnable bottles, spray-paint graffiti, and hijacking of aircraft are all memes. This therefore raises complex questions as to what they are if not, in part at least, brain, too. Are they mind, and is mind then wholly separate from brain after all? Memes are paradoxical. They can leap from brain to brain by the ordinary interactive processes of culture, bypassing some of its members altogether. Yet without brains to cognize them, memes would not exist, for consciousness perennially implies something for the brain to be conscious of. Unsurprisingly, the meme idea has brought strong attack from many quarters. As a concept it is interesting, but is very hard to pin down and ironically therefore is still easy to use in lax fashion.

Finally there is Roger Penrose's view that consciousness comes not from brain at all but from quantum mechanics.[16] The nervous system operates algorithmically, as do computers. But much in mathematics is subtler than the algorithm. Since mathematics is itself a kind of thought—to its adherents the purest kind—then it follows that the nervous system can't account for all the kinds of thought that humans are capable of. And the quantum particle is too small to affect the nervous system, so it must work elsewhere. Penrose's candidate is the "micro-tubule" (part of the "skeleton" of brain cells). Furthermore, the quantum can be in two places at once and can be activated by being observed. Such energy or mobility at the heart of matter itself might be something to do with consciousness right outside the neural system, and even be universal.

The problem with all such views is that what they say isn't really explanation. They merely indicate the contending areas that any theory of consciousness would have to take into account. It gets more promising with a certain refinement within the consciousness idea. For we can be conscious of consciousness itself; and that fact begins to nudge us toward language. Here is a simple example. One is conscious of a pinprick but also conscious of a proposition about it. My reaction may be both "ouch!" and "I know what that was, it was a pin." The first is pure reaction, the second is syntactical, articulated. The difference appears in many phenomena of mind and brain at work.

Suppose I see an apple and then turn away. My mind/brain remembers the object. Yet the real apple can't have entered the brain. But there can't be nothing at all either. So there must be some "representation" of an apple in some way or other, somewhere in between. Current neuroscience data supports the idea of representations. The question then is, is this representation visual or nonvisual? Or suppose I see my dog's tail sticking out from under the bed. Do I make sense of this by visualizing the whole of the dog, or do I just infer it by straight cognition? Again the former would be further experience, or quasi-experience; the latter would be syntactical, cognate with language. Again opinion is divided on the matter.

There is a further factor when something is seen whole from the outset, like the apple was. Evidence suggests that outflowing signals from the prefrontal cortex must be matched by incoming signals from the eye's retina, if actual seeing, rather than mere imagining or remembering, is to occur. Yet it seems that one must also be actively looking for the apple, positively seeking it, in order to see it, even when the incoming retina signals are available. (It is common experience to pass our eyes right across some item in a room or landscape and yet not register it. Numerous laboratory experiments have elucidated this.) Once more two levels of consciousness are implied. The stimulus may be available, but our conscious articulation of that to ourselves takes the experience to a different order of meaning.

And the same distinction applies to what we have discussed already. The brain may have "plural activity" rather than a "central intender." Yet for existence, identity, and responsibility to proceed at all, humans will need some kind of integration into "selves," too, and this applies whether selves are illusory or not (Dennett 1991, chap. 13). Again Fodor puts the general point interestingly. If everything really is so separate and plural, meeting this need here and that threat there, then "there had also better be somebody in charge; and, by God, it had better be *me*."[17] The neural equivalent of this is the "binding problem"; how the brain joins outputs from spatially separate groups of neurons into the perception of a unified object. Oscillation, "Hz firing," and other modes have been suggested. The firing of synapses at the nerve-ends gives the nervous experience but not the perception.

At last, if tentatively, we approach our own topic. The "mental representations" already referred to—of the apple or the half-hidden dog—may themselves be some sort of mental language. Some call this "mentalese." Externally we may have a language correlative, like speech or a sign-system; but the brain has to do it differently, with only its own neural materials. Now, whether there are "sentences in the head" or, as Ruth Garrett Millikan has suggested, an orthography for mentalese and apt to it, is again a matter of whether the mental experience is felt "pure" or in some way as syntactical, articulated. For Millikan a mental representation contains "tacit suppositions," "intentional icons" (I take these to be tendency-icons), actual representations, and mental sentences.[18] Yet all of these are covalent; unlike language they have no hierarchy and are not rule-governed. The materialist brain can have no overriding axioms governing the arranging of these things, for what in turn would decide those axioms? Rather, these brain-tokens just set up connections via middle terms of some kind, of no more or less value than what they connect. They could be like mnemonics— which, perhaps, evolve to the proverbs we saw reported by Kwame Gyewye. As Millikan says, mental sentences have not picture-representation but composition, which is like saying they have no lexicon, only syntax. Others however believe that this itself may introduce a "commonsense-psychology module," by which skill we can recognize a face or even desire what doesn't exist, for example, a mountain made of dollars.

We can't be said to "sense" our conscious thoughts, for there is no sense organ for doing so. Rather we have further thoughts about them, and these are best called "higher order" thoughts. This sounds reasonably encouraging, for as we said earlier, "thoughts about thoughts" is something the abecedary's equability handles rather efficiently. But this overall distinction, between pure-brain response and syntactic response, has led to polarized views as to what is fundamentally entailed. At one extreme, beliefs and intentions are held not even to exist—a remarkable view from those who "believe" such theories, although in the event it is not quite so absurd as it sounds. At the other extreme are such as Susan Haack, who has strongly defended traditional epistemology against such progressive positions.[19] Haack contends that for example "He did B because he believed A" (syntactical) is a more plausible explanation than "He did B because he had a B-disposition" (pure reaction). The first proposition is "thought about thought," the second sounds like tautology. Haack infers that evolution of language is what has enhanced these cognitive abilities. Reasoning, deliberating, and inquiring grow only when language mastery grows. This view squares with that of Deacon as indeed that of the primitive peoples we discussed in chapter 1. People say things like "I was thinking aloud" or "I speak French but I think in English." *Pace* Chomsky, language is at least in part an external phenomenon. It recalls the remark of Joseph Graham cited many times already. "Words do not take the place of thoughts. They occupy a different space." Syntax has something like the shape of the brain's activities. The lexicon introduces objects from the outer world.

In now trying to get at the role of the abecedary in these matters, I would like to introduce here a notion of my own. I wonder whether consciousness-researchers may be finding no mind-brain link because they are predefining consciousness in a certain way. One might instead try looking at the space where language came from, where primitive humans found it, and, in our context here, the features of the abecedary we have discerned already.

Consciousness is not a "thing" at all. I suggest it is more like a surface. Like consciousness, surfaces are perfectly real and not illusory, but they aren't the metal or the air that meet; they just are the flat location, the Euclidean "area without thickness" at which the sheets of metal and air are in contact. For this reason a few philosophers and scientists of cognition, such as David Rosenthal, see no problem in consciousness.[20] It just is the person awake and responsive to sensory input. The mind/brain just is an awareness of reality rather as water just is wet. Of course, correlation between variants of this awareness may be sought in neural variants. But it often reads like someone examining the battery, bulb, and wires in the hope of finding out what a torch is being pointed at. Rather, we should think of consciousness/mind as a point that brain has come to. Imagine walking toward the edge of a high cliff and reaching its own (vertical) surface, the sheer drop to the rocks below. Suddenly previous programs abruptly cease; the freedom to go one foot before another heedless, to wander along enjoying the day without being too attentive, swigging your bottle looking right and left. A new frame of apprehension is instantly opened up. There is sheer space, emptiness; yet the result is not an ending of consciousness but a sharp heightening of it. Parallels to this empty-state scenario by analogy might be coming out of a decade's prison-sentence to freedom; the continuous noise we become aware of only when it stops;[21] or being told we are terminally ill. The sudden shock of simply "no more" of something; confinement to a dark cell; endless din; or more years of life, all produce an intensifying of consciousness, not its disappearance, but not a newly evolved mental entity, either. These are analogues for human development, in search of survival, of consciousness itself.

If the species that evolved into Homo sapiens at some point acquired consciousness, as we must suppose it did, the question is of what happened. Maybe they "came to the edge of the cliff"; came to the surface of themselves. By this I mean that brain evolved to such a particular pitch or level of complexity, subtlety, or whatever else, that there was suddenly nothing more at its own level of challenge left to confront. It could find engagement only in its own self. It suddenly *just was cognizing that it was there.* The growth of the cortex and its functions; the firing of the synapses; the networking of the neurons; the evolution of the processors; the externalities, the computation, the innateness, and all the rest; all of this was suddenly at a point at which it just did have the capacity to apprehend that it was itself doing so, too. It was merely one more new state.

In this drastic, unprecedented, "empty" situation, the sentient being had a huge cognitive abyss in front of it, like the person on the cliff top, and comparable to the sheet of metal at its surface. This ME is trying to witness this ME. At first it might have been like an electrical short circuit or a snake trying to eat its tail. The problem then is, what sphere of action is there, what does the sentient being actually do, in this new predicament?

It comes across, or invents, language. For none of this entails some kind of disrespect either for consciousnesses or for surfaces. On the contrary, if there were no surfaces we wouldn't have the slightest awareness of anything whatever—colors, beautiful objects, interesting people, food, the contents of books, the interface between silent air and music. Here is what early peoples might have meant by their belief that "the gods gave us language." The craving of the new consciousness to have some counterpart to itself may have been met when it first dawned on humans that the out-there could be seen, heard, consciously remembered, and therefore perhaps in some ways recorded. It was not merely that a large seashell when banged makes an echoing noise, or that flesh when scratched or bleeding would change its appearance. That was known already. It was that appearance and sound could absorb this new consciousness, take meaning, be linked to aspects of what consciousness now knew.

Language is an objective correlative "out there" that can, or can seem to, fill the abyss met at the end of proto-experience, and into which this experience-excess or consciousness-excess can be poured. It marks the "surface" that the new consciousness just is, and there is little else in the material world that can do that. All other material experience is just that; just more material experience, which any ant or ivy-tree would receive accordingly. The next question was of what sort of thing these marks and noises could be. They were at first maybe crude correlates; a drawing of a cup meant something like "I think cup." The evolution and sophistication up to the abecedary is a long process. Many questions are entailed.

For example, some cognitive scientists believe that the "plurality" suggested earlier as having evolved for survival purposes was the developing of specialized intelligences. A generalized intelligence evolved only later. This might have arisen via the "cognitive fluidity" that Steven Mithen has suggested appeared in humans about forty thousand years ago.[22] Specialized neural modularities found a way of flowing into each other to mutual enrichment. This first produced art, then language, but the essential overflowing and externalizing on to the receiving-capacity and inscribability of matter was of the same principle. The problem then was one of linguistic mediation. The question "How do you get from specialized to generalised concepts?" turns into that of "How do you get from specialized concepts to *words for* generalized concepts?" (Fodor's emphasis).[23] The capacity of matter to become signal, symbolic, now comes to the center. Mark Greenberg, writing about Fodor, has put it that since symbols are both physical and semantic at once, we confront "the question of how concrete physical items, like ink marks, electronic signals or, more to the point, neural structures, get to have meaning—can be *symbols*" (Greenberg's emphasis).[24] This problem raises exactly our distinction between the abecedary as physical and as virtual. To put it differently, one might wonder whether consciousness went out toward matter to seek out matter's mark-possibilities, or whether, conversely, matter somehow got drawn in to mind, to fill up or even write on the "surface" that consciousness had by now become. This latter idea does not refer to Locke's tabula rasa, a different conception altogether. It is more a question of whether marks go looking for matter to write on, or whether consciousness in itself is the discovery that, if it is to attain symbolic status, matter needs to get marked. Again there is a parallel at the level of the abecedary and intention. For we might similarly wonder whether intentions are a raft of things to which letters give body, or whether letters are a raft of things to which intentions give body. On the consciousness question, Fodor's own answer is computational as already said, but that itself leaves too much unanswered, and perhaps mysterious.

All these considerations recall for me those cases of language we found in the poets: Herbert's words of mutually exclusive spelling *(feeble/spirit: look/right)*, Eliot's clusters kept rare (*-tch, -st, Waste Land* 19, 30), Wordsworth's "distance-doubles" like *cataract* and *murmur*. What I want to know is, how can the brain possibly ever actually avoid taking note of such things and their positions when scanning the whole message. We have said that every object, like an apple, has a brain-representation that isn't an apple itself but isn't nothing either. So then, must there not be a brain-representation not only for an apple but also for the rolle "apple"; not only for actual murmuring but also for the rolle "murmur"? If we believe, with Chomsky and Pinker, that the sign is merely arbitrary, then does the brain-representation for *murmur* annihilate itself in the moment of arrival and substitute the brain-representation for murmuring on the instant? Furthermore, the sound "murmur" fades a little in the second syllable, while the rolle *murmur* on the page has three letters identically repeated. Again alphabetical stability is relevant, for again the written version may long have parted company from the oral experience. So, quite aside from what *murmur* "means," do not our brain's micro-apprehensions sense its oral-written difference, these two aspects, too? And then there are the cases of Herbert and Eliot. If we say the brain automatically ignores Herbert's mutually exclusive spellings or the rarity of Eliot's syllables switching straight to the brain-representations of "feeble" and "spirit" and of "clutch" and "dust," and instead goes to their meanings direct, then were Herbert's and Eliot's practices all just a waste of effort?

Consciousness, newfound, in the end reaches out not just to words but to words in particular; some long some short, some spelled centrifugally some centripetally, some with ascenders some with descenders, some strongly consonanted some mainly voweled. It was suggested in chapter 8 that individual letters could act like "hooks" for neural receptors to hang on. Perhaps rather the letters are looking for these hooks in the receptors. Of course, Pinker is in one sense right. It could be—this is entirely speculative on my part—that when the reader sees "cattle," he/she does indeed inevitably also recall "battle," but also, that an overriding intelligence-monitor of some kind for intention just knows that "cattle" is there and is what the author meant. But then, the possibility of any "battle"-residue remaining arises.

There is also the tempting analogy with color. Color it seems doesn't exist outside of our seeing it. According to current physics there are no "colors" as such; color is an evolved focusing, for survival purposes certainly—selection of nontoxic fruits to eat, for example—but not by selection of wavelengths that somehow already each have a color, say red or green, tied to each. Rather, color occurs when an aspect of brain locks in with an aspect of wavelength. It is like the way that, if you tear a piece of paper in half, you have two edges that exactly and uniquely fit. That is to say, "Colors and color-vision were made for each other" (Dennett 1991, 376). Now if, as just noted above from Fodor, the problem of how symbols are both physical and semantic at once applies both to "ink marks" and to "neural structures," we have a possibility. Could it be that brains and alphabetical properties were also "made for each other"? Are "me," and my personal selection from the abecedary, somehow entailed in its supposed "arbitrariness"? Since we have emphasized all along that "words do not take the place of thoughts, they occupy a different space"—there was even the view of some that they are as separate as "yesterday" and "tortoise"—it might seem the reverse. But there is no contradiction. Being made for each other does not mean they are twins or clones, but that there is perfect fit in their interrelation.[25]

As a result, or perhaps concomitantly with this, words can be seen as in a state of perennial readiness, on the lookout for chances to "get themselves said" (Dennett 1991, 242), in a way that crabs are *not* simply waiting to get themselves eaten or trees to get themselves chopped down. A word, on this view, has simply no existence except as waiting to get itself said. A letter bbbbb just is a letter bbbbb; we can't say "we only see it as a bbbbb." It is self-proving. What one sees it as, is just what it is. In this sense perhaps "language speaks us," or thought comes unsummoned to the brain, or is already in the brain and surfacing in consciousness, in that thought and words, to humans, are inseparable. On such arguments the poets were always first to the cliff-edge.

18

The Aesthetic

IF THERE ARE TWO LEVELS OF CONSCIOUSNESS, THE PURE-REACTION and the syntactical, then one effect of their merger is the aesthetic experience. So it is to the aesthetic that we must now go. As before, we seek the place of the abecedary in the experience. Again, it will take a little while to get there.

Notoriously indeed, the aesthetic is ungraspable. As Kant said, it has no concept;[1] and Kant's formulation has pervaded most of the debate ever since, to a point where for two or three decades historical/political criticism has evaded the aesthetic in the literary altogether. Yet this elusive category has been sought for centuries, long before the two-hundred-year mark often accorded to it in recent accounts.

For Plato it fell short of the ideal. For Aristotle it was cathartic. For Sidney it was delight. Vasari had ignored it altogether, content to praise its embodied works. For the nineteenth century it was both perfection exemplified (John Stuart Mill) and imperfection allowing the approachable (Ruskin, Hardy). For Kant it was precisely the elusive equilibrium between two stillnesses (the contemplative and the practical); for Hegel it embodied the Absolute alone. For W. H. Auden and Somerset Maugham it could not long hold the attention, for Keats it lasted forever. In our century it has been dislodged altogether as anything either static or teleological. For Paul Valery the work of art is not finished but abandoned, for Andre Breton the waking state is "a phenomenon of interference." Finally, in bleak paradox, for Theodore Adorno there is no aesthetic and no language after Auschwitz, and for just that reason, in desperate irony, language must aspire to the fullest aesthetic possible.

There is also the aesthetic's slippery nature morally. For Susanne Langer art was "virtual" and for Mary Mothersill beauty is a good, while for Terry Eagleton, Stanley Fish, and others it is somehow always complicit with evil. Beauty would remain merely insipid without the dark side that morally might seem to contradict it. But the idea is equally elusive conceptually. For Langer "What Is Beauty?" was the wrong question; the right one was to ask what it is that works of art create. In a seminal article Morris Weitz argued that theories of art are impossible, because no work of art can have either necessary or sufficient conditions. Aesthetic theory is "a logically vain attempt to define what cannot be defined."[2] But these very dualities may be key to the aesthetic. Perfection and imperfection, matter and form, the object and our conception of it, division and unity, good and evil—it is almost as though our suspense between any oppositions at all is itself what leads to the aesthetic fascination, the magnet to what always remains unattainable but seems undeniably still there. Even today it recalls the Kantian position, precisely because Kant's view itself, paradoxically, grasps the aesthetic object's very suspension between contraries, and so seems to acknowledge all such responses in all their diversity.

For Kant the opposition between our cognitions and our actions left a gray area between them. Our cognitions cannot "desire" their objects any more than we can desire two and two to make four, which is already a direct intuition. Our actions by contrast do come from desire, but one that at least in principle can be fulfilled; for example, to help a child, or mend a broken fence. But when we run up against the aesthetic object, the "work of art," we are halfway between these two positions. The aesthetic object's consoling or disturbing power does draw us toward it, but not for any instrumental use outside itself, as with a moral or a tool. The aesthetic object attracts me, yet I stop short of it in order to leave it intact. We can't reach it, exactly because we want it left as it is. All that is left to do, Kant thought, is to judge it (Kant 1952, 3–39). Whatever the truth of that, it is this halfway suspended animation that seems so cognate with our contemporary dilemmas on this topic, and indeed that seems to capture the elusive nature of virtually all theories of the aesthetic and their uneasy relationship with each other.

With some irony, the pattern of this "elusive middle" marks the aesthetic commentary of one of the most politically oriented theorists, Terry Eagleton. "Sensibility seems at once the surest foundation, and no foundation at all" (Eagleton 1990, 44, on Jane Austen). "At once source and supplement, creator and leftover" (76, the noumenal subject in Kant). "At once an astonishingly optimistic and bitterly pessimistic doctrine (76, Kant on the aesthetic). "So boundlessly eloquent as to be speechless" (109, on Schiller's aesthetic). "Achieving your goal and falling short of it thus occur in the same instant" (137, on Hegel). "This very proposition cancels itself out" (165, on Schopenhauer). "Marx preserves this distinction in the act of transgressing it" (202, subject/object distinction). "The commodity is densely corporeal and elusively spectral at the same time" (208). "At once turbulently vital and blankly meaningless" (243, reality for Nietzsche). "The universal truth is that there is no universal truth" (248). "Both a subject and not a subject" (97, Heidegger's *Dasein*). "Bloom is at once sunk in gross particularism and abstractly cosmopolitan" (322, on Joyce's *Ulysses*). "The truth of contradiction is accordingly unity" (330, referring to Lukacs). "A valid theory could be one which thinks against itself" (347). "[Art represents] an arational reason confronting an irrational rationality" (351). Art is also "at once precious and worthless" (357) and the "consummation and ruin of philosophy" (360), while music is "nothing but the expression of its inexpressibility." To crown it all, "The only cure for our sickness is that it should grow worse" (362).

Hardly surprisingly also then that "The aesthetic is thus turned against the aesthetic" (330). It is as though, in attempting to cut out the Kantian oppositions, Eagleton has left himself with an even more bewildering set of mergers. If this is Marxist dialectic eating itself alive, it might also illustrate how easily political criticism has entered the void left by Kant's suspendedly appreciative state. For the political charge against Kant has been that his "judgment," halfway between contemplation and practice as the spot where the aesthetic is encountered, itself savors too much of cognition and reason alike. It led Kant to believe that judgment could attain universal validity (Kant 1952, 50–60). The view that judgment neatly bridges the space between abstract cognition and practical reason seems to take all three too much out of the land of organic living. Judgment replaces a wider kind of response. Naturally this view collapses today, for we are too involved altogether; if we are to "judge" art, we must judge ourselves judging at the same time; our situations oppress us. The supposed (bourgeois) attempt to see works of art as silently suspended above everyday life simply makes for inertia. Social and political action are drawn off into an uplifting emotion that is left with no external targets.[3]

Yet Kant's "elusive middle" does seem to situate itself very well in between so many of our difficulties. As we said of consciousness, it has two levels, the pure-reaction and the syntactical, which don't seem to meet. The aesthetic may exactly interplay between them. On the literary-political front, we are left either respecting the aesthetic experience as it stands or else incorporating it into whatever approaches to art—feminism, historicism, and the rest—we have evolved for wider, nonaesthetic purposes. As said already, to have our sense of the artwork's overwhelming power go along with an equal sense that we may never fully know that effect's cause is itself aesthetically awesome, itself a further case of the same kind of dilemma. For such reasons there have been increasing and indeed interesting attempts to refloat the aesthetic in our time in something like traditional terms, if under a new conception. So far the breakdown of values generally, the arrival of major new kinds of art, and their kinetic natures have prevented this from getting widespread intellectual acceptance. In the aesthetic field, all is still relative.

And yet—here comes the real surprise. The authenticity of the aesthetic is found at its most startling today in mathematics and science. If true, this surely destroys any notion that, whatever "works of art" may be, the aesthetic itself is merely an area of enjoyment for the privileged; unimportant in the serious practices of human existence. Mathematics and science are at the heart of our economic calculations, our medicine, our understanding of climate, our knowledge of sexual conception and life itself, our now all-pervading electronic technologies, our demographic movements, our neurological observations, our geographical habitat and the evolutionary chain that got us here; in short, how we survive on this insignificant rolling planet at all. If the aesthetic response is entailed in mathematics and science at their very heart, that must kill dead any idea of the aesthetic as merely marginal.

The most famous case of the aesthetic as guarantor of scientific discovery in recent times was the discovery of the structure of the DNA molecule in 1963 by James Watson and Bernard Crick. Watson and Crick had no doubt their model was correct, for in Watson's words it was "too pretty not to be true."[4] The cluster of parts for the task (transmitting the genetic code) fell into explanatory place with no remainder; and it was via aesthetic apprehension, and nothing else, that this elegant simplicity was seen to correspond to reality itself. Matter and the universe were simply like that, and there was just no need to go looking for some more complex model even if, logically, one might conceive of one. The quantum physicist Paul Dirac stated this position categorically. "It is more important to have beauty in one's equations than to have them fit experiment . . . the discrepancy may be due to minor features that are not properly taken into account and that will get cleared up with further developments in theory . . . If one is working from the point of view of getting beauty in one's equations, and if one has really a sound insight, one is on a sure line of progress." Writing rather later, Michael Polanyi noted evidence of "aesthetic recognition by contrast to a systematic recognition based on key features" in the successful discovery of new species in botanical fieldwork. In a chapter on mathematics and art, Morris Kline wrote that "For about a hundred years now mathematicians have come to recognize what was felt and asserted by the Greeks but had been lost sight of in the intervening centuries: mathematics is an art and mathematical work must satisfy aesthetic requirements."[5] The last three words are exactly formulated. As well as being a feeling, the aesthetic has requirements, and they are cognate with the universe's structure.

In the 1980s and 1990s, scientists took the implication even further. The aesthetic is inextricably entwined with chemistry, physics, and mathematics as aspects of the created universe. The current claim of cosmologists that our minds resonate with the fundamental nature of the universe comes with the aesthetic nature of our apprehensions of it—and that aesthetic dimension is fundamental. Scientists could hardly be farther apart than Paul Davies and Peter Atkins on the existence of a divinity or the role of fundamental chance. Yet both see the aesthetic as central. Davies observes that "all great scientists are inspired by the subtlety and beauty of the natural world that they are seeking to understand," and then appends a catalog of testimonies by scientists, including Dirac, as to how elegance and satisfaction must mingle with observable fact when one seeks material truth (Davies 1983, 220–21). Atkins agrees. But Davies and Atkins even use the same example as prototype of this experience. Davies: "The collection of c-dots [computer applications for mapping rules for complex numbers] forms the Mandelbrot set. This set has such an extraordinarily complicated structure that it is impossible to convey in words its awesome beauty." Atkins, too, sees the Mandelbrot images as "of such endless beauty that in them we have transcended the tetraktys [a discovery of Pythagoras] and its harmonies and have touched perhaps the springs of our perception of beauty. Mathematical physics and aesthetics have merged, and science is ready to become whole."[6]

Atkins, however, ties this most radical of observations to consciousness itself. Our apprehending minds are products of the very universe they seek to understand more deeply. "The deep structure of the brain may be in resonance with the deep structure not only of mathematics but also of the physical universe" (121). Again Davies takes the same position (Davies 1992, 232). It sounds close to Dennett's suggestions noted earlier, that the brain and external phenomena like color "were made for each other." And if brain and abecedary were also made for each other, as we suggested there, too, then the relations between the abecedary, the aesthetic, consciousness, and science become crucial.

How is the aesthetic more than pleasurable, "pleasurable-plus," and where are the links between consciousness, speech/writing, and science? In fully aesthetic response the pleasure seems to lie, not just in itself, but also somewhere in the apprehension of it. The pleasure at harmony, disturbance, or whatever else brings with it a conscious sense of it as valuable, but via depths or feelings we weren't aware of and cannot always formulate. Perhaps this authenticity is what led Kant to firm it up as needing "judgment" exclusively; but such process of judgment does not have to follow for a truly aesthetic, perhaps highly disturbing—certainly not pleasurable solely—experience to have happened. If the universe and the human brain were indeed "made for each other," if it is indeed awesome that a universe can evolve to a point where tiny parts of it (humans) actually know it is a universe and wonder about its nature *and also find that very experience profoundly beautiful and satisfying*, then maybe that says something about "works of art." Perhaps works of art are special occasions where that deepest apprehension is somehow intensified round a tiny spot, a superstar next to all space, or are like the neutrino that weighs hundreds of times as much as the atom it inhabits while actually being hundreds of times smaller.

On this argument our "works of art"—whether of Rachel Whiteread or John Donne—are points of intense concentration, special renderings of what it is to apprehend existence at all, in exactly the way that most distinguishes human neural consciousness from the animal kingdom, organic matter, or indeed, so far as we yet know, any other being out there in the universe. That being so, too, a more radical or more disturbing art—today, a postmodern, violent, and self-shattering art—equally intensifies that universe/human observer made-for-each-other confrontation but in its darker aspects. Nature is red in tooth and claw, and there are human actions that the most relativist of atheists can still only call "evil." After the Dunblane Primary School massacre in Scotland in 1996, Peter Atkins, for years a believer in the purposelessness and value-absent character of the cosmos, couldn't keep words like "wicked" and "evil" out of his comment on the event.[7] Postmodernist critics have reincorporated the Burkean term "sublime" for the aesthetic rendering of such occasions.

Consequently the questions "what is beauty?"; "what is art?" are still relevant, and consciousness-theory, physics, and other sciences may be indispensable to any sort of answer. Mary Mothersill has acknowledged that no aesthetic theory could be the guarantor of an aesthetic choice. That is to say, there could be no law of the form "an object containing the curves x will aesthetically please viewer of the type y." One might say "I really like those curves" or even "curves always seem so central in sculpture"; but no more than that. But, she therefore argues, no such theory could refute that choice either. There could equally be no law of the form "an object containing the curves x will never, on any occasion, aesthetically please viewer of the type y." That is to say, there may be no standards by which to measure the aesthetic, but equally there are none that can dislodge it (Mothersill 1984, chaps. 4 and 5). It is not just a feeling; it is an epistemological category. We continue to find certain things "beautiful" rather than just made of metal, five feet long, looking like a fish, not to be stolen, good fun, rich, dangerous, and a lot more besides, all of which descriptions also severally apply to countless non-work-of-art objects. Between these two extremes we need some conception like "beauty" because without it, we couldn't speak of the aesthetic experiences we do have. As Mothersill puts it (247), we should not know how to proceed.

In then formulating the concept of beauty, as a kind of good; made out of anything at all; and linked causally with pleasure and inspirational to love (Mothersill 1984, chap. 9) Mothersill takes the aesthetic to a generality that could be tied to the responses of science we have already discussed. Our experience of artworks entails something else about what we are, here in this universe. The question "What is art?" may well be one of those standard philosophical questions like "How do I know when I'm dreaming?"; "Might I have been somebody else?"; or indeed Nagel's "What is it like to be a bat?" But, I would now argue, the what-is-art question can be rearranged yet again. "What *are* these high-intensity points at which the creatures—humans—who own universe-consciousness seem most to focus it with the deepest awe, disturbance, and satisfaction?"

At last, again, we get back to the abecedary. To apprehend ourselves and the universe as linked by consciousness raises usefully again the idea of the virtual. We are not grossly conscious, but virtually/virtuously conscious, of ourselves as having perhaps a special place in the universe by our very consciousness of it. But literary art may be especially "virtual" by its use of the abecedary. Susanne Langer developed a theory, already alluded to, of what works of art create. She concluded that they create "virtual realities." These are symbols of feeling. In its virtuality the work of art neither give us those feelings nor draws them off; it symbolizes them. Langer suggested that paintings create virtual space, music creates virtual time, dance creates virtual power, and sculpture creates virtual body. Music isn't its notes or periods, painting isn't its pigments or its subjects depicted, poetry isn't its words or the feelings expressed. Those are just the materials from which a virtuality is made. But for literature the expression is more various. Literature creates virtual life, virtual experience, and virtual memory (chaps. 13–15). Langer wrote too early to deal complexly with film but recognized its future and saw it as virtual authenticity. Film is omnivorous.

But we suggested earlier too that virtuality is a feature of the abecedary in some way that it is not a feature of stone, raw sound, images from light-through-celluloid, and the rest. Art's virtuality, on this theory, would seem to imply an unusual place for the abecedary. In this connection Langer made a couple of notable points about literature in contrast to the plastic arts. By being made of words, literature can be treated, at mundane level, as not "literature" but merely another body of work within the humanities. Saul Bellow—or one of his characters—once made the savage comment that "the educated people of modern countries are a thinking rabble [whose] business is to reduce masterpieces to discourse."[8] If true, this would have to be strongest for literature. But the ease of mingling the literary words with our commentary on them also makes literature radically different from the other arts. The truism, if true at all, that "poetry is discourse" has for many come to mean that poetry is nothing else; it is merely continuous with one or other mode of language already in place in society and secreting ideology knowingly or otherwise.[9] Biographical and political critics of left and right treat it accordingly. Traditional hermeneutics too, as of Schleiermacher and Dilthey, often seemed to approach any written text whatever along the line of a one-dimensional "understanding" rather than a full-bodied aesthetic response. But for Langer poetry is not utterance. Rather it uses utterance to create a virtual memory. This virtual memory may be disturbing; sweet and consoling; or invigorating and muscular, inspiring to action. It is still any of those by attaining universality, which in the context we now have of the last few pages, means literally in touch with the points where consciousness itself touches the universe as consciousness's own origin. The universe is material, our consciousness of it is virtual, and our body-and-mind language for that, namely the abecedary and devised for use at consciousness's cliff-edge, is physical and virtual at once.

Whatever else, there is a notable outcome. In this unique case the same medium, language, provides both the literary work itself and the abecedarial lexicon of aesthetic response to it. Literary-critical terms embody the same medium as that of the works they comment on; they "sponge up" in second-order fashion what literary words have captured in the first place. We have just used a few here: *sweet, consoling, muscular, inspiring to action.* Countless could be added. *Great, super, smash, brill, wow* are ejaculations, with *really lovely, really good, really-really great* just a more easeful version. On a straight sublime/beautiful distinction would come *terrific, tremendous, shocking, striking, stunning, shattering, staggering,* with *amazing, awe-inspiring,* and *awesome* similar but with smaller metaphor of physical violence. On the "beautiful" side are *beautiful, delightful* with *graceful, delicate, dainty, neat, soothing,* and others reaching for the character of the experience. *Gripping, arresting, heartrending, spellbinding, tear-jerking, touching, sobering, absorbing, thought-provoking, uplifting, elevating, liberating, wonderful, spine-tinglingly beautiful*—the aesthetic thesaurus is extensive enough to be subjected to its own critical scrutiny. Fuller expressions from the last three decades have come and gone or stayed as they tried to fill out the response while remaining still indivisibly idiomatic: *gets me, sends me, roots you to the spot, knocks you out, gave me a buzz, could listen to this forever, run out of superlatives, a wholly successful piece, a real shaker, simply divinely gorgeous, most enjoyable, pure joy.* Thumbs-down counterparts include *escapist, bourgeois, mere rhetoric, tripe, emotional outpourings, self-indulgence, deadly, garish, merely pretty, incy-wincy, horrendous.*

The common factor in such terms is that they remain conscious of both the advantages and the danger of sharing literature's own medium. They all seem to project the literary themselves, even when referring to nonliterary arts. So they try to ensure that this overlap between the language of both the work and the criticism of it, always veers in favor of being drawn back toward the aesthetic sphere. It is of the work's same medium but can't belong to it, so it praises it. If it doesn't, it will dilute the aesthetic and draw it out into something else; biography, for example, or politics. Ordinary nonaesthetic terms from daily life—*honest, disorganized, highly competent, tedious*—get drawn, in aesthetic context, into the same ambivalent status. This is neither a failing nor a claim that literature is superior to other arts. It merely suggests the right accuracy of the relationship. Langer's view of literature as easily lending itself to treatment as just one more discourse within the humanities more widely has become widespread.

Indeed, in the history of the debate about what is the supreme art form—now surely redundant with the arrival of film, action-art, concept art, and the like—Walter Pater and Langer herself advocated music. By contrast Kant and Georg Wilhelm Freidrich Hegel opted for literature, for the very reason that the supposed insignificance of the sign could allow thought and the idea to emerge triumphantly in the subject. Yet from the abecedary's nature Langer infers something special. With verbal language "this pregnance of the physically trivial form with a conceptual import verges on the miraculous" (52). But the "virtuality" of both what art creates (Langer) and of the abecedary has further import. It means, not that poetry is necessarily the supreme art form literary or otherwise, but a) that it has a special position within literature, b) that its virtuality is specially associated with the abecedary's virtuality via the nature of language in itself.

For the miraculous-seeming feature that Langer adduces is just what occurs when the signifier meets the signified. In discussing Saussure, Elizabeth Wright formulated the idea as precisely as one could wish. "The link between [the signifier and the signified] is entirely arbitrary, for any sound can be linked with any concept. Once bonded in use, however, the combination is secure, as firmly bonded together as the two sides of a single sheet of paper."[10] We might question her term "entirely," but in general, Wright's is the point about the "arbitrary" we have tried to underline all along. This indissoluble bond must reintroduce the poetic rather than the literary as the key conception, since of all writers it is poets who most work and foreground language's palpable medium. And if the abecedary is main medium between our consciousness of universal reality and our presumed place within it as maybe unique embodiments of such consciousness, which latter many scientists are now suggesting, then the poetic, in some form or another, becomes fundamental again. Surprisingly no doubt, this view is at one with not just the likes of Paul De Man but also those critics who designate literature, too, as an invention. That is to say, a socially and technologically emerging possibility in the sixteenth century for Foucault, or an ideological one for numerous critics of that persuasion of the last two or three decades.

And this, really, is the inference of this discussion for the aesthetic. The abecedary is at one with what it evokes; the signified is inseparably bonded to the signifier. Yet as we have stressed all along too, the abecedary can only call up mind itself via the abecedary's own system. Words do not match the mind, they occupy their own space. In this paradoxical duality lies equally the space in which, used by the poets, we also find the (Kantian) aesthetic elusiveness. In the plastic arts, the mode of attachment between form and content, that is to say the medium used and the evoked result, is just as elusive. But the two components in each case are always distinguishable. We can see the difference between the paint and the tree that the paint looks like even if—delightfully or disturbingly—we can't see how they meet.[11] But with the abecedary, we can't similarly say that the rolle "pain" is matched with—pain, because the second term still clones the first.

This too brings out the how the abecedary is aesthetic as a medium. The poet/painter David Jones once suggested that nothing that has not been in some sense loved can be transposed into a work of art.[12] It is easy to see how one can "love" a dishful of gorgeous cobalt blue watercolor powder, a grand old rotting tree trunk, or a shiny steel girder, music's raw materials in birdsong, a city's deep rumblings, or the sounds of waves at sea. But I believe that we love the abecedary, too; indeed, it is quite obvious, from our pleasure at all those word games, puzzles, puns, conundrums, and everything else. We love typing, we love handwriting, we love our personal word processors, we love those carefully chosen letter-fonts rolling up the credits in high-budget films. We love it too in its gentle suppleness, its level harmony of small forms rendered by ink or print, and its willingness to hover in the background. But this endearment is always as to the abecedary's pregnant readiness for its naming work, without which in the end it is nothing. Our double-level consciousness, already described, depends on this elusiveness. Science gives us its details, its raw components.

Naming is the poetic form of what, for all writing, has been called exemplification.[13] If all writing is naming, literary writing—whatever may count as "literary"—could loosely be called naming through imagination. But poetry's naming highlights the abecedarial name-substance itself. In doing so it is bound to make present, both the not-yet-named things or relations it will evoke according to their natures, and the different, internally systematized parts of the abecedary. These last are its fewness, stability, equability, physicality, and virtuality, and the continuous distributions by which these are exploited. These parts seem to have, if nothing so metaphysical as a permanence, certainly a longevity that suggests their structure might be important. The abecedary's few components are distributed by the thousand or million. It is stable in time and equable in space. It joins the material and nonmaterial in its physical and virtual aspects.

The equability limits the abecedary to naming and nothing else. It doesn't aspire to match real-world items in their own kind, like painting a leaf green or copying the heart's passions in musical cadence. Speech-acts and intentions, libidos and subconscious thrusts, the stored lexicon or the generative grammar, and the things we run up against in the external world; simply everything has to be rendered down to the combinations of the abecedary. They are all subjected to the one process. This unity is supported by abecedarial fewness, for fewness keeps the texture within the same one plane of reality even more firmly. Yet the same fewness makes the writing idiosyncratic to itself, rather than any exact match with the mind, because the combinations repeat themselves and come round again even when the "meanings" of any two identical or near identical rolles are quite different. That the naming exploits the signifier/signified inseparability is what ensures, however, that we don't just have a word-and-thing match. The rolle lends its own texture and feel—length or brevity, spiky consonants, nasal hum, rare letters, double letters, and the rest—to the mental or neural nonnamed experience that the resulting word embodies. And all of this can survive as the work of art's desired permanence, just because the abecedary is also stable. But finally, our experience of universal reality as both obdurately material and also a felt consciousness, is evoked by the abecedary's physicality and virtuality. It can say "butterfly" yet "perhaps," "psychology" yet "cityscape," and "haven't" but "George"; it can say "bottle" and "bottling," or "food" and "my gosh—we've run out of food." Rolles can absorb or "sponge up" outlines of what the physical senses know separately, and they can, if hazily, do so in matters of syntax when no such physical reality is involved. The whole world of our experience can be met. The virtuality is not and can't be just a whimsical notion on our part, for the sign-function of the abecedarial lines, angles, and squiggles that make it up are radically different from the noises, substances, and colors that go to fund the other plastic arts.

The five poets we considered earlier deployed all these features, as we saw. Their poetry was a virtual consciousness well before recent science arose with its own view of that consciousness. Yet the "belatedness" that so many critics have seen in the work of T. S. Eliot throws the whole matter open again, on to the wider texture of life and existence in the postmodern world. To which we turn next and finally.

19
The Postmodern

BELATEDNESS MAY HAVE BEEN MODERNISM'S PROPHECY. THE POST-modern condition has been variously characterized. The simulacra; the suspicion of metanarratives; the permanent present; the carnival; the violence and the noise; the overwhelming ethos of consumption; all affect and are affected by language with traceable influence on poetry now being written. Yet with postmodernist theory itself arguing that there can be no theory, people are divided about it. Some see a panic culture, others a new kind of evolution, yet more a set of huge technological changes that, however, it is for society to find out how to control.[1] In that dilemma, tentatively, one has to drill down to what at least feels solid, even in the illusions of the time.

If it is to survive at all, poetry must both exploit and resist a world of electronics, a merging of languages and cultures, and a science that pervades everything from worldviews down to daily life. Science's truths are not normally transmitted in abecedarial form. The fear that poetry may be ending goes at least back to Keats (*Endymion* 2:723-32), yet to retort that such fear always proves groundless and that poetry always gets through somehow may be too easy. Perhaps Keats stood on the middle rung of a wharfside ladder down which today we can go no lower without entering the water. And yet there is room for optimism, too. Poetry seems always to get itself written, somehow or other, and the greatness of the new usually lies exactly in that its particular mode and cast were never even remotely predicted.

Again we need a rather extended account before coming to our own topic. Everything stems from the shrinking of the planet. The present period of burgeonings and eruptions is paradoxical in effect. An explosion, whether of a bomb or an overstretched carton of office equipment, hurls its material as far as the first velocity sends it, and it lies there. But there is no longer room in our world for everything to be flung as far as its initial power sends it. So the explosion in any area is stopped short, implodes on itself, or curiously entails its own opposite elsewhere. For example, we have our bodies. They can now be taken to pieces mentally and in part physically and reassembled. Artificial limbs, facial rebuilds, organ transplants, false breasts, hormone injection, hair-color switches, fingertip transmission of electronic messages, sports fitness techniques, and every type of genetic engineering all burst open the notion that anyone is uniquely associated with the "body" they occupy. That is the explosion. Yet the fallout is not mere fragmentation but a newly synthetic sense of ourselves, including our consciousnesses. There is a different explosion-implosion in business and capital. The myth of King Midas takes on new meaning. Virtually nothing avoids being turned into an item of consumption or being swamped by its promotion. Not just clothes, fridges, suburban houses and cars, but also holidays, university courses, languages, love matches, psychiatric treatments, insurance schemes, sport, water, air, time, and numerous other things almost too rarefied to name are so affected. An entire house can be furnished and equipped from accumulated prizes offered on top of purchases or bank loans. We await the first MMMM Life Assurance Evensong from Westminster Abbey and may yet see the NNNN Allied Newspapers Monarchy. Again though the fallout implodes into itself. Capitalism converts opposition, whether of uncouth politics or radical clothes, into merely one more new product. We become what we view and watch what we buy; to update the poet Stephane Mallarme, everything exists to be made into a television program. Ordinary-speak and advertising-speak met long ago. Free enterprise finds its entropy in monopoly and world-resources cross the horizon as finite.

Those rogue elements noise and violence also get cultural valence. The amplification explosion allows self or group to intrude on the personal decibel-space we might have cherished like personal body-space. Motorbikes discard silencers and full-volume rock thumps from lowered car windows: my body-presence in my car must radiate. The aesthetic effect of such things deliberately disrupts mainstream culture and its choice refinements based on stasis. High-powered trucks, cranes, earthmovers, police sirens, and pneumatic drills whine and thunder near parks, churches, hospitals, and schools. Violence itself is a bolt-on event for a daytrip, a pub evening, a sports fixture, not because everyone is just brutal but because the centrifugal force of the explosion is self-perpetuating. Yet again in confined space the implosion follows. As George Steiner has put it recently, silence is now expensive.[2] This is meant literally. Only the well-to-do can afford the calm spaces where stress is relieved and peace regained, or where deeper progresses, innocent or more sinister, can continue. But this high premium on silence also works at the deepest level of the sublime and the subliminal. The great symbol of silence is Auschwitz. The great symbol of explosion is Hiroshima.

Other areas entail agriculture (soil as synthetic invention), ecology, and weather (which we now alter all-embracingly); electronic computerizing, and language itself. The debris turns from fallout to excrement, a problem notably recorded by Milos Kundera; that which is waste.[3] This implosion is self-disgust, but also that nothing may go to waste in a resource-precious world. The origin of all these categories is the first great explosion of population itself, imploding too in that the fallout has neither space nor resources to receive the fragments. The planet is now literally too small, yet we haven't expanded into outer space. And we are ourselves within the exploding process; our detonated culture is in the air and has not yet landed. Here is found what Fredric Jameson has formulated as the "permanent present" of postmodernism.[4]

The permanent present is itself a sea change in how political and historical time were until recently understood. Marxism held that ideology distorted truth while being necessary to it, and traditional society held that ideology wasn't known to mass populations. But war, that great arranger of history, may (despite some recent events) just possibly be mercifully over as a major realigner of nations, themselves obsolete. In postmodernism, truth and its origins vanish into their own message. Even Foucault's entirely new epistemes needed some kind of organic rationale in each case for their takeover bids to succeed.[5] But now, so the theory goes, history fades as an organic source of reality for millions of people, for it appears side by side with society's pervasive self-picturing in television and advertising. The historical image becomes the product image. Television interviews its own personalities and recycles previous footage in a kind of appearance-history constructing and replacing reality at once. Serial killing can become a grim magnet: at least something is being done sequentially. Perhaps similarly, so is sport. Film—that marvelous new medium of our age—presents all in its own grammar. The political triumph and the winning touchdown, replayed instantly four times, in slow motion and from several angles, are all impossible in ordinary human experience. We can collect historical moments on video, like George W. Bush's delayed electoral victory or Princess Diana's sad death. All this leaves the real "permanent present" then to suspect its own grounding. "Ends" appear; the End of History, the End of the Book, maybe or maybe not the end of poetry.[6]

The traditional modes of knowledge (now called metanarratives) also become suspect, as Jean-Francois Lyotard seminally suggested.[7] The means of their understanding have merged in the historically still new medium of film, also an exploding force. One suspects that this doesn't fully apply for science and mathematics, because their truths, real or presumed, do emerge in obdurate changes in real life. We really do transplant hearts and a thousand dollars really is ten times a hundred. But "at the human level," insofar as that can be disentangled, all else epistemologically disappears into "cultural studies," that erupting project in which we monitor and express just anything at all, ourselves immersing ourselves in the culture's own modes of expression as we do so. I take this to be Richard Rorty's import (Rorty 1980), although Rorty observes mainly at the level of discourse.[8] Philosophy becomes the ongoing conversation of the thoughtful in the race, and there are interesting things to say. Yet most commentators bar various "specialists" adopt television idioms and slangy vernaculars. The academy, like capitalism, incorporates. The consumer consumes; but all are producers, all are consumers.

And this "permanent present" stands oddly toward the Derridean perpetual deferral, based as that is on the linearity of writing and the constant movement of script to the right. For film and photography have exploded a riot of paradoxically static images into our apprehending world. We appraise people, events, issues of the day, and the rest in nests of images, transposing them into words only to reaffirm or point up such images themselves. Less and less, it sometimes seems, are old-style lexicon and syntax the means to our epistemologies. Film has its own orderings; it devours all and, as Langer suggested, conveys total authenticity. Sight and its applied sound-track are the only senses. Dennett (1991, 55–56) noted the domination of the eye exactly as Augustine did in the *Confessions*; but film, unlike opera, has no smell, taste, touch, or third dimension. As to the detonation of the formal arts, Baudrillard's four-stage account gives art's move from depiction of reality through to no reality, then no depiction, and finally sheer simulacra with no distinction between reality and representation.[9] I personally am not convinced that this explosive/implosive environment, in which everything is drawn into its own black hole of hysteria and incomprehension, is the human lot for the next few decades until we destroy ourselves (lest all this be misunderstood, I'm equally unconvinced that it's all bad). Millions of people, by choice or otherwise, continue to live an albeit arduous yet still unhindered life, in which food is grown, small groups met and befriended, huts or houses maintained, and local jobs quietly done. Millions equally live in large cities with much corporate cordiality, good living conditions, and intellectually and humanly rich activities of a truly high order. (Millions more starve, but that is "cultural" only with an aroma of irony.) Be all this as it may though, if our concern is with language, abecedary, and poetry, then the sweep of language up from the printed page into the whole range of media is certainly having deep effects on language use, and the outcome is not predictable.

Here are a couple of middle-range homely glossy magazines. They are neither soft-porn nor upmarket affluent. The cover of one of them has letters in six different colors and twelve different typefonts. This continues inside. Every page has at least four colors not including those in the photographs, and at least six type fonts. These are in different sizes; titles or headings are stuck across like baggage labels with drawings of paper clips at the top, or seemingly come out from under whatever is adjacent. The other magazine has mixed fonts with mixed sizes within a single message. The framed text-items are the size of and seem at one with the photographs. Certainly here, as elsewhere in the world of print, the main text of single items we earlier called the abecedary's "microbillion" comes in ordinary, small, level, evenly-spaced words in black on white. Yet the effects described break reading up into small bytes. Every item seems to hail from a different source, like the multifarious lights in a city at night, as though whoever is generating it all is either a group of people joking among themselves on a sprightly jaunt or a single mind in bedlam.

In the postmodern world different terms enter the language with inorganic roots or none. The sponsoring firm's name is tacked on to the sporting event; indeed more and more often physically intervening, as when the cricket bowler crosses the insurance company's logo for every delivery, and the rugby player touches the ball down (the game's key moment) on the name of the building society. The British TV channel 4 racing commentator hesitated, momentarily, before referring to the "two hundred and eighteenth Vodafone Derby" at Epsom on 7 June 1997 while competitions in professional British team sports tolerate a strange dance of names as their sponsors come and go. The Synthetic Lager League becomes the Dairy Product League which becomes the City Bank League which becomes the Saloon Car League, all in the space of a few seasons, the same teams all the time and seemingly with no sense of the ridiculous. Insurance, soft drinks, and electronic apparatus appear on the tracksuits and singlets of international contestants, while snooker players have a newspaper or aftershave named on their evening suits. The telephone time clock is "sponsored" by a watchmaking firm, whose name is metronomically repeated at every ten-second interval. One intriguing outcome of all this is that the statistically rarer letters of the alphabet are used more often, a point illustrated by other names that have entered the language; *zoom, quosh, xerox, kwik-save,* and others. Business chooses impactive logos that hit via these rarer signs. The explosive power of the postmodern shoots into the abecedary's "fewness" via its centrifugal nature and then implodes into the inertia of visible letters without meaning.

This curious result appears too in the acronym, or indeed the set of initials unpronounceable and the more visual accordingly. NATO, NUM, QASAR, FORTRAN, QUANGO, RADAR, OXFAM, MCC, TLS, PLC, VISA, VAT, PGCE, GCSE, BBC, ITV, NYPD, M&S, IRA, ERM, ECU, DVLC, P&O, P O BOX, V&A, OFGAS, CD, and so many others more join the couple of car registration numbers, minimum two phone numbers, and at least one zip code shared by most families. The power of acronyms to absorb the sacred in earlier times is matched here by their equal power to become true name-substitutes even when they remain unpronounceable, for of course they too are visual. Since, too, whole sentences like "Fax those effing laser yuppies up in Admin a.s.a.p., OK?" (not a real term among them) can now be heard daily in company corridors and editorial offices, the abecedarial balance of frequency-use, and certainly visual presence, of its twenty-six members may be changing. There are numerous other phenomena, far too many to examine here. There is the "small print" in contract documents; computer language; the century's explosion of word games and puzzles; and what Jean-Jacques Lecercle has called "dubious synthesis," coinages like *hotline* and *feedback*.[10]

More semantically, two phenomena may be exemplary; the slogan and the headline. The slogan is typically found on advertisement and T-shirt. The T-shirt slogan varies from the confessional ("I feel outrageous/pubertal/terrific") through to the political demand ("Stop the Whaling," "New Labour New Danger") with almost anything possible in between. The advertisement slogan is a quasi-proverb. We looked at the proverb in chapter 1 and then in the work of George Herbert. The slogan equally has the proverbial structure, the balance of letters, and the brevity, but with the product replacing the recommended moral term. "I've started so I'll finish," from the British TV quiz game *Mastermind*, entered the language because it captured a real nuance. But "Brilliant Cleaning Starts with Finish" (a dishwasher powder) echoes, however unintentionally, the hint of a universal principle. Intriguingly, the letters of "Starts" have all but disappeared in "Finish," orally totally so. With "Allied Dunbar—for the Future You Don't Yet Know" (life insurance), the letters of the company name sturdily contrast the open-ended inference of the last seven words, where the fffffs, ooooos, and yyyyys do what is now a centripetal work. In some promotions there is a deliberate double take. The caption "We Aren't Here to Help You" turned out to mean the product was so perfect that no help would be needed. None of this is to doubt that such claims are sincerely believed by their companies and may indeed commonly be true. What is interesting is the transfer of the proverbial form and its abecedarial structure from general folk wisdom to the strictly narrower world of commerce. Traditional proverbs closed down thought as they opened it up, but resolved that limitation by their overall presence as philosophy by interlocking network. These commercial slogans equally, like proverbs, often seem to offer to teach us something useful for life, but the gains come separately from the isolated product in question. If as Coleridge said the greater part of our knowledge lies in aphorisms, then it might seem that modern commerce sometimes offers the merits of its products as near-epistemological certainties.

The headline is something else. It modifies proverb not by brand name but by letter-overlap and pun. Letter-overlap and pun, we recall, stem from the fewness of the abecedary. The headline pun may be overt or cryptic, but it has a double entendre in one word or across the phrase. *No Nudes Is Good News* (objections to nude artwork), *Bring Back Hanging* (game birds in gourmet cuisine), *Fangs Aren't What They Used to Be* (old horror films as classics), *Trance Would Be a Fine Thing* (value of hypnosis), *All That Glitter Is No Longer Gold* (pop singer Gary Glitter's ratings), *No Smoke without Ire* (anticigarette campaign). But the pun has become so ubiquitous in newspaper headline compiling that some detail is needed if we are to sense the effect. On most days most newspapers contain a minimum of four or five important pun headlines. The question is therefore of what purpose it fulfills, why it is attractive, whether it can be serious, what its variants contribute.

There is great variety of both topic and complexity in the punning headline. For example, *Under Lock and Quay*, for an article on canal holidays, is brilliant, but no salient point is made. In others the point can cause offense. The headline *Selling Saddam His Arms* referred not to armaments but to the bronze arms cast for a statue of the Iraqi leader, and the foundry wrote in protest to the newspaper concerned.[11] Punned headlines in fact, despite their jokey nature, are by no means confined to lighthearted topics or the leisured side of life. On race, *London Pride and Racial Prejudice* (racism in London), *It's All White for Some* (critique of program on racism), *A Nazi Piece of Work* (book on Goebbels), and *Le Pen Is Mightier* (French right-wing politician) have all appeared in recent years.

Yet bereavements private or public, missing children, and similar heartrending events do not attract puns. Perhaps a terse verbal irony is allowed even in serious cases so long as no immediate grief or fear is entailed. Some commentators see such language-use as power, and certainly the pun's abecedarial fixity allows little leeway in interpreting what is intended. Or is the headline then part of the postmodernism explosion, too, part of the carnival, with nothing serious and just real or affected detachment on the part of the writer? The following all headed stories or features of national importance on any serious definition, but the mild inward grin still accompanies: *Gentlemen Prefer Bonds* (old-boy ties in city investment), *Czechs Starting to Bounce* (power battle in Czechoslovakia), *John's Bull* (Prime Minster John Major on Britain), *Labour-Saving Devices* (getting Tony Blair elected), *Midwife Crisis* (shortage of hospital nurses), *The Devil and the BBC* (criticism of broadcasting official), *King Kongs* (Hong Kong power-holders), *Brain Transplants* (emigrating academics), *Patents Is a Virtue* (lucrative spin-offs from science), *Tunnel Vision* (skillful funding for Channel project), *Diseases Straight from the Cow* (danger of untreated milk), and *Come Out, Wherever You Are* (homosexuals in professions to declare themselves).

Great skill is often on view. Often there is a double pun, as in *Nuts and Bolts* (escapees from mental homes) and *Fare and Franc Exchange* (travel bargains in France), but also *Playing To The Gallery*, about not just art but getting children to look at art. So the "playing" is enriched also. Often too the headline hides the topic, so we learn that only by reading what follows. *Settling Old Scores* kept its secret perfectly, turning out to be about the hazards of editing music manuscripts made illegible by age. Sometimes a punctuation shift or words added at the end makes the difference: *Where's the Spice, Girls?* (tame all-woman short list for Turner art prize), *How The West Was One Long Disaster* (bad cowboy movie), and *Can You Keep a Secret Garden?* (walled gardens). Both these last recall our earlier syntax-shift example "Pete went to work on his motorcycle (project)." A proper noun bears the weight in *Is This a Degas that I See before Me?* (value of exhibiting traditional art), and *Early Tibet, Early To Rise* (old Tibetan artifacts gain in popularity). Yet the skill itself suggests some degree of art for art's sake.

All these cases—type font variation, acronyms, commercial logo intrusion, advertising slogan, and punned headline as well as TV program openers and countless other applications—use aspects of the abecedary and the traditional figures of speech that most employ it. But they omit the naming function the abecedary's equable nature fits it for so well. Nothing is named but the name itself. These applications are commonly skillful and, strictly anyway, of morally neutral import. Yet that innocence itself may suggest a hollowness matching an equal gap in the postmodern sense of what language is for, if indeed it is for anything. No newspapers existed in the time of Herbert and Milton, and no advertising as expanded as our own until well after Eliot. The daily drenching of our consciousnesses with the abecedary's parts makes a context far from the verbally less uncluttered worlds in which the earlier poets wrote. It is as though poetry has had its raiment stripped for sheer demonstration purposes. Yet that metaphor of poetry as clothing, once taken for granted by Thomas de Quincey, Jacob Burckhardt, H. D. F. Kitto, and others has long since been held obsolete for poetry.[12] Poetry has a closer relation between form and content. Yet in our time, in public and highly visible letterings of this kind, what Benedetto Croce saw as the inherently aesthetic nature of all language has been skinned from its content altogether. It might seem to leave poetry dead in the water, simply no longer a viable mode of expression at all. George Steiner (1989, 114) feared for poetry because our central truth-findings today come not as words but in the numbers and symbols of mathematics and science. If he is correct the outlook for the poetic might seem bleak indeed.

Writing was a tool, the gift of the gods. Speech was echo, the voice of the gods. These things seem to have dissolved in front of us. The primitive awe at the single sacred word is pushed aside—or itself harnessed—by the demands of brand name, monogram, and logo. Traditional warnings at excess in the use of words seem simply irrelevant. Plato's fear that writing would destroy memory goes ambivalent when we are unsure just what there is out there worth remembering. These phenomena are not speech acts from a mental impulse direct. The abecedary's centrifugal nature is exploited by the word's mobility and the acronym's rarer letters. Its equable and physical aspects may be compromised by advertising if what is named is a self-named product with the name several inches high.

The abecedary's distributive power is threatened by the different distributions of mixed type fonts, layouts, multidesign periodicals, and logos. Its virtuality is virtually forgotten. The letter is even motif or design, on wallpaper, linen, and china—and often very beautifully, too, as indeed some ads are certainly beautiful. And this last also underlines one of the most notable but unnoted aspects of the abecedary in the postmodern era. Despite all, it remains stable. In the seismic shifts of our time no one has suggested we add or remove a single letter. Other quite basic objects change: armaments, garments, buildings, roads. The abecedary still quietly survives, perhaps precisely because we ignore its features. Perhaps poetry will survive as well.

ELECTRONICS

It is too early to know the import of such things. If the aesthetic is elusive it becomes easier both to create and to hijack. Maybe we are indeed at a "great hinge in history, where we are going beyond writing." If so, such a shift is probably strongest in the new world of the electronic computer, the more impressively so by its functioning silence. The situation changes so rapidly that anything one says may already seem tired by the time it reaches daylight. But with luck we may stumble on a few, more durable points.

Most obviously there are the changes before us as we sit at the word processor, staring at our screens, manipulating our texts as never before. All this is now familiar of course to most people who do any writing at all. I can insert, delete, shift text around, enumerate, paginate, indent, center, tabulate, double-space, and shape all as to columns, divisions, and margins. But I can also italicize, capitalize, embolden, or underline, and at the press of a button witness those changes happening before my eyes. That is really new, and it vaporizes the abecedary's solidities, perhaps enhancing its virtuality in a quite new way. I can also change fonts, my feelings and thoughts shifting between Times Roman, Perpetua, Courier, Goudy, Copperplate, Algerian, Colonna, Garamond, and a couple of hundred others, with all the cultural memories I might find in those forms. I can shrink or enlarge them so that they jump back from or forward to my gaze, and I can color them with like results. I can copy a whole file and put it safely away on disk into a drawer. By covering a line and pressing the return key I can repeat a line of poetry at will. This last saves me from retyping the stanza-closing lines of Thomas Hardy's poem "The Garden Seat" (text in appendix 2), suggesting maybe that Hardy too pressed a mental repeat-button when he composed the poem in the first place.

But there is more. I can swing whole sentences about, split them up, add qualifiers, change my mind, see on the instant how an argument feels if its phrases are reordered or modified, and generally tie thinking to writing more flexibly than was ever possible with the one-sequence typewriter or ink. Plato's objection, that when you ask a piece of writing what it means it just lies there repeating the same answer, remains true, but it is somehow no longer the whole story. And I can copy a paragraph so that lo!—suddenly there it is twice before me. All of this correlates with the letter as not ink but electronic pulse, sheer form rendered as energy. If the electronic book comes about, ink and paper may form a somewhat smaller part of our literary apprehension than they have hitherto.

But all such things, though central, are only the onscreen parts of this revolution. Insofar as it affects literature, something curious is already afoot in the world of computer electronics. Just like people who stay with the codex, computer technology users already exhibit their own conservative/radical divide. This growing debate is familiar but we need a brief summary here for our own concerns with letters. First, there are the traditionalists. Some computer users employ the technology in service of something close to traditional reading and literary criticism.[13] Blocks of text can be retrieved from anywhere in the computer memory and online worldwide, and arranged in windows onscreen for comparison. These may be variations on a literary text, dictionary entries on key terms, or arrays of critical commentary. These shapings enhance the text as coming in small bytes; quite simply, small rectangular blocks of multisource print rather than the continuous work. A sense of homogeneity will also appear. As the individual works begin to blur and merge with each other, the very idea of canon undergoes revision. Much has been made of an even more radical-seeming innovation. The viewer can adjust the text him/herself, put in new suggestions, change the poem, and pass it down the Internet line—with some comparison, admittedly, with what happened to some handwritten texts in former times.

Yet all this is still essentially conservative. It is still text to be read; still key critical passages on Shakespeare from Johnson, Bradley, and Stanley Wells, still bits of "literature" humanly interpreted, with the plays' excerpts themselves still center of attention. Some commentators indeed, while gladly accepting the new electronic medium, argue that human reading is always what controls any shifting of text. Intertextuality must dominate hypertextuality. Even more traditionally, criticism and in effect intellectual life are still human narrative and critical argument, which is something that the breakdown into bytes can't contribute to. "As a vehicle for the narrative voice, the book cannot be bettered."[14] As with the abecedary, stability is untouched.

The opposing position is more truly radical. No longer a mere rearrangement of what is already there, it undermines the very idea of humanism itself. As Sadie Plant has put it, "digitalization is re-engineering the media, economics, the arts and sciences with a complete lack of discretion or regard for the differences in kind which once kept them apart" (Plant 1996 33). That is to say, these processes do not consult humanist notions of order, agency, reason, progress, or indeed benevolence, although they have no destructive aim either. They have no aim at all. This is of no sinister intention; it simply reflects the self-organizing nature of the electronic world now unleashed. Like the Internet, "none of these complex assemblages are discrete, unified, or guided by some form of central strategy." Rather "they are engineering themselves from the bottom up." Computer-electronic processes do not consult humanism—"the special status and privileged role of the human species"—upon which criticism and philosophy have traditionally depended. The quasi-neural activities of fourth-generation computers replace the practices and indeed values of traditional humanism with their own processes, and stem from the physical nature of electronic computer-systems. The key inference is that "humans are no longer the sole agents of intelligence" (39).

This more radical intervention has profound import for human theory generally. Theory itself becomes inextricable from the new software engineerings it attempts, in vain detachment, to comment on. Indeed, even the search for artificial intelligence (AI) is obsolete insofar as it tried to be a controlled humanist project. Late-generation computers elaborate their own intelligences. However, our concern here again is with language and our civilization's way of embodying it, namely, the abecedary. The foundation principle of early computing was Alan Turing's requirements for an artificial intelligence. These have been summarized as a) a serial process, b) a severely restricted workspace, c) with available data and instructions, d) from an inert but infallible memory, e) to be worked by a finite set of operations.[15] And this could be important, for these five aspects seem to correspond, if crudely, to the six aspects of the abecedary we have elaborated. The serial process corresponds to the abecedary's equable nature. The restricted workspace is its few-ness. The "data" is the abecedary's physicality, the "instructions" its virtuality. The "inert but infallible memory" is its stability. And the "set of operations" clearly is the abecedary's distributive as-pect. It is as though the original alphabet, millennia back, was made with some kind of artifice of intelligence somewhere in mind from the start.

For if this scheme of pairings holds even roughly, it would seem that the ancient evolution of language through letters itself began with a "machine" containing the fundamental principles that, ac-cording to Turing, any intelligent machine must possess. As we have argued, the abecedary's structure has an ambiguous relation-ship with the human mind. In sum, the subconscious (Freud and Jung), the intentional act (Austin, Searle, and the hermeneuticists), and the evolved small-problem-solving consciousness (Dennett, Fodor, et al.) interact with the abecedary but are different from it. Words do occupy their own space, yet abecedary and mind were indeed made for each other. But if, as is now the case, the later generation of far more sophisticated computers can build direct on our understanding of human consciousness after all, then we have an entirely new situation. We refer here of course to neurocomput-ers as opposed to digital (or Turing-based) ones. For "naturally in-telligent systems" are based on connectionism just as the brain is, are taught rather than programmed, and can then learn autono-mously and have memories that themselves lead to growth rather than being just store-places.

Such computering brings up over the horizon the faint chance that the abecedary itself could one day be redundant. The brain acts on the parallel-distribution process of "excitement/inhibition" (Caudill and Butler 1991, 15), whose two aspects correspond to two opposed forms of synapses, the sensitized points on the nerve ends that come off a single brain cell. Excitement/inhibition is a neural filter system by which some stimuli are accepted, others rejected. So it is by excitement/inhibition that I can reject various alterna-tives and accept the correct one, when seeking a rolle to fit a mean-ing "on the tip of my tongue." By excitement/inhibition, "intention" can select among objective—in this sense truly "arbi-trary"—signs instead of being swamped by them. By excitement/inhibition I know that "raincoxt" is a misspelling while "raincoat" is correct. The same thing enables a rolle to "sponge up" its mean-ing, a word its physiognomy. This has worked well enough for three thousand years and could be behind what gives poetry disturbance or delight. The tension between what is excited or inhibited, what is "intended" yet what is offered as alternative, enriching meaning(s) in the same words, is what the poem organizes to fullest effect.

But what if this same new process generates powers so similar to those of the human brain that it can make contact direct? What if at least some advanced computer systems come to exactly match the neuro-chemical processes in human consciousness? A technology is currently being developed at IBM in San Jose, California, called Personal Area Networks.[16] By touching fingertips with someone you can instantly transfer to them code or bank numbers, security details, and indeed any kind of signifiable information. A small pocket transmitter containing these details harnesses body sanity to pass a current up to my skin and across to whatever receiver—your skin—it touches. Body sanity is a good conductor of electricity. Conceivably then, the electrical discharges from the brain itself could similarly be harnessed. This sounds very like telepathy. It might mean some sort of "alphabet" of its own, by which neuro-impulses were conveyed; indeed, in part the brain does this already.

There is another development. Within "desubstantiation" generally we can already "volatize our whole sense of artistic quiddity."[17] Music and paintings can be digitally decomposed, rearranged, added to, and indeed produced by computer process. But the abecedary too has long been desubstantiated. A rectangular dot-matrix with a crosspiece inside it can generate all twenty-six letters thousands at a time on the instant. What looks like an eight: |⁼| —yields all the rest: |⁼||⁼||‾ ⎕||⁼|⁻|⁼|¦ |⁻| —and so on. The solidity of the centuries-old individual sign is lost. The monk-calligrapher's human touch disappeared with printing; now the loss is within the very signs that are printed. The abecedary is "virtual" with a vengeance, its quiddity vanished altogether. But there is a gain, too. The abecedary lies neurally ready for new kinds of permutation or combination. Maybe, inversely, thoughts themselves could be "desubstantiated" at least to the point of being rendered in some such neural alphabet. Be that as it may, and taking these two innovations together, our traditional and wonderful abecedary might turn out, after all, a sadly clumsy device next to the refinements the future may offer.

Not everyone thinks all this need happen. In a personal communication to myself, Michael Heather has suggested that although the "unwritten written" (maybe the "mental representations" referred to in chapter 17 above) may yield "an even more generalized form of text than we have hitherto thought of," yet even so "the alphabet we already have can do it all." Again we see testimony to the alphabet's stability. David Diringer, pioneer of alphabet studies, wrote firmly on this issue of stability and modernity half a century back. "The fact that alphabetic writing has survived with relatively little change for three and a half millennia, notwithstanding the introduction of printing and the typewriter, and the extensive use of shorthand writing, is the best evidence for its suitability to serve the needs of the whole modern world. This simplicity, adaptability and suitability has secured the triumph of the alphabet over the other systems of writing" (Diringer 1947, 214). Clearly, if in different terms, Diringer is also referring to aspects of the equability and virtuality we have also discussed. But the abecedary is already a form of digitalization. Such interesting speculations are imponderable while we wait to see how the self-teaching neurocomputer develops. The possibilities are far-reaching. One might wonder what poets will make of them.

20

Conclusion: Poetry

W<small>E</small> BEGAN THIS BOOK WITH A QUESTION: "WHAT IS IT, TO CONSTI-tute or communicate all that we know, mean, think, and feel, and turn that into an art (poetry), by countless rearrangements of a mere twenty-six nonpictorial and seemingly meaningless material signs?" That question now seems (unwittingly) prophetic in terms of what we have been discussing in this part 4. The bit in the middle there, about "know, mean, think, and feel," seems close to what the earlier chapters of this part severally tried to consider, via the specialized attention those matters have received in the twentieth century. "Turning it into poetry" is quite evidently an aesthetic issue; and the remaining chapter examined those "countless re-arrangements" at a new level; namely, the rather drastic events, mainly later-twentieth-century, that may have modified poetry's en-terprise in good or bad ways. Here are just a few final remarks.

One might wonder whether poetry can continue in present condi-tions. Yet such speculation, though always interesting, is likely to be inconclusive if not futile. Poetry sells little, and there are strong jeremiads to persuade us it is over. Yet literally millions write it, and if only a top few become best-sellers then that is much as things have always been. It is hard to see an art declining for all time when its medium is perennially so available, so cheap, so simple. Ironi-cally, too, while the dominant literary criticism of the last quarter century, namely the historical/political, has bent its efforts to the demolition of "literature" as a category, it has done so almost en-tirely in context of the literature of the past. Much of Terry Eagle-ton's work can be seen as "End of . . ." texts to add to the eschatological canon; but what is regarded as having "ended" is not literature but its status as an autonomous category. That is to say, Eagleton has often seemed unconcerned about whether writing of poems and novels will now go on; maybe literature can be de-fined right out of the semiautonomy it has sometimes been ac-corded. That way other things, let's say politically active projects, can absorb it as mere exemplary detail. As Eagleton wrote back in 1983, "The embarrassment for literary criticism (is) that it defines for itself a special object, literature, while existing as a set of techniques which have no reason to stop short at that object at all."[1] No reason indeed, except that its practitioners might just want to, through a sense that literature is a locus of the sacred, the aesthetic, and the human, with extremely special characteristics arising out of the medium of words and letters rather than, for example, stone, sound and paint. Any technology whatever can be employed beyond its original purpose without that origin necessarily becoming obsolete or redundant itself. For David Bromwich, motives such as Eagleton's are themselves signal of theory's failure. The determination not to "stop short at that object" is pretentious, for it betrays the real agenda, the critic's own targets. That Eagleton should then return to the aesthetic in his longest work could be variously interpreted; either way, though, the aesthetic that had refused to go away has to be subsumed under the political. Some critics see literary criticism as broken up altogether. Denis Donoghue states that "in my experience it has become extremely difficult to persuade students even to imagine what an aesthetic reading of a novel or a poem might be. For the most part, literature is taught not as rhetoric and poetics but as politics." Graham is blunter still: "Most of the doubt voiced about the method of [traditional] literary theory is less than serious; it is frankly ludicrous."[2]

This is all part of the general postmodern explosion sketched out earlier. Branches of literary criticism no longer stand in coherent disagreement, they simply fly out in all directions. But as we have implied all along, the heart of real attention to literature must be some kind of poetics, because the materials with which literature is written—the language, lexicon, syntactical structure, and in the end the abecedary—go back millennia. They cannot depend solely on the political shifts, veerings, and divisions of even the last three centuries, let alone the last three decades. They carry with them a cargo of embodied import or image that will always be at least part, at least the materials, of what is written, no matter what is the undeniable freight of contemporary inference, political, sexual, ecological, or anything else. Deconstruction has its own problems, being rather too keen on dissolving presence; but at least it notes the sign, that, as Barthes said, is where the true reader always lives.

A good way in to this conclusion, then, might be the aesthetic. It has this suspension between contraries that we said seems to mark the aesthetic experience in all cases, regardless of era or prevailing culture. And poetry is seated in the aesthetic as are all the arts.

Many other things may be incidentally or indeed significantly aesthetic, and we said as much of science. But art's very ambience is of letting the object rest, or live, in a kind of permanent equilibrium between whatever contraries press upon it in any one case. Any pair of contraries may be entailed; perfection and imperfection, what is and what might have been, matter and form, the object and our conception of it, division and unity, good and evil. In present context one might add, power and freedom from power.

But that list can go wider still. It can move out into the domain of epistemology generally. For example, there is the root contrast between the aesthetic experience we have and our subsequent consciousness of it. The two elements, a) the strong power of any unique work, b) yet the fact that we may never know what caused that power, are themselves contraries, obviously of a very general nature. As to science, it is not that scientific experiments and findings are themselves works of art, though we needn't deny certain affinities. The parallel lies in the fact that the successful scientific theory, by which some previous intellectual burden is lifted, dissolves the two or more factors that were "contrary"—as yet unrelated to each other—before the theory neatly and elegantly drew them into a clear unity. And if, as some say, science is possible only because the human brain and the entire cosmos are somehow "made for each other," then similarly works of art may be the tiny spots where that fitting consciousness, held in equilibrium in the aesthetic experience, reaches its highest human intensity. That indeed is where a more apt target for critical response might lie. But most important of all here, the abecedary also seems to hang halfway between its own contraries. Its contraries are its gross material existence and the purposes to which that is then put. It is thus the artist's "medium"—exactly the middle bit in between—more than are the materials used for other arts. Noise, pigment, stone, and the rest already have their place in the natural physical world and don't, in themselves, insist on being taken further. The abecedary, by contrast, is already designed for something else; it could not have come up in any such form via nature's ordinary processes. It is thus in some sense already aesthetic, which is no doubt why we love it.[3] Of course, the abecedary is used in all language—the contrast between Augustine and Aquinas already posed the wider "prose-poetry" contrast in a general way—but poetry foregrounds the medium as medium from the start. Finally, and again, none of this is to describe poetry as the superior of all arts; but, in this sense, it does seem to be an especially exemplary one.

Which takes us back to our earlier sections on language and

mind. Our topics were the language instinct; the lexicon and its neural storage; intention and the illocutionary force; psychoanalysis; and consciousness. I would argue here that all these five topics can be related to poetry because, in our context and in the poets, they all secreted a kind of potential reaching-out for the abecedary. Again, they and the abecedary seem to be "made for each other" in a way that does not apply to contingent historical and political events. Any poet is implicated in all these areas, but it might help explanation if we conveniently take the briefest look at each of our five poets from part 3 in light of one of each of these five areas. (It is of course sheer coincidence that there are "five and five" here; we are certainly not embarking on any further system-building at this stage.)

Emily Dickinson's "abyss" could be seen as emerging from the depths of a language instinct that isn't—in the view of its supporters—tied to any one contingent sign-system whatever. This abyss could thus be the "unnameable" the abecedary deals with ambivalently. Dickinson's poems are short, sharp matrices, but she doesn't particularly go for the repetitions, sacred words, proverbial forms, or even, with no derogation of herself implied, the "humanism" that got its strongest seventeenth-century voice in Shakespeare. In that case her poetry relies most on the sheer stability of the abecedary and makes whatever abecedarial distributions occur to her as pressing. George Herbert has a stored noun-verb lexicon whose very letters press on him as saying something rather important about the way Scripture itself could be held sacred, the very Word of God. So he uses the fewness, physicality, and distributive powers of the abecedary to positively resist Scripture in the same act as he reveres it. A strong sense of the work's intention comes through in John Milton's *Paradise Lost*. Critics have called this his "will," and the poem forthrightly declares its aim in its first paragraph. The poem embodies all six aspects of the abecedary with equal authority: yet with Milton more than anyone we feel he could have ten times as many letters as the "few" twenty-six, such is his power of command, and his overt illocutionary force. William Wordsworth has often been thought of as overtly anticipating the provenance examined by psychoanalysis. Lacan-wise, he raises up his past experiences into the language—*verbe*—which his poetry requires when he writes it. His abecedary is strongly equable and virtual, and, although he distributes his letters as much as any other poet, this seems unconscious or unawares, as his own critical comments often suggest. T. S. Eliot's poetry is eminently one of literary self-consciousness. *The Waste Land* knowingly raids existing texts from the past and cites them unchanged; indeed, the poem often feels mainly like a cunning pastiche of just these items. And this unexpectedly survives, as we saw, into the overtly more traditional *Four Quartets*. Eliot's explicit monitoring of both his own methods, and of language's workings generally, gets one entire section out of the five that comprise each quartet. Furthermore, this facet seems expressed in Eliot's criticism, for his emphasis on the poet's impersonality suggests that the poem itself, not the poet, is the locus of what is expressed; it is the "surface" between self and outside, which is what human consciousness also appears to be. Any poem's images—we move beyond Eliot now—its figures, tropes, and syntax—correspond to the "representations" the brain needs in order to accommodate the outside into the neural process. And, as we have said, these five matchings are for convenience here only. Much more—so very much more—could be added to these five summaries. And other poets could have been used instead—Chaucer, Pope, William Blake, Emily Bronte, Walt Whitman, Auden, or any other. This book could have been written around them, too.

The poem seeks the abecedary. In that sense the abecedary looks for chances to "get itself said," poetically, to its fullest intensity. The trappings of contemporary communications—the ads, headlines, word processor gizmos, and the rest—similarly go for such intensity but by external means. They exploit the single word, repetition, and proverbial form for temporary, not to say instant reception. They scoop the abecedarial characteristics that are most adaptable locally, that is to say its fewness, physicality, and distributive options—and somewhat ignore the rest. That isn't wholly true, for the abecedary's equability is actually all the more required if these strangely oversized and fragmented utterings are to be tolerated at all. Rather it is even that abecedarial equability gets drastically underused. It is also true, as said already, that abecedarial stability survives unscathed, for no ad, however revolutionary, could invent a new set of letters or even a random sample of such. But the general stability of usage is threatened. As to virtuality, headlines and slogans may well include emotional or spiritual reference, but their encapsulated and physically extreme nature makes any entry into the reader's wider thinking somewhat feverish.

Yet all this need be no threat to poetry, which works quietly away with full reliance on its deeper abecedarial foundations. If there should be tendencies that might militate against poetry's continuance, they would appear to come from the wholly new inventions of film and the later-generation computer. If later-generation computers do attain independence, if they can eschew consulting humanist notions of order, agency, progress, reason, and even benevolence—not that they aim to—they may dispense with the Turing set of requirements for artificial intelligence altogether. We suggested that Turing's requirements paralleled the characteristics of the abecedary; but the computer has no in-built responsibility ever to use the abecedary at all. But that would not prevent ordinary humans going on speaking and writing just as they always have done. The later-generation computer would have to evolve— probably will evolve—its own ways of meeting the stabilities, equabilities, and virtualities that writing meets on the page.

As to film, the position seems broadly comparable. Here it is worth giving an example in more detail, because film has so impressively enriched our culture with its new injections. The film *Accident* (director Joseph Losey, screenplay Harold Pinter, 1967) begins with a still of a large many-windowed house set well back from the road and the camera in late twilight. Against a background of pure silence come two noises; a car approaching and, from somewhere inside the house, the faint tapping of a typewriter. The sound of the car becomes alarmingly loud. When it ends with its dreadful mangling crash, there is silence, and an instant switch. The typewriter is replaced by a dog's continuous barking, equally distant. We are suddenly conscious of the sounds of birds in the trees; a single train is heard going by in the distance. After a moment a man comes out the front door. He walks out along the road. This extraordinarily beautiful orchestration of sound secretes in itself the deep rhythms that for centuries have been called poetic. They are nearer to poetry than to music—though suggestive of both—because they are immediately and inherently interpretable as to their utilitarian or animal sources. In this and other films and TV programs the interplay of human speech with the array of world-sounds that the microphone cannot fail to record—just as the camera cannot lie— make for a kind of new mixed-medium altogether. The immense spread of recorded music in our time is, naturally, a great competitor to the more self-committed task of reading poetry. But music isn't new. The amalgamation of these sounds of the passing world, in the soundtracks of films, is a reality newly evoked.

But again, such magnificent works needn't cut across poetry or other arts, because they inhabit entirely different areas of our appreciation. Film can as easily stimulate poetry as overshadow it. The poem's matrix speaks to a different sample or arrangement of our responses from that of the moving and visual film. It touches the sacred, the proverbial, the unnameable in quite different ways. By analogy, the huge differences we found between the one-level, fated epics of Homer and the emergent dialectical-based disciplines—drama, dialogue, formal philosophy, oratory—of later ancient Greece did not put an end to the epic or to poetry at all. Yet one might have expected such an outcome precisely because the same medium was used for both kinds of genre, broadly speaking poetry and prose. It never happened. All the less then need it happen in any inexorable fashion when the two technologies, writing and film, have so little mutual resemblance. We can salute the age of the great film while cherishing the continuation of language's own art. In everyday terms, sometimes we feel like one, sometimes the other. Again then, as far as poetry's future is concerned we can only stay to see; the position is entirely open.

One wonders how far the inventors of the first alphabets knew what they had invented. Letters are light-receptors, pure surface, so no part of them exists except in light. So too are colors, but colors aren't human inventions. Letters take what is in darkness and make it available to the light. In darkness resides fertility. Roots of plants, female ovum and male seed, ideas and images in the brain all need darkness for survival and their very existence. Judaism's original fiat *let there be light* encapsulated the handover, the god's voice commanding light where the god's words could then be recorded. As a result, formalized knowledge and understanding could grow. In Milton's words at the start of *Paradise Lost*, *What in me is dark illumine, what is low raise and support*: the literal meanings of low-high in human life may also, as metaphor, reinforce the sense of darkness beneath and light on the surface.

There is an ambiguity if letters are thought of this way. Humans can't look directly at the sun, it is too strong for the eyeball to bear. But if light is the traditional symbol for understanding, how then are knowledge and understanding themselves to be recorded? By something for the light to shine on; namely, the abecedary or other alphabet, which however isn't that light itself. This ambiguity is borne out by our sense that letters both are and are not objects; solidly physical yet still only virtual; things but without quiddity; one of the "microbillions" like ants, cells, and grains of sand, yet exceptional among such in having no organic inner principle of burgeoning reproduction and multiplication. There are still only twenty-six letters despite our millions of recombinations of them. This elusive, poised ambiguity suggests that letters could still be seen as something close to sacred, in a sense comparable to what the earliest anthropologists found in certain forms in nature. Sacredness and ambiguity were inseparable. Mary Douglas noted how primitive peoples dealt with the ambiguous in the natural world, things that couldn't be classified according to normal principles.[4] Bats, anteaters, and duck-billed platypuses seemed like mammals with wings, mammals with shells, and mammals that laid eggs respectively. Ear wax, excrement, and saliva seemed both part of and separable from the human body at once. In their different sphere letters sometimes seem equally unable to be categorized. We use them every day of our lives and unconsciously depend on them as we do on air and water; yet, unlike more solid forms of sign, they have often seemed unable to tolerate too much attention. Writing and speech are life-essential, yet a verbose person is more socially offensive than a taciturn one. Both the abecedary's letters and their combinations in words can be tedious and lovely at once.

The alphabet's first users must have found out certain things quickly. What couldn't be named must remain permanently so. The holy (including the ambiguous), the "one god," must not be too readily voiced, along with "qualia" of every kind and the "unnameable" itself. The fourteenth-century European mystics found that such things could only be self-referred, *suchness, thisness, isness* (Davies 1992, 227–28), the replay of the abecedary's parts in their own terms. The alphabet could only add to itself; literally, only go on adding more and more letters and words, in Hebrew to the left, in our abecedary to the right. It must forever miss the center it seeks to capture. Yet the abecedary's massive distributions could also capitalize on their use by different people, and different kinds of people, in a society at any one time. As writers from Bakhtin to Levinas have emphasized, the "address" of the letter, its speech to the Other therefore varies according to who is using it. In a remarkable passage in *The Brothers Kamarazov*, Aloysha states that "We are all responsible for everyone else, but I am more responsible than all the others." That sentence has its truth whoever is speaking, yet the referent "I" will have changed. It underlines that the abecedary's relentless sideways shift can take on three-dimensional properties, through its distributive capacity, according to its social location and direction. Such is poetry's challenge now.

The alphabet existed before our religion, our sacred texts, our monarchies, our parliaments, our global explorations, our political systems, and the institutions of the people. It was in place before the Jews came out of Israel or the Greek and Roman Empires established even the beginnings of their own lastingly influential institutions. It makes our political attitudes toward literature seem somewhat recent. Yes, we may reply, but even that too is young. The Lascaux cave paintings in France are dated at not three thousand years but twenty thousand; the Chauvet paintings are dated at over thirty thousand. If the subtle lines of the cave paintings express equally sophisticated perception on the part of their artists, we can hardly claim any timeless status for writing, for writing no more claims the original mark-on-matter status than drawing does. That can be answered, maybe, by those who believe with Hegel that literature is the most advanced of the arts, following in the wake of architecture, music, and drama. But it shrinks the idea of the sacred as itself timeless. The alphabet is recent. The sacred is not infinite or indestructible. Furthermore—and this book has tried to bear this in mind throughout although we have seldom said it—our own abecedary is far from universal. The Chinese and Arabic scripts work in different ways even though they also fundamentally emanate from the same universal principle of inscription.

In our own time production of the alphabet has multiplied to the point of the indigestible. It is neither abominated nor revered but simply blown apart. This is an unprecedented situation for the poets, certainly since the invention of printing and perhaps since that of writing itself. For the poets, too, don't take their inscriptions, word added on word, forever to the right. They constantly take forward the earliest practice of inscription since before language recorded just speech, and rather wrote two-dimensionally, in the matrix form across and down at once, as said earlier. In that practice they were comparable to the sacred text. But poems weren't sacred texts, or not necessarily so; rather they embodied and expressed the sacredness of the alphabet itself. It is traditionally said either that poetry always protests against the godhead, or that it evokes what the godhead declines to utter or answer. If either is true, then poetry itself may become expendable when the godhead either disappears or is so distended as to equate with no more or less than ultimate intention and, one trusts, benevolence. Alternatively some new dispensation, so far barely conceivable, may arise for poetry altogether.

Such is surmise; the electronic and genetically engineered world seems to move so fast but in another sense it is taking its time. There is a fair way to go yet before the shape of the longer future is clear even remotely. For the present, we can only hear poetry old and new, look after our planet, and wait on anything that seems like further instruction.

Appendixes

Appendix 1. Changes in Twentieth-Century Linguists' Views on the Relation between Writing and Speech

(This appendix summarises the debate in twentieth-century linguistics briefly alluded to in the introduction.)

THE DISCIPLINE OF LINGUISTICS DEALS WTH MOST ASPECTS OF LANguage, including the relationship between writing and speech. There was a profound shift of emphasis in the twentieth century. In the established philological tradition of the eighteenth and nineteenth centuries, writing was central and speech counted for little. Early-twentieth-century linguists reversed this. They stated that speech was fundamental while writing had an entirely secondary role. This was often asserted with strong feeling. Leonard Bloomfield and Ferdinand de Saussure, the two founding fathers of modern linguistics, shared this stance despite their markedly different traditions in other respects. It should again be emphasized that they were both, in their turn, responding to the earlier positions.[1]

Saussure was thus highly skeptical of the importance of writing, even when reluctantly acknowledging it. "Writing, though unrelated to its inner system, is used continually to represent language. We cannot simply disregard it." But Saussure would have been glad of the tape recorder in his time, for then writing could have been ignored:

> Language and writing are two distinct systems of signs; the second exists for the sole purpose of representing the first. The linguistic object is not both the written and spoken forms of words; the spoken forms alone constitute the object. But the spoken word is so intimately bound to its written image that the latter manages to usurp the main role. People attach even more importance to the written image of a vocal sign

than to the sign itself. A similar mistake would be in thinking that more can be learned about someone by looking at his photograph than by viewing him directly. (Saussure 1959, 23, 24)

When Bloomfield wrote his *Language* twenty years later in 1933, he virtually borrowed Saussure's terms. Writing merely records language in visible marks. "A language is the same whatever its writing system, just as a person is the same no matter how you may take his picture. . . . In order to study writing, we must know something about language, but the reverse is not true."[2] There is the same reluctant concession to written records, and even the comparison with the photograph.

Not formally a linguist, Fr. Walter Ong published his study of the subject in 1967. Ong equally subordinated writing to speech yet equally acknowledged its daily domination. "We are the most abject prisoners of the literate culture in which we have matured. . . . For certain uses of language, literacy is not only irrelevant but a positive hindrance."[3] Ong wrote when the influence of his fellow-Torontonian Marshall McLuhan was at its height, expounding his theories of the return, via electronic media and global village, to a world renewedly oral, the culture of the printing press simultaneously coming to its close. Yet by taking a metaphysical line on sight and sound, Ong clarified certain matters in the writing-speech debate. The spoken word empowers, yet being temporal it leaves no discernible effect in space. Speech lasts only so long as it is going out of existence. It comes from all round and therefore cannot be escaped—while it lasts. Writing lasts. Writing makes word and meaning seem exact and fixed. Similarly with sight and sound generally. Sight lasts but is thin; sound, though evanescent, packs more presence. Ong believed that the printed culture is what has desacralized the world. It is true that, although writing will in one sense always be supplementary—one cannot imagine us always writing and never speaking—its existence is inevitable in the very structure of reality because sound is fleeting. But equally, although writing will indeed survive, its supplementary status will be shown up by the new electronic orality.

In the decades since these writers, things have changed yet again. For Jack Goody "It is strange that a group of human beings [i.e., linguists] who probably spend more time reading and writing than they do speaking and listening, have been so oblivious to the social and psychological implications of their craft" (Goody 1987, 261). Roy Harris, commenting on Bloomfield in 1990, states flatly that "the notion that all written texts are records of words spoken prior to their inscription is manifestly absurd."[4] Countless government and company reports, textbooks, and manuals were never spoken and never will be. Harris believes too that seeing language as necessarily linear forced Bloomfield into his view of speech's priority. Michael Garman, also in 1990, noted the dominant tradition of phonetics. "It is unfortunate that linguistic science has . . . not devoted comparable efforts towards the study of the visible forms of language" (Garman 1990, xiv). Barry Powell, cited earlier on the invention of the Greek alphabet at Homer's time, writes comparably. "Writing is not 'secondary' to other expressions of uniquely human mental processes, especially language (as often held); writing exists in its own right as a form of expression of human thought" (Powell 1991, 69). Most telling though is what might on first reading seem to be a change of emphasis recorded by a leading linguist of our time, David Crystal. In 1965, Crystal wrote that "the phonetician studies the sounds of speech from a number of different points of view. What he does *not* do is study writing. Writing is a conventional, visual representation of speech; it is of secondary importance. . . ." (Crystal's emphasis).[5]

Twenty years later Crystal's emphasis was different. On the foregoing debate he writes: "It is understandable but regrettable that writing and speech should have been allowed to confront each other in this way. There is no sense in the view that one mode of communication is intrinsically 'better' than the other. Whatever their historical relationship, the fact remains that modern society makes available to its members two very different systems of communication, each of which has developed to fulfill a particular set of communicative needs, and now offers capabilities of expression denied to the other. Writing cannot substitute for speech, nor speech for writing, without serious disservice being done" (Crystal 1987, 178).

In fact, this switch in Crystal's emphasis is not the whole change it might at first seem to be, for there was also a change of context. Crystal's earlier remark was referring to phoneticians, not linguists, and so he is not in fact contradicting himself in these two positions.[6] The question then would be regarding any overall change of view as to what is most important. But we really need to ask what was being asserted most fundamentally in this whole debate. The earlier linguists were concerned with writing's political implications, and again they too were responding to an earlier debate situated in its own time and cultural context. But since writing was so long the provenance of only a few people, they were the ones who controlled knowledge, and therefore power, too. Writing seemed like a material seizure of power. And, while one honors the ethics of this position, it still doesn't fully get to grips with the actuality Ong conceded. Suppose writing becomes universally available; is it then still inferior to speech? The expansion of literacy has taken some of the pressure off the problem of exclusion, much as that is still far from eradicated. The fact again to be emphasized is that writing is as inherent in material reality as is speech. Current linguistics treats language as a rich, seamless web, teeming with details, vocabularies and structures, modes of expression, vernacular, visual display, color, noise, silence, and cultural form of all kinds. The relation between reading and spelling has been much researched but is still not well understood (Aitchison 1994, 236). The great vogue of the work of Jacques Derrida in the last twenty years stems as much from his innovatory theory of *ecriture* as from his resultant rereadings of seminal texts in European culture. *Ecriture* is "writing" in its most pervading sense, metaphysical and material, aural and visual at once. As said earlier, in Derrida's long-famous phrase, it is the mark, trace, hinge, rupture entailed in any intervention on bland unity of any kind at all.

So the question of just what happened when the alphabet was invented, has taken a more sophisticated turn. Writing has gradually been seen to play back on to speech as much as, just as validly at one level, it merely records it. Writing trails speech but also modifies it. Speech patterns of literate speakers are observably altered, maybe (while retaining their vernaculars) enriched, by long reading experience. And writing may have helped, settled, and extended speech. Clearly writing's extension into syntactical length right out of speech's range is a major effect. This extension then moves from page to voice, with a major inference resulting.

The suggestion is that our very power to consider language at all, our self-consciousness of it, was enabled by the invention of the alphabet. Speech could become conscious of itself only by the invention of a different medium, still language but different, by which speech itself could be externalized as an object for consideration. The invention of the alphabet firms up the exact selection of noises that variants on it are to count as and correspond to. Variants in English are numerous and familiar: aaaaa *(and, bar, day)*, nnnnn *(dent, coming, rien*—French), ttttt *(them, take, better*—Cockney glottal stop), hhhhh *(those, hair, caught*—silent), rrrrr *(roll, fire*— silent or pronounced), ggggg *(through, gentle, coming, gift)*, ccccc

coming, peace, chance), ppppp *(person, philosophy, psyche—*
silent), sssss *(was, stone, shaved),* kkkkk *(baking, knowledge—*
silent), bbbbb *(baking, comb—*silent), and so on for almost every
letter of the abecedary.

The thrust toward the invention may indeed have been powered
by this impulse. For writing does not merely tell us what utterances are utterances of. That was something speakers already
knew. Rather, writing "provides a basis for saying what, thereafter, utterances would be counted as utterances of."[7] It is the
"thereafter" that matters. The invention of the alphabet, for the
first time tying writing and utterance fully and closely together,
was therefore a historical event of major importance, perhaps one
of the three or four most significant to occur in our entire history.
It enabled the very examination of language, because writing itself points to a range of utterances with which, thereafter, it will
be associated.

The implication is striking, indeed astonishing. The invention of
the alphabet could not have been what it now all too easily seems,
namely, the assignment of fixed sounds to already agreed words.
For, without the alphabet, such assigning could not first have taken
place. In the oral world the nuances of both sound and meaning
would vary, by much or little, on each occasion of their speech, but
without something like the alphabet there would have been nothing
to say which of these variants constituted the true version. But once
the row of letters is fixed, the word is fixed, or at least can culturally
be so regarded. As a result, a new form of language, namely alphabetical writing, has come into existence. Letters do not just record
speech; in part they enable it, and human consciousness of it. Writing cannot possibly just record speech, for all occasions of any
word or phrase in speech; "meet you at the cafe," or "beyond further consideration," are different in each enunciation both phonetically and in context. Writing them, therefore, does not actually
record them; rather it gives a central focus for their several unique
occasions to be measured against.

Nigel Love points out (113) that, by virtue of this distancing of
speech in the invention of writing, linguistics even became possible
itself. Perhaps this also applies to criticism. The suggestion supports the position taken in this book, namely, that silent reading of
poetry is general, and reading it aloud is specific. Much of what we
have cited passim from David Olsen puts the same position, and in
greater detail.

APPENDIX 2. POEMS REFERRED TO IN THE TEXT BY GEORGE HERBERT AND THOMAS HARDY

George Herbert

VERTUE

Sweet day, so cool, so calm, so bright,
The bridall of the earth and skie:
The dew shall weep thy fall tonight;
    For thou must die.

Sweet rose, whose hue angrie and brave
Bids the rash gazer wipe his eye:
Thy root is ever in its grave,
    And thou must die.

Sweet spring, full of sweet dayes and roses,
A box where sweets compacted lie;
My musick shows ye have your closes,
    And all must die.

Onely a sweet and vertuous soul,
Like seasoned timber, never gives;
But though the whole world turn to coal,
    Then chiefly lives.

THE ELIXER

Teach me, my God and King,
  In all things thee to see,
And what I do in any thing,
  To do it as for thee:

Not rudely, as a beast,
  To runne into an action;
But still to make thee prepossest,
  And give it his perfection.

A man that looks on glasse,
  On it may stay his eye;
Or if he pleaseth, through it passe,
  And then the heav'n espie.

All may of thee partake:
Nothing can be so mean,
Which with his tincture (for thy sake)
Will not grow bright and clean.

A servant with this clause
Makes drudgery divine:
Who sweeps a room, as for thy laws,
Makes that and th' action fine.

This is the precious stone
That turneth all to gold:
For that which God doth touch and own
Cannot for lesse be told.

Thomas Hardy

THE GARDEN SEAT

Its former green is blue and thin,
And its once firm legs sink in and in.
Soon it will break down unaware,
Soon it will break down unaware.

At night when reddest flowers are black
Those who once sat thereon come back;
Quite a row of them sitting there,
Quite a row of them sitting there.

With them the seat does not break down,
Nor winter freeze them, nor floods drown,
For they are as light as upper air,
They are as light as upper air!

APPENDIX 3.   GERARD MANLEY HOPKINS' *The Wreck of the Deutschland*

(Hopkins takes the abecedary to such lengths that it seemed unwise to give him full treatment in part 3. His unique practice might seem to endorse our notions far too easily for general application not to be risky. It is equally a matter of space. I have done a detailed study of The Wreck of the Deutschland *from the abecedarial point of view, but it would take fifty pages to report it in full detail.*

A study of Hopkins by John Robinson (1978) is entitled In Extremity. *The term captures the poetry and the spiritual life alike. Hopkins' poetry is rich indeed, like that of any major poet; but it is marked by extravagance. Here are some miscellaneous observations on* The Wreck of the Deutschland. *They are as systematic as possible but far from exhaustive. They are chosen to illustrate this extravagance. Some comparisons are made with* Tintern Abbey.)

1) The Letter eeeee

Eeeee appears over eleven hundred times in the poem, yet only twenty-two of them begin a word. If "the first letter owns the word," then perhaps Hopkins was trying to subdue eeeee's ubiquity. In any case he often preferred to begin, and end, words with consonants. Ten lines in the poem have no eeeee: intriguingly, five of these open their stanzas. One is an oft-cited line, *Thou hast glory of this nun?* (stanza 30).

2) Sexuality and Gender

> Jesu, heart's light,
> Jesu, maid's son,
> What was the feast followed the night
> Thou hast glory of this nun?
> Feast of the one woman without stain
> For so conceived, so to conceive thee is done . . .
>
> —from stanza 30

The omission of "that" and "when" intensifies the stanza. The last three lines contain clear sexual innuendos with the pun on *conceive* climactic.

The words *God* and *Lord* appear in the poem five times each. Five nouns drowned in the wreck, and these are compared to the five wounds of Christ. The poem is about five nuns, yet the word *nun* appears only twice throughout. The three most frequent six-letter words are *Christ, father,* and *master.* Whether this is overtly intentional, subliminally so, or sheer coincidence is anybody's guess, but Hopkins certainly enjoyed playing around with the qualities of individual words, as his notebooks clearly show. Hopkins' regard both for the nuns and for the Virgin Mary is quite undeniable, but the inscription of maleness is marked.

3) Monosyllables

Contrasting the verbal richness and extravagance are the mono-syllabic lines, stretching to the point of bursting:

> And she beat the bank down with her bows and the ride of her keel
> The girth of it and the wharf of it and the wall
> Or is it that she cried for the crown then?
> To flash from the flame to the flame then, tower from the grace to
> the grace
>
> —from stanzas 3, 14, 25, 32

Gentle, thin lines abound—here with the "thin" iiiii prominent: *Over again I feel thy finger and find thee* (stanza 1). Is this spiritual, sexual, or about writing itself? *Is it love in her of the being as her lover had been?* (stanza 25); forty letters here, but only fifteen of the alphabet are used.

Numerous runs of three or four lines in succession are almost entirely monosyllabic. Monosyllabic words declog, look pure on the page with a diaphanous quality like smooth pebbles, and thus strikingly contrast the richly lettered lexicon that pervades the poem elsewhere.

4) Alliteration

Bar the usual rarest four (jjjjj, qqqqq, xxxxx, and zzzzz), every single letter of the alphabet is massively alliterated in the poem on several occasions. Just a few comments here.

The letter mmmmm alliterates around the triple theme of Mary, mercy, and master. *Miracle-in-Mary-of-flame* is the poem's longest hyphenated sequence. Successive stanzas 11 and 12 have the two highest mmmmm-counts, with stanzas 9 and 10 only a few less.

The rarest letters have a kind of broad alliteration, a wider proximity. Qqqqq appears only six times, yet *quails* and *quickly* come in successive lines. Jjjjj appears only seven times in the poem, yet all of them appear in twelve successive stanzas out of the poem's thirty-five.

Types of alliteration. i) Semantic contrast: *Lightning and love . . . winter and warm.* ii) Doubled within two words: *heeds but hides, bodes but abides.* iii) Alliteration anticipated. In *With a mercy that outrides / The all of water . . . ,* after the force of the sea off the Kent coast, it is easy to supply *wall—the wall of water*—to make the alliteration complete. iv) Oral alliteration with inexact or no visual counterpart: *ocean of a motionable wind* (stanza 32), *cipher of suffering Christ* (stanza 22). In the second phrase here ccccc/phph-phphph alliterates sssss/fffff. v) Dense alliteration: *I did say yes* (stanza 2), the poem's shortest line, has four pairs of letters with only eeeee and aaaaa left single, and they are both vowels.

5) Punctuation

Stanzas are visual on the page, often through punctuation:

> But how shall I . . . make me room there:
> Reach me a . . . Fancy, come faster –
> Strike you the sight of it? look at it loom there,
> Thing that she . . . there then! the Master,
> Ipse, the only one, Christ, King, Head,
> He was to cure the extremity, where he had cast her;
>
> —from stanza 28

Punctuation is heavily present in the poem. Types of punctuation are frequent in *The Wreck of the Deutschland* most of which do not appear in *Tintern Abbey* even once: sixty-six hyphens, fifteen question marks, three rows of dots, and twenty-seven possessive apostrophes including a spate of six in the poem's last line. *Tintern Abbey* contains almost no dashes; in Hopkins' poem there are twenty-four. No punctuation mark of any kind appears more often in *Tintern Abbey* than in *The Wreck of the Deutschland*.

6) "Exotic" Words

What we called the "centrifugal effect" pervades the poem and is famously one of its most striking features. *Anvil-ding, waft, bugle, cinquefoil, token, swivelled, fleece, dreadnought, coifed, brim,* and numerous others all contain letter combinations uncommon in English. These are supported by Hopkins' numerous coinages, hyphenated words, and resurrections from older dialects; *quickgold* (from *quicksilver*), *burl, quain, wimpling; plush-capped, moth-soft*; the *–le* words like *brandle, buckle, ruddle, scuppled,* and many more. All these usually contain a higher ratio of the abecedary's less frequent letters and are all further acts of uniqueness in writing.

7) Letter-Frequencies and Word-Frequencies

As one might have expected, Hopkins uses far more harsh consonants and far fewer vowels and liquid consonants than does Wordsworth in *Tintern Abbey*. Calculating as though both poems were of identical length letterwise, we find the visually and orally abrasive kkkkk (discussed in detail in chapter 8 above) has overwhelmingly the highest increase, with proportionately nearly four times as many appearances as in *Tintern Abbey*. There is, of course, a strong sound-symbolism and sight-symbolism around the word *wreck*. Much lower but still next is bbbbb, followed by ddddd, wwwww, rrrrr, ccccc, and ggggg in that order. The *lowest* appearances in Hopkins' poem relative to Wordsworth's are (descending rank order) lllll, nnnnn, ooooo, uuuuu, vvvvv, mmmmm, yyyyy, and ppppp. Mmmmm is massively more extensive in Wordsworth's poem; again though, Hopkins' great use of mmmmm is sacramental, as suggested above.

In plain lexicon—leaving "exotic" words aside—*Tintern Abbey* is actually richer than *The Wreck of the Deutschland*. That is to say, a higher percentage of the words in Wordsworth's poem appear only once. However, Hopkins makes up this "discrepancy" lower down the list, for more of his words appear only three or four times more than do Wordsworth's.

8) Other Word-Distribution and Wordplay

Puns sometimes have to be intuited. *Guessed* and *maid* do not appear to pun *guest* or *made* (stanzas 26, 30), yet in *And they the prey of the gales . . .* a pun with *pray* seems to hover, and the nun's desperate prayer follows three lines later.

The word *the* appears on average nearly six times per stanza, yet in two successive stanzas, 9 and 10, it disappears entirely.

There is a high rate of words with consonants at start and finish. This separates the words sacramentally, that is to say it enhances their status as "sacred," i.e., set apart.

The spiky, harsh appearance of *The Wreck of the Deutschland* might have led us to expect far more letters with ascenders and descenders—"uppers and lowers"—in it than in *Tintern Abbey*. In fact, the difference is slight, with just over a third of both poems consisting of such letters. The strong appearance of *The Wreck of the Deutschland* lies elsewhere: in the unusual shape of the stanza; the frequent punctuation marks; the many hyphenated words and unusually exotic terms; the contrast between those and the many very short words; the places where both long and short words appear in any one stanza; the many hard consonants in short words; and possibly most striking of all, the many words with consonants at start and finish.

Hopkins often stated that his poetry was rhythmic and meant to be spoken. His belief that the case against onomatopoeia had widely been overstated may have been directed at the theories of the eminent philologist Max Muller, who was friendly with Hopkins' father. Yet this emphasis on sound seldom seems a real opposition to writing. Hopkins' note "Poetry and Verse" seems to suggest speech/verse, not speech/writing, is the antithesis he has in mind.[8]

He wants the tone of common dialect, not the educated poet of conventional opinion, and this perhaps is why he was fond of monosyllabic words. Hopkins preferred the Saxon to the Latinate: *child* not *infant, house* not *residence,* and so on. His list of favored words, although not always the most used ones, is largely monosyllabic.[9] But his own practice is on the page; he was a good and well-read scholar, and most important his list-making in his notebooks is an obsession not with syntax and expressive articulation but with lexicon and philology. Cary Plotkin calls this Hopkins' "isolation of the word at the expense of syntactic relations."[10] In his highly influential work *On The Study Of Words* (1851), Richard Chevenix-Trench wrote that "many a single word also is itself a concentrated poem, having stores of poetical thought and imagery laid up in it." Hopkins may well have read this work.

Hopkins lived at the high point of the nineteenth century philological debate on dialect and the status of language, and he probably attended Muller's famous series of lectures at Oxford. Hopkins also may well have studied Hensleigh Wedgewood's etymological dictionary as well as other similar works (Milroy 1977, 44). Nineteenth-century etymological research had established previously unknown links between words such as *loft/lift, sieve/sift, drift/drive,* and numerous others. According to Hillis Miller, Hopkins supposed that, by a continuous process of subdivision, all words descend from a first original, an ur-word. Hopkins' notebook-lists of linked words, *school, shoal, shell—gulf, golf, gulp, gula, hollow, hold, hilt—tweak, twitch, twig, earwig, wicker,* etc., etc., were in effect an attempt to get back to this ur-word, by a compulsive and impossible effort to trace the links between every existing word there is.[11] The ur-word was created by God; it is not itself the Word for it is created. There is no "masterword" for the Word. On this argument words were not the mere breathing of subjective expression; they were creations of God. Hopkins wrote that "words are like other creatures: they have inscapes beautiful in themselves."[12] The tendency is eloquent as to how Hopkins' poetry related to his religion. He often expresses the two realms as antagonistic, but this usually seems a moral matter; one of conflicting claims on the disciplines of the vocational life. But in language, Hopkins' sense of the uniqueness of words squares exactly with his espousal of the Duns Scotus view of the individuation of reality. The opposing, Thomist view that prevailed among the Jesuits was that reality is unified. Aquinas had a sense of God's "not"-qualities, God-sameness.

The Wreck of the Deutschland is a commemoration of five nuns who drowned; but it is also Hopkins' largest rendering of his linguistic extravagance and excitement. Elisabeth Schneider emphasizes Hopkins' insertion of himself into this process in the poem's opening words, *Thou mastering me God*.[13] Here Hopkins inverts normal syntax in the act of submitting himself to God, for God was the origin of language in its ever-expanding nature. The poem begins with Hopkins' conversion to Catholicism and ends with the same hoped-for conversion of Britain. In between these is the wreck itself, but also the death of the tall nun. Her tragedy entailed a direct visitation of Christ, whose gift of his unique, one-shot flesh and blood in the sacrament was divinely analogous to the gift of unique language. *The Wreck of the Deutschland* is a poem that risks yet survives its own wreckage. The stanzas look like ships, and each is "wrecked" by the hyphenated terms, broken syntax, and brittle punctuation. But the wreck is internal. The stanza outline survives in each case. Hopkins thus anticipates poetic modernism with its fragmentation, but modernism lost the religious dispensation that would survive it. The breakdown of language continues in our own time.

APPENDIX 4. ALEXANDER POPE AND OLIVER GOLDSMITH

(Our selection of poets in part 3 went from the seventeenth century to the twentieth, but it included no poet from the eighteenth. So here are two passages from Pope and Goldsmith, by which to make a few observations on that period from the viewpoint of our topic.)

Alexander Pope

> Who first taught souls enslaved, and realms undone,
> The enormous faith of many made for one;
> That proud exception to all Nature's laws,

To invert the world, and counter-work its cause?
Force first made conquest, and that conquest, law;
Till Superstition taught the tyrant awe,
Then shared the tyranny, then lent it aid,
And gods of conquerors, slaves of subjects made:
She midst the lightning's blaze, and thunder's sound,
When rock'd the mountains, and when groan'd the ground,
She taught the weak to bend, the proud to pray,
To power unseen, and mightier far than they:
She, from the rending earth and bursting skies,
Saw gods descend, and fiends infernal rise:
Here fix'd the dreadful, there the blest abodes:
Fear made her devils, and weak hope her gods;
Gods partial, changeful, passionate, unjust,
Whose attributes were rage, revenge or lust;
Such as the souls of cowards might conceive,
And, form'd like tyrants, tyrants would believe.
Zeal then, not charity, became the guide;
And hell was built on spite, and heaven on pride.
Then sacred seem'd the ethereal vault no more;
Altars grew marble then, and reek'd with gore:
Then first the flamen tasted living food;
Next his grim idol smear'd with human blood;
With heaven's own thunders shook the world below,
And play'd the god an engine on his foe.

—Essay on Man, 3:241–68

Donald Davie said that the heroic couplet as used by Dryden and Pope was capable of rendering "only one sort of movement through the mind; it is committed by its very nature to a syntax of antithesis and razor-sharp distinctions." The couplet has been called classical, rational, and mechanical, rightly enough. Geoffrey Tillotson and Winifred Nowottny examined it in detail, and Davie cites an anonymous *Times Literary Supplement* writer from 1936: "In Pope a couplet will often suggest a difficult figure in Euclid, its vowels and consonants, its sense-oppositions and sense-attractions, fitted together like arcs and lines." [14]

Yet the passage from Pope just cited has a different tenor. It is fierce, savage; indeed apart from the detachment of objective description, it is rather like the George Gordon Byron who wrote *Manfred*. Superstition, tyranny, lightning's blaze and thunder's sound, fiends and devils, rage, revenge and lust, spite, gore, and human blood—none of these much recalls Euclid. The passage is extreme in terms of Pope, but some of his other poems too, notably in *The Rape of the Lock* and the epistolary mode generally, stand back in their smile of reason from poems like the *Essay on Criticism*. The passage has containment; huge forces are held in check by the couplet form that also issues them. Near-mutually exclusive spellings are everywhere.

Equally powerful forces are needed to achieve this. The very word *force* is controlled: *Force first made conquest, and that conquest, law*. Orally, the puffing fffff and seething ccccc, here sounded as sssss, are taken out of the counterbalancing term *law* even as the vowel-sound stays the same. Yet on the page, *law* is quite different from *force*. Its intellectual connotation is not just opposed but taken right away elsewhere, for the two words have no letters in common. Both orally and visually *force* gets its comeuppance. More dramatically, alliteration gives strong order to what ought to be mayhem. After *lightning's blaze and thunder's sound,* the phrase *groan'd the ground* stops just short of burlesque, and Superstition's irrational power can thus actually bring calm to these earthquake movements. In teaching *the weak to bend, the proud to pray,* the rhyme-word opens out to no consonant and level wonderment. But most of all, when superstition's failure to base power on principle is relentlessly unfolded, the spate of gruesome events at the end has not only disaster but acceptance:

> Then sacred seem'd the ethereal vault no more;
> Altars grew marble then, and reek'd with gore:
> Then first the flamen tasted living food;
> Next his grim idol smear'd with human blood;
> With heaven's own thunders shook the world below,
> And play'd the god an engine on his foe.

The reason is that the caesura has largely disappeared. The single clear contrast is between lines, not within them: *. . . first . . . Next.* The caesura in the heroic couplet has only limited options by which to apply it. By the range of his thought and reference Pope's skill can play the same few changes forever: *the . . . the . . . ; And . . . and . . . ; Here . . . there . . . ;* yet the mode has to be called reactionary, without that being pejorative and nothing else. Thomas Sprat and the Royal Society hover strongly in the background, wanting word and thing to stand tidily opposite each other in a tidy cosmos with caesura and couplet rhyme commanding the relations between such entities. Yet the binary idea of word-thing had originally grown out of the separation of human language from the realities it articulated. But without Foucault's "middle term" the word-thing relation can become convention, perhaps power.[15] Royal Society–science and the French Academy will later try to enforce this.

With a couple of exceptions, the letters in the passage appear in the standard frequency of English. Only iiiii drops below the usual "etaison" dominance; hhhhh, rrrrr, ddddd, and lllll are dutifully next; jjjjj, qqqqq, xxxxx, and zzzzz clear at the bottom, and so on. The violent stirring vocabulary is held very tightly by the common connectors, *the, and, her, his, on,* and others. *If* with its modifying sense of condition doesn't appear in the passage at all. The strong words stand out by their very rarity. There is also the letter ddddd, noted elsewhere in this book already and rather important in Auden (appendix 5). Commonly ddddd's pressure arises from its incessant pressure in *and* and the past tense. But in this passage it has a different use, or at least a variant on it.

Ddddd appears sixty-three times. Thirty of them come in words that are neither *and* nor ddddd's common use as past tense ending: *abodes, aid, bend, blood, cowards, descend, devils, dreadful, fiends, food, gods* (five, including *god* once), *ground, guide, idol, midst, pride, proud* (two), *rending, sacred, sound, thunders* (two, including *thunder's* once), *undone, world* (two) and *would.* This is an important lexicon, reinforced by powerful alliterations: *thunder's sound; gods descend, and fiends; dreadful . . . abodes; devils . . . gods; And play'd the god;* the rhymes *guide/pride* and *food/blood*; and others. *Gods descend, and fiends* has ddddd five times in four words.

The force in the repeated *gods* throughout is central to the passage's power, and it is located centrally in a key line with no real caesura: *Gods partial, changeful, passionate, unjust.* The line departs Pope's abecedarial conservatism. Eeeee appears only twice, both times silently. The preceding line sets up this line's emphasis by virtue of the passage's most marked caesura: *Fear made her devils, and weak hope her gods.* Pope makes strong but only local play with the harsh rough consonants usually employed: *fffff, kkkkk, ggggg, ccccc,* and such. The robustness of Beowulf and Tyndale is under heavy control. The gods thud and thunder.

Oliver Goldsmith

> At church, with meek and unaffected grace,
> His looks adorned the venerable place;
> Truth from his lips prevailed with double sway,
> And fools, who came to scoff, remained to pray.
> The service past, around the pious man,
> With steady zeal each honest rustic ran;

Even children followed with endearing wile,
And plucked his gown, to share the good man's smile.
His ready smile a parent's warmth exprest,
Their welfare pleased him, and their cares distrest;
To them his heart, his love, his griefs were given,
But all his serious thoughts had rest in Heaven.
As some tall cliff that lifts its awful form,
Swells from the vale, and midway leaves the storm,
Tho' round its breast the rolling clouds are spread,
Eternal sunshine settles on his head.
—The Deserted Village, 1770 (177–92)

This passage is included as a contrast to Pope's. It is from the description of the parson in *The Deserted Village*, and it is far milder even than Pope's "Man of Ross" passage in the *Moral Essays* 3 (also about a rural benefactor), let alone Pope's lines just considered. At the level of letters Goldsmith's dilution emerges rather exactly. Allowing for the passages' different lengths, one finds that on the vowels Goldsmith uses the thin iiiii proportionately more often and the visually strong yyyyy less so. On the gentle and liquid wwwww, rrrrr, and lllll (strictly labial, trill, and lateral aveolar), Goldsmith is up, using the lllll in particular half again as often as Pope. Yet on the stronger consonants, Pope goes well ahead on the plosives ddddd, ttttt, and bbbbb and the guttural ggggg, and slightly ahead on the orally abrasive and visually spiky kkkkk, xxxxx, and zzzzz, although absolute numbers, as always, are low for those last three letters. In such letters Goldsmith is only up markedly on sssss. The most striking contrast lies in the nasals, for Pope has proportionately nearly twice as many nnnnn, but a fifth fewer mmmmm. Nnnnn can—though it needn't—whine and keen, while mmmmm is almost always inward. The picture isn't exact—wwwww is angular, too, and nnnnn and mmmmm look alike—but the overall trend is there.

It all comes from Goldsmith's use of the heroic couplet in Pope's manner and with similar tricks, but those much diminished. There are only three clear caesuras, and the run of four substantives that was so strong in Pope's *Gods partial, changeful, passionate, unjust* shrinks to three monosyllabic nouns in Goldsmith's *To them his heart, his love, his griefs were given*. So, comparing the gentle parson with the "awful" tall cliff seems out of place, and Goldsmith keeps it down to four lines. The passage isn't automatically inferior, and Goldsmith's reputation as an ineffectual and at times rather ridiculous person didn't leave him less than an astute observer of humanity. Rather, the century is moving on, the poetry of sensibility is arriving, and the need to melt down the more terse boundaries of expression doesn't sit easily with the heroic couplet's virtues. Goldsmith seems less to evoke sensibility's sometimes unfounded emotion, than to generalize. His parson is rather ideal, and this accounts for some of the sssss's in the prototype plurals. The repetition of *smile* is revealing, a pronouncement that lexicon-precision isn't always where poetry is to be found.

APPENDIX 5. W. H. AUDEN'S "IN MEMORY OF SIGMUND FREUD"

(Auden's poem well illustrates the potential of the letter ddddd in poetry as we have noted that periodically in this book. Readers are invited to accompany what follows with a copy of the text of the poem, which cannot be reproduced here. Auden's use is a long way from Pope's [see appendix 4].)

Exactly a quarter of the lines in the poem, 28 out of 112, end with a word containing the letter ddddd. In sixteen of these ddddd is also the last letter and so ends the line, too. The resulting effect is both enhanced and diluted by ddddd appearing at other key points; for example in a line's starting-word; or where a phrase begins, or ends. All such cases are marked by punctuation. Since there are about twenty-five of these other occasions, too, and since the letter ddddd appears just over 150 times in the poem, it seems, on the face of it at least, that every third ddddd in the poem is in some kind of prominent position. It is this prominence that is used as resource to achieve the poem's remarkable effect.

This effect is a very low-key resonance that the reader gathers as it accrues. It is always just subdued enough to seem ever about to surface fully while never quite doing so. The effect comes from the start, but gently, and the first line contains no ddddd at all. But we then see that three lines of the poem's first nine have ended with this letter: *exposed*, *good*, and *wished*. The line-endings have begun to toll quietly in the background. They help underscore as key phrase what might otherwise have seemed indifferent, indeed hardly poetry at all: *Such was this doctor* . . . in the ninth line.

The gentle chanting then proceeds throughout, coming and going, never oppressive but never far off:

> They are still alive, but in a world he changed
> able to approach the Future as a friend . . .
> have felt the change in their bones and are cheered . . .

Often the quietly treading ddddd is internal:

> all he did was to remember
> like the old and be honest like children . . .

There is often more than one ddddd in a line, but it never comes across as excessive. The voice ends the poem, still playing on the same letter, in one of poetry's quieter and deeper climaxes:

> One rational voice is dumb. Over his grave
> the household of Impulse mourns one dearly loved:
>   sad is Eros, builder of cities,
> and weeping anarchic Aphrodite.

In this final stanza of the poem the appearances of ddddd rise markedly against their standard frequency in English; namely from tenth place to seventh. It is as though Auden is gently clinching what he has hitherto practiced more evenly; or, maybe, at last overtly acknowledging what he has been doing more tacitly all along. For previously in the poem ddddd's appearances are not above their standard frequency for English. Indeed, they are just a little under that norm—not that the difference is significant statistically. Rather it is ddddd's use and placing that has achieved the poem's deadpan yet strongly meditative effects. There are 135 words containing ddddd in the poem. More than four in five begin, end, or both begin and end with this letter. Of course, thanks to the common "and" and the equally common use of an end-ddddd to make past tenses, it isn't difficult to find ddddd-endings in English; indeed it might be hard to avoid them. Far the majority (85 percent) of the poem's words that end with ddddd come from those two categories. But because of such prominent positioning of the letter in any word—the Kabbalists' *notarikon* or study of first and last letters—there is an opportunity to place gentle accent or stress on such words in their places in the line. Yet Auden's subtlety, his underplaying rather than overplaying, are what count. And words that contain ddddd elsewhere, that is to say neither at the start nor at the end of the word, are often quietly leaned on through their lexical significance: *wonder, children, garden, obedience*. In fact, *wonder* is only the second word in its stanza, which contains no other ddddd-word. Since this stanza is just halfway through the poem— twelfth out of twenty-eight—it offers just a suggestion of alleviation to the main resonance, itself already subliminal enough. In this respect that stanza picks up the opening line's ddddd-absence, which of course at that early stage wasn't noticed as an absence at all. In other places two or three ddddd-words come close together without, however, this forcing itself on us as "alliteration" in too obvious a way: *in a world he changed*; *deeds that must be punished*, and in the final stanza, already quoted.

As said already then, it is not that ddddd appears more often in Auden's poem than it usually does in English, as we found it did when used for comparable effects in *The Waste Land* (chapter 15). Indeed, the spread of the abecedary in the poem generally is more or less standard: the *etaison* group comes first, hhhhh/lllll/rrrrr/ddddd next, the bottom four the usual suspects. Again then, the poem's restrained mood as far as ddddd is concerned comes from the positions in which the letter finds itself, both in word and line.

"In Memory of Sigmund Freud" was probably the first Auden poem consciously wrote in full discursive style and public voice. He had aspirations to this formal urban role and, as has sometimes been suggested, maybe attempted it as result of his long reading of Marianne Moore's syllabic poems. Auden found the mode difficult but persevered, "sensing the integrity of her rule."[16] The result was his choice of alcaics, the form borrowed by Horace from the exiled Greek poet Alcaeus. Freud and Auden were both, in a sense, also exiled; Auden in America and Austria, Freud in Britain.

The poem speaks with the authority and gravitas of civic mourning. Since in our own time Freud is, to some, discredited (see chapter 17), Auden's detached appraisal (lines 60 and 65) was farsighted. Its suavity might have meant insincerity but for the weighting of each term, placed in each case to invest it with the memory of the departed over time.

For the critic just cited (note 16 above) the poem "sounds prosy . . . [its rhythms are] trained more on speech than on song." But one might equally say that the poem was conceived as speech but then leaves that behind. From silent intellectual sifting and the calculated discarding of alternatives, the poet has found exactly the right terms and the poem begins to stir. It is low-key but could well be set to music. To aver that the bass-theme of the ddddd seems to be muttering *Sigmund Freud, Sigmund Freud*, could easily—put so pat—seem absurd, but the strain works because, unlike the case cited with Pope, it is always only just within earshot.

Notes

(NB—throughout this book's notes, when a page number is not given in any citation, the cited author discusses the topic in question frequently or passim.)

INTRODUCTION

1. Hans-Georg Gadamer, *Truth and Method,* trans. by William Glen-Doepel (London: Sheed & Ward, 1975), 145; Susanne K. Langer, *Feeling and Form: A Theory of Art* (London: Routledge & Kegan Paul, 1953), 52.

2. *Poetry Review* 83:4 (winter 1993–94): 83.

3. Steven Mithen, *The Prehistory of the Mind* (London: Orion Books Phoenix, 1998).

4. See note 5 to chap. 6. Spelling is currently being reformed in Germany. Adjustment of the alphabet is not on the agenda.

5. Camilla Paglia, *Sexual Personae* (New Haven: Yale University Press, 1990), 17–18.

6. Tom Paulin, "In The Workshop" (review of Helen Vendler's *The Art of Shakespeare's Sonnets*) *London Review of Books* (22 January 1998): 3–8.

7. Isobel Armstrong, "Thatcher's Shakespeare?" in *Textual Practice* 3:1 (spring 1989): 1–14.

8. Terry Eagleton, *The Ideology of the Aesthetic* (Oxford: Basil Blackwell, 1990).

9. Kiernan Ryan, "Don't Look Back: *Hamlet*, Theatre, and the Future of Criticism," at the After the New Historicism Conference, Birkbeck College, University of London, 14 March 1998.

10. *The Times Higher (London),* 2 Oct 1998.

11. Morris Kline, *Mathematics in Western Culture* (Harmondsworth: Penguin, 1972 [from 1953]), chap. 26.

12. Harold Bloom, *Kabbalah and Criticism* (New York: Seabury, 1979), 76.

13. Ludwig Wittgenstein, *Philosophical Investigations,* trans. G. E. M. Anscombe (Oxford: Basil Blackwell, 1958), 60e-80e, especially pp. 67e ff., offers probably his most detailed reflections on the principle of letters and their relation to meaning.

14. E. R. Curtius, *European Literature and the Latin Middle Ages*, trans. Willard R.Trask (London: Routledge and Kegan Paul, 1953), chap. 3.

15. For instance, Seamus Heaney, "Glanmore Sonnets VII," in *North*, (London: Faber & Faber, Ltd. 1975), and Carol Ann Duffy, "Prayer," in *Mean Time* (London: Anvil Press, 1993).

16. Octavio Paz, *Alternating Current* (London: Wildwood House, 1974), 66.

17. I am grateful to my colleague Glyn Purseglove for this point.

18. See especially the comments of Nigel Love as well as of David Olsen throughout this book.

19. Jerome J. McGann, *The Textual Condition* (Princeton, N.J.: Princeton University Press, 1991).

20. T. J. G. Harris, *P N Review* (Manchester) 19:2 (November–December 1992): 29.

21. Suzanne Reynolds "The Sounding of Texts," *Times Literary Supplement* (25 July 1997): 33.

22. Philip Larkin, *Required Writing* (Londonz; Faber, 1983); 61.

23. Geoffrey Hartman, *The Unremarkable Wordsworth* (London: Methuen, 1987), chap. 7.

24. Eric Gill, *Autobiography* (London: Jonathan Cape, 1940), 120.

25. Harriet Martineau *Autobiography* (London: Virago Press, 1983), 1:119; C. S. Lewis *Surprised By Joy: The Shape of My Early Life* (London: HarperCollins, 1977), 113–14; Roland Barthes, *The Pleasure of the Text*, trans. Richard Miller (New York: Hill & Wang, 1975); Peter Redgrove, "A Poet in Teaching," *Helix* (Australia), 9–10 (double issue): 88–102. Jonathan Miller spoke of "the joys of the purely manual handling of books . . . there is something about the idea of turning pages backwards and forwards very quickly . . . the texture of the paper, the pleasure of typography, the bindings, the taking it down from a shelf." George Steiner spoke of the "inward dialogue with oneself and with (books) which no other form can replace" (BBC program "Brains Trust," quoted in *Times Literary Supplement* (12 January 1996): 14).

26. Saunders Lewis, "David Jones's Inscriptions," *Poetry Wales* 8:3 (winter 1972): 56.

PART 1. THE ABECEDARY; AND CHAPTER 1. BEGINNINGS

1. The many facts adduced in this opening statement are not referenced in the footnotes. Quite simply one would have to reference virtually every sentence. Even if that were possible or desirable, it would be difficult to choose one source over another, for all this material can be found in one or other—commonly more than one—of the many introductions, handbooks, and guides available on the various areas covered. I hope no reader experiences any inconvenience.

2. Ferdinand de Saussure, *Course in General Linguistics*, trans. Wade Baskin (London: Fontana/Collins, 1959), 24; Leonard Bloomfield, *Language* (London: George Allen & Unwin, 1933), 21.

3. Renownedly in our time, Richard Dawkins, *The Blind Watchmaker* (Harlow: Longmans, 1986), eyeball discussed.

4. David Crystal, *Cambridge Encyclopedia of Language* (Cambridge: Cambridge University Press, 1987), 288–91; Leanne Hinton, Johanna Nichols, and John J. Ohala, eds., *Sound Symbolism* (Cambridge: Cambridge University Press, 1995).

5. Robin Dunbar, *Grooming, Gossip, and the Evolution of Language* (London: Faber & Faber, 1995); "Grey Natter" in *Times Higher* (London), 26 January 1996, 13; Mircea Eliade, *The Myth of the Eternal Return* (London: Penguin Arkana, 1989); John Reader, *Missing Links: The Hunt for Earliest Man* (London: Penguin Books, 1981), esp. 55–56; Myra Shackley, *Neanderthal Man* (London: Duckworth, 1980), esp. 111–13.

6. "Chinese Researchers Find Evidence of Earliest Writing," *Independent* (London), 17 March 1993; Crystal, *Cambridge Encyclopedia*, 196.

7. For useful and detailed accounts, see Jack Goody, *The Interface between the Written and the Oral* (Cambridge: Cambridge University Press, 1987); Georges Jean, *Writing: The Story of Alphabets and Scripts*, trans. Jenny Oates (London: Thames & Hudson, 1992).

8. Henri Bergson, *Creative Evolution*, trans. Arthur Mitchell (London: Macmillan, 1911), 168.

9. David L. Edwards, *A Key to the Old Testament* (Glasgow: Collins, 1976), 82.

10. Robert Warren, "Perceptual Basis for the Evolution of Speech," in *The Genesis of Language*, ed. Marge E. Lansberg (The Hague: Mouton, 1988), 101–10; Steven Pinker, *The Language Instinct* (London: Penguin Books, 1995).

11. Richard A. Firmage, *The Alphabet Abecedarium: Some Notes on Letters* (London: Bloomsbury, 2000), 175.

12. Ibid., 107, 111, 205, 168.

13. Umberto Eco, *The Search for the Perfect Language*, trans. James Fentress (Oxford: Blackwell, 1994), 148. The letter H (in the word for the god Ptah) was "the image of the god Heh with his arms raised." Even as the alphabet emerged, the writing was still ideographic. Chris Stray kindly pointed out to me interpretations for the letters A and B that have been suggested.

14. But here is another interesting one. "'Our house is full of tulips, if you want any,' said Charles inexplicably. . . . .*Tulips*, I thought, staring at the jumble of letters before me. Had the ancient Greeks known them under a different name, if they'd had tulips at all? The letter *psi*, in Greek, is shaped like a tulip." Donna Tartt's novel *The Secret History* (London: Penguin, 1993), 343–44.

15. Michael D. Coe, *Breaking the Maya Code* (New York: Thames & Hudson, 1992).

16. Joseph F. Graham, *Onomatopoetics* (Cambridge: Cambridge University Press, 1992), 108.

17. David R. Olsen, *The World on Paper* (Cambridge: Cambridge University Press, 1994).

18. Nigel Love, "The Locus of Languages in a Redefined Linguistics," in *Redefining Linguistics*, ed. Hayley G. Davies and Talbot J. Taylor (London: Routledge, 1990), 110, my emphasis.

19. Kwame Gyekye, *An Essay on African Philosophical Thought: The Akan Conceptual Scheme* (Cambridge: Cambridge University Press, 1987).

20. *From Primitives to Zen: A Thematic Sourcebook of the History of Religions*, ed. Mircea Eliade (London: Collins, 1967), 83. Some of the other references in this chapter are cited from this work; others are from *Sacred Texts of the World: A Universal Anthology*, ed. Ninian Smart & Richard D. Hecht (London: Macmillan Reference Books, 1992), 9.

21. A. C. Bouquet, *Sacred Books of the World* (Harmondsworth: Penguin Books, 1951), 132.

22. Smart and Hecht, *Sacred Texts*, 11.

23. Claude Levi-Strauss, *The Savage Mind* (London: Weidenfeld & Nicholson, 1972), 184–85.

24. Cited in Alberto Manguel, *A History of Reading* (London: HarperCollins Flamingo, 1997), 67.

25. Daniel Cohn-Sherbok, *The Crucified Jew* (London: HarperCollins Fount, 1992), 59–60; Berjouhi Bowker, *The Word as Image* (London: Studio Vista 1970),

8; Firmage *Alphabet,* 95; Nora Chadwick, *The Celts* (Harmondsworth: Pelican Books, 1970), 248–49; Bowker, *Word as Image,* 8.

26. Christmas Humphreys, *Buddhism* (Harmondsworth: Penguin Books, 1951), 233.

27. Michel Foucault, *The Order of Things* (London: Tavistock, 1970), 207.

28. On the nasals, see John Ray, reviewing Merritt Ruhlen, *On The Origin of Languages* (Stanford: Stanford University Press, 1993) in *Times Literary Supplement* (London), 11 November 1994, 34. "'Mama', 'papa', negatives in 'n' and interrogatives with 'm' . . . are probably determined by basic physiology. . . ." "There is a pattern in the old world which uses 'm' in the first person and t/s in the second. Similarly, the American languages are united in preferring 'n' in the first person and 'm' in the second."

29 The poet Edward Thomas once illustrated this point particularly well. He quoted the poet Algernon Charles Swinburne as calling Shakespeare's *As You Like It* "one of the most flawless examples of poetic and romantic drama that ever cast its charm upon eternity." Thomas's comment: "Those last seven words are of no use except that they lengthen the sentence and make it more high-flown. . . . [they] *fall without an echo into the brain*" (my emphasis). Edward Thomas, *A Language Not to Be Betrayed: Selected Prose,* ed. Edna Longley (Manchester: Carcanet, 1981), xxxvii.

30. Humphreys, *Buddhism,* 127.

31. *Bhagavad Gita,* trans. Juan Mascaro (Harmondsworth: Penguin Books, 1962), 14.

32. W. E. H. Stanner, "Religion, Totemism, and Symbolism," *Aboriginal Man in Australia,* ed. R. M. Berndt and C. H. Berndt (Glasgow: Angus & Robertson, 1965), 231.

33. See for example Peter Atkins, *Creation Revisited* (London: Penguin Books, 1992), 129 and passim.

34. Thomas à Kempis, "Of Avoiding Superfluity in Words," 1: chap. 10 of *The Imitation of Christ* (London: Dent, 1960); Thomas Henry Huxley, *Thomas Henry Huxley on Education,* ed. C. Bibby (Cambridge: Cambridge University Press, 1971), 105 ("How revolting it is to meet someone who knows nothing but what others have written"); William Wordsworth, "A narrow girdle of rough stones and crags" line 72 *The Poems,* edited in 2 volumes by John O. Hayden (Harmondsworth: Penguin Books 1997) 1: 430) Gyekye, *Essay,* 64; Humphreys, *Buddhism,* 14; Stanley Cavell, *Must We Mean What We Say?* (Cambridge: Cambridge University Press, 1976), 85–86. Cf. also Proverbs 18:27: "He that knoweth, spareth his words."

Chapter 2. Ancient Greece

1. Barry B. Powell, *Homer and the Origin of the Greek Alphabet* (Cambridge: Cambridge University Press, 1991).

2. Homer, *Iliad,* trans. Richmond Lattimore (Chicago: University of Chicago Press, 1951), 21, 31.

3. Gerald F. Else, *The Origin and Early Form of Greek Tragedy* (New York: W. W. Norton, 1972), 47. Else's emphasis. Else adds: "This contest established the solid base of all Attic literature to come; for that literature remains close to Homer and is based from beginning to end on firm expectation of love of the poet and close knowledge of his text by the whole Athenian people."

4. Denis Feeney, "All Talk, No Substance," *Times Literary Supplement,* 28 April 2000, 9.

5. *The Oxford Companion to Classical Literature,* comp. Paul Harvey (Oxford: Oxford University Press, 1984), 206.

6. Sir Philip Sidney "An Apologie for Poetrie," in *The Prelude to Poetry,* ed. Ernest Rhys (London: Dent, Everyman Library, 1927), 44; Percy Bysshe Shelley, "A Defence of Poetry," in Ibid., 213.

7. Edith Hamilton, *The Greek Way to Western Civilization* (New York: Mentor Books, 1948), chap. 4.

8. Nicholas Denyer, *Language, Thought, and Falsehood in Ancient Greek Philosophy* (London: Routledge, 1995).

9. Quoted in Brian Vickers, "Skills to Move Men's Minds" *Times Literary Supplement* (London), 11 February 2000, 10.

CHAPTER 3. AUGUSTINE, AQUINAS, AND OTHERS

1. Augustine, *City of God,* trans. Henry Bettenson (Harmondsworth: Penguin Classics, 1972), 315. Augustine also states that at age twenty he read Aristotle's *Ten Categories* and gained little from it. *Confessions* IV 16.

2. A. M. Renwick, *The Story of the Church* (Grand Rapids, Mich.: Eerdmans 1958), 25, 39–41.

3. Henry Chadwick, *Augustine* (Oxford: Oxford University Press 1986), 35.

4. Garry Wills, *Saint Augustine* (London: Weidenfeld & Nicolson 1999), 29.

5. For example, Rabbi Julia Neuberger in the *Independent Magazine* (London), 7 December 1991, 94. Neuberger sees Augustine as one who "set the stage both for the torture of the Inquisition and the adulation of monasticism," and as "the product of repressed sexuality, a man whose energy and power could have been put to much better use."

6. David Knowles, *The Evolution of Medieval Thought* (London: Longmans 1962); 34.

7. For a brief useful summary of Augustine's influence down the centuries, see Chadwick, *Augustine,* 1–3.

8. M. H. Abrams, *Natural Supernaturalism* (New York: W. W. Norton, 1971), 84.

9. Rowan Williams, *On Christian Theology* (Oxford: Blackwell, 2000), 7.

10. Jacob Burckhardt, *The Civilization of the Renaissance in Italy* (London: Phaidon Press, 1940), 322.

11. "The great poets . . . who have first brought into consciousness, and next have clothed in words, those grand catholic feelings that belong to the grand catholic situations of life," in Thomas de Quincey, *Recollections of the Lakes and the Lake Poets,* ed. David Wright (Harmondsworth: Penguin English Library, 1970), 143. "No doubt this classical garment . . . served to clothe much that was foul and malicious," in Burckhardt, *Civilization,* 229, on Renaissance Italian. "Clothes the whole thing in magnificent poetry," H. D. F. Kitto, *Form and Meaning in Drama* (London: Methuen, 1959), 9, discussing the *Agamemnon.* De Quincey's distinction of thought and word into temporal stages makes explicit the deep distinction in all such formulations.

12. John Henry Newman, *The Idea of a University,* ed. I. T. Ker (Oxford: Clarendon Press, 1976), part 2, essay 3, "English Catholic Literature," sect. 4.

13. The example outside the *Confessions* is Augustine, *De Vera Religione,*

22:42. The idea is that although a line of verse occupies time, it is timeless also. "That is how a line can have a lovely meter that seems quite natural even though you can't say any two of its syllables at once. A syllable is uttered only when the previous one is over, and it goes on like that to the end of the line. So when the last one is said by itself, with no residue from the sounds of the others, it can still clinch the line's beauty and shape, because it is still part of the whole texture."

14. Karl Barth, *The Doctrine of the Word of God*, vol. 1, *Church Dogmatics* (Edinburgh: T. & T. Clark, 1936).

15. In fact, this is not the first case ever recorded. As early as the fourth century B.C., Alexander the Great silently read a letter from his mother—to the bewilderment of his soldiers—while in 63 B.C., Julius Caesar is recorded as silently perusing a note from Cato's sister. But the case of Ambrose is certainly the earliest found in Western literature. Manguel, *History of Reading*, 43.

16. "Sight so dominates our intellectual practices that we have great difficulty conceiving of an alternative. In order to achieve understanding, we make visible diagrams and charts, so that we can 'see what is happening' and if we want to 'see if something is possible,' we try to imagine it 'in our mind's eye.' Would a race of blind thinkers who relied on hearing be capable of comprehending with the aid of tunes, jingles, and squawks in the mind's ear everything we comprehend thanks to mental 'images'?" Daniel C. Dennett, *Consciousness Explained* (London: Penguin, 1991), 56.

17. R. W. Southern, *The Making of the Middle Ages* (London: Hutchinson, 1953).

18. For text of this letter, see ibid., 60.

19. James Anthony Froude, *Essays in Literature and History* (London: J. M. Dent, Everyman Edition, 1906), 147.

20. Anthony Kenny, *Aquinas* (Oxford: Oxford University Press, 1980), 9; Williams, *On Christian Theology,* 146n.

21. Walter Hilton, *The Ladder of Perfection,* trans. Leo Sherley-Price (Harmondsworth: Penguin Books, 1957), 59–60; Wittgenstein, *Philosophical Investigations,* 4–5; Dionysus (anon), *The Cloud of Unknowing,* trans. Clifton Wolters (Harmondsworth: Penguin Books, 1961), sects. 37–39; Kempis, *Imitation of Christ,* chap. 10.

22. Allan B. Wolter, *The Philosophical Theory of John Duns Scotus* (Ithaca: Cornell University Press, 1990), chap. 4.

23. Leo Schaya, *The Universal Meaning of the Kabbalah,* trans. Nancy Pearson (London: Allen & Unwin, 1971), 16.

24. Harold Bloom, *The Anxiety of Influence* (Oxford: Oxford University Press, 1973), and his *A Map of Misreading* (Oxford: Oxford University Press, 1975).

25. *La Disparition* has been translated into English by Gilbert Adair *(La Void),* also with no eeeee.

26. See note 12 to introduction.

27. Ninian Smart, *The Religious Experience of Mankind* (Glasgow: Collins Fontana, 1971), 541.

CHAPTER 4. THE REFORMATION AND HUMANISM

1. David Daniel, "Translating the Bible," in *The Nature of Religious Language* (London: Roehampton Institute, Sheffield Academic Press, 1996), 68–87.

2. Curtius, *European Literature;* Foucault, *Order of Things.*

3. Recently the present writer was fortunate enough to see and handle the Lichfield Gospels, a manuscript in that cathedral and which probably dates from the seventh century. Fine as undoubtedly are the illuminated pages and so-called "carpet pages"—reversible geometric diagrams—it was the superlative unadorned script of some near-genius monk, page after page, that had the most stunning effect.

4. See Curtius *European Literature,* but also J. Huizinga, *The Waning of the Middle Ages* (Harmondsworth: Penguin Books, 1955).

5. Dante Alighieri, *The Divine Comedy* trans. and intr. C. H. Sisson (Manchester: Carcanet New Press, 1980).

6. Francois Wendel, *Calvin,* trans. Philip Mairet (London: Collins Fontana, 1963), 116.

7. Eamonn Duffy, *The Voices of Morebath: Reformation and Rebellion in an English Village* (London and New Haven: Yale University Press, 1996).

8. Surely the first line here is behind Edmund Blunden's lines written to commemorate the British twentieth-century war dead, and recited every year at the 11 November ceremony at the Cenotaph in London:

> We shall grow old, as they will not grow old.
> Age shall not wither, nor the years condemn.
> At the going down of the sun and in the morning,
> We shall remember them.

CHAPTER 5. LETTERS ARE FEW

1. "It is in cultural life as in speech; selection is the prime necessity. The numbers of sounds that can be produced by our vocal cords and our oral and nasal cavities are practically unlimited . . . (yet) a language that used even a few hundred of the possible—and actually recorded—phonetic elements could not be used for communication." Ruth Benedict, *Patterns of Culture* (London: Routledge & Kegan Paul, 1935), 16. I am grateful to David Crystal for a personal communication stating that we use several *phones* even though we use few *phonemes.*

2. Elissa Newport et al., discussed in Terrence Deacon, *The Symbolic Species* (London: Penguin Books, 1997), 128–35.

3. John A. C. Greppin, "In the Beginning was the Mark," in *Times Literary Supplement,* 19 April 1996, 13.

4. Francis Thompson, *Crofting Years* (Western Isles: Luath Press, 1984), 122.

5. Powell, *Homer,* 78. Powell adds that although this hieroglyphic system contained a basic twenty-four "uniliterals" (signs standing for a single consonant plus unspecified vowel)—yet the typical Egyptian writer "never showed the slightest interest in using this simplification, though it had been implicit in his signary from the beginning."

6. Samuel Taylor Coleridge, *Aids to Reflection,* ed. John Beer (London: Routledge/Princeton; Princeton, N.J.: Princeton University Press, 1993), 34.

7. The change of prefix—more than one letter though here—can also change a part of speech, as in the rhyme *tigress/progress,* from Wilfred Owen's poem "Strange Meeting."

8. George Puttenham, *The Arte of English Poesie,* ed. Gladys Doidge Willcock and Alice Walker (Cambridge: Cambridge University Press, 1936), 2:108.

9. However, Geoffrey Hartman (1987) and Mark Taylor (Taylor 2002) cite

cases where the word-within-a-word does seem to have literary presence. Hartmann sees "loud" in "clouds" in a key Wordsworth passage where sight and sound have special contrast (Wordsworth, *Prelude*, 1805, 1:350). Taylor notes "die" inside "adieu" as a telling moment in the Hamlet's play-within-a-play before Claudius (*Hamlet*, 5.1.300).

10. Joseph Addison, in *The Spectator* (London: J. M. Dent, 1945), 10 May 1711, 186.

11. Graham, *Onomatopoetics*, 102; Michael Garman, *Psycholinguistics* (Cambridge: Cambridge University Press, 1990), chap. 5; Pinker, *Language Instinct*, 73–82.

12. Sigmund Freud, *Totem and Taboo* (Harmondsworth: Penguin Books 1938 [from 1919], chap. 1; also see Emile Durkheim, *The Elementary Forms of the Religious Life*, trans. Joseph Ward Swain (London: Allen & Unwin, 1915), 2, chaps. 1–7; Peter Worsley, "Groote Eylandt Totemism and *Le Totemism Aujourd'hui*" *The Structural Study of Myth and Totemism*, ed. Edmund Leach (London: Tavistock, 1967).

13. Ina-Stina Ewbank, "Shakespeare and the Arts of Language," in *The Cambridge Companion to Shakespeare Studies*, ed. Stanley Wells (Cambridge: Cambridge University Press, 1986), 49–66, 57.

14. Pinker, *Language Instinct*, 152; later however I will consider this view from a different angle.

15. For the references here cited earlier, see note 34 to chap. 1.

16. "Only once" strictly means "one-ly once," so it is tautology. Of course, that is a purist view, because of the different nuance that "only" has long accrued. Even so, the American use "just once" is often better.

17. John R. Searle, *Speech Acts* (Cambridge: Cambridge University Press, 1969), 59–60. Two of Zipf's main laws of language are as follows. a) The frequency rank of words in a text, and the number of appearances of each, descend by a constant ratio. (If you rank words by appearance—highest, second, third, etc.—and then count the frequencies of each—108, 59, 38, etc., multiplying these two numbers together always brings roughly the same figure. The inference of this evenness of ratio is that there is a kind of subconscious pull to distribute words by a sense of their natural usefulness in the language. b) The shorter the word, the greater its frequency. This works dynamically, too, for long words used often tend to get abbreviated: "mike" for microphone, "soccer" for association football, etc. Both principles might be used to support a theory of "least effort"—which would leave "excess" in language as something to be accounted for as unusual psychological or cultural indulgence.

CHAPTER 6. LETTERS ARE STABLE

1. Alfred Fairbank, *A Book of Scripts* (Harmondsworth: King Penguin, 1949), plates 18, 19, 22, 35, 38.

2. Peter Forbes, "A Struggle for Survival," in *The Independent* (London) 5 November 1988.

3. Martineau, *Autobiography*, 1:302.

4. I am grateful to Glyn Pursglove for alerting me to this point.

5. Timothy Buck, "No happyend in sight" [*sic*], in *Times Literary Supplement*, 10 October 1997, 14.

6. Geoffrey Leech, *Principles of Pragmatics* (London: Longmans 1983), 2 (my emphasis).

7. For discussion see for example Charles Altieri, "The Hermeneutics of Literary Indeterminacy: A Dissent from the New Orthodoxy," in *New Literary History* 10:1 (autumn 1978).

8. Samuel Johnson, *Lives of the English Poets,* ed. in 3 volumes by G. B. Hill (Oxford: Clarendon Press, 1905), 1:19; Martineau, *Autobiography,* 2:239; Matthew Arnold, *Essays in Criticism* (New York: A. L. Burt, 1865), 300; W. Somerset Maugham, *Cakes and Ale* (London: Heinemann, 1930), 107 ("He was for long thought to write very bad English, and indeed he gave you the impression of writing with the stub of a blunt pencil; his style was laboured"). The character of Edward Driffield in *Cakes and Ale* is usually held to have been modeled on Thomas Hardy.

9. Jorge Luis Borges, *Labyrinths* (Harmondsworth: Penguin Books, 1970), 62–71.

CHAPTER 7. LETTERS ARE EQUABLE

1. R. H. Robins, *General Linguistics* (London: Longmans, 1993); D. A. Cruse, *Lexical Semantics* (Cambridge: Cambridge University Press, 1986).

2. Stephen Hawking, *A Brief History of Time* (London: Bantam Press, 1988), 128–29.

3. However, repetition of a syntactical category can be tolerated when the individual terms vary. "You have been noisy, lazy, stupid, obstructive, obtuse, bossy, interfering. . . . ." But even here further variation will set in before long: ". . . insolent to your seniors, emotionally up and down, wildly extravagant with money, . . . " An interesting trope is found in English with the string of nouns as adjectives. *The murder, the beach murder, the beach murder trial, the beach murder trial aftermath, the beach murder trial aftermath furore,* and so on.

4. George Steiner, *Real Presences* (London: Faber & Faber Ltd 1989): 56.

5. Ian McEwen, *Enduring Love* (Vintage Books, 1998), 170; Walter Scott, *Guy Mannering* (London: J. M. Dent & Sons, 1968), chap. 54, 395); *The Heart of Midlothian* (Oxford: Oxford University Press, 1991), chap. 32, 317.

6. Ludwig Wittgenstein, *Tractatus Logico-Philosophicus,* trans. D. F. Pears and B. F. McGuinness (London: Routledge & Kegan Paul, 1961), 13:3.221.

7. Garman, *Psycholinguistics,* chaps. 4–7. Manguel, *History of Reading,* (37 and n) also notes that in the late nineteenth century the French ophthalmologist Emile Javal had already discovered that the eye leaps about the page as it reads; indeed, writing's sequential linearity has to cope with this.

CHAPTER 8. LETTERS ARE PHYSICAL

1. Mary Shelley, *Frankenstein* (Oxford: Oxford University Press, World's Classics, 1969), 8.

2. Auden: "If I type out a poem, I immediately see defects which I missed when I looked through it in manuscript. When it comes to a poem by someone else, the severest test I know of is to write it out in longhand." W. H. Auden, *The Dyer's Hand* (London: Faber & Faber, 1963), 17. In a TV interview many years

ago, Noel Coward said that typing a script was always dangerous because it made you think you had finished.

3. I am indebted to Peter Larkin for suggesting this phrase for this aspect of the matter.

4. "Using long words" was once a frequent plaint of uneducated people against show-offs. Not always unjustified, of course, but it was sometimes felt forceful enough to need answering. Frank Swinnerton wrote of Aldous Huxley that, "He uses long words because he thinks in long words; and not because he is aware they are long words." Nicholas Murray, *Aldous Huxley: An English Intellectual* (Little, Brown, 2002), 278. Such talk scarcely appears in the late twentieth or early twenty-first century. But those of smaller vocabulary needn't have worried too much, for many quite ordinary words are fairly long; e.g., *terrifying, afternoon.*

Chapter 9. Letters Are Virtual

1. Thomas Nagel, *The View From Nowhere* (Oxford: Oxford University Press, 1986), 33.

2. Anthony Flew and Alasdair MacIntyre, eds., *New Essays in Philosophical Theology* (London: S.C.M. Press, 1955), 99–105.

3. William Faulkner, *As I Lay Dying*, cited in Malcolm Bradbury and James McFarlane, *Modernism* (Harmondsworth: Penguin Books, 1976), 462. Article author Melvin J. Friedman stated that this novel "is as much about language and its limitations as it is about a mock-burial procession in rural Mississippi."

4. I. A. Richards, *The Philosophy of Rhetoric* (Oxford: Oxford University Press, 1936); Max Black, *Models and Metaphors* (Ithaca: Cornell University Press, 1962).

5. Winifred Nowottny, *The Language Poets Use* (London: Athlone Press, 1962).

6. Paul Ricoeur, *The Rule of Metaphor* (London: Routledge & Kegan Paul, 1978).

7. A. J. Ayer, *Language, Truth, and Logic* (Harmondsworth: Pelican Books, 1971). See especially page 60.

8. Ted Cohen, "Metaphor and the Cultivation of Intimacy," in *Critical Enquiry* 5 (autumn 1978): 3–12 and p. 6; Donald Davidson, "What Metaphors Mean," in Ibid., 31–47, esp. pp. 37–38.

Chapter 10. Letters Are Distributive

1. We have mentioned this topic already. But there are a couple of curious outcomes of this discreteness. One is that a sound-tape can't be run backward, like a film can. There is no oral counterpart to seeing the high-diver come backward up out of the water and end up standing on the high board (Garman 1990, 12). Another outcome is that printing is almost universally noncursive. Cursive typefonts are now widely available in word processor printers, but they seldom get extended use. The word processor has cut out the labor of handwriting, so one might expect cursive typefonts to replace them in personal letters; yet people seem to know that discrete letters are easier on the eye than cursive ones.

2. For example, Wittgenstein 1958, 16, sect. 330; Mary Mothersill, *Beauty Restored* (Oxford: Clarendon Press, 1984), chap. 11.

3. Other poems that notably play the double-letter are Wordsworth's "Simplon Pass" passage (*Prelude,* 1805, VI 553–72) and Thomas Hardy's "On the Departure Platform."

4. Mark Taylor, "Voyeurism and Aposiopesis in Renaissance Poetry," in *Exemplaria* (SUNY, New York): 4: 2: 267–92.

5. J. Mukarovsky, "Standard Language and Poetic Language," in *A Prague School Reader* ed. P. Garvin (Washington: Georgetown University Press, 1964), 17–30, esp. p. 19.

6. Roman Jakobson, "Linguistics and Poetics," in *Style in Language,* ed. T. Sebeok (Cambridge: MIT Press), 350–77, esp. p. 353.

PART 3. THE ABECEDARY IN THE POETS
CHAPTER 11. GEORGE HERBERT

1. For a recent discussion of this aspect in Wordsworth, cf. Leon Waldoff, *Wordsworth in his Major Lyrics* (University Press of Missouri, 2002). The book gives major treatment to "Tintern Abbey."

2. John Carey, *John Donne: Life, Mind, and Art* (London: Faber & Faber, 1981), 24; Amy M.Charles, *A Life of George Herbert* (Ithaca: Cornell University Press, 1977), 56–65, 104–11.

3. George Herbert, *The English Poems of George Herbert,* ed. C. A. Patrides (London: Dent, 1974 [from 1633]), 31.

4. Chana Bloch, *Spelling the Word: George Herbert and the Bible* (Berkeley and Los Angeles: University of California Press, 1985), pt 1.

5. It recalls an old proposal to emend the word in *Macbeth*: "And all our yesterdays have lighted fools / The way to dusty death." Theobald, Cunningham, and others proposed "dusky"; but the parched dirt of the trodden ground surely already captures human sin and/or wretchedness better than either "dusky" there or "(guiltie of) lust (and sinne)" would in Herbert's poem. *Macbeth,* ed. Kenneth Muir (London: Methuen [Arden Shakespeare], 1984), 153–54.

6. See Alan Llywd, "Cynghanedd and English Poetry," *Poetry Wales* 14:1 (summer 1978): 23–58.

7. Helen Vendler, *The Poetry of George Herbert* (Cambridge: Harvard University Press, 1975), 275–76.

8. William Empson, *Seven Types of Ambiguity* (London: Chatto & Windus, 1956), 226.

9. Ggggg and uuuuu have three appearances each; bbbbb, ccccc, sssss, and wwwww have two each; and fffff, lllll, vvvvv, and yyyyy appear only once each. Jjjjj, kkkkk, ppppp, qqqqq, xxxxx, and zzzz do not appear at all.

10. Among them Vendler, *Poetry of George Herbert,* chaps. 3, 7; Bloch, *Spelling the Word,* part 3 John Hollander, *Vision and Resonance: Two Senses of Poetic Form* (New Haven: Yale University Press, 1985), 263–68; Joseph H. Summers, *George Herbert: His Religion and Art* (London: Chatto & Windus, 1954), 123.

11. Geneva Bible, 1560, part 1, folio 267.

12. George Herbert, *The Country Parson, The Temple,* ed. John N. Wall, Jr. (New York: Paulist Press, 1981), 62.

13. Richard Todd, *The Opacity of Signs: Acts of Interpretation in George Herbert's THE TEMPLE* (University Press of Missouri, 1986).

14. As well as Vendler, A. D. Nuttall writes on this point. A. D. Nuttall, *Overheard By God* (London: Methuen, 1980).

15. Louis L. Martz, "Donne and Herbert: Vehement Grief and Silent Tears," in *John Donne Journal* 7:1 (1988): 21–36.

CHAPTER 12. JOHN MILTON

1. Cited in John T. Shawcross, ed., *Milton: The Critical Heritage* (London: Routledge & Kegan Paul, 1970), 101.

2. Johnson, *Lives of the English Poets* 1:189–90.

3. Discussed passim in John Leonard, *Naming in Paradise: Milton and the Language of Adam and Eve* (Oxford: Clarendon Press, 1990).

4. Milton's newness, of language at least, hardly needs debate. However, his close use of sources is sometimes interesting. Cary Plotkin (1989) cites a passage from John Josias Conybeare (in Charles Knight, *Old England*, 1854), which quotes from the Old English poem of the seventh century, about the creation. (This poem is sometimes attributed to Caedmon but the authorship is not certain.) Here is the passage cited by Conybeare:

> Then was the Mighty angry,
> The highest ruler of heaven
> Hurled him from his lofty seat;
> Hate had he gained at his Lord.
> His favour he had lost,
> Incensed with him was the good in his mind.
> Therefore he must seek the gulf
> Of hard hell torment,
> For that he had warr'd wit heaven's Ruler.
> He rejected him then from his favour,
> And cast him into hell,
> Into the deep parts,
> When he became a devil:
> The fiend with all his comrades
> Fell then from heaven above,
> Through as long as three nights and days,
> The angels from heaven into hell.

The parallel in Milton is *Paradise Lost,* I 44–53:

> Him the Almighty Power
> Hurl'd headlong flaming from th'ethereal sky,
> With hideous ruin and combustion, down
> To bottomless perdition, there to dwell
> In adamantine chains and penal fire,
> Who durst defy th' Omnipotent in arms.
> Nine times the space that measures day and night
> To mortal men, he with his horrid crew
> Lay vanquish'd, rolling the fiery gulf,
> Confounded though immortal.

Knight's comment is: "Mr. Conybeare says that the resemblance to Milton is so remarkable . . . that much of this portion might be almost literally translated by a cento of lines from that great poet." Referring admittedly to another passage (the great speech of Satan) Knight continues: "Who can doubt that when the music of that speech of Satan . . . swelled upon Milton's exquisite ear, the first note was struck by the rough harmony of Caedmon?" (Cary H. Plotkin, *The Tenth Muse* [Carbondale & Edwardsville: Southern Illinois University Press, 1989]: appendix, "The Saxon Connection," 150–51). This is a very early passage in Milton's epic, and he may have depended on transliteration more than usually. But of course Milton's newness lies in his invention of his own language by which to render the old material analogously to the way Shakespeare used Plutarch and Holinshed; often equally close materially but with exactly the changes of word that make the poetic difference. As Christopher Hill points out, Milton's enthusiasm for the "chosen people" did not last. He did write a history of England, but it seems to have been largely borrowed, again even transcribed, from others, and it doesn't figure strongly in Milton's writings (A. N. Wilson, *The Life of John Milton* [Oxford: Oxford University Press, 1983], 229–30). No doubt Milton's prodigious memory for both history and the older poets, his flair for languages, and his involvement in contemporary politics, produced a mix from which his "new language" using old material resulted. Incidentally, some of Milton's spellings were peculiar to himself. Writing in 1734, Jonathan Richardson remarks especially on *sent, thir, perfet, soule, eeven, minde, don,* and the two-letter words *hee, mee, yee—scent, their, perfect, soul, even, mind, don, he, me—*in *Paradise Lost.* Jonathan Richardson, "Explanatory Notes and Remarks on Milton's Paradise Lost," in Helen Darbyshire, ed., *The Early Lives of Milton* (London: Constable, 1932), 305).

5. Christopher Hill, *Milton and the English Revolution* (London: Faber & Faber, 1979), 268.

6. Wilson, *John Milton,* 136.

7. For a skeptical commentary on seventeenth-century political readings of *Paradise Lost,* see Howard Erskine-Hill, "On Historical Commentary: The Example of Milton and Dryden," in *Presenting Poetry: Composition, Publication, Reception,* ed. Howard Erskine-Hill and Richard A. McCabe (Cambridge: Cambridge University Press, 1995), 52–74.

8. Hill, *Milton,* chap. 26.

9. ". . . this fitness, this presence, this condensation, this self-constraint" . . . "(Milton) is too full-stored to show us in much detail one conception, one piece of knowledge. He just shows it to us in a pregnant allusive way, and then he presses on to another." Matthew Arnold, *On Translating Homer* in *On the Classical Tradition,* ed. R. H. Super (Ann Arbor: University of Michigan Press, 1960), 145.

10. Stanley Eugene Fish, *Surprised by Sin: The Reader in Paradise Lost* (Berkeley and Los Angeles: University of California Press, 1971), 107–22.

11. T. S. Eliot, *On Poetry and Poets* (London: Faber & Faber, 1957), 157.

12. Richard Bradford, *A Linguistic History of English Poetry* (London: Routledge, 1993), 78.

13. Thomas de Quincey, *De Quincey as Critic,* ed. John E. Jordan (London: Routledge and Kegan Paul, 1973), 450; Empson, cited in Ricks (note 14, this chapter), page 35 162.

14. Christopher Ricks, *Milton's Grand Style* (Oxford: Oxford University Press, 1963), 35.

15. Richardson, "Explanatory Notes," 199–330; 291, 315.

16. Ninety percent of people registered in Britain as blind today are in fact partly sighted (information provided by Kent Association for the Blind, U.K.).

17. Stevie Davies, *Milton* (Hemel Hempstead: Harvester/Wheatsheaf, 1991).

CHAPTER 13. WILLIAM WORDSWORTH

1. *The Letters of William and Dorothy Wordsworth,* in seven volumes, ed. Ernest de Selincourt, Mary Moorman, Chester L. Shaver, Alan G. Hill, and others (Oxford: Clarendon Press, 1967–88, plus Supplement, 1993), 1:586.

2. William Wordsworth, *The Poems,* edited in two volumes by John O. Hayden (Harmondsworth: Penguin Books, 1977), 2:36.

3. I am most grateful to my watchful colleague Peter Larkin for suggesting this cautionary phrase.

4. J. P. Ward, *Wordsworth's Language of Men* (Brighton: Harvester Press, 1984), 39.

5. Stephen Gill, *William Wordsworth: A Life* (Oxford: Clarendon Press, 1989), 152.

6. Marjorie Levinson, *Wordsworth's Great Period Poems: Four Essays* (Cambridge: Cambridge University Press, 1986), 41, her emphasis.

7. John Barrell, "The Uses of Dorothy," in *Wordsworth,* ed. John Williams (Basingstoke: Macmillan Casebooks, 1993), 150.

8. Harold Bloom, *Poetry and Repression* (New Haven: Yale University Press, 1976), 59; Geoffrey Hartman, *The Unremarkable Wordsworth* (London: Methuen, 1987) chap. 7.

9. As to Yeats, the point is almost worth an appendix to itself. Here are a few examples from Yeats's best-known poems. *He that made this knows all the cost, / For he gave all his heart and lost,* from an early poem "Never Give All The Heart"; *I saw, before I had well finished, / All suddenly mount* ("The Wild Swans at Coole"); *All, all are in my thoughts tonight being dead* ("In Memory of Major Gregory"); *I balanced all, brought all to mind* ("An Irish Airman Foresees his death"); *But in the grave all, all shall be renewed* ("Broken Dreams"); *And prove of all imaginable things / The most unlike, being my anti-self. . . . all that I seek* ("Ego Dominus Tuus"); *Why should not you/Who know it all ring at his door. . . . .?. . . . The strange reward of all that discipline* ("The Phases of the Moon"); *All's changed, changed utterly / A terrible beauty is born* ("Easter 1916"—the phrase *all's changed* also appeared in "The Wild Swans at Coole"); *That all her thoughts may like the linnet be. . . . / Where all's accustomed, ceremonious* ("A Prayer for my Daughter"); *For I would ask a question of them all. . . . / As I would question all, come all who can* ("The Tower"); *Such thought—such thought have I that hold it tight / Till meditation master all its parts* ("All Souls' Night"). The last-named example—and its title—make the point about Yeats and his life-long project to, as he put it, hammer his thoughts into a unity. His "all" is inclusive; Wordsworth's aspires to general universality unnamed. Both exploit the rolle "all," which could have been spelled other ways in English; surely to lesser effect.

10. Kenneth R. Johnson, "The Politics of 'Tintern Abbey'" in *The Wordsworth Circle* 14:1 (winter 1983): 7; *The Hidden Wordsworth: Poet, Lover, Rebel, Spy* (New York: W. W. Norton, 1998), 596.

11. The passage talks of fever in a tone of fervor. I am not aware that the two terms are connected etymologically. Certainly the Latin noun *fervor* (boiling heat, ardor, vehemence) has no counterpart in Latin like "fevor," but they could perhaps have reached overlap in Old or Middle English.

12. No doubt the point shouldn't be labored, but it is surely striking now to note together the four letters that have greatest increase in *Tintern Abbey* over their frequency in all English. The letters are mmmmm, uuuuu, wwwww, and yyyyy. The last-named is the only one with either ascender or descender. All four are open

orally and quiet in visual design. The poem's gentle gradualism and hesitant movement forward are marked by such means.

13. Jerome J. McGann, *The Romantic Ideology: A Critical Investigation* (Chicago: University of Chicago Press, 1983), 85–88.

14. Anne K. Mellor, *Romanticism and Gender* (New York: Routledge, 1993), 19; Barrell, "Uses of Dorothy."

15. Jared Curtis, ed., *The Fenwick Notes of William Wordsworth* (Bristol: Bristol Classical Press, 1993), 4.

16. John O. Hayden, "The Road To Tintern Abbey," in *The Wordsworth Circle* 12:4 (autumn 1981): 211–16.

17. Letters reveal Wordsworth calling the poem "the Wye &c" to Coleridge in 1803 (Letters 1:425); "the Poem upon the Wye" to close family friend Catherine Clarkson in 1815 (3:188); "my own Lines upon the Wye" to an Edinburgh librarian R. P. Gillies in 1817 (3:384); and "the blank verse poem on the river Wye" to Henry Taylor in 1823 (4:237). William's brother John calls it "the Poem on *The Wye*" (his emphasis) in 1805 (1:535). Johnson himself notes that years later Sara Coleridge refers to "the Nightingale and the River Y" [*sic*] when telling her husband which poems in *Lyrical Ballads* were proving the most popular (Johnson 1998, 677). And in the love letters of William and Mary of summer 1812, the line *O Sylvan Wye thou Wanderer through the Woods* is gently chanted back and forth between them in four successive letters (Darlington 174, 197–98, 227, 241–42). The letters of that summer mention the Wye at least twenty times. Tintern Abbey is mentioned only three times, two of them cursory and none in connection with the poem, though in one case Mary clearly had it in mind (Darlington 166, 219, 220). Wordsworth usually only refers to the poem as "Tintern Abbey" when classifying his poems or dealing with printing or publishing (1809, 2:335; 1814, 3:177; 1826, 4:444). To Charles Lamb and Thomas de Quincey, once each, he calls the poem "Tintern Abbey" (1801, 1:316, 1804, 1:455). These are virtually all the references to the poem in the lifetime's letters.

In an earlier article Kenneth Johnson (1983) appears to claim that the poem was known to Wordsworth and his circle as "Tintern Abbey." This is "evidenced most recently" (said Johnson) "in Beth Darlington's edition of Wordsworth's love letters to his wife, where he speaks of 'the Tintern Abbey . . . of all my poems The one [in] which I speak of it will be the most beloved by me'" (page 9). In fact the full text from Darlington runs: "You cannot think how much dearer the Wye is to me since you have seen it: I loved it deeply before on most tender remembrances & considerations but now that you have seen it also & know it, & we [now] can talk of it together what a sanctity will it attain in my mind, and of all my poems The one [in] which I speak of it will be the most beloved by me" (Darlington 241–42). Tintern Abbey is not mentioned anywhere; the "it" clearly refers to the Wye. Johnson has dropped the point from his recent book (1998, 590–98).

This long note has been necessary to underline the clear sense, to the poet and his wife, and usually to others except in formal cases, that the poem is about the river.

18. Like wwwww, the letter mmmmm has ancient ties with water. The Phoenician word for "water" was "mem" and most scholars agree this was originally a pictograph for water (Firmage, *Alphabet,* 150). Mmmmm's strong presence in the poem underlines this point although it is certainly true too that much of Wordsworth's poetry deeply requires and evokes the presence of water as the occasion of its truth.

Chapter 14. Emily Dickinson

1. Joan Kirkby, *Emily Dickinson* (Basingstoke: Macmillan, 1991), 137; Harold Bloom, *The Western Canon: The Books and Schools of the Ages* (London: Macmillan, 1995), 291; James Reeves, "Introduction" in *Selected Poems of Emily Dickinson* (London: Heinemann, 1959), ix-lii.

2. Jan Montefiore, *Feminism and Poetry* (London: Routledge & Kegan Paul/ Pandora, 1987), 168, 175; Helen McNeil, *Emily Dickinson* (London: Virago, 1986), 3.

3. Sandra M. Gilbert and Susan Gubar, *The Madwoman in the Attic* (New Haven: Yale University Press, 1979); Montefiore, *Feminism,* chap. 3; Adrienne Rich, "When We Dead Awaken," in *On Lies, Secrets, and Silence* (London: Virago 1980); Margaret Homans, *Women Writers and Poetic Identity* (Princeton: Princeton University Press, 1980).

4. For standard letter-frequencies in English see chap. 5. The ranking in detail for the list of words just given is E 16, O 10, G 9, A 8, D 7, B and Y 6, S and W 5, L P R and U 4, I and N 3, H K and M 2, C J T X and F 1, Q V and Z 0. Total 105 letters.

5. Maybe Dickinson is recalling Donne's "Hymn to God my God, in my Sickness." Both poems see death as narrowing to a small room in which one encounters God (Dickinson's "King"). Dickinson's Fly replaces Donne's equally three-letter "map" and its buzzing his more classical "I shall be made thy music." The parallels could be taken deeper.

6. Patrocinio P. Schweickart, "Reading Ourselves: Toward a Feminist Theory of Reading," in *Speaking of Gender,* ed. Elaine Showalter (London: Routledge, 1989), 17–44; 30.

7. Roman Jakobson, *Fundamentals of Language* (The Hague: Mouton, 1971), pt. 2.

8. Again pursuing the word-length issue in Dickinson, there is an interesting distribution in this poem 480, which may add to the strange feeling of disorganization it emits. I know of no average or typical word-length distribution in English, but one might suggest two or three likely patterns. Words might decrease in number the longer they get (with one-letter words of course an exception anyway); they might hold up in roughly equally numbers up to about the six-letter mark and then get regular decline; or there might be varying rates depending on outside factors such as vernacular, degree of speaker's education, and the nature of the topic in hand. In this poem the second rule seems to apply, but only up to six letters, at which point it breaks down entirely. The totals are: one-letter words 3, two letters 20, three letters 25, four letters 14, five letters 8, six letters 5; and then crucially— seven letters 8, eight letters 1, nine letters 6, ten letters 1 (total 91 words). This seems hardly accounted for by the variation likely in any short sample because the ups-and-downs for the four longest words are so marked. I sense this rather, if it is anything at all, to be again an expression of Dickinson's tiny-immense pairing.

9. Jacques Derrida, *Of Grammatology*, trans. Gayatri Chakravorty Spivak (Baltimore: Johns Hopkins University Press, 1974); *Writing and Difference* translated by Alan Bass (London: Routledge & Kegan Paul 1978).

10. Claude Levi-Strauss, *The Raw and the Cooked* (London: Jonathan Cape, 1970).

11. In *Winter Pollen,* ed. William Scammell (London: Faber & Faber, 1994), 158.

CHAPTER 15. T. S. ELIOT

1. "Incremental repetition" is F. O. Matthiesen's phrase. Cf. also the very marked presence of the letter ppppp in the early quatrain poems, especially "Sweeney Erect," "A Cooking Egg," "The Hippopotamus," and "Mr Eliot's Sunday Morning Service."

2. For "spellbound," see Grover Smith, *The Waste Land* (London: Allen & Unwin, 1983), 52.

3. Jessie L. Weston, *From Ritual to Romance* (Cambridge: Cambridge University Press, 1920).

4. Presented in 1917 in T. S. Eliot, "Tradition and the Individual Talent" in *Selected Essays* (London: Faber & Faber, 1951).

5. David Trotter, *The Making of the Reader* (Basingstoke: Macmillan, 1984), 41.

6. Maud Ellmann, *The Poetics of Impersonality: T. S. Eliot and Ezra Pound* (Brighton: Harvester Press, 1987), 100.

7. Edmund Wilson, *Axel's Castle* (New York: Scribner, 1931), 106.

8. Cited in Erik Svarny, *"The Men Of 1914": T. S. Eliot and Early Modernism* (Milton Keynes: Open University Press, 1988), 23.

9. Peter Ackroyd, *T. S. Eliot* (London: Sphere Books/Abacus, 1984), 119.

10. On 2 October 1919. *The Letters of T. S. Eliot,* vol. 1, ed. Valerie Eliot (London: Faber & Faber, 1988), 336.

11. T. S. Eliot, *The Use of Poetry and the Use of Criticism* (London: Faber & Faber, 1933), 144–5.

12. T. S. Eliot, *To Criticize the Critic* (London: Faber & Faber, 1965), 126.

13. Helen Gardner, *The Composition of Four Quartets* (London: Faber & Faber, 1978), 5.

14. T. S. Eliot, *After Strange Gods* (London: Faber & Faber, 1934), 40–1.

15. Stephen Medcalf, "The Shaman's Secret Heart," in (*London*) *Times Literary Supplement,* 2 October 1992: 10–12; 10.

16. Eliot, *To Criticize the Critic,* 132; his emphases.

PART 3. THE ABECEDARY
CHAPTER 16. LANGUAGE-MIND THEORIES

1. See notes 7 and 8 to introduction.

2. Cited in McGann, *Textual Condition,* 95.

3. Graham, *Onomatopoetics,* 199–214; David Bromwich, *A Choice of Inheritance* (Cambridge: Harvard University Press, 1989), 264–91.

4. Noam Chomsky, *Selected Readings,* ed. J. P. B. Allen and Paul Van Buren (London: Oxford University Press, 1971), 43.

5. Jean Aitchison, *Words in the Mind: An Introduction to the Mental Lexicon* (Oxford: Basil Blackwell, 1994), 8.

6. J. L. Austin, *How To Do Things With Words,* ed. J. O. Urmson and Marina Sbisa (Oxford: Oxford University Press, 1971).

7. Searle, *Speech Acts,* 66–67.

8. C. S. Lewis and E. M. W. Tillyard, *The Personal Heresy: A Controversy* (London: Oxford University Press, 1939); W. K. Wimsatt, "The Intentional Fallacy" in *The Verbal Icon* (London: Methuen, 1970), and others.

9. Richard Ohmann, "Speech, Literature, and the Space Between," in *Essays in Modern Stylistics,* ed. Donald C. Freeman (London and New York: Methuen, 1981), 367; Stanley Eugene Fish, *Is There A Text in This Class?* (Cambridge: Harvard University Press, 1980), 222, 69; Wolfgang Iser, *The Act of Reading* (London: Routledge & Kegan Paul 1978): 60.

10. Freidrich Schleiermacher, "The Hermeneutics (Outline of the 1819 Lectures)" in *New Literary History* (autumn 1978): 1–16; Wilhelm Dilthey, "The Rise of Hermeneutics," trans. H. P. Rickman, in W. Dilthey, *Selected Writings* (Cambridge: Cambridge University Press, 1976), 246–63.

CHAPTER 17. UNCONSCIOUSNESS AND CONSCIOUSNESS

1. Sigmund Freud, *The Interpretation of Dreams,* trans. James Strachey (Harmondsworth: Pelican Books, 1976), part VI A–E.

2. Sigmund Freud, *The Psychopathology of Everyday Life,* trans. Alan Tyson (London: Ernest Benn, 1960), 125.

3. Anthony Storr, *Jung* (London: Collins/Fontana 1973), 52–53, 58–59.

4. The very first stanza of Dante's *Divine Comedy* was written over six hundred years earlier:

> When I came to the middle part of life
> I found myself in an obscure forest
> And at once realized I had lost my way
>
> (*Inferno,* 1:1–3)

5. From *Finnegans Wake*; cited in Richard Ellmann, *James Joyce* (Oxford: Oxford University Press, 1983), 466. Joyce's destructiveness has been suggested elsewhere. "Today I am much nearer seeing Joyce as a purely disintegrating force, a sacred monster. . . . Writers who give themselves up to the destruction of language are, as far as they know, innocent of the impulse to destroy civilization. But the roots of the impulse run underground a long way, to the point where the smoke from burning books becomes the smoke issuing from the ovens of death camps. . . ." Storm Jameson, *Journey from the North* 2 vols. (London: Virago Press, 1984), 1:245.

6. Jacques Lacan (i), "The mirror stage as formative of the function of the I" (1949), in *Jacques Lacan: Ecrits, A Selection,* trans. Alan Sheridan (London: Tavistock, 1977), 1–7; esp. p. 2.

7. Jacques Lacan (ii), "The function and field of speech and language in psychoanalysis." In Ibid., 30–113; 48, 86.

8. Jacques Lacan (iii), "The agency of the letter in the unconscious or reason since Freud." In Ibid., 146–78; 153.

9. Raymond Tallis, "The Shrink from Hell," (*Times Higher,* 31 October 1997, page 20; Richard Webster, *Why Freud Was Wrong* (London: Harper/Collins, 1995); Richard Webster, "The Bewildered Visionary" *Times Literary Supplement,* 16 May 1997, 8–9; Frederick Crews, *The Memory Wars* (London: Granta Books, 1996); Anthony Clare "The Final Analysis" *Sunday Times,* 17 September 1995.

10. " . . . my selfbeing, my consciousness and feeling of myself, that taste of myself, of *I* and *me* above and in all things, which is more distinctive than the taste of ale or alum, more distinctive than the smell of walnutleaf [*sic*] or camphor, and is incommunicable by any means to any man . . . Nothing else in nature comes

near this unspeakable stress of pitch, distinctiveness and selving, this selfbeing of my own. Nothing explains it or resembles it, except so far as this, that other men to themselves have the same feeling." From "Notes on the Spiritual Exercises," in *Gerard Manley Hopkins,* ed. Catherine Phillips (Oxford: Oxford University Press, 1986), 282.

11. David Chalmers, *The Conscious Mind: in Search of a Fundamental Theory* (Oxford: Oxford University Press, 1995).

12. Susan Greenfield, "Dances with neurons," in *(London) Times Higher,* 2 February 1996, 22; also see her *The Private Life of the Brain* (London: Allen Lane, 2000), 180.

13. Jerry Fodor, "Do we have it in us?" in *(London) Times Literary Supplement,* 16 May 1997, 3–4; "The Trouble with Psychological Darwinism," in *London Review of Books,* 22 January 1998, 11–13.

14. Cited in Patricia Churchland, "Does consciousness emerge from quantum processes?" in *Consciousness,* supplement in *(London) Times Higher,*) 5 April 1996, i-xii; vi; Philip Johnson-Laird, *The Computer and the Mind* (London: HarperCollins Fontana, 1988), 388.

15. Susan Blackmore, *The Meme Machine* (Oxford: Oxford University Press, 1999).

16. Roger Penrose, *The Large, The Small, and the Human Mind* (Cambridge: Cambridge University Press 1994); Stuart Hameroff and Roger Penrose, "Does consciousness emerge from quantum processes?" in *Consciousness,* 5 April 1996, i-xii, vi.

17. Jerry Fodor, "The Trouble with Psychological Darwinism," in *London Review of Books,* 22 January 1998, 11–13, Fodor's emphasis.

18. Ruth Garrett Millikan, "On Mentalese Orthography," in *Dennett and his Critics,* ed. Bo Dahlbom (Oxford: Basil Blackwell, 1993), 97–123.

19. Susan Haack, *Evidence and Inquiry: Towards Reconstruction in Epistemology* (Oxford: Basil Blackwell, 1993).

20. *Consciousness* 5 April 1996, i-xii, esp. p. ii.

21. Ibid., p. vii.

22. Mithen, *Prehistory of the Mind.*

23. Jerry Fodor, "It's the thought that counts," in *London Review of Books,* 28 November 1996, 22–24.

24. Mark Greenberg, "What connects thought and action?" in *(London) Times Literary Supplement,* 23 June 1995, 8, his emphasis.

25. The following may seem far-fetched, but the well-known sense that the vowels each tie to a color might be worth remarking on. The colors differ from person to person. Rimbaud stated that his were "A black, E white, I red, O blue, U green" (Arthur Rimbaud, *A Season in Hell,* Oxford: Oxford University Press, 1973, 77). In a radio broadcast some years back, C. B. Cox said that when he was young he saw words as colored. Letters were colored, too, but he gave no details ("Opinions," channel 4, 8:00 p.m., 28 February 1993). A novel by A. S. Byatt has characters discussing the phenomenon. "Crowe said there was an odd passage in Proust where he associated letters of the alphabet with colors. He claimed that the letter 'i' was red . . . Lady Rose immediately said no, no, i was ice-blue, and Anthea said no, silvery-green . . . (Crowe) asked the others about the letter i . . . Jeremy Norton said 'silver,' Alexander said 'sage,' Wilkie said 'inky' and Caroline muttered 'green'." They then relate colors to other things like clothes, and gender itself. A. S. Byatt, *Still Life* (Harmonsworth: Penguin Books, 1986), 79–80. Recently, poet Roger McGough has attested to the same general phenomenon *(The*

(London) Independent, 18 March 1999). For what it is worth, my own sense of it since childhood has been: a = red, e = blue, I = white, o = yellow, u = gray-white. Readers can doubtless identify their own patterns.

CHAPTER 18. THE AESTHETIC

1. Immanuel Kant, *The Critique of Judgement.* trans. James Creed Meredith (Oxford: Clarendon Press, 1952).
2. Langer, *Feeling and Form,* Mothersill, *Beauty Restored;* Eagleton, *Ideology;* Fish, *Surprised by Sin*; Morris Weitz, "The Role of 'Art' in Aesthetic Theory," in *Journal of Aesthetics and Art Criticism* 15 (1956): 27–35.
3. Paul Hamilton, "'A Shadow of a Magnitude': The Dialectic of Romantic Aesthetics," in *Beyond Romanticism,* ed. Stephen Copley and John Whale (London: Routledge, 1992), 11–31.
4. J. D. Watson, *The Double Helix* (Harmondsworth: Penguin Books, 1970), 174.
5. Paul Davies, *God and The New Physics* (Harmondsworth: Penguin Books, 1983), 220–21, my emphasis; Michael Polanyi, *Personal Knowledge: Towards a Post-Critical Philosophy* (New York: Harper & Row, 1964), 351; Kline, *Mathematics,* 520.
6. Paul Davies, *The Mind of God* (London: Penguin, 1992), 143; Atkins, *Creation Revisited,* 123.
7. Peter Atkins, *The (London) Independent,* 15 March 1996, 17. The Dunblane massacre happened two days earlier.
8. Saul Bellow, *Humboldt's Gift* (Harmondsworth: Penguin Books, 1976), 34.
9. Anthony Easthope, *Poetry as Discourse,* (London: Methuen New Accents, 1983).
10. Elizabeth Wright, *Psychoanalytic Criticism* (London: Methuen New Accents, 1983), 109.
11. The art critic Kenneth Clark repeatedly tried the experiment of walking away from or toward a painting to see if he could establish the instant at which the paint merged into the object represented, or the object represented dissolved into paint. He never succeeded. There was always either object or paint clearly. "I thought I might learn something if I could catch the moment at which this transformation took place, but it proved to be as elusive as the moment between waking and sleeping." Kenneth Clark, *Looking at Pictures* (London: John Murray, 1960), 36–37. The painting Clark always used was Velasquez's "Las Meninas," to which Foucault devoted so much attention at the start of *The Order of Things.*
12. David Jones, *Epoch and Artist* (London: Faber & Faber, 1959), 29.
13. Graham, *Onomatopoetics,* 214–29.

CHAPTER 19. THE POSTMODERN

1. Arthur Kroker and David Cook, *The Postmodern Scene: Excremental Culture and Hyper-Aesthetics* (Basingstoke: Macmillan Education, 1988) has much on the panic theme.
2. BBC "Brains Trust" (cf. supra introduction note 9). Steiner also alluded to

a survey on adolescent reading. Of those interviewed, 85 percent could not read without background noise of some kind. See also note 25 to introduction.

3. Milos Kundera, *The Unbearable Lightness of Being* (London: Faber & Faber, 1984), 6:4.

4. Fredric Jameson, "Postmodernism, or the Cultural Logic of Late Capitalism," in *New Left Review* 146 (1984): 53–92.

5. Sadie Plant, "Connectionism and the Posthumanities," in *Beyond the Book: Theory, Culture, and the Politics of Cyberspace,* ed. Warren Chernaik, Marilyn Deegan, and Andrew Gibson (London: Centre for English Studies, University of London), 33–41; 37–38.

6. For example, Francis Fukuyama, "The End of History?" in *The National Interest* (Washington: I. Kristol, 1989), 3–18; Bill McKibben, *The End of Nature* (London: Penguin Books, 1990); Derrida 1974, pt. 1, chap. 1, "The End of the Book and the Beginning of Writing."

7. Jean-Paul Lyotard, *The Postmodern Condition: A Report on Knowledge,* trans. Geoff Bennington and Brian Massumi (Manchester: Manchester University Press, 1984).

8. Richard Rorty, *Philosophy and the Mirror of Nature* (Oxford: Basil Blackwell, 1980).

9. Jean Baudrillard, *Simulations,* trans. Paul Foss, Paul Patton, and Philip Bleitchman (New York: Semiotext(e), 1983).

10. Jean-Jacques Lecercle, "Postmodernism and Language," in *Postmodernism and Society,* ed. Roy Boyne and Ali Rattansi (Basingstoke: Macmillan, 1990), 76–96.

11. Letter, *(London) The Independent,* 6 February 1991.

12. See note 11 to chap. 3.

13. George F. Landow, "We Are Already Beyond the Book," in *Beyond the Book,* 23–32.

14. John Pickering, "Hypermedia: When Will They Feel Natural?" in Ibid., 43–55; 54.

15. Maureen Caudill and Charles Butler, *Naturally Intelligent Systems* (Cambridge: MIT Press, 1991), 9–11; Dennett, *Consciousness Explained,* 212.

16. "Quite a Buzz," in *Network Plus* supplement, *The Independent,* 25 February 1997, 2–3.

17. Richard A. Lanham, "The Electronic Word: Literary Study and the Digital Revolution," in *New Literary History* 20:2 (winter 1989): 265–90; 273.

CHAPTER 20. CONCLUSION

1. Terry Eagleton, *Literary Theory: An Introduction* (Oxford: Basil Blackwell, 1983), 201–2.

2. Bromwich, *Choice of Inheritance,* 264–91; Eagleton, *Ideology;* David Donoghue, "Doing Things with Words," in "Critical Theory" feature, *(London) Times Literary Supplement,* 15 July 1994, 4–6; Graham, *Onomatopoetics.*

3. Materials like industrial waste and so on are of course also "designed for something else," but they have already achieved that status before being used in art. Plastic bags and iron girders are already plastic bags and iron girders, whereas the abecedary is not consummated until it is distributed in words and sentences.

4. Mary Douglas, *Purity and Danger* (London: Routledge & Kegan Paul, 1966). See also Durkheim, *Elementary Forms.*

Appendixes

1. I am grateful to David Crystal for alerting me to this important point.

2. Saussure, *Course,* 23, 24; Bloomfield, *Language,* 21.

3. Walter Ong, *The Presence of the Word* (University of Minnesota Press 1967), 19, 21.

4. Roy Harris, "On Redefining Linguistics," in *Redefining Linguistics,* ed. Hayley G. Davies and Talbot J. Taylor (London: Routledge, 1990), 18–52; 39.

5. David Crystal, *Linguistics, Language, and Religion* (London: Burns & Oates, 1965): 70–71.

6. In a communication to the present writer, David Crystal explained as follows: "The change of view is this. In the 1965 book I hardly mention writing at all. It doesn't figure. Today it is strongly present. . . . To a phonetician, writing is still secondary. Linguists are different from phoneticians!"

7. Love, "Locus of Languages," 53–117; 110.

8. Full text in *The Journals and Papers of Gerard Manley Hopkins,* ed. Humphrey House and Graham Storey (Oxford: Clarendon Press, 1959), 289–90.

9. James Milroy, *The Language of Gerard Manley Hopkins* (London: Andre Deutsch, 1977), 6.

10. Cary H. Plotkin, *The Tenth Muse* (Carbondale and Edwardsville: Southern Illinois University Press, 1989), 103.

11. J. Hillis Miller, "The Linguistic Moment," in *Gerard Manley Hopkins: Modern Critical Views,* ed. Harold Bloom (New Haven: Chelsea House, 1986), 147–62, esp. 159. If any two chains of words could find even one link between them—something in common between just one term from each list—the two chains themselves were united. The process of accretion went on up from there.

12. Margaret R. Ellsberg, *Created to Praise: The Language of Gerard Manley Hopkins* (Oxford: Oxford University Press, 1987), 81.

13. Elisabeth W. Schneider, "The Dragon at the Gate," in *Gerard Manley Hopkins: Modern Critical Views,* 35.

14. Donald Davie, *Articulate Energy* (London: Routledge & Kegan Paul, 1955), 79, 94.

15. Foucault, *Order of Things,* 42; we discussed his "middle term" in chap. 4.

16. Rosanna Warren, "Alcaics in Exile: W. H. Auden's 'In Memory of Sigmund Freud'," *Philosophy and Literature* 20 (1996): 111–21; 113.

Bibliography

This bibliography includes all works substantially discussed and/ or consulted. Works alluded to more briefly are referenced in the Notes. Dates refer to the edition used.

Abrams, M. H. 1971. *Natural Supernaturalism*. New York: W. W. Norton.

Ackroyd, Peter. 1984. *T. S. Eliot*. London: Sphere Books/Abacus.

Aitchison, Jean. 1994. *Words in the Mind: An Introduction to the Mental Lexicon*. Oxford: Basil Blackwell.

Altieri, Charles. "The Hermeneutics of Literary Indeterminacy: A Dissent from the New Orthodoxy." *New Literary History* 10:1 (autumn 1978).

Anselm. 1962. "Proslogium." *St. Anselm Basic Writings*. Translated by S. N. Deane, 2–34. La Salle: Open Court.

Aquinas, Thomas. 1972. *An Aquinas Reader*. Edited by Mary T. Clark. London: Hodder & Stoughton.

Aristotle. 1926. *Ethics*. Translated by H. Rackham. London: Heinemann Loeb Library.

—— 1927. *Poetics*. Translated by W. Hamilton Fyfe. London: Heinemann Loeb Library.

Arnold, Matthew. 1865. *Essays in Criticism*. New York: A. L. Burt.

Atkins, Peter. 1992. *Creation Revisited*. London: Penguin Books.

Auden, W. H. 1969. *Collected Shorter Poems, 1927–1957*. London: Faber & Faber.

Augustine. 1961. *Confessions*. Translated by R. S. Pine-Coffin. Harmondsworth: Penguin Classics.

——. 1972. *City of God*. Translated by Henry Bettenson. Harmondsworth: Pelican Classics. Austin, J. L. 1971. *How To Do Things with Words*. Edited by J. O. Urmson and Marina Sbisa. Oxford: Oxford University Press.

Barrell, John. 1993. "The Uses of Dorothy." *Wordsworth*. Edited by John Williams. Basingstoke: Macmillan Casebooks.

Barthes, Roland. 1975. *The Pleasure of the Text*. Translated by Richard Miller. New York: Hill & Wang.

Baudrillard, Jean. 1983. *Simulations*. Translated by Paul Foss, Paul Patton, and Philip Bleitchman. New York: Semiotext(e).

Bergson, Henri. 1911. *Creative Evolution*. Translated by Arthur Mitchell. London: Macmillan.

Bhagavad Gita. 1962. Translated by Juan Mascaro. Harmondsworth: Penguin Books.

Black, Max. 1962. *Models and Metaphors*. Ithaca: Cornell University Press.

Blackmore, Susan. 1999. *The Meme Machine*. Oxford: Oxford University Press.

Bloch, Chana. 1985. *Spelling the Word: George Herbert and the Bible*. Berkeley and Los Angeles: University of California Press.

Bloom, Harold. 1973. *The Anxiety of Influence*. Oxford: Oxford University Press.

——— 1975. *A Map of Misreading*. Oxford: Oxford University Press.

——— 1976. *Poetry and Repression*. New Haven: Yale University Press.

——— 1979. *Kabbalah and Criticism*. New York: Seabury.

——— 1995. *The Western Canon: The Books and Schools of the Ages*. London: Macmillan.

Bloomfield, Leonard. 1933. *Language*. London: George Allen & Unwin.

Bouquet, A. C. 1951. *Sacred Books of the World*. Harmondsworth: Penguin Books.

Bowker, Berjouhi. 1970. *The Word as Image*. London: Studio Vista.

Bromwich, David. 1989. *A Choice of Inheritance*. Cambridge: Harvard University Press.

Burckhardt, Jacob. 1940. *The Civilization of the Renaissance in Italy*. London: Phaidon Press.

Carey, John. 1981. *John Donne: Life, Mind, and Art*. London: Faber & Faber.

Caudill, Maureen and Charles Butler. 1991. *Naturally Intelligent Systems*. Cambridge: MIT Press.

Cavell, Stanley. 1976. *Must We Mean What We Say?* Cambridge: Cambridge University Press.

Chadwick, Henry. 1986. *Augustine*. Oxford: Oxford University Press.

Chadwick, Nora. 1970. *The Celts*. Harmondsworth: Pelican Books.

Chadwick, Owen. 1964. *The Reformation*. Harmondsworth: Penguin Books.

Charles, Amy M. 1977. *A Life of George Herbert*. Ithaca: Cornell University Press.

Chomsky, Noam. 1971. *Selected Readings*. Edited by J. P. B. Allen and Paul Van Buren. London: Oxford University Press.

Coe, Michael D. 1992. *Breaking the Maya Code*. New York: Thames & Hudson.

Cohen, Ted. "Metaphor and the Cultivation of Intimacy." *Critical Enquiry* 5 (autumn 1978): 3–13.

Cohn-Sherbok, Daniel. 1992. *The Crucified Jew*. London: HarperCollins Fount.

Coleridge, Samuel Taylor. 1993. *Aids to Reflection*. Edited by John Beer. London: Routledge/Princeton; Princeton, N.J.: Princeton University Press.

Consciousness. 1996. Supplement in *(London) Times Higher*. 5 April 1996, i-xii.

Croce, Benedetto. 1909. *Aesthetic: As Science of Expression and General Linguistic*. Translated by Douglas Ainslie. London: Macmillan.

Cruse, D. A. 1986. *Lexical Semantics*. Cambridge: Cambridge University Press.

Crystal, David. 1965. *Linguistics, Language, and Religion*. London: Burns & Oates.

——— 1987. *The Cambridge Encyclopedia of Language*. Cambridge: Cambridge University Press.

Curtius, E. R. 1953. *European Literature and the Latin Middle Ages*. Translated by Willard R. Trask. London: Routledge & Kegan Paul.

Daniel, David. 1996. "Translating the Bible." *The Nature of Religious Language: A Colloquium*. Edited by Stanley E. Porter, 68-87. London: Roehampton Institute: Sheffield Academic Press.

Dante Alighieri. 1980. *The Divine Comedy*. Translated by C. H. Sisson. Manchester: Carcanet New Press.

Davidson, Donald. "What Metaphors Mean." *Critical Enquiry* 5 (autumn 1978): 31–47.

Davie, Donald. 1955. *Articulate Energy*. London: Routledge & Kegan Paul.

Davies, Hayley G., and Talbot J. Taylor. 1990. *Redefining Linguistics*. London: Routledge.

Davies, Paul. 1983. *God and The New Physics*. Harmondsworth: Penguin Books.

——— 1992. *The Mind of God*. London: Penguin Books.

Davies, Stevie. 1991. *Milton*. Hemel Hempstead: Harvester/Wheatsheaf.

Dawkins, Richard. 1986. *The Blind Watchmaker*. Harlow: Longmans.

Deacon, Terrence. 1997. *The Symbolic Species*. London: Penguin Books.

Dennett, Daniel C. 1991. *Consciousness Explained*. London: Penguin Books.

Derrida, Jacques. 1974. *Of Grammatology*. Translated by Gayatri Chakravorty Spivak. Baltimore: Johns Hopkins University Press.

——— 1978. *Writing and Difference*. Translated by Alan Bass. London: Routledge & Kegan Paul.

Dickens, A. G. 1967. *The English Reformation*. London and Glasgow: Collins/Fontana.

Dickinson, Emily. 1975. *The Complete Poems*. Edited by Thomas H. Johnson. London: Faber & Faber.

Dilthey, Wilhelm. 1976. "The Rise of Hermeneutics." *W. Dilthey, Selected Writings*. Translated by H. P. Rickman, 246–63. Cambridge: Cambridge University Press.

Dionysus (anon). 1961. *The Cloud of Unknowing*. Translated by Clifton Wolters. Harmondsworth: Penguin Books.

Diringer, David. 1947. *The Alphabet: A Key To the History of Mankind*. London: Hutchinson.

Donoghue, David. "Doing Things with Words." "Critical Theory" feature, *(London) Times Literary Supplement*. 15 July 1994, 4–6.

Douglas, Mary. 1966. *Purity and Danger*. London: Routledge & Kegan Paul.

Duffy, Eamonn. 1996. *The Voices of Morebath: Reformation and Rebellion in an English Village*. London and New Haven: Yale University Press.

Dunbar, Robin. 1995. *Grooming, Gossip and the Evolution of Language*. London: Faber & Faber.

——— "Grey Natter." *(London) Times Higher*. 26 January 1996, 13.

Durkheim, Emile. 1915. *The Elementary Forms of the Religious Life*. Translated by Joseph Ward Swain. London: Allen & Unwin.

Eagleton, Terry. 1990. *The Ideology of the Aesthetic*. Oxford: Basil Blackwell.

Earliest English Poems. 1966. Translated by Michael Alexander. Harmondsworth: Penguin Classics.

Easthope, Anthony. 1983. *Poetry as Discourse*. London: Methuen New Accents.

Eco, Umberto. 1994. *The Search for the Perfect Language*. Translated by James Fentress. Oxford: Blackwell.

Edwards, David L. 1976. *A Key to the Old Testament*. Glasgow: Collins.

Eliade, Mircea, ed. 1967. *From Primitives to Zen: A Thematic Sourcebook of the History of Religions*. London: Collins.

———. 1989. *The Myth of the Eternal Return*. London: Penguin Arkana.

Eliot, T. S. 1933. *The Use of Poetry and the Use of Criticism*. London: Faber & Faber.

——— 1923. *The Waste Land*. London: Hogarth Press.

——— 1951. *Selected Essays*. London: Faber & Faber.

——— 1957. *On Poetry and Poets*. London: Faber & Faber.

——— 1959. *Four Quartets*. London: Faber & Faber.

——— 1965. *To Criticize the Critic*. London: Faber & Faber.

——— 1988. *The Letters of T. S. Eliot*. Vol. 1. Edited by Valerie Eliot. London: Faber & Faber.

Ellmann, Maud. 1987. *The Poetics of Impersonality: T. S. Eliot and Ezra Pound*. Brighton: Harvester Press.

Ellsberg, Margaret R. 1987. *Created to Praise: The Language of Gerard Manley Hopkins*. Oxford: Oxford University Press.

Fairbank, Alfred. 1949. *A Book of Scripts*. Harmondsworth: King Penguin.

Firmage, Richard A. 2000. *The Alphabet Abecedarium*. London: Bloomsbury.

Fish, Stanley Eugene. 1971. *Surprised by Sin: The Reader in Paradise Lost*. Berkeley and Los Angeles: University of California Press.

——— 1980. *Is There A Text in This Class?* Cambridge: Harvard University Press.

Forche, Carolyn. 2003. *Blue Hour*. Tarset: Bloodaxe Books.

Foucault, Michel. 1970. *The Order of Things*. London: Tavistock.

Freud, Sigmund. 1938. *Totem and Taboo*. Harmondsworth: Penguin Books.

——— 1960. *The Psychopathology of Everyday Life*. Translated by Alan Tyson. London: Ernest Benn.

——— 1976. *The Interpretation of Dreams*. Translated by James Strachey. Harmondsworth: Pelican Books.

Froude, James Anthony. 1906. *Essays in Literature and History*. London: J. M. Dent, Everyman.

Gadamer, Hans-Georg. 1975. *Truth and Method*. Translated by William Glen-Doepel. London: Sheed & Ward.

Gardner, Helen. 1978. *The Composition of Four Quartets*. London: Faber & Faber.

Garman, Michael. 1990. *Psycholinguistics*. Cambridge: Cambridge University Press.

Gilbert, Sandra M., and Susan Gubar. 1979. *The Madwoman in the Attic*. New Haven: Yale University Press.

Gill, Eric. 1940. *Autobiography*. London: Jonathan Cape.

Gill, Stephen. 1989. *William Wordsworth: A Life*. Oxford: Clarendon Press.

Goldsmith, Oliver. 1966. *The Collected Works of Oliver Goldsmith*. Edited in 5 volumes by Arthur Friedman. Oxford: Clarendon Press.

Goody, Jack. 1987. *The Interface Between the Written and the Oral*. Cambridge: Cambridge University Press.

Graham, Joseph F. 1992. *Onomatopoetics*. Cambridge: Cambridge University Press.

Greenfield, Susan. 2000. *The Private Life of the Brain*. London: Allen Lane.

Gyekye, Kwame. 1987. *An Essay on African Philosophical Thought: The Akan Conceptual Scheme*. Cambridge: Cambridge University Press.

Haack, Susan. 1993. *Evidence and Inquiry: Towards Reconstruction in Epistemology*. Oxford: Basil Blackwell.

Hamilton, Edith. 1948. *The Greek Way to Western Civilization*. New York: Mentor Books.

Hamilton, Paul. 1992. "'A Shadow of a Magnitude': The Dialectic of Romantic Aesthetics." *Beyond Romanticism*. Edited by Stephen Copley and John Whale, 11–31. London: Routledge.

Hardy, Thomas. 1976. *The Complete Poems of Thomas Hardy*. Edited by James Gibson. London: Macmillan.

Harris, Roy. 1990. "On Redefining Linguistics." *Redefining Linguistics*. Edited by Hayley G. Davies and Talbot J. Taylor, 53–117. London: Routledge.

Hartman, Geoffrey. 1987. *The Unremarkable Wordsworth*. London: Methuen.

Hayden, John O. "The Road To Tintern Abbey." *The Wordsworth Circle* 12:4 (autumn 1981): 211–16.

Herbert, George. 1974. *The English Poems of George Herbert*. Edited by C. A. Patrides. London: Dent.

———— 1981. *The Country Parson, The Temple*. Edited by John N. Wall, Jr. New York: Paulist Press.

Hill, Christopher. 1979. *Milton and the English Revolution*. London: Faber & Faber.

Hilton, Walter. 1957. *The Ladder of Perfection*. Translated by Leo Sherley-Price. Harmondsworth: Penguin Books.

Hinton, Leanne, Johanna Nichols, and John J. Ohala, eds. 1995. *Sound Symbolism*. Cambridge: Cambridge University Press.

Hodgart, Matthew, ed. 1965. *The Faber Book of Ballads*. London: Faber & Faber.

Hollander, John. 1985. *Vision and Resonance: Two Senses of Poetic Form*. New Haven: Yale University Press.

Homans, Margaret. 1980. *Women Writers and Poetic Identity*. Princeton: Princeton University Press.

Homer. 1951. *Iliad*. Translated by Richmond Lattimore. Chicago: University of Chicago Press.

———— 1965. *Odyssey*. Translated by Richmond Lattimore. Chicago: University of Chicago Press.

Huizinga, J. 1955. *The Waning of the Middle Ages*. Harmondsworth: Penguin Books.

Humphreys, Christmas. 1951. *Buddhism*. Harmondsworth: Penguin Books.

Huxley, Thomas Henry. 1971. *Thomas Henry Huxley on Education*. Edited by C. Bibby. Cambridge: Cambridge University Press.

Iser, Wolfgang. 1978. *The Act of Reading*. London: Routledge & Kegan Paul.

Jakobson, Roman. 1960. "Linguistics and Poetics." *Style in Language*. Edited by T. Sebeok, 350–77. Cambridge: MIT Press.

———— 1971. *Fundamentals of Language*. The Hague: Mouton.

Jean, Georges. 1992. *Writing: The Story of Alphabets and Scripts*. Translated by Jenny Oates. London: Thames & Hudson.

Johnson, Kenneth R. "The Politics of 'Tintern Abbey'." *Wordsworth Circle* 14:1 (winter 1983): 6–14.

———— 1998. *The Hidden Wordsworth: Poet, Lover, Rebel, Spy*. New York: W. W. Norton. Johnson, Samuel. 1905. *Lives of the English Poets*. Edited in 3 volumes by G. B. Hill. Oxford: Clarendon Press.

Johnson-Laird, Philip. 1988. *The Computer and the Mind*. London: HarperCollins Fontana.

Jones, David. 1959. *Epoch and Artist*. London: Faber & Faber.

Kant, Immanuel. 1952. *The Critique of Judgement*. Translated by James Creed Meredith. Oxford: Clarendon Press.

Kempis, Thomas à. 1960. *The Imitation of Christ*. No translator given. London: Dent, Everyman.

Kenny, Anthony. 1980. *Aquinas*. Oxford: Oxford University Press.

Kermode, Frank. 1971. *Modern Essays*. London: Collins Fontana.

King James Bible (1611). 1949. London: Collins.

Kirkby, Joan. 1991. *Emily Dickinson*. Basingstoke: Macmillan.

Kline, Morris. 1972. *Mathematics in Western Culture*. Harmondsworth: Penguin Books.

Knowles, David. 1962. *The Evolution of Medieval Thought*. London: Longmans.

Kuhn, T. S. 1970. *The Structure of Scientific Revolutions*. Chicago: University of Chicago Press.

Lacan Jacques. 1977i. "The Mirror Stage as Formative of the Function of the I." *Jacques Lacan: Ecrits, A Selection*. Translated by Alan Sheridan, 1–7. London: Tavistock.

———— 1977ii. "The Function and Field of Speech and Language in Psychoanalysis." *Jacques Lacan: Ecrits, A Selection*. Translated by Alan Sheridan, 30–113. London: Tavistock.

———— 1977iii. "The Agency of the Letter in the Unconscious or Reason since Freud." *Jacques Lacan: Ecrits, A Selection*. Translated by Alan Sheridan, 146–78. London: Tavistock.

Landow, George F. 1996. "We Are Already beyond the Book." *Beyond the Book: Theory, Culture, and the Politics of Cyberspace*. Edited by Warren Chernaik, Marilyn Deegan, and Andrew Gibson, 7. Oxford: Office for Humanities Communications Publications.

Langer, Susanne K. 1953. *Feeling and Form: A Theory of Art*. London: Routledge & Kegan Paul.

Lanham, Richard A. "The Electronic Word: Literary Study and the Digital Revolution." *New Literary History* 20:2 (winter 1989): 265–90.

Larkin, Philip. 1983. *Required Writing*. London: Faber & Faber.

Leavis, F. R. 1932. *New Bearings in English Poetry*. London: Chatto & Windus.

Lecercle, Jean-Jacques. 1990. "Postmodernism and language." *Postmodernism and Society*. Edited by Roy Boyne and Ali Rattansi, 76–96. Basingstoke: Macmillan.

Leech, Geoffrey. 1983. *Principles of Pragmatics*. London: Longmans.

Leonard, John. 1990. *Naming in Paradise: Milton and the Language of Adam and Eve*. Oxford: Clarendon Press.

Levinson, Marjorie. 1986. *Wordsworth's Great Period Poems: Four Essays*. Cambridge: Cambridge University Press.

Levi-Strauss, Claude. 1970. *The Raw and the Cooked*. London: Jonathan Cape.

——— 1972. *The Savage Mind*. London: Weidenfeld & Nicholson.

Love, Nigel. 1990. "The Locus of Languages in a Redefined Linguistics." *Redefining Linguistics*. Edited by Hayley G. Davies and Talbot J. Taylor, 53–117. London: Routledge.

Lyotard, Jean-Paul. 1984. *The Postmodern Condition: A Report on Knowledge*. Translated by Geoff Bennington and Brian Massumi. Manchester: Manchester University Press.

Manguel, Alberto. 1997. *A History of Reading*. London: HarperCollins Flamingo.

Martineau, Harriet. 1983. *Autobiography*. 2 vols. London: Virago Press.

Matthiesen, F. O. 1935. *The Achievement of T. S. Eliot*. New York: Oxford University Press.

McGann, Jerome J. 1983. *The Romantic Ideology: A Critital Investigation*. Chicago: University of Chicago Press.

——— 1991. *The Textual Condition*. Princeton, N.J.: Princeton University Press.

McNeil, Helen. 1986. *Emily Dickinson*. London: Virago.

Mellor, Anne K. 1993. *Romanticism and Gender*. New York: Routledge.

Miller, J. Hillis. 1986. "The Linguistic Moment." *Gerard Manley Hopkins: Modern Critical Views*. Edited by Harold Bloom, 147–62. New Haven: Chelsea House.

Millikan, Ruth Garrett. 1993. "On Mentalese Orthography." *Dennett and his Critics*. Edited by Bo Dahlbom, 97–123. Oxford: Basil Blackwell.

Milroy, James. 1977. *The Language of Gerard Manley Hopkins*. London: Andre Deutsch.

Milton, John. 1952. *Complete Poetry and Selected Prose*. Edited by E. H. Visiak. London: Nonesuch Press.

——— 1971. *Paradise Lost*. Edited by Alastair Fowler. London: Longmans.

Mithen, Steven. 1998. *The Prehistory of the Mind*. London: Orion Books, Phoenix.

Montefiore, Jan. 1987. *Feminism and Poetry*. London: Routledge & Kegan Paul/Pandora.

Mothersill, Mary. 1984. *Beauty Restored*. Oxford: Clarendon Press.

Mullen, Harryette. 2002. *Sleeping with the Dictionary*. Berkeley and London: University of California Press.

Nagel, Thomas. 1986. *The View from Nowhere*. Oxford: Oxford University Press.

Nowottny, Winifred. 1962. *The Language Poets Use*. London: Athlone Press.

Nuttall, A. D. 1980. *Overheard By God*. London: Methuen.

Ohmann, Richard. 1981. "Speech, Literature, and the Space Between." *Essays in Modern Stylistics*. Edited by Donald C. Freeman. London and New York: Methuen.

Olsen, David R. 1994. *The World on Paper*. Cambridge: Cambridge University Press.

Ong, Walter. 1967. *The Presence of the Word*. Minneapolis: University of Minnesota Press.

Paglia, Camilla. 1990. *Sexual Personae*. New Haven: Yale University Press.

Paz, Octavio. 1974. *Alternating Current*. London: Wildwood House.

Pinker, Steven. 1995. *The Language Instinct*. London: Penguin Books.

Plant, Sadie. 1996. "Connectionism and the Posthumanities". *Beyond the Book: Theory, Culture and the Politics of Cyberspace*. Edited by Warren Cherniak, Marilyn Deegan, and Andrew Gibson. London: Office for Humanities Communication Publications. 33–42.

Plato. 1921. *Thaetetus* and *Sophist*. Translated by Harold North Fowler. London: Heinemann Loeb Library.

———— 1930/1935. *Republic*. Translated in 2 vols. by Paul Shorey. London: Heinemann Loeb Library.

———— 1971. *Timaeus* and *Critias*. Translated by Desmond Lee. Harmondsworth: Penguin Books.

———— 1973. *Letters VII* and *VIII*. Translated by Walter Hamilton. Harmondsworth: Penguin Books.

———— 1973. *Phaedrus*. Translated by Walter Hamilton. Harmondsworth: Penguin Books.

Polanyi, Michael. 1964. *Personal Knowledge: Towards a Post-Critical Philosophy*. New York: Harper & Row.

Pope. Alexander. 1956. *Alexander Pope's Collected Poems*. Edited by Bonamy Dobree. London: J. M. Dent.

Powell, Barry B. 1991. *Homer and the Origin of the Greek Alphabet*. Cambridge: Cambridge University Press.

Puttenham, George. 1936. *The Arte of English Poesie*. Edited by Gladys Doidge Willcock and Alice Walker. Cambridge: Cambridge University Press.

Quincey, Thomas de. 1973. *De Quincey as Critic*. Edited by John E. Jordan. London: Routledge & Kegan Paul.

Reader, John. 1981. *Missing Links: The Hunt for Earliest Man*. London: Penguin Books.

Reeves, James. 1959. "Introduction." *Selected Poems of Emily Dickinson,* ix–lii. London: Heinemann.

Renwick, A. M. 1958. *The Story of the Church*. Grand Rapids, Mich.: Eerdmans.

Rich, Adrienne. 1980. "When We Dead Awaken." *On Lies, Secrets, and Silence*. London: Virago 1980.

Richards, I. A. 1936. *The Philosophy of Rhetoric*. Oxford: Oxford University Press.

Richardson, Jonathan. 1932. "Explanatory Notes and Remarks on Milton's Paradise Lost." *The Early Lives of Milton*. Edited by Helen Darbishire, 199–330. London: Constable.

Ricks, Christopher. 1963. *Milton's Grand Style*. Oxford: Oxford University Press.

Ricoeur, Paul. 1978. *The Rule of Metaphor*. London: Routledge & Kegan Paul.

Robins, R. H. 1993. *General Linguistics*. London: Longmans.

Rorty, Richard. 1980. *Philosophy and the Mirror of Nature*. Oxford: Basil Blackwell.

Saussure, Ferdinand de. 1959. *Course in General Linguistics*. Translated by Wade Baskin. London: Fontana/Collins.

Schaya, Leo. 1971. *The Universal Meaning of the Kabbalah*. Translated by Nancy Pearson. London: Allen & Unwin.

Schleiermacher, Freidrich. "The Hermeneutics (Outline of the 1819 Lectures)." *New Literary History* (autumn 1978): 1–16.

Schneider, Elisabeth W. 1986. "The Dragon at the Gate." *Gerard Manley Hopkins: Modern Critical Views.* Edited by Harold Bloom. New Haven, Connecticut: Chelsea House.

Schweickart, Patrocinio P. 1989. "Reading Ourselves: Toward a Feminist Theory of Reading." *Speaking of Gender.* Edited by Elaine Showalter, 17–44. London: Routledge.

Searle, John R. 1969. *Speech Acts.* Cambridge: Cambridge University Press.

Shackley, Myra. 1980. *Neanderthal Man.* London: Duckworth.

Shawcross, John T., ed. 1970. *Milton: The Critical Heritage.* London: Routledge & Kegan Paul.

Shelley, P. B. 1927. "A Defence of Poetry." *The Prelude to Poetry.* Edited by Ernest Rhys, 207–41. London: Dent, Everyman Library.

Sidney, Sir Philip. 1927. "An Apologie for Poetrie." *The Prelude to Poetry.* Edited by Ernest Rhys, 9–60. London: Dent, Everyman Library.

Smart, Ninian. 1971. *The Religious Experience of Mankind.* Glasgow: Collins Fontana.

Smart, Ninian, and Richard D. Hecht, eds. 1992. *Sacred Texts of the World: A Universal Anthology.* London: Macmillan Reference Books.

Smith, Grover. 1983. *The Waste Land.* London: Allen & Unwin.

Southern, R. W. 1953. *The Making of the Middle Ages.* London: Hutchinson.

Stanner, W. E. H. 1965. "Religion, Totemism and Symbolism." *Aboriginal Man Australia.* Edited by R. M. Berndt, and C. H. Berndt, 207–37. Glasgow: Angus & Robertson.

Steiner, George. 1989. *Real Presences.* London: Faber & Faber.

Storr, Anthony. 1973. *Jung.* London: Collins/Fontana.

Summers, Joseph H. 1954. *George Herbert: His Religion and Art.* London: Chatto & Windus.

Svarny, Eric. 1988. *"The Men Of 1914": T. S. Eliot and Early Modernism.* Milton Keynes: Open University Press.

Taylor, Mark. 2002. *Shakespeare's Imitations.* Newark: University of Delaware Press.

Thomas, Edward. 1981. *A Language Not to Be Betrayed: Selected Prose.* Edited by Edna Longley. Manchester: Carcanet Press.

Thompson, Francis. 1984. *Crofting Years.* Western Isles: Luath Press.

Todd, Richard. 1986. *The Opacity of Signs: Acts of Interpretation in George Herbert's THE TEMPLE.* Columbia: University Press of Missouri.

Trotter, David. 1984. *The Making of the Reader.* Basingstoke: Macmillan.

Vendler, Helen. 1975. *The Poetry of George Herbert.* Cambridge: Harvard University Press.

Waldoff, Leon. 2002. *Wordsworth in His Major Lyrics.* Columbia: University Press of Missouri.

Ward, J. P. 1984. *Wordsworth's Language of Men.* Brighton: Harvester Press.

——— "Poetry and Sociology." *Human Studies* 9 (1986): 323–45.

Warren, Robert. 1988. "Perceptual Basis for the Evolution of Speech." *The Genesis of Language*. Edited by Marge E. Lansberg, 101–10. The Hague: Mouton.

Warren, Rosanna. "Alcaics in Exile: W. H. Auden's 'In Memory of Sigmund Freud'" *Philosophy and Literature* 20 (1996): 111–21; 113.

Weitz, Morris. "The Role of 'Art' in Aesthetic Theory." *Journal of Aesthetics and Art Criticism* 15 (1956): 27–35.

Wendel, Francois. 1963. *Calvin*. Translated by Philip Mairet. London: Collins Fontana.

Williams, Rowan. 2000. *On Christian Theology*. Oxford: Blackwell.

Wills, Garry. 1999. *Saint Augustine*. London: Weidenfeld & Nicolson.

Wilson, A. N. 1983. *The Life of John Milton*. Oxford: Oxford University Press.

Wilson, Edmund. 1931. *Axel's Castle*. New York: Scribner.

Wittgenstein, Ludwig. 1958. *Philosophical Investigations*. Translated by G. E. M. Anscombe. Oxford: Basil Blackwell.

———— 1961. *Tractatus Logico-Philosophicus*. Translated by D. F. Pears and B. F. McGuinness. London: Routledge & Kegan Paul.

Wolter, Allan B. 1990. *The Philosophical Theory of John Duns Scotus*. Ithaca: Cornell University Press.

Wordsworth, Dorothy. 1971. *Journals of Dorothy Wordsworth*. Edited by Mary Moorman. Oxford: Oxford University Press.

Wordsworth, William. 1977. *The Poems*. Edited in 2 vols. by John O. Hayden. Harmondsworth: Penguin Books.

———— 1979. *The Prelude 1799, 1805, 1850*. Edited by Jonathan Wordsworth, M. H. Abrams, and Stephen Gill. New York: W. W. Norton.

———— 1993. *The Fenwick Notes of William Wordsworth*. Edited by Jared Curtis. Bristol: Bristol Classical Press.

Wordsworth, William, and Dorothy Wordsworth. 1967–69, 1993. *The Letters of William and Dorothy Wordsworth*. Edited in 7 vols. variously by Ernest de Selincourt, Mary Moorman, Chester L. Shaver, Alan G. Hill, and others. Oxford: Clarendon Press.

Wordsworth, William, and Mary Wordsworth. 1982. *The Love Letters of William and Mary Wordsworth*. Edited by Beth Darlington. London: Chatto & Windus.

Worsley, Peter. 1967. "Groote Eylandt Totemism and *Le Totemism Aujourd'hui*." *The Structural Study of Myth and Totemism*. Edited by Edmund Leach. London: Tavistock.

Wright, Elizabeth. 1983. *Psychoanalytic Criticism*. London: Methuen New Accents. *Macbeth* V. v 15-46

Index